# WOMEN TELLING NATIONS

# *Women Writers in History 1*

# WOMEN TELLING NATIONS

Edited by
Amelia Sanz
Francesca Scott
Suzan van Dijk

Rodopi

Amsterdam - New York, NY 2014

Cover image top: Faustina Sáez de Melgar, in *La lira del Tajo*, Madrid: Imprenta de D. Bernabé Fernández, 1859. The portrait is signed by J. Vallejo; lithograph made by J. Donon (Madrid).

Cover image middle: Selma Lagerlöf, portrait by A. Blomberg 1906. National Library in Stockholm.

Cover image bottom: Princess Zinaïda Alexandrovna Volkonskaia, aquarel by Jean-Désiré Muneret, 1814, State Historical Museum, Moscow, Russia.

The paper on which this book is printed meets the requirements of "ISO 9706: 1994, Information and documentation - Paper for documents - Requirements for permanence".

ISBN: 978-90-420-3870-7
E-Book ISBN: 978-94-012-1112-3

Printed in The Netherlands

## CONTENTS

## INTRODUCTION

*AMELIA SANZ AND SUZAN VAN DIJK*

WE AGREE: THE NATION HAS BEEN ONE OF THE MOST MOBILIZING MYTHS of the modern world and nationalism has been the most constant and pervasive, owing to its great potential for adaptation and survival. In political terms, since the First World War we have been living in a world where the 'international legitimate order' is the nation state. It could be asked why such a concept has obtained such great political power. We propose to verify that 'nation' is a trans-cultural, trans-social and trans-gendered concept.[1]

We have followed the guidance of authors such as Hobsbawm, Anderson, Giddens, Thiesse, Casanova and Smith[2] who, over the last three decades, have emphasized that this idea of nation (with its correlates, nationality and nationalism) is a product of modernity that dates back no further than the late $18^{th}$ century. They have shown us that nationalism comes before nations and is the product of a collective imagination constructed through selective memory, but they omit gender from their framework. We no longer consider the nation as a closed set of observable facts, and even less a transparent category, but rather as a belief in a collective, a major form of identification and a cultural artifact. The idea of a self-enclosed national literature first generated national histories, then national literary histories where language, literature and nation have melded together into an unproblematic union, in which geographical, political and linguistic borders coincide, a spirit that was

---

[1] We are grateful to Laura Sánchez for her collaboration in editing and reviewing this volume.

[2] E.J. Hobsbawm, *Nations and Nationalism since 1780: Programme, Myth, Reality*, Cambridge: Cambridge University Press, 1990; Anthony Smith, *National Identity*. London: Penguin, 1991; Benedict Anderson, *Imagined Communities: Reflections on the Origin and Spread of Nationalism*. New York [etc.]: Verso, 1994; Anthony Giddens, *The transformation of intimacy: sexuality, love, and eroticism inmodern societies*. Stanford: Stanford University Press, 1992; Anne-Marie Thiesse, *La création des identités nationales: Europe XVIIIe-XXe siècle*. Paris: Seuil, 1999; Pascale Casanova, *La République mondiale des Lettres*. Paris: Seuil, 1999; Anthony Smith, *National Identity*. London: Penguin, 1991.

supposed to have found its highest expression in the works of great male writers. We now think the 'nation' should be considered a "space that is internally marked by cultural difference and heterogeneous histories of contending peoples, antagonistic authorities and tense cultural locations".[3]

But historiography has rarely been gendered; what is more, history as a discipline has been hardened by the masculinisation of history-writing and the exclusion of women and women writers. The lack of engagement between 'masculinist' writings on nationalism and recent feminist work has been denounced by a number of scholars, particularly in the political sciences[4]. The first to look for gendering nations were feminist historians, whose denunciation was clear: the "nation" constructs minorities and excludes deviants from important power resources.[5] The claim that the creation of national canons excluded women was one that became familiar. In the development of nation and modernity, the exclusion of multiplicity implied a wish for uniformity, certainty and decisiveness: the hegemony of homogeneity.

In recent decades, scholars have shown how the national project affected women and men differently, thereby engendering different degrees of enthusiasm. They have done this by (i) providing evidence of the varying but often large commitment to the national project of women, and indeed of different groups of women differentiated by class, education and urban-rural residence,[6] (ii) looking at the differential integration of women and men into national projects,[7] (iii) claiming that transnational entities can only be understood by analysing gender relations,[8] and (iv) finding feminist demands shaping nationalistic demands in the Third World.[9] It is definitely time for

[3] Homi Bhabha, *Nation and Narration*. London-New York: Routledge, 1991: 299.

[4] Sita Ranchod-Nilsson and Mary Ann Tétreault, *Women, States, and Nationalism. At home in the nation?* London and New York: Routledge, 1982.

[5] Nira Yuval-Davis, *Gender and Nation*. London: Sage Publications, 1997: 11, for example.

[6] Yuval-Davis and Anthias, *Woman-Nation-State*, London: MacMillan, 1989: as biological reproducers of members of national collectivities, as reproducers of the boundaries of national groups, as participating centrally in the ideological reproduction of the collectivity as reproducers, as signifiers of national differences, as participants in national, economic, political or military struggles.

[7] Sylvia Walby, "Woman and Nation" in *International Journal of Comparative Sociology*, XXXIII, 1-2, 1992: 81-100.

[8] Cynthia H. Enloe, *Bananas, Beaches and Bases: Making Feminist Sense of International Politics*. London: Pandora, 1989.

[9] Kumari Jayawardena, *Feminism and Nationalism in the Third World*. London: Zed Press, 1986.

nations to be seen for what they are: gendered for the sake of multiple histories and multiple modernities.

Academia has traditionally conceived cultures, writings and literatures in terms of nations, within the framework of printed books and based on a (male) canon. Nowadays, however, nations are no longer the only identity card, and all kinds of world voices, even those using manuscripts, are available to readers on the Internet. Moreover, in the last hundred years, literary studies have shifted from an *author-centred* perspective (those of Raymond Picard in the French school) to a *text-centred* perspective (those of Barthes and of structuralisms from the 1960s on), to attain more *reader-centred* perspectives (those of Cultural, Postcolonial and Gender Studies) that have clearly allowed for a greater inclusiveness, accommodating different voices, especially those of women.

More specifically, this refers to a series of questions concerning the status of women's writing in Europe: What were women doing from the 16$^{th}$ to the 19$^{th}$ centuries while national identities were being forged? In what way were women, as readers and writers, contributing to these imaginary communities, or refusing to build them? Could nations be built without taking into account what women thought and wrote? To what extent were they invisible? Was the time of nations a time for women? And were national territories those of women? What other kinds of 'nations' were women building as a result of the circulation of literary material through reading and writing? Was there any common or shifting form of gender differentiation and inequality across different nations? How were boundaries defined in a political and intellectual sense in times of national construction? If we go back to the etymological sense of 'nation' (birth), what were women's literary nations?

*Women Telling Nations* attempts to face these challenges and contribute address the gap as part of a networking research project, which has been financed as a COST Action entitled *Women Writers in History: Toward a New Understanding of European Literary Culture* (2009-2013),[10] involving twenty-five countries and more than a hundred researchers. Its aim is to study the circulation of women's writings before 1900, beyond the canon, on a

[10] Suzan Van Dijk, Anke Gilleir, Alicia C. Montoya, "Before NEWW (New Approaches to European Women's Writing): Prolegomena to the Launching of an International Project" in *TULSA Studies in Women's literature*, 27, I, 2008: 151-157.

large European scale, thus beyond the nation and, with the help of our Virtual Environments,[11] beyond the culture of print.

From its very beginning, the project was a reaction against an idea that was widespread in historiography and textbooks, according to which the participation of women in the literary world was marginal until 1900. Enough evidence of a real circulation of women authors is provided by data that captures the readings of women's writing, and by collecting it we are heeding Mario Valdés's call for an "effective literary history" based on data gathering, as opposed to a monumental literary history,[12] effective history requiring collaborative work, similar to that already carried out at international level in science laboratories. We also subscribe to the proposals advanced by Franco Moretti in 2005, when he threw out a similar challenge, inviting literary scholars to look beyond the 200 or so literary works they work on during their lifetime with a 'close reading' method. He suggested, instead, a quantitative approach that he called 'distant reading', using graphs from quantitative history, maps from geography and trees from evolutionary theory.[13] Finally, we follow Gerda Lerner's call, not for 'compensatory history' (looking for women missing from history and writing the history of notable women), but for 'contributary history', which describes women's contribution to the male-defined world and their subjection to it, judging the contribution firstly with respect to its effect on the movement and, secondly, by standards appropriate to men.[14] *Women Telling Nations* is an example of how to transform women's writing from monuments into documents.

We have chosen to work on women's writing before 1900, prior to the 20th century triumphs of feminism and the critical apparatus built around it. It can be a salutary experience at the beginning of the 21st century to work on the heteronomy of early modern Europe, more specifically, at a time when nationhood had been born, but nationalism had yet to appear – in other words, in pre-modern times in the context of different empires, such as the Habsburg and Ottoman Empires in the 16th and 17th centuries, or the Austro-

[11] See *Women Writers Networks*. On line at http://www.womenwriters.nl and *Women Writers Database* at http://www.databasewomenwriters.nl.

[12] Mario Valdés and Djielal Kadir, *Literary Cultures of Latin America: A Comparative History*. Oxford: Oxford University Press, 2004: XIX and XXI.

[13] Franco Moretti, *Graphs, Maps, Trees : Abstract Models for a Literary History*. New York: Verso, 2005: 4

[14] Gerda Lerner, "Placing Women in History: Definitions and Challenges" and "The Challenge of Women's History" in *The Majority Finds its Past.Placing Women in History*. Chapel Hill: The University of North Carolina Press, 2005: 115-126, 133-143.

Hungarian, Ottoman and Russian Empires in the 18th and 19th centuries, in which constructed patterns of membership and belonging overlapped (kingdoms, fiefdoms, languages, religious practices, family, cities, sects, shires, occupations, associations…). In this context, we feel obliged to consider discursive constructions that have strong metaphorical power, such as Nation, Balkans, Orientalism, Europe... Our emphasis is, therefore, on the diversity of nationalisms.

Contributions to *Women Telling Nations* come from twenty countries, which have very different agendas in terms of their historical, academic and technical domains. This presents important challenges: in the first place, not all the dates relating to Pre-Modern/Modern/Post-Modern Times coincide, so we have been forced to accept different forms of modernity, not just the current occidental; secondly, academic traditions are filled with political, economic, even religious heritages, some using a very positivistic methodology, others being heavily influenced by the latest claims, and we have to accept all of them; thirdly, not all technical skills and computing infrastructures are shared by researchers to the same degree – some of them have access to their entire digitised patrimony, while the archives of others are under threat. In order to avoid the monopolisation of just three or four core countries, we decided not to adopt the standard centre-centred approach (usually based on France, England and Germany as dominant European powers), but consider different positions from the fringes, focusing on the circulation of fairly closely connected sets of writings that change in time and space. This enables a kind of 'entangled history' (*histoire croisée* in Michel Espagne's words)[15] to be developed from *Women Telling Nations* that criticises the habit of referring to traditions in an impacted, monolithic way. In fact, these junctions are already a familiar characteristic of gender studies, which have been comparative and transcultural from the very beginning.[16] As

[15] Michel Espagne, "Au-delà du comparatisme" in *Les Transferts culturels franco-allemands*, Paris: PUF, 1999: 35-49; Michael Werner and Bénédicte Zimmermann, "Penser l'histoire croisée: entre empirie et réflexivité", *Annales HSS*, 1, 2003 : 7-36 ; Ursula Keller and Ilna Rakussa (dir). *Writing Europe. What is European About the Literatures of Europe? Essays form 33 European Countries*, Budapest/New York: CEU Press, 2004.

[16] As we can see in some journals such as *Signs, Feminist Studies, Journal of Women's History, Feministische Studien*; or some anthologies such as Renate Bridenthal et Claudia Koonz, *Becoming Visible: Women in European History* 1977, or Jean Quataert and Marilyn Boxer, *Connecting Spheres: Women in the Western World, 1500 to the Present* , 1987. See also Deborah Cohen and Maura O'Connor (ed.).

a result, contributions to *Women Telling Nations* adopt both a transnational approach, focused on relationships and event chains that cross and transcend borders, and a comparatist approach. This way, it is possible to understand women's conditions with respect to the similarities and differences found in different cultures, and also the interaction of general trends with particular cases.

*Women Telling Nations* aims to underline the quantitative importance of the circulation of women's writings and to demonstrate the extent of the international cross-fertilisation of nations, especially for women. This is a constructive way of countering the widely held idea that the reception of women's writings was largely reduced to a female audience, and to avoid the risk of essentialising the separation of spheres, in other words, labelling an author 'a woman writer' and discussing her works exclusively in relation to other members of the same group. Studying this circulation allows us to decompartmentalise women's time and space and draw constellations that transcend national boundaries.

By so doing, we are moving towards other conceptual metaphors, which means other scientific paradigms and anthropologies. The biological stance of the 19th century (rooted in birth, development and death) provided a vague scientific background to race, milieu and time. Nowadays, we adopt terms like 'circulation', 'networks' and 'transculturality', not only to keep ourselves up-to-date, but because we are aware of the epistemological displacements produced by these metaphorical schemas: 'trans' (rather than 'multi' or 'inter'), whose Indo-European root means 'across' and 'beyond'. National imaginary adopts a kind of 'vertical' strategy of representation and legitimation; global imaginary uses the 'horizontal': the more your papers, your commodities and your works circulate, the more value they are given.

Our starting hypothesis is that, faced with the *archaeological* paradigm of a history of literature that seeks its origins vertically, looking for unity, we can work from a horizontal, reticular paradigm that looks for routes and connections. Let us say that our question would not be so much Where do you come from? but rather Which way are you coming from? Which way are you circulating? We therefore want to move away from an archaeology of

---

*Comparison and History: Europe in Cross-National Perspective*. New York: Routledge, 2004.

origins to a representation of circulation, because circulation brings as much meaning as origin.[17] We are interested in routes rather than roots.

Since the main channel of circulation for writing and research is no longer the printed book, and large data collections, data volumes and computing resources for analysis and high performance visualisation are provided by virtual libraries and digital tools, now is the right time for collaborative work and the right place for virtual environments that allow the circulation of women's writing to be studied. It is for this reason that the contributions of this volume are rooted in our Virtual Collaborative Environment, the *WomenWriters Database*, and there are numerous references to this data throughout the volume. As Mario Valdés puts it: "The meaning of a historical event in traditional literary history is determined by its role in a linear development; but in a comparative history of literary culture there is a weblike construct that is proposed as the context of production and reception and that establishes the dialectic framework for a debate of the conflict of interpretations".[18] More than ever, there is a need for practices with available data that are interpretative, recursive and questioning, in order to reason about sources and develop deep reading: the time has come for a new hermeneutic turn in which different interdisciplinary and transcultural points of view are located. The aim of *Women Telling Nation* is to publish the result of collaboration and contribution to the interpretation of data.

## Women belonging to nations

Women were not excluded from the nation, nor did they exclude themselves. Through their writing and publishing they could actually represent territories and political or religious communities in their own way. This could be likened to the effect of a burka; on the one hand, writing hid the identity of women who wanted to develop what were considered to be male activities, and on the other hand, writing liberated them and allowed them to participate in the literary game, a social and public act that made them visible and historical. *Women Telling Nations* presents some of these alternative identities.

In early modern times, in a context of nascent nationhood, we were a long way from Isabelle de Charrière's assessment: "Je voudrais être du pays de

[17] James Clifford, "Travelling cultures" in Laurence Grosberg et al. (ed.). *Cultural Studies*. London: Routledge, 1992: 6-116.
[18] Op. cit.: XXI.

tout le monde" [19] or from the Virginia Woolf's famous quote: "As a woman I have no country. As a woman I want no country. As a woman my country is the whole world".[20]

In contrast, from the 15th century, and against the background of the Hundred Years' War, some women (queens, princesses and *trobairitz*) developed a sense of belonging to a territory, identifying themselves at the same time to a sovereign and the emblematic image of a lineage. As Madeleine Jeay points out in *Medieval Women Networking Before the* Appearance of Nations, the prevalence of the notion of lineage in the Middle Ages did not exclude certain tension with respect to the sense of territorial entity and the community it was supposed to embody and identify with.

In fact, although deprived of *potestas*, some women were not deprived of *auctoritas* by writing. In *Latine Loquor: Women Acquiring Auctoritas (Portugal 1500-1800),* Inês de Ornellas stresses the role of those women who became part of a transnational cultural space because they could write in Latin or hide their own ideas behind the translated Latin text, Latin being the only language until the mid-18th century that unified the European intelligentsia. The few learned women who were educated like men,

---

[19] Isabelle de Charrière in a letter to her secret correspondent David-Louis Constant d'Hermenches (27-3-1768). However, the similarity to what she wrote much later to Benjamin Constant: "Vous et moi, nous n'étions d'aucun pays quand nous étions ensemble" (6-1-1795), and to what she had written earlier to James Boswell: "écrivez-moi […] tout ce qui vous viendra dans la tête. J'entendrai les pensées nées en Angleterre comme celles qui sont nées en France, elles sont toutes compatriotes des miennes, les miennes sont de tout pays" (18/19-6-1764), is, perhaps, suspicious: these were men she loved, platonically or in any other sense, and who were of a different nationality to her. See Isabelle de Charrière, *Oeuvres complètes,* ed. by Jean-Daniel Candaux e.a. Amsterdam: Van Oorschot, respectively vol. II (1980), p. 80; vol. V (1983), p. 27; vol. I (1979): 194. We thank Madeleine van Strien-Chardonneau, Rob Gielen and Trix Trompert for discussing together this question.

[20] Virginia Woolf, *Three Guineas.* Oxford: Oxford University Press, 1992 [1931]. The context of this quote, which is generally left aside, is indeed important here also. Woolf imagines a man speaking to a female 'outsider', saying that "he is fighting to protect her body, she will reflect upon the degree of physical protection that she now enjoys when the words 'Air Raid Precaution' are written on blank walls. And if he says that he is fighting to protect England from foreign rule, she will reflect that for her there are no 'foreigners', since by law she becomes a foreigner if she marries a foreigner. And she will do her best to make this a fact, not by forced fraternity, but by human sympathy. All these facts will convince her reason (to put it in a nutshell) that her sex and class has very little to thank England for in the past; not much to thank England for in the present; while the security of her person in the future is highly dubious."

generally in an aulic context, used Latin consciously in order to become part of the *Respublica litteraria* that transcended the limits of frontiers.

Women could ignore these political boundaries and show a social identity based on religion. This is demonstrated in the context of the Habsburg Empire and the territory of the Iberian peninsula by Nieves Baranda in her contribution *Beyond Political Boundaries: Religion as Nation in Early Modern Spain.* By living in their own space, for example, behind the permeable walls of Catholic convent communities or as descendants of a prestigious tradition of cultivated noble women, women could link themselves to a transnational institution: either their religious order or the Spanish language, which was an international language at that time.

Along the same lines, the development of monastic foundations and the preservation of Catholic communities of Englishwomen in the convents and schools of France and Flanders, which were composed of French, English, Flemish, Dutch and Spanish nuns, were studied by M. Jesús Pando in *Expatriates: Women Communities, Mobility and Cosmopolitanism in Early Modern Europe: English and Spanish Nuns in Flanders*. In revealing the difficulties implicit in the management of these multilingual transcultural communities, textual evidence poses a challenge to the national discourse on 'Englishness' and opens up new ways of approaching the formation of national and cultural identities in the early modern period.

As we can see, stripped of their national, religious and cultural identity, some women positioned themselves in interstitial spaces. They appropriated a language foreign to them, which empowered them to engage in a narrative of identity repair. This is the case of the *prophetesses des Cévennes* studied by Henriette Goldwyn: under a monarchy claiming to be monolithic, homogeneous and unitary, an ecstatic language emerged and infused part of southern France when a teenage girl, Isabeau Vincent, became a prophetess who espoused an anti-absolutist discourse in recognising only one form of authority: God.

## Women writing the nation

Women's voices had a role in modern times within the framework of Nations and Nationalism, at a time when a monocultural, homosocial literary canon was rising. Appropriation of speech by women was not systematically transgressive, particularly during the development of nationalism in smaller countries, when writing was put at the service of the foundation of a unique and inalienable national culture. Women were placed in the reproductive normativity that supports nationalisms, as mothers holding the future of the nation in their wombs and going on to give birth. In *Women Telling Nations*, researchers examine the gradual progression of different practices: from the devotion to nationalism, led by men, to going beyond the threshold of what is acceptable, expressible and practicable. Whatever the case, access to restrained citizenship on the part of women after revolutionary periods (without voting rights, among many others), as well as the emergence of the nations themselves, led to the birth of the category of authoress in all the 'countries' of Europe in the 19th century. Indeed, the development of print culture, the rise of literacy and the growth of a broad reading public in the early modern period fostered more pluralist writing (periodicals) and dissent.

This was the case in Serbia. Even if asymmetrical access to literacy and schooling shaped different paradigms and values over the centuries, Biljana Dojcinovic and Ivana Pantelic show that there is a clear relationship between national independences and the creation of female schools, women's access to reading/writing activities and their subsequent demands for their rights, in *Early Modern Women Intellectuals in 19th Centuries Serbia: Milica Stojadinovic, Draga Dejanovic and Milica Tomic*. The first Serbian women writers were aware of their nationality and were devoted to writing and the rise of the Serbian Nation.

During the Czech and Slovak National Revivals in the late 18th and early 19th centuries, relatively few women participated in cultural initiatives and, of those who did, most did so to support men. By the mid-19th century, a new generation of women writers were called to serve the country as women were expected to do: by having children and educating them as a new generation of patriots. This is the private situation of Božena Němcová, described by Alejandro Hermida in *Women Writers and the Rise of Czech and Slovak Modern Identity*, but Němcová's literary career was not about renunciation, but about (sometimes dramatic) self-realisation.

Bearing these contributions in mind, we should regard with caution the synergic effect between discourses on emancipation and nation-building with respect to women writers and activists, a denunciation made by Nadezhda Alexandrova in *A Queen of Many Kingdoms: The Autobiography of Rayna Knjaginja*. The heritage of this Bulgarian woman writer is less cherished than the symbolic, monolithic image of her female hero, created by means of biographical accounts and with the support of a previously existing fictional character of the same name, 'Rayna'. Alexandrova proposes a critical rethinking of such cultural phenomena in order to restore the missing parts of complex identities, and she shows Knjaginja as an example of a very common practice: while male authors encouraged women to publish their own work in journals, the price for contributing to the common national goal was that the image of the protagonist was purified of any contamination with improper feelings: female figures functioned as metonymies for a sacrificed and victimised motherland, preserving a patriarchal model of femininity.

Slovenian men also invited Slovenian women to join them in asserting Slovenian culture more strongly. In the context of a multinational empire (the Austro-Hungarian) and the Pan-Slavic movement, Katia Mihurko reflects on *The Representations of Slavic Nations in the Writings of Josipina Turnograiska*, whose work, with its themes from the history of Slavic nations, can be interpreted as her wish to go beyond narrow national limitations, as it shows a tendency towards the openness of Slovenian culture to other literatures.

However, she was not the only one to go beyond frontiers in writing their nation. Another example is Ileana Mihaila's *Dora d'Istria and the Spring Southeast European Nations*. Even though she remained almost unknown in Romania, Dora d'Istria was involved through her writings in the movement to have Balkan people recognised as nationals following the 1848 revolutions. As she never wrote in Romanian, her fellow countrymen could only access her writings via translations or in the original French. This way, she became a true intercultural mediator.

In this process of telling the Nation, the position and role of female citizens in the nation was negotiated by early feminist thinking. This is the case of Marie Linder's Gothic novels, which were studied by Kati Launis in *Towards More Equal Nations: Russian-Finnish Author Marie Linder (1840-1870)*. In the political debate of the time, the novel as a genre offered women writers the possibility of expressing their views on issues such as family, women and marriage, issues that in Finland and Sweden were not just private but also public and national.

Jenny Bergenmar analyses the works of two Swedish writers debating on the relationships of home and state as a false dichotomy in *The Author and the Spinster: Serma Lagerlöf, Frederika Bremer and Women as Nation Builders*. Although in this case the authorship has been overshadowed by the more official reception, reading within female communities and the use of their texts as children's literature on the one hand, and the parallel reading of important women's magazines and readers' letters to Selma Lagerlöf on the other, give a glimpse of the depth of horizontal comradeship. This does not come from any shared idea of the nation and the more vertical real power structure of patriarchal authority; it can be more adequately described as a common response to the public and political crises brought about by the Woman Question.

Women took a step forward in de-transcendentalised nationalism at the end of the 19th and the beginning of the 20th century through literary imagination, when the 'people' became a puzzle for middle class patriots. Viola Parente studies a gendered strategy of telling nation in Finland from neither above nor below, but from 'in between', in accordance with the decadent strategy of ambivalence in *Decadent Women Telling Nations: L. Onerva and Her 'Upstarts'*. If the highly valued 'Kalevalian' epic tradition, which usually figured as a 'male' genre, did not appeal to Onerva as much as the women's lyrical tradition, she used the figure of 'nousukas' (upstarts) to highlight complexities about aspects of gender: on the one hand there was a wish to participate in the way the *fin de siècle* questioned fixed gender roles, while on the other hand there was an urge to speak out on behalf of women, to ponder perennial women's issues from a pronouncedly female viewpoint, all *vis à vis* the issue of (women's) artistry.

## Women in networks

Histories of literature are a paradigmatic example of the manipulation of our memories: the very few women writers who appear in them are presented more as 'curiosities' than authors who deserve to figure in a representative *corpus* of canonical literature. Nevertheless, women writers whose authority would later be denied did manage to find a way of being involved in a network of relationships that was not necessarily national or territorial. Maps, yearbooks, inventories and imaginary genealogies were always sources of legitimation for women writers, while manuscript circulation, translation waves and periodical publications are nowadays considered as an argument for legitimation.

For this reason, in *Women Telling Nations*, we pay special attention to the circulation of reviews, catalogues of exemplary women and collective biographies as a kind of common literature found throughout Europe. Such celebrations of historic womanhood reinforced the idea of gender difference, helping to expand the praiseworthy roles that were available beyond the European upper classes and traditional occupations. At the same time, they were 'selected traditions' based on representative women as a sort of synecdoche, a model womanhood for an imagined community.

From the outset, a survey of compilations on women over six centuries reveals that women have always moved easily across national boundaries: Hilde Hoogenboom, in *The Community of Letters and the Nation State: Bio-Bibliographic Compilations as a Transnational Genre*, demonstrates that these compilations were national in content, their international roots in the classics and the ancient world having been abandoned. They were launched in the tradition of *translatio studii et imperii* in Italy, France, England, Denmark, Germany and Russia. However, from the Renaissance onwards, in the two and a half centuries that separated the works of Christine de Pizan and Brantôme, a major difference arose, which led to the creation of a new category: women writers.

More specifically, in *Anthologies of Female Italian Authors and the Emergence of a National Identity in 19th Century Italy*, Rotraud Von Kulessa compares the roles of compilations in Italian and French literary fields, taking into account the large number of women's dictionaries in Italy throughout the 19th century. She concludes that Italian criticism at the end of the century showed a certain acceptance of women's writing as part of the process of forging Italy's national identity, unlike post-revolutionary France, where an extremely hostile discourse developed towards women who wrote.

A parallel could be drawn between Italy and Finland. In *Histories of Women, Histories of Nation: Biographical Writing as Women's Tradition in Finland, 1880-1920s*, Maarit Leskela shows that biographical writing was one important genre where non-academic women writers took part in constructing national history.[21] The early Finnish biographical tradition of women writers, and more precisely the work of Helmi Krohn, acted as a critic to underline women's input in the culture and history of Finland.

At the same time, as from the 18th century, the tremendous success enjoyed by periodicals, now being published in great numbers, provoked anxious reactions against the plurality of opinions, divergence and debate. Literary magazines were quick to open up space for women to contribute and even edit their own work, partly because, for women, the world of the periodical press bridged the divide between public and private at the very moment the public sphere was being created. Magazines were rooted in a real network of personal relations and performed the function of a bridge. *Women Telling Nations* describes two specific parallel cases.

---

[21] As Alison Booth does in *How to Make It as a Woman. Collective Biographical History from Victoria to the Present*. Chicago: The University of Chicago Press, 2004.

With reference to Greece, and based on the image promoted by female literary magazines published as from 1847, Sirmoula Alexandridou, in *Early Women's Press (three female magazines): A Challenge for the 19$^{th}$ Century East and Greece,* examines the special relationship between women and the nation: taking action instead of submitting; distinguishing themselves through education instead of accepting rigid racial differences; establishing clear goals with regard to their service to the nation, all with a well-rounded personality. What they were in fact asserting was a right to the authority of the intelligentsia.

In the case of Spain, in *Connecting People, Inventing Communities in Faustina Sáez de Melgar's Magazine La Violeta (1862-1866)*, Henriette Partzsch studies how this periodical publication tried to create within its pages a sense of community among a disperse readership. A different narrative, which partly overlapped and partly collided with hegemonic discourse formations on the Spanish nation and women, was created by texts perceived as suitable for women but also by themes that opened up the possibility for them to intervene in society as women, for example, in the fight against slavery. *La Violeta* experimented with a different kind of imagined community, one in which the connection between the public and the private sphere was never completely severed.

## Women looking elsewhere

Women lived in a closed and humanised place (a quiet center of set values) but some of them also needed open space as a domain for unrestricted movement and adventure. Very often, women who read or wrote were branded as different, to the extent of being called not just strange, but foreign or expatriate. Their tendency to learn foreign languages was also thought of as 'ill considered' and an obstacle to efforts made to secure their pure and solid national character. Women were assumed to have a tendency to daydream through the reading of foreign novels, and were not considered to be focused on reality. As a result, rather than being different at home, some of them preferred to be foreigners elsewhere.

This is the case studied by Joanna Partika in *Overpassing State and Cultural Borders: A Polish Female Doctor in 18$^{th}$ Century Constantinople. Regina Salonea Pilsztyn.* Regina Salonea Pilsztyn was a kind of "doctoress of medicine and ophthalmologist", who felt lost and cheated in her native Poland and found her *place* in the Turkish Empire. In the Muslim world, she was allowed to speak in public, to have dealings with both men and women, to travel and collect true-life stories and to tell nations through her diary.

Four Russian women, Catherine II, Ekaterina Dachkova, Mme de Krüdener and Zinaida Volkonskaia also had to look elsewhere. Elena Gretchanaia, in *Between National Myth and Trans-national Ideal: The Representation of Nations in the French Language Writings of Russian Women (1770-1819)* shows these women writing in French and working on the discourse of the Russian nation and its place among other nations, in order to display to all of Europe a country that had long been unknown. Their contribution to the national mythology would not lead, as was often the case with male writings, to mistrust of the western pattern.

Later on, Regina Maria Roche looked for influential ideas and expressions of national identity in Gothic romances set mainly in Ireland, but also in France, Spain and Italy. Begoña Lasa, in *Regina Maria Roche and Ireland: A Problematic Relationship*, studies how implicitly these romances alluded to the benefits of union between Britain and Ireland and urged her audience to pay more attention to women's opinions.

In fact, women often had to read elsewhere. This is what happened in Romania, where French novels became an authoritative form of social and cultural analysis imbued with the highest prestige. Novels by Isabelle de Montolieu, Sophie Cottin, Stephanie de Genlis, Adélaïde de Souza, Juliane von Krüdener and Germaine de Staël were critically acclaimed and became bestsellers of their time. In *Amor Vincit (R)om(a)nia: Reshaping Identities in Romanian mid-19$^{th}$-century Culture*, Carmen Dutu reveals the 'underground' revolution triggered by women's emancipation, when some narrators complained that women's behaviour was to the detriment of national literature, a local adaptation of the broader network of mentalities emerging throughout the space of modern Europe. Reading practices completely transformed intimacy in mid-19$^{th}$-century European culture.

As we have seen, women's freedom has been one of the components of the nationalist movement. This is also true in the case of Turkey, as Senem Timuroglu shows in *Women's Nation from Ottoman to the New Republic in Fatma Aliye and Halide Edip Adivar's Writing*. She focuses on how these two women writers experienced the transition from a multicultural, multilingual and poly-ethnic empire that for centuries encompassed a vast geography, to a nation state based on a monolingual, mono-religious and mono-ethnic society. As they dreamed of a free world for the women of their country, they suggested solutions in their novels and papers.

Readers and writers overcome limits through their own reading and writing of texts. Women readers and women writers live in 'literary nations', where they can choose their neighbours, travel and decide to be born. *Women Telling Nations* presents a public display of these alternative collective identities.[22]

[22] We are greatly indebted to the members of the LEETHY Research Team, at the Complutense University, and particularly to Dolores Romero (ed.), *Naciones Literarias*. Barcelona: Anthropos, 2006, and "La identidad velada: el uso del pseudónimo en algunas literatas de la Edad de Plata" in Joaquín Alvarez Barrientos (coor.), *Imposturas literarias españolas*, Salamanca: Ediciones de la Universidad de Salamanca, 2011:151-170.

# Part I.

# Women Belonging to Nations

# Medieval Women Networking before the Appearance of Nations

*Madeleine Jeay*

ABSTRACT In the 12-13th centuries, well before the emergence of the concept of nation, certain women were given the opportunity to be involved in the political and religious issues of the time. With Ermengard of Narbonne and Eleanor of Aquitaine we see how feudalism, which is based on the prestige of lineages and the ties of vassalage, gave to heiresses the opportunity to participate on the political and cultural level. Devotional writings from and about women reveal strategies of legitimization related to these women themselves and those who supported them: dynasties such as the Plantagenêts and the Capetians or spiritual authorities such as the Preachers and the Mendicants.

WHAT FOLLOWS DEALS WITH AN ERA, the 12-13th centuries, well before the emergence of the concept of nation which, at least for France and England, appears in the 15th century in the context of the Hundred Years' War.[1] The social and political conditions of the period gave to certain women the opportunity to be involved in political and religious issues until the end of the Middle Ages when limitations were imposed on this prerogative. The 12th century can be seen as the apogee of the feudal organization of society, whereas the 13th experiences the establishment of networks of power with the development of towns and the supervision of the Church over the different segments of society through the mendicant orders, especially the Franciscans and Dominicans. The operating principles of feudalism, which are based on the prestige of lineages and the ties of vassalage, in other words the relations of protection and service between fief holders, gave to heiresses the opportunity to participate at the political and cultural levels. We will see with Ermengard of Narbonne and Eleanor of Aquitaine, the two heiresses on whom we will first focus, how these two aspects are interconnected.

---

[1] About the development of nationalisms at the end of the Middle Ages, see Colette Beaune, *Naissance de la nation France*. Paris: Gallimard, 1985.

Supporting poets, such as troubadours or trouvères and sponsoring works of art or literature contributed to the prominence of a court and its lords: one can speak of the ideological use of writers, of forms of a diffuse propaganda from powerful houses and dynasties.[2] Ermengard and Eleanor were experts in this political game in which women had their part to play.

Among the poets who gravitated in their circles, women, the trobaïritz, competed with their male counterparts, the troubadours, in the courts of what is now Southern France, especially around Ermengard. Eleanor's double status of Duchess of Aquitaine and Queen of England put her in an ambiguous position, since she was sometimes Henry II Plantagenêt's partner in his political endeavours and sometimes his opponent, confronting him and even fighting against him in order to advance the rights of her lineage. Saints lives composed by the nuns of the Abbey of Barking which was in the king's orbit, were not without impact in the legitimization of his power over England, as we will see secondly. The writings related to 13$^{th-}$century devout and mystic women on which we will concentrate thirdly, also reveal strategies of mutual legitimization. I will just provide two examples. The first one is the case of beguines from Belgium whose experiences were validated by renowned preachers such as Jacques de Vitry and Thomas de Cantimpré celebrating them in order to decry the Cathar heresy. The second one is illustrated by another beguine, the visionary Douceline de Digne whose life was written by Felipa Porcelet. Felipa who belonged to the Provençal aristocracy, combined to the objectives of the community of pious women established by the mystic, with those of the Franciscans who supported her and those of the Angevin dynasty in Provence and Sicily.

In the cultural environment which allowed the blossoming of troubadour poetry, the women who emerged were eminent members of the aristocracy acting as their protectors. They understood the importance of these poets' production for the reputation of their courts and their lineages. In the context of the present reflection, the few *trobaïritz* who gravitated in their orbit are more interesting by their contribution to this enterprise than by the substance of their poetry.[3] They conformed to the conventions put in place for the

---

[2] According to Jacques Le Goff, this kind of not yet fully planned ideological use of writers and artists can be considered as "pre-propagandist". See Jacques Le Goff, "Conclusions" in Cammarosano, Paolo (ed.). *Le forme della propaganda politica nel due e nel Trecento*. Rome: École française de Rome: 519-520

[3] William D. Paden (ed.). *The Voices of the Trobairitz. Perspectives on the Women Troubadours*. Philadelphia: University of Pennsylvania Press, 1989; Matilda Tomaryn Bruckner, "The Trobairitz" in Akehurst, F.R.R. and Judith M. Davis (eds). *A*

expression of *fine amour* or courtly love, whereas through polemical genres like the *sirventès*, several troubadours sided with their protectors in the battles in which they were engaged. Ermengard of Narbonne's example will allow us to determine the nature of these conflicts and what was implied by the identification with a parentage and a court.

Ermengard was only five when she inherited the county of Narbonne.[4] At the centre of struggles between surrounding powers for its control, Narbonne was weakened by the young age of the heiress who became a prey for marriage candidates. In the 11th century, a few aristocratic families had fought to ensure their domination over the area. The Counts of Barcelona had purchased the title of Counts of Carcassonne and became Counts of Provence by marriage, then again by marriage, kings of Aragon. They had formed strong alliances with the viscounts of Narbonne, the lords of Montpellier, and the Trancavels who were viscounts of Albi, Béziers, Agde, Nîmes and lords of the Carcassès. Facing these alliances, the counts of Toulouse and Saint-Gilles also claimed by marriage the county of Provence; since the beginning of the 11th century. Raymond IV expected to be called count of Toulouse, duke of Narbonne and marquis of Provence. However, even in his town of Toulouse, his sovereignty was not guaranteed because the counts of Poitiers claimed the county for themselves as a result of Willliam IX's marriage to Philippa, daughter of William IV of Toulouse. It was she and not Raymond IV who had inherited the county at their father's death. Her right over the county passed to her son, William X and from him to Eleanor of Aquitaine. Then it was claimed on her behalf by her two husbands, the king of France, Louis VII, and Henry II, king of England.

One can see in this brief overview the importance of the role played by matrimonial strategies and how being an heiress could be both a factor of vulnerability and an advantage as soon as she is not a simple instrument and acts in her own name. Ermengard's marriage at the age of twelve or thirteen to Alphonse Jourdain, count of Toulouse, who wanted to control Narbonne as its legitimate suzerain, was dissolved following the opposition of the count of Barcelona and of Roger I Trancavel to this claim. They arranged for her to marry Bernard of Anduze, a widower with several children, who did not take part in the government of the viscounty. Narbonne was administered by

---

*Handbook of the Troubadours*. Berkeley-Los Angeles: University of California Press, 1995: 201-233.

[4] Fredric L. Cheyette, *Ermengard of Narbonne and the World of the Troubadours*. Ithaca and London: Cornell University Press, 2004.

Ermengard for more than fifty years, from 1143 to 1197. She inspired troubadours who sojourned at her court, praised her beauty and her generosity, and dedicated songs to her. Among them were trobaïritz, possibly the Countess of Die and Azalaïs of Porcairagues who dedicated to the viscountess the only song known from her. The reputation of Ermengard made her a legend. An example can be found in the *vita* of the troubadour Peire Rogier telling how she welcomed him at her court in Narbonne, how he fell in love with her and celebrated her in his songs, so much so that she had to ask him to leave. She was regarded as a paragon of *fine amour*, mentioned by Andreas Capellanus in his *The Art of Courtly Love* among others arbiters of love debates, one of them being Eleanor of Aquitaine.

Eleanor's role in the circulation of courtly lore doctrine is well known: she is the object of a cycle of poems from Bernard of Ventadour, perhaps the most famous of the troubadours.[5] Among the works dedicated to her, Wace's *Roman de Brut* based on Geoffrey of Monmouth's *Historia Regum Britanniae*,[6] is meant to contribute to the genealogical glorification of the ruling houses of Normandy and England who had been linked since the 1066 Conquest.From 1154 when Henry II ascended the throne, until 1173 when his sons and their mother rebelled against him, Eleanor assumed her role of queen which implied being the dedicatee of works finding their raison d'être in issues related to the Plantagenêt empire. The strength of the Plantagenêts but also their weakness came from the number and the diversity of their possessions. They consisted of Henry's own provinces of Anjou and Normandy together with England which he obtained by inheritance and Eleanor's own possessions, Poitou and Aquitaine, she had inherited in 1137. For Eleanor, the need to hold her rights over her territories was a constant preoccupation in her career. This objective can explain why, after having been married at fifteen to the king of France Louis VII, and after a divorce she initiated in great part, she offered her hand to Henry Plantagenêt just two months after the separation. In doing so, she circumvented offers of marriage

---

[5] On Eleanor, see special issues of *Cahiers de civilisation médiévale*, 29, 1986 et 37, 1994; Martin Aurell, "Les Plantagenêt, la propagande et la relecture du passé" in *Culture politique des Plantagenêt (1154-1224)* : 9-34. Poitiers: Université de Poitiers, 2003. Martin Aurell and Noël-Yves Tonnerre (eds). *Plantagenêts et Capétiens: confrontations et héritages*. Turnhout: Brépols, 2006; Jean Flori, *Eleanor d'Aquitaine. La reine insoumise*. Paris: Payot, 2004.

[6] See their respective entries at Wikipedia: http://en.wikipedia.org/wiki/Geoffrey_of_Monmouth, and http://en.wikipedia.org/wiki/Historia_Regum_Britanniae.

that followed immediately and, by giving birth to eight children, she prevented her Aquitaine from being taken by the French king on behalf of their two daughters. It was also her interest for her possessions that determined her to fight with her sons against their father, particularly with Richard the Lionheart who was meant to inherit them.

Legitimizing his accession to the throne and opposing the prestige of his dynasty against the Capetians was crucial for Henry II. Among other clerics commissioned for this enterprise, the nuns of the Abbey of Barking played their role with the writing of saints lives destined for the monastic community and the Plantagenêt court.[7] They are accredited with the *Life of Saint Catherine* by Clemence of Barking, the anonymous *Life of Edward the Confessor*, and the *Life of Saint Audrée* signed by a certain Marie, identified by some critics with Marie de France.[8] Since its foundation in the 7th century, the female monastery of Barking was known for its high level of culture and the possession of a number of Latin and French manuscripts. Its abbess had feudal rights over the Abbey's important possessions. In the middle of the 12th century, it benefited from strong connections with the court since several of its abbesses had lineage alliances with the king's entourage. Following the crisis that confronted Henry II with his former counsellor Thomas Becket after he became archbishop of Canterbury, a conflict which resulted in Becket's murder, his sister Mary was appointed as abbess by the king in contrition for the killing. He later nominated his illegitimate daughter Mathilda to the same position. Such appointments make it clear that the texts written in French in the Abbey were aimed beyond the narrow circle of the nuns, to an audience of high social and cultural level with a good command

---

[7] Aurell, « Les Plantagenets », 9-34; Amaury Chauou, *L'idéologie Plantagenêt. Royauté et monarchie politique dans l'espace Plantagenêt (XIIe-XIIIe siècles)*. Rennes: Presses universitaires de Rennes, 2001, and "*Arthurus redivivus*: royauté arthurienne et monarchie politique à la cour Plantagenêt (1154-1199)" in *Culture politique des Plantagenêt (1154-1224)*. Poitiers: Université de Poitiers, 2003: 67-78.

[8] Dominica Legge, *Anglo-Norman Literature and its Background*. Oxford: The Clarendon Press, 1971; Jocelyn Wogan-Browne, "'Clerc u lai, muïne u dame': Women and Anglo-Norman Hagiography in the Twelfth and Thirteenth Centuries" in Meale, Carol M. (ed.) *Women and Literature in Britain, 1150-1500*. Cambridge: Cambridge University Press, 1993: 61-85; Emma Campbell, *Medieval Saints' Lives: the Gift, Kinship and Community in Old French Hagiography*. Woodbridge: D.S. Brewer, 2008; Carla Bellotto Rossi, *Marie de France et les érudits de Cantorbéry*. Paris: Classiques Garnier, 2009.

of the language of the elite, particularly aristocratic women who did not have access to Latin.[9]

Clémence of Barking may have belonged to the same background since she has been identified with Clémence de Fougères, a sister of Henry II's chaplain. Her *Life of Saint Catherine*, the first known text in French by a woman, was actually dedicated to "gentils pulceles / E vus, nobles barnesses beles" (v. 2537-38).[10] The popular legend of St Catherine of Alexandria could be a source of inspiration for them not only as an example of martyr to the Christian faith, but as a learned woman whose knowledge competed with that of the philosophers and scholars of her time and who managed to convert to Christianity the fifty doctors against which she had been ordered to engage in a public debate by the emperor Maximian. With the *Life of St Audrée* and the *Life of St Edward the Confessor*, we see a combination of hagiographic legend and the history of English dynasties. In the 7th century, saint Audrée or saint Ethelrede, remained virgin in spite of her two marriages, imposed on her by her father, the king of East Anglia. An example of chaste marriage, like Edward the Confessor, she emblematized the sacred dimension that kings claimed for themselves. In her prologue, Marie draws attention to the saint's royal blood and to the number of holy women who descended from her. Her mother Herswitha was baptised at the time of the conversion of her father, the king of Northumbria, and she ended her life in a French Benedictine convent she had endowed with her dower. Herswitha's three other daughters were also declared saints, as well as her sister saint Hilde. We will see with Douceline de Digne that this notion of the sacredness of royal dynasties was still alive at the end of the 13th century.

Two lives of St Edward the Confessor were intended for Henry II, one in Latin by the Cistercian abbot Aelred of Rievaulx which is dedicated to him, and the one in French by the anonymous nun of Barking who praises the "gloriüs rei Henri / Ki de ceo saint lignage eissi" (v. 107-108).[11] Henry's

---

[9] About this audience, see David N. Bell, *What Nuns Read: Books and Libraries in Medieval English Nunneries*. Kalamazoo: Cistercian Publications, 1995; Anne Clark Bartlett, "Reading Medieval Women Reading Devotional Literature" in *Male Authors, Female Readers: Representation and Subjectivity in Middle English Devotional Literature*. Ithaca: Cornell University Press, 1995: 1-33.

[10] "Gentle maidens and you noble fair baronesses". See also the electronic edition of these lives: http://homepage.mac.com/dianejak/MARGOTtest/campsey/cmphomef.html

[11] The "glorious King Henry / Who came from this holy lineage". In Aelred's *Genealogia regum Anglorum* ("Genealogy of the Kings of the English") written

interest in reviving the memory of the king thanks to whom William the Conqueror could reign over England, is easily understandable. As a result of conflicts over the succession to the throne and the invasion of the country by Danish pretenders, Edward had taken refuge with his maternal uncle in Normandy, where he stayed twenty years or so. When he finally acceded to the throne, he married Edith of Wessex, but not having consummated their marriage, he designated his grandnephew William of Normandy, the future Conqueror, as his successor. Edward's canonization in 1161 gave to Henry II the possibility to confirm the continuity of the dynastic link with the Anglo-Saxon monarchy and, thanks to this predecessor, to reinforce and sanctify a sovereignty over England which had still to be legitimized. This simple count of Anjou, who inherited Normandy that had been conquered by his father, became king of England through his mother Mathilda who was the daughter and heir of king Henry I, after a struggle to have his rights recognized. The worship of Edward the Confessor echoes the veneration in which the kings of England held St Edmond who died at the end of the 9$^{th}$ century and who had symbolized the Anglo-Saxon resistance to the Danes. The *Life of Edward the Confessor* by the nun of Barking begins with a brief genealogy of the English kings, an indication of the desire of the Normans living in England to build an English identity through its inscription in the Anglo-Saxon past.While he worked to be recognized as the Confessor's legitimate successor, Henry II had to carry out the unity of the two entities. A copy of the *Life of Edward the Confessor* circulated in France during the reign of St Louis who can be himself considered as a descendant of the holy king through his mother Blanche of Castile, Henry II and Eleanor's granddaughter.

We will return later to St Louis since chronology invites us to first consider the development of beguine communities in Belgium. Their appearance at the beginning of the 13$^{th}$ century corresponds to the evolution of society I described earlier, namely the expansion of an urban culture characterized on the one hand, by the increasing importance of trade and consequently the beginning of a monetary form of wealth, and on the other by consideration given to lay spirituality, especially to women. This lay spirituality movement was accompanied by access restrictions to traditional monastic orders, especially for women. It benefited from the expansion of new ones like the Preachers and the Mendicants whose purpose was precisely to take care of lay spirituality. In doing so, these orders provided an answer to

---

around 1153-54, we find saint Margaret of Scotland, the devout king Alfred and Edward the Confessor among the descendants and family.

what appeared to the Church to be a danger, the propagation of heretic movements like the Cathars who welcomed women. The combination of these elements explains why the new orders, particularly Franciscans and Dominicans, took interest in beguines, these women from urban classes of artisans and merchants who wanted to devote themselves to a religious life. Either because they were not allowed to enter a convent or by choice, they lived together in communities without taking vows. They led active lives in the towns where they gave themselves up to occupations often related to the weaving and clothing trades. Not being part of an official institution, family or convent, the beguines were seen as somewhat marginal and ran the risk of upsetting ecclesiastical authorities. In such a context one can understand the mutual benefit that important religious figures such as Jacques de Vitry and Thomas de Cantimpré could get from their collaboration: they wanted to promote as examples of orthodox feminine behaviour the biographies they wrote on their mystic subjects. When Jacques de Vitry undertook Marie d'Oignies's Life that would be used as a model for many biographies of mystic women until the end of the 15$^{th}$ century, he explicitly introduced her as an instrument of the fight against heresy.[12] In return, he won recognition of the beguines from the pope. The Dominican Thomas de Cantimpré carried on this effort with a continuation of Marie d'Oignies's Life and biographies of Christina of Saint-Trond, famous for her astonishing manifestations of mystic frenzy, of Margaret of Ypres and Lutgard of Aywières. Their kind of vocation and spiritual devotion, founded on asceticism and characterized by charismatic episodes such as visions and ecstasies, would become the norm for a great number of women whose experiences became publicized either by their own testimony or by their biographers' account.

Among these women, Douceline de Digne's journey combined the aspects we have seen so far. She came from the family of a rich merchant in the Provençal town of Digne who, as soon as the Franciscans settled in Provence at the very beginning of the thirteenth century, devoted themselves to helping the poor and the sick as St Francis had recommended. Hugues, Douceline's brother, was a distinguished Franciscan preacher admired by St

---

[12] About the influence of these mystics and their biographies, see Madeleine Jeay and Kathleen Garay, "'To Promote God's Praise and her Neighbour's Salvation'. Strategies of Authorship and Readership among Mystic Women in the Later Middle Ages" in Gilleir, Anke, Alicia C. Montoya and Suzan Van Dijk (eds). *Women Writing Back / Writing Women Back. Transnational Perspectives from the Late Middle Ages to the Dawn of the Modern Era.* in *Intersections. Interdisciplinary Studies in Early Modern Culture* 16, 2010: 23-50.

Louis who conferred with him on his way back from the seventh crusade in 1254. She herself engaged in practices of devotion and asceticism according to the model described in the biographies of beguines, and received in return the usual God's graces such as revelations, the gift of prophecy and ecstatic experiences, and even in her case, levitation. She gathered around her, first in Hyères around 1240, then in Marseilles around 1250, a group of devout women following the beguines' example. It is possible that her brother and spiritual advisor who had spent time in Paris just before she established her first house, had informed her about the communities in Belgium. Her reputation as a mystic, with the dramatic manifestations characteristic of her ecstatic episodes, determined the significant role she played in Provence, politically as well as at the religious level. Her renown allowed her to build with the Count of Provence, Charles I, a relationship that, once again, was advantageous to both. It was triggered by a dream in which the Countess, who was pregnant, saw a beguine comforting her in assuring that she would give birth without difficulty. Douceline was called to the Count's court where she experienced one of her ecstasies. After the Countess's safe delivery, she benefited from a privileged status as Charles's counselor. They exchanged letters in which she advised him about ruling the kingdom of Sicily, bestowed on him as the result of a negotiation where the views of his brother the king of France St Louis and the pope had been determining factors. In exchange, Douceline found support for her communities in Hyères and Marseilles. She also managed to restore the Count's links with the Franciscans who had provoked his hostility because they had sided with Marseilles when the town rebelled against the authority of this count of Anjou who ruled the county of Provence as the result of his marriage with its heiress Beatrice.

The details of Douceline's biography and her mystic manifestations come from the account written by a fellow beguine, Felipa Porcelet who belonged to a Provençal aristocratic family. The only witness of the text, the manuscript Paris BnF fr. 13503, is the result of the updating around 1315, of a first version that can be dated in 1297. With the *Life of St Douceline*, Felipa wrote one of the most remarkable works of Occitan literature. Her personality and the date of its composition provide some indications about her objectives. Moreover they are a convincing illustration that the experiences of these women and the accounts reporting them were related the structure of high medieval society and the ways it represented itself.

Felipa came from an influential family that had been drawn to Sicily by Charles I who, in attracting the Provençal nobility to the kingdom, found a way to control it while cutting it from its roots. As a consequence, he was also able to strengthen his power over Provence. When Felipa lost her husband, she joined Douceline's community where she immediately began to play an important role. While the mystic was its spiritual mother, Felipa concentrated on its administration. She provided for its material prosperity through her investments with artisans and merchants of Marseilles, the purchase of land and the rental of properties to the beguines. The 1297 version of the *Life* was probably written after consultation with the members of the community.[13] Its first audience were the beguines themselves with the objective of promoting the mystic's holiness and bringing her memory to the younger ones who did not know her and would then have at their disposal an official version of her journey. The narration of several miracles of the saint, like a healing that occurred during a public reading of Douceline's *Life,* shows moreover that Felipa looked for ways of validating her own work. In order to understand what was at stake, the *Life of St Douceline* must be related to Louis IX's canonization on August 6, 1297 and to the death of his grandnephew Louis of Anjou, a Franciscan and bishop of Toulouse, who was himself canonized in 1307. It appears that Felipa wanted to associate Douceline with these Capetian saints, a probable hypothesis if we consider that Charles I had been engaged in the promotion of the Capetian dynasty as a sacred lineage. He had campaigned for his brother's canonization and asked to Agnes of Harcourt, a lady-in-waiting of their sister Isabelle who was a nun in the Abbey of Longchamp, to write the *Life of Isabelle de France* in order to promote her holiness. His purpose was in fact to confirm his legitimacy as founder of his dynasty in Sicily, an objective that was carried on after him by his son Charles II whose marriage with Mary of Hungary contributed to reinforce the notion of sacred dynasty. The Arpadian dynasty in Hungary itself drew on the existence of saints in the royal family, especially Elisabeth of Hungary who was revered for her life of mortification and dedication to the poor.

Even if identifying oneself to a sovereign or the emblematic image of a lineage represents the main unifying factor in the Middle Ages, one cannot totally deny the importance of the 'proto-nationalist' sense of belonging to a territory. In Eleanor and Ermengard's cases that goes without saying since, as

---

[13] Madeleine Jeay, "La Vie de sainte Douceline par Felipa Porcelet: les mobiles d'une hagiographe du XIII$^{e}$ siècle" in Guy Poirier (ed.). *Dix ans de recherche sur les femmes écrivains de l'Ancien Régime: influences et confluences. Mélanges offerts à Hannah Fournier*. Québec: Presses de l'Université Laval, 2008: 17-36.

legitimate heiresses, they both emanate from their land. The situation is different for Henry II and his ancestor William the Conqueror who had to be legitimized through validating campaigns in which women took part either as patronesses such as Eleanor or as authors in the case of the nuns of Barking. Originating from Normandy or Anjou, and having established French as the language of the court and the elite, both William and Henry had to confront a strong sense of identity emanating from the Anglo-Saxon rulers. In the 13th, Charles of Anjou, St Louis's brother, faced the same kind of situation first in Provence when he became count after his marriage with Beatrice of Provence, then in Sicily granted to him by pope Clement IV. In both cases the mystic Douceline de Digne acted as mediator and advisor. When several towns rebelled against him in Provence, especially Marseilles where she had settled one of her communities of beguines, she contributed to his reconciliation with the Franciscans who had sided with the town. At the time of the discussions about Sicily, the holy woman encouraged him strongly, saying that he should not hesitate to accept this undertaking which had been offered to him by the will of God. [...] She said he could be sure of victory and would triumph, with the help of the Lord and his mother, and of Christ's standard-bearer, My Lord Saint Francis. But she told him that, after those things that God would do for him and through him, he should be careful not to be carried away with pride, as the first king of Israël had been in his ingratitude. For if he did that, God would reproach him as he had done to Saul when he took his kingdom away from him.[14]

In spite of her warnings, Charles's exacting administration led to a revolt that ended in the massacre of the Sicilian Vespers in which Felipa's brother, William, was the only Frenchman who was not killed. These examples illustrate that the prevalence of the notion of lineage in the Middle Ages does not exclude a tension with the sense of territorial entity and the community it is supposed to identify and embody, a tension that would persist in the centuries to come since the preponderance of national identities does not rule out more archaic forms of solidarity. They show how women played their part in that complex texture of identifying structures.

[14] Kathleen Garay and Madeleine Jeay (tr.). *The Life of Saint Douceline, a Béguine of Provence.* Woodbridge: Boydelll and Brewer, 2001: 78.

## Select Bibliography

### A. Primary Sources

Field, Sean L. 2003. *The Writings of Agnes of Harcourt. The "Life of Isabelle of France" and the "Letter on Louis IX and Longchamp"* Notre Dame: University of Notre Dame.

Garay, Kathleen and Madeleine Jeay. (tr.). 2001. *The Life of Saint Douceline, a Béguine of Provence.* Woodbridge: Boydelll and Brewer.

MacBain, William. (ed.). 1964. *The Life of St Catherine by Clemence of Barking*. Oxford: Anglo-Norman Text Society.

McCash, Hall, June and Judith Clark Barban (eds). 2006. *The Life of Saint Audrey, a Text by Marie de France*. Jefferson and London: McFarland.

Newman, Barbara and Margot H. King, (eds). 2008. *Thomas of Cantimpré. The Collected Saints' Lives: Abbot John of Camtimpré, Christina the Astonishing, Margaret of Ypres, and Lutgard of Aywieres.* Turnhout: Brepols.

Södergård, Östen. (ed.). 1948. *La vie d'Edouard le Confesseur; poème anglo-normand du XII^e^ siècle.* Uppsala: Almqvist & Wiksell.

—. 1955. *La vie seinte Audree, poème anglo-normand du XIII^e^ siècle.* Uppsala: Lundequistska bokhandeln; Wiesbaden, Harrassowitzt.

Vitry de, Jacques and Thomas de Cantimpré. 1998. *Two Lives of Marie d'Oignies,* (tr. Margot H. King and Hugh Feiss). Toronto: Peregrina.

### B. Secondary Sources

Aurell, Martin, (ed.). 2003a. *Culture politique des Plantagenêt (1154-1224).* Poitiers: Université de Poitiers.

—. 2003b. "Les Plantagenêt, la propagande et la relecture du passé" in *Culture politique des Plantagenêt (1154-1224)*, 9-34. Poitiers: Université de Poitiers.

—. and Noël-Yves Tonnerre. (eds). 2006. *Plantagenêts et Capétiens: confrontations et héritages*. Turnhout: Brépols.

Beaune, Colette. 1985. *Naissance de la nation France*. Paris: Gallimard.

Bell, David N. 1995. *What Nuns Read: Books and Libraries in Medieval English Nunneries*. Kalamazoo: Cistercian Publications.

Bellotto Rossi, Carla. 2009. *Marie de France et les érudits de Cantorbéry.* Paris: Classiques Garnier.

Campbell, Emma. 2008. *Medieval Saints' Lives: the Gift, Kinship and Community in Old French Hagiography.* Woodbridge: D.S. Brewer.

Chauou, Amaury. 2001. *L'idéologie Plantagenêt. Royauté et monarchie politique dans l'espace Plantagenêt (XIIe-XIIIe siècles)*. Rennes: Presses universitaires de Rennes.

—. 2003. "*Arthurus redivivus*: royauté arthurienne et monarchie politique à la cour Plantagenêt (1154-1199)" in *Culture politique des Plantagenêt (1154-1224)*. Poitiers: Université de Poitiers: 67-78.

Cheyette, Fredric L. 2004. *Ermengard of Narbonne and the World of the Troubadours*. Ithaca and London: Cornell University Press.

Clark Bartlett, Anne. 1995. "Reading Medieval Women Reading Devotional Literature" in *Male Authors, Female Readers: Representation and Subjectivity in Middle English Devotional Literature*. Ithaca: Cornell University Press: 1-33.

Flori, Jean. 2004. *Eleanor d'Aquitaine. La reine insoumise*. Paris: Payot.

Jeay, Madeleine and Kathleen Garay. 2010 "'To Promote God's Praise and her Neighbour's Salvation'. Strategies of Authorship and Readership among Mystic Women in the Later Middle Ages" in Gilleir, Anke, Alicia C. Montoya and Suzan Van Dijk (eds). Women Writing Back / Writing Women Back. Transnational Perspectives from the Late Middle Ages to the Dawn of the Modern Era. in *Intersections. Interdisciplinary Studies in Early Modern Culture* 16: 23-50.

—. 2008. "La Vie de sainte Douceline par Felipa Porcelet: les mobiles d'une hagiographe du XIIIe siècle" in Poirier, Guy (ed.). *Dix ans de recherche sur les femmes écrivains de l'Ancien Régime: influences et confluences. Mélanges offerts à Hannah Fournier*. Québec: Presses de l'Université Laval: 17-36.

Legge, Dominica. 1971. *Anglo-Norman Literature and its Background*. Oxford: The Clarendon Press.

Le Goff, Jacques. 1994. "Conclusions" in Cammarosano, Paolo (ed.). *Le forme della propaganda politica nel due e nel Trecento*. Rome: École française de Rome: 519-520.

Paden, William D. (ed.). 1989. *The Voices of the Trobairitz. Perspectives on the Women Troubadours*. Philadelphia: University of Pennsylvania Press.

Tomaryn Bruckner, Matilda. 1995. "The Trobairitz" in Akehurst, F. R. R. and Judith M. Davis (eds). *A Handbook of the Troubadours*. Berkeley-Los Angeles: University of California Press: 201-233.

Wogan-Browne, Jocelyn. 1993. "'Clerc u lai, muïne u dame': Women and Anglo-Norman Hagiography in the Twelfth and Thirteenth Centuries" in Meale, Carol M. (ed.). *Women and Literature in Britain, 1150-1500*. Cambridge: Cambridge University Press: 61-85.

# *Latine Loquor*: Women Acquiring *Auctoritas* (Portugal 1500-1800)

*Inês de Ornellas e Castro*
UNIVERSIDADE NOVA DE LISBOA

ABSTRACT This chapter examines the trajectory of some Portuguese women who belonged to court life in the 16th and 17th centuries, and reflects on the way they chose to enter into literature. The prefaces to their translations and works written in Latin, but presented as citations and translations, reveal they felt connected to the canonic literature they studied and that this shaped their work. When studying translation, we find women revealing their *auctoritas inter pares*, participating in the public debates of their own time without losing the feminine qualities required of them by society.

## 1. *Auctoritas* as a literary concept

*«ut quae apud hominem et gratia et auctoritate vales plurimum» [as among men your merit is immense due to your grace and authority] João Rodrigues de Sá Menezes*

AS AN EPIGRAPH, I chose a brief citation from an undated letter written by the famous Portuguese Renaissance poet Sá de Menezes[1] addressed to Joana Vaz (fl. 1535) where he recognizes her intellectual faculties with two interesting substantives: grace, in the strict sense of merit, and authority. Although *gratia* is not unusual for a lettered woman, and we can find it in the special context of lives of illustrious women as well as in hagiographies, *auctoritas* could seem rather unexpected. The name of Joana Vaz is widely unknown; only a handful of late 20th century scholars have shown interest in her work. She belongs to a number of marginalised women that we, in the

[1] See Manuscript F.G. 6368 at Biblioteca Nacional de Portugal.

Portuguese Women Writers project,[2] intend to rescue from oblivion. If female authors have remained silent, such silence is more constrained when we remember that for many centuries it was generally accepted that women from the post-classical world had no linguistic competence for an acquired and gendered language such as Latin.

The Latin word *auctoritate,* applied to Joana's talent by Sá de Menezes and other contemporary writers and scholars,[3] leaves no doubt: women can be empowered by *auctoritas*, an *auctoritas* they never claim for themselves, but others, generally male, praise. But what do we mean by *auctoritas?*[4] Can we merely translate it as 'authority'? Although there are several meanings to consider, such as 'model, influence, advice, prestige' etc, the semantics are always clarified by the context. We are obliged to distinguish between traditional notions of authority, textual and institutional, intellectual and empire and church related.

In a pre-modern socio-political European context, framed by the period from the Renaissance until the 18th century (the centuries we intend to focus on here), women were disempowered in public life. Excluded from public power, women were not even considered citizens, and therefore benefited from no real authority in the public sphere, unless they were rulers by right, and these rare cases are always perceived as exceptions. But besides being deprived of *potestas*, an enlarged concept of power understood as an *auctoritas* with social functions, were women also deprived of *auctoritas*? While the concept of *potestas* is restricted to a social function, *auctoritas,* that Cicero (*Top.* 19.73) considered also as a kind of natural *authority* lying especially in the *virtus,* can be used in the private and familiar spheres. What kind of *auctoritas* was, then, a woman allowed to exercise? We are obliged to perceive this concept in a literary context as a kind of restricted 'authority' in the republic of letters based on the recognition of intellectual skills, supported by having direct access – via Latin – to the authority of ancient authors,

---

[2] All the Latinate women referred in this chapter are in *Women Writers.* On line at http://www.databasewomenwriters.nl.

[3] In the same Manuscript collection we can find letters address to Joana Vaz and correspondence between scholars referring to her knowledge by Rodrigo Sanches, Baltazar de Teive and António Pinheiro (dated from 1533-34). Her achievements in Portuguese court as the princesses' tutor are comparable to those of Doña Beatriz Galindez, known as La Latina, queen's Isabel of Castile tutor.

[4] *Auctoritas,* a technical socio-juridical meaning first found in law, is a typical Roman concept, used in the political and moral contexts with no Greek equivalent. The etymology of this substantive abstract derives from *augeo* (to increase) and is connected to *auctor* (the one who increases or is responsible by).

Church Authorities church fathers and the Bible. In a Europe where Humanistic values were increasingly becoming the foundation of all knowledge and the *Respublica litteraria* transcended the limits of political frontiers, the few learned women who were educated like men, generally in aulic contexts, *Latine loquuntur* [spoke Latin]. This aulic context and its entourage can be explained by the fact that when women were expected to be in charge of political power, to handle royal authority, they were encouraged to speak, read and write in Latin – examples include the daughters of Isabel of Castile[5] and Habsburg princesses in general.[6]

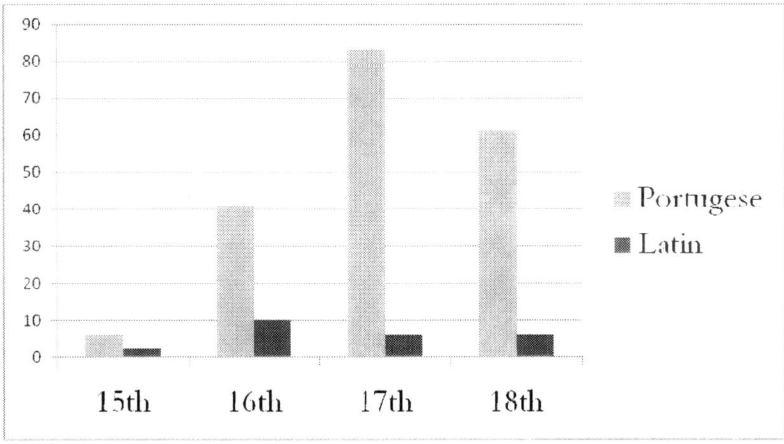


Table 1: Portuguese female writing Portuguese and Latin between the 15th and 18th centuries.

By mastering the language that allowed access to both literary and scientific knowledge, between the 15th and 18th centuries, some 24 women, (a provisory number see percentage in Table 1 and final Index), became indeed part of a transnational cultural space due to the fact that they could write in Latin or translate Latin, and were thus recognized by male scholars as equals, being sometimes considered superior *auctoritates*, like Joana Vaz. It is the political

[5] For numerous references to Catharine of Aragon's language skills, in particularly the use of Latin, see Antonia Fraser, *The Wives of Henry VIII*, New York: Vintage, 1994: 9-48. She commissioned the *Institutio mulieris chrsitiannae* to Luis Vives for the education of her daughter Maria Tudor.

[6] Jane Stevenson, *Woman Latin Poets: language, gender, and Authority, from Antiquity to the Eighteenth Century*. Oxford: Oxford University Press, 2005: 205.

and social context of each European country that defines the real opportunity to exercise intellectual *auctoritas*.

## 2. Sources and methodology

Do we know many female authors before the 19th century? Where can we find their works? How many mastered Latin? We could begin with questions, and, indeed, my task has been to answer these questions. In order to find women proficient in Latin, I was obliged to enlarge my scope with the help of members of this project.[7] I had to work with very flexible criteria: some testimonies would not be considered sufficient to prove the existence of a male author. To be an author, or to be perceived as an author, are, indeed, two different realities, especially if we add gender into the equation. As a fact, the further we go back in time the more we find second hand evidence of these women's production. Sometimes I had to rely on traces of female authorship sustained by reception – usually by erudite and bibliophiles – hoping that one day I would be able to find the real texts. Such is the case for the works of 8 of our 24 female writers. Fortunately, titles can also be helpful to begin constructing an itinerary according to subjects and, above all, they show that women were active, listened to, and admired in circles of likeminded female and male scholars.

Table 2 presented below (combined with the Index of authors, centuries and works at the end) may, indeed, be considered a starting point for discussion.

Until now we have found 24 Latinate women whose work can be distributed – and may be classified – as above:

---

[7] *Portuguese Women Writers project I and II* financed by the Foundation for Science and Technology hosted by FCSH – Universidade Nova de Lisboa.

| Manuscript texts (total 16) | | | Printed texts (total 16) | | |
|---|---|---|---|---|---|
| Subjects | | | Subjects | | |
| Original In Latin | 10 | Poetry: 4<br>Epistles: 5 (authors)<br>Religion: 3<br>Commentaries on the classics: 1 | Original In Latin | 7 | Poetry: 4<br>Epistles: 1<br>Biography: 1<br>Philosophy: 1 |
| Adaptation In Latin | 5 | Religion: 2<br>History: 2 | Adaptation In Latin | 1 | Religion: 1 |
| Translation | 0 | | Translation From Latin | 8 | Religion: 3<br>History: 2<br>Classical texts: 3 |

Table 2: Total manuscripts and printed texts by genre

## 2.1 Manuscripts/ printed texts

At a first glance, the number of manuscripts equals the printed works. However, if we distinguish posthumous editions, the result differs: indeed three Renaissance authors were published only in the 19th century, and one of Marquise of Alorna's (1750-1839) translations, *The abduction of Proserpine [O roubo de Proserpina]*, also received a posthumous edition (1844). Manuscript or 'scribal writings' became slightly more dominant. In Portugal, as in most of Europe, from the Renaissance onwards, only a minority of women learned, wrote, or translated in Latin, and, obviously, very few published in Latin; furthermore, circulation was mainly by manuscript. Nevertheless, this does not mean they could not have reached major audiences: manuscript circulation was very common in Europe and, especially in Portugal and Spain, which were considerably affected, and would be up to the end of the 18th century, by harsh Inquisitorial censorship,[8]

[8] Inquisition is the name by which is generally known the *Tribunal do Santo Oficio*, created by a bull dating from 23 May 1536. The persecutions were intensified in 1539 when King John's III brother, Infante D. Henrique, became the Inquisitor General. In Portugal also had a council of local bishops called *Ordinario*, and the King's censorship, designated by *Desembargo do Paço*. Due to the reforms operated in the

as manuscripts allow faster dissemination while eluding institutional surveillance.

This fact explains why few texts written by Portuguese Latinate women – as we shall refer to those proficient in Latin – did not survive, but direct evidence, such as epistolography, like the quote on Joana Vaz we began with, and poems written by illustrious men, remain and must be considered valuable testimony – as should engraved stones be found in old churches. Other well-known proofs, which we cannot always trust, are those compendia or catalogues of Illustrious Women,[9] a kind of literature common throughout Europe, mainly from the Renaissance onwards, and modelled on Plutarch's *Parallel Lives* and Valerius Maximus *Facta et dicta memorabilia* [*Memorable Deeds and Sayings*], which reflect the anomalous status attributed to learned females. Nevertheless, for some learned ladies, these are the only kinds of sources available. Can we put these women aside just because the sources are scarce and differ from what we usually find for more recent periods, in particular the 19th century? If we do so, we are perpetuating the silence imposed upon them by society, by time and by traditional scholarship. As a fact, and especially until the 19th century, female literary discourse has been almost invisible, both in contemporary testimonies and in those posterior '*monumenta*' of national literatures configured by anthologies and histories of literature, written by men, who continue to reveal the same paternalistic pattern of the 16th century catalogues. Histories of literature, all the way down to the most up-to-date internet site, are a paradigmatic example of manipulation of our memory, and they have played a major role in projecting the image of women writers: the very few who appear are presented rather as 'curiosities' than authors deserving to figure in a representative *corpus* of canonical literature.

---

18th century by King Joseph I, in 1768 was created the *Real Mesa Censória*, that assimilates the previous three organisms.

[9] In Portugal these compendia are more popular in the 17th and 18th centuries. Good examples are Frei Luiz dos Anjos, *Jardim de Portugal em que se da noticia de alguas Sanctas, & de outras molheres illustres em virtude, as quais nascerão, ou viuerão, ou estão sepultadas neste Reino, & suas coquistas.* Coimbra: Impresso em casa de Nicolao Carualho Impressor del Rey, 1626; and Damião de Froes Perim, *Theatro Heroino, Abecedário Histórico e Catálogo das Mulheres Ilustres em Armas, Letras, Acções Heróicas e Artes Liberais,* Lisboa Ocidental, Officina Sylvania e Academia real, 1736-40, 2 vols. In the last title, the name 'heroino', from the Latin feminine 'herois', in vogue after Ovid's *Heroides*, signifies, as in other contexts from Renaissance on, a female writer.

Were they really so few until the 19th century? If we want an answer for this, we have to ask more questions (a classical hermeneutic): Did they consider themselves writers? What literary genres were they cultivating and what were their subjects? As our common aim is to put women writers on the map of European literature, the specificity of our sources as well as the non-existence of traditional categories capable of contextualizing these women's works in histories of literature prompt us to consider that methodologies, which, obviously, directly reflect the type of sources available, cannot be the same for all periods.

## 2.2 Originals, adaptations and translations

Once we agree on the importance of adopting methodologies according to sources and available materials, we will be ready to change concepts. The first would be the concept of authorship, because it is connected to the importance of reception in the perception of what an author is.

Although the distinction between manuscript and published text has been relevant to external criticism, when analyzing the concept of authorship (for both sexes), the categories 'original', 'adaptation' and 'translation' can also involve problems connected to authorship, or, at least, to the perception of authorship that these women acknowledge for themselves. When resorting to internal criticism, we began to analyze some published texts presented as adaptations or even translations by female writers and came across two distinct options: either they simply do not consider themselves writers because they are not presenting originals but assuming a process of rewriting, or they vindicate a subtle authorship as they present the intention of rewriting a text belonging to a codified genre[10] (genres that have a poetical tradition edified in Ancient canons), according to personal norm. The work of D. Leonor de Noronha (1488 – 1563), a female translator in the Renaissance under court patronage, is a good example. She applied to historiography (her historical translations deserve more discussion ahead) translating humanist Marcus Antonius Sabellicus [11] (1436 – 1506). By no means does she present herself as a conservative translator. Although she announces that it is a word-

[10] For the concepts of norm and generic code, see Gian Biagio Conte, *The Rhetoric of Imitation: Genre and Poetic Memory in Virgil and Other Latin Poets*. Translated By Charles Segal, New York: Cornell University Press, 1996.

[11] This is the Latinized name of Marcantonio Sabellico, who explored various genres and remained famous as a Renaissance Venice historian.

for-word translation, she intervenes, cutting parts and adding others, practices that allow her to find her own poetical norm in a codified genre:

> I translated, Madam, the Sabellicus's chronic this way because it is very general and he arrived in narrating until the time of the Kings your grandparents [...]; and as it is good Latin and those who were taught will profit from collating their Latin with our language. Because the intention that presided this work was translating word for word, putting aside a few words which were unnecessary in our language but needed for the elegance of Latin, and adding others needed for the language and pointless for maintaining Latin elegance. I divide it into chapters to cause less boredom to readers. And because in some aspects Sabellicus is too short, I add a little more [of my own] and put it in the margins of this first Aeneid, and in the others I introduce the additions right inside the chapters.

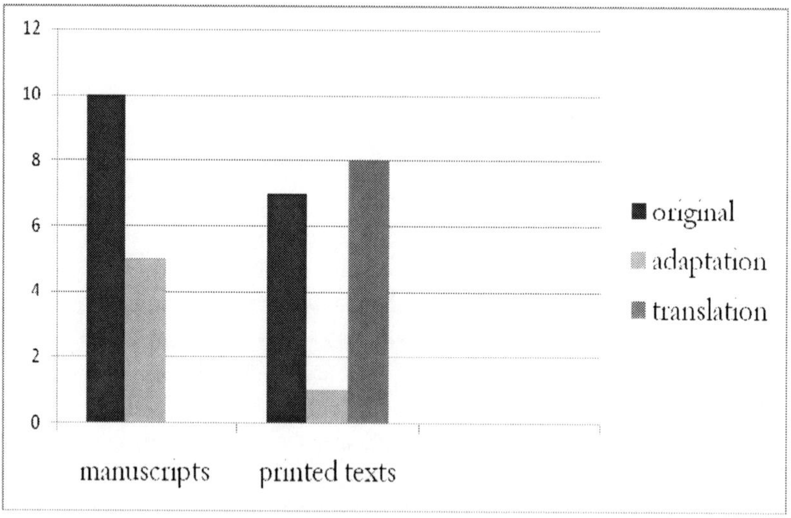


Table 3: Manuscripts/ printed texts: originals, adaptations and translations.

Between the Renaissance and Enlightenment, as we can see by the numbers in the Table 3, the universe of Portuguese Latinate females who presented themselves as translators is very restricted, only 7 cases, but it increases to 12 when we add the 5 adaptations (4 in manuscript versions and 1 printed). But where does translation end and adaptation begin? There is another possibility deserving attention, especially while analyzing female production: D. Leonor de Noronha could be a good example, that, whether consciously or not, both processes, translation and adaptation, are strategies to become authors. This fact explains why most printed texts are presented as adaptations or translations, as if these are minor works. Translation, as we all know, has been traditionally considered by criticism to be a derivative activity. The importance of translation to spread ideas, to edify knowledge and shape our cultural values, began to be recognized by scholars – mostly with the increase of cultural studies – only two decades ago. Translation Studies became autonomous only in the 1980s.[12]

During the periods focused on here, especially until Enlightenment, with most texts translated under royal patronage (as those by D. Leonor de Noronha, Luisa Sigeia or Publia Hortencia de Castro) or by princesses, we can observe a common objective: women wanted to educate themselves and others and also to participate in contemporary intellectual debates. But while in the Renaissance Latin writing as well as translation allowed them to take part in a transnational cultural movement expressed in Latin, as we approach the Enlightenment, and Latin is supplanted by the teaching of vernacular languages, translation came to be perceived as a useful tool, and subjects elected for translation – with more emphasis on the classics – are a good insight into their motivations.

## 2.3 Literary genres and subjects of originals and translations

Printed texts offer a greater variety of subjects than manuscripts. Indeed the latter, where the category 'originals' is more thoroughly represented (10), evoke what could be perceived as the female restricted world of intimacy: epistles (5), poetry of various subjects (4) and religious themes (4). Is this accurate? Were the epistles in the vernacular we might associate them with mere communications between relatives and friends, but once written in Latin, they say much more about these women: they are communicating with the world. That is why those who received them (the main percentage are letters addressed to male scholars) generated publicity among their correspondents and fixed them for posterity.

This episode with the celebrated Latinate Joana Vaz, one of the most respected humanists of her time, known as The Philosopher, is revealing: she was considered an authority and consulted by several published male

[12] For this subject see André Lefevere, *Translating, Rewriting and the Manipulation of Literary Fame*. London and New York: Routlege, 1992.

authors.[13] Baltasar de Teive, in a letter from Salamanca (on September 28th 1532) to Rodrigo Sanches, Queen Catherine'schaplain, praises her exceptional knowledge – the *topos* on her supremacy is not uncommon – but complains: "I frequently hear about Joana Vaz, from Coimbra, mentioned by many persons [...] she is a miracle of our time, an exception among her sex, designed by Minerva to eloquence, so that in due time no one should take the place of the goddess. I don't write to her because I don't want to wait for her letter." Moreover, according to epistolary sources, we know that she never wrote Latin letters without her father's permission and scholars had to address her orally in court.

The poetry represented by 8 cases (4 manuscripts and 4 published) all under the category 'original' comprehends three main registrations: personal, panegyric under classical influence (mostly epigrams) and religious. The religious texts, the dominant theme (9) in both sections (manuscripts and printed works), illustrate a strategy for women to establish themselves as authors in their own name. Only 3 are original (the manuscripts), and 6 are either adaptations or translations. Consciously or not, these processes of adaptation/ translation use literal manipulation of the text and denounce those women who do not want to be perceived as entering the male space; they prefer to face society as competent Latinists by displaying an elegant style (intellectual identity) and simultaneously find a way to affirm their personality and religious convictions (ideological identity). Such is the case of princess D. Catarina (1436- 1463), the daughter of King Duarte, who embraces the monastic life at Saint Clara's convent after the death of her fiancé, the prince Charles of Navarra. Among the works attributed to her, only one was printed, a translation of two treaties by St Laurence Justinian[14]

---

[13] Ms F.G. 6368, Fol. 285 (transcription by A.C. Ramalho and translated here by Inês de Ornellas e Castro). See Américo da Costa. Ramalho, "Joana Vaz, femina doctissima", *Estudos sobre a época do Renascimento.* Lisboa: Fundação Calouste Gulbenkian –JNICT 1997: 346- 352.

[14] *Ho liuro que se escreue da regra e perfeyçam da conuersaçam dos monges: ho qual liuro foi copilado per ho reuerendo senhor Lourenço Justiniano primeryro patriarcha de Veneza, que foy dos primeyros fundadores da cõgregaçam de Sam Jorge em Alga*; at the end of the volume one can read it had been edited at Santa Cruz Monastery at Coimbra in 1531.A second edition was made by the end of the 18th century: *Da Perfeição da vida Monastica e da Vida Solitaria: dous tratados de S. Lourenço Justiniano, traduzidos do Latim em Portuguez pela Serenissima Senhora Infanta D. Catharina Filha do Senhor Rei D. Duarte de Feliz Memória. Segunda Edição, sem discrepancia da primeira, feita no Real Mosteiro de Santa Cruz de Coimbra, anno de 1531* – Lisboa, na Officina de Simão Thaddeo Ferreira, Ano 1791.

from Latin into Portuguese, known as *Da Perfeição da vida Monastica e da Vida Solitaria* [*On the Perfection of the Monastic life and Solitary Life*]. Her choices, as well as her way of translating, reveal her intellectual and confessional identity.

But, if the strategy of hiding behind rewriting is valid for all translated genres, here we are dealing with a gender-valorized factor: spiritual themes were considered appropriate for women. And who were the women who wrote about religion? We have 4 nuns and two 'recolhidas' at convents: Princess Catarina and Públia Hortensia de Castro, who wrote *Flosculucus theologiae* and the Paraphrases of Psalms. We also have D. Maria Guadalupe, who wrote a poetical spiritual testament, and Filipa Nunes, whose identity is quite unknown. Although the Paraphrases of Psalms were a genre cultivated by many illustrious figures throughout Europe, the other translated religious works have no equivalent in male production.

But was history appropriate to female authors? We find 2 adaptations among manuscripts, *The life of the first five Portuguese Kings* by Agostinha Barbosa da Silva, a woman who, we suspect, felt she was invading male territory because her other work was published under a male pseudonym,[15] and the *Epitome Regum Francorum,* dedicated to Madame de Dacier, by a very erudite nun, Soror Sebastiana de Magalhães, the only Portuguese author, as far as we know, to be interested in the *Gesta Regum Francorum* (Anonymous). She is also the author of commentaries on ancient historians – more precisely abbreviators of late Latinity: Florus, Aurelius Victor and Eutropius. Once more one can see the choice of authors has a way of affirming her profile as author/adaptor. The classics she adopted and commented on can be perceived as a statement, a way of bypassing the classical canon of her own time. Florus and Aurelius Victor were not among the text books used in Portuguese schools at this time, and that might be one of the reasons why they never received specific attention from male authors, and Eutropius, who only entered the Portuguese curriculum in the 19th century (1857),[16] waited until then for his first translation with commentaries by José Félix Pereira.[17]

---

[15] *Tractado de Architectura, e Arithmetica*, pseud. Pedro de Albornoz, published in Castile.

[16] Manuel Simões Dias Cardoso, *Lugares selectos de escriptores latinos, com a tradução interlinear, para uso das escolas*, Coimbra: 1857.

[17] José Félix Pereira, *Resumo da História Romana de Eutrópio.* Tradução do original latino. Lisboa: Tipografia Rua da Vinha, 1872. He shows no knowledge of Soror Sebastiana de Magalhães.

The two historical works translated, or at least presented as such, belong to D. Leonor de Noronha, alluded to before. She translated *Enneades sive Rhapsodia historiarum* (1504),[18] a world history from Antiquity to the author's time, by the humanist Marcus Antonius Sabellicus[19] (1436 – 1506) that Leonor de Noronha entitles *Coronica geral de Marco António Cocio Sabelico Des ho começo do mundo ate nosso tempo.* As the title and the dedicatory to Queen Catherine confirms, we have here much more than a translation. Her explicit purpose is the alibi she needs to present herself as an author: to instruct the Ladies of court with didactic literature instead of mere fiction, thus suggesting that her practice of translation is linked to gender issues, as we can read:

> ...I translated a general chronic from Latin into Portuguese language for Her Majesty's ladies so that they wouldn't waste their blessed time – as it is blessed while your Highnesses reign – reading fables but the truth, and it will be very beneficial, because knowing the past they will know the present better. And at least we gain by reading history as being participants in praising the deserving alien virtue and intending to imitate it.

She is thus following the ideological frame dominant among *Quattrocento* historians – and inherited from the Classics – that History's main objective was educational. Her other historical translation pursues the same purposes, as in the title she mentions the book was translated for consolation of those who cannot read Latin: *Este livro he o começo da historea de nossa redençam que se fez pêra consolação dos que nam sabem latim; pede ho autor della aos leitores que se nella acharem lhe digam por amor de deos hu pater noster polla alma.* [This is the beginning of the History of our redemption made for the consolation of those who do not know Latin; the author of this work asks the readers who came across that they pray a Pater Noster upon her soul.]

D. Luisa de Azevedo (1579-1655) published her husband's biography, a sub-genre of historiography, entitled *De morte maritii praeclarissimi, ac nobilissimi viri Sebasiani Vieira da Silva* aimed with the same motivation of *exempla* for future generations. Her case is singular; no other woman wrote about her husband, she follows the model of the *Vitae siue Viris illustribus.*

---

[18] Also known as *Ab orbe condito*, retaining Titus Livy's title *Ab urbe condita.*
[19] The Latinized name of Marcantonio Sabellico, who explored various genres and remained famous as a Renaissance Venice historian.

She has been attributed other works, mainly Latin poetry, but for the time being it remains a conjecture. Singular are also the works by the most celebrated peninsular humanist Luisa Sygea (1522- 1560). Although she was born in Toledo, Luisa[20] and her sister Ângela, a musician, came to Portugal and later entered the service of the Portuguese court where she remained for 13 years (1542 -1555). The Infant D. Maria Chambers and all her literary production dates from that time: the poem *Cintra* (edited in Paris, 1546), and the philosophical and didactical dialogue *Duarum Virginum Colloquium – Dialogum de Differentia vitae rusticae, & urbanae*[21] (printed only in 1901) dedicated to her Portuguese patron, in addition to 23 Latin epistles. Like a few other women, she did not restrict her activity to translation, but chose Latin (and also Greek, Syrian, Hebrew and even Arab) as the language of publication, the reason why her publications announced her as 'Luisa Sigeia from Toledo, polyglot'.

We have to wait for the Enlightenment to find female translations of the classics. Reflecting the decline of Latin learning, especially in the second part of the 18th century, several translations appear. It is "le temps des traductions",[22] according to Henri-Jean Martin, not only in France, but also in the rest of Europe, including Portugal. We must keep in mind that the need to exchange ideas and the new need to disseminate knowledge are closely related to this passion that leads authors to also master the vernacular languages in order to translate contemporary works.

Claude Maffre's survey[23] on Portuguese translations in Portugal in the 18th century shows that between 1706, the beginning of the reign of John the V, and 1807 – when Napoleonic troops invade Portugal – we find a total of 1282 translations. A huge number for an estimated population of 3 million by the end of the 18th century, whose potential readers do not exceed the two hundred, or at most, the two hundred and fifty thousand; the number becomes

---

[20] Luísa Sygeia came to Portugal when she was 8 years old. Her father was the preceptor of D. Jaime, Duque of Bragança. She served the princess for 13 years and left to Spain in 1555, after marrying, to dye only five years later at 38.

[21] *Dialogue de Deux Jeunes Filles sur la vie de cour et la vie de retraite*. Paris: PUF/ Fundation Calouste Gulbenkian, 1970.

[22] Cited by Françoise Waquet, *Le latin ou l'empire d'un signe : XVIe –XXe siècle*. Paris : Albin Michel, 1988 : 10.

[23] Claude Maffre, "Les Portugais lisent l'Europe: panorama des traductions au Portugal au XVIIIe siècle" in *Lire l'autre dans l'Europe des Lumières/ Reading the Other in Enlightenment Europe*. Textes recueillis par Thomas Bremer et Andréa Gagnoud. Coll. Le spectateur européen/ The European Spectator, vol.8, Un. Paul-Valéry – Montpellier III, 2007 : 101-119.

more interesting if one adds the considerable weight of censorship to obtain a license for publishing.

Until 1750, most of the books (60%) are about religion and the language most translated is Castilian with 40%. Latin occupies 17%. From 1750 on – certainly in relation to the change in education and the evolution of ideas – only 19% of the books have Religion as the subject, 12% are devoted to Science, 5% to History, 3% to Philosophy, 15% are distributed in a variety of topics, and finally, 46% are creative (which could claim only 15% of the editions before 1750). During this period, the French took the lead with 49% of the translated books, and Latin, the language we are concerned with, can claim only 14% of the translations. An analysis of the translated Latin themes allows us to find 3 fields: Theology (declining), a few scientific essays and especially the classics – Ovid, Horace and Quintilian.

We find two ladies 'competing' with male translators:[24] D. Rita Clara Freire de Andrade and D. Leonor de Portugal, Marquise of Alorna. They published while alive the *Ars Poetica,* translating Horace directly from Latin. There is a fundamental reason for the several translations[25] *Ars Poetica* received in the 18th century: if the Aristotlean literary theory, reassembled in the *Poetic* and in the *Rhetoric*, is considered the foundations of the baroque poetic creation, in the 18th century, Horace and his *Epistula ad Pisones*, which had already provided the Renaissance Poetics with its main principles, reassume a major influence.

Author of a vast poetic production, the Marquise was also dedicated to the translation of epistles and odes by Horace and *The abduction of Proserpine* by Claudianus (395-397). Her version of the *De Raptu Proserpine* dates back to 1815, when she was 65 years old, but was only published posthumously in the 5th volume of her *Complete Work* (1884). An examination of the 3 manuscript versions she left shows that she intended to publish her translation. The only other translation available in Portugal dates to 1991.

---

[24] We have 9 male translators of Horace by the time: Francisco José Freire (1758), Miguel Couto Guerreiro (1772), João Rosado de Vilalobos e Vasconcelos (1777), Pedro da Fonseca (1790), Jerónimo Soares Barbosa (1791), Padre Tomás José de Aquino (1793), Joaquim José da Costa e Sá (1794) and Thomaz José de Aquino (1796).

[25] The *Ars Poetica* by Horace begins to be translated only in the 18th century, Aníbal Pinto de Castro, "Alguns aspectos da teorização poética no neoclacissismo Português" *Bracara Augusta* 28, 65-66 (77-78), 1974: 10-11, alludes to some translators and commentators from the 18th.

All this makes us think that Portuguese female production did not set out to 'compete' with male authors. They were original, even when they chose to hide their talent behind translations and adaptations. Much is still to be discovered, but I do not think we will encounter materials that will change these provisory results. I believe, on the contrary, that future contributions will fortify this conviction.

## 3. The social condition of Latinate female

In our *corpus* of 24 Latinate women, only 5 were nuns (see final Index), although some others chose to spend the end of their lives in convents as 'recolhidas' without becoming novices. According to Stevenson, a reality very different from our Spanish neighbors among whom "almost all of the women who published or left records in manuscript were nuns, and a substantial proportion were visionaries, though there was also a flourishing genre of religious autobiography, often elicited by confessors as part of a process of self-examination".[26]

In Portugal, while in the Renaissance the education of the royal family affected the entourage and humanist circles at court, including women (they were very well represented at Garcia de Resende's *Cancioneiro Geral*), in the $17^{th}$ and $18^{th}$ centuries we find learned women from noble families who were educated at home (see Table 4). Not even nuns were taught Latin; those who wrote or translated Latin had already received an education before entering the convent. The correspondence found in monasteries[27] show that those who could read Latin were in the minority and felt obliged to translate the rules of the order or spiritual literature for the benefit of the community. Most written lives demanded by confessors for self-examination we have found so far are in vernacular.

---

[26] Jane Stevenson, *Woman Latin Poets: language, gender, and Authority, from Antiquity to the Eighteenth Century*. Oxford: Oxford University Press, 2005: 203.

[27] A survey on the reading habitudes in female convents of the Santa Clara order in Portugal is elucidative on this subject. See José Adriano de Freitas Carvalho, «Do recomendado ao lido. Direcção spiritual e prática de leitura entre franciscanas e clarissas em Portugal no século XVII» in *Via Spiritus*, nº4, 1997: 7-56.

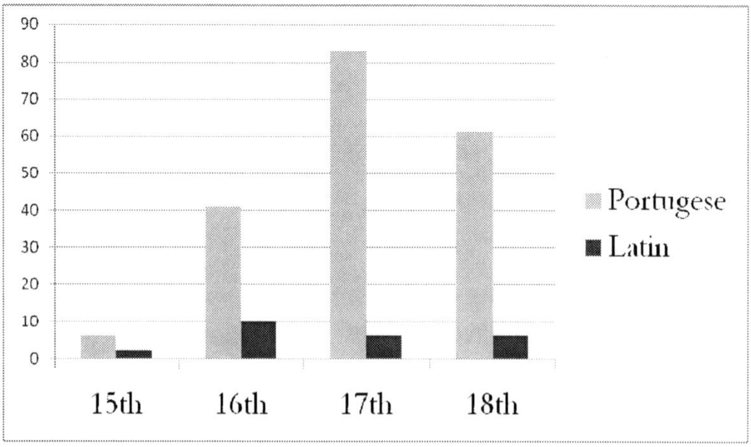


Table 4: The social condition of Latinate female and their knowledge

The percentages reflect a social reality that cannot be separated from places of education. Latin studies in Portugal underwent an evolution. In the 15th century, and in particular from 1485 on, due to the efforts of Cataldo Parisius Siculus (1455- 1517), Portugal participated more and more in the movement that congregated all European countries in a *Respublica literaria* united by Humanistic values shared by the mastership of written and oral Latin. Cataldo, a famous scholar of Sicilian origin invited by king John II, like other Italian humanists, as the Geraldini brothers or Lucio Marineo in Spain under the Catholic Monarchs, stressed the importance of verbal fluency and his educational techniques encouraged Latin speaking.[28] Cataldo introduced new pedagogical methods for the study of Letters with the contribution of the Latin classics, mainly Quintilian (*Institutio oratoria*) and Cicero (*Orator*, *De oratore* and *Brutus*), and proposed a humanist *ratio studiorum* structured towards progressive knowledge according to age and student development.

As we know, in most European countries (Italy, France, Spain, England, Germany) from the Renaissance until the middle of the 17th century, Latin was taught in schools from early years. Children began to learn to write and

[28] A technique also embraced by Jesuit schools and followed all over Europe, even in later protestant countries. For Jesuit education rules and techniques, see Fernando Patrício José de Lemos, *A Reforma Pombalina da Escola Secundária e o Ensino do Latim. Política de educativa, enqudramento curricular, métodos, agentes e instrumentos de ensino.* Dissertação de doutoramento em Literatura Latina apresentada à Faculdade de Letras da Universidade de Lisboa, 1998.

read first in Latin and only later in their own language. Latin would be, indifferent to beliefs – whether catholic or protestant – the only language unifying the European *intelligentsia* until the mid-18$^{th}$ century, as a *lingua franca*, like English today. In Portugal, especially during the Renaissance under the patronage of the Infant D. Maria (1521 – 1577), the ladies of the court took part in that movement, allowing them to read the new translations of the Greek classics and the works of the great humanists of their time, such as Erasmus. Like their male companions they were able to read, write and speak fluently in Latin. Male testimonies, mostly Cataldo's correspondence[29] and laudatory poems, allude to ladies to whom one could address in Latin, either in epistles or in oral discourses. Among them were queen D. Leonor, the wife of king John II, infant D. Joana, the king's sister, and her ladies[30], queens D. Isabel and D. Maria, king Manuel's first and second wife, and noble ladies such as D. Maria Freire, Marquise of Vila Real, and her daughter, D. Leonor de Noronha, Cataldo's favourite disciple, who dedicated herself to history. As a fact, the testimonies of humanists travelling in Portugal, like Nicolaus Clenardus,[31] spoke in this way of the Portuguese court: "this court pleases me immensely. It has, and in great number, scholars who are expert in Greek and Latin languages: not even in Salamanca one would have been able to speak Greek or Latin with less effort". By the same period, King John III's half-sister, princess D. Maria, assembled around her a small intellectual group of ladies celebrated by posterity for their erudition and poetical skills, such as Joana Vaz, who taught Latin to the princess and her niece.[32]

---

[29] *Epistolae et orationes quaedam Cataldi Siculi*, Lisboa, Valentim Fernandes da Morávia, 21 de Fevereiro de 1500.

[30] Cataldo dedicated epigrams to her and her fellow ladies, the sisters Clara and Catarina da Silva, from the count of Abrantes family, to whom he addresses: «Clara ex Siluarum generosa gente creata» or in this small epigram « Hesterno Catherina die sermone benigno / Rettulit a domina carmina nulla legi,/ Anxia propterea, subida quae febre cubaret, /Et quae uix fieriet copia parua sui». [Yesterday Catherine, with good words, gave me the message that Her Lady wouldn't read poems, Catherine so anxious, because she was lying in bed, with a sudden fever, and barely responding. »

[31] Excerpt from a letter by Nicolaus Clenardus to Johanes Vaseus dated from 1534, about King John III and his sister court intellectual life: "Mire mihi placet haec aula. Habet enim doctos et graece et latine non paucos: ne Salmanticae quidem reperias qui aut graece aut latine tam loquantur expedite" (my translation). Latin transcription in Américo da Costa Ramalho, *Estudos sobre a época do Renascimento.* Lisboa: Fundação Calouste Gulbenkian –JNICT, 1997.

[32] D. Maria daughter of King John III.

During the period of dual monarchy (1580- 1640), and later on, the circles were more circumscribed to the domesticity of the great noble houses. In the 17th century, as opposed to the Renaissance, Latin writing was not connected to the aulic circles, although most women from our *corpus* belonged to nobility. Apart from Bernarda Ferreira de Lacerda (1595- 1644), who left a prominent work in Latin and in Castilian, the epic poem *La España liberada,* or D. Luisa de Azevedo's husband biography – *D. Aloysiae de Azevedo, de morte maritii praeclarissimi, ac nobilissimi viri Sebasiani Vieira da Silva* –, whose works were printed, these women seemed to be confined to their domesticity and wrote only for small entourages.

Everything changed with the Enlightenment. Women like Feliciana Soutomayor or Teresa Luísa Febrónia da Silva, were recognized in laudatory anthologies.[33] At the same time, translation, like all rewriting processes, became a singular strategy of public exhibition of feminine authorship, as exemplified by D. Rita Freire de Andrade and the Marquise of Alorna, the most celebrated Portuguese woman writer of the 18th century. The latter translations, written under no patronage, were always produced with the intention of publishing, suggesting that she understood the role of transmission, and therefore dissemination, due to the translated text. With the exception of *Elegia à morte de S.A.R. o príncipe do Brasil, D. José* (Lisbon, 1788) most of the texts published while D. Leonor was alive were translations, and in addition to Latin (Horace and Claudian), she also translated from English the *Ensaio sobre a crítica* [*Essay on criticism*] by Pope, and French *De Bounaparte e dos Bourbons e a necessidade de nos unirmos aos nossos legítimos príncipes* [the famous opuscule *De Buonaparte et des Bourbons*] by F.- R. Chateaubriand (1814) and the *Ensaio sobre a indiferença em matéria de religião* [*Essai sur l'indifference en matière de religion*] by Lammenais (1820). The reasons for such translations are not only didactic ones; if we analyze them carefully we can also find political and social purposes. Times had changed and a 'docta femina' demanded to

[33] They were both published in Frei Francisco da Cunha. *Oraçam Académica, Panegyrica, histórica, Encomiastica, Profano-Sacra que pelos felices succesos, e vitoriosas armas da Augustissima, e Sereníssima Rainha de Hungria, e Bohemia, etc Com a descripção do mesmo Reyno, e Corte de Praga, e das duas victorias do Panro, e Meno; adornada de varias poezias, e muntos versos dos milhores engenhos portugueses. Consagra, Tributa, e Oferese à mesma Soberana Senhora D. Maria Thereza Augusta, Christina, Amelia, Walburga da Austria,* Lisboa na oficina Alvarense, 1743.

be more than 'an exception among her sex'; she wanted her intellectual skills recognized as a contribution to society.

As we verified, between the 15th and 18th centuries in Portugal, only a small percentage of women, mainly from the aristocracy, had contact with Latin, the gendered language of Humanities (the concept of *Humanitates* or *Litterae humaniores* incorporated since Antiquity all the literary and scientific knowledge, that is to say all forms of scholarship[34] that distinguished man from the rest of nature and animals), until the second half of the 18th century. Although some embraced monastic life or become nuns, their humanistic education was previously acquired at home, under masters contracted by the family or in a court environment. Perceived in their own time as exceptions to which intellectual *auctoritas* were recognized, Latinate ladies, like women in general, seldom interiorized literary authorship as a female domain. Although Latinate females imposed themselves easier when working under patronage or belonging to royalty, they rarely published; nevertheless, women produced a lot and they were read in manuscript circulation, a way of diffusion in Portugal and Spain, until the end of the 18th, due to difficulties to obtain licenses under censorship. For that reason, especially when studying women before the 19th century, we must rely on second hand testimonies – mainly by males – and accept them as the only proof of their existence. The fact that they preferred to use translation and adaptation as a strategy to claim authorship can be interpreted as recognition that they were invading a territory traditionally masculine. But, on the other hand, we must understand the choices of subjects (architecture or history), or classical authors for commentaries, as a statement, because as we have been able to verify that religious themes (printed and manuscripts) were a small percentage of Latinate female production.

If the Latinate ladies of Renaissance, generally under royal patronage, could have pedagogy as an alibi and use Latin in order to became part of the international *inteligentsia*, those who wrote or translated in both the 17th and 18th centuries were rather moved to impose themselves as members of the Republic of Letters; their effort to translate and disseminate new ideas was a new alibi that allowed them to hide their own ideas under the translated text.

---

[34] See R. S Crane, "The ideia of Humanities» in *The Ideia of Humanities and Other Essays Critical and Historical*. Chicago: Chicago Press, 1967. Aulus Gellius, *Noctes Atticae* 13.16 refers to the use of *humanitas* by Cicero explaining it was *"eruditionem institutionemque in bonae artes"* [education and training in good ars].

## Select Bibliography

### A. Primary Sources

Alemparte, Jaime Ferreiro. 1991. *La leyenda de las Once Mil Virgenes, sus relíquias, culto e iconografia*. Múrcia.

Cardoso, Manuel Simões Dias. 1857. *Lugares selectos de escriptores latinos, com a tradução interlinear, para uso das escolas*. Coimbra.

Carvalho, José Adriano de Freitas. 1997. "Do recomendado ao lido. Direcção spiritual e prática de leitura entre franciscanas e clarissas em Portugal no século XVII" in *Via Spiritus* 4: 7-56.

Conte, Gian Biagio. 1996. *The Rhetoric of Imitation: Genre and Poetic Memory in Virgil and Other Latin Poets*. (Tr. Charles Segal). New York: Cornell University Press,

Crane, R. S. 1967. "The ideia of Humanities" in *The Ideia of Humanities and Other Essays Critical and Historical*. Chicago: Chicago Press.

Ditchfield, Simon. 2000. "An early Christian School of Sanctity in Tridentine Rome" in *Storia d'Italia*. Torino: Annali 16.

Fraser, Antonia. 1994. *The Wives of Henry VIII*, 9-48. New York: Vintage.

Lefevere, André. 1992. *Translating, rewriting and the manipulation of Literary Fame*. London and New York: Routlege.

Lemos, Fernando Patrício José de. 1998. *A Reforma Pombalina da Escola Secundária e o Ensino do Latim. Política de educativa, enquadramento curricular, métodos, agentes e instrumentos de ensino*. PhD thesis. Faculdade de Letras da Universidade de Lisboa.

Maffre, Claude. 2007. "Les Portugais lisent l'Europe: panorama des traductions au Portugal au XVIIIe siècle" in Bremer, Thomas et Andréa Gagnoud. Coll (eds). Lire l'autre dans l'Europe des Lumières/ Reading the Other in Enlightenment Europe, in *Le spectateur européen/ The European Spectator*. 8: 101-119.

Méndiz, Maria Carmen Pallares. 1993. *A vida das mulleres na Galicia Medieval (1100- 1500). Bibliotéca Divulgación*. Santiago de Compostela: Universidade de Santiago de Compostela.

Osswald, Maria Cristina. 2004. "The Society of Jesus and the diffusion of the cult and iconography of Saint Ursula and the Eleven Thousand Virgins in the Portuguese Empire during the second half of the 16th century" *16th Century Organization and Conferences*. Toronto: 601-609.

Pereira, José Félix. (tr.). 1872. *Resumo da História Romana de Eutrópio.*. Lisboa: Tipografia Rua da Vinha.

Ramalho, Américo da Costa. 1997. *Estudos sobre a época do Renascimento.* Lisboa: Fundação Calouste Gulbenkian –JNICT.

Stevenson, Jane. 2005. *Woman Latin Poets: language, gender, and Authority, from Antiquity to the Eighteenth Century*. Oxford: Oxford University Press.

Waquet, Françoise. 1998. *Le Latin ou l'empire d'un signe, XVIe – XXe siècle*. Paris: Albin Michel.

# Beyond Political Boundaries: Religion as Nation in Early Modern Spain

*Nieves Baranda*
UNED

ABSTRACT The emergence of women writers in Spanish culture of the $16^{th}$ and $17^{th}$ centuries is accompanied by characteristics that differentiate it from what happened in other European countries. The author presents several Spanish women writers who showed concern for their social identity, which they grounded in the notions of history and religion. In fact, religion can be established as one of the most important social identity categories and a key element when talking about transnational influences or culture.

NATION HAS BECOME SUCH AN IMPORTANT CONCEPT in understanding our collective identity, that it can be difficult to imagine scholarship without it. As noted by Álvarez Junco,[1] an expert on Spanish nationalism, "Among the mobilizing myths of the modern world, nationalism has been the most constant and pervasive, because of its great potential for adaptation and survival, the better able to serve different purposes and operate in different contexts". Writing in a pioneering study on the subject, Anthony D. Smith[2] defined nation "as a named human population sharing an historic territory, common myths and historical memories, a mass, public culture, a common economy and common legal rights and duties for all members". This suggests that a nation is not a real entity, but a symbolic concept, essentially a myth that reinforces the politics of state and allows it to perform multiple functions legitimately: to broaden its influence on society, to homogenize the culture, to intervene in the economy, to redistribute income, and, in brief, to dominate society and provide individuals with the ability to integrate into an imaginary community, giving up part of their identity, or at least mitigating it.

---

[1] José Álvarez Junco, *Mater dolorosa. La idea de España en el siglo XIX.* Madrid: Taurus, 2001: 97.
[2] Anthony D. Smith, *National Identity*, London: Penguin Books, 1991: 14.

Nationalism – the ideology that sustains the legitimacy of nations – is a product of modernity that can be dated back to the late 18th century. It emerged as a response to the identity crisis produced by the attempt to create a "scientific state" to substitute absolute monarchies, replacing the old religious and traditional legitimacy with a new one based on the use of reason and scientific observation. This crisis profoundly affected the intellectuals who had to produce alternative concepts, developing new myths and symbols to support human action and thought.[3] Referring to a nation in the days before that historical moment, therefore, poses a conceptual problem, because, although we can refer to countries, kingdoms or states, nations did not exist – at least in the modern sense. Nor is there any element that can be named as essential in creating a nation, because neither one language, one religion, race or even the historical consciousness of belonging to the same state is a requisite for the transformation into a modern nation.[4] Nonetheless, that does not mean that people did not have a sense of belonging to a common and shared social identity, Nonetheless, that does not mean that people did not have a sense of belonging to a common and shared social identity, but as unless culturally motivated natural loyalties tend to proximity, Hobsbawm underlines how proto-national identities were differently understood by the popular classes and the elites. For those who were illiterate, and who in our sources rarely verbalize their conceptions, these relations extended little beyond the place where they lived, while the elites had political ties and a vocabulary that we directly linked to institutions and states. Our writers are part of these privileged classes, and so we find in their writings expressions of belonging to a state, albeit appearing only occasionally and sporadically, outside of a structured discourse of political reasoning.

## Women writers and nation

The emergence of women writers in the Spanish culture of the 16th and 17th centuries has its own characteristics that differentiate it from what happened in other European countries.[5] Broadly speaking, there were very few women

[3] Alberto Rosa Rivero, Guglielmo Bellelli and David Bakhurst.*Memoria colectiva e identidad nacional.* Madrid: Biblioteca Nueva, 2000: 59.

[4] Eric Hobsbawm, *Nations and Nationalism since 1780: Programme, Myth, Reality.* Cambridge: Cambridge University Press. 1990: 49-79.

[5] The following summary is based on Nieves Baranda, *Cortejo a lo prohibido. Lectoras y escritoras en la España Moderna.* Madrid: Arco Libros, 2005, and shows

writers during the 16th century: some poets in the royal court and the Madrid area, about two authors of secular printed works and three or four nuns. Among religious writers, Teresa of Ávila is the most influential (†1582) having started the Discalzed Carmelites religious order, and founded several new convents throughout the Peninsula. During her lifetime she enjoyed great prestige and soon after her death became a highly respected figure; less than sixty years after her death she was officially recognized as a saint by the Catholic Church. Teresa of Avila was a prolific writer, she never published her works but some were widely read in manuscript during her lifetime. She wrote a religious autobiography, a history of her convent foundations, and several meditation books. Soon after her death some of these works were printed, first in Portugal and, in 1588, in Spain. Thereafter, they were often reprinted and translated and she became a very well-known and even popular female writer, which surely helped to change some of the most critical objections to women who wrote and their culture, so the implicit condemnation that followed them lost its force. In fact, from the early 17th century onwards, there was a significant increase of women writers (religious and profane) and their visibility largely remained until 1700. Thus, most Spanish female writers of the Early Modern Period wrote in this century. The majority of them were nuns and accordingly their works dealt with religious subjects. Fewer women wrote about secular topics (theatre, novel, poetry) and of these, less than a handful were interested in matters that might be termed intellectual,[6] none can be said to have written about politics as such.

But engaging with politics is not the only way of expressing one's feelings of belonging and identifying with a supra local community. In fact, to find a sense of proto-national belonging we do not need political works with a coherent theory of state or society; autobiographical texts, historical accounts, or treatises of various kinds can elucidate this, especially if the state or group identity is in some way at stake – for example, if it is threatened, challenged or subject to tension. Indeed, as has repeatedly been argued, threat, whether real or fictional, is a crucial element and subject to this pressure. Some Spanish women writers of this period demonstrate the limits of their collective identity and identify characteristics they feel to be their own or alien.

---

some of the conclusions reached following extensive research into Spanish women writers up to the 18th century.

[6] Nieves Baranda, *Cortejo a lo prohibido*: 123-174.

## A nation of nations

Spain belongs to a group of European countries whose state identity remained largely stable before they became a nation. That does not mean that citizens (or strictly speaking, 'subjects') had a homogenous identity, because the country consisted of several nations. During the 16$^{th}$ and 17$^{th}$ centuries, the official title of rulers was not the 'king of Spain' but of 'Castile', 'Aragon', 'Portugal', 'Naples', and so on,[7] and while from abroad the country was identified as *Spain,* inside there was an awareness of different nations.[8] Thus, when we talk about Spanish women writers we are applying anachronistic concepts to define subjects who never conceived themselves in that way or at least not in the same terms now in use. Generally speaking, in present literary histories, we group under Spanish authors those who wrote in Castilian, but this approach is unstable because it is not evenly applied. For example, Jorge de Montemayor, who was born in Portugal but wrote mainly in Castilian, is included, while Bernarda Ferreira de Lacerda, a similar case, falls under Portuguese history. Authors born in Latin America (as important as Sor Juana Inés de la Cruz) are segregated as "Latinamerican literature", even though they were the same king's subjects like anybody born in Seville or Madrid. These sample cases serve to underscore how artificial constructions of literary history are. Language is preferred as the selective category, but around it other inclusions/ exclusions accumulate with very little or no explicit argument. Moreover, the women writers I shall discuss are defined in terms of having written in Castilian, but some of them come from the kernel of the Monarchy (Castile) and others come or live in the periphery. Their different points of view, when collective or political identity tensions arise, enrich the perspectives and hence the argument. As such, there is a writer born in Portugal when that kingdom belonged to the Spanish crown; a Spanish aristocrat who watches the territory with the awareness of being Castilian; nuns who move from one place to another and become aware of the limits of religious conflict; and a Portuguese Jewish writer who must emigrate in order to achieve religious freedom and lives in a cultural multilingual ghetto.

---

[7] Henry Kamen. *Spain, 1469-1714: A Society of Conflict.* Harlow: Longman, 1991: 9-16.

[8] Laura Manzano Baena, "Inventando al enemigo: imágenes de España en las Provincias Unidas" in *A. Crespo and M. Herrero, eds., España y las 17 provincias de los Países Bajos. Una revisión historiográfica (XVI-XVIII).* Córdoba: Universidad, 2002: 781.

Bernarda Ferreira de Lacerda (1595-1644) was born in Oporto, Portugal. She wrote *Hespaña Libertada* ('Liberated Spain', Lisbon, 1618) a verse history of the re-conquest of the Peninsula from Muslim rule during the Middle Ages. She published only the first part, the years 711 to 1109, but always intended to continue it; her daughter eventually published the second part in 1673. Bernarda Ferreira's main source was one of the most famous Spanish chronicles of the time, *Historia general de España* ["General history of Spain"], by the Jesuit priest, Father Mariana.[9] This history was a milestone in the construction of Spanish history, and would be a crucial reference source for the next 250 years. Mariana's work provides Ferreira with the basic narrative plot and selected events. Following this structure, she recasts some episodes that negotiate a Portuguese perspective on the same affairs using another famous history of that time, the *Monarchya Lusitana* ["Portuguese Monarchy"] by Bernardo de Brito (Lisbon, 1609).

Writing history was a powerful tool for propaganda, which was rarely detached from political programs and power aims. It has been shown that historians in the 16th century deliberately confused the identities of Castile and Spain so the contribution of other kingdoms to the common deeds, and the historical myths created to forge a joint past, were blurred.[10] Bernarda Ferreira's work enters this controversial arena with a very expressive title ['liberated Spain'], alluding to a common Spanish identity and to the most powerful historical myth of the time – the liberation of the Iberian Peninsula from a Muslim rule that had lasted from 711 to 1492. This myth had a very deep religious meaning and was emphasized in the work by the adjective *libertada,* pointing to the title of Tasso's most famous poem *Gerusalemme liberate* which was about the crusades and was well known and imitated all over Europe at that time. Ferreira's work deals with the foundational myth of the Spanish monarchy and its identity, which had political and religious meaning. Her poem reworks this *Castilian* point of view to reintegrate a Portuguese perspective by which her kingdom, recently united to the Spanish crown (1580), was a prominent contributor to the present situation. Under that very programmatic title she is not complying with the *official* account which Mariana's chronicle represents, but negotiating a Portuguese position within that history so Castilian readers would be compelled to understand

---

[9] It was first written and published in Latin (Toledo, 1592; etc.) and later translated into Castilian going through many editions after 1601. In 1699 an English translation was published in London.

[10] Henry Kamen *Imagining Spain: historical myth and national identity.* New Haven: Yale University Press, 2008: 18-20.

their own national history under a new light; as their heroes and most emblematic episodes are reduced or replaced by Portuguese deeds without previous notice, so the main role has to be shared with Portuguese heroes.

What was the purpose? From 1580, Portugal formed part of the kingdoms of the Spanish Crown, which meant that the heart of power had shifted from the royal court in Lisbon (now without a king and converted into a viceroyalty) to an only court in Madrid, where the Portuguese position was not strong enough to enforce its particular interests or groups.[11] Finally, in 1619, after several delays, the king of Spain visited Lisbon. This became an opportunity to attract his interest in the Portuguese kingdom and highlight services to the Crown. In modern Europe, royal power was based on an exchange of favours for services, so the relation between valuable acts for the Crown was done in order to receive a reward. It might be easier to understand the way in which *Hespaña libertada* interweaves history by considering it in this context: because of its courage in helping to achieve *freedom* (and banishing Muslims), Portugal, like Castile, deserves to be taken into account, implying that families who actively participated in the task should be rewarded. At the beginning of Canto V (stanzas 1-22) a brief excursus is introduced to discuss the Judges of Castile lineages. These mythical characters belong to a number of legends about Castile's origin, which came to symbolize independence and justice during the time before it became a kingdom (in the 10th century). Vaguely related to these Judges through a Portuguese branch (the Porcelos) are the lineages of Herrera (or Ferreira), the Leytaõ, Castro and Meneses, who stem from the same branch that leads to the Spanish royal house and to the house of Sandoval, Francisco de Sandoval, the King's favourite and the most powerful man in Spain. The mention of these Portuguese lineages and the connection with royal power in Castile in the early 17th century, has a very clear meaning as some are lady Bernarda's

[11] One of the most important ways of integrating a territory to the crown was incorporating its elites into the Royal court as this was the place where concessions could be got. For Portuguese aristocracy and privileged classes not having a court in Lisbon was a clear drawback for their interests. See Fernando Bouza, *Portugal no tempo dos Filipes: política, cultura representações (1580-1668)*. Lisboa: Cosmos, 2000 and *Las redes del imperio. Elites sociales en la articulación de la Monarquía Hispánica, 1492-1714*. Madrid: Marcial Pons/ Historia, Universidad Pablo de Olavide, 2009.

family names: his father was Herrera (the same as Ferreira) and Leytaõ, Meneses her maternal grandmother.[12]

The new political situation after 1580, by which Portugal was part of a transnational monarchy, forced elite groups to renegotiate their position in the social network, especially attending to their links with the ruling dynastic house. The liberated Spain that Ferreira depicts in her poem integrates Castile and Portugal as equals by making both originally part of the crown and by intermingling their noble lineages. This symbolic integration entitles families who remain in Portuguese territory to have the same rights as those in Castile. Thus, by showing that the reconquest was a shared task, Bernarda Ferreira's work does not present the link between Castile and Portugal as domination (which it largely was), but as an equal co-existence between realms, where the newly incorporated elites are entitled to keep (or improve) their privileges, given that they have the same origins. Political and family circumstances also help to clarify the author's position. Lady Bernarda's father, Ignacio Ferreira, was a prominent member of the Council of Conscience and Orders, and made the welcoming speech to King Philip III when the latter arrived in Lisbon, which proves his relevance. Her daughter's book was published a year earlier when she was 19, so we should see the decision not as an individual choice but as familial, trying to procure visibility in their milieu by associating their name with a poem on a highbrow topic, surprisingly composed by a young woman,[13] dedicated to the King, about a current political issue and published only a year before the royal visit. Flattery, through the use of a young girl's literary skills, in order to procure the king's or his favourite's attention, could have been the purpose of Bernarda's family, and it did not go unnoticed. Her work arrived to the royal library, where it is mentioned in the 1637 inventory (Bouza, 2005: 403), and her name mentioned by Portuguese and Spanish poets (in Madrid) between 1629 and 1639.

Spain and Portugal became open enemies in 1640 when Portuguese nobility, with the help of a *coup d'etat,* elected a new king, rebelling against the Habsburg dynasty. After several defeats, the Treaty of Lisbon was signed,

---

[12] The Meneses origin in Canto IV, stanza 94. Her husband's surname was Sousa, a lineage that is said to descend from a Portuguese Count or Judge from the same remote period (Canto V, stanza 19). The nobility of a lineage is also measured by its antiquity.

[13] Other woman writers comments, such as Isabel de Liaño, demonstrate that they were talked about when their writing activity became publicly known: Nieves Baranda, *Cortejo a lo prohibido*: 102-103.

accepting Portuguese independence in 1668. The aristocrat Maria de Guevara (c.1620-1683), concerned with the kingdom's difficulties (war, and political and economic crises), addressed a work to king Phillip IV proposing solutions. Her work, *Tratado y advertencias hechas por una mujer celosa del bien de su rey y corrida de parte de España* ["Treatise and warnings by a woman concerned for the good of her king and affronted by part of Spain"] was written in 1663 at the height of Spanish defeats[14] and attempts to highlight the ills that plague the country, its causes and possible solutions. It is not a political theory text, but when exposing positive values that have been lost and explaining Spain's decline, her identity concepts are revealed. She believes that the king, as the country's unifying symbol, is beyond all questioning and consequently reasons that his advisors must be blamed for the country's decadence and disgrace. Pointing at current ills, Guevara highlights the identity values that turned Spain into Europe's most powerful country under Phillip II's rule – namely a war vocation that transformed every Spaniard into a hero and a soldier ready to protect his territory from alien threats. In her view, women share this essential *national* quality, and her work is there to prove that while men have lost it women have not, so they dare to speak their mind when everybody else keeps silent.

Her second work, *Desengaños de la corte y mujeres valerosas* ["Disenchantments of the court and valorous women"], written a year later, stresses the same point,[15] and the cases of exemplary women she mentions are noted almost entirely for their courage in wielding weapons. She uses history as a source for characters that can demonstrate this trait as essential to Spanish women. Enemies offer great opportunities to define one's own identity,[16] so when she rejects Portuguese people and tries to justify war against them she "bases her attacks on strong ethnic-religious beliefs, speaking from her dominant class position (as a noble conservative woman)".[17] She justifies war because Portugal is being helped by England (heretics),[18] and plebeians are mainly Jews who arrived in the kingdom after

---

[14] Nieves Romero-Díaz, *Warnings to the Kings and Advice on Restoring Spain A bilingual edition.* Chicago; London: The University of Chicago Press 2007: 50-62.

[15] Nieves Romero-Díaz, *Warnings to the Kings*: 73.

[16] Stefano Andretta, "Note sulla natura dell'immagine del nemico in età moderna tra identità e alterità" in *Cantù, Francesca; Giuliana Di Febo; and Renato Moro* (eds.), *L'immagine del nemico. Storia, ideologia e rappresentazione tra età moderna e contemporanea.* Roma: Viella, 2009: 32-35.

[17] Nieves Romero-Díaz, *Warnings to the Kings*: 27.

[18] In this essay I use the words *heresy* and *heretics* in much the same way they were used by Spaniards at the time, i.e. meaning those who are not Catholic, mainly

being chased from Spain. Lady Maria is defining her country's identity mainly as Catholic (non Jew/ non protestant), but also as brave, which is a feature that demonstrates nobility, as derived from the old medieval chivalric concept that was deeply rooted in the class ideology of her time.

According to Álvarez Junco,[19] "The only cultural field that really worried 16th and 17th century rulers was religion",[20] but it could not be considered as a country identity feature because it had a transnational nature, and in fact, could expand imaginary identity boundaries beyond political ones. The entire Catholic world could be part of the same imaginary 'nation'. In her book, *The Way of Perfection,* Teresa of Avila says:

> At this time news reached me of the damage that Lutherans had done in France and how this unfortunate sect was spreading. I felt great fatigue and, as if I could do something, I cried to the Lord and begged remedy for so much evil. It seemed to me that I was ready to put a thousand lives to save one soul of many that were being lost there. And as I was conscious of being a woman and a mean one... I determined to do this little bit that was in me, that is to follow the evangelical counsels as perfectly as I could ... and that all of us, occupied in prayer for the defenders and preachers and lawyers of the church who defend it, would help This Lord of mine as much as we could, because he was being abused by them.[21]

---

Protestants and Lutherans in the North of Europe. The word had a very negative semantic load.

[19] José Álvarez Junco, *Mater dolorosa*: 77.

[20] "El único terreno cultural que realmente preocupaba a los gobernantes de los siglos XVI y XVII era la religión, no la lengua" (José Álvarez Junco, *Mater dolorosa*: 77). Mª Victoria López-Cordón, "Enemigos, rivales y contrarios: formas de antagonismo en los tiempos modernos" in *Cantù, Francesca; Giuliana Di Febo; and Renato Moro* (eds.), *L'immagine del nemico. Storia, ideologia e rappresentazione tra età moderna e contemporanea.* Roma: Viella, 2009: 61-62, notes that during the sixteenth century the religious maverick turns into a state public enemy (*hostis*), because professing Catholic faith was the cornerstone of the political system, so limits between state reason and religious principles became blurred.

[21] "En este tiempo vinieron a mi noticia los daños de Francia que habían hecho estos luteranos y cuánto iba en crecimiento esta desventurada secta. Diome gran fatiga y, como si yo pudiera algo, lloraba con el Señor y le suplicaba remediase tanto mal, Parecíame que mil vidas pusiera yo para remedio de un alma de las muchas que allí se perdían. Y como me vi mujer y ruin... determiné de hacer esto poquito que era en mí, que es seguir los consejos evangélicos con toda la perfección que yo pudiesse, ... y que todas, ocupadas en oración por lo que son defendedores de la iglesia y predicadores y letrados que la defienden ayudásemos en lo que pudiésemos a este Señor mío, que tan apretado le traen", *Camino de perfección* 1,2.

Evidently, Teresa of Avila ignores political boundaries and considers Catholic territory to be her own space; thus, threats to that faith, wherever they happen, are a menace to her identity. The text also shows how she transfers the political structures of the monarchy to that Catholic nationality: God is the Lord of that kingdom, defended by an army of priests. Men are at the forefront: preachers, lawyers, scholars ... etc., as they have an active position against the enemy which they face directly. At the rear are women who defend this kingdom through prayer, locked in monasteries. All of them play the same role: to defend the true God's realm, which is threatened by Lutheran heresy. This conception prevails amongst the writings of other nuns.[22]

In 1627 the *Relación de cómo se ha fundado en Alcántara de Portugal junto a Lisboa, el muy devoto monasterio de N.S. de la Quietación,... para las monjas peregrinas... venidas de la Provincia de Alemania Baxa, después de los hereges las aver perseguido y desterrado de tierras en tierras por quatro vezes* ['Story of how it was founded in Alcantara in Portugal near Lisbon, the most devout monastery Our Lady of the Quietness ... for the pilgrim nuns... coming from the Low German Province, after the heretics persecuted and banished them from one land to another four times'] appeared in Spain. It was written by Sister Catherine of the Holy Spirit, a nun living in that convent, and dedicated to Princess Margarita de la Cruz, Phillip II of Spain's sister, a nun too, in a monastery in Madrid. The events recalled in the book had taken place forty years before, and to explain the publication we must remember how, after the Twelve years' truce ended in 1621, hostilities broke out again in the Low Countries between the United Provinces and the Spanish controlled southern states. In a way, bringing the history to light

[22] María de San José, one of Teresa's closest disciples, reflects this ideological climate in the preface to *Libro de las recreaciones* (Book of recreations), in which she exhorts other nuns to pray and discipline themselves to oppose "two wicked heretics", and adds: "[Our Lord] chose you, so it can be said what was said at the time of that brave Deborah: 'New way of battling was chosen by the Lord'" ([el Señor] os escogió a vosotras por que se pueda decir lo que en el tiempo de aquella valerosa Débora se dijo: 'Nueva manera de batalla ha elegido el Señor'", María de San José, *Escritos espirituales*, Roma: Postulación General O.C.D., 1979: 48). Nonetheless, it is not completely clear if she is referring to Calvinists or to the newly elected heads of her religious order against whom she defended Teresa of Avila's spirit and the rights of nuns (Mª Pilar Manero Sorolla, "Exilios y destierros en la vida y en la obra de María de Salazar" in *Actas del VII Simposio de la Sociedad Española de Literatura General y Comparada.* Madrid: Castalia,1988). In any case, it shows that heresy was considered to be the main trait in defining enemies and in praying a womanly weapon against them.

must be considered part of the propaganda campaigns that helped to create a favourable public opinion about war, as resources and men were demanded to maintain it.

The book narrates the attacks on Franciscan convents and against Franciscan friars in some cities in the Netherlands. The events took place between 1566 and 1581, and are arranged in geographical order, by listing the plight of nuns and monks in different towns. Narrative focus highlights the goodness and suffering of Catholic priests and nuns and heretic cruelty, which is on a par with the devil, sin and hell, deprived of any virtue. Friars suffering penalties, or even brutal torture, act as martyrs, and if saved from peril, God's hand and protection explain it. In this respect, as expected, the work follows a Manichean rhetoric of good and evil with no shades of grey, as in popular propaganda leaflets. Collective identity requires a collective memory that highlights glories but never more than grievances, military defeats, and atrocities suffered by the ancestors.[23] The narration manages to do this, as it creates an atmosphere of continuous violence against the Franciscan friars and nuns. Although the book refers to events that took place nearly fifty years before, the war situation in the Low Countries makes them alive once more for the reader, who can understand that the same things are happening again. He can identify himself with the suffering friars and nuns and have a first-hand account of what this distant war implies for his Catholic identity. The account explains reality in religious terms, leaving aside political angles of the problem.

Even when referring to herself, Catherine of the Holy Spirit does not believe herself to be an exile, because her social identity is linked to the convent community and its way of life. A Nun's nation, that is, the territory to which she belongs, is the convent, no matter the country where it is situated, as long as that enclosed space is ruled by the norms of the religious order she chose when professing. While in the preface Fray Juan de las Llagas says that nuns "gave up the sweet taste of home and their parents and relatives support (...)",[24] sister Catherine is concerned about "the sad and miserable state of our homeland when we left, where there are so many cities, towns and villages, so abandoned by heaven and so dominated by the Devil that there are neither sacraments, nor priests or friars to administer them apart

---

[23] José Álvarez Junco, *Mater dolorosa*: 98.

[24] "renunciaron a los gustos de la dulce patria y lo que de sus padres y deudos podían esperar..." (Catalina del Espíritu Santo, 1627).

from a few ones secretly dressed in secular garb".[25] In contrast, they are "in such a peaceful and Catholic country as Portugal, where we can restfully and peacefully serve God and live according to our profession",[26] moreover, she is grateful for God's protection when bringing her "to this haven of Christendom amidst Portuguese kingdom Catholics".[27] Religious orders were in many cases transnational institutions that expanded their networks moving people and promoting their cultural agenda in several countries.[28]

Cloistered life for women meant living within convent walls; however, it did not imply a lack of communication with the outside world, as through visits, letters, and the network of favours and benefits that nuns enjoyed in the urban society where their families frequently lived, the convent was considered to be an active part of the much larger lay community. They could, in fact, be an asset in politics – as demonstrated by the Discalced Carmelite. Nuns of this order were part of the political propaganda and dissemination of Catholicism in France and the Low Countries, where they moved before friars of the same order were seen by people in a less hostile light and thus were able openly engage in their activities without

---

[25] "el triste y miserable estado en que dexamos nuestra patria, donde ha [*sic*] tantas ciudades, villas y lugares, tan desamparadas del cielo y tan tyranizadas del demonio que no ha sacramentos ni sacerdotes o religiosos que los administren, si no son algunos muy encubiertos en trage seglar..." (Catalina del Espíritu Santo, *Relación de cómo se ha fundado en Alcántara de Portugal junto a Lisboa, el muy devoto monasterio de N.S. de la Quietación,...*. Lisboa: Pedro Craesbeeck, 1627: 2)

[26] "...en tierra tan pacífica y cathólica como es Portugal, donde con descanso y quietud podemos servir a Dios y vivir conforme a nuestra professión" (Catalina del Espíritu Santo, *Relación de cómo se ha fundado en Alcántara de Portugal junto a Lisboa*: 1-2).

[27] "...hasta me traher a este remanso de la christiandad entre los cathólicos del reyno de Portugal" (Catalina del Espíritu Santo, *Relación de cómo se ha fundado en Alcántara de Portugal junto a Lisboa*: 31v.). This was one of the ideas that propaganda relished. Leaving the Catholic Church had resulted in destruction and calamities for kingdoms in Germany, France, England, and the Low Countries, while peace in Spain was due to the perfect accord between the true faith and the monarchy (José María Jover Zamora, Mª Victoria López-Cordón, "La imagen de Europa y el pensamiento político internacional", in *El siglo del Quijote (1580-1680). Volumen I. Religión,* filosofía, ciencia. Madrid: Espasa-Calpe, 1988: 372; Yolanda Rodríguez Pérez, "Los neerlandeses en el teatro de la primera fase de la Guerra de Flandes (1568-1609)", in A. Crespo and M. Herrero (eds.*) España y las 17 provincias de los Países Bajos. Una revisión historiográfica (XVI-XVIII*). Córdoba: Universidad, 2002: 811-831).

[28] The Catholic Church, and especially some of the religious orders like Jesuits, had one of the best transnational networks for information and propaganda, and included priests but also laymen and laywomen that pursued the same goals.

opposition.[29] The first foundation was in Pontoise (France) in 1605, followed by others in Tours and Paris and everywhere the nobility was ready to accept them, so girls from the high ranks of local society professed in these convents demonstrating their success. Following the same purpose and trying to draw population near to Catholicism, Isabel Clara Eugenia, the Low Countries' governor on behalf of the King of Spain, called them to Brussels in 1612. Ana de Jesús [Anne of Jesus] (1541-1621) and Ana de San Bartolomé [Anne of Saint Bartholomew] (1549-1626) were the founders, although it was Ana de San Bartolomé who more closely followed the ruler's ideology.

Spanish nuns in France and the Low countries show in their letters the anxiety of living in an environment that they may not have understood, so they occasionally feel isolated and place the blame on being in another country. In her autobiography Ana de San Bartolomé says to God: "My Lord, neither exile nor the lack of friends nor poverty nor these French people intricacies will drive me away me from Thee".[30] In her case, as in others, the permeability of convent walls (metaphorically speaking) was very noticeable, and she is conscious of being culturally immersed in an alien surrounding which made her feel anxious, always alert to signs of alterity. Ana of San Bartolomé is constantly aware of living in a foreign territory, but language barriers do not necessarily separate; conversely, they can also be an asset:

> We have not mastered the French language, although most of us understand it, but we do not speak it well, apart from a few sentences. We have been mortified by Our Lord. I think it is for our good, and that talking a little has not been bad for us, because every nation has its customs and those in it have their condition and they do not always want to change or think it is good to change them. And so it has been better that we have not been able to talk about everything, because things run more smoothly. It does not have to do with our religious Rule, ... but things in which there is fault are not related to it. So silence is good for everyone.[31]

---

[29] Concha Torres Sánchez, "Conventualismo femenino y expansión contrarreformista: el carmelo descalzo español en Francia y Flandes", in *I Congreso internacional del monacato femenino en España*. León: Universidad de León, 1993: t. II, 237-248.

[30] "Señor mío, ni el destierro ni la falta de los amigos ni la pobreça ni los embrollos destos Falçeses [*sic* instead of "franceses"] me apartarán de ti", Ana de San Bartolomé, *Obras completas de la beata Ana de San Bartolomé*, Roma: Teresianum, 1981: 467.

[31] "...no hemos salido maestras [en la lengua francesa], aunque las más la entendemos, mas no la hablamos bien si no es pocas razones; Nuestro Señor nos ha mortificado. Yo creo es por mejor, y que el hablar poco no nos ha sido malo, porque las naciones cada una tiene sus costumbres y los que están en ella y poseen su

As deep, human understanding is impossible between people from different countries because their habits cannot match, Ana prefers silence to avoid dispute. Religion was common ground for all the sisters in the convent and other questions were deemed less important.[32]

Ana de San Bartolomé was especially involved in political affairs in Brussels, and she kept in touch with Princess Isabel Clara Eugenia, governor of the Southern Low Countries. She opposed the truce and her private writings show that she felt anxious about war affairs – not because of her safety, but because heresy meant that thousands of souls would be condemned to hell without a chance of eternal salvation. Like Teresa of Avila, her friend, she considered herself a praying soldier and would write to her sisters: "My child, tonight I have strongly fought in prayer against all the hell, I think the Church needed it".[33] She was not worried about the interests of Spain or Castile in the Low Countries, but only about the religious faith of those territories; the Catholic Church was her nation, the one she really served and fought for. This view was shared by political powers and society in general, as Princess Isabel Clara Eugenia, the Low Countries' Regent, believed Ana de San Bartolomé's praying had saved Antwerp. Years later, when Ana's beatification process started, all the witnesses would agree.

Religion was not a cultural barrier for all women. Rebeca Isabel Correa challenges almost all the limits of national literature and traditional criticism dealing with post-national categories. According to Barbosa Machado,[34] the great bibliographer of Portuguese literature, Isabel was born in Portugal. She is, however, also mentioned in 1764 by the first author of a Spanish literary history and appears in some Sephardic literature histories. She was probably born in Portugal, but in her adulthood she belonged to Amsterdam's

---

condición, no quieren siempre ni tienen por bueno mudarlas, y así les ha sido más a propósito que no hablemos todo, porque se va más dulcemente. No es por lo que toca al rigor y guarda de la Regla, que eso lo guardan muy en su punto y para eso bien nos entienden; mas las cosas que faltan no es en eso. Y así es bien para todas el silencio" (Ana de San Bartolomé, *Obras completas*: 227).

[32] Mª Victoria López-Cordón, "Enemigos, rivales y contrarios": 66, notes that by the beginning of the seventeenth century Europe was not only a map but a living organism with the inhabitants of each country sharing a set of fixed and timeless characteristics determined by nature. In this way cultural patterns were not so different.

[33] Julien Urkiza, "Soldados españoles de Flandes y sus mujeres bajo el amparo espiritual y solidario de Ana de S. Bartolomé", in *Monte Carmelo*. 2008, 116: 168.

[34] Barbosa Machado, *Bibliotheca Lusitana historica, critica, e cronologica na qual se comprehende a noticia dos authores portuguezes e das obras que compuserao*, Lisboa: Antonio Isidoro da Fonseca, 1741-1759: II, 850.

Sephardic community,[35] where she was living at the end of the 17th century.[36] Her work, *El pastor Fido* ['Fido the shepherd'], is a translation of a dramatic poem from Italian into Spanish. In 1694, the book was apparently printed in two places, Amsterdam and Antwerp, although the Antwerp edition is counterfeit – a usual practice when trying to meet the Hispanic market in Europe and the Iberian Peninsula.[37] She was certainly read in Spain as there are many copies of the book in country libraries. Readers of the time could not identify the work as culturally alien as the text lacks any marks of religious ideology and the original Italian poem can be termed a product of Renaissance upper culture, and therefore suitable for educated readers throughout Europe.[38] Her work belies any kind of national identity tie as she uses a language that was spoken only by a minority in the Low Countries, although it was not her mother tongue (we can assume), but a literary tool employed by many Portuguese writers. She is a Jew but dedicates the translation to Manuel de Belmonte, the Regent of the Catholic King, and one of Amsterdam's cultural patrons, so her social relations is above religious barriers. The original work cannot be referred to a particular cultural milieu and all of Europe was able to re-read it one way or another for a long time.

Curiously enough, these disturbing peculiar questions (to us) are not mentioned in her preface, which is entirely dedicated to her gender identity in the *querelle des femmes* tradition ,[39] asserting her right to write. She resorts to the usual list of wise women, in which the Duchess of Aveiro (Maria de

---

[35] Sephardic Jews were the descendants of Jews who lived in the Iberian Peninsula before their expulsion in the late 15th century. This includes both the descendants of Jews expelled from Spain or Portugal before 1500 and the descendants of crypto-Jews who left later.

[36] Francisco López Estrada, "Una voz de la Holanda hispánica sefardí: Isabel Rebeca Correa" in Monika Bosse, Barbara Potthast and André Stoll (eds.), *La creatividad femenina en el mundo barroco hispánico. María de Zayas – Isabel Rebeca Correa-Sor Juana Inés de la Cruz,* Kassel: Reichenberger, 1999: 395-417.

[37] Harm den Boer, *La literatura sefardí de Amsterdam,* Alcalá de Henares: Universidad de Alcalá, 1996: 52-56.

[38] The work was translated into Spanish by Suárez de Figueroa, and published in Naples in 1602 (a Spanish kingdom at the time), and Valencia in 1609. The original poem by Giovanni Battista Guarini was first printed in Venice in 1590 and went through many editions. The work was turned into a play by the famous Spanish playwright Calderón and there were many musical versions, one of them by Haendel in 1712.

[39] Ursula Jung, *Autorinnen des spanischen Barock. Weibliche Autorschaft in weltlichen und religuiösen Kontexten.* Heidelberg: Universitätsverlag Winter.2010: 61-67.

Guadalupe de Lencastre y Cardenas) is included. Correa might have met her as she knew she is writing a book on China; nonetheless, she says nothing about other women writers living in Amsterdam at the time.[40] How, then, did Correa define her social group identity? What was her *national* feeling? The question is not answered by her words, so it can be discovered in her silence. Boer[41] has noticed contradictions in the identities of Spanish and Portuguese Jews in Amsterdam's exiled society: loyalty to the original land that had banned them, love of that language, identification with its literary culture, friendship and service to Spanish and Portuguese nobility and politicians or defence of aristocratic values which served to discriminate them. Isabel Correa, as a cultivated member of that society, could not ignore these contradictions, so I believe she consciously puts them aside by silencing them and positioning herself on the margin or above the conflict. Religion, territory, culture, politic loyalty, history, group identity features were fingerprints she erased from her book, in which only the problem of being a woman writer in a male milieu is mentioned, and this question places her as a descendant of a prestigious tradition of cultivated noble women.[42] In her case, language was the only identity trait she could not avoid, although it could be viewed as an asset, since Spanish was the most international language in Europe after Latin, even at that time.

Although nations did not exist in the Early Modern Period, educated people considered themselves part of a supra-local community with which they had feelings of collective belonging. Hobsbawn[43] looks for these proto-national feelings in language, ethnicity, common territory, common history, cultural traits, among others, but he demonstrates that none of them are imperative in developing a nation. The women writers we have observed

---

[40] Kennet Brown, "La poetisa es la luna que con las de Apolo viene: nuevos datos sobre y textos de varias poetisas sefardíes de los siglos XVII y XVIII", in Monika Bosse Barbara Potthast and André Stoll (eds.), *La creatividad femenina en el mundo barroco hispánico. María de Zayas – Isabel Rebeca Correa- Sor Juana Inés de la Cruz,* Kassel: Reichenberger, 1999: 439-480.

[41] Harm den Boer, "Las múltiples caras de la identidad. Nobleza y fidelidad ibéricas entre los sefardíes de Amsterdam", in *Familia, religión y negocio. El sefardismo en las relaciones entre el mundo ibérico y los Países Bajos en la Edad Moderna,* Madrid: Fundación Carlos de Amberes, 2002: 95-112.

[42] Boer, *La literatura sefardí de Amsterdam:* 19, divides Sephardic editions into Jewish and non-denominational works. He thinks that counterfeit editions were meant for non-Jewish readers looking for a more extensive reception; Correa's translation can be classified as part of this group.

[43] Eric Hobsbawn, *Nations and Nationalism since 1780: Programme, Myth, Reality.* Cambridge: Cambridge University Press, 1990: 7-8, 48-79.

belonged to the elites, and even though they did not directly state their feelings of community, their ideas are shown in their expression. Political and cultural concepts permeate their works, so their understanding of this collective identity can be traced. As expected, allusions to this question arise when it is being challenged, threatened or when faced with its ideological boundaries, and the answer is either for reaffirmation or opposition. In creating nationalism or any other group identity, definite enemies are essential, because they are modelled to invert community values and so strengthen them, as demonstrated by studies on the subject.

All the writers discussed here show concern for their social identity and express on the grounds of two concepts– history and religion. The country's history is understood as a way to find permanent values and establish rights. These common grounds offer a great opportunity to select and retell the past, which is used to design a different present and give basis to support the writer's position. Ferreira's history revision is built from the point of view of the family so her group can have a place among the illustrious families of Portugal, where they are positioned by creating a new past shared with Castile. Guevara's treatises offer a gendered interpretation of history in line with the *querelle des femmes* debate, as bravery is one of her country's main identity traits. But as only women keep have been able to maintain it this makes them superior to men. This interpretation is used as a way of affronting men and making them aware of their duties to the country, but it is also used as a means of pointing out how both genders share essential qualities with Castile people too.

As stated previously, collective identity is nourished by grievances and Sister Catherine's *Relación* is created on that basis. Her personal history is narrated as part of a group united by a common religious trait and the selection of events underscores their positive characteristics. The wide range of historical sufferings creates an identity of extreme semantic oppositions: Protestant / Catholic, cruel / kind, damnation / salvation, dangerous / peaceful territories, conflict/ coexistence, freedom/ oppression. In the end this is associated with each religious option and is defined as we-Catholics positive *vs*. them-Protestants negative. Within this frame, sister Catherine cannot feel foreign as Lisbon is not the land of exile, but a country she can identify with, the "Portuguese kingdom Catholics" she refers to. She uses history to define a religious transnational identity that can be associated with any Catholic country. This same feeling of religious belonging which crosses political borders can be found in the writings of Spanish Carmelite nuns living in

France or Brussels as they try to put aside linguistic or cultural differences for the sake of Catholicism, making it the most important bond.

We can contrast Guevara's and Correa's positions as both are the only writers to put forward a gender identity. Correa avoids any other identity signs possibly because she has left behind country and language and lives in a politically and culturally minority community which does not want to call attention to itself. On the other hand, Guevara hoists the Castile flag against Portuguese people and it is then that she uses the religious question by describing them as Jews. It is interesting to note that this kind of distinguishing tag was put forward possibly because language, politics or territory could not be used to define them as *alien,* as these traits were not shared by Castilians, Aragonese, Basques or Neapolitans, even though they were part of the Spanish crown and not enemies.

Under this light religion can be established as one of the most important social identity categories, and we must probably consider it to be a key element when talking about transnational influences or culture. If religion was more important than territory or language, defining writers after our national identities without considering this trait can distort our analysis. At least during the Early Modern Period, as seen from Spain, it was probably the hardest boundary to cross, segregating two worlds so women writers who are to be termed as essential for our culture, such as Teresa of Avila, would never be read in Luteran countries, and on the other hand, books coming from those countries were banned in Spain. Even when talking about fiction, were Catholic writers read in protestant countries or vice versa? Did they write the same kind of works? In the same way? Was this due to religious influence? To censorship restrictions?

Nations did not exist during the Early Modern period, although the word use is well documented. Searching for this non-existent concept has not been a futile hunt as it has shown other social identity categories that might be difficult to understand nowadays but if not taken into account could allow the historical perspective to become blurred. If nothing else, this trap must make us aware of existing methodological pre-conceptions that should be tackled very careful.

## Select Bibliography


### A. Primary Sources

Catalina del Espíritu Santo. 1627. *Relación de cómo se ha fundado en Alcántara de Portugal junto a Lisboa, el muy devoto monasterio de N.S. de la Quietación,... para las monjas peregrinas... venidas de la Provincia de Alemania Baxa, después de los hereges las aver perseguido y desterrado de tierras en tierras por quatro vezes.* Preface and epilogue by fray Juan de las Llagas. Lisboa: Pedro Craesbeeck.

María de San José Salazar, 1979. *Escritos espirituales*, (ed. Simeón de la Sagrada Familia) Roma: Postulación General O.C.D.

Ana de San Bartolomé. 1981. *Obras completas de la beata Ana de San Bartolomé,* (ed. Julián Urkiza) Roma: Teresianum.

### B. Secondary Sources

Álvarez Junco, José. 2001., *Mater dolorosa. La idea de España en el siglo XIX.* Madrid: Taurus.

Andretta, Stefano. 2009. "Note sulla natura dell'immagine del nemico in età moderna tra identità e alterità" in *Cantù, Francesca; Giuliana Di Febo; and Renato Moro, eds., L'immagine del nemico. Storia, ideologia e rappresentazione tra età moderna e contemporanea.* Roma: Viella: 31-40.

Baranda, Nieves. 2005. *Cortejo a lo prohibido. Lectoras y escritoras en la España Moderna.* Madrid: Arco Libros.

Barbosa Machado. 1741-1759. *Bibliotheca Lusitana historica, critica, e cronologica na qual se comprehende a noticia dos authores portuguezes e das obras que compuserao,* Lisboa: Antonio Isidoro da Fonseca. 4 vols.

Boer, Harm den. 1996. *La literatura sefardí de Amsterdam,* Alcalá de Henares: Universidad de Alcalá.

—. 2002. "Las múltiples caras de la identidad. Nobleza y fidelidad ibéricas entre los sefardíes de Amsterdam", in *Familia, religión y negocio. El sefardismo en las relaciones entre el mundo ibérico y los Países Bajos en la Edad Moderna,* Madrid: Fundación Carlos de Amberes: 95-112.

Bouza, Fernando. 2000. *Portugal no tempo dos Filipes: política, cultura representaçóes (1580-1668).* Lisboa: Cosmos.

—. 2005. *El libro y el cetro. La biblioteca de Felipe IV en la Torre Alta del Alcázar de Madrid.* Salamanca: Instituto del Historia del Libro y la Lectura.

Brown, Kennet. 1999. "La poetisa es la luna que con las de Apolo viene: nuevos datos sobre y textos de varias poetisas sefardíes de los siglos XVII y XVIII" in *La creatividad femenina en el mundo barroco hispánico. María de Zayas – Isabel Rebeca Correa- Sor Juana Inés de la Cruz.* Bosse, Monika, Barbara Potthast and André Stoll (eds). Kassel: Reichenberger: 439-480.

Hobsbawm, Eric. 1990. *Nations and Nationalism since 1780: Programme, Myth, Reality.* Cambridge: Cambridge University Press.

Jover Zamora, José María, Mª Victoria López-Cordón. 1988. "La imagen de Europa y el pensamiento político internacional" in *El siglo del Quijote (1580-1680).* V. I. *Religión, filosofía, ciencia.* Madrid: Espasa-Calpe (*Historia de España*, dir. por Ramón Menéndez Pidal, XXVI, I).

Jung, Ursula. 2010. *Autorinnen des spanischen Barock. Weibliche Autorschaft in weltlichen und religuiösen Kontexten.* Heidelberg: Universitätsverlag Winter.

Kamen, Henry. 1991. *Spain, 1469-1714: A Society of Conflict.* Harlow: Longman.

—. 2008. *Imagining Spain: historical myth and national identity.* New Haven: Yale University Press.

López Estrada, Francisco. 1999. "Una voz de la Holanda hispánica sefardí: Isabel Rebeca Correa" in *La creatividad femenina en el mundo barroco hispánico. María de Zayas – Isabel Rebeca Correa- Sor Juana Inés de la Cruz,* Bosse, Monika, Barbara Potthast and André Stoll (eds). Kassel: Reichenberger: 395-417.

López-Cordón, Mª Victoria. 2009. "Enemigos, rivales y contrarios: formas de antagonismo en los tiempos modernos" in Cantù, Francesca; Giuliana Di Febo; and Renato Moro (eds). *L'immagine del nemico. Storia, ideologia e rappresentazione tra età moderna e contemporánea.* Roma: Viella: 57-76.

Manero Sorolla, Mª Pilar. 1988 "Exilios y destierros en la vida y en la obra de María de Salazar" in *Actas del VII Simposio de la Sociedad Española de Literatura General y Comparada.* Madrid: Castalia: 51-59.

Manzano Baena, Laura. 2002. "Inventando al enemigo: imágenes de España en las Provincias Unidas" in A. Crespo and M. Herrero (eds.) *España y las 17 provincias de los Países Bajos. Una revisión historiográfica (XVI-XVIII).* Córdoba: Universidad: 775-796.

Redes 2009. *Las redes del imperio. Elites sociales en la articulación de la Monarquía Hispánica, 1492-1714.* Madrid: Marcial Pons/ Historia, Universidad Pablo de Olavide.

Rodríguez Pérez, Yolanda 2002. "Los neerlandeses en el teatro de la primera fase de la Guerra de Flandes (1568-1609)" in A. Crespo and M. Herrero (eds). *España y las 17 provincias de los Países Bajos. Una revisión historiográfica (XVI-XVIII*). Córdoba: Universidad: 811-831.

Romero-Díaz, Nieves, (ed.).(tr). 2007. *Warnings to the Kings and Advice on Restoring Spain A bilingual edition.* Chicago; London: The University of Chicago Press (The Other Voice in Early Modern Europe).

Rosa Rivero, Alberto, Guglielmo Bellelli and David Bakhurst.2000. *Memoria colectiva e identidad nacional.* Madrid: Biblioteca Nueva.

Smith, Anthony D. *National Identity,* 1991. London: Penguin Books.

Torres Sánchez, Concha. 1993. "Conventualismo femenino y expansión contrarreformista: el carmelo descalzo español en Francia y Flandes" in *I Congreso internacional del monacato femenino en España.* León: Universidad de León, t. II: 237-248.

Urkiza, Julen. 2008. "Soldados españoles de Flandes y sus mujeres bajo el amparo espiritual y solidario de Ana de S. Bartolomé" in *Monte Carmelo.* 116: 165-202.

# Expatriates. Women's Communities, Mobility and Cosmopolitanism in Early Modern Europe: English and Spanish Nuns in Flanders

*María Jesús Pando-Canteli*

ABSTRACT The Spanish Netherlands were, during the 17th century, the destination of English Catholics escaping from the restrictions of the Penal Laws. The exile of English women and the displacement of their Spanish coreligionists made difficult the adscription of cultural practices to a single national tradition. Through their intense correspondence, a complex set of alliances was created in Flanders between religious Spanish and English women. This epistolary activity contributed to permeating the imagined borders of national groups by constructing a sense of collective identities around common cultural practices. The foundation enterprise of the first English Carmel in Antwerp is a case in point that illustrates how transnational women networks managed to negotiate proper, if not always legitimate, channels of influence that indicate the fluid and ubiquitous nature of power in early modern communities.

IN 1598, AN ENGLISH AGENT recorded the profession of English nuns at the heart of a Habsburg court:

> There are 16th English Gentlewomen in this town who wish to set up a nunnery. The Archduke gave them 2000 pounds, and they bought a house. On the instant a daughter of Sir John Berkeley, and sister of Nicholas Pointz, was solemnly created Abess by the Archbishop of Malines, and the next Sunday, the Lady Mary Percy, Mrs Dorothy Araundell, and six other English ladies took the habit. The ceremony was very solemn; the Infanta, who was their godmother, the Archduke and all the Court, and the Pope's Nuncio being present ... The eight were most bravely apparelled ... and adorned with rich jewels like brides. The Infanta brought them into Church, leading the Lady Mary Percy and Mrs Dorothy (Araundell)... The ceremony over, they returned in pairs apparelled as nuns, the Abbess following. The Infanta embraced them all, and assured them she would be a mother to them. The Archduke promised them all assistance. The Infanta made a

> banquet for 100 persons, the great ladies, Abbess and nuns dining at one of the tables. It was one of the solemnest things that was seen this hundred years. [1]

This episode, registered in the *Calendar of State Papers,* recalls the profession of Lady Mary Percy and Joanna Berkeley as Benedictine Nuns in the first convent for English ladies in Brussels, known then as the Spanish Netherlands. The prominence given to this event by the English agent shows that, for the intelligence services, 'nunneries' were far from the trivial affairs of women. The presence of the Archdukes and the Papal Nuncio speaks by itself of the political transcendence of the enterprise, and reveals the anxieties of compatriots it inspired on the other side of the Channel.

A similar episode took place a few years later in 1607, when the Archdukes founded the first convent of Discalced Carmelites in Flanders, also in Brussels:

> The year of 1607, on March 25th, their Serene Highness Archduke Albert and Infanta Isabella Clara Eugenia came in the evening to the very place they had chosen to erect the building of this Royal convent of Carmelites, where everything had been disposed and ready for this matter [...] for despite being a Royal work fit for Princes, they wanted to build it according to their Constitutions. [2]

Situated immediately beside the Infanta's palace, these convents stand as the hallmark of femal e agency in counterreformation Europe. Determined in their commitment to support monastic expansion in Europe, this is an unequivocal sign of Habsburg's strategy against the growing pressure of Lutheranism and Calvinism in neighboring territories:

---

[1] *Domestic Calendar Elizabeth* 1598-1601, Edmondes to Salisbury, Brussels, April 17, 1607. PRO Flanders Correspondence, vol.8 f.279.

[2] "El año de 1607 a 25 de marzo, sus Altezas Serenísimas el Archiduque Alberto y la Infanta Isabel Clara Eugenia [...] vinieron a la tarde con toda su corte al sitio que habían tomado para hacer la fábrica de este Real convento de las Carmelitas, donde estaba todo dispuesto y acomodado para esto [...] que aunque era obra real como hecha de Prinzipes, quisieron que se hiciese como dice la Constitución", "Teresa de Jesús: Sobre la Fundación del Monasterio", in Concha Torres Sánchez, *La clausura imposible. Conventualismo femenino y expansión contrarreformista.* Madrid: Asociación cultural Al-Mudayna, 2000: 70.

> The place that I have chosen for the monastery is beside our house, and that is what I always wanted, so we can receive the good influence of your house.[3]

Why is the English spy concerned about a community of cloistered women? What interest, if any, can be gleamed from the contemplative life of a few women? And how can the Infanta's personal involvement in these enterprises be interpreted? The above examples also demonstrate that these cloistered communities were mostly comprised of foreign women: English and Spanish, but also Dutch and French. This presence of foreign communities of women in Flanders may pose an interesting case at work in the formation of transnational religious and cultural identities, thus destabilizing pre-existing notions of national allegiances.

This paper aims to illustrate the complex conglomerate of transnational and multilingual monastic ventures in Flanders at the turn of the 17th century by examining the intense epistolary activity taking place between these cloistered women and contemporary persons of influence, and also through evidence found in some of their autobiographies and convent chronicles. In particular, I will illustrate the case of the cross-national network that enabled the foundation of the first Carmelite convent for English ladies in Antwerp in 1619, and in doing so, I intend to highlight the importance of these female discursive practices in negotiating cultural and national identities and allegiances.

From the 1590s until the 1630s, partly coinciding with the *Twelve years truce*, the Spanish Netherlands was a real *terra franca* in the transit and meeting of persons among different European territories, which makes this territory as a true *third space* of cosmopolitanism and trans-nationalism in the early modern period. Two forces, among others, contributed to this phenomenon: the English exile, on the one hand and the counter-reformist expansion on the other.

Flanders was the destination of English Catholics escaping from the hard restrictions of Penal Laws, and also the first step in the post-tridentine expansion of reformed religious orders from Spain into the Continent. Due to the permanent financial support of the Spanish crown, many English settled in Flanders, whether as Spanish pensioners and agents, or as officials of some

---

[3] "el sitio que tengo para el monasterio es junto de nuestra casa, que es lo que yo he pretendido siempre, para que se nos pegue algo de lo bueno que tendréis en la vuestra." "De la Infanta a Ana de Jesús", in Concha Torres, *La clausura imposible*: 58-59.

Spanish army. Some benefited more indirectly, through the politics of patronage for nuns and priests in convents and seminaries. The commitment began as early as 1586 with the Duchess of Parma as governor of the Low Countries. The pension system provided by the Spanish crown to assist the English exiled on the continent was the beginning of a financial apparatus that would also involve the English Mission of the Society of Jesus, the foundation of new colleges and seminaries for English priests, and the maintenance of a number of religious enterprises, like the Bridgettines of Syon, and the English Benedictines in Brussels. The foundation movement of Catholic convents was thus carried out at the expense of the private fortunes of many of these ladies, the generous dowries of their novices, the patronage of the Catholic nobility and, above all, the unconditional commitment of the Spanish Catholic monarchy with its various ramifications.[4]

From 1580 to 1630, Augustinians, Jesuits, Benedictines, Carmelites, and Poor Clares multiplied their convents and schools in the Catholic territories of France and Flanders, contributing to the transformation of the social fabric, the establishment of new centers of power and, consequently, to the creation of contested identities. Some of these founders came all the way from Spain, as is the case of the Jesuits and the Discalced Carmelites. The two founding mothers in France and Flanders, Ana de Jesús and Ana de Bartolomé, had been direct collaborators, disciples and close friends of Teresa of Avila, and from 1604 to 1614 they set up at least ten new convents, from Paris to Antwerp, whose cloisters were formed by French, English, Flemish, Dutch and Spanish nuns. Others, like the Benedictines in Brussels, had been there since 1592. This circumstance made Flemish convents truly cosmopolitan places where various nationalities shared common spaces and

---

[4] The topic of the English pensioners and the politics of monastic foundation for English Catholics on exile were first explored as early as 1914 by Peter Guilday. In the sixties, the works of Albert Loomie, such as *Spain and the Jacobean Catholics, 1613-1624.* London: Publications of the Catholic Record Society, 1978, on the Spanish connection of Elizabethans and Jacobeans were providing rich textual evidence of this intensive and extensive contact. More recently, Cristopher Highley, *Catholics Writing the Nation in Early Modern Britain and Ireland.* Oxford: Oxford University Press, 2008, and Ronald Corthell, Frances Dolan, and Arthur Marotti, *Catholic Culture in Early Modern England.* Notre Dame, Indiana: University of Notre Dame Press, 2007, reassessed the secular exclusion of Catholics in the configuration of English national culture in the early modern period. Claire Walker, *Gender and Politics in Early-Modern Europe. English Convents in France and the Low Countries.* New York: Palgrave-Macmillan, 2003, and Concha Torres, *La clausura imposible*, explored at length the politics involved in the foundation movement of both English and Spanish nuns abroad.

religious practices. But they also became sites of intense political activity[5] and conflict, which required management skills and a leadership that transcended the walls of the cloister. This complex circulation of people implies a frantic activity that overcomes national borders and creates a transcultural space of transit and influence, a 'contact zone', conditioned by permanent exchange and mobility. Many of the agents at work in the formation of these spaces are women, who actively contributed, from within and beyond, to the cultural and social transformation of these communities. But, how did all this happen? Are these conditions of displacement productive for the construction of, for example, alternative alliances and allegiances than of those with their compatriots back home?

Texts – of different quality and origin – written by women can provide answers to these questions. Although these discourses (letters, autobiographies, records and chronicles of convents) have not traditionally been subject to the interest of literary scholars, they materialize women's active and direct contribution to cultural production. In this sense, recent scholarship on early modern women's writing has drawn attention to their intense activity in textual production, consumption and circulation, and shifts the emphasis from the conventions and channels of traditionally male genres to textual communities built upon peer collaboration and exchange.[6] This activity has already been widely studied in terms of Catholic territories, where female monastic life allowed for a regular involvement in writing and study activities.[7] Among these, letter correspondence was one of the most

---

[5] It is commonly assumed that the Counter-Reformation expansion carried out by religious orders in France and Flanders served the political purpose, among others, of restraining the advance of Protestantism by growing seeds of Catholic piety among the children of the local gentry and English exiles. Claire Walker, *Gender and Politics in Early-Modern Europe,* illustrates how later in the century, during the Civil War and protectorate, English convents played an important role in the restoration of the English monarchy.

[6] See Julie D Campbell and Anne R. Larsen (eds). *Early Modern Women and Transnational Communities of Letters.* Burlington VT: Ashgate, 2009 and Vicente, Marta V. and Luís R. Corteguera (eds). *Women, Texts and Authority in the Early Modern Hispanic World.* Burlington VT: Ashgate, 2003.

[7] The groundbreaking study of Electa Arenal and Stacey Schlau (eds). *Untold Sisters: Hispanic Nuns in their Own. Works.* Alburquerque: University of New Mexico Press, 1989, on religious women writing in the Hispanic world gave way to further studies on individual. See Allison Weber, *Teresa of Avila and the Rhetoric of Femininity.* Princeton: Princeton University Press, 1990, or collective agency in both the English such as Claire Walker, *Gender and Politics in Early-Modern Europe*, and Hispanic worlds: Elizabeth A Lehfeldt. *Religious Women in Golden Age Spain. The Permeable*

powerful means of participating in contemporary life. Despite the strict observance of the reformed orders, nuns kept a fluent communication with their families and acquaintances in England and Spain, Church authorities in Flanders and Rome, disciples and correligionists in other convents, and with fellow English priests, who were also exiled.

By the time the Spanish Infanta was leading Lady Mary Percy to the altar on the occasion of the foundation of English Benedictines in Brussels, as stated above, a Spanish noble woman devoted to the cause of English martyrs, Luisa de Carvajal, was writing to her friend in the Flemish court (Magdalena de San Jerónimo) regarding her offer to found a monastery for Spanish nuns in Brussels:

> Do tell her Highness if she would like me to go and at my cost establish a convent of Spanish nuns; I am told she found most agreeable one for English ladies, whom she encountered at that court some time ago. One of these ladies being the daughter of the most glorious martyr Thomas Percy, Earl of Northumberland.[8]

Carvajal never founded that convent. Instead, she donated her dowry some years later to the foundation of a Jesuit Seminary for English priests in Louvain. Yet her offer highlights the centrality of the Spanish Infanta in the foundation enterprise,[9] the complicity of political and religious forces, and the importance of female networks in their accomplishment. Carvajal arrived

---

*Cloister*. Aldershot: Ashgate, 2005, and Jodi Bilinkoff, *Related Lives. Confessors and their Female Penitents, 1450-1750*. Ithaca: Cornell University Press, 2005.

[8] "Dígale vuestra merced a su Alteza, que si gustará de que le vaya a hacer un monasterio de españolas a mi costa; que me dicen holgó mucho con uno de señoras inglesas que se ha fundado de poco acá en esa corte, hija una dellas del gloriosísimo Tomás Percy, mártir, conde de Northumberland." "Luisa de Carvajal to Magdalena de San Jerónimo", March 1600. Venerable Dª Luisa de Carvajal y Mendoza, *Epistolario y poesías*. Madrid: Biblioteca de Autores Españoles, 1965: 100.

[9] Isabel Clara Eugenia is of utmost importance in understanding the development of anti-Protestant politics among English Catholic exiles. She was the candidate proposed by some English exiles to occupy the throne of England after the death of Elizabeth I. There was a movement among these English Catholics, alongside the diplomacy in Spain, Italy and Flanders, to urge Philip III and the Holy See to intervene in claiming the throne of England for Isabel Clara Eugenia, whom they considered as the only 'safe' candidate to the throne given their distrust of Scottish Stuarts. She and her husband Albert never showed any interest in this enterprise, which they saw as dangerous and destabilising for the peace of the region, and declined the offer. See "Father Robert Parsons to Martin de Idiaquez", in *Calendar of State Papers*, Eliz, Domestic 648, 1588-1601: 628-631.

in London during the turbulent times that followed the Gunpowder Plot, and remained there until her death in 1614. From the powerful family of the Mendozas, Carvajal grew up in the closed circle of the royal family in the Monastery of Descalzas Reales (Madrid) and soon became engaged in the activities of the Society of Jesus, whose influence was central in her decision to move to London as an active apostle against the expansion of Protestantism and in support of the persecuted Catholic community.[10] Her letters, addressed to some of the most powerful and influential people in England at that time, provide an extraordinary source of information about the condition of Catholics in Jacobean England and abound in recommendations for sons and daughters of English families travelling to the continent to join seminaries or nunneries.[11]

In another letter to Magdalena de San Jerónimo, from London, Carvajal introduces Lady Mary Lovel, an English widow travelling to Flanders with the purpose of setting up new convents for English women. At the end of 1606 she was writing from London:

> I think that it is there a widowed lady, called Milady Lovel, whom I came to know well here and from whom I received charity and shelter when I was in London alone and ill. I pray you please befriend her, because her constancy is worthy of it, since she has always been a true Catholic and hosted regularly fathers and priests, and I believe she would please you, had she the chance.[12]

---

[10] Glynn Redworth, *The She-Apostle. The Life and Death of Luisa de Carvajal y Mendoza*, Oxford: Oxford University Press, 2008; María J. Pando-Canteli, "*Tentando vados:* The Martyrdom Politics of Luisa de Carvajal y Mendoza", in *Journal of Early Modern Cultural Studies*. 10(1), 2010: 117-141.

[11] Together with Carvajal's collection of letters, the letters of the Spanish Carmelites – Ana de Jesús (edited by C. Torres 1995), Ana de San Bartolomé (edited by J. Urkiza 1983, 1998), Leonor de San Bernardo, and Beatriz de la Concepción (edited by Serouet in 1981 and 1967 respectively) – have also been published. There is no published record of English contemporary nuns, although some biographies include fragments or references to letters (Claire Walker, "'Doe not supose me a well mortifyed Nun dead to the world': Letter Writing in English Early Modern Convents" in Daybell, J. (ed.). *Early Modern Women Letter Writers*. New York: Palgrave-Macmillan, 2001: 159-176), and there are allusions to women's epistolary activity in the chronicles of their convents (Carmelites at Brussels and Antwerp; Sta Monica, Louvain; Benedictines in Brussels, English Carmelites now in Lanherne, England, etc).

[12] "Ahí creo está ya una señora viuda, que se llama Milady Lovel, a quien acá conocí muy bien y recibí della muy grande caridad y acogimiento en tiempo que estaba en Londres, sin tener a quien volver la cabeza, y bien mala. Suplico a vuestra merced

Involved in several controversies with the Benedictines and the Carmelites, Lovel was an acquaintance of Carvajal herself, who a month later, pleaded again to her friend San Jerónimo on her behalf: "please approach her and befriend her ".[13] Lady Mary Lovel was "[one] of the best-known and most fervent recusants of their era,"[14] widowed around 1606 – just the time when she decided to move to the Spanish Netherlands. It seems likely that Lady Lovel might have used some of the channels facilitated by Luisa de Carvajal and her close acquaintances at court, because in 1608 she entered a Benedictine convent in Brussels. This was the first convent founded for English women under the protection of the Infanta, with the financial support of the Flemish court, but it was also closely scrutinised by English agents, as the opening episode of this paper illustrates. Lady Mary Lovel left soon afterwards, however, due to major differences with the prioress, Mary Percy. Lovel strove for many years to use her money and influence to found other convents, but she did not succeed until 1619, when she founded the first English Carmelite convent in Antwerp, with Anne of the Ascension (Anne Worsley) as prioress, and the somewhat reluctant approval of the Carmelite superiors, Ana de Jesús and Ana de San Bartolomé.

Although very poorly documented, the record of Lovel's enterprise in founding English convents and her liaisons with Carmelites, English Jesuits, and the Spanish political and religious establishment, is a fascinating case at work of how these cross-national female communities worked, and their importance to the circulation of goods and people in early modern Europe.

By the time Lovel finally managed to settle in Antwerp with a small group of English nuns in 1619, St Teresa's disciples – Ana de Jesús and Ana de San Bartolomé – and three other companions, had already been trying to establish the Carmel in France and Flanders for more than fourteen years: since their initial journey from Spain to France in 1605, they had founded convents in Mons, Paris, Pontoise, Dijon, Amiens, Tours, and Rouen, all peopled with daughters of the local nobility. The arrival of Ana de Jesús in

---

cuanto puedo, le haga toda amistad, porque lo merece su constancia, que ha sido muy verdadera católica siempre y tenía ordinaria hospedería de padres y sacerdotes, y ella creo yo sabrá dar gusto a vuestra merced en cualquier ocasión." "To Magdalena de San Jerónimo", Londres, 3 de noviembre de 1606, in Venerable Dª Luisa de Carvajal Y Mendoza, *Epistolario y poesías.* González, Marañón Jesús and Camilo María Abad (eds). Madrid: Biblioteca de Autores Españoles, 1965 (179): 192.

[13] *Ibid.*, 194.

[14] Colleen M Seguin, 'Lovel, Mary, Lady Lovel (*c.*1564-1628)', in *Oxford Dictionary of National Biography*. Oxford: Oxford University Press, 2008.

Brussels in 1609 had been the first step towards establishing the Carmelites in Flanders and had been solemnly welcomed and supported by the political and religious authorities, particularly the Spanish Infanta:

> Although I wished you were here for long, and see the daughters of our Mother Teresa in these our states, Our Lord did not fulfill my will until now, and I wish you cannot decline the offer of coming and found a monastery here. [15]

Being direct disciples of Teresa of Avila, her closest collaborators and companions in her final years, Ana de Jesús and Ana de San Bartolomé were the perfect ambassadors to secure the expansion of the order for the Spanish monarchy in strategic territories. After the foundation in Brussels came the foundation in Mons (1607), Lovain (1607), Antwerp (1612), Malines (1616), and Ypers (1623). These communities were recruiting women of Flemish origin but also French and English, and were often ruled by the Spanish foundresses and under the jurisdiction of the local clergy, until the Carmelite friars later settled in the country. The first Carmelite convent for English women in Antwerp was founded in 1619 by Lady Mary Lovel, under the guidance of Mother Anne of the Ascension, first prioress of the English Carmelites at Antwerp (originally Anne Worsley, daughter of an English Catholic exile, who had settled in Flanders fleeing from the Elizabethan persecution of Catholics). The multinational, multilingual environment was a challenge for community life. Hardman reports how Anne of the Ascension would "mortify her desire to be taken for what she was, an English gentlewoman, for, at that time, she was living among Spanish, Flemish and Dutch nuns".[16] This poses interesting questions as to how national allegiances may or may not condition basic aspects of monastic life, such as the politics governing these institutions, the recruitment processes, and all the human capital involved in the support of these houses, as well as the dissemination to the world of their contemplative vocation. The foundation of the English Carmelites in Antwerp shows the global machinery at work in setting an institution that, paradoxically, shelters women with the vocation of 'dying to

---

[15] "Aunque ha muchos días que os he deseado aquí y ver en estos estados a las hijas de la Madre Teresa de Jesús, Nuestro Señor no ha sido servido de cumplirme este deseo hasta ahora, que espero no me negaréis el venir a fundar aquí un monasterio. "*De la Infanta a Ana de Jesús*", 1606, in Concha Torres, *La clausura imposible*: 58.

[16] Anne Hardman, *English Carmelites in Penal Times*. London: Burns Oates & Washbourne, 1936: 154.

the world'. As some scholars[17] have already noted: "far from separating from society and dying to the world and its concerns, the convent is considered an integral part of the early modern state, economy, social fabric and culture".[18]

Lady Mary Lovel had been negotiating with the local clergy about the possibility of founding a new convent herself. Her disputes with the Benedictines in Brussels had mainly been caused by her radical opposition to renounce Jesuit confessors. It is no coincidence that she moved from England to Flanders led by the powerful hand of the Jesuit William Baldwin, who in turn had been sheltered by Carvajal in London and assisted by her during his imprisonment in Newgate after the Gunpowder Plot, and was well known in the political circle of recusant Catholics and political agents close to Spanish imperial circles. In the Chronicles of the English Carmel in Antwerp, composed of the autobiographical records of prioresses and other testimonies, Anne of the Ascension explains how Lady Mary Lovel first got in touch:

> Madam Lovel in England then widow, being moved and inspired to employ herself and means to the service of God, being in the spiritual exercise under the direction of a father of the Society [...] was moved to come over to these countreys to doe some particular service to our blessed lady which she understood was to found a Monastery most dedicated to our Lady. Being in these parts she took the Spiritual Exercise under the direction of a father of the Society of Jesus, English at Louvain, who informed her of our Order, and that it would be a work most agreeable to God.[19]

Baldwin, and other prominent English Jesuits like Holt, Hoskins or Gerard,[20] were key in enhancing cosmopolitan networks through their

[17] Electa Arenal and Stacey Schlau (eds). *Untold Sisters: Hispanic Nuns in their Own. Works.* Alburquerque: University of New Mexico Press, 1989: Allison Weber. "The three lives of the Vida. The uses of convent autobiography" in Vicente and Corteguera (eds). *Women, Texts and Authority in the Early Modern Spanish World,* London: Ashgate, 2008, and Magdalena Sánchez, *The Empress, the Queen and the Nun. Women and Power at the Court of Philip III of Spain.* Baltimore: Johns Hopkins University Press, 1998.

[18] Claire Walker, *Gender and Politics in Early-Modern Europe*: 5.

[19] *Chronicle of the English Carmel in Antwerp*, 82-84, MS. I want to thank Julen Urkiza for providing me with a copy of the original manuscript of these Chronicles.

[20] In Gerard's autobiography there is evidence of the acquaintance with Mary Lovel. He, John Gerard, was sent to Flanders in 1609 "to help in the foundation of the first novitiate of the English province at Louvain" (Philip Caraman. *John Gerard. The Autobiography of an Elizabethan.* London: Longman, 1951: 277) which was erected thanks to the donation of Carvajal herself. Likewise, Carvajal coincided with Hoskins

constant interaction with these women, who were strategically located in continental convents or English households, and conveniently protected by the powerful machinery of imperial Spain. Lady Lovel might have relied on both Baldwin and Carvajal to enter the circle of the English Catholic elite on the continent, the circle of the daughters of renowned families such as the Araundels, Percies, Vavasour, Digbys or Vaux – she herself being a Roper, a descendant of Thomas More.

Mary Lovel is also mentioned several times in the correspondence between the Spanish Carmelite Ana de San Bartolomé and her English disciple Anne of the Ascension, about the foundation of the first English Carmel.[21] A convent of Carmelites had already been founded in Antwerp in 1612 by Ana de San Bartolomé, with nuns of different origins, speaking different languages: Spanish, Flemish, English and French. The initial joy at having in Lovel a financial sponsor ("good news of a prosperous and happy event, that I have been told an English lady is going to found a monastery")[22] was soon overshadowed by misgivings about her authoritarian stance and difficult personality ('terrible mujer' as San Bartolomé calls her). Lovel was a woman of good contacts and better means, a convenient partner, but also a troublesome person considering the way in which she failed to integrate her self into different communities (the Benedictines in Brussels and the Austin Cannoneses in Louvain before). "Terrible mujer ... y si la enojo, temo lo sabra todo el mundo" [terrible woman, and if annoyed, everybody will know],[23] writes Ana de San Bartolomé to Anne of the Ascension as early as 1617, when conversations for the foundation began. It was also established that Lovel did not spare any energy in getting as much support as possible

in Madrid, who might have informed her still in Madrid about the activities of English Catholic women in exile. Hoskins was a close collaborator of Mary Percy, as was the Jesuit Holt, with whom she was engaged in translation activities). The close and intense liaisons between the Jesuits cosmopolitan network and these women in the dissemination of Catholic culture deserve a separate analysis.

[21] More than 130 letters written by Ana de San Bartolomé to Anne of the Ascension are preserved and published by Julián Urkiza in his excellent edition of *Obras completas de Ana de San Bartolomé* (1998). As far as I know, no letters of Anne of the Ascension to Ana de San Bartolomé are preserved, although her autobiography refers unambiguously to the intense and deep relationship between the two nuns and, of course, abounds in details on the Lovel affair and the foundation process.

[22] "Buenas nuevas de un próspero y feliz hecho que me dicen que una dama inglesa va a fundar un monasterio" "A las Carmelitas Descalzas de Malinas" [1617] letter 195, in Julián Urkiza, *Obras completas de la Beata Ana de San Bartolomé*. Burgos: Editorial Monte Carmelo 1998: 1104.

[23] *Ibid,*. 1119.

from the Carmelite superior in Brussels, Tomás de Jesús, when the English convent faced a cold reception from the authorities at Antwerp: "Harto me pesaque los de la villa no quieran aquí las inglesas" [I regret that the English nuns are rejected by the villagers],[24] and some days later: "La fundación de las inglesas no la han admitido aquí... ella [Lovel]es ida a Bruselas a nuestro padre" [the English foundation was not admitted here [...] and she [Lovel] went to Brussels to visit our Father].[25] Anne of the Ascension's autograph in the convent chronicles also dwells on this episode:

> The provincial who was then Father Thomas a Jesus ... the next ... sent for the Lady Lovel to know her resolution and make agreement with her; after which he went himself to the Infanta with whom he was in great credit, and told her God would have him further a Monastery of English, desired her assistance and leave. She granted that he should choose any place in her country.[26]

Anne of the Ascension's autobiography, as well as the letters between her and Ana de San Bartolomé during these years, show a difficult relationship with Lovel from the very beginning.[27] These texts reveal the tensions derived from power struggles. On the one hand, the zeal to expand the order and found new convents in Flanders required the financial support of the Catholic gentry; on the other, though, orders distrusted these lay people whose financial support was crucial but whose direct potential control upon the foundations could endanger the autonomy of monastic life. Although Lovel intended this foundation to be subject to the local clergy and not to the Carmelite Superiors, she had to yield initially and accept the authority of the Spanish Carmelite Tomás de Jesús. Later on, however, problems continued at her radical opposition to regular confessors and her refusal to admit non-English nuns into the cloister. Most cloisters were peopled with women from different countries. Walker mentions how in the Flemish cloister at Louvain, the English prioress had "many sorts of nations under her government (...) all

---

[24] Letter 241, *ibid.*, 1152.
[25] Letter 243, *ibid.*, 1155.
[26] *Chronicle of the English Carmel in Antwerp*, 84, MS.
[27] This difficulty is also recorded in her relations with other persons. Guilday, for instance, notes that her difference with Mary Percy made her abandon de convent shortly after she entered, and the Earl of Salisbury also complains of her attitude when still in England, she applied for a visa to travel to the Continent. See Peter Guilday, *The English Catholic Refugees on the Continent, 1558-1795*. London: Longman,1914: 360-361.

in one house",[28] and before the foundation of English convents, women of different languages and origin lived under the same roof. This means that most of these women could speak more than one language, and some were poliglottal. Ana de San Bartolomé writes her 130 letters to Anne of the Ascension in Spanish, and this one eplies in Flemish, while using French in her autobiography, which was translated in a late 18th century English transcription. Likewise, Leonor de San Bernardo, another Spanish Carmelite involved in the foundation movement in Flanders and France, was writing indistinctively in Spanish and French.[29] Why, then, was Lovel so reluctant to allow Flemish women to profess in the English convent? Was it a matter of national allegiance? When Carmelite authorities threatened to stop sending vocations to the convent if she did not comply with the rules, she replied that she would recruit them in England herself.[30]

The Lovel controversy ended in an open confrontation with the prioress, Anne of the Ascension, and the superiors of the Order. The consequent crisis provoked by the choice of confessors, and the English nuns' demand to remain outside the jurisdiction of the Order, moved beyond the scope of the convent and became a political issue that demanded the direct intervention of the Infanta, Isabel Clara Eugenia. In April 1625 Ana de San Bartolomé was urging her friend in Brussels, Beatriz de la Concepción, to inform the Infanta about the ill behaviour of these English nuns who, despite being alien, seemed to be willing to *rule over these earthly princes as though they were locals.*[31] Later, in 1626, San Bartolomé herself wrote directly to the Infanta requesting action:

> They got me angry; and I plead that your Highness will oppose them or put them out of your land if they do not obey the Order, because they are foreigners and so free that they do not respect your Highness, and they do not deserve your courtesy, and their liberty will make them bring the customs of their land, and then they may bring heresy,

---

[28] Claire Walker, *Gender and Politics in Early-Modern Europe*: 40.

[29] Pierre Serouet, *Leonor de San Bernardo. Lettres.* Bruges: Desclée de Brouwer, 1981.

[30] Peter Guilday, *The English Catholic Refugees on the Continent*: 361.

[31] "que siendo extranjeras, parece quieren mandar sobre los príncipes de la tierra con más libertad que los naturales" *"A Beatriz de la Concepción"* (1625), letter 648, in Julián Urkiza, *Obras completas de la Beata Ana de San Bartolomé*: 1597.

> may God not allow; but all can be expected from their daring behavior.[32]

The episode illustrates a controversy, the free will of confessors, that had underpinned the expansion and management of monastic communities from the very beginning, and, moreover, the way in which it had affected the authority and control of the clergy over the consciousness of hundreds of women, whose role in social and political life should not be underestimated. It also reveals the complex liaisons within the walls of the cloister and the permeability of these communities to worldly structures of power. In the end, the English Carmelites of Antwerp and those of Louvain succeeded in their aim of remaining under the Jurisdiction of the Bishop, eluding the control of the friars.

Financial funding, religious license, political approval, and intense recruitment campaigns carried out in England and on the continent were all actions accomplished by women that crossed borders and defied national allegiances. The process involved the circulation of people, goods and messages from London to Brussels, from Madrid and Valladolid to Louvain or St Omer, and in these circuits of power women were not only efficient, but absolutely necessary: a complex network of allegiances and patronage involved Church authorities, wealthy nobility and political personages of the highest rank. Carvajal's active engagement as facilitator in the transnational circulation of persons is exceeded by the role played by the Infanta Isabel Clara Eugenia who, in the Low Countries, provided the soil for the establishment of the English community, and paved the way for the extraordinary monastic expansion that took place during her rule. Her commitment to this cause makes her a great mediator, supporter, facilitator, and patroness *par excellence* – the piece that brought together religious women and allowed feminine cross-national religious activity to flourish in Flanders. The narrative constructions of national identities and allegiances that emerge in the discourses produced by these women reveal the importance of focusing on 'processes' and 'in-between' spaces as sites of

---

[32] "Que me tienen harto enojada; y deseo que vuestra Alteza ponga su poder en resistirlas o mandarlas ir de su tierra si no se ponen en la Orden, que pues son extranjeras y tan libres que le pierden el respeto a vuestra Alteza, no merecen que las tenga cortesía, y con esta libertad podrán poner costumbres de su tierra y meter otro día una herejía, lo que Dios no lo quiera; mas todo se puede temer de sus atrevimientos". "A la Infanta Isabel Clara Eugenia" (1626), letter 650, in Julián Urkiza, *Obras completas de la Beata Ana de San Bartolomé*: 1599.

contestation in cultural production, as "terrain for elaborating strategies of selfhood – singular or communal – that initiate new signs of identity, and innovative sites of collaboration, and contestation, in the act of defining the idea of society itself".[33]

Even though recent English scholarship has re-established the importance of Catholic communities in the construction of an English identity (see note 1 above), it is equally true that insularity and chauvinism often condition this approach, as exiles are still approached as a natural extension of the island – Britain – and women's discourses are generally excluded from the analysis. Shifting the perspective towards these transnational networks as *interstitial spaces,* productive sites where the articulation of difference does not presuppose pre-given ethnic or cultural traits, opens up new ways of approaching the formation of national and cultural identities in the early modern period, and acknowledges the agency of women in these processes.

---

[33] Homi Bhabha, *The Location of Culture*. London: Routledge, 2004: 1-2.

## Select Bibliography

Arenal, Electa and Stacey Schlau. (eds). 1989. *Untold Sisters: Hispanic Nuns in their Own. Works.* Alburquerque: University of New Mexico Press.

Bhabha, Homi. 2004. *The Location of Culture.* London: Routledge.

Bilinkoff, Jodi. 2005. *Related Lives. Confessors and their Female Penitents, 1450-1750.* Ithaca: Cornell University Press.

Campbell, Julie D. and Anne R. Larsen. (eds). 2009. *Early Modern Women and Transnational Communities of Letters.* Aldershot: Ashgate.

Caraman, Philip. (tr). 1951. *John Gerard. The Autobiography of an Elizabethan*. London: Longmans.

Carvajal y Mendoza, Venerable Dª Luisa de. 1965. *Epistolario y poesías.* González, Marañón Jesús and Camilo María Abad (eds). Madrid: Biblioteca de Autores Españoles (179).

Corthell, Ronald, Frances E. Dolan, Christopher Highley, and Arthur F. Marotti. (eds). 2007. *Catholic Culture in Early Modern England.* Notre Dame, Indiana: University of Notre Dame Press.

Donahue, Darcy. (ed.). 2008. *Ana de San Bartolomé. Autobiography and other Writings.* Chicago: University of Chicago Press.

"Father Robert Parsons to Martin de Idiaquez". 1588-1601. *Calendar Of State Papers,* Eliz, Domestic. 648: 638-41.

Guilday, Peter. 1914. *The English Catholic Refugees on the Continent, 1558-1795.* London: Longmans.

Hardman, Anne. 1936. *English Carmelites in Penal Times.* London: Burns Oates & Washbourne.

Highley, Christopher. 2008. *Catholics Writing the Nation in Early Modern Britain and Ireland.* Oxford: Oxford University Press.

Klingenstein, L. 1910. *The Great Infanta Isabel, Sovereign of the Netherlands.* New York, London: Mehtuen.

Lehfeldt, Elizabeth A. 2005. *Religious Women in Golden Age Spain. The Permeable Cloister.* Aldershot: Ashgate.

Loomie, Albert J. 1978. *Spain and the Jacobean Catholics, 1613-1624.* London: Publications of the Catholic Record Society.

—. 1963. *The Spanish Elizabethans. The English Exiles at the Court of Philip II.* New York: Fordham University Press.

—. 1973. *Spain and the Jacobean Catholics, 1603-1612.* London: Publications of the Catholic Record Society.

Pando-Canteli, María J. 2010. "*Tentando vados:* The Martyrdom Politics of Luisa de Carvajal y Mendoza" in *Journal of Early Modern Cultural Studies.* 10(1): 117-141.

Redworth, Glynn. 2008. *The She-Apostle. The Life and Death of Luisa de Carvajal y Mendoza.* Oxford: Oxford University Press.

Sanchez, Magdalena. 2009. "Sword and Wimple. Isabel Clara Eugenia and Power" in Cruz, Anne J. and Mihoko Suzuki (eds). in *The Rule of Women in Early Modern Europe.* Urbana & Chicago: University of Illinois Press.

—. 1998. *The Empress, the Queen and the Nun. Women and Power at the Court of Philip III of Spain.* Baltimore: Johns Hopkins University Press.

Seguin, Colleen M. 2004 'Lovel, Mary, Lady Lovel (*c.*1564-1628)' in *Oxford Dictionary of National Biography.* Oxford University Press. online Oct 2008 http://www.oxforddnb.com/view/article/69036, [accessed 26 Feb 2012].

Serouet, Pierre. (ed.). 1967. *Beatrix de la Conception. Lettres Choissies.* Bruges : Desclée de Brouwer.

—. 1981. *Leonor de San Bernardo. Lettres.* Bruges : Desclée de Brouwer.

Torres Sánchez, Concha. 2000. *La clausura imposible. Conventualismo femenino y expansión contrarreformista.* Madrid: Asociación cultural Al-Mudayna.

Torres Sánchez, Concha. (ed.). 1995. *Ana de Jesús. Cartas (1590-1621). Religiosidad y vida cotidiana en la clausura femenina del Siglo de Oro.* Salamanca: Ediciones Universidad de Salamanca.

Urkiza, Julián. 1998. *Obras completas de la Beata Ana de San Bartolomé.* Burgos: Editorial Monte Carmelo.

Vicente, Marta V. and Luis R. Corteguera. (eds). 2003. *Women, Texts and Authority in the Early Modern Hispanic World.* Burlington VT*:* Ashgate.

Walker, Claire. 2003. *Gender and Politics in Early-Modern Europe. English Convents in France and the Low Countries.* New York: Palgrave-Macmillan.

—. 2001. "'Doe not supose me a well mortifyed Nun dead to the world': Letter Writing in English Early Modern Convents" in Daybel, J. (ed.). *Early Modern Women Letter Writers.* Balsingstoke: 159-176.

Weber, Allison. 1990. *Teresa of Avila and the Rhetoric of Femininity.* Princeton: Princeton University Press.

—. 2008. "The three lives of the Vida. The uses of convent autobiography" in Vicente and Corteguera (eds). *Women, Texts and Authority in the Early Modern Spanish World.* Aldershot: Ashgate.

# Strange Language and Practices of Disorder: The Prophetic Crisis in France following the Revocation of the Edict of Nantes in 1685

*Henriette Goldwyn*

ABSTRACT My article aims to analyze the eruption of entranced pronouncements in the public sphere at the end of the 17th century in France and how these prophetic utterances – mostly by lay young women – kept Calvinism alive in spite of the revocation of the Edict of Nantes in 1685. With the edict of tolerance and its numerous articles revoked, the Calvinists found themselves barred of their social identity, freedom of conscience, and civic rights. During this watershed period, prophesying provided Huguenot women a unique discursive space where, in the wilderness, appropriating a language foreign to them, their tales of deliverance sustained the spirit of their coreligionists, and thereby engaged in a narrative of identity repair.

AT THE END OF THE 17TH CENTURY, a troubling and complex phenomenon[1] appeared which offers insights into the narrative of identity repair articulated by entranced prophesying during illicit and clandestine worship services in Protestant France. Following the revocation of the Edict of Nantes in 1685, under a monarchy claiming to be monolithic, homogenous and unitary, an ecstatic language erupted and infused parts of southeastern and southwestern France.[2]

Focusing on the climate of dissent during that period, I will show how the persuasive nature of prophetic speech, which had been barred from the public arena, sustained the Huguenot community remaining in France and gave them a continued sense of cultural and religious identity. Through their ecstatic utterances in the midst of prohibited assemblies, a handful of mostly uneducated young people, women in particular, continued to speak despite

---

[1] The outbreak of prophetic pronouncements by 'lay people' divided the Huguenot community at the time and remains a controversial topic to this day.

[2] The manifestations of prophesying were located mostly in the Dauphiné, Vivarais, Velay, Lower Languedoc and the Cévennes (in what is called the Huguenot Midi).

having been reduced to silence. Telling of frontiers and dislocation, they confronted authority, questioned notions of nationhood and sovereignty,[3] and claimed their place as subjects whose rights had been banned by a monarchist, absolutist and wholly Catholic France[4] that had revoked the Edict of Nantes and pushed the logic of dehumanization to the extreme in its attempt to eradicate the Calvinist minority. This controversial discursive form, which culminated and turned violent with the Camisards insurrection,[5] sowed disorder in France from 1688 to 1716. Although the earliest prophetic-ecstatic pronouncements are generally traced to Isabeau Vincent,[6] the first recorded prophetess, there were some who preceded her.[7] The year 1716 sounded the death knell for prophetism and the restoration of institutional Calvinism by Antoine Court.[8]

---

[3] In *The Cult of the Nation in France: Inventing Nationalism 1680-1800*, David Bell writes that "it is only when the French ceased to see themselves as part of a great hierarchy uniting heaven and earth, the two linked by an apostolic church and a divinely ordained king, that they could start to see themselves as equal members of a distinct, uniform, and sovereign nation" (Cambridge, MA: Harvard UP, 2001:7-8).

[4] Louis XIV, the sun king, whose ultimate goal was monarchical power and religious homogeneity, came to represent the single most powerful unifying force in France. Any exception to the religious unity of the kingdom endangered its political unity as well, by virtue of the often-invoked adage: "one faith, one law, one king" [*une foi, une loi, un roi*]. See Elizabeth Labrousse, "Calvinism in France, 1598-1685", in *International Calvinism 1541-1715*, Menna Prestwich (ed.).Oxford: Clarendon Press, 1985: 285-313.

[5] The Camisards (because of the white shirt they wore to distinguish them at night) is the name given to French Huguenots who, in the mountains of the Cévennes region, led an insurrection against the royal forces between 1702 and 1704. At first, the prophetic movement was pacifist, but became violent with the Camisards.

[6] Yves Krumenacker, "Siefar", *Dictionnaire Siefar,* On line at http://www.siefar.org/dic tionnaire/fr/Isabeau_Vincent

[7] See Emmanuelle Carpuat's, "Le vin du malheur et le feu de la langue. Les procès du prophétisme dans l'intendance de Montpellier, 1685-1715", Master's thesis, Toulouse, 2003. She traces the rise of prophetism to the years preceding the Revocation. It should also be noted that in the first four years following the Revocation, voices were heard singing psalms to airs composed by Clément Marot and Théodore de Bèze near places where Protestant churches had earlier stood. See Hubert Bost, "Orthez ou le chant des anges, La VIIe Lettre pastorale de Jurieu," *BSHPF* 135 (1989) : 403-23.

[8] Although his mother was a prophetess, Antoine Court (1695-1760) worked to suppress the prophetic movement, dedicating his life to the restoration of rigorous Calvinist discipline and the training of pastors.

Since its promulgation in 1598, the Edict of Nantes[9] – considered a charter of tolerance – had been the symbol of the Huguenots' place within the French national community and the recognition of their religious specificity, as underscored by Hubert BoSt[10] When the Edict was revoked at the end of the 17th century, it was ironically the outbreak of prophetic discourse that gave a voice to plural identity: a religious, social and cultural 'diversity' that advocated freedom of religion, freedom of conscience, and the coexistence of two religions in France – and it did so by the most unlikely of characters.

## The divided self and the rise of entranced pronouncements

In reflecting upon the rise of entranced pronouncements by 'lay persons' in Reformed communities, it would be helpful to situate the place of the Huguenot in the construction of the French nation.[11] As a political organization, a nation-state is the juxtaposition of a nation and a state; that is, a set of individuals who share a communal identity (the nation), and the political and administrative institutions that exercise sovereignty over those individuals within a given set of borders (the state). To be a Huguenot in the 17th century was to belong to a specific cultural universe that had fashioned a singular personality: resisting, compromising, negotiating, and often re-negotiating to maintain its threatened identity. But from one day to the next, the Huguenots saw their legal recognition revoked and their religious specificity stripped away. So how could they proceed once they were barred from all legal status? How do you survive within a nation-state that denies your legal existence as well as your basic identity (the one inherited from your parents) and forcefully imposes another one upon you?

---

[9] Signed on 13 April 1598, the Edict of Nantes is a unique edict of tolerance in Europe. It appeared as the first milestone in the long history of the conquest for public and individual liberties, aiming to make it possible for two religions, Catholic and Protestant, to coexist with the same rights in a Catholic state. Besides freedom of conscience, the Edict afforded Protestants the freedom to worship as they pleased. In the juridical realm, an amnesty restored Protestants' civic rights in their entirety.

[10] Hubert Bost, "Des porte-parole protestants au chevet de l'édit de Nantes moribond," in *Revue de synthèse 5e série* 126, no. 1 (2005) : 70 : "Le symbole de l'appartenance des Huguenots à la communauté nationale française et de la reconnaissance de leur spécificité religieuse." In this article, see especially Claude Brousson's comments about the relationship between the state, the individual, and his freedom of conscience (78).

[11] Bell, *The Cult of the Nation*, 3-4.

As they mourned the loss of their status, Protestant discourse – that is, the better-known discourse of pastors, theologians, jurists, historians and philosophers engaging in the Huguenot diaspora and its philosophical vocation – confronted issues concerning the relationships between the state, the individual, and freedom of conscience from their places of refuge.[12] But another Protestant discourse, foreign to the discourse of rationality and strict Calvinist orthodoxy, also erupted into the public sphere. Uttered by those who did not emigrate, it manifested itself in prophesying, preaching and exhorting. Proclaiming that the 'spirit of God' spoke through their mouth, the 'young prophets' (*petits prophètes*), as opposed to the 'major prophets' (*grands prophètes*) in the Bible, found fertile ground and addressed assemblies of their coreligionists. They were the offspring of those who had abjured their faith and remained in France.

The inspired speeches of these young Protestants – in a strange language which seemed imperfect, fragmented, lacking in rhetorical strategies, and disorderly to the exiled enlightened orthodoxy – were accompanied by other practices of disorder, such as holding illicit assemblies, singing psalms, reciting passages of scripture and praying. In spite of strict punitive royal decrees and the fear of the dragoons,[13] they gathered in a highly symbolic space, the 'wilderness' (*le désert*),[14] thereby conveying the spiritual desolation of the devastated Calvinist community, captivating its imagination and saving it from eradication against the attempt to suppress Protestantism in France.

---

[12] Hubert Bost, "Des porte-parole protestants," 70.

[13] The dragoons were royally appointed infantry units that carried out persecutions against Protestants in the years surrounding the Revocation of the Edict of Nantes.

[14] The word "désert," which will be further developed, stands as a metaphor for the Huguenot's "interior exile" and also designates the illicit space where the gatherings were held at night. See Charles Bost, *Les Prédicants protestants des Cévennes et du Bas-Languedoc 1684-1700,* Montpellier: Presses du Languedoc, 2001); Hubert Bost, "Le désert des huguenots : une poétique de l'épreuve", *Le Désert, l'espace et l'esprit,* in *Revue des sciences humaines* II, no. 258 (2000) : 177, 183; Solange Deyon, "La résistance protestante et la symbolique du désert", in *Revue d'histoire moderne et contemporaine* XVIII (1971) : 237-249; Hillel Schwartz, *The French Prophets,* Berkeley : University of California Press, 1980 : 14; and Henriette Goldwyn, "Les espaces du Désert où 'les pierres mêmes crieront,'", in *Intersections. Biblio 17* 161 (2005) : 271-283.

## The prophetic shepherdess

"It all began in the Dauphiné with a shepherdess."[15] This is hardly surprising in a century enamored with shepherds and shepherdesses. We may recall in passing the intellectual hold of *L'Astrée* on the mores and mentalities of an entire era. But this shepherdess speaks, and it is her speech, the memory of her pronouncements, and how they were recorded that is of particular interest here.[16]

The prophetic crisis is linked, in the first place, with trauma. The mass apostasy of French Protestants, the exiling of pastors, the razing of temples, the prohibition of Protestant worship services, the confiscation or destruction of Protestant Bibles and Psalters, imprisonments, deportations and galley sentences, rapes, billeting of dragoons in Protestant homes: all of these stripped the Calvinists in the Huguenot Midi of their religious, cultural and social references. Every link to a Protestant identity was broken and every spiritual framework dismantled. In the midst of these ruins and this desolation, where the order of worship and the bonds with the Lord appeared to have been annihilated, the voice of Isabeau Vincent arose, followed by the voices of other prophets or *inspirés*. How did these public and inspired pronouncements manifest themselves? Although a new generation of very active women did participate in many intellectual and cultural domains in France throughout the 17th century, sermons and preaching remained staunchly masculine territory because they were considered expressions of divine truth through which the voice of God and his teaching could be heard. Feminine discourse in the sphere of religion was generally restricted to nuns, cloistered sisters, grand abbesses, or mystics, who wrote poetry, letters, memoirs, hymns, plays and mystical texts.

---

15 "*Tout a commencé dans le Dauphiné avec une bergère*," declares Jean-Pierre Richardot in his introduction to the new edition of *Le Théâtre sacré des Cévennes ou récit de diverses merveilles nouvellement opérées dans cette province du Languedoc*, François-Maximilien Misson and Jean-Pierre Richardot (eds). 1978, Brignon : Presses du Languedoc: 9.

16 Henri Manen and Philippe Joutard. *Une Foi enracinée* : *La Pervenche. La Résistance exemplaire d'une paroisse protestante ardéchoise*. (pref. Lucien Schneider), Valence : Imprimeries réunies, 1972. Manen insists on the importance of the discovery of a copy of Isabeau Vincent's *Abrégé de l'histoire de la bergère du Saou près du Crest dans le Dauphiné*, as it represents the best testimonial of the first phase of prophetism, from which all subsequent phases derived. This deposition, written in comprehensible French, consists of a small seven-page notebook containing a letter, her proclamations, and the recording of one of her speeches by an eyewitness who was a lawyer (56-57).

In the Dauphiné in 1688, however, in the absence of legitimate pastors, in the midst of a modest rural community, an unprecedented phenomenon occurs: a teenage girl, Isabeau Vincent, speaks publicly and delivers an ecstatic predication. For four months, this illiterate young shepherdess, who was just 15 years old, and whose father had repudiated his faith in exchange for money even before the Revocation, styled herself as the organ of the divine message through visions, oracles and above all, through public utterances. This event engendered a movement that engulfed the region,[17] ultimately reaching the lands of refuge where French Protestants were already established, notably Geneva, Amsterdam and London.[18]

Prophetism provided a unique discursive space for Huguenot women. Mostly illiterate and relying on an oral tradition, they left no texts signed by their own hand. Paradoxically, their speeches – some of which exist in the form of eyewitness transcriptions and depositions – display, to everyone's surprise, knowledge of certain biblical fragments,[19] psalms, prayers, and sermons written by Protestant ministers such as Pierre Jurieu[20] and Claude

---

[17] For lists of other *inspirés* see Daniel Vidal, *Le prophète et son malheur*, Paris: Payot, 1983, 19-23 and Carpuat, "Le vin du malheur."

[18] On the reception of the Prophetic movement in Switzerland, Germany, Holland and London, see Clarke Garrett. 1987. *Spirit Possession and Popular Religion*, Baltimore: Johns Hopkins UP: 40-51.

[19] In *Une Foi enracinée*, 49, Henri Manen and Philippe Joutard underscore the consequences of nightly Bible reading for the young '*inspirés*', and evoke the manner in which the Reformed community fooled the illiterate dragoons by tearing out the first page of the Bible. See also Clarke Garrett, *Spirit Possession and Popular Religion,* 19-21.

[20] The exiled Calvinist's *Lettres pastorales adressées aux fidèles de France qui gémissent sous la captivité de Babylone (1686-1689*) were to become one of the most significant texts circulating clandestinely amongst the Reformed community in France. In contrast to other pastors who instructed the Protestant minority to flee, Jurieu incited them to remain in France and to continue to hold their assemblies, and he also supported the ministry of lay preachers, women and visionaries. The original purpose of the *Lettres pastorales* was to maintain contact with the Protestants of France, to give them news "from afar," to encourage their resistance, perseverance and activism, all while fortifying their faith and, finally, to bear witness to the injustice of their fate to Protestant Europe. See Robin Howells' excellent introduction to the *Lettres pastorales*, Hildesheim: Georg Olms Verlag, 1988 : vii-lxxvii; Patrick Cabanel, «Le Dieu inaudible", in *Les Camisards et leur mémoire, 1702-2002:* Cabanel and Joutard (ed.). *Colloque du Pont-de-Montvert des 25 et 26 juillet 2002*, Montpellier: Les Presses du Languedoc, 2002 : 262-63 ; and Henriette Goldwyn, "Censure, clandestinité et épistolarité : *Les Lettres pastorales* de Pierre Jurieu", in *Le Savoir au XVIIe siècle. Biblio 17* 147 (2003) : 285-294.

Brousson.[21] Unlike other pastors, they exhorted their coreligionists to undertake what Daniel Vidal calls "a new nativity of the word."[22] The *petits prophètes*' discourse therefore differed greatly from that of the institutional Calvinist pastors, especially with respect to the duty to obey the sovereign. One of their major detractors, the exiled pastor Elie Merlat,[23] held political opinions favorable to absolute monarchy and respect for authority. For the prophets on the other hand, who drew their inspiration from the Bible, sovereignty belongs to God alone, for it is divine in essence. If the king is called sovereign, it is only because he is the guardian of sovereign authority, not because he is the proprietor.

According to extant sources – that is, stenographic transcriptions of one of Isabeau's prophetic frenzies recorded by an eyewitness[24] – we know that she prophesied while asleep covered by a sheet. Addressing new converts – 'new Catholics', those who had abjured without resistance like her father –, Isabeau, like her followers, insists on the fact that her proclamations emanate from the Holy Spirit.[25] Inspired by Joel's prophecy in the Bible (Joel 2:28), she declares, "it is not I who speaks, [it] is the Spirit that is in me [;] these last days your young people will prophesy and your old men will dream dreams."[26] At certain moments she would extend her arms from under the

---

[21] In *Les Prédicants protestants des Cévennes et du Bas-Languedoc 1684-1700*, Montpellier: Presses du Languedoc, 2001, 1 : 262-64, Charles Bost asserts that Brousson insisted on the necessity of clandestine assemblies and secret organizations even before the Revocation. See also Georgia Cosmos, *Huguenot Prophecy and Clandestine Worship in the Eighteenth Century*, Burlington, VT: Ashgate, 2005, 41-42, especially on Brousson's sermons read aloud and preached in the "désert," initially published in Amsterdam in 1695 under the title *La Manne mystique du désert*.

[22] Daniel Vidal, "De l'insurrection camisarde : une prophétie entrée en révolte, " in Cabanel and Joutard, *Les Camisards et leur mémoire*, 41-42.

[23] Author of *Le Traité du pouvoir absolu des souverains. Pour servir de consolation et d'apologie aux Églises Réformées de France qui sont affligées*, Cologne : Jacques Cassander, 1685. Like Merlat, many pastors continued to preach in favor of the duty to obey the sovereign as long as they thought there was some advantage to be drawn from their loyalty.

[24] All references to this document are to be found in *Une Foi enracinée: La Pervenche. La Résistance exemplaire d'une paroisse protestante ardéchoise*, in which Henri Manen republishes with copious commentaries and analysis the original document printed in Amsterdam in 1688 entitled *L'Abrégé de l'histoire de la bergère du Saou, près de Crest, en Dauphiné*.

[25] Carpuat, "Le vin du malheur," 301-303, establishes a list of prophetesses who, just like Isabeau, confirm "having received the Holy Spirit" ("avoir reçu le St Esprit").

[26] I am using the English translation of the transcription by Clark Garret found in *Spirit Possession and Popular Religion*, 19. For the original French citation, see "*Ce*

sheet and shake them; sometimes her chest would heave and swell. She first prophesied in patois, lying in her bed, but later, during gatherings, and even in prison, she would prophesy in French. The fact that Isabeau and the other young prophets were occitanophones (speakers of patois), yet prophesied, exhorted and preached in proper French, seemed strange and even suspect, especially to detractors. A closer investigation, however, reveals that it was actually an antiquated form of French from the 16th century. According to historians who have studied prophetism, this can be explained by the fact that the Bible was read in spite of prohibitions and exactions, and that these young people had memorized fragments from the Olivetan Bible published in 1535. The most ardent detractors, David de Brueys[27] and Esprit Fléchier,[28] maintained that these young "fanatics"[29] were pushed to rebellion and militancy by Jurieu's *Lettres pastorales* and were instructed by another pastor, a certain De Serre, who would come from Switzerland to train them.[30] Isabeau disappeared. All manner of hypotheses have circulated surrounding what happened to her following her arrest and imprisonment. Some say she converted to Catholicism, others that she was sent to a convent, or was paid for her silence, but no proof exists for any of this. It is more important, however, that prophetism spread, reaching the Vivarais in 1689, and the Cévennes and Lower Languedoc in 1701, after the terrible massacre at Serre de la Palle where an assembly of three hundred Protestants was murdered by the royal forces. Finally it swept to the lands of refuge, especially in the early eighteenth century, after the routing of the Camisards in 1704. In London, they would be dubbed 'The French Prophets.'

On the one hand, the prophets were supported by pastors like Jurieu, who encouraged their action with singular fervor. He was the first to recognize

*n'est pas moi qui parle, (c)'est l'Esprit qui est en moi, ces derniers temps, vos jeunes gens prophétiseront et vos anciens songeront des songes*," quoted in Manen, *Une foi enracinée*, 70.

[27] Converted by Bossuet in 1681, this 'new catholic' became the most virulent of the detractors.

[28] The Bishop of Nîmes, whose correspondence paints a particularly negative and accusatory picture of prophetism.

[29] Faced with the rapid spread of prophetism (there were some 8,000 prophets in the Cévennes and Lower Languedoc), Bâville asked the faculty of the Montpellier medical school to examine the inspired youths. They were the first to use the term "fanatic," according to Patrick Cabanel and Philippe Joutard, *Les Camisards et leur mémoire*, 17.

[30] Cilette Blanc, "Genève et les origines du mouvement prophétique en Dauphiné et dans les Cévennes", in *Revue d'histoire suisse* 23 (1943) : 234-249.

and to articulate the importance of prophetic inspiration, especially for the preservation of an oral religious culture.[31] Valorizing the contribution of Isabeau Vincent in his third *Lettres pastorales*, he writes: "for many months [God] has been using the ministry of a simple shepherdess who knows neither how to read nor to write."[32] Aside from the *Lettres pastorales*, Brousson's writings also praise and give an account of the prophets' actions. In recent years, female prophetism and the role of women during the Camisards' insurrection has gained scholarly interest as well.[33]

On the other hand, there were quite a few detractors, many Catholic writers and converted Protestants, but above all pastors from the enlightened orthodoxy who denounced women's appropriation of pastoral speech and rational Calvinism. The danger of sliding toward illuminationism and millenarianism[34] alarmed the detractors. Ultimately Antoine Court, under the influence of Basnage de Pictet and Samuel Turettini, would impose synodal discipline in the clandestine churches and put an end to prophetism.

## The performative body and entranced speech

This transformation of pastoral discourse by women – this new form of transmitting the master's word, now delivered in a fractured language laced with stylistic disparities and repetitions, and opposed to all rhetorical logic – was all the more shocking because it emerged from a convulsive, entranced

---

[31] Henri Bosc, "Les prophètes cévenols" in *BSHPF* 126 (1980), 8; E. G. Léonard, *Histoire générale du protestantisme*, Paris : PUF, 1964, 3 : 15-16; and Patrick Cabanel, "Le Dieu inaudible. La Réception du prophétisme cévenol (1685-1715)," quoted in Cabanel and Joutard, *Les Camisards et leur mémoire*, 261-281.

[32] "depuis tant de mois [Dieu] se sert du ministère d'une simple bergère qui ne sait ni lire ni écrire " (I, iii, 20-22).

[33] There is a reductionist interpretation of prophetism and the role of visionaries in France, who are frequently depicted as inspired women and children who assembled to prophesy without liturgy. However, several recent studies have argued for the essential role of prophetesses, most notably, Marguerite Soulié's "Les femmes pendant la période du désert," in *VIIe colloque, Musées protestants: Deuxième rencontre européenne 30 avril – 3 mai 1992* (s.p., s.d.), 16-24; Vidal, *Le Malheur et son prophète*; Garrett, *Spirit Possession and Popular Religion*; Greg Monahan, "Prophétesses et rebelles : le rôle des femmes dans la guerre des Camisards," quoted in *Les Camisards et leur mémoire,* 69-83 ; and Emmanuelle Carpuat, "Le vin du malheur."

[34] For an analysis of the millenarian ethos, see Hillel Schwartz, *The French Prophets,* 2-6 and Jean-Paul Chabrol, *Élie Marion le vagabond de Dieu*, Aix-en-Provence: Édisud, 1999.

body. A disordered, suffering and visually powerful body: their eyes bulging, their chests heaving, some prophets would lose consciousness before they spoke, throw themselves to the ground seized by terrible fits of shaking and contortions, or cry tears of blood.[35] The performative dimension of prophetism would reach its apogee in London when some of the Camisard prophets became the darlings of fashionable London salons fiercely vying for the opportunity to see them fall into a trance.

The whole bodily and gestural ritual of prophetism was depicted and described in minute detail in the depositions gathered by François-Maximilien Misson in a powerful and seminal text published in London in 1707. This archive is a collection of testimony given under oath by survivors[36] and is entitled: *Le Théâtre sacré des Cévennes, ou récit des diverses merveilles, Nouvellements opérées dans cette partie de la province du Languedoc.*[37] The intriguing expression "*Le Théâtre sacré des Cévennes*" is taken from the deposition given by one of the many eyewitnesses, Mathieu Boissier, who speaks of "many prodigious things, marvels that it pleased God to reveal [...] in the sacred theater of the Cévennes."[38] Other testimonials describe the manner in which the prophetic body is suddenly 'seized' with shaking and convulsions and thrown to the floor before the magical words, spoken in comprehensible French, alternate with long periods of silence. In her deposition, Sibylle de Brozet recounts meeting two '*inspirées*' and attests that: "there was one who was suddenly seized, and became extremely pale [...] her head and stomach shook violently. The first words she spoke were

---

[35] Deposition of Élie Marion in Misson and Richardot, *Théâtre sacré des Cévennes*, 129 : "*Je répandis des larmes de sang en abondance.*"

[36] Associated with a literature of atonement, *Le Théâtre sacré* presents the testimonials of those eyewitnesses (especially the Camisards) who, fleeing France, had made it to London. See chapter 8 Cosmos, *Huguenot Prophecy*, 159-175, as well as the list of depositions, 195.

[37] The term "Cévennes" refers to the entire region of the Huguenot Midi. *Le Théâtre sacré* was translated in English the same year by John Larcy under the following title: *A Cry from the Desart, or Testimonials of the Miraculous Things Lately come to pass in the Cévennes, Verified upon Oath and other Proofs.*

[38] *Ibid.*, 66 : "beaucoup de choses prodigieuses, des merveilles qu'il a plu a Dieu de faire éclater [...] sur le théâtre sacré des Cévennes."

'My child, I say to you.' She strongly exhorted us to repent."[39] "While under the influence, both spoke French otherwise they only spoke patois."[40]
Like the preceding example, Sarra Dalgone's testimonial highlights both the bodily and linguistic transformation experienced by a young girl: "I saw her many times when she had her inspirations [...] She breathed only in sighs, her chest shook and her whole body trembled [...] She always spoke in proper French."[41]

At first glance, these prophetic utterances seem disconnected, consisting of un-orderly phrases without formal coherence. There is no continuity of thought, and these fragments appear to be juxtaposed, repeated, devoid of any rational element and structurally unrelated to traditional pastoral predication. By adopting an ecstatic style that is unedited and free of rhetorical artifice, the *petits prophètes* claim that their prophecies flow directly from God and must be heard and understood by all those present at the assembly. However, the very repetitious quality of their speeches, which follow a certain recurrent modality, rhythm, order of delivery and choice of symbolic imagery, point to how these "*inspirés*" appropriate pastoral discourse to create persuasive messages intended to restore and repair the Calvinist identity which was at stake.

The Huguenot community's validation and recognition of women's prophecies is an extraordinary event in the history of French Protestantism. It shows the degree to which women – beyond the traditional roles given to them in the domestic sphere (as the teachers who ensured the transmission of a religious conscience) and in the domain of conversion – played a preponderant role within prophetism, wielding authority over language in the religious domain.

---

[39] *Ibid.*, 116 : "il y en eut une qui fut saisie tout d'un coup, et qui devint extrêmement pâle [...] elle eut de grandes agitations de la tête et de l'estomac. Les premières paroles qu'elle prononça furent : ' Mon enfant, je te dis '. Elle exhorta fort à la repentance."

[40] *Ibid.*, 117 : "Elles parlaient français dans l'Inspiration et jamais dans un autre temps." The prophetic movement is also linked to glossolalia, an intense mystical phenomenon allowing some people to express themselves in a language foreign to them but comprehensible to the audience they are addressing.

[41] *Ibid.*, 122 : "Je l'ai vue plusieurs fois pendant qu'elle avait ses inspirations [...] Elle ne respirait que par soupirs, sa poitrine était agitée et tout son corps était tremblotant [...] Elle parla toujours bon français."

Yet, for a long time, the positions they attained as prophetesses[42] and their narrative of identity repair went unrecognized. Often associated with sorcery, possession and even prostitution, their influence was suppressed and they were frequently relegated to the background of the Camisard insurrection, despite prophetism's important contribution to the war. Because they were too closely related to neurosis, hysteria, paranoia and epileptic seizures,[43] these displays of collective exaltation during gatherings – ecstatic experiences, trances, convulsions – quickly provoked critical reactions, which were further fueled by rumors mentioning sleepwalking, magnetism and hypnotism. It was necessary, then, to put a stop to the linguistic disorder, and to the abnormality of this prophetic body, which was moreover doted with a strong erotic charge. Lamoignon de Baville, the intendant of Languedoc, mentions the debaucheries in his correspondence. Esprit Fléchier, the bishop of Nîmes, speaks of immorality, libertinage, and the blissful cohabitation of young prophets and prophetesses. According to their description, it was something like a big performance art 'happening'.

## The prophet and the wilderness

Thus, the principal actor within the scene of the performance (the prophet) and the symbolic space in which the ecstatic utterance occurs (the wilderness), merit further reflection. The prophet refers to him- or herself as the 'instrument', the 'organ', or rather the 'ectoplasm'[44] of God, the body, the vessel, through which the divine word passes. Whether it be prediction (discourse on the future) or predication (exhortation), this speech constitutes the prophetic figure. The prophet is bound to God, since it is from him that he receives his mission.[45]

---

[42] The Bible cites the names of women who transmitted the word of God: Agar, Miriam (the sister of Moses and Aaron), Deborah, Hulda, Anne, and the four daughters of Phillip the Evangelist.

[43] Manen and Joutard, *Une Foi enracinée*, 58, and Dominique Colas, "Fanatisme, hystérie et paranoïa : le prophétisme camisard" in *Les Temps modernes* 36, no. 410 (1980) : 478-79, allude to sexual repressions. As for food deprivation, Élie Marion himself asserts that the Spirit would order him to fast in *Le Théâtre sacré*, 140-41.

[44] Colas, "Fanatisme, hystérie et paranoïa : le prophétisme camisard," 482.

[45] Carpuat, "Le vin du malheur," 211-212, drawing from existing arrest and interrogation reports, emphasizes that all the prophets respond in a similar fashion: "they were following the will of God who was giving them words, grace and inspiration."

However, prophetism is also a social phenomenon. The one who literally "speaks for" God becomes the acute conscience of the devastation of his or her time, and of the community's sin and stains. The Reformed community had repudiated its faith without resistance: the elders were called upon but were leading a double life, Catholics by day and Protestants by night. Moreover, not only had the fathers abjured, most often in exchange for money, the pastors had as well, either renouncing their faith, fleeing, or remaining silent. Faced with the failure of fathers and pastors, it is the word of the first prophetess – and of those who follow her – that nourishes and cements a devastated community. An active agent of consolation, the chosen prophet of God finds him- or herself woven into 'the history of a people', the Huguenot people. In his analysis of prophetism and the relationship between Moses and God and the restoration of faith, André Néhér remarks: "A dialectic of the people and the prophet is added to the dialectic between the prophet and God."[46]

Finally, prophetism is a political phenomenon, since it espouses an anti-absolutist discourse in recognizing only one form of authority, that of God. In its essence, this discourse is opposed to the discourse of pastors prior to the Revocation (of which the most striking example is Merlat who insists on recognizing the divine power of the monarch). In his deposition in *Le Théâtre sacré*, Élie Marion[47] (the best educated of the Camisard prophets who writes almost thirty years after Isabeau) emphasizes the need to overthrow the "Pharaoh": "terrasser le Pharaon."[48]

The term 'wilderness' (both a spatial designation and a spiritual organization of space) has a particular resonance within the Huguenot imagination. First, it is associated with the Old Testament: the wanderings of the chosen people in the desert, the test of their faith, their punishment, their atonement, but also their rebirth. Second, it is associated with the geographical dimension of the isolated, clandestine, illicit place where the Reformed minority gathered to observe their worship services in spite of the prohibitions and exactions. Their open-air gatherings were held in these churches without walls, since the churches had been destroyed. As Jurieu explains, "the Reformed faith needs neither a church nor pastors so long as

---

[46] André Néhér, *Prophètes et Prophéties*, Paris: Payot, 2004 : 230 and 200.

[47] See also Jean-Paul Chabrol, *Élie Marion le Camisard aux semelles de vent*, Nîmes : Alcide, 2008.

[48] *Le Théâtre sacré*, 161.

the word passes between the believers",[49] and it is in the wilderness that the destiny of the Protestants is shaped and that ecstatic predication arises. Filled with the prophets' incantatory voices and their extraordinary bodies, the Cévenol wilderness became the propitious place for the transmission of a form of magic (the terms 'wonder' (*merveille*), marvel, and 'miraculous' repeatedly appear) that brought solace to the community's divided existence and fractured psyche.

## Conclusion

Isabeau the prophetess and her followers positioned themselves in this interstitial space, an example of what Michel Foucault calls "heterotopia of crisis;"[50] that is, privileged, sacred or forbidden places, where bonds could be reformed in the midst of a devastated community. In addressing their audience, they called above all for 'metanoïa' (penitence, repentance), for atonement, for confession (an internal transformation), for deliverance and for the destruction of Babylon (the hope of a new Jerusalem), thus participating at a crucial moment in the reconstruction of a fragmented identity. By assuming and internalizing the sins of the elders – to the point of martyrdom[51] – it is through their inspired prophecies that they exhorted their coreligionists to persevere and to resist, sustaining their spirit and strengthening their faith. It is therefore in the wilderness that this transmutation carried by the word allowed women to rise and tell tales of deliverance. This watershed moment in which religious and political events coalesced was foundational in the creation of new identities for Protestant women as prophetesses. Stripped of their national, religious and cultural identity, these women appropriated a language foreign to them, empowering themselves to engage in a narrative of identity repair.[52]

---

[49] In his letter I, iv, 27, Jurieu insists that: "la foi réformée n'a besoin ni de lieu de culte, ni de pasteur consacré, du moment que la parole circule parmi les croyants : La mission d'un pasteur [...] n'est qu'une forme [...] dont on peut se passer dans les cas de nécessité."

[50] Michel Foucault, "Des espaces autres (conférence au Cercle d'études architecturales, 14 mars 1967)" in *Architecture, Mouvement, Continuité* no. 5 (October 1984) : 46-49.

[51] Carpuat, "Le vin du malheur": 311 insists that these prophets who had not emigrated were ready to sacrifice themselves.

[52] Translated with the help of Stephen Crumb and Kathrine La Porta.

## Select Bibliography


### A. Primary Sources

Field, Sean L. 2003. *The Writings of Agnes of Harcourt. The « Life of Isabelle of France » and the « Letter on Louis IX and Longchamp »*. Notre Dame: University of Notre Dame.

Garay, Kathleen and Madeleine Jeay. (tr.). 2001. *The Life of Saint Douceline, a Béguine of Provence*. Woodbridge: Boydelll and Brewer.

MacBain, William. (ed.). 1964. *The Life of St Catherine by Clemence of Barking*. Oxford: Anglo-Norman Text Society.

McCash, Hall, June and Judith Clark Barban (eds). 2006. *The Life of Saint Audrey, a Text by Marie de France*. Jefferson and London: McFarland.

Newman, Barbara and Margot H. King, (eds). 2008. *Thomas of Cantimpré. The Collected Saints' Lives: Abbot John of Camtimpré, Christina the Astonishing, Margaret of Ypres, and Lutgard of Aywieres*. Turnhout: Brepols.

Södergård, Österı. (ed.). 1948. *La vie d'Edouard le Confesseur; poème anglo-normand du XIIe siècle*. Uppsala: Almqvist & Wiksell.

—. 1955. *La vie seinte Audree, poème anglo-normand du XIIIe siècle*. Uppsala: Lundequistska bokhandeln; Wiesbaden, Harrassowitzt.

Vitry de, Jacques and Thomas de Cantimpré. 1998. *Two Lives of Marie d'Oignies*, (tr. Margot H. King and Hugh Feiss). Toronto: Peregrina.

### B. Secondary Sources

Aurell, Martin, (ed.). 2003a. *Culture politique des Plantagenêt (1154-1224)*. Poitiers: Université de Poitiers.

—. 2003b. "Les Plantagenêt, la propagande et la relecture du passé", in *Culture politique des Plantagenêt (1154-1224)*, 9-34. Poitiers: Université de Poitiers.

—. and Noël-Yves Tonnerre. (eds). 2006. *Plantagenêts et Capétiens: confrontations et héritages*. Turnhout: Brépols.

Beaune, Colette. 1985. *Naissance de la nation France*. Paris: Gallimard.

Bell, David N. 1995. *What Nuns Read: Books and Libraries in Medieval English Nunneries*. Kalamazoo: Cistercian Publications.

Bellotto Rossi, Carla. 2009. *Marie de France et les érudits de Cantorbéry*. Paris: Classiques Garnier.

Campbell, Emma. 2008. *Medieval Saints' Lives: the Gift, Kinship and Community in Old French Hagiography*. Woodbridge: D.S. Brewer.

Chauou, Amaury. 2001. *L'idéologie Plantagenêt. Royauté et monarchie politique dans l'espace Plantagenêt (XIIe-XIIIe siècles)*. Rennes: Presses universitaires de Rennes.

—. 2003. "*Arthurus redivivus*: royauté arthurienne et monarchie politique à la cour Plantagenêt (1154-1199)", in *Culture politique des Plantagenêt (1154-1224)*. Poitiers: Université de Poitiers: 67-78.

Cheyette, Fredric L. 2004. *Ermengard of Narbonne and the World of the Troubadours*. Ithaca and London: Cornell University Press.

Clark Bartlett, Anne. 1995. "Reading Medieval Women Reading Devotional Literature", in *Male Authors, Female Readers: Representation and Subjectivity in Middle English Devotional Literature*. Ithaca: Cornell University Press: 1-33.

Flori, Jean. 2004. *Eleanor d'Aquitaine. La reine insoumise*. Paris: Payot.

Jeay, Madeleine and Kathleen Garay. "'To Promote God's Praise and her Neighbour's Salvation'. Strategies of Authorship and Readership among Mystic Women in the Later Middle Ages", in Gilleir, Anke, Alicia C. Montoya and Suzan Van Dijk (eds). Women Writing Back / Writing Women Back. Transnational Perspectives from the Late Middle Ages to the Dawn of the Modern Era. in *Intersections. Interdisciplinary Studies in Early Modern Culture*, 16 (2010): 23-50.

—. 2008. "La Vie de sainte Douceline par Felipa Porcelet: les mobiles d'une hagiographe du XIIIe siècle", in Poirier, Guy (ed.) *Dix ans de recherche sur les femmes écrivains de l'Ancien Régime: influences et confluences. Mélanges offerts à Hannah Fournier*. Québec: Presses de l'Université Laval: 17-36.

Legge, Dominica. 1971. *Anglo-Norman Literature and its Background*. Oxford: The Clarendon Press.

Le Goff, Jacques. 1994. "Conclusions", in Cammarosano, Paolo (ed.) *Le forme della propaganda politica nel due e nel Trecento*. Rome: École française de Rome : 519-520.

Paden, William D. (ed.). 1989. *The Voices of the Trobairitz. Perspectives on the Women Troubadours*. Philadelphia: University of Pennsylvania Press.

Tomaryn Bruckner, Matilda. 1995. "The Trobairitz", in Akehurst, F. R. R. and Judith M. Davis (eds). *A Handbook of the Troubadours*. Berkeley-Los Angeles: University of California Press: 201-233.

Wogan-Browne, Jocelyn. 1993. "'Clerc u lai, muïne u dame': Women and Anglo-Norman Hagiography in the Twelfth and Thirteenth Centuries", in Meale , Carol M. (ed.). *Women and Literature in Britain, 1150-1500*. Cambridge: Cambridge University Press: 61-85.

# Part II.

# Women Writing the Nation

# Early Modern Women Intellectuals in 19th-Century Serbia: Milica Stojadinović, Draga Dejanović and Milica Tomić

*Biljana Dojčinović and Ivana Pantelić*

ABSTRACT Three Serbian women intellectuals – Milica Stojadinović Srpkinja, Draga Dimitrijević Dejanović and Milica Miletić Tomić – are presented in this chapter. Although their lives were different, all three were very much aware of their nationality, considering it a decisive part of their identities: Milica Stojadinović made it the subject of her patriotic poetry, it permeated Draga Dejanović's writings, and it was the main motif of Milica Tomić's political efforts. Their lives and works represent the evolution of independent thinking and acting of Serbian women – from the wish of Milica Stojadinović to work as a woman of letters exclusively, to the feminist awareness of Draga Dejanović, all the way to the clearly defined political struggles of Milica Tomić.

THE BALKAN PENINSULA WAS UNDER the rule of the Ottoman Empire for more than 350 years, from the 15th to the 19th century. The enslaved Balkan peoples had no rights, and were isolated from the contemporary modernization processes happening in Western Europe. At the beginning of the 19th century, Serbia was the first Balkan state to become independent from the Ottoman Empire. During the Serbian revolution (1804-1815), an independent state was formed on a part of the Serbian territory. The dramatic suppression of Serbian uprisings was followed by decades of slow autonomy gains. The first autonomous rule was established in 1815, and internationally acknowledged fifteen years later; soon after, Serbia adopted its first constitution. In 1856, the Great Powers warranted Serbian autonomy, while the Principality of Serbia finally received international recognition of independence in 1878.

Only after having acquired its autonomy in 1830, did Serbia gain the right to open its first schools. In 1836, there were only 227 pupils, 16 of who were female (making up 7% of the total amount).[1] In 1844, a school law was passed, which laid the foundations of the schooling system in the Principality of Serbia. Only two years later, in 1846, an Act on female schools was passed, entitled *The Nomination of the Schools for Girls*. According to the Act, girls were supposed to attend three-grade primary schools, starting from the age of six. Apart from public schools, private schools for children and adults were also established in the 1840s, as well as private female schools. The first female school was founded in Belgrade, in 1846. The principal aim of these schools was to highlight the importance and the necessity of more than just basic education for female children. The schooling of female children was first accepted by public servants and affluent traders, who were already used to sending their daughters to educational institutes abroad, or to hiring private tutors from Vojvodina,[2] and other parts of the Austro-Hungarian Empire, instead. It was those girls whose parents could not pay for their education abroad, who attended the first private schools for girls. The first public school for women was opened in 1845, in Paraćin, a town in central Serbia, while the second was established in Belgrade, the capital of Serbia, in 1846. According to the available statistics, there were 558 primary schools for boys and 17 for girls, in the school year of 1879-80. Girls constituted around 20 % of the total number of pupils, in 1889-90.[3] The first secondary school for women was founded in 1863 in Belgrade, and girls started attending high schools as of the academic year 1874-75.

Although the Serbian society of the 19th century was rather poor and underdeveloped, a few educated, brave, women intellectuals stood out. We are presenting such three outstanding women – Milica Stojadinović Srpkinja, Draga Dimitrijević Dejanović and Milica Miletić Tomić. The poetess, the actress and journalist, and the politician, respectively, epitomize the educated and the modern European woman of the 19th century. Through their work they had proven that they deserved to be counted among the educated and the emancipated British and French women. Their struggle for social identity and their own rights was based on the national spirit. When they spoke of their nation and national feeling, their attitudes were almost identical to those of their male colleagues, but, on the other hand, when the issue of the position of women arose, their views were very different. As Draga Dejanović wrote:

---

[1] Neda Božinović. *Žensko pitanje u Srbiji u XIX i XX veku* (*Women's Issue in Serbia in the 19th and 20th centuries*). Beograd: Žene u crnom., 1996: 55.

[2] Vojvodina is a part of Serbia which had been under the Austrian-Hungarian Empire until 1918.

[3] *Ibid.*, 57.

> The fate of the women is the fate of the people, and therefore the freedom of women must be looked upon as the freedom of all our people from the backward laws that have been holding us in chains for so long. This is why the future of women must not be taken for granted. The poverty, the everlasting issue of the unmarried status, and then the typical female flaws, such as curiosity, gossiping, stupidity, sentimentality, prink, fashion-addiction etc., are not women's faults, but the faults and evils of the unemployed, the unskilled, or lazy people, who simply have too much spare time. These characteristics do not apply to the working women any more.[4]

## Milica Stojadinović Srpkinja – The tragic foremother

The very word *feminism* was never actually used in the writings of Milica Stojadinović Srpkinja.[5] The notion of feminism itself became problematic much later, at the beginning of the 20th century. As an example of the confusion around this term, it would be enough to read the meanings of and relations to the term in the magazine *Srpkinja*, published in 1913.[6] However, this publication clearly represents Milica Stojadinović as the foremother of Serbian women's writing and activism of the 19th century. In her life and writings, the growing gap between traditional society and modern times is obvious. Milica Stojadinović considered herself to be a poet and a writer exclusively; refusing to get married or work as a governess, which was one of the few available vocations for an educated woman of her time. The result was sad – after her father's death, she lost her home, could not support herself, and was forced to live in bitter poverty, until her own untimely death. Her position may also be considered 'liminal' in geopolitical terms: she belonged to the Serbian community within the Austrian and Austro-Hungarian Empire, and her national feeling was a very important part of her identity. The struggle of the Serbian people for complete autonomy, and the

---

[4] Draga Dejanović, *Emancipacija žene* (*Emancipation of woman*). Kulturni centar, 1869, no. 34 – 35: 83-84.

[5] Radmila Gikić, *Život i književno delo Milice Stojadinović Srpkinje*. Novi Sad: Dnevnik, 2010: 45.

[6] *Српкиња: њезин живот и рад, њезин културни развитак и њезина народна умјетност до данас. (Serbian Woman: her life and work, her cultural development and her folklore art up to date).* Edited by Serbian women writers, printed by Dobrotvorna zadruga Srpkinja u Irigu (Humanitarian Society of Serbian Women in Irig), Sarajevo: Štamparija Pijuković i drug, 1913.

political battles going on inside her *mother country,* influenced her life and work strongly.

'The Fairy from Vrdnik', as Milica Stojadinović was called, was born in Bukovac, in Srem (former Austrian empire), in 1828 or 1830, and died in Belgrade (Serbia), in 1878. Her first poems were printed in Pest, which is now a part of the Hungarian capital, Budapest, and afterwards in the Austrian Empire, in 1847. She continued to publish, as a signed author, in literary magazines in Serbia, like *Sedmica, Vojvođanka, Šumadinka, Fruškogorka, Danica*, and, without signature, in *Putnik* and *Komarac*.[7] She was praised by the well-known Serbian language reformer and folk literature collector, Vuk Karadžić, as well as by the Austrian poet, Ludwig August Frankl.[8]

According to the testimonies of her contemporaries,[9] Milica Stojadinović was fluent in German, and most probably in Slovakian, and was self-taught in Italian and French. Some of translations from these languages are entered into her diary, including the works by Balzac and Ludwig August Frankle. Her diary also tells us that she read a German woman writer, Düringsfeld, in addition to Schiller and Goethe, whose genius she admired.[10] Further to this, she wrote down Serbian folk songs, chants and stories for Vuk Karadžić. In her correspondence with Vuk Karadžić, Milica thanked him for a present he sent her, a collection of *Serbian Folk Poems*, concluding that without his contribution the "innumerable and invaluable pieces of folk tradition would

---

[7] None of these were specialized women's magazines.

[8] The first book of her poems, *Pesme* (*Poems*), was published in 1850, and later on two expanded editions were issued in 1855 and 1869. She also published a diary, entitled *U Fruškoj gori 1854* (In Fruška Gora, 1854), in three volumes, issued in 1861, 1862 and 1866. The diary, printed in the city of Novi Sad, 433 copies sold out in advance to subscribers, out of which 200 copies were bought by the Serbian duchess, Julia Obrenović, in Vienna. Other copies were distributed in Belgrade, and other smaller towns in Serbia and Austria. Vienna – 200 (bought by duchess Julia Obrenović); Budim – 20; Belgrade – 84; Šabac – 20, Vukovar – 40 Karlovci – 49, of which 16 for professors, Mitrovica 20.

[9] According to Đorđe Rajković, see in Radmila Gikić, *Život i književno delo Milice Stojadinović Srpkinje*: 74.

[10] She was prescribed to a great number of books, as the data in Library of Matica Srpska show, among which are included works by Schiller. See Radmila Gikić, *Život i književno delo Milice Stojadinović Srpkinje*: 80.

be lost forever".[11] In her diary she described how she collected the folk customs and poems, merging life and fiction.[12]

This shows that Milica possessed both the knowledge of Western literatures, as well as a deep interest in the folk tradition of her own people. In 1843, at the age of 15 (or 13, if she was indeed born in 1828), she attended a German school in the city of Varadin. It would be interesting to compare her education with the other possibilities offered in Serbia at that time. Actually, as Gikić points out, at the time when Milica Stojadinović lived, the systemic education for girls had not yet been established. As such, Milica had no opportunity for education in Serbia, nor did she express any grief for not having gone to school there.[13] Her knowledge about her own national identity came from the oral tradition – the poems her mother Jelisaveta read and narrated to her children. Therefore, the oral tradition remained intertwined with her national feeling throughout her whole life, which was most strikingly visible in her effort to help Vuk Karadžić record the Serbian folk tradition.

For Milica Stojadinović, the issue of nationality was also the issue of personal identity, language, religion. In a letter to Dimitrije Matić she clearly stated her views on the national issue, but also on the relationship between Serbs the church, faith and their native language, which she considered to be the basis of the national identity. She claimed that:

> It is one of our greatest misfortunes, that the majority of the learned upper class disregards the importance of the church and the faith! They show their vanity by saying that faith and church mean nothing. But the Lord will help them come to their senses, for has not our mother, the church, saved our nationality? [...] This vanity is killing us, for it numbs the senses of the people, just like opium does. I look at Novi Sad, it has such a foreign spirit, that one must think twice before knowing whether one is among the Serbs. Wherever one goes, the foreign wind blows. One can hear Serbian women speak a foreign language, or a twisted Serbian, that sounds foreign! I asked one of

---

[11] *Ibid.*, 33.

[12] On this topic see, Biljana Dojčinović-Nešić, "Transcribing the Voice of the Mother: The Diary of Milica Stojadinović-Srpkinja", http://www.zenskestudie.edu.rs/index.php?option=com_content&task=view&id=241&Itemid=45.

[13] Even her efforts to secure scholarship for her brother Ljubivoje were focused on cities within the Austro-Hungarian Empire, Vienna and Budapest.

> them, why? She answered that one can learn Serbian even in the street![14]

The name of the nation is also a part of the identity, as much as religion and language are – Milica complained in her diary that the Serbs south of the Danube were called Turks, while those on the north bank were called Germans: "And when will all of them be called Serbs?",[15] she asked, noting the liminal position of her nation – between the Austrian and the Ottoman empire, and the danger of being 'swallowed' by these two big entities. In July 1862, she went to Belgrade while it was being bombed by the Turks, and wrote a report about the events, which was then published by *The Hungarian Journal* under the title *Heart and Barricades*, making her the first Serbian "female war correspondent".[16]

Milica Stojadinović was the first Serbian woman writer completely devoted to writing and to the rise of her Serbian nation. Despite this, she died miserable and forgotten in 1878, ironically the same year when Serbia gained international recognition as an autonomous country.

## Draga Dimitrijević Dejanović – The first Serbian feminist

Draga Dimitrijević Dejanović is recognized in Serbian historiography as the first Serbian feminist, woman journalist and actress. She was born in 1840, in Southern Hungary. She began her education in the place of her birth and continued it at the Vinchikov Institute in Timisoara, and then in Pest.In 1862 she joined the acting ensemble of the Serbian national theater in Novi Sad. It was a bold break with the established rules, a move resisted by her family. One year later, Draga Dejanović moved to Belgrade where she translated some plays for the National Theatre. Despite her private obligations, she did not abandon public work and the task she had devoted herself to: 'prosvećivanje Srpstva' (the enlightenment of Serbdom), was an expression she often used in her texts. While she was in Pest, Draga Dejanović met the leaders of *Ujedinjena omladina srpska* (the United Serbian Youth /USY/). Dejanović was a prominent member of the USY, which existed from 1866 to

---

[14] Milica Stojadinović Srpkinja. *Pesme* (*Poems*), Bačka Palanka, 2008: 14-15.

[15] Milica Stojadinović Srpkinja. 1985. *U Fruškoj gori 1854* (In Fruška gora 1854), Beograd: Prosveta, 1854: 59.

[16] Radmila Gikić (ed.), *Prepiska Milice Stojadinović Srpkinje* (*Correspondence of Milica Stojadinović Srpkinja).* Novi Sad: KZ, 1987: 7.

1872. The United Serbian Youth, founded in 1866, was an organization based on the model of Mazzini's Young Italy. Their goal was the promotion of education and culture of the Serbian people. The founders of the USY were the first Serbian socialists and liberals, Svetozar Marković, Svetozar Miletić and Vladimir Jovanović. The USY was among the first organizations to raise the question of women's emancipation, including the women's section as its constituent part which coordinated various related activities. At the USY meetings Draga openly advocated women's equality. She called for the USY to stand behind the demand for an equal education for both boys and girls. Her first texts about the emancipation of women were published in *Matica* (a journal published by the USY). In the mid 19th century, the originators of the idea of women's liberation in Serbia mostly addressed the legal and ethical side of the issue, whereas whenever the national issue arose, the ideals of wifehood, motherhood and sisterhood prevailed over all other aspects of women's freedom.

Draga Dejanović began her work as a literary publicist in 1862, by publishing several poems and articles in the *Danica* magazine. In the poems of Draga Dejanović the main themes were, of course, patriotism and love. For her there was nothing dearer than a 'kind Serb', while the Turks she 'hated as a freezing grave', and was comforted by the very thought of help from the 'brigands':

For the holy cross, the name of a Serb
I would shed my blood
And for my dear Serbian mother
I would gladly die.[17]

Draga Dejanović's most significant texts are feminist.She advocated the complete independence of women, saw the enlightenment of women as necessary to "the awakening of the people's self-consciousness",[18] and sought out ways to contribute to this 'awakening'. The role of a woman in family life as a 'teacher of children' was burdened with great responsibility, since it was women who determined whether or not the family home prospered or was ruined. Although she openly criticized patriarchal education

---

[17] Julka Hlapec Đorđević, *Omladinka Draga Dejanović, Studije i eseji o feminizmu*, (Youth Draga Dejanović, Studies and essays on feminism). Beograd: izdanje, Života i rada, 1935: 170.
[18] *Ibid.*, 173.

as superficial and backward nonsense, these texts abound in her observations and conclusions about her rights and obligations towards the Serbian people and herself. As a spirited supporter of the USY she considered that it was her duty to contribute to the awakening of the national consciousness. As such, she kept up the message to the Serbian women to love and revere their own people and fight to stop its ruin. In her texts she makes many references to the question of maternity, defining it as a woman's obligation towards her nation:

> And what is the current state of affairs. Are we still dedicated to the sacred cause of our nation's progress? Are we still harbored by that fare and for our nation useful costume, which had guarded our old mothers? Do we intend to bestow our good names and future generations to our nation [...] If only I could, oh my dear sisters, I would ring all the alarm bells. If only I could, I would scream for every true Serbian heart to hear, that it is us, the women, who are solely responsible for the ever decreasing number of our people.[19]

Draga Dejanović was imbued with romantic patriotism, but also aimed to highlight the formidable problems with which women were faced in society. She considered poor education to be the greatest obstacle to women's emancipation. In her article "Zla sreća devojačka" (The Ill Fortune of Girls), she concluded that financial independence and modern education were the basics of women's independence. In all of her texts, Draga Dejanović also expressed dissatisfaction with what she considered to be the passivity of Serbian women. She publicly criticized the majority of women who believed that the responsibility for the material support of the family should rest entirely with men. She pointed out that women had the legal right to a public education and argued that there were no formal obstacles preventing them from acquiring education, and from becoming equally trained for both intellectual and manual work. Draga Dejanović criticized women for not being organized, for being satisfied with men's alleged superiority, and for not undertaking anything to change their situation.

Some of Draga Dejanović's writings remained unpublished. The most important of these include her play *Deoba Jakšića* (The Succession of the Jakšićs), *Svećenik u Morlaku* (The Priest of Morlak), and a pedagogical study

---

[19] Draga Dejanović, *Srpskim majkama (To Serbian mothers)*, Mlada srbadija, 10.april 1871: 85, 86.

*Mati* (Mother).[20] Draga Dejanović loved her family (children and husband) and suffered a sense of great personal tragedy when her son died in infancy, in 1867. She died in 1871, while giving birth to a daughter.

## Milica Miletić Tomić – The politics of library and beyond

Milica Miletić Tomić (1859-1944) was an author, politician and journaliSt[21] She was born in Novi Sad, the daughter of a Serbian politician, Svetozar Miletić.[22] Her husband, Jaša Tomić, was also a politician, a journalist and a publicist.Milica Tomić grew up in an atmosphere of national and political strife, and was brought up in the national spirit. She was even given the name Milica, in memory of Milica Stojadinović Srpkinja.[23] Milica Tomić was educated in Novi Sad, Pest and Vienna. She entered public life at the age of eighteen, at the time when her father was arrested for the first time because he opposed the "undemocratic" Habsburg authorities. She was in charge of her father's correspondence and first began publishing political articles in the newspaper *Zastava* (*The Flag).*[24] Young Milica was received by the emperor Franz Joseph, and succeeded in accelerating her father's release. She vividly described this meeting in the *Flag*:

> Then I forgot all that I had been taught, because it all seemed artificial and inappropriate, and I told the king about all the things laying at the bottom of my heart. I told him everything about my misfortunes, but I've mentioned this as well, that the Serbian people share Miletić's destiny.[25]

---

[20] Ivana Pantelić, *Draga Dejanović (born Dimitrijević) (1840-1871)*, in F. de Haan, K. Daskalova, A. Loufti (eds). *A Biographical Dictionary of Women's Movements and Feminisms, Central, Eastern and South Eastern Europe, 19th and 20th Centuries*, Budapest-New York, Central European University Press, 2006: 107.

[21] http://neww.huygens.knaw.nl/authors/show/4001

[22] Svetozar Miletić (1826-1901) was a lawyer and the leader of *People's Serb Freethinkers Party.*

[23] Sofija Božić, "Milica Tomić: stremljenje ka modernom" (Milica Tomić: striving towards the modern) , in Latinka Perović (ed.), *Srbija u modernizacijskim procesima 19. i 20. veka, 2: Položaj žene kao merilo modernizacije (Serbia in the Modernization Processes of 19th and 20th Century, 2: Position of Woman as a Measure of Modernization, a conference)*. Beograd: Institut za noviju istoriju Srbije, 1998: 456.

[24] *The Flag* was a newspaper founded in 1866. It was the most widely read and the most influential daily within the Serbian community in Austria-Hungary.

[25] Milica Jaše Tomića, *Očevo pomilovanje (*Father's Pardon*)*, Zastava, 23.09.1906, no. 198: 15.

Milica Tomić is remembered in the *Herstory* of the feminist movement as the first woman in Serbia who, together with her friend Julka Ilić, showed the power of female activism in practice. In 1907, at a gathering in Veliki Bečkerek, these two collected 30,000 signatures against Apolonius's law which demanded the introduction of Hungarian into all schools in Hungary, including Serbian schools:[26]

> And when schools in our native tongue became endangered, and when they intended to replace our native tongue with the Hungarian language, then our narrow circle had arisen, we went all around our cities and towns, our Hungarian land, and in a short period of time we collected more than 30,000 signatures from the Serbian women. The Hungarian Members of Parliament were eager to see those signatures, because they were astounded by the attitude of our women.[27]

Thanks to her, the *Poselo Srpkinja* (The Gathering of Serbian Women) was founded in 1905 in Novi Sad, which later turned into a female reading-room named *Posestrima* (Sister-by-choice). Milica Tomić said that the idea was born in 1904, when women begun to meet on Thursdays – they would knit and talk (gossiping was forbidden), while men were banned from entering the room and had to pay fines if they did. The number of members quickly grew to 17, highlighting the need for such gatherings. Later on, Milica Tomić wrote:

> I already know that many eyebrows will be raised when the women's reading room is mentioned. My personal belief is that the foundation of the women's reading rooms should only be the beginning of the intensive enlightenment of our women. I should point out that these women's reading rooms, as originated in Novi Sad, are noting like the men's reading rooms, as I imagine, nor do they resemble the women's reading rooms as they exist in the WeSt[28]

In its first year, the library collected 300 books. In February 1910, there were 96 members, and in November, 170, but then their activities were stopped by

[26] Gordana Stojakovic (ed.), *Znamenite žene Novog Sada* (Famous women of Novi Sad), vol I, Novi Sad: s.n., 2001: 52.

[27] Milica Jaše Tomića, *Ženska čitaonica* (Women's reading room), *Žena*, 1921, no. 1: 20.

[28] *Ibid.*, 21.

the First World War. However, the Library was renewed in 1919, with 300 members, and the last article on the activity of *Posestrima* was published in the Novi Sad newspapers, on December 6, 1935.

Some rules of the women's public library, *Posestrima,* clearly show that the marks of modernization related to the women's social positions For instance, the aim of the society was to create a space where adult women, the citizens of Novi Sad, would meet on Sundays and in the holidays, to improve their social life and education. The library would collect books, newspapers and magazines. The important thing was that politics was also a part of the library's domain, which meant that politics was not only actively discussed among its members, but also that these women were politically engaged. Political engagement lay in the very foundation of the library. Announcing that only 'role-model women' (Hungarian citizens) could become members, the rules also included the idea of (in) properness, connected to the education and emancipation of women. And, of course, the library was meant to be a female sanctuary that men were barred from, while female guests were allowed, making it, thus, a semipublic or a semiprivate space.[29]

Milica Tomić was a great advocate of female suffrage. She was among seven women who were elected members of the Great Parliament in 1918,[30] and very shortly afterwards women got the right to vote.[31] In 1911, she started the magazine *Woman*, where she worked as an editor. The magazine focused on the political and cultural emancipation of women, while the dominant topics were suffrage and the right to political engagement. Milica Tomić emphasized the emancipatory role of this magazine:

> The *Woman* will primarily have our Serbian home in mind, as well as the Serbian social circumstances, but it will also try to introduce our

[29] That libraries were cultural centers for women was also determined by the fact that the author of the first review of feminism in Serbia was Ljubica Marković – the first Serbian woman librarian. In 1933, at the yearly assembly of the Association of the University Educated Women, Ljubica Marković spoke about the beginnings of feminism in Serbia and Vojvodina and later published a text on the subject (in 1933 and 1934). This text is the first comprehensive review of feminist thought in Serbia.

[30] Representatives of the people of Srem, Bačka, Banat and Baranja, which today are the northern territories of Serbia and Croatia, gathered on 25 November 1918, and declared the joining of those territories to the Kingdom of Serbia (some years later the bigger state of the Kingdom of Serbs, Croats and Slovenes was formed).

[31] Women gained political rights under the communist Yugoslavia in 1945.

> readers to the progress women of other nationalities are making in their own countries. [32]

Milica was the first woman to pay attention to the "unworthy position of Serbian women" in her texts, the burden of their every-day lives, and the impossibility of dedicating themselves thoroughly to their children. She also wrote about other backward aspects of the Serbian family: superstition, unhygienic living conditions, fear of doctors, etc. For Milica Tomić, the introduction of foreign, particularly western, customs and the neglect of one's own folk tradition, symbolized the alienation from one's own nation. The old Serbian heritage was holy for her, and it had to be respected and looked after. She kept reminding her female readers that they should remain critical of Western and Ottoman influences, in all segments of life. Therefore, the *Woman* published texts which emphasized that foreign culture, language and customs must serve as an impetus and inspiration for refining, and not for forgetting, one's own culture, language and customs.

## Conclusion

Although their lives were rather different, Milica Stojadinović, Draga Dejanović and Milica Tomić have important things in common. First, all three were completely aware of their nationality, considering it to be a decisive part of their identity. Second, each made at least one significant break with patriarchal tradition. It was Milica Stojadinović who first claimed that being a poet is enough of a vocation for a woman. She felt, tragically, the impossibility of that position, becoming both a madwoman and a foremother – a kind of Judith Shakespeare of Serbian literature. Just like Milica's, the fate of Draga Dejanović is imbued with a certain degree of romanticism, induced by her untimely death. However, Dejanović was an outspoken activist, both in her private and public life as an actress, as well as in her writings. Her awareness of the status of women was much clearer and better structured than Milica Stojadinović's, which is why her struggle for women's education makes her the Serbian Mary Wollstonecraft. Finally, Milica Tomić's strong political engagement, along with her extraordinary practicality, was reflected in the establishment of *Posestrima* as a semipublic space in which women could form a political force. Her role in the women's suffrage can be compared to those of Millicent Garrett Fawcett.

[32] Sofija Božić, "Milica Tomić: stremljenje ka modernom": 465.

Therefore, the lives and works of Milica Stojadinović, Draga Dejanović and Milica Tomić represent the evolution of independent thinking and acting of Serbian women – from the dearly paid wish to be a woman of letters exclusively, all the way to the clearly defined political struggle. This line starts with the struggle for national independence, in which all three were involved: Milica Stojadinović with her patriotic poetry, Draga Dejanović through the theatre and her writings, and Milica Tomić via her political engagement. All three women saw the chance to live an authentic life, striving to modernize the deeply patriarchal Serbian nation, as in both aspects – gender and nation – liberation was the main issue, and the final goal was freedom.[33]

[33] This text is written within the project *Knjiženstvo, Theory and History of Women's Writing in Serbia until 1915* (No. 178029) of the Ministry of Education and Science of the Republic of Serbia.

## Select Bibliography

Božić, Sofija. 1998. "Milica Tomić: stremljenje ka modernom" (Milica Tomić: striving towards the modern) in Latinka Perović (ed.). *Srbija u modernizacijskim procesima 19. i 20. veka, 2: Položaj žene kao merilo modernizacije (Serbia in the Modernization Processes of XIX and XX Century, 2: Position of Woman as a Measure of Modernization, a conference),* Beograd: Institut za noviju istoriju Srbije.

Božinović, Neda. 1996. *Žensko pitanje u Srbiji u XIX i XX veku* (*Woman's issue in Serbia in the 19th and 20th centuries*). Beograd: Žene u crnom.

Dejanović, Draga. 1869. *Emancipacija žene* (*Emancipation of woman*). Kulturni centar: 34 – 35.

—. 1871. *Srpskim majkama (To Serbian mothers).* Mlada srbadija, (10. April): 85- 86.

Dojčinović-Nešić, Biljana, "Transcribing the Voice of the Mother: The Diary of Milica Stojadinović-Srpkinja" in http://www.zenskestudie.edu.rs/index.php?option=com_content&task=view&id=241&Itemid=45

Gikić, Radmila "Milica Stojadinović Srpkinja" in *Zavera nečitanja na* http://www.zenskestudie.edu.rs/index.php?option=com_content&task=view&id=244&Itemid=45

—. (ed.). 1987. *Prepiska Milice Stojadinović Srpkinje* (*Correspondence of Milica Stojadinović Srpkinja).* Novi Sad: KZ.

—. 2010. *Život i književno delo Milice Stojadinović Srpkinje*. Novi Sad: Dnevnik.

Hlapec Đorđević, Julka. 1935. *Studije i eseji o feminizmu (Studies and essays on feminism)*. Beograd: izdanje, Života i rada.

Pantelić, Ivana. 2006. *Draga Dejanović (born Dimitrijević) (1840-1871)*, in F. de Haan, K. Daskalova, A. Loufti (eds). *A Biographical Dictionary of Women's Movements and Feminisms, Central, Eastern and South Eastern Europe, 19th and 20th Centuries*. Budapest-New York: Central European University Press.

Stojadinović Srpkinja, Milica. 1985. *U Fruškoj gori 1854 (In Fruška gora 1854).* Beograd: Reprint Prosveta.

—. 2008. *Pesme* (*Poems*). Bačka Palanka: 14-15.

Stojaković, Gordana. (ed.). 2001. *Znamenite žene Novog Sada (Famous women of Novi Sad).* vol I. Novi Sad: s.n.

Tomića, Milica Jaše. 1906. *Očevo pomilovanje (Father's Pardon)*. Zastava. (198): 15.

—. 1921. *Ženska čitaonica. (Women's reading room), in Zena,* no. 1: 20.

# The Role of Božena Němcová in the Construction of Czech and Slovak Cultural Identity

*Alejandro Hermida de Blas*

ABSTRACT In this chapter, the author presents those women who participated in the cultural initiatives of Czech and Slovak National Revivals by supporting men. Rather than develop a voice of their own, women generally played a modest role. But the most important of these women was Božena Němcová (1820?-1862). More than half a century, before the rise of this state, Němcová, the first canonic Czech woman writer, helped to strengthen Czech-Slovak relations at a critical moment.

THE CZECHS AND THE SLOVAKS, like many other European people, had their National Revival in the late 18th and early 19th centuries. This resurgence focused on the restoration (the Czechs) or introduction (the Slovaks) of the written use of the national language. To reach this goal, they had to overcome a number of obstacles both material – the allophone education, the restrictions of the authorities of the Habsburg Monarchy – and mental – the prejudice of identifying Czech and Slovak languages with lower, peasant or working classes, and foreign languages (mostly German) with social promotion.

Women generally played a modest role in both National Revivals. Besides barriers common to men, women had to overcome their particular position in society, which emphasized their dedication to family above any personal and professional ambition. For these reasons, relatively few women participated in the cultural initiatives of Czech and Slovak National Revivals, and most did it to support men rather than with a voice of their own.

In Bohemia, where the urban middle class was more developed than in Slovakia, the conditions for the cultural activity of women were more favourable. The first well-known Czech woman writer was Magdalena Dobromila Rettigová (1785-1845). Rather than having a particular artistic value, her works, the best known of which is a *Home Cookery Book* (*Domácí kuchařka*, 1826), have a practical or didactic nature. Nevertheless,

Rettigová's cultural role was later vindicated by younger Czech women writers – like Božena Němcová.[1] At that time, the lack of women writers was felt in men's patriotic circles, which led to several literary mystifications.[2] The best known of them is that of the leading poet and scholar František Ladislav Čelakovský, who invented the fictitious poet Žofie Jandová so successfully that even the English translator John Bowring included one of 'her' poems in his *Cheskian Anthology* (1832). The gap was only partially filled from 1838 by songs published in literary magazines by Marie Čacká (a pseudonym of a real woman, Františka Božislava Svobodová-Pichlová, 1811-1882).

At the end of the National Revival, by the mid-19th century, things began to change in Czech literature and society. A new generation of women writers approached their work with the same literary ambition as men. Their contribution was welcome, and some of them achieved recognition and even became very prominent figures of Czech culture. The most important of these women is Božena Němcová (1820?-1862). She played the role of the great woman writer the Czech nation was waiting for, and she has retained it even to the present day.[3] Paradoxically, her origin and education did not predispose her to devote herself to Czech culture. She was born in Vienna, her parents were German or germanized, and she received a German education.[4] How, then, did she, contrary to her family and social

---

[1] "What for me is strange is that no one has referred at length to Rettigová, after all, she also deserves a honouring picture, why do not anyone publish a portrait of her? (...) Write about that to your sister, after all, only women could publish it (...). We, the housewives, are somehow obliged to her.", Letter to A. B. Čelakovská on December the 19th, 1847, in B. Němcová, *Čtyry doby (Výbor z díla III)*. Prague: Československý spisovatel, 1974$^2$: 45-46.

[2] Macura Macura, V. *Znamení zrodu (České národní obrození jako kulturní typ), 2.* Jinočany: Rozšířené vydání, H&H. 1995:110 ff.

[3] A general survey of the recent researches on the Němcová myth can be found in Horčáková, V. "Život a dílo Boženy Němcové v novější literatuře (Legendy a skutečnost)" in *Sdružení knihoven České republiky*. Brno: Sdružení knihoven ČR, 2009: 67-71. See also contributions to this subject in Piorecký, K. (ed.). *Božena Němcová a její Babička (Sborník příspěvků z III. Kongresu světové literarněvědné bohemistiky, Praha 28. 6. – 3. 7. 2005, svazek 3)*. Prague: Ústav pro českou literaturu AV ČR, 2006.

[4] As is well known, the official biography of Božena Němcová says her parents were two servants of the famous Duchess Wilhelmine von Sagan (known among Czechs as Kateřina Zaháňská): Johann Pankl, a coachman from Lower Austria, and Terezie Novotná, a germanized Czech laundress. However, there is solid evidence that the

circumstances, become a Czech writer? The author herself explains that it was in youthful "pretty bad verses, but I did not know how to make them better":

> Czech land did not give birth to me,
> but it is my dear homeland,
> and of calling myself a Czech
> I am proud, I am delighted.
> (...)
> And this beautiful, euphonic language
> how it could not be dear to me?
> Since my mother taught me to pray,
> to speak, to sing only in Czech.
> (...)
> I gave my heart to a Czech man,
> a patriot is my husband,
> and I will bring up Czech children
> as sturdy sons of the homeland.[5]

The influence of her maternal grandmother Magdalena Novotná, who lived with the family for a few years, seems to have been decisive in sewing the seeds of love for the Czech country and Czech language in Barunka, the seeds that would germinate years later. As the writer herself explains in a letter to a friend:

---

baby, who was named Barbora, could have been born earlier, in 1817 or even 1816, and she may be the illegitimate daughter of a member of the aristocratic circle of the Duchess von Sagan (perhaps the Duchess' herself, as it has often been suggested, or her sister's Dorothea, as the scholar Helena Sobková thinks. The 4th edition of her book *The Mistery of Barunka Panklová*, Sobková, 1997: 115 ff., mentions other scholars' most recent hypotheses including the curious theory, defended by a great-grandson of the writer, which claims Božena Němcová was the daughter of Spanish painter Francisco de Goya and his young model, the aristocrat Sabasa García). Thus the Pankls would be only her adoptive parents, and Božena Němcová would have no Czech origin at all. Shortly after birth, the family moved to the realm of the Duchess in Ratibořice (northern Bohemia), where Barbara, who was in favour with the Duchess, received an education in German, higher than could be expected given the humble status of her parents. Thus, little Barunka, as they called Barbora in her childhood, became Miss Betty, who borrowed German books from the Duchess' library in the nearby mansion in Chvalkovice.

[5] B. Němcová, *Čtyry doby (Výbor z díla III)*: 33-34.

> I was also educated mostly in German, and only my grandmother – a sincere old-Czech woman you can still find anywhere, although they go unnoticed – instilled in me the love for the fatherland; she told me episodes from the Czech history – mostly about Libuše and Přemysl[6] – and she always tried to dissuade me from speaking German. When I was little, I obeyed her, but when I grew up, I rebelled against this animosity toward German language; I defended it, because I enjoyed very much reading German books, while reading in Czech and this language seemed very vulgar to me. It's true that I spoke more and better Czech than German, but despite this fact I liked more German. I had been quite a few years married, when I got in my hands the collected works of Tyl.[7] They moved my heart and reminded me vividly of my good grandmother. [...] My love for the mother language and for the nation I come from grew stronger in this gradual way.[8]

In her most famous work, *The Grandmother* (*Babička*, 1855), the author pays tribute to the two women who had the most influence on her education: the one who entitles the novel, and the Duchess. The fictitious, cordial meeting between these two women, one of them a Czech peasant, and the other one a German aristocrat, symbolizes the reconciliation between two conflicting forces in Němcová's social and national identity. In this sense, the influence of her Czech teachers and her husband Josef Němec, a Czech patriot who will suffer reprisals after the failed revolution of 1848-1849 has also been highlighted; but her first stay in Prague (1842-1845) seems to have been much more decisive. There she became acquainted with patriotic intellectual circles. They welcomed her with enthusiasm and gave her the encouragement to devote herself to writing that she did not find in her family environment. Following usual practice at that time, Barbora Němcová took the more Slavic pen-name of Božena.

At first, the idea of cultural activities, as defended by Božena Němcová, was in agreement with the role of women in the society of the time. In 1843, Němcová published in *Květy*, the magazine edited by Tyl, a poem entitled To

---

[6] Libuše and Přemysl are the main characters of the legend about the foundation of the first Czech dynasty, the Premysls.

[7] Josef Kajetán Tyl (1808-1856), a dramatist, prose writer and journalist, one of the main representatives of Czech patriotic romanticism.

[8] Letter to V. Vrbíková on January the 22th, 1851, in B. Němcová, *Čtyry doby (Výbor z díla III*: 225-226.

Czech Women, in which she calls them to serve their country as only women can do – having children, educating them as patriots and giving them in sacrifice to the homeland:

> Czech women, Czech mothers!
> Let's make and keep a promise!
> For the good of our dear homeland
> let's sacrifice all our strength!
> (…)
> Man, oh, has got his sharp sword,
> his arm, his strength – he's got everything;
> but delicate, weak woman
> just her heart – and her kid.[9]

The same spirit of devotion to the homeland led Němcová to advise her friend Antonie Reissová (known in patriotic circles as Bohuslava Rajská) not to accept the proposal of marriage of the young Slovak poet Samo Bohdan Hroboň – unless her heart says otherwise – but that of the renowned Czech scholar and also poet František Ladislav Čelakovský, an older widower with four children, because it was of better service to the Czech nation:

> If it is real love, a passion because of which you forget each obstacle put in the way, because of which the beloved object is the only goal of happiness, if it is such a love you feel for Hroboň, then my words are vain; I know the desire for the voluptuous rose which we reach for, even though its thorns prick us. But if it is a love you want to sacrifice for the homeland, for our cause, if you honour him only as a martyr of the Slavic nation, because of which we here should suffer the great loss of you, then, please, do not do it, incline to go to the other side, where you can work more, where you will keep the glory of the Czech nation, a father for his family and the family for the joy of the father; just think what you can do for us in that role; you know that a man, even if he is the greatest celebrity, is not capable of doing as many as a sensible woman, and you with your talent, with your ardent love for the dear homeland (…) [10]

---

[9] B. Němcová, *Čtyry doby (Výbor z díla III)*: 31.

[10] Letter to B. Rajská on August the 8th, 1844, in B. Němcová. *Čtyry doby (Výbor z díla III)*: 32.

However, these early statements do not reflect the essence of Němcová's literary and cultural activity. Her desire to contribute to the Czech national cause was not limited to a quiet supporting role of men, nor giving birth and bringing up new generations of patriots, but became a conscious cultural project full of personal ambition, social impact, and political implications. Němcová's literary career was not about renunciation, but about (sometimes dramatic) self-realization. The writer was a tireless worker, who suffered from a lack of time and funds to devote herself fully to writing, and who did not hesitate to run away from time to time from her family to carry out her literary projects. Her letters are full of sharp comments on political events, social and cultural life. She criticizes, for instance, the excessive and shallow patriotism of some contemporaries, as well as cultural and pedagogical initiatives influenced by religion:

> Nevertheless the chauvinism, the flirtation of our patriotic girls disgusts my soul; every third word is 'love for the fatherland', they are full of red-blue, white-red bows, without which if they were seen in the streets, they would think that the Czech country will suffer destruction, but when you see it close up, you can see a total emptiness, just pretence. – You have also heard and read about Mrs Amerling's girls institute;[11] we put great hopes in it, though who knows her better had already predicted how it will end. The girls there learn many things, but they do not know anything about all that, and the things on which depends all our future well-being are not taken into account. When the soul must become corrupted, what does it matter if it happens in Czech or in German? It might be better even if it would happen in German, perhaps the children would not catch it so strongly. A Jesuit runs Mrs Amerling, Mrs Amerling runs the institute where our hopes are educated! I do not need to explain further to you what kind of education is there, where a Jesuit sneaked in. – What a poor thing, my dear soul, what a poor poor thing![12]

---

[11] Natural scientist and educationalist doctor Karel Slavoj Amerling (1807-1884) founded a Utopian school called Budeč in Prague, and later a pedagogical institute, the women's section of which was run by his wife Františka Svatava Michalcová-Amerlingová.

[12] Letter to V. Vrbíková on January the 22th, 1851, in B. Němcová, *Čtyry doby (Výbor z díla III)*: 226.

One of the fields to which Němcová devoted her energy were the relations between the Czechs and the Slovaks. It was a recurring theme in literature and culture of the first half of the nineteenth century, especially among the Slovaks, who, cornered in the mountainous regions of the so-called Upper Hungary, tried to strengthen contacts with other Slavic peoples; in particular, those who were the closest historically and linguistically. For most of the Czech intelligentsia, the Slovaks were an unredeemed branch of a single Czech – or Czechoslovak – nation. For this reason, many Czechs were offended when, in 1846, Ľudovít Štúr published a new Slovak grammar and got the Slovaks – even those, who traditionally wrote in Czech – to accept it. Despite this language 'schism' (rozkol), as it came to be known among the Czechs, the mutual relations remained strong during the second half of the nineteenth and early twentieth centuries.

Němcová knew Slovakia shortly after the language 'schism', at first by chance: in 1850 her husband, a customs officer, was transferred to Hungary, first to the city of Miskolc (in Slovak Miškovec) and then to Balassagyarmat (Balážske Ďarmoty), near present-day Slovakia.[13] In the first of her four trips to Hungary in 1851, Němcová met Slovaks, but she had no time to enter, strictly speaking, the territory of Slovakia. This she did in 1852 and in 1853, when she visited the Banská Bystrica area – one of the most 'authentic' according to cultural canons – and contacted many Slovak intellectuals. Particularly intense was her fourth and final trip in 1855. It was a long prepared working trip, made by Němcová without her family. In previous correspondence with the professor Alois Vojtěch Šembera, the author makes clear her motives and ambitions. She wanted to contribute to the reciprocity between the two peoples by making known the Slovak cultural heritage to the Czechs. As a woman, she felt particularly qualified for this task:

> There are some things which only woman's eyes can see. A stranger is not allowed to know all the secrets of domestic life, not even men of the household are allowed, as I see. [...] You know what we need, you know the state of Slovakia and the Slovaks. Maybe my travel could

[13] At that time Slovakia did not exist as an administrative unit in Hungary, and therefore its borders were not defined. In the northern Carpathian region (Upper Hungary) the population was almost exclusively Slovak (or, in the north-east, Ruthenian), while in the Danube plain (Lower Hungary) there was a mixed population of Magyars, Slovaks and other ethnic groups.

> bring many other benefits, could move many stones out of the way to rapprochement. [14]

Proof of how seriously Němcová took her task is that the literary fruits of the four trips to Slovakia occupy a significant part of her work: a series of travel and ethnographic reports, an important collection of *Slovak Tales and Legends* (*Slovenské pohádky a pověsti*, 1857-1858), whose texts were mostly first edited by her, as well as a set of Slovak characters and topics in her prose fiction, especially in her novel *A Mountain Village* (*Pohorská vesnice*, 1857), and in the story *The House at the Foot of the Mountains* (*Chyže pod horami*, 1858), subtitled "A Description of Local Customs of Slovakia." We cannot discuss all these topics here.[15] Němcová shows an image of Slovakia as a mountainous country with beautiful landscapes. It is inhabited by farmers and herders who live an idyllic, simple and traditional life. Slovak people are described as cordial, hospitable, quite superstitious, but cheerful, always willing to sing a popular song. This way, Němcová, besides other authors, contributed in fixing the cliché about Slovakia as was popular in Czech literature in the second half of the nineteenth and early twentieth centuries. We must, nevertheless, remember that Němcová had a real knowledge of Slovakia, even though this knowledge related only to a small part of the country.

As illustrated by this passage from the story *The House at the Foot of the Mountains*, the author considered Czechs and Slovaks as two brotherly peoples, two branches of the same Czechoslovak nation:

> "The Sir is not Slovak?" asked the farmer's wife with surprise.
> "I am Czech," replied the hoSt
> "Czech, I like that!" exclaimed the old farmer. "And here I thought that the Sir was Slovak, from the Trnava area."
> "The Sir speaks Slovak as if full-blooded," said the astonished son-in-law.

---

[14] Letter to A. V. Šembera on May the 4th, 1855, in B. Němcová, *Čtyry doby (Výbor z díla III)*: 475-477.

[15] For a comprehensive description of them, based on previous studies by B. Haluzický and M. Tomčík, see K. Rosenbaum, *Vzťahy slovenskej a českej literatúry 19. a 20.* Bratislava: Storočia, Obzor, 1989: 91-105. An alternative interpretation of Slovak inspiration in the works of Němcová can be found in Janáčková, *Božena Němcová: příběhy, situace, obrazy*. Prague: Academia, 2007: 143-150.

> "And why couldn't he speak, if Slovaks and Czechs are leaves of the same tree, and they easily understand each other?" said the farmer.[16]

Like her lover doctor Dušan Lambl, Němcová was one of the few Czech intellectuals who showed understanding of the Slovak decision to preserve their distinct language, some details of which she reproduced in the dialogues of her Slovak-themed writings and in the letters to her friend Gustáv Kazimír Zechenter. Her first purpose – which she finally could not carry out – was to edit in Prague Slovak folk tales in their original language.

Besides her sense of observation, Božena Němcová formed her image of Slovakia on the basis of the information and opinions of the local intelligentsia. She met or corresponded with many members of the Slovak romantic generation: Ján Francisci-Rimavský, Janko Kráľ, Samo Chalupka, Gustáv Kazimír Zechenter-Laskomerský, Samo Tomášik, Andrej Sládkovič and others. In letters to the closest friends, among them Zechenter, Chalupka, Němcová complains of the distrust of some Slovaks towards the Czechs, and of the passivity of the Slovaks to their own affairs, a passivity which makes them more vulnerable to Germanization than the Czechs. However, she also criticizes Czechs for their arrogant attitude towards the Slovaks. She complains that she is criticized in her own country because of her sympathy towards the Slovaks (letter to A.V. Šembera on December the 11th, 1857).[17]

Němcová's interest in Slovakia was not only culturally justified; it had practical and economic reasons. She believed that mutual relations could benefit both peoples – the more developed (the Czechs) and the relatively backward (the Slovaks). As she explains in a letter:

> The strength of the people of Bohemia is going to America, and this is certainly bad, because these people are lost to us, while, on the contrary, with a similar settlement in Hungary or Slovakia we would just win, and Slovaks as well, and Hungarians.[18]

She knew what she was talking about: the reasons for which her husband sought a transfer to Hungary were to do with a better chance of promotion

---

[16] B. Němcová, *Čtyry doby (Výbor z díla III)*: 166-167.

[17] *Ibid.*, 498.

[18] Letter to J. Dlabač on May the 8th, 1852, in B. Němcová. *Čtyry doby (Výbor z díla III)*: 420.

and the fact that their children could go to a Slovak language school (he got neither one nor the other).

The historical situation in the second half of the 19th century was favourable to the realization of Němcová's ideas on Czech and Slovak brotherhood. From the late 1850's onward Czech and Slovak patriots revived cultural activity with more modest and concrete goals. Realism in politics and literature gradually replaced the remains of Romanticism. The Austro-Hungarian Compromise of 1867 divided the empire into two separate administrative units. Unlike the Hungarians, the Czechs did not regain their self-government, but, thanks to their own ability and greater tolerance of the Austrian authorities, their cultural revival was unstoppable. On the other side, in the territory under Hungarian administration, the authorities tried to build a Magyar nation-state by means of subjecting national minorities in an almost unveiled acculturation process. The Magyarization, a danger Němcová had underestimated only a decade earlier, replaced Germanization in Slovakia. That situation aroused again the sense of solidarity of Slovaks among Czech intellectuals, and finally led to the creation of the Czechoslovak Republic in 1918.

It remains to be established the extent of the influence of Němcová's ideas and works on Slovak culture, but her importance as an editor of folk tales is undeniable. Her collection preceded the great Slovak compilation by Pavel Dobšinský, who included some of her tales. It is more difficult to follow the possible influence of Božena Němcová on the group of Slovak women writers who emerged in the second half of the 19th century. In the list of her Slovak friends and correspondents there are practically no women, with the exception of Pepa Szablaková. By the mid-19th century, women barely participated in literature or in public cultural activities in Slovakia. At that time, their contribution to the patriotic movement focused on philanthropic and fund-raising initiatives.[19] They made the leap into literary creation a generation later, in a different social and artistic context. The early women intellectuals generally came from families of teachers or evangelical priests.[20] In 1869, the Association of Slovak Women 'Živena' – Spolok

[19] Gregorová, H. Ženy slovenské v dobe matičnej in Š. Votrubová (ed.). *Letopis Živeny, V. (II. vyd.),* Turčiansky Svätý Martin: "Živena" Spolok slovenských žien, 1928: 89 ff.

[20] Mráz, A. *O slovenských realistických prozaikoch.* Bratislava: Slovenské vydavateľstvo krásnej literatúry, 1956: 205 ff.

slovenských žien – was founded in the town of Turčiansky Svätý Martin, then the cultural centre of Slovakia. It played an important role in the cultural activation of Slovak women and in the Slovak culture in general. As explained in a summary article by Elena Maróthy-Šoltésová (1855-1939), which would later become its chair and renowned figure, one of the main goals of Živena was to create women's Slovak language secondary schools, which would prevent the acculturation of girls in Hungarian schools.[21] This goal could not be performed because of the repressive policy of the Hungarian authorities. Only a few years later, even the few Slovak language secondary schools – there were only three, all of them for men – as well as the cultural association of Matica Slovenská, were closed. Paradoxically, the repressive policies provided Živena with unexpected importance, by making it the only Slovak cultural institution whose activity was allowed after 1875. For many years, its annual festival in August was the main national cultural event. Also noteworthy are its homonymous almanacs and reviews. In 1887, Živena organized an exhibition of Slovak handicrafts, which opened a new field of work. Even an activity as innocuous as the sale of folk embroideries under the Slovak brand acquired political significance under a scheme in which the Slovaks did not exist as a people with their own identity, but only as second-class inhabitants of Upper Hungary. It was also a source of income for the women who manufactured them.[22]

According to all sources, the initiative of creating Živena was of Ambro Pietor (1843-1906), a journalist who became its first secretary. This post was held by a man, while the chair and vice-chairs were women. As Pietor himself explains in an article in 1869,[23] he conceived the idea of founding a Slovak women's association in Prague, where the first women's associations had, by this time, appeared: Czech Production Society (Český výrobní spolek) in 1863, the American Club of Ladies (Americký klub dam) in 1865, and the Czech Women's Production Society (Ženský výrobní spolek český) in 1871. As Šoltésová admits, and not without irony, the appearance and operation of Živena would not have been possible without the cooperation of men such as Pietor, who at the same time imposed limits on its performance:

---

[21] Maróthy-Šoltésová, E. "O 'Živene' z prvého jej obdobia" in Š. Votrubová (ed.). *Letopis Živeny*, V., II. vyd. Turčiansky Svätý Martin: "Živena" Spolok slovenských žien, 1928: 7-8.

[22] *Ibid.*, 9-10.

[23] Cited by Gregorová, "H. Ženy slovenské v dobe matičnej" in Š. Votrubová (ed.). *Letopis Živeny*, V. II. vyd.: 92.

"understanding the new women's movement in a healthy way, certainly, without recognizing us what was not suitable to our conditions"[24]. Which conditions did she mean? The struggle "against acculturating terror of Hungarian fanaticism. [...] Meanwhile, women's rights were achieved by women of free nations living their own cultures, and they achieved them also for us – especially our closest Czech sisters, which were always in the front line of this struggle" [25]

In another article, also in 1869[26], Pietor quoted as a model for Slovak women three Czech she-writers: Božena Němcová, Karolina Světlá and Žofie Podlipská. He says "they are authentic Slavic mothers, educators and aware persons, who any Slavic woman can always point out with pride". The sisters Karolina Světlá (a pseudonym of Johanna Mužáková, 1830-1899), and Žofie Podlipská (1833-1897), whose maiden name was Rott, came from a wealthy family in Prague. As in the case of Božena Němcová – with whom they had a close friendship in the early 1850s, but later distanced themselves – their decision regarding the literature and the Czech language was an act of will against their conventional German education. Both sisters participated in the voluntary movement of Czech women. The most well-known to Slovaks remained, however, Božena Němcová, although she died a few years earlier. One of the first vice-chairs of Živena was Jozefina Sablaková (Pepka Szablaková) from Banská Bystrica, a friend of the Czech writer, whom she provided with records of Slovak folktales. Slovak review *Orol,* published in the 1870s, is a series of literary portraits of Czech writers including both Němcová and Světlá.[27]

Ambro Pietor probably vindicates the three famous authors rather as a model of awareness than as a literary model. However, prose fiction of the women writers of the Živena group – the aforementioned Šoltésová, Terézia Vansová (1857-1942) – shows some typological similarities with that of their older Czech counterparts. These similarities (qualified in each individual case) could be due to a direct influence of Czech authors on Slovak authors, or to common readings and concerns: the novels of George Sand, German

[24] Maróthy-Šoltésová, E. "O 'Živene' z prvého jej obdobia" in Š. Votrubová (ed.). *Letopis Živeny*, V., II. vyd.: 8.
[25] *Ibid.*, 10-11.
[26] Gregorová, "H. Ženy slovenské v dobe matičnej" in Š. Votrubová (ed.). *Letopis Živeny,* V. II. vyd: 93-94.
[27] O. Čepan et al. *Dejiny slovenskej literatúry III.* Bratislava: Vydavateľstvo Slovenskej akadémie vied, 1965: 347.

sentimental literature and so on.[28] Slovak women writers of the 1880s and 1890s were part of the so-called *descriptive* or *ideal realism*, which can be defined as a combination of realistic descriptions (of domestic and social life, of 'peasants' life including ethnographic details) and utopic conflict resolutions (both in personal and national sphere). For instance, in Šoltésová's novel *Against the Tide* (*Proti prúdu*, 1894), the hero, a magyarized aristocrat, is persuaded to regain his Slovak roots because of his love for a cultured and patriotically committed woman. Because of this idealism the novel was criticized by the two leading fiction writers of that time (S. H. Vajanský and Martin Kukučín). As Ján Števček explains, Šoltésová defended herself with rational arguments; the idealization of her characters was deliberate, due both to the artistic purpose of the author (a woman) and to the expectations of the (mainly women) readers, and it did not mean a rejection of reality, but an extension of the concept of reality in order for it to include the positive effects of human action.[29]

More evident is the influence of Němcová on Vansová, a more sentimental and less political author than Šoltésová. She translated *Babička* into Slovak[30] and there have been noted similarities between the foolishness of her character Veronika – from the novel *The Orphan of the Podhradský Family* (*Sirota Podhradských*, 1889) – and that of Němcová's Viktorka.[31] Alongside Vansová's admiration for Němcová, their affinities have been explained by applying the concept of *late Biedermeier* to the Slovak cultural situation which was under increasing Magyarization.[32]

The influence of Němcová's personal example – and to a lesser extent, of her literary work – was felt in the works of the first Slovak women writers. Both Šoltésová and Vansová had greater problems than their Czech

---

[28] An analogy between B. Němcová and G. Sand was highlighted by several scholars, beginning with J. Kopal (*George Sandová a Božena Němcová*, 1937). Much less frequent is the study of their concrete literary relations (an example can be seen in J. Janáčková, *Božena Němcová: příběhy, situace, obrazy*: 242-249). There are several contributions regarding Němcová's relations with German literature in K. Piorecký (ed.). *Božena Němcová a její Babička (Sborník příspěvků z III. Kongresu světové literarněvědné bohemistiky, Praha 28. 6. – 3. 7. 2005, svazek 3)*. Prague: Ústav pro českou literaturu AV ČR, 2006.

[29] J. Števček, *Esej o slovenskom románe*. Bratislava: Tatran. 1979: 163 ff.

[30] O. Čepan et al. *Dejiny slovenskej literatúry III*: 561.

[31] *Ibid.*: 564.

[32] Marcela Mikulová, in K Piorecký (ed.). *Božena Němcová a její Babička (Sborník příspěvků z III*: 117-126.

predecessor in being accepted as part of the literary canon, but they are, now, recognized authors. Despite these literary connections, Božena Němcová's ideas regarding Czech-Slovak relations produced no response among the Slovak intelligentsia, including its section of women. In the new socio-political conditions of the Dual Monarchy, the Slovak and Czech cultural differentiation was already an irreversible process. Němcová's approach was essentially that which would later be called *Czechoslovakism*, which, from 1918, became the official ideology of the Czechoslovak Republic, although it was never accepted by the majority of Slovaks. In 1914, the magazine *Prúdy* conducted a survey among Czech and Slovak intellectuals on mutual relations. Due to the outbreak of World War I, it was not published until 1919. One of the Slovak writers who took part in the survey was Šoltésová, at that time the chair of Živena. Her answer clearly shows the majority point of view of the Slovak intelligentsia:

> We Slovaks have without any doubt the closest relationship to Czechs, but only if we include among them the even closest to us Moravians. It is evident in our mutual cultural history. It is nevertheless also a fact that we are two, and not the same people. If we were the same, the reciprocity would be settled. We are two people with the same origin, but not with the same character; each one has its own aptitudes and attributes. The aim to ignore or, more accurately, to deny this duality would not lead to agreement, but with certainty to discord. [33]

It seems as if Šoltésová, in these statements, had anticipated the tensions that would accompany the coexistence of Czechs and Slovaks in a common state for three quarters of the twentieth century (1918-1993). More than half a century before the rise of this state, Božena Němcová, the first canonic Czech woman writer, helped to strengthen Czech-Slovak relations at a critical moment. She was not the only women writer, but she was the best known. She made a real effort to become acquainted with Slovak folk culture and language, and to reflect it in her works. She was so open-minded enough to accept the differences between the two people. She proposed not to eliminate them, but to build a brotherly relationship on the basis of mutual understanding, coexistence and cooperation. However, in the end, her ideal of unity was defeated by the reality of historical facts.

---

[33] K. Rosenbaum, *Vzťahy slovenskej a českej literatúry 19. a 20.* Bratislava: Storočia. Obzor. 1989: 207.

## Select Bibliography

Čepan, O., I. Kusý, S. Šmatlák and J. Noge. 1965. *Dejiny slovenskej literatúry III*, Bratislava: Vydavateľstvo Slovenskej akadémie vied.

Gregorová, H. 1928. "Ženy slovenské v dobe matičnej" in Š. Votrubová (ed.). *Letopis Živeny, V. (II. vyd.)*, Turčiansky Svätý Martin: "Živena" Spolok slovenských žien: 89-94.

Horčáková, V. 2009. "Život a dílo Boženy Němcové v novější literatuře (Legendy a skutečnost)" in *Sdružení knihoven České republiky*. Brno: Sdružení knihoven ČR: 67-71.

Janáčková, J. 2007. *Božena Němcová: příběhy, situace, obrazy*. Prague: Academia.

Macura, V. 1995. *Znamení zrodu (České národní obrození jako kulturní typ), 2.* Jinočany: Rozšířené vydání, H&H.

Maróthy-Šoltésová, E. 1928. "O 'Živene' z prvého jej obdobia" in Š. Votrubová (ed.). *Letopis Živeny, V., II. vyd.* Turčiansky Svätý Martin: "Živena" Spolok slovenských žien: 7-11.

Mráz, A. 1956. *O slovenských realistických prozaikoch*. Bratislava: Slovenské vydavateľstvo krásnej literatúry.

Němcová, B. 1974[1]. *Dobrý člověk (Výbor z díla I)*. Prague: Československý spisovatel.

Němcová, B. 1974[2]. *Čtyry doby (Výbor z díla III)*. Prague: Československý spisovatel.

Piorecký, K. (ed.). 2006. *Božena Němcová a její Babička (Sborník příspěvků z III. Kongresu světové literarněvědné bohemistiky, Praha 28. 6. – 3. 7. 2005, svazek 3)*. Prague: Ústav pro českou literaturu AV ČR.

Rosenbaum, K. 1989. *Vzťahy slovenskej a českej literatúry 19. a 20.* Bratislava: Storočia, Obzor.

Sobková, H. 1997. *Tajemství Barunky Panklové. Portrét Boženy Němcové*. Prague: Mladá fronta.

Števček, J. 1979. *Esej o slovenskom románe*. Bratislava: Tatran.

Tille, V. 1947. *Božena Němcová*. Prague: Družstevní práce.

# A Queen of Many Kingdoms: The Autobiography of Rayna Knyaginya (1877)

*Nadezhda Alexandrova*

ABSTRACT The name Rayna Knyaginya means Queen Rayna, but this woman was just a teacher in a provincial town on the South of the Balkan mountain. She wrote her life-story, entitled *The autobiography of the Bulgarian teacher Rayna Popgeorgieva, called by the Turks the Bulgarian Queen Rayna* (1877). Besides the use of autobiography as means for self-creation, there are other premises for the creation of the myth of Queen Rayna. The Bulgarian literary history of the mid 19th century reminds us of a sentimental novel and drama which promoted the character of the medieval Bulgarian Queen Rayna who, according to the plot of these literary pieces, was part of Bulgarian royal history from the 11th century. Literature helped in the creation of the model of this charismatic woman-leader who became a provincial school-teacher with the same first name – Rayna.

AT THE CELEBRATION CEREMONY OF THE OFFICIAL HOLIDAY in Bulgaria, there is always a speaker who recites solemnly the names of the country's national heroes. The name of Rayna Knyaginya is one of the few female names on this list.She was the first woman to published her autobiography, but it is not this that stabilized her image in cultural memory; rather, she is remembered as a devoted revolutionary and a survivor in the struggle of Bulgarians for independence from Ottoman rule.

The name Rayna Knyaginya means Queen Rayna, but she did not originate from royalty. Her real name was Rayna Popgeorgieva Futekova (1856-1917). In the 1860s she lived in a small town on the South of the Balkan mountain – the town of Panagyurishte. Soon after becoming a teacher in her hometown, she joined the conspiracy movement for the preparation of what was later called "the April uprising against the Ottoman power of 1876".[1] She embroidered the flag of the local revolutionary group and when the uprising started she became a standard-bearer, riding a horse with a sword

[1] J.A. MacGahan, *The Turkish Atrocities in Bulgaria. Letters of the Special Commissioner of the Daily News*. London: Esq. 1876.

on her belt and a gun in her hand. These moments of illusionary freedom, however, ended as soon as local armies and Ottoman troops arrived and defeated the revolutionaries. After the failure of the uprising, Rayna Popgeorgieva was imprisoned, interrogated, tortured and would hardly have escaped with her life if it had not been for the support of local representatives of the foreign consulates in the Ottoman Empire. One year after these events, as a refugee in Moscow, she put on paper her autobiography, called: "The autobiography of the Bulgarian teacher Rayna Popgeorgieva, called by the Turks the Bulgarian Queen Rayna, translated into Bulgarian language by the Bulgarian M."

The name Queen Rayna gained symbolic status in Bulgarian culture over the course of the century. From the middle of the 19$^{th}$ century on, the royal title was attributed to a fictional character and then given to a real person – the Bulgarian schoolteacher and female writer Rayna Popgeorgieva. The fluctuation between real and symbolic was based on the sameness of the name 'Rayna'. It served the purpose of building an exemplary image of a woman-revolutionary that was required for the ideological reproduction of the Bulgarian national identity. In accordance with the nationalistic imperatives of the time, the exemplary woman was one who put the interest of the nation before her personal wishes, and expressed loyalty to her family and nation by her readiness for sacrifice.[2] The case of Queen Rayna presents an example of the impact of symbolic reincarnations on the legacy of the female authorship. The symbolic image was more durable than the self-asserting efforts of Rayna Popgeorgieva's writing. The potential of her autobiography to recall the events of the uprising from the perspective of the standard-bearer was used only partially when new (fictional) and biographical accounts of her life appeared in the 20$^{th}$ century.[3] Rayna Popgeorgieva's own text remained in the shade of Bulgarian literary history.

---

[2] The brief sketch of the characteristics of the 'exemplary Bulgarian woman' fits well with the terms of the inclusion of women in the ethnic and nation building process, specified by Floya Anthias and Nira Yuval Davis in their study on women and nationalism: *Women-Nation-State*. London: Macmillan, 1989.

[3] There are a number of novelettes or biographical essays on Rayna Popgeorgieva-Rayna Knjaginja. Some of them are written by women authors who were members of the Club of Bulgarian women writers in the Interwar period, such as Fani Popova-Mutafova. See Fani Popova-Mutafova, "Rayna Knyaginya" in *Veliki Senki. (Rayna Knyaginya.* in *Great Shadows of the Past).* Sofia: s.n., 1935, and Magda Petkanova, *Rayna Knyaginya*, Sofia: Nationalen SAvet na OF, 1962. New biographies and fictional pieces on the same topic appeared during the Socialist period in Bulgaria

Rayna Popgeorgieva's autobiography contains a denouncement of the name Queen Rayna because it was a nickname, given to her by her interrogators. There are also other controversial facts in her text that present the story of her inclusion and participation in the April uprising differently from those associated with her personality as a hero in the national history. In order to entail a critical rethinking of the production of such monolithic images and to bring back the voice of the woman author, it is necessary to reveal these controversial facts and situate them in the context of Bulgarian literary history in the 19th century, when the symbolic image of Queen Rayna was born. Revealing the history behind that symbol is crucial for the explanation of the role of literature in the circulation of cultural memory.

There are several moments in the process of symbolization of the stages in the figuration and re-figuration of the image of Rayna. The first is situated in the 1850s, when the name of Rayna Knyaginya entered the Bulgarian cultural context with the influence of Old-Slavonic and Russian manuscripts and historical books. The second is related to the events of the April uprising of 1876 and the life of the woman writer Rayna Popgeorgieva. She wrote an account of her life in her efforts to clarify her connection with the title "Queen Rayna" and to position herself in current events. The third moment of symbolization is the post-Ottoman period when the grant national narrative was built. In it the two names-Rayna Popgeorgiva- Rayna Knyaginya-achieved synonymity as a result of the biographies and historical novelettes, written in favour of the invention of the national pantheon of Bulgarian heroes. The royal title was attributed unquestionably to the real person; the symbol was successfully created whereas the real woman writer ended her life in misery. The images of those women writers who were related to suitable symbolic domains, such as that of the devoted revolutionary, or that of the angelic muse,[4] had a more of a chance to be remembered. Rayna

(1945-1989). They were a gesture of nationalistic commemoration of the above-mentioned April revolt (Krastev 1967, Karaleeva 1969, Paskaleva and Patyrchanova 1976, Hrusanov, 1976). In the post-socialist period, new and more critical perspectives of the agitated life of Rayna Popgeorgieva appeared. See Krassimira Koeva, "V Tarsene Na Rayna Knyaginya (in Search of Rayna Knyaginya)" in *Azbuki* V 44: 16, 1995; Bonka Stefanova, "Tragichnata Sadba Na Potomcite Na Rayna Knyaginya. (The Tragic Fate of the Ansestors of Rayna Knyaginya)" in *Prelom* VIII, (38): 5, 1998; Hristo Dipchev, *Rayna Knyaginya. Biograficheski Ocherk. (Rayna Knyaginya. Biographical Essay)*. Sofia: Izdatelstvo Georgi Pobedonosetz, 1996.

[4] It is common in mainstream literary history for women writers to be contextually situated in literary circles where their writing is 'cultivated' by male writers. Usually

Popgeorgieva's case fitted the former symbolic domain of the exemplary woman–revolutionary.

## Kingdom of literature

The Bulgarian literary history of the mid 19th century contains several literary works that include the character of the medieval Bulgarian Queen Rayna. At first her image appeared in a sentimental novel by the Russian writer Alexander Veltman, translated two times into Bulgarian language in the 1850s.[5] The novel inspired the Bulgarian playwright Dobri Voinikov to stage it as a drama and present it a number of times in different versions.[6] Although the fictional texts located the existence of the queen in the Bulgarian royal court of the 11th century, this is still questionable, as there is no definitive evidence that she really existed. At that time there were just a few well-educated historians who could prove the succession of Bulgarian rulers on the basis of old-Slavonic manuscripts. There was a lack of historical evidence, which was compensated by fictional writings that fueled the production of national confidence and supported the revival of a state that had existed on the map of Europe before the Ottomans came to the Balkans.

---

the story includes the roles of the 'the mentor in writing' and his 'muse'. In the Bulgarian literary history of 19th century, such a role was attributed to the first woman poet and translator of the novel "Rayna, the Bulgarian queen"- Elena Muteva (1825-1854). As part of a literary circle of Bulgarian students in Odessa, she became an inspiration for one of the distinguished poets of the time –Nayden Gerov (1823-1900).

5 The novel was written by the Russian writer Alexander Veltman in 1843 and was in favour of spreading the common idea that Bulgarians and Russians were of Slavic origin. One of its main plot lines is the attraction between King Svetoslav of Kiev and Rayna, the daughter of a Bulgarian King Peter from the 11th century. In the 1850s two translations of this novel from Russian into Bulgarian appeared. See Veltman, Alexander. *Rayna Bulgarska Tzarkinja. Prikazka Ot A.F. Veltman (Rayna, the Bulgarian Queen. A Tale by Alexander Veltman)*, Elena Muteva (tr.). StPeterburg: Izdanie na Kaloferskoto uchilishte, 1852.

6 In the 1870s the Bulgarian amateur theatre cast from the lands of Walachia in Braila enthusiastically embraced the idea of creating a historical drama out of the novel. The playwright Dobri Voinikov wrote several drafts of script. It was staged in 1868 for the first time and it was also the first time that women appeared on the stage of a Bulgarian theater performance. See Nikolaj Zhechev, *Bukuresht – Kulturen Center Na Bulgarite Prez Vazrazhdaneto (Bucharest – a Cultural Setting of the Bulgarians During the Time of the National Revival)*. Sofia: Bulgarian Academy of Science Publishing House, 1991.

The production of such texts initially started in Orthodox monasteries in the second half of the 18th century. Those manuscripts were compilations of old Greek and Slavonic chronicles. They mostly presented the glorious moments of the Bulgarian medieval kingdom, keeping quiet about the episodes of defeat. [7] By the 19th century, Bulgarian writers had already taken inspiration from those manuscripts and started publishing schoolbooks, novelettes and dramas, that spoke of charismatic kings, titanic battles, dynastic marriages, and courtly intrigues. Characters, such as Queen Rayna, supported the process of building historical continuity and natural succession from the medieval past to the prospect of a restored Bulgarian kingdom. The female characters in such fictional texts of Bulgarian medieval history were envisioned as submissively loyal to the patriarchal order, yet as educated and open-minded women. In most cases these female characters functioned as representations of a sacrificed, victimized motherland, whose defeat was a result of courtly intrigues and diplomatic wars between Bulgaria and Byzantium. Similarly, the sentimental novel Rayna, the Bulgarian queen by A.Veltman and the drama by Dobri Voinikov present a beautiful noble princess who is left without her father's protection and forced to marry the son of her father's political rival, who usurps the Bulgarian throne. Rayna rejects the marriage with the 'Armenian-Greek' prince Samuil and seeks support from the Russian King Svetoslav. The latter is described as a benevolent and handsome ruler who is strongly attracted both to Rayna and to what she represents – 'the beauty of the Bulgarian land'.

According to more recent historical evidence, Svetoslav came to Northeast Bulgaria because he was hired by the Byzantine emperor to weaken the Bulgarian kingdom. In 968-969 A.D. he conquered the medieval capital of the country and subjugated the ruling Bulgarian kings. However, in the above-mentioned fictional works "Rayna, the Bulgarian Queen", Svetoslav is envisioned as the friend and saviour of Bulgarians. The contrast between the facts and the fictional representation of the character is due to the evolving expectations of Bulgarian intellectuals who considered that the

---

[7] "Istoria slavyanobulgarska" ("The history of Slavo-Bulgarians"), by the monk Paisius from Hilendar is a manuscript from 1762, accomplished in the Zograph monastery at the Mount Athos. It is considered a cornerstone text of the Bulgarian national history and one of the first efforts of retrieval of the Bulgarian medieval history. The evidences report that over 50 copies of the manuscript were circulating among Bulgarians until the late 19th c. See Petar Dinekov, *Parvi Vazrozhdenci (the First Figures of Enlightenment)*. Sofia: Bulgarsko otechestvo (Doverie), 1944.

Russian empire should be ready to support and protect Bulgarians on the basis of the common Slavic origin.[8] The sentimental infatuation between the Russian King Svetoslav and the Bulgarian Queen Rayna was parallel to the construction of a Russian-Bulgarian common ethnic and cultural past, based on the usage of the old-Slavonic language, and the common religious affiliation to Orthodox Christianity. Moreover, the common Slavonic heritage was used as a means for political influence by the Russian empire over her allays in the Christian Orthodox communities, still living under Ottoman rule.

The Russian influence on Bulgarians was both ideological and financial. Over the course of the 19th century, Russian professors in linguistics and philology were crossing the Balkans in search for manuscripts that explained the origins of their Cyrillic alphabet and strong attachment to the Eastern Orthodox Church. Russian and Ukrainian philanthropic organizations and private donors started giving financial support to young Bulgarian boys and girls to study in Russia.[9] A clear example of this influence can be seen in the fact that the first translator of the novel "Rayna, the Bulgarian Queen" was in fact the first woman poet in Bulgarian literature – Elena Muteva. She was born in a small Bulgarian town, but spent her years of study in Odessa, surrounded by a circle of young Bulgarian intellectuals. Similarly, the women writer and revolutionary who inherited the name "Queen Rayna", Rayna Popgeorgieva, also spent around two years in Russia after surviving the dramatic aftermath of the April uprising. In 1877, in Moscow, she studied to be a midwife with the support of the Ladies Department of the Russian Slavophile Committee. It was exactly this period of her life when she wrote and published her autobiography.

It would be a mistake to suggest a direct correlation between the appearance of this plot in 19th century Bulgarian literature and the attribution of nobility to the provincial schoolteacher Rayna Popgeorgieva. Yet, the fictional representations of the female character were very popular among the Bulgarians from late 19th century onwards, and there were even litho-

---

[8] Nikolai Aretov, *Nacionalna Mitologia I Nacionalna Literatura (National Mythology and National Literature)*. Sofia: Kralica Mab. 2006; Nikoleta Pytova, *Dramaturgia Na Bulgarskoto. Nationalnata Identichnost Vyv Vazrozhdenskata Drama. (Staging Bulagaria: National Identity in the Drama from the Time of the Enlightenment)*. Sofia: Kralitza Mab, 2012.

[9] Maria Todorova, *Imagining the Balkans*. London and New York: Oxford University Press, 1997; Elena Nalbantova, *Odesa V Istoriata I Literaturata Na 19 Vek (Odessa in the Bulgarian History and Literature of the 19th C.)*. Odessa: Druk, 2006.

graphical reprints of her image, created on the basis of the novel.[10] The cultural context had the potential to create a memorable historical figure by means of literature, because the sameness of the names of the fictional character and the real schoolteacher – Rayna – could function as a trigger for this interplay of nominations. This potential was exercised with a very controversial effect during the April uprising of 1876 but later, throughout the 20th century, it lost its controversy and the representation of Queen Rayna was adopted to new social and political context in Bulgaria which, by then, was already an independent state. Despite the changes in political regimes during the 20th century, the nationalistic discourse acquired and kept exemplary individuals, such as Queen Rayna, who put the common goals of the community before their personal wills.

It is difficult to trace their history, as it is not a history of subsequent identifications but one of forced entitlement and conscious refusal of certain nominations. Due to the mischievous nature of memory, the controversies and disjunctions between the preexisting image and the real woman disappear as time marches on. Gradually, the Bulgarians stopped questioning the correctness of the nomination 'Knyaginya' and accepted it as an honour for the emerging new national heroes in history.

## A kingdom under attack: Rayna Popgeorgieva's autobiography

The notion of autobiography as "a figure of reading"[11] serves the present case of Rayna Knyaginya well. Paul de Man discusses the historical and aesthetic functions of the autobiographical text that support the match between the protagonist and the author of the text. The same 'proper name' unifies the protagonist with its creator – the author. By means of the historical function of the autobiographical text, which is invested in the facts and details of the author's life, the text is capable of securing the figurative image of its creator for future generations. Due to the capacity of the writer of the autobiographical text, who can arrange the story of his/her life with aesthetic means and according to a certain desired image of him/herself, the autobiography can be re-figured with any new given reading. Thus, the autobio-

[10] See the paintings of Nikolay Pavlovic (1835-1894) in Nikolay Raynov, *Nikolay Pavlovich*. Sofia: Izdatelstvo na BAN, 1955.

[11] Paul de Man, "Autobiography as Defacement" in *MLN*. 94 (5), 1979: 919-930.

graphy expresses its creator's will to influence and determine the future readings of his/her life after his physical death.[12]

Likewise, Rayna Popgeorgieva, a witness of historic events and a skilled teacher, put on paper her recollections of the April uprising in 1876 and noted the way in which her own name should be connected to the title "Rayna Knyaginya". The text is called "The autobiography of the Bulgarian teacher Rayna Popgeorgieva, called by the Turks the Bulgarian Queen Rayna, translated into Bulgarian language by the Bulgaran M. (1877)". As is evident from the title, the author distinguishes between her family name and the nickname "Queen Rayna". Moreover, even on the front cover of the book, it is clear that the nickname 'queen' was used in mockery by the Turkish soldiers and officials who interrogated her. Rayna Popgeorgieva did describe herself as a devoted and brave Bulgarian woman, hostage of the governing Ottomans, yet she denounces the title 'queen' both in the title of the autobiography and a few times in the narrative itself.

The efforts of this woman writer to distinguish herself from the image of Rayna Knyaginya and to provide an account of the forceful ways which were used to make her join the conspiracy movement had little effect on the construction of the nationalistic version of Bulgarian history. Typically, these facts were put aside, or left only for devoted researchers of the April uprising or of the literary history of the 19$^{th}$ century. The power of the image of the exemplary female queen adopted for the sake of the revolutionary struggle overruled the epistemological legacy of Rayna Popgeorgieva's autobiography. Rayna Popgeorgieva's own self-asserting gesture, to be the author of her own life, did not prevent the metamorphosis of her real life into a life of a woman-revolutionary. The proper name remained but its noble connection was frozen for the sake of creating a symbol of normative femininity in Bulgarian national history.

The autobiography of Rayna Popgeorgieva can be regarded as an exemplary life-story of an outstanding social figure. It created an image of the author as patriotic, courageous, yet weak and emotional woman, a true martyr of the April uprising. The title is long and descriptive in the manner of the titles of Bulgarian texts from that period. It includes information about the author, the origins of the text and provides a notion of its contents and goals. There are three chapters in the book. The first one "My upbringing and

---

[12] Jacques Derrida, *Memories of Paul De Man*. New York: Columbia University Press, 1989.

serving for the motherland" lays emphasis on the image of Rayna as a dutiful schoolgirl, and then as a teacher and an initiator of the women's association in her hometown. The second chapter "The Panagyurishte uprising and my participation in it" is devoted to the preparation of local revolt against Ottoman rule. The third chapter is the longest.It is called "The aftermath of the uprising and my subsequent destiny" and retells from a personal perspective the defeat of the revolt. It presents in detail the difficulties she suffered when she witnessed the death of her compatriots and relatives. She reconstructs her dialogues with Turkish officials and describes the horrible conditions of the prisons where she stayed while awaiting sentence. In the final pages of the autobiography, in several very emotional paragraphs, she expresses her gratitude to the foreign consulates in the Ottoman Empire, whose representatives practically saved Rayna Popgeogrieva from dying behind the bars.

The overall portrait of the protagonist seems to fulfill the purpose of safeguarding an account of an exceptional person for future generations – a Bulgarian woman who witnessed and survived the dreadful events of the April uprising in 1876. This autobiography was designed to support the nationalistic national narrative, and at first glance it apparently does not contain any indication to the contrary. Yet, the autobiographical text was not put into circulation and the story of Rayna Knyaginya was usually retold without special reference to the text of Rayna Popgeorgieva. One of the reasons for this could be because the text was published in Russian and translated into Bulgarian in just two editions of the book throughout the 20th century.[13] Besides this, however, there are also some moments in the narrative that challenge the general perception of Queen Rayna and some chiefs of the Bulgarian conspiracy movement.

As aforementioned, the title of the autobiography indicates that the name Rayna Knyaginya was used in mockery, a nickname given to the Bulgarian woman by the 'Turks'. She recollects that during the interrogations Turkish officials laughed at her, calling her *'kral kız'* (a woman queen) in Turkish. The narrator recalls the painful memory when she was tied and exposed to

---

[13] Teodora Peykova, (ed.). *Rayna Knyaginya. Avtobiografia (Rayna Knyaginya. Autobiography)* Sofia: Knipegraf, 1935. Virzhinia Paskaleva and Ruska Patyrchanova (ed.). *Rayna Knyaginya. Autobiografia, Dokumenti I Mateirali, Prevel Luben Milev. (Rayna Knyaginya. Autobiography, Documents and Evidences. tr. Luben Milev).* Sofia: Nauka i izkustvo, 1976.

the mockery by the crowd of people standing aside while her cart, escorting her along the city streets. They would laugh at her, calling her (ironically) 'the Bulgarian queen'. The degrading origin of the nickname is also mentioned in one of the most popular chronicles about the April Uprising, written by the Bulgarian post-Ottoman politician and writer Zahari Stoyanov.[14] It appears that Rayna Popgeorgieva and other witnesses of the same event do not approve of the synonymy between the name of the standard-bearer and Queen Rayna, which is enacted today. They do not consider the vision of the Bulgarian woman riding a horse with a flag in her hands as direct reminiscence of the medieval Queen Rayna; rather, there is a willingness to differentiate the writer and woman teacher from a label that sounded degrading and abusive when it was used to denounce the efforts of the Bulgarians to gain independence.

Another interesting observation to be seen in the title of the autobiography is that the original is written in Bulgarian and then translated into Russian by somebody called Bulgarian M. Historians who have investigated the biography of Rayna Popgeorgieva cannot recognise who this person is, but assume that the text has been adapted to suit the expectations of the Russian audience. The gender of the adjective 'Bulgarian' M. suggests that this is an initial of a male's name. The title of the autobiography already states that this is a translation, which might have been done to promote better understanding, compassion and support toward Russian society and the victims of the Turkish massacre, and in view of the approaching Russian-Turkish war (1877-1878).

Could the mediation of language influence the contents of the text and be considered a reason for its minor place in the corpus of evidence regarding Rayna Knyaginya? The answer to this question can never be certain. However, regarding the question of authorship and the place of women writers in the creation of a literary canon, the autobiography of Rayna Popgeorgieva presents another example of male interference in women's writing. At that period male authors usually encouraged women to publish their own work. This is a common phenomenon in worldwide literary history and has lucid examples in the Bulgarian context of the 19th and early 20th

---

[14] Zachary Stoyanov, *Zapiski Po Bulgarskite Vastania (Cronicles of the Bulgarian Uprisings)*. Vol. I., Plovdiv: Oblastna pechatnitza, 1884.

century. It is usually regarded as support of the 'fair sex' to appear in the 'kingdom of literature'. Besides its interpretation as being emancipatory for women, there is also another, much darker consequence of such 'pygmalionism'. The male literary mentorship (usually in the form of editing, translating, or publishing a woman's text under a different name) endangers the authenticity of women's writing and could be a reason for the exclusion of certain women writers from the literary canon.[15] Women writers were often in a familial or intimate relationship with their mentors, and even if they were famous for their appearance in journals and public events, literary history has frequently discarded the woman's own voice by replacing the story with a juicy tale of infatuation. Moreover, women's public activism did not guarantee acknowledgement of the autonomous status of the first Bulgarian women writers. In the best-case scenario, their subjectivity had to evolve so that it could be identified with the cause of the Bulgarian nation. The protagonists of their texts did not dare to express intimate feelings other than love for the fatherland and devotion to the family and community. The topics of upbringing, education and marriage were the most common, as a reflection of the nationalistic atmosphere of the time. But just as can be seen in the autobiography of Rayna Popgeorgieva, the price for contributing towards this common national goal was that the image of the protagonist was censored, purified of any improper feelings or actions.

A very remarkable fragment from the autobiographical narrative is when Rayna Popgeorgieva enters the conspiracy movement and agrees to embroider the flag of the uprising. Contrary to the expectations of the general public, the narrator describes a dialogue in which the schoolteacher from Panagyurishte is forced to join the conspiracy movement by the chief of the conspiracy committee – Georgy Benkovski. He threatens her with a gun saying that he could shoot her if she refuses to collaborate.

This moment comes as a surprise to Bulgarians today who are taught to believe in a general upheaval and enthusiasm for inclusion of Bulgarians to the movement for national liberation. Her personality is frequently closely

---

[15] Some of Bulgaria's most distinguished poets and writers were acting as editors and promoters of the major works of the first women writers. For instance, the most distinguished Bulgarian writer Ivan Vasov was a friend of, and in close intellectual exchange with Evgenia Mars. As a consequence, literary enemies suggested that Ivan Vazov was the actual author of her works. See ZhivkaSimova, *Obichana I Otrichana.Kniga Za Evgenia Mars (Loved and Hated. A Book about Evgenia Mars)*. Sofia: Sofia University Publishing House, 1998.

connected with the heroic image of the revolutionary Georgi Benkovski, and during interrogations Turkish officials often asked her if they were romantically involved. She denounced that possibility, yet many of her later biographical and fictional reverberations of Bulgarian culture hint at a love infatuation. Therefore, the text of Payna Popgeorgieva presents a very different and striking perspective of this relationship between Georgi Benkovski and herself. In this situation, just like in many others, Rayna Popgeorgieva presents herself as a victim of circumstances, as a qualified teacher, as a skillful embroiderer, but not as a passionate revolutionary. If the autobiography of this woman expresses her own will in conveying the state of her recollections to future generations, then the memory of Rayna Popgeorgieva wants to diverge from the 'nobility' status of a Queen Rayna, and embrace the status of 'victim' of Ottoman arbitrariness.

The autobiography of this woman writer is preserved and cherished as the heritage of a national hero. It is familiar to historians and literary scholars but not as much to the general public. Considered in light of Paul de Man's notion of the autobiography as a text comprising historic and aesthetic function, this autobiography does not sufficiently penetrate mainstream (literary) history. Perhaps this is due to the above-mentioned uncertainties – the status of the author, the language of the original text and the moments in the narrative that denounce the easy attribution of the title 'queen'. The 'reign' of the proper name from the kingdom of figural transformations was more powerful than the 'reign' of the autobiography in the kingdom of subjective recollections. The contemporary image of this woman is idealized and purified. The name of Rayna Knyaginya has successfully secured her reign in the kingdom of cultural memories.

## Kingdom of cultural memories

There is no 'shortcut' between the kingdom, inhabited by the fictional medieval Queen Rayna, and the "ten days long kingdom" in Panaguyrishte[16] that Rayna Popgeorgieva wrote about in her autobiography. The repetition that generated the invented memory of Rayna Knyagiyna as a national hero is

[16] The Ten Days Freedom is the time when Bulgarian revolutionaries overtook the city's governance and were celebrating their momentary victory euphorically. See Atanas Shopov, *Desetdnevnoto Tzaruvane (The Ten Days Long Kingdom)*. Sofia: Petchatnicata na Bulgarski gla, 1881.

a result of the cohesion of two cultural phenomena from the second part of the 19th century. They accumulated the potential to contribute to the creation of the Bulgarian imagined community. The circulation of stories about the medieval queen Rayna at that time was intensive due to the theatre performance of the drama, based on the novel "Rayna the Bulgarian queen". Furthermore, since the beginning of the independent Bulgarian state in 1878, Payna Popgeorgieva's autobiography was regarded as part of a substantial wave of memoir production, which contributed to the creation of a 'requiem' for the victims of the defeat of the April uprising in 1876. This tragic defeat by the Ottoman army quickly became a cornerstone moment in Bulgarian national history. It is evident that the name Rayna belonged to several exemplary female figures, that served the same nationalistic discourse in different ways. Despite these differences, and the obvious desire of the woman writer Rayna Popgeorgieva to leave her memoir as a self-defense tool against the currents of forgetfulness, the symbolic charisma of Queen Rayna devoured the factual controversies and the multiple characters under the same name.

In this tricky game of referents, the potential of the cultural memory of Queen Rayna in sustaining the power of the national narrative was activated many times throughout the 20th century. Rayna Knyaginya became the representation of monolithic exemplary femininity. As such, the memory of her (yet not her own memoir) became an integral part of the cultural memory of Bulgarian society.[17] The life of the charismatic queen in the kingdom of cultural memories inspires abundant interpretations in the form of biographies, novellas, museum collections, monuments, paintings, etc. The glory of Rayna Knyaginya spread over different political and social contexts. Her biography was cherished and promoted in the first part of the 20th century, when Bulgaria was a monarchy, and in the second part of the century (1945-1989), when the country adopted a Socialist ideology in all aspects of life.

---

[17] The term 'cultural memory' is used in the paradigm of Jan Assman "Collective Memory and Cultural Identity" in *New German Critique* 65, 1995: 132. It refers to artifacts of objectified culture, such as texts, images or monuments, which are designed to recall fateful events in the history of the collective memory and is adopted in different historical and social contexts.

Among the many authors of biographical texts about Rayna Knyaginya there are several distinguished Bulgarian women writers.[18] Fani Popova-Mutafova[19] and Magda Petkanova[20] were famous for their historical novels and their affiliation with the influential "Club of Bulgarian women writers", existing in the interwar period in Bulgaria. Their fictional representations of Rayna Knyaginya preserve the sense of fearlessness and stoicism seen in the autobiography of Rayna Popgeorgieva. The character's strength is revealed in the dialogues with her interrogators, which are retold at length. The irony of the Ottoman officials in using the nomination 'queen' is kept in the new versions of Rayna's life. Their function is to underline her image as a bold and dedicated revolutionary.

A frequent episode in all biographical versions of Rayna Knyaginya's life is the moment when the leader of the revolutionion invites her to join the secret organization and to embroider the flag of the uprising. Yet, the detail that Georgi Benkovski threatened to kill her if she refused is almost always omitted. On the contrary, some biographies imply an infatuation between Georgi Benkovski and Rayna Popgeorgieva. For instance, in a later essay about Rayna Knyaginya by the contemporary Bulgarian poet Valentina Radinska,[21] the episode with the gun is justified by the emergency of the situation. Furthermore, the offer to embroider the flag of the uprising is regarded as an opportunity bestowed on her by Georgi Benkovski. He is presented as a clever man with a vision, who foresaw the effect of her 'coronation' and paved her way to immortality.

Due to those historical and fictional accounts of Rayna Knyaginya, her monolithic image is in active circulation in the cultural memory of contemporary Bulgarians. The general public does not question the equation between 'Queen Rayna' and Rayna Popgeorgieva. The woman is most often associated with the flag that she embroidered and then carried across the city,

---

[18] The genres of the accounts about Rayna Knyaginya vary between 'a biography', 'a biographical novella', or 'a biographical essay'.

[19] Fani Popova-Mutafova, "Rayna Knyaginya" in *Veliki Senki. (Rayna Knyaginya. in Great Shadows of the Past)*. Sofia: Drevna Bulgaria, 1935.

[20] Magda Petkanova, *Rayna Knyaginya (Rayna Knyaginya)*. Sofia: Nationalen SAvet na OF, 1962.

[21] Valentina Radinska, "Rayna Knyaginya" in E. Andonova N. Karamfilov (ed.). *Bulgarki. Biografichni Ochertzi S Predgovor Na Efrem Karamfilov (Bulgarian Women. Biographical Essays with an Introduction by Efrem Karamfilov)* Sofia: OF, 1982.

and much less as a woman writer. In order to preserve this exceptionality Rayna Popgeorgieva and most of her later biographers did not mention any facts or descriptions of drastic treatment, such as physical torture and rape. In presenting the author in the text as an exceptional woman, Rayna needed to maintain her silence about the many details that could have polluted her heroic image; later on, this auto-censorship was preserved in the biographies about her. Some accounts of foreign journalists and witnesses of the defeat of the revolutionaries contain horrific scenes of the mass rape of local women and violence. It is possibile that Rayna Popgeorgieva was raped herself and perhaps humiliated for several months until the foreign consuls could arrange shelter for her.[22] Neither her autobiography, nor the later biographies mention such a scene. The omission of such description in the autobiography could be the result of psychological suppression. Furthermore, the recreation of a symbolic figure out of the real woman could be suspended if the life-story of Rayna Knyaginya included episodes of rape. Such an episode would represent an ultimate domination over the woman's body by the Ottoman oppressors, but it would also harm the symbolic corpus of physical and moral virtue, reaffirmed by the autobiography of Rayna Popgeorgieva. Reasons for reducing the scenes of torture and humiliation to just verbal expressions, mockery and smaller acts of violence like a slap on the face, could be that the translation of the original text into Russian intended to promote the image of its author as a person with strong national consciousness who was just a victim of circumstances.

The kingdom of cultural memory is not particularly receptive to the factual and authentic life-story of Rayna Popgeorgieva – the writer of the first Bulgarian women's autobiography. In contrast, it is a comfortable dwelling for the symbol of Rayna Knyaginya – the celebrated revolutionary. Feminist history regards cautiously the synergic effect between discourses of emancipation and nation-building in regard to women writers and activists. Often, the complexity of their identity is limited by the requirements of female excellence that are imposed in accordance with the national ideology. The case of Rayna Knyaginya indicates that the heritage of the woman writer

---

[22] This hypothesis has recently been outlined by the Bulgarian literary critic Nikolai Aretov in his critical study examining the myth of Russia in Bulgarian culture. See Nikolai Aretov, *Izkovavaneto Na Mita Za Rusia. Rayna Bulgarska Knyaginya. (Coining of the Myth About Russia. Rayna the Bulgarian Queen)*. 2,147. 2012.

is less cherished than her symbolic, monolithic image of a female hero, created by means of biographical accounts and with the support of a previously existing fictional character of the same name, 'Rayna'. Therefore, a critical rethinking of such cultural phenomena is needed in order to restore the missing parts of their complex identities. A way of doing this for the sake of women's literary history is to use a kaleidoscopic method: gathering the various sources that detail their social and literary interactions. It is not an easy task and requires the efforts of networks of researchers in women's literature. The aim is not to reach the ultimate truth, but to present the processes that lead to the exclusion of certain women writers from literary history and the actions that can be performed to restore their names and review their writings anew.

## Select Bibliography

Anthias Floya, Yuval-Davis, Nyra, (eds). 1989. *Women-Nation-State*. London: MacMillan.

Aretov, Nikolai. 2006. *Nacionalna Mitologia I Nacionalna Literatura (National Mythology and National Literature)*. Sofia: Kralica Mab.

—. 2012. *Izkovavaneto Na Mita Za Rusia. Rayna Bulgarska Knyaginya. (Coining of the Myth About Russia. Rayna the Bulgarian Queen)*. 2, 147. [LiterNet, Accessed february 2013].

Assman, Jan. 1995. "Collective Memory and Cultural Identity." *New German Critique* 65 : 132.

Derrida, Jaques. 1989. *Memories of Paul De Man*. New York: Columbia University Press.

Dinekov, Petar. 1944. *Parvi Vazrozhdenci (the First Figures of Enlightenment)*. Sofia. Bulgarsko otechestvo (Doverie).

Dipchev, Hristo. 1996. *Rayna Knyaginya. Biograficheski Ocherk. (Rayna Knyaginya. Biographical Essay)*. Sofia: Izdatelstvo Georgi Pobedonosetz.

Hrusanov, Georgi. 1976. *Znamenoskata.I V Oganya Zhiv. Povesti Za Aprilskoto Vastanie (the Woman Standard-Bearer. Alive in the Flames. Novellas About the April Uprising)*. Sofia: Izdatelstvo na BZNS.

Karaleeva, Lubomira. 1969. *Rayna Knyaginya. Istoricheska Povest (Rayna Knyaginya. A Historical Novella)*. Sofia: Darzhavno voenno izdatelstvo.

Koeva, Krassimira. 1995. "V Tarsene Na Rayna Knyaginya (in Search of Rayna Knyaginya)" in *Azbuki* V 44: 16.

Krastev, Dimitar. 1967. *Rayna, Knyaginja Bulgarska. Povest.(Rayna, the Bulgarian Queen. A Novella)*. Sofia: Darzhavno voenno izdatelstvo.

MacGahan, J.A. 1876. *The Turkish Atrocities in Bulgaria. Letters of the Special Commissioner of the Daily News*. London: Esq.

Man, Paul de. 1979. "Autobiography as Defacement" in *MLN*. 94 (5): 919-930.

Nalbantova, Elena. 2006. *Odesa V Istoriata I Literaturata Na 19 Vek (Odessa in the Bulgarian History and Literature of the 19th C.)*. Odessa: Druk.

Offen, Karen. 2000. *European Feminisms, 1700-1950. A Political History*. Stanford: Stanford University Press.

Paskaleva Virzhinia, Patyrchanova Ruska, (ed.). 1976. *Rayna Knyaginya. Autobiografia, Dokumenti I Mateirali, Prevel Luben Milev. (Rayna Knyaginya. Autobiography, Documents and Evidences. tr. Luben Milev)*. Sofia: Nauka i izkustvo.

Petkanova, Magda. 1962. *Rayna Knyaginya (Rayna Knyaginya)*. Sofia; Nationalen SAvet na OF.

Peykova, Teodora. (ed.). 1935. *Rayna Knyaginya. Avtobiografia (Rayna Knyaginya. Autobiography)* Sofia: Knipegraf.

Popova-Mutafova, Fani. 1935. "Rayna Knyaginya" in *Veliki Senki. (Rayna Knyaginya. in Great Shadows of the Past)*. Sofia: Drevna Bulgaria.

Pytova, Nikoleta. 2012. *Dramaturgia Na Bulgarskoto. Nationalnata Identichnost Vyv Vazrozhdenskata Drama. (Staging Bulagaria: National Identity in the Drama from the Time of the Enlightenment)*. Sofia: Kralitza Mab.

Radinska, Valentina. 1982. "Rayna Knyaginya" in *Bulgarki. Biografichni Ochertzi S Predgovor Na Efrem Karamfilov (Bulgarian Women. Biographical Essays with an Introduction by Efrem Karamfilov)* Andonova N. Karamfilov E. (ed.). Sofia: OF.

Raynov, Nikolay. 1955. *Nikolay Pavlovich*. Sofia: Izdatelstvo na BAN.

Shopov, Atanas. 1881. *Desetdnevnoto Tzaruvane (The Ten Days Long Kingdom)*. Sofia: Petchatnicata na Bulgarski gla.,

Simova, Zhivka. 1998. *Obichana I Otrichana.Kniga Za Evgenia Mars (Loved and Hated.A Book About Evgenia Mars)*. Sofia: Sofia University Publishing House.

Stefanova, Bonka. 1998. "Tragichnata Sadba Na Potomcite Na Rayna Knyaginya. (The Tragic Fate of the Ansestors of Rayna Knyaginya)" in *Prelom* VIII, (38): 5.

Stoyanov, Zachary. 1884. *Zapiski Po Bulgarskite Vastania (Cronicles of the Bulgarian Uprisings)*. Vol. I, Plovdiv: Oblastna pechatnitza.

Todorova, Maria. 1997. *Imagining the Balkans*. London and New York: Oxford University Press.

Veltman, Alexander. 1852. *Rayna Bulgarska Tzarkinja. Prikazka Ot A.F. Veltman (Rayna, the Bulgarian Queen. A Tale by Alexander Veltman, tr. Elena Muteva)*. St Peterburg: Izdanie na Kaloferskoto uchilishte.

—. 1952. *Rayna Knyaginya Bulgarska. Povest Ot Veltmana. Prevedena Ot Yoakima Grueva (Rayna the Queen of Bulgaria. A Novella by Veltman, tr. Yoakim Grueva)*. Belgrade: Pravitelsvetna knigopechatnja. (2nd ed.1866).

Zhechev, Nikolaj. 1991. *Bukuresht – Kulturen Center Na Bulgarite Prez Vazrazhdaneto (Bucharest – a Cultural Setting of the Bulgarians During the Time of the National Revival)*. Sofia: Bulgarian Academy of Science Publishing House.

# The Representations of Slavic Nations in the Writings of Josipina Turnograjska

*Katja Mihurko Poniž*

ABSTRACT Josipina Turnograjska was the first Slovenian woman writer who wrote in the years after the March revolution of 1848. During that period, the national consciousness of the Slovenians living under the Austro-Hungarian domination began to strengthen. Her male contemporaries, who were beginners in the field of Slovenian prose as well, wrote nationalist literature where the figure of the Slovenian peasant was placed in the limelight. Josipina Turnograjska used the events from the histories of Slavic nations as the subject matter for her stories. In her works women were depicted as the figures who surpassed the male protagonists in courage when fighting for their homeland on the battlefield. Turnograjska wanted to awaken the love for the Slav homeland through her work and sought the integration of all Slavs in the common homeland.

A COMMON LANGUAGE ORIGIN IS what connects Slovenian literature to literatures of other Slavic nations, and a similar history of a so-called 'nation without a state', or a non-dominant nationality, is what ties the Slovenian nation to other nations of the aforementioned Slavic group.[1] Historically, most Slavic nations, such as those of the Czechs, the Slovaks, the Polish, the Bulgarians and the Croats (amongst others), lived under the rule of at least one of the great three multinational empires: Austro-Hungarian, Ottoman or Russian. During the process of nation-building in the 19th century, the Slavic nations began to connect their political rights[2] and the opportunity for

[1] In 1848, of all Slavic nations, only the Russians, Serbians and Montenegrins lived in an independent state.

[2] After the March Revolution in 1848 and the Spring of Nations, demands rose on the Slovenian ethnical territory for a so-called *United Slovenia*, an independent administrative unit in which the official language of schools and offices would be Slovenian. See Janko Prunk, *A Brief History of Slovenia*, (tr. Wayne Tuttle and Majda Klander). Ljubljana: Založba Grad, 1996: 63-66. Slovene population numbered about a million in 1848.

freedom to their artistic endeavours, focussing mostly on national identity issues. The political and social subordination of many Slavic nations encouraged the emergence of the so-called movement of Pan-Slavism. Its beginnings reach back into the period after the fall of Napoleon. The first Pan-Slavic Congress was held in 1848 in Prague, and it established legitimate demands for the complete equality of all nationalities in Austria.[3] Pan-Slavic ideas were also received in the Slovenian ethnic territory.[4] This movement affected not only political, but also cultural life. The influence of poets and writers of Slavic descent is especially noticeable in literature during this period. In the Slovenian and Croatian territories, not only Pan-Slavism, but also the Illyrian Movement was established. This was a south Slavic literary and cultural, as well as national and political movement, established as an interpretation of Ján Kollár's (1793-1852) conception of Slavic reciprocity.[5] It also defended Slavic autochthony in the Balkans and connected South Slavs to descendants of the antique Illyrians.

## Slavic themes in Slovenian literature

Slovenian secular prose and poetry developed in the early 19th century and was partly influenced by the works of Polish (for example Adam Mickiewicz, 1798-1855) and Slovak (for example Ján Kollár) writers.[6] Slovenian male writers in the first half of the 19th century, especially the leading poet of Slovenian Romanticism, France Prešeren (1800-1849), praised the brotherhood of Slavic nations[7] in their works; however, they did not take their literary figures from the histories of those nations even though Slovenia

---

[3] Anna A. Grigorieva, "Pan-Slavism in Central and Southeastern Europe" in *Journal of Siberian Federal University. Humanities & Social Sciences.* (1). 2009: 13-21.

[4] Furthermore, the *United Slovenia* program was successfully incorporated into the final memorandum of the Prague Congress: see Oto Luthar, (ed.). *The land between: a history of Slovenia.* Frankfurt am Main: Peter Lang, 2008: 285.

[5] Kollár advocated the concept of four great Slavic languages: Russian, Polish, Czech and Illyrian: *Ibid.*, 277.

[6] Janko Kos, *Primerjalna zgodovina slovenske literature.* Ljubljana: Partizanska knjiga, 1987: 73.

[7] In his poem *Zdravljica* [A Toast], today's Slovenian anthem, Prešern wrote the following verses: "May unity, joy, blessing,/ Return, may we be reconciled!/ And, brotherhood professing,/ Close linked be Slava's every child, / That again/ we may reign/ And honour riches now regain!" France Prešeren, *Poems*. Tom Priestly and Henry Cooper (tr.), Kranj: Municipality; Klagenfurt- Ljubljana- Vienna: Hermagoras, 1999: 159.

itself lacked charismatic historical personalities. While Slovenian poetry reached its first artistic peak with France Prešern, Slovenian prose bore no literary qualities until the 1850s and was also extremely simple in its themes.[8] In fact, the works of male authors depicted mostly Slovenian rural life, as the Slovenian bourgeoisie reached its social and economical status only in the late 19th century.

The period after the March Revolution, in which the first Slovenian female prose author[9] Josipina Turnograjska (1833-1854) wrote, saw the escalation of the national issue in the Habsburg Monarchy. The expectations of the March Revolution were not realized, and thus the question of the national rights remained very current and demanded a strong response. Nationally conscious Slovenians sought various patriotic activities, since all organized political activities were forbidden. In 1851, the politician Matija Majar Ziljski wrote: "It is impossible to start politics now – we just must be conscious of what is happening and raptly undertake literary writing. This is our politics now (…)"[10]

With this, literary creativity lost its aesthetic autonomy since it became the means of expressing, however indirectly, national, social and political demands.[11] The principle of nationality blocked the devlopment of literature causing it to lose its literary aestheiticism and become an ideology.[12] After 1848, nationally affirmative themes prevailed in Slovenian literature, which in prose were perceived in the works which revived folklore motifs on the one hand and in texts with Slavic themes on the other. Such was the literary situation in 1851, when Josipina Turnograjska published her first work.

---

[8] Gregor Kocijan, *Kratka pripovedna proza od Trdine do Kersnika.* Ljubljana: Državna založba Slovenije, 1983: 61-78.

[9] Before her entrance to the literary public, there were only two female poets, namely Fanny Hausmann and Jela Tomšič. The first Slovenian play written by a woman is the tragedy *France Prešerin* (1877) by Luiza Pesjak, which was never published.

[10] Pogačnik, Jože. *Zgodovina slovenskega slovstva I.* Ljubljana: Cankarjeva založba, 2001: 226.

[11] *Ibid.*, 226.

[12] Dušan Pirjevec, "Pri izvirih slovenskega romana" in *Problemi*, (109): 31–35, 1972: 35.

## The entrance of female writers in Slovenian literature and the position of Slovenian women around 1850

Josipina Turnograjska's first publication was not only the consequence of her own decision to reveal her literary works to the public, but also of the social situation which was, for the first time in Slovenian literary history, in favour of female literary authorship. Slovenian men invited Slovenian women to join them in their cultural activities in a greater show of Slovenian culture, which would legitimatise the need for the greater political independence of the Slovenian nation. The representatives of the male elite called for female voices and asked them to contribute to male, nationalist cultural activities. In 1838, the poet Matevž Ravnikar Poženčan encouraged women to join male poets and awaken the national consciousness in their compatriots in his poem *Slovenkam* [To Slovenian Women].[13] Ten years later, in 1848, the poet Lovro Toman – who later became the husband of Josipina Turnograjska – summoned Slovenian women to patriotic works in his poems *Edinost* [Unity] and *Slovenskim dekletom* [To Slovenian Girls]. The first response to Toman's poems was the poem *Prijaznost* [Kindness], published in 1849 by Jela Tomšič.[14] For female authors, publishing in newspapers was not the only option for public presentations of their works. After 1848, cultural life was in full swing with social events called *bésede*. These were educational and entertainment events where women as well as men could participate in singing and reciting. Patriotic Slovenians were addressed by the politician, cultural worker and Slavic aficionado Radoslav Razlag (1826-1880). He presented the female poets Leopoldina (Lavoslava) Kersnikova (1833-1850), Josipina Turnograjska, Antonija Oblak in Ljudmila Gomilšak as an example of patriotism.[15] The historian Stane Granda explains how Slovenian women entered the public sphere:

---

[13] He followed the Croatian representatives of the Illyrian Movement who similarly invited their compatriots, for example Babuhić in his text *Domorodkinjam ilirskim za leto 1838* (To Illyrian Compatriots for 1838) in the magazine *Danica*. In 1838, in Zagreb, Count Drašković published the German book *Ein Wort an Illyriens hochherzige Töchter* in order to encourage women who had not yet learned Croatian to listen as well.

[14] Dates of birth and death can no longer be found.

[15] The dates of birth and death of Antonija Oblak and Ljudmila Gomilšak could not be found.

> The political activity of women in the revolutionary years of 1848/49 was influenced not only by the traditional forms of their public activities, which mainly covered welfare, cultural activities in clubs (Kasinos), reading societies, and bourgeois and aristocratic parlours, but also by their material circumstances. More than ever before, their rights to trade activity and to hold property titles became important. The latter was especially so in a country where the main criterion for public activity was the possession of a farm. In some places women as title holders had the right to vote at pre-elections. We can find them in the same social role among the signatories of the petitions for a United Slovenia.[16]

In accepting some women (e.g. Luiza Pesjak (1828-1898) Marija Murnik Horak (1845-1894), Marica Nadlišek Bartol (1867-1940)), as important public workers, Slovenes followed in the footsteps of larger Slavic nations, especially the Czechs, where men supported women in even more progressive activities, such as the founding of secondary schools and campaigns for higher education (seeing female education as a matter of national pride), and later, in the nineties, by debating the 'female question' seriously.[17]

## The writing beginnings of Josipina Turnograjska

Among the first women to react to the invitations of nationally-conscious Slovenian men was, as already stated, Josipina Urbančič Turnograjska. She was the daughter of Janez Nepomuk Urbančič, the owner of the castle Turn, which she later chose as her pseudonym. Josipina's father died when she was eight years old. Following this, her mother took care of her upbringing and made private schooling possible for her by hiring a private teacher and a language teacher, who taught Josipina Latin and Italian. The writer of the first lengthy article about Turnograjska (1884), Andrej Fekonja, wrote that Turnograjska knew German and Slavic, as well as classical Greek and

[16] Stane Granda, "Ženske in revolucija 1848 na Slovenskem" (Women and the 1848 Revolution on the Slovene territory) in Nataša Budna Kodrič and Andreja Serše (eds). (tr. Marija Vera Erjavec) *Splošno žensko društvo*. Ljubljana: Arhiv republike Slovenije, 2003: 515.

[17] Katherine David, "Czech Feminists and Nationalism in the late Habsburg Monarchy" in *Journal of women's history*. 2 (Fall).1991: 26-45.

Latin.[18] The young Turnograjska also demonstrated musical talents – four preserved compositions testify to this. In 1849, the priest Lovro Pintar, who studied in Croatia, assumed the role of her teacher and inspired Turnograjska's interest in the Illyrian Movement. The latter appeared as an adaptation of Ján Kollár's theory of Pan-Slavism. Pintar encouraged Turnograjska to write short stories and he must have passed on to her his views about the future of Slavic culture and the Slovenian nation, as Turnograjska later chose the material for many of her short stories from Slavic history. As early as 1850, the young writer expressed her belief in a letter to her friend and future husband that poems by Slavic poets should be translated and published in order to show the Germans and other adversaries how rich Slavic poetry was.[19]

When she started writing and publishing, Turnograjska turned towards new themes and developed them into the innovative genre of short prose which she called *povestica* (short tale). Her short tales are usually between 500 and 2000 words. In January 1851, she sent a story, *Nedolžnost in sila* [Innocence and Force], to the magazine *Slovenska bčela* [The Slovenian Bee].[20] The theme of the story is unrequited love between a married aristocrat and an innocent girl, which Turnograjska took from the history of the Counts of Celje.[21] Count Friderik was said to have murdered his first wife, the Croatian noblewoman Elizabeta, so that he could marry a pretty Croatian noblewoman called Veronika. For political reasons, his father Herman

---

[18] Andrej Fekonja, "Josipina Turnogradska" in *Ljubljanski zvon* (6): 345-352, 1884: 346.

[19] NUK (National and University Library), Manuscript Department, *The Correspondence of Josipina Turnograjska and Lovro Toman*, Ms 1446, folder 2a, letter number 8 (12.12.1850), page 8.

[20] In the Slovenian ethnic territory, between the years 1851-1854 when Josipina Turnograjska wrote, only one literary magazine was published, namely *Slovenska bčela* (The Slovenian Bee) (1850-1853). When the first Slovenian poem by a woman was published – by the poet Fanny Hausmann (1818-1853) – no literary magazine existed in the Slovenian public sphere. Fanny Hausmann published her first poem in 1848 in the weekly *Celske novine* (Celje News) (1848-1849). Her other love and patriotic poems were also published in this newspaper as well as in the newspaper *Slovenija* (Slovenia) (1848-1850). In 1849, the Ljubljana daily *Novice* (News) published the aforementioned poem *Prijaznost* (Kindness) by Jela Tomšič.

[21] Counts of Celje represented the most important medieval aristocratic and ruling house with roots and territory in the 14th and 15th century in present-day Slovenia. Their rise began in the 14th century and ended in 1456 when the last male member of the family died without descendants.

opposed the match and accused Veronika of witchcraft. Despite his efforts, he was unable to have her convicted, and, instead, had her murdered. Josipina Turnograjska was one of the first to depict Veronika Deseniška in Slovenian literature; she later became a staple character.[22] Although the text by Turnograjska, from a stylistic and narratological point of view, is very simple, it is also the first Slovenian literary work in which the main character is a woman who is at the same time also an historical figure. This means that her nationality can also be attested. The writer writes about Veronika with admiration, and is compassionate about her destiny which is a consequence of political intrigues: the ruler's power ultimately defeats the innocence of a young woman.

The story was published in the following issue of *Slovenska bčela*, on the 1st of February 1850. This encouraged the young author to become a prolific writer. In the relatively short period of four years, in which she also got married and established a home in the Austrian city of Graz, she wrote four poems and thirty-eight stories, only eight of which were published during her lifetime. The first publication already shows the direction in which the prose of Josipina Turnograjska was developing: love in a historical, Slavic background and a female character as the protagonist of the story. Female characters in her works are always the carriers of justice, tolerance, wisdom and courage. Her first success encouraged Josipina to send in another work. She wrote these words with it:

> Honourable Sir!
> The day of the Mother Sláva has glimmered. Her sons hurry to bring each their own gift; they all want to prove they are her worthy sons. And why would not her daughters as well have this same wish? This thought is the cause of my trying to write in my gentle language.[23]

With these words, Josipina Turnograjska qualified as a writer who stressed her Slavic and Slovenian provenance. She signed the letter with the words 'the honest Slovenian woman Josipina Urbančič'. The words from the quote above could also be read as a miniature literary programme of the young author who depicted her works within the broader context of the struggle of

---

[22] Bruno Hartman. *Celjski grofje v slovenski dramatiki* (Counts of Celje in Slovenian dramas), Ljubljana: Slovenska matica, 1977.

[23] A letter from Josipina Turnograjska to Anton Janežič, the editor of *Slovenska bčela* (published in *Slovenska bčela*, 11.2.1851).

Slovenians, as a Slavic nation living under foreign rule, to enjoy the freedom of their own language.

As such, I will revisit Turnograjska's works, directing my attention to the following questions: Why is the nation such an important issue for the first Slovenian female writer? Why does she depict other Slavic nations in her works, as well representing the Slovenian nation? What role do female protagonists from the histories of Slavic nations play in her texts? Does her choice of themes cause her contemporaries to see her as the glory of the Slovenian nation? What were her international contacts and what was the reception of her works abroad?

## Slavic themes in the works of Josipina Turnograjska

Protagonists from Slavic history were often depicted in her works, which is why Radoslav Razlag wrote as early as 1852 in his magazine *Zora* [Dawn] that Josipina Turnograjska was a Slovenian prophet and, furthermore, that she was an enthusiastic Slovenian. He even called her a great wonder amongst Slavic daughters since she did not fail her nation as many other representatives of Slavic nations did.[24] Her enthusiasm for Slavism was also noticed by the authors of articles which were published after her death. In the Catholic literary magazine *Dom in svet* [Home and World], an article about her was published in 1899 by F. Rebol, who stressed that her works were mostly taken from Slavic history and depict her as an honest, witty, and religious Slovenian woman.[25] The author of the first Slovenian literary overview, Karel Glaser, had a similar opinion. He stressed the concision of her works and the thematic connection to Slavic life.[26] The author of the first, if very brief monograph about Turnograjska, Ivan Lah, wrote that beside "national tendency, love for freedom, homeland, and her nation – the echo of time – is also reflected in the works of Josipina Turnograjska. Her words about brotherly harmony, forgiveness and love are heard".[27]

[24] Radoslav Razlag, "Životopisi. Slovanske domorodkinje" in *Zora:* 161-165, 1852: 164.

[25] Franc Rebol, "Josipina Turnogradska Tomanova" in *Dom in svet:* 321-326, 1899: 322.

[26] Karel Glaser, *Zgodovina slovenskega slovstva*. Ljubljana: Slovenska matica, 1894: 82.

[27] Ivan Lah, *Josipina Turnograjska: Njeno življenje in delo*. Maribor: Mariborske tiskarne, 1921: 31.

In more than half of her stories,[28] the protagonists are the representatives of different Slavic nations – Slovenians, Croats, Czechs, Slovaks, Poles, Serbians, Bulgarians, and Russians. Turnograjska took the topics for these stories, which are set in different historical periods, from Illyrian and Slavic newspapers which were given to her by her teacher Lovro Pintar.[29] In all the stories in which Turnograjska uses the themes from the history of Slavic nations, the principal characters – female as well as male – are examples of righteousness, honesty, and are the carriers of patriotic emotions and ideas.

In the time of pan-Slavism and the Illyrian Movement, Slavic identity was understood as a concept which did not exclude national identity. On the contrary – Slavic identity enabled a small nation under the rule of a larger, more culturally rich community, to define its demands for independence and defy the dominant Germanic nation. Although some Slovenians rejected the Illyrian Movement in the 19th century out of fear that the Slovenian identity would gradually disappear if blended with larger South Slavic nations, Josipina Turnograjska's works, with themes from the history of Slavic nations, can be interpreted as her wish to surpass narrow national limitations and as a leniency towards the openness of Slovenian literature, in comparison to other national literatures.

Slavic history, especially the history around the Turkish invasion, was sometimes also used by Turnograjska's male contemporaries – like Janez Trdina (1830-1905) and Luka Svetec (1826-1921). However, in her time, Josipina Turnograjska was the only Slovenian female writer who used historical motifs. Her first successor to do the same was Lea Futur (1865-

---

[28] Stories with this theme include the following: *Popotnik* (Traveller) (1850), *Domoljubje* (Patriotism) (1850), *Očetova kletev* (Father's Curse) (1850), *Sodba Bretislavova* (Bretislav's Judgement) (1850), *Nikola Zrinji* (1850), *Izdajstvo in sprava* (Betrayal and Reconciliation) (1850), *Nesrečen prepir* (Unfortunate Quarrel) (1850), *Svobodoljubna Slavjanka* (Freedom-loving Slavic Woman) (1850), *Poljski rodoljub* (Polish Patriot) (1850), *Zvestoba do smerti* (Loyalty until Death) (1851), *Carigrajski patriarh* (The Istanbul Patriarch) (1851), *Marula* (1851), *Vilica* (1851), *Slavjanski mučenik* (The Slavic Martyr) (1851), *Katarina, ruska carica* (Katarina, the Russian Tsarina) (1851), *Rožmanova Lenčica* (Rožman's Lenčica) (1851), *Nepoznani dvobojnik* (Unknown Duellist) (1851), *Svatoboj pušavnik* (Svatoboj the Hermit) (1851), *Moč vesti* (The Power of Conscience) (1851), *Tverdislav* (1851) *Spitignjev in vdova* (Spitignjev and the Widow) (1851) and *Boris* (1851).

[29] France Koblar, "Josipina Toman" in *Slovenski biografski leksikon*. Vol. 4. Ljubljana: SAZU, 1980-1991: 99.

1943),[30] who also used the Turkish invasion as a theme in several works. What is interesting is the question of why this theme was so prevalent in Slovenian literature in the 19th century, and why Josipina Turnograjska commonly depicted it.

The Turkish invasion of Slovenian territory was one of the most traumatic periods in Slovenian history,[31] and fear of the Turks was still evident in collective memory during the time of Josipina Turnograjska. Furthermore, Slovenians projected the fear of the foreign and unknown onto the image of a Turk. Even in the 19th century, nobody questioned such stereotypes; what is more, with the increase of works with motifs of Turkish violence, poets and writers anchored such stereotypes in the cultural memory. Turnograjska did not avoid this because she needed an historical background in which the heroism of her female character could be as effective as possible. Thus, the heroism of her female characters was that much greater if they defeated the Turkish army, an entity that was still frightening for her readers in the 19th century. Another reason for her decision is probably the exposure to censorship.[32] Since the Turks were enemies of the Austrian nation, they were not problematic as opponents of Slavic people and the historical events were so deep in the past that the heroic image of a woman did not allude to the actual position of women in the 19th century in Slovenian territory.

In Turnograska's stories, psychologization is still foreign to the author, although she does try to motivate the protagonist's actions with heroic character traits in some works, for example in *Musa izdajnik*. She adapts historical accuracy in some works in order to create a character that would enthral the readers, for example *Katarina, ruska carica* [Katarina, the Russian Tsarina]. Slavic history is more than just background plot to the author. She understands her literary work as raising readers' awareness about

---

[30] The theme of the Turkish invasion was also depicted many times in the 2nd half of the 19th century by male authors.

[31] Turks invaded the territory of today's Slovenia during the 15th and the 16th century. The first invasion took place in 1408. The Battle of Sisak (1593) marked the end of the Turkish threat to the Slovene lands. See Vasko Simoniti, *Turki so v deželi že.* Celje: Mohorjeva družba, 1990.

[32] Following the brief freedom of the press after the March Revolution, a repressive law 'against the misuse of press' was passed on the 13th of March which regulated press conditions in the monarchy. See Janez Cvirn, "Naj se vrne cenzura, ljubša nam bi bila." *Avstrijsko tiskovno pravo in slovensko časopisje* in Mateja Režek (ed.). *Cenzurirano. Zgodovina cenzure na Slovenskem od 19. stoletja do danes*. Ljubljana: Nova revija, 2010: 24.

the prominent history of Slavic nations who should be motivated by the national struggle. The most important contribution of Josipina Turnograjska to Slovenian literary history is on the way in which her female characters play an active role in her works and are, just like men, the carriers of ideas about Slavic courage, persistency, and justice. Considering the development of Slavic prose, her female and male characters are not likely to be based on real people, but are idea carriers, sometimes even symbols or allegories of courage. If they are compared to the female characters depicted in the same period by representatives of literature with a rich tradition, Josipina Turnograjska's female as well as male characters appear characteristically unaccomplished. However, her decision to set a female character in the centre of action, which is clearly portrayed in many of the aforementioned stories, is a complete novelty in Slovenian literature, and is worthy of close scrutiny.

## The role of Slavic female protagonists in Turnograjska's stories

Ivan Lah stressed that a characteristic of Turnograjska's works is that the author loves "especially female heroines and she loves to show the female winning force, as if she wanted to enthuse the Slovenian women for a national struggle"[33] While literary historians stressed her fondness for Slavic themes,[34] they did not focus on her attempt to provide an image of a woman as a special ideological starting point, which was different from the image of a mother – a dominant image in Slovenian public discourse at that time.[35]

---

[33] Ivan Lah, *Josipina Turnograjska: Njeno življenje in delo.* Maribor: Mariborske tiskarne, 1921: 31-32.

[34] Anton Slodnjak, *Pregled slovenska slovstva.* Ljubljana: Akademska založba, 1934; Matjaž Kmecl, *Od pridige do kriminalke.* Ljubljana: Mladinska knjiga, 1975; Gregor Kocijan, *Kratka pripovedna proza od Trdine do Kersnika,* Ljubljana: Državna založba Slovenije, 1983.

[35] The role of the mother was persistently praised in Catholic publications. The authors warned their readers that neglecting motherly duties was the most dreadful sin. The good mother was presented as a figure who, in the interest of her children, relinquishes all of her own interests and desires, and devotes her time entirely to the wellbeing of the family. This suggested that any activities she engages with outside the home necessarily mean neglecting her duties as a mother. Publications that promoted the image of the sacrificial mother solidified this characterization and, furthermore, compelled and stimulated women towards this ideal. See also Katja

Until now, Turnograjska's writings have not been examined from a gender perspective. In 1996, the literary historian Silvija Borovnik briefly wrote about the connection between Turnograjska's female characters and national identity. In her words, Turnograjska wanted to:

> Ignite in the Germanised Slovene women an interest in the common past through "national heroines" – beautiful, strong and invincible maidens from "Slavic history" – and, influenced by the demands of the nascent Slovene bourgeoisie, also a feeling for the Slovene "national cause" or national identity, or at least an interest in reading and writing in Slovene.[36]

Interestingly, with the exception of Borovnik's short remarks, the way in which Turnograjska's female protagonists are defined by their gender identity and their nationality had only been mentioned in the monographs about Turnograjska written by Mira Delavec in 2004 and 2009.

Turnograjska's extraordinary interest in female characters and their destiny is especially noticeable when they are a part of historical events. In five stories, the name of the protagonist is also the title. It is very likely that her works were well accepted by her contemporaries because she depicted her female characters as courageous women who fight the common enemy for the common good. Thus, it is important to examine which texts and in what way Turnograjska combines Slavic history, Turkish invasion and female characters.

The first work that combines these themes is entitled *Svobodoljubna Slavljanka* [Freedom-Loving Slavic Woman]. The work depicts the gathering of Christian warriors for their march towards the Turkish city of Istanbul in 1471. The Christians come close to Istanbul and are overcoming various obstacles, but must seize the city of Atalia. The fight by the walls of the city is hard, and the Christians are just about to give up, when, suddenly on the walls, a woman slave of the Turks appears. Turnograjska introduces her as "the freedom-loving Slavic woman", who strongly raises her sword, and

---

Mihurko Poniž, *Evine hčere. Konstruiranje ženskosti v slovenskem javnem diskurzu 1848-1902*. Nova Gorica: Založba Univerze v Novi Gorici, 2009 : 170-171.

[36] Silvija Borovnik, *Pišejo ženske drugače?* Ljubljana: Mihelač, 1996: 32-33.

"heroically addresses the confused ones in the language of her nation",[37] saying that they are all cowards who should fight with greater determination. However, the Christians have lost their courage and the Slavic woman realises that they will give up and that she will remain a slave, and thus she jumps off the wall and dies. In this short story, Turnograjska does not depict the protagonist as an individual character, but as the allegory of courage and dedication to the idea of a free nation. Although the author does not individualise the protagonist, her decision to set a female character as a rebel was extremely progressive for Slovenian literature at the time, since women had always played a passive role in works by male authors, even those with a Turkish theme.[38]

Another woman who has more courage than an entire army fighting against the Turks is depicted in Turnograjska's story *Zvestoba do smrti* [Loyalty until Death]. Here, another fight with the Turks is again described. At the beginning of the story, it appears that the Turks will defeat the Croatian hero Nikola Zrinjski and his army. One of his soldiers wants to 'protect' his wife from the Turkish violence and rushes home to kill her before the city is taken over by the Turks. But his wife determinedly stands up to him and goes to the battlefield where they are killed together in the fight against the enemy. As seen in this early story, Turnograjska used the motif of a soldier's wife,[39] which is known to other literatures as well. In 1824, the Slovakian poet Ján Kollár, in his poem *Slávy Dcera* [The Daughter of Sláva], describes Slavic heaven in which there are heroines who accompanied their husbands and sons in battle and bravely fought the enemy there. Among these heroines there is also Marula, who was depicted by Turnograjska as well.

Marula is the title character from a story that depicts the battle between the Turks and the Christians in 1457 on the island Lemnos. The Christians lose their commander and thus their motivation to fight, and, as a

---

[37] Josipina Urbančič: "Svobodoljubna Slavljanka" in Mira Delavec, *Moč vesti: Moč vesti: Josipina Turnograjska: prva slovenska pesnica, pisateljica in skladateljica.* Brežice: Primus, 2009: 280.

[38] Compare the characters of IlkaJanez Trdina: *Pretres slovenskih pesnikov in pisateljev* (The Distress of Slovenian Poets and Writers) (1850), Fran Levstik: *Popotovanje od Litije do Čateža* (Journey between Litija and Čatež) (1858).

[39] The motif of a girl soldier appears in the folklore of the Balkans, the Apennine and Iberian Peninsulas, Provence and even Brazil. See Zmaga Kumer et al. *Slovenske ljudske pesmi: pripovedne pesmi.* Ljubljana: Slovenska matica, 1970: 63.

consequence, the Turks nearly beat them. In that moment, Marula appears on the battlefield as a *deus ex machine.*[40] She is the daughter of the dead Slavic commander. Bravery and courage shine from her eyes. She exchanges her own clothes with her father's and appeals to the warriors not to allow themselves to be outdone in bravery by a girl unused to fighting: "Heroes, brothers! Are you going to let a weak girl, not used to fighting, outdo you? Oh you will not let that! Be heroes! Do not cast a shadow upon the glory of our nation! The spirit of my dead father shall lead you! Get the fiend! Follow me!"[41] This empowers the soldiers and they defeat the Turks.

Josipina Turnograjska took the protagonist of *Katarina, ruska cesarica* [Katarina, the Russian Tsarina] from Russian history. In this historical frame she inserts a female figure in order to show her virtues, not in the sphere of private life, but again on a battlefield. She also adapts the actual historical events by introducing Catherine the Great as a simple girl and not as the princess she was by birth. Turnograjska idealizes the love between her and Tsar Peter the Great whom she dazzles with her beauty and grace. However, Turnograjska wished to depict Catherine as an intelligent and brave woman, and so her female character asks the Tsar whether she can accompany him to war against the Turks. It is she who finds a solution on the battlefield with which Peter the Great's army forces the retreat of the Turks. Although the solution is unconvincing – Catherine gives the Turks her jewels and her fur coat – and although the love between the spouses is depicted pathetically and ideologically, the story shows Turnograjska's wish to prove, by using important historical figures, that women can be an example of courage and wisdom.

In the story *Rožmanova Lenčica* [Rožman's Lenčica] Turnograjska again takes the motif about a girl soldier from folk literature. The story about Rožmanova Lenčica is different from the rest of her stories not only in length, but also because it demonstrates a more skilled storytelling technique, an interesting plot and more original metaphoric language. Rožmanova

---

[40] Turnograjska summed up the character of Marula according to a motif which was known in the broader Slavic space. The Slovak poet Ján Kollár, who wrote in Czech, depicted her in the aforementioned work *Slávy Dcera* (*The daughter of Sláva*) (1824), and the Croat Andrija Kačić Miošić (1704-1760) in his work *Razgovor ugodni naroda slovinskoga* (Pleasant Conversation of Slavic People) (1756).

[41] Josipina Urbančič, "Marula" in Mira Delavec, *Moč vesti*: *Moč vesti: Josipina Turnograjska: prva slovenska pesnica, pisateljica in skladateljica.* Brežice: Primus, 2009: 292.

Lenčica dresses up as a soldier because otherwise her old and feeble father would have to go to war. It is difficult for her to leave since she loves a boy named Pavel who stays at home. The author does not state why Pavel does not go to fight the Turks; however, in so doing, Turnograjska definitely provides her own, perhaps even ironic view of a Slovenian man who stays at home while his lover fights the Turks. On the battlefield, Lenčica more than proves herself: "Lenčica is in the imperial army. The gentle hand of the splendid Slovenian heroine brandishes the sharp sword as if it were a toy. Lenčica is joyful and happy among the soldiers".[42] There is a twist in the narrative when the emperor gives the order that whoever rides through the wide Danube may return home. Lenčica tries, succeeds, and returns home. Soon she marries Pavel on the idyllic Bled Island dominated by the symbol of Slovenia – the mountain Triglav. The writer concludes with these words: "And the sun smiles at them more gently than even in a bright sky, and old Triglav happily bursts into the sky, announcing to the Slovenian nation the eternal union of his earnest heroine with the gentle Pavel.[43]

## Turnograjska's reception in her lifetime

Turnograjska's contemporaries accepted her works with enthusiasm. Her stories were read and commented on positively.[44] In April 1851, an article was published in the magazine *Slovenska bčela* [The Slovene Bee], signed with the male pseudonym Zoridan. In this article, Turnograjska was praised as "the loyal daughter of Mother Sláva", as a Slavic woman of a 'gentle, strong heart'. It further exclaims at the end of the article: "Glory to you, gentle Slovenian woman!" The poetess Milica Žvegelj[45] was the first to follow her lead. She stressed Turnograjska as an example in her letter (1852) to the editor of *Slovenska bčela*: "Receive the awakened voice of Mother

---

[42] Josipina Urbančič, "Rožmanova Lenčica" in Mira Delavec: *Moč vesti*: 309.

[43] *Ibid.*, 310.

[44] Anton Janežič, "V spomin Josipine Turnogradske" in *Slovenski prijatelj* (5) 1856: 15; Radoslav Razlag, "Životopisi. Slovanske domorodkinje" in *Zora,* 1852*:* 161-165; and Janez Muršec, "Iz austrianskih krajev. Iz Gradca" in *Novice* 12/1854, 47, 14.6, 187.

[45] Milica Žvegelj was Josipina Turnograjska's contemporary. The dates of birth and death are unknown.

Sláva also from our parts. Far away in our mountains, I heard the gentle voice of Josipina, the flower of our gender".[46]

Turnograjska's success was based on the fact that her male contemporaries comprehended her stories as entirely fictional and did not feel threatened in the way that they did a few decades later when works written by women writers depicting independent, strong women appeared in the Slovenian cultural sphere. These writings (written in the late 19th century and at the beginning of the 20th century) were frequently criticised by male critics,[47] who felt uncomfortable when confronted with such female characters. In the 19th century, Slovenian society only accepted women who were submissive, passive and loyal wives, mothers and daughters. By placing her female characters in the past, and in distant, foreign countries, Turnograjska could depict their strength, activism and independence. For this reason, her works do not appear to be feminist at first sight; however, even so, her protagonists enable her readers to identify with the image of a strong woman, which was most likely one of the reasons for the positive reception she received from female readers. The second reason for the positive reception of Turnograjska's stories is probably connected to the strengthening of a positive image of good Christians, since the majority of Slovenians were Catholic. Due to this, Turnograjska did not have to fear attacks from the Church, which interfered with cultural life whenever artists critically depicted the Church or its clergy.

In her lifetime, Turnograjska's glory reached ever further. In 1852, the Slovenian almanac *Zora* [Dawn] was read by the ladies-in-waiting of the Russian countess Antonina Dmitrijeva Bludova's (1813-1891) literary club.[48] In that almanac, Turnograjska's work *Boris* was published. Letters sent by

---

[46] Milica Žvegelj, "U spomladi" in *Slovenska bčela*, 11(3), 1852: 80.

[47] The responses of female readers were not preserved, with the exception of Zofka Kveder's letter to Fran Govekar, in which she mentions Pavlina Pajk and stresses the importance of her work as an encouragement for her own writing career: "I want to write, write a lot. And I will fulfil that ideal of mine, which arose so coyly within me when I read the first book by [Pavlina] Pajk, with her portrait, and so rapturously wished to be a writer" , Zofka Kveder in her letter to Fran Govekar, 10 August, 1926. Legacy of Zofka Kveder, National and University Library of Slovenia, Ms 1113. By "the first book by Pajk," Kveder presumably referred to the first book of Pajk's Collected Works (*Iz zbranih spisov Pavline Pajkove*, 1893).

[48] K.D. Petkovič in the letter (19.8. 1852) to M.F. Rajevski: Iskra Vasil'evna Čurkina, *Rusko-slovenski kulturni stiki: od konca 18. stoletja do leta 1914.* Ljubljana: Slovenska matica, 1995: 68.

Bludova to the Bulgarian K.D. Petkovič, show that Turnograjska and the countess possibly met each other, which could be considered a sign of enthusiasm of the reader for the author.[49] Petkovič also personally met Turnograjska and admired her.[50] He wrote about Turnograjska and her love of Russia which had often been seen as a symbolic Slavic homeland to the countess Bludova by the representatives of Slavic nations:

> She loves saint Russia with all the fanaticism of a Slavic heart, and I am convinced that when she sings the melancholic melodies of a Russian song and when the glorious Triglav, the mighty peak of Slovenians, is covered in snow in the background, the young countess Josipina Urbančič will remember her fellow brother of Mother Sláva and especially the noble Russian countess who strives for the good of humanity and the brotherhood between all Slavic people.[51]

The enthusiasm about Turnograjska was confirmed by Petkovič, but can also be seen in the way that he translated her story *Boris* into Bulgarian and published it in a Bulgarian magazine. As the magazine *Slovenska Bčela* reported, Bulgarian-Russian journalist Nikolay Palauzov (1821-1899) sent three of his works to Josipina as a sign of appreciation of her story *Boris*.[52]

The reactions to Turnograjska's writing are also seen in St Petersburg's magazine *Северная пчела* [Northern Bee] in which the following was written in 1852: "Her European education did not separate her from her nationality and although she appreciates foreign literatures, she writes in the national language. This is rare in her country."[53] The author wanted to emphasize that Turnograjska chose to write in Slovenian even though she was well educated and could write in other languages, as some of her Slavic contemporaries in the Habsburg Monarchy did.[54]

---

[49] Bludova visited Graz in 1852, where Turnograjska lived after her wedding: *Ibid.*, 69.

[50] Mira Delavec, *Moč vesti*: 152

[51] Bludov cited in Iskra Vasil'evna Čurkina, *Rusko-slovenski kulturni stiki: od konca 18. stoletja do leta 1914*: 69.

[52] "Zmes" in *Slovenska bčela* 16.9.1852: 309-310.

[53] Северная пчела 21.3.1852, p. 265, quoted from Iskra Vasil'evna Čurkina, *Rusko-slovenski kulturni stiki : od konca 18. stoletja do leta 1914*. Ljubljana: Slovenska matica, 1995: 68.

[54] An article on Turnograjska is also found in Slovakia. The Slovak male writer M. J. Hurban wrote about Turnograjska's text *Slavljanski mučenik* [The Slavic Martyr]

After giving birth prematurely, Turnograjska caught a cold and later became seriously ill. Following her death in 1854, many commemorative accounts and eulogies mentioned Turnograjska's beauty and wrote about her work and what a great loss her death was for Slovenian culture and literature.[55] In the report of her death, the newspaper *Novice* stressed not only that she was a Slovenian writer, but that her death was a loss for the entire Slavic world: "And all the Slavs, who knew her sincere patriotism, and who found joy in her pleasant stories which were written in the local language by our hopeful writer, shall truly pity a great loss."[56] Her husband Lovro Toman wrote in the newspaper *Novice*: "Surely each Slav shall be joyful when they learn that Josipina, although she passed so early, left many treasures of her mind and heart to her nation".[57]

In 1884, Andrej Fekonja published an article about Turnograjska in the only Slovenian literary magazine of that time, *Ljubljanski zvon*. He concluded it with a paragraph about her reception by Slavic people with the following words: "And thus our Slavic brothers, the Slovaks and Russians, published and spread the praise and the glory for the daughter of a small Slovenian nation, our noble Josipina Turnograjska.[58]

Josipina Turnograjska was a unique figure in Slovenian 19th century storytelling and her stories depicting battles with Turks were enriched by the literary character of an extraordinary female writer, thus adding a new dimension to the female protagonists from other stories on similar topics. Moreover, Turnograjska stressed the national affiliation of these protagonists by adding questions of gender and nationality to the formerly rather passive female characters portrayed in Slovenian stories, especially those describing

about the Slovak national hero Vilko Šilek in the magazine *Slovenské Pohlady* in 1851 and gave her "a deep bow, full of gratitude, full of praise and respect." Slovenské Pohlady, 1851, Vol. 4, quoted from Andrej Fekonja, "Josipina Turnogradska" on *Ljubljanski zvon* (6). 1884: 352.

[55] In the 19th century, the term Slovenian literature became an important factor in the struggle for the recognition of the rights of the Slovenian nation. For this reason, works appear after 1848 in which their authors write about the tasks of Slovenian literature, about what the corpus is and which works are in it. Compare: Janez Trdina, *Pretres slovenskih pesnikov in pisateljev* (The Distress of Slovenian Poets and Writers) (1850), and Fran Levstik: *Popotovanje od Litije do Čateža* (Journey between Litija and Čatež) (1858).

[56] From Ljubljana in *Novice*, 7.6. 1854, Nr. 45: 180.

[57] Toman, Lovro. "O literarni zapuščini Josipine Turnogradske Tomanove" in *Novice* 12/1854. 26.8, 270-271; 30.8., 274: 68-69.

[58] Andrej Fekonja, "Josipina Turnogradska" in *Ljubljanski zvon* (6) 1884: 352.

the Slavic-Turkish battles. Josipina Turnograjska consciously chose her themes. With the exception of the characters Rožmanova Lenčica and Marula, who are Slovenian, her female protagonists belong to other Slavic nations. In the context of the battle for Slavic independence, strong, independent and autonomous female characters working according to their own will and beliefs were acceptable. Due to the distinct pro-Slavic orientation of her work, as well as her bourgeois and Christian moral values, Josipina Turnograjska long remained the personification of a Slovenian writer who actively participated in the fight for Slovenian national emancipation. Turnograjska had contacts with male and female representatives of other Slavic nations (ranging from royalty to journalists, writers, artists, etc.), which speaks of her desire to gain broader recognition, beyond the Slovenian cultural space. In this way, she exceeded the narrowness of the Slovenian ethnic space of the 19$^{th}$ century.

## Select Bibliography

### A. Primary Sources

Urbančič, Josipina. 2009. "Svoboduljubna Slavjanka" in Delavec: *Moč vesti*: 279-280.

—. 2009. "Zvestoba do smerti" in Delavec: *Moč vesti*: 285-286.

—. 2009. "Marula" in Delavec: *Moč vesti*: 291-292.

—. 2009. "Katarina, ruska cesarica" in Delavec: *Moč vesti*: 300-302.

—. (2009): "Rožmanova Lenčica" in Delavec: *Moč vesti*: 305-310.

### B. Secondary Sources

Borovnik, Silvija. 1996. *Pišejo ženske drugače?* Ljubljana: Mihelač.

Cvirn, Janez. 2010. "Naj se vrne cenzura, ljubša nam bi bila." *Avstrijsko tiskovno pravo in slovensko časopisje* in Mateja Režek (ed.). *Cenzurirano. Zgodovina cenzure na Slovenskem od 19. stoletja do danes*. Ljubljana: Nova revija: 13-44.

Čurkina, Iskra Vasil'evna. 1995. *Rusko-slovenski kulturni stiki : od konca 18. stoletja do leta 1914.* Ljubljana: Slovenska matica.

David, Katherine. 1991. "Czech Feminists and Nationalism in the late Habsburg Monarchy." in *Journal of women's history*. 2 (Fall): 26-45.

Delavec, Mira. 2009. *Moč vesti: Josipina Turnograjska: prva slovenska pesnica, pisateljica in skladateljica.* Brežice: Primus.

—. 2004. *Nedolžnost in sila, življenje in delo Josipine Urbančič Turnograjske (1833-1854).* Kranj: Gorenjski glas.

Fekonja, Andrej. 1884. "Josipina Turnogradska." in *Ljubljanski zvon* (6): 345-352.

Granda, Stane. 2003. "Ženske in revolucija 1848 na Slovenskem" (Women and the 1848 Revolution on the Slovene territory). in Budna Kodrič, Nataša and Andreja Serše (eds). (tr. Marija Vera Erjavec) *Splošno žensko društvo*. Ljubljana: Arhiv republike Slovenije: 515.

Grigorieva, Anna A. 2009. "Pan-Slavism in Central and Southeastern Europe." in *Journal of Siberian Federal University. Humanities & Social Sciences.* (1):13-21.

Haan, Francisca de, Daskalova, Krassimira and Loutfi, Anna (eds). 2006. *A Biographical Dictionary of Women Movements and Feminisms. Central, Eastern and South Eastern Europe, 19th and 20th Centuries.* Budapest, New York: Central European University Press.

Jayawardena, Kumari. 1986. *Feminism and Nationalism in the Third World.* London: Zed Books.

Janežič, Anton. 1856. "V spomin Josipine Turnogradske." in *Slovenski prijatelj*. (5): 15.

Koblar, France. 1980-1991. "Josipina Toman." in *Slovenski biografski leksikon*. Vol. 4. Ljubljana: SAZU: 99-100.

Kocijan, Gregor. 1983. *Kratka pripovedna proza od Trdine do Kersnika*. Ljubljana: Državna založba Slovenije.

Kos, Janko. 1987. *Primerjalna zgodovina slovenske literature*. Ljubljana: Partizanska knjiga.

Kmecl, Matjaž. 1975. *Od pridige do kriminalke*. Ljubljana: Mladinska knjiga.

Kumer, Zmaga (et al.). 1970. *Slovenske ljudske pesmi: pripovedne pesmi*. Ljubljana: Slovenska matica.

Lah, Ivan. 1921. *Josipina Turnograjska: Njeno življenje in delo*. Maribor: Mariborske tiskarne.

Luthar, Oto, (ed.). 2008. *The land between: a history of Slovenia*. Frankfurt am Main: Peter Lang.

Mihurko Poniž, Katja. 2009. *Evine hčere. Konstruiranje ženskosti v slovenskem javnem diskurzu 1848-1902*. Nova Gorica: Založba Univerze v Novi Gorici.

Muršec, Janez. 1854. "Iz austrianskih krajev. Iz Gradca." in *Novice* 12/, 47, 14.6: 187.

Pirjevec, Dušan. 1972. "Pri izvirih slovenskega romana." in *Problemi*, (109): 31–35.

Pogačnik, Jože. 2001. *Zgodovina slovenskega slovstva I*. Ljubljana: Cankarjeva založba.

Prešeren, France. 1999. *Poems*. Kranj: Municipality; Klagenfurt-Ljubljana-Vienna: Hermagoras.

Prunk, Janko. 1996. *A Brief History of Slovenia*, (tr. Wayne Tuttle and Majda Klander). Ljubljana: Založba Grad: 63-66.

Razlag, Radoslav. 1852. "Životopisi. Slovanske domorodkinje." in *Zora:* 161-165.

Rebol, Franc. 1899. "Josipina Turnogradska Tomanova." *Dom in svet:* 321-326.

Simoniti, Vasko. 1990. *Turki so v deželi že*. Celje: Mohorjeva družba.

Slodnjak, Anton. 1934. *Pregled slovenska slovstva*. Ljubljana: Akademska založba.

Svetec, Luka. 1851. "Vladimir in Kosara." in *Slovenska bčela*, 2, 1: 4–7; 2: 19–23; 3: 35–38; 4: 51–54; 5: 69–72.

Trdina, Janez. 1998. *Janez Trdina*, Ljubljana: DZS.

Toman, Lovro. 1854. "O literarni zapuščini Josipine Turnogradske Tomanove." in *Novice* 12/, 26.8: 270-271; 30.8: 274.

Walby, Sylvia. 1992. "Women and Nation." in *International Journal of Comparative Sociology*. (33): 1-2.

West, Lois A. (ed.). 1997. *Feminist Nationalism*. London: Routledge.

Yuval-Davis, Nira. 1997. *Gender & Nation*. London: Sage Publications.

"Zmes". 1852. *Slovenska bčela* 16(9): 309-310.

Zoridan. 1851 "Perva beseda v Gradcu 23. marca 1851." in *Slovenska Bčela.* (April): 111.

Žvegelj, Milica. 1852. "U spomladi." in *Slovenska bčela*, 11(3): 81.

# Dora D'Istria and the Springtime of the Peoples in South-Eastern European Nations

*Ileana Mihailă*

ABSTRACT Following the revolutions of 1848, Romania, as most of the countries of South Eastern Europe, succeeded, by diplomatic or even by violent means, in forming a separate nation state. This chapter examines the determining role Dora d'Istria's writings played in the movement to have Balkan people recognised as nationals. In spite of her importance, Dora d'Istria remains almost unknown in Romania because she never wrote in Romanian. Dora d'Istria's fellow countrymen could only have had access to her writings via an 1876 translation of some of her works.

WHILE WELL RECOGNIZED IN HER OWN TIME,[1] despite the prejudices against her gender (from which she was not exempt),[2] Dora d'Istria is now little known. In spite of the effort to assign women writers and scholars a different place from that which was infamously assigned by Molière's comedy, *Les Femmes savantes*, Dora d'Istria deserves to have her work considered in a

---

[1] See, for exemple, what Swedish author Frederika Bremer wrote on her: "La nouvelle Corinne" in her book *La vie dans le vieux monde* (quoted in Romanian translation in *Operile dómnei Dora d'Istria,* trans. Gregorie G. Peretz, t.I, Bucureşti, Typographia Curţii: 1876: 364-368), or Mario Ruffini: "spirito universale lottante per gli ideali di liberta del suo tempo, rispettata nel mondo intellettuale della seonda metà del secolo scorso como lo era stata in antecedenza George Sand", Mario Ruffini, "Il golfo della Spezia nella descrizione di una principessa romena" in *Il Commune della Spezia*, anno XII, 1934, n. 4: 3-4.

[2] Even her most well-known biographer, B. Cecchetti, whom she herself had picked as the writer to introduce her to Romanian readership, begins his presentation (see "Despre viaţa şi operile principesei Dora d'Istria", *Operile dómnei Dora d'Istria,* Gregorie G. Peretz(tr.) , Bucuresci, Eforiei Spitalelo, 1876-1877, vol. I: 3-6), by overtly declaring that a woman's place is at home with her family, and only after having completed all her motherly and wifely duties should she think of her „social life". As for the exceptional case of Dora d'Istria, the key-phrase that he uses to justify her lifestyle is: "for her marriage had been neither happy, nor fertile" (*ibid.*, 14).

new light. Through her writings, she became involved in the movement to have Balkan people recognised as nationals. Following the revolutions of 1848, a period usually known as the 'Spring of Nations', most of the people of South Eastern Europe succeeded, by diplomatic or even by violent means, in forming separate nation states. It is high time Dora d'Istria's voice was examined as playing a determining role in this process.

Dora d'Istria, born Princess Elena (or Ileana)[3] Ghica (1828, Bucharest – 1888, Florence), was a Romanian writer who often wrote in French. She had been exiled, along with her family, arriving in Potsdam in 1848, eventually returning to Moldavia in 1849, where she married the Russian prince Alexandr Koltsov Massalski, and lived in Russia until 1855. After they separated, she went first to Switzerland, and then to Italy, where she lived for five years in Turin, Genoa, and, finally, Florence, where she died. Through her truly remarkable literary contribution, she helped inform the readership of her time in the most accurate and complete manner she could of the national identity issues of South Eastern European people (Romanians, Greeks, Albanians, Serbs, Bulgarians and Turks). Her writings, frequently published in *Revue des deux mondes* or *Il Diritto*, as well as in individual volumes – the best known of these being *Des femmes en Orient* (1859) and *Des femmes par une femme* (1869) – translated and annotated in several European languages[4]

---

[3] According to a Greek source: *Hai Ionioi Nēsoi hypo tēn despoteian tēs Henetias kai tēn Anglikēn prostasian: kai hē en autais Hellēnikē poiēsis (Hē Hellēnikē poiēsis en tais Ioniois Nēsois ... (La poésie grecque dans les Îles-Ioniennes .., griech./neugriech.) meta perilēpseōs tinos tēs archaias autōn historias (Hai Ionioi Nēsoi pro tēs Anglikēs prostasias. (Aus d. Ms. übers.), hypo tēs Komēsoēs Doras d'Istrias (Countess Dora d'Istria, d.i. Ileana Ghica; d. i. Elena Kol'cova Massalskaja, metaphrasthenta ek tu Galliku hypo M.K. Rhallē [M.K. Rallēs], ekd. hypo Th. Thermogiannē kai D[ēmētriu] Eirēnidu,* M.K. Rallēs (tr.); Th.Thermogiannēs, Athènes: 1859; *Peri tōn en tē Anatolē gynaikō: syngramma,* Athènes, Chrēstou Douka: 1861.

[4] *Des femmes en Orient,* Zürich: Meyer & Zeller Year, 1859, and *Des femmes par une femme,* Paris: Librairie internationale / A. Lacroix, 1869. For an essential bibliography (extremely vast even in her lifetime), see Katharina M. Wilson (ed.), *An encyclopedia of continental women writers*, vol. I. A-K, New York-London: Garland Publishing, 1991: 465; Helena Verdel and Traude Kogoj (eds). *Die hundert bedeutendsten Frauen europäischen Ostens*, Klagenfurt: Wieser Verlag, 2003: 105-108; Francisca De Haan, Krassimira Daskalova and Anna Loutfi, *A Biographical Dictionary of Women's Movements and Feminisms. Central, Eastern, and South Eastern Europe,* Budapest & New York, Central European University Press: 2006; Antonio d'Alessandri, *Il pensiero e l'opera di Dora d'Istria fra Oriente Europeo e Italia*, Roma: Gangemi, 2007. See the excellent website, www.ghyka.com/Divers/Dora d'Istria/Dora

(such as Albanian, English, Greek, Italian, Romanian and Turkish), some of which appeared during her lifetime, and others after her death, contributed to a better dissemination and understanding of these peoples' history in the West.The folk poetry of these people (which was sparsely studied at the time) was also further disseminated, being regarded by Dora d'Istria as an exclusive testimony of their strong ethnic spirit and historical path.

The long road that European civilisation travelled towards the consolidation of national identities into nation states is manifested in the centrifugal movement which defined the end of the *Ancien Régime* in Europe. These transformations mainly targeted the Habsburg Monarchy and the Ottoman Empire, but the balance of European powers demanded that the majority of great nations in the Old Continent take an explicit stance, on one side or the other of the very real fight on the barricades, among the peoples concerned with every moment of this long process of dissolution of the vast imperial administrative systems.[5]

Even though politics belonged, as always, more to the cabinets of ministers and summit meetings rather than to newspaper columns and book pages, one must not overlook the weight of public opinion regarding the leaders' political choices. In this sense, we now consider the efforts of those romantic quills,[6] male or female, who, through their writings, stirred up sympathy within their readers, subsequently exerting pressure on political decisions, as worthy of attention. Starting in the late 18th century, Romanticism had devised a complex system of depicting the concept of personal, as well as collective identities, which, at the level of nationality, found its best and most authentic representation in folk poetry, as an

---

d'Istria.htm and all the information about her reception in http://www.womenwriters.nl.

[5] On this matter, I checked the following sources: Charles and Barbara Jelavich, *The formation of the national Balkan states*, Washington: University of Washington Press, 1977; Georgios Prevelakis, *Les Balkans. Cultures et géopolitique*, Paris: Ed. Nathan, 1994; Maria Todorova, *Imagining the Balkans*, Oxford: Oxford University Press, 1997; Stevan K. Pavlowitch, *A History of The Balkans*, London: Addison Wesley Longman Limited, 1999; Mark Mazower, *The Balkans. From the End of Byzantium to the Present Day*, London: Phoenix Press, 2002; Gheorghe Zbuchea, *Românii şi Balcanii în epoca modernă*, Craiova: Ed. Scrisul Românesc, 2003. None of these works mentions Dora d'Istria, but her views and her information are most often confirmed.

[6] For instance, the translation of Romanian folk poetry, *Les Doinas – poesies moldaves*, J. E. Voïnesco (tr.), Paris: de Soye et Bouchet, 1853.

exclusive means of expressing a person's soul. In Herder's view,[7] for instance, writers must find their inspiration in the language and culture of their people. The entire world of letters, and most notably poets, regrouped themselves into casual folklorists and ethnologists, enthusiasm sometimes eclipsing their competence, making room for actual collections of folk songs and local traditions that would establish the foundations of a new branch of discipline with a bright future: ethnology, ethnography and folklore.[8]

The approach which Dora d'Istria chose for her series of articles concerning the Balkan people, and their reflections in folk poetry, published in *Revue des Deux Mondes,*[9] falls perfectly under the discourse in favour of the national rights of these peoples. To each article, she adds a subtitle which specifies the name of the collection of folk poetry she relies on for her demonstration. Looking to promote these people favourably, she begins her articles each time with a short history destined to acquaint the Western reader with the specific issue of each group of people in the region, then moving on to a selective and personal presentation of the material she makes use of, on which she comments in her own manner:

> Had this rebirth of Romanian poetry not been preceded by the really original trials of unknown poets who maintained in the soul of the multitudes a very keen feeling of nationality and the legitimate hope of seeing it overcome all kinds of obstacles that paralysed its awakening? [...] Deeply convinced that the race to which he belongs is inferior to no other, that he is even superior to the neighbouring Austrian, Russian and Turkish peoples, through his illustrious origins and highly ancient civilization, the peasant proudly answered whoever talked to him about the coming enslavement of his country: 'I fear not, because I am Romanian'. Even beyond the Danube [...] when one of

---

[7] *Une autre philosophie de l'histoire pour contribuer à l'éducation de l'humanité*, Max Rouché (tr.), Paris: Aubier/Montaigne, 1943.

[8] On the connection between Dora d'Istria and the emergence of these disciplines in the second half of the 19th century, see: Liviu Bordas, "Etnologia ed orientalistica romantica nei nuovi stati Italia e Romania. Angelo de Gubernatis, Dora d'Istria e gli studiosi romeni nella secunda metà dell'Ottocento", in *AION. Annali dell'Università degli Studi di Napoli "L'Orientale"*, Napoli, 65, nr. 1-4, 2005 : 103-119.

[9] "La nationalité roumaine d'après les chants populaires" in 1859, "La nationalité serbe d'après les chants populaires" in 1865, "La nationalité albanaise d'après les chants populaires" in 1866, "La nationalité hellénique d'après les chants populaires", in 1867 – although preceded by "La poésie grecque dans les Iles-Ioniennes" en 1858 "La nationalité bulgare d'après les chants populaires" in 1868.

> these rough shepherds meets a Vlach, without hesitation he gives him the beautiful name of *frate* (brother), which has remained so Latin, that its mere pronunciation is a protest in favour of Romanian nationality.[10]

She thus summarises or quotes from translations of popular ballads which praise the exploits of national heroes, whether they be princes like Marko Kralevich, the Serbian *cneaz* Lazar, Stephen the Great of Romania, or much loved brigands, such as the Wallachian *haiducs* and the Greek *klepts*, to whom the popular imagination attributed the role of defenders of the people. Of course, given the purpose she had in mind, one should expect syntheses, rather than original research or personal contributions. She does indeed record real events and local traditions in her travel writings, which are studded with charming descriptions of folk tales, ballads and lore, later put to good use in her most famous books, such as *Les Femmes en Orient* or *La vie monastique dans l'église orientale.*[11] Her only endeavours in historical research are leafing through the pages of archives and chronicles, mainly concerned with glorifying her family's past, in the published outcomes of which she introduces herself as Romanian, Greek or Albanian, depending on her momentary needs.[12] Yet, the comments which accompany this exhibit a

[10] "La Nationalité roumaine d'après les chants populaires" in *Revue des deux mondes,* 15 mars 1859 : 430; sub-title: *Ballades de la Roumanie,* in t. 1: 1852, and t. 2: 1853. *Les Doïnas*, the Moldavian poems of Vasile Alecsandri, translated from the Romanian by J.-E. Voïnesco, Paris: Imprimerie de De Soye et Bouchet, 1853. The second edition (Paris: Cherbuliez, 1855) mentions *three* translators, Vasile Alecsandri, J.-E. Voinescu and Georges Bell.

[11] *La vie monastique dans l'église orientale*, Paris/Geneva: Cherbuliez, 1855; Paris: Cherbuliez, 1858.

[12] *Gli Albanesi in Rumenia, storia dei principi Ghika nei secoli XVII, XVIII e XIX su documenti inediti degli archivii di Venezia Vienna, Parigi, Berlino, Constantinopoli, etc.*, Francese di B. Cecchetti (tr.), Firenze, Tipografia editrice dell'associazione: 1873 (partially taken from *Rivista europea*, 1871-1873). This book was to cause a scandal within her family, as they had considered themselves Romanians for many centuries (her uncle had been elected *Romanian* reigning prince of Wallachia in 1821), or, at least, Greeks (in the 18th century, the Ottomans had accepted the Ghica, as Phanariot princes of the Romanian Principalities, that is to say as members of the Greek community of Constantinople). As for their 'Albanian' origins, they had considered themselves as belonging to the Aromanians of Albania (also known as Vlachs), which explained their perfect integration among Romanians after only one generation, according to 17$^{th}$ century sources. Moreover, Dora d'Istria herself speaks warmly of these ambassadors of the Roman East, whom she calls "the great, powerful

genuine talent for writing which outshines the overflow of rich and varied information, which is not always sufficiently understood and often expressed in a foreign language (most notably in French). Historian Nicolae Iorga , the greatest and most famous Romanian historian (1871-1940), noted that:

> It is true that writing in languages other than her native tongue, *ban* Mihail Ghica's daughter could not have had the profound vibration of a true writer's words in the entirety of her vast oeuvre [...] But it is astonishing to see the amount of knowledge this exceptional woman's mind has gathered and how effortlessly she could bring it to the front every time there was a battle to fight. For she was a preacher of militant credo. Anticlerical liberalism found a tireless defender in her. And so did the nations' right to live. Has this theory of hers sprung out of love, as shown by her histories, presentations and romantic formulations, for the nation from which, not forgetting the distant Albanians, she drew her origins? Or did this genuine love, although poorly disclosed, or, at least, rarely acknowledged, lead her to general her considerations concerning the sufferings of nations and their legitimate aspirations? We believe the latter to be true. Therefore, a belated feeling of heartfelt gratitude goes to Elena Ghica, a descendant of Romanian princes.[13]

At her death, one of her many Italian admirers wrote that "[there was] never another person in the whole of Europe to represent them [the Balkan nation, its Principalities and populations] more brilliantly than this woman of noble descent"[14].

The first articles she dedicated to the Romanian cause are dated 1856-1859, a time of diplomatic conflict concerning the unification of Romanian Principalities. The collection of *Romanian Ballads* (Iaşi, 1856-1859), compiled by the poet Vasile Alescandri and published in Paris in 1855, served as an opportunity and basis for Dora d'Istria's study *La nationalité roumaine*, in which she resumes her endorsement of romantic theories

---

Romanian-Greek tribe of the high valleys of Albania", in "La nationalité hellénique": 595.

[13] Nicolae Iorga, "Prefaţă", in Magda Nicolaescu Ioan, *Dora d'Istria*, Cartea Româneasca: Bucureşti, 1932: 7-8.

[14] Enrico Pazacchi, "Dora d'Istria" in *Nuova Antologia*, vol XVIII, 1888: 772.

regarding the meaningful link between the rebirth of a nation and the (re)connection to its folklore:

> Wasn't the rebirth of Romanian poetry preceded by truly original essays written by unknown poets who preserved in the hearts of so many a burning national sentiment and a legitimate hope of seeing it triumph over obstacles of all kind currently paralyzing its awakening? The *Hellenes*' great national revolution of 1821 was salvaged only by the crowd's generously stubborn devotion; In *Servia*, the intrepid shepherds who had risen along Karageorge were careful not to approve of the perilous concessions to which their leaders had given in. National poetry had therefore stirred, to some extent, a noble impulse. Were the Romanians less happy than the Greeks and the Serbs? [...] Among Romanians, at the worst of times in their history, the vigorous mountaineers of the Carpathians sang the glory of Mircea, of the Hunyads, of Stephen the Great, of Michael the Brave. Deeply convinced that the race to which he belonged is no way inferior to any other, him being actually superior to the neighbouring peoples, the Austrians, the Russians, the Turks, by illustrating his origins and the high antiquity of his civilization, the peasant would proudly reply to those speaking of the imminent enslaving of his country: 'I have no fear, for I am Romanian'. [...] Even beyond the Danube [...] whenever one of these fierce pastors meets a Wallachian, without hesitation, he beautifully calls him *frate* (brother), a noun which has stayed so Latin that its very pronunciation makes up an argument in favour of Romanian national identity.[15]

The symmetry of the titles in this series clearly suggests that her interest revolves around the people from this part of Europe. As such, "La nationalité serbe d'apres les chants populaires"[16] was inspired, particularly, by Vuk Stephanovitch Katadijitch's successful *National Poems*. It has already been noted that the Serbs were an object of concern for her, as an inherent part of Balkan reality, where folklore often played the role of a collective consciousness: "If the Serbs have been hardly able to preserve by means of methodical procedures the memories of their great figures, they have nevertheless found within their poetic genius a faultless way of

[15] "La nationalité roumaine d'après les chants populaires" in *Revue des deux mondes*, March 15, 1859: 430.

[16] "La nationalite serbe d'apres les chants populaires" in *Revue des deux mondes*, 15 janvier 1865: 315-360.

immortalising, along with the names of theirs heroes, the stories, the struggles and the sorrows of their race."[17]

As for the Bulgarians, to whom she also dedicates a study, she notes that:

> Bulgarian national poems are so foreign to Western Europe, that we can only hope that a study on the matter will be met be greeted by chance in a time in which deal so frequently with the aspirations of the Bulgarian people. We felt it was better to interview naïve poets who represent the people's very core, rather than to lend it ideas and feelings which are more often than not unfamiliar to its spirit. This study, which will not prove useless to those concerned with the still very little known literary history of the East, will also be of interest to politicians.[18]

Here, however, her efforts are still far from being appreciated by scholars. To this day, there is very little reference in Bulgarian literature to Dora d'Istria. Could it be that readers might have disapproved of her displaying little confidence in the future of their political struggle? This is certainly what she suggests on the subject:

> Revolts are not the main means of regaining a contested independence. Getting rid of the language imposed by the conquest, and the foreign manners, reawakening national intelligence numbed by centuries of ignorance, recovering the sound thought of one's ancestors, calling the attention, by generous efforts, of all those who have mind of their own to be part of the general movement of ideas and the liberal aspirations of elevated souls. [...] admitting by all means that there are no other motives other than the independence, happiness and freedom of one's country, these are the better non-violent means of reclaiming a lost place in a civilized world.[19]

---

[17] Admittedly, Serbian experts are not convinced by Dora d'Istria's efforts in approaching their historical and cultural realities. Thus, Zivomir Mladenović, considers the opinions expressed in this article either compilations, or mere fabrications. See "Dora d'Istrija i srpska narodna poezija" in *Zbornik Matice Srpske za kwizevnost i jezik*, Beograd, vol. XLVII, n. 2-3, 1999: 201-220.

[18] "La nationalité bulgare d'après les chants populaires" in *Revue des deux mondes*, July 15, 1868: 319.

[19] *Ibid.*

Lastly, and in order to remain faithful to Dora d'Istria's reasoning, the Turks must also be included among the people of this region who interested her, being full members of the Balkan world, and having brought a rich cultural heritage which fruitfully coexisted with other cultures in the region. She writes detailed, well-regarded studies of Ottoman poetry.[20]

Certainly, the same could be said of Greece, even though they had, at this point, already succeeded in creating their own nation state.[21] After having taken a stance in her articles *La poésie grecque dans les Iles-Ionienne* and *Les Iles-Ioniennes sous la domination de Venise et sous le protectorat britannique*[22], militating for the restitution of the seven islands to Greece, Dora d'Istria, resumed the cause of her dear Greece in 1867 with "La nationalité hellénique d'après les chants populaires", written on the occasion of the Cretan revolt (August 1866). This time, the object of her comments was Claude Fauriel's remarkable work, *Chants populaires de la Grèce moderne*, which, having been published in 1824, two years after the massacres on Chios Island and the defeat of the first Greek uprising against the Ottoman Empire, was nothing less than a manifesto for this nation's right to independence.[23] In her comments, Dora d'Istria expresses her ideas freely, but not without some bitterness:

---

[20] "La poésie populaire des Turcs orientaux" in *Revue des deux mondes*, 1 feb. 1873: 513-583.

[21] Nothing could be found in the literature suggesting that her pen name, "d'Istria", was inspired not only by the former name of the Danube (Istros), as it is generally believed, but also by the name of the first leader of the modern state of Greece, Ioannis Antonios Kapodistrias, Giovanni Cappo d'Istria in Italian, assassinated in 1831.

[22] These articles were very favourably received in Greece and also translated: *Hai ionioi nēsoi hypo tēn despoteian tēs Enetias kai tēn anglikēn prostasian, kai hē en autais hellēnikē poiēsis*, tr. M.K. Rallēs; Aristotelēs Valaōritēs, Athènes: Typographeion D. Eirēnikon, 1859; *Hai Ionioi Nēsoi hypo tēn despoteian tēs Henetias kai tēn Anglikēn prostasian: kai hē en autais Hellēnikē poiēsis (Hē Hellēnikē poiēsis en tais Ioniois Nēsois ... (La poésie grecque dans les Îles-Ioniennes ..., griech./neugriech.) meta perilēpseōs tinos tēs archaias autōn historias (Hai Ionioi Nēsoi pro tēs Anglikēs prostasias hypo tēs Komēsoēs Doras d'Istrias (Countess Dora d'Istria, d.i. Ileana Ghica; d. i. Elena Kol'cova Massalskaja), metaphrasthenta ek tu Galliku hypo M.K. Rhallē, ekd. hypo Th. Thermogiannē kai D[ēmētriu] Eirēnidu*, M.K Rallēs (tr.), Athènes: Th.Thermogiannēs, 1859; additionally, she collaborated extensively with the Greek press at the time, publishing especially for *L'Espérance* paper in Athens.

[23] Anne-Marie Thiesse, *La création des identités nationales: Europe XVIIIe- XXe siècle*, Paris: Seuil, 1999: 61-67.

> Through this study, and by resorting to several new publications, I would like to outline an idea, if not entirely new, at least more complete, of this people, the Greeks, throughout the long trials which have changed them. Their bold life, their beliefs, their moors, all these are reflected in their songs; therefore let us examine successively, in this order, this vast *romancero*.[24]
>
> The oldest Greek folk songs date back to a time when the Turks were threatening the Byzantine Empire [...] My understanding of a Greek muse is that of a folk muse. The upper classes, in fact, endured the insults of the Turks quite patiently and did not resent helping them lay down without too many impediments, their domination over Europe.[25]

Here she also refers to Turkish domination of Romanian territories in the 18th century, made possible with the help of the Greek 'princes' of the Phanar quarter (amongst whom were some of Dora d'Istria's ancestors), and the oppressors' invaluable allies. It is true, however, that the cooperation of the Ghica family with the Turks had met a bloody end. The last member of the family to reign as a Phanariot prince was assassinated by a Turkish emissary, late in September 1777, for having protested too vocally against the Austrian occupation in northern Moldavia. The sultan had offered Mary-Therese the territory as a reward for the support she had given the Ottoman Empire during the Russo-Turkish war of 1769-1774. Dora d'Istria would always proudly remember this episode, where a member of her family had sacrificed himself for the Romanian people (an episode which was rewarded with the election of her paternal uncle as reigning prince of Moldavia): "Ah! I said to myself, if a vivacious patriot, if Grigore III Ghica, if the indomitable prince of Moldavia, or Grigore IV the Restorer Ghica would then reign in Bucharest, Michael the Brave's crown would not have served as a toy for diplomats and degenerate despots from Stamboul!"[26]

She also focused on the Albanians and the richness of their folk poetry in the very same spirit, and by consulting a rich bibliography in Italian, French and German, as well as quoting from works in Albanian. With undeniable warmth, she states that:

---

24 "La nationalité hellénique d'après les chants populaires", in *Revue des deux mondes*, August 1, 1867: 588.

25 *Ibid.*, 589.

26 *Des femmes par une femme:* 53.

> Albania's past, as it reveals itself to us through its folk songs, touches upon present issues more than we would think, and moreover, it always makes an interesting spectacle to follow a small people through the trials of being conquered and exiled without ever losing the qualities which make up their powerful national spirit. [...] Their zealous way of preserving national traditions, their eagerness to inquire about Western scientific progress, their desire to get the civilized nations interested in their Eastern would make a powerful able contribution to the awakening of their nation.[27]

Dora d'Istria's history of connections to the Albanian people cannot, however, be summarized so neatly. Even though she took joy in writing the first letter in *Des Femmes par une femme* as a first-person account of an Albanian woman from Parga, this does not make her that particular woman. As far as she is concerned, she was born in Bucharest, as shown by her official papers, and often declared herself Romanian, in her writings. If she had gone to look for a different ethnic identity, her mother's Greek origin would have been closer to her than that of her distant ancestors, who had left Albania more than two centuries before. Indeed, despite the past and present efforts of a few scholars,[28] Dora d'Istria remains almost unknown in Romania. The cause is simple: having never written in Romanian, her fellow

---

[27] "La nationalité albanaise d'après les chants populaires" in *Revue des deux mondes,* May 15 1866: 382.

[28] See Radu Ionescu, "Doamna Dora d'Istria" in *Revista română*, vol. I, 1861: 427-448, 783-806 and vol. II, 1862: 17-44; Cezar Bolliac, "Doamna Dora d'Istria" in *Trompeta Carpaților*, 22 July and 26 August 1873: 2; Vasile Gr. Pop, *Conspect asupra literaturei române*, Bucureşti: Editura Eminescu, 1876, vol. 2: 147-148; Claudia D.C. Zaharia, *Dora d'Istria. Viața şi opera sa*, Bistrița, s.n., 1932; Magda Nicolaescu Ioan, *Dora d'Istria*, Bucureşti: Cartea Româneasca, 1932; Nicolae Iorga, "Lettres de Dora d'Istria" in *Revue historique du sud-est européen,* Paris – Bucarest, IX, no. 4-6, April-June 1932: 153; Petre Ciureanu, "Dora d'Istria" in *Revue des Études Roumaines*, n. 2, 1954: 169-192; n. 3-4, 1957: 82-110; Adrian Fochi (ed.). *Bibliografia generală a etnografiei şi folclorului românesc, I (1800-1891),* Bucureşti: EPL, 1968: 11 entries (3, 92, 152, 216, 823, 824, 3637, 6073, 6707, 6977, 7048); Iordan Datcu, "Dora d'Istria si unitatea românilor" in *Memoriile sectiei de filologie*, seria IV, tom X, 1988: 91-96; Cristia Maksutovici and Georgeta Penelea-Filitti, *Dora d'Istria*, Bucuresti: Criterion, 2004; *Dicționarul general al literaturii române*, Bucureşti: Ed. Univers Enciclopedic, 2004: 719-721; Liviu Bordas, "O insulă exótică a culturii române: Dora d'Istria" in *Revista de istorie şi teorie literară*, n.1-4, IV, 2010: 317-328.

countrymen could only have had access to her writings via an 1876 translation of some of her works. Dora d'Istria's works in the original can only be found in major libraries. In response to Charles I's act of moral compensation,[29] she offered a very generous gift and donated part of her fortune to the city of Bucharest.It seems, also, that a school was named after her. If there are testimonies assuring us that for a while it had been known as "Dora d'Istria" School, this name is now long lost.[30]

---

[29] Reigning Prince Charles I of Romania offers her a BENE MERENTI gold medal (*Monitorul Oficial*, 4-16 May 1876).

[30] It still appears with its old name (later changed to *Şcoala Silvestru*) in several articles, published on the Internet on September 30, 2009. See: http://foaienationala.ro/tag/cotul-donului.

## Select Bibliography

### A. Primary Sources

Ghica, Elena. 1855. *La vie monastique dans l'église orientale*. Paris/Geneva: Cherbuliez; Paris: Cherbuliez, 1858.

—. 1859. "La Nationalité roumaine d'après les chants populaires" in *Revue des deux mondes,* 15 mars: 430.

—. 1859. *Hai Ionioi Nēsoi hypo tēn despoteian tēs Henetias kai tēn Anglikēn prostasian: kai hē en autais Hellēnikē poiēsis (Hē Hellēnikē poiēsis en tais Ioniois Nēsois ...., hypo tēs Komēsoēs Doras d'Istrias,* M.K. Rallēs (tr.). Athènes: Th.Thermogiannēs.

—. 1859. *Hai ionioi nēsoi hypo tēn despoteian tēs Enetias kai tēn anglikēn prostasian, kai hē en autais hellēnikē poiēsis,* M K Rallēs (tr.). Athènes: Typographeion D. Eirēnikon.

—. 1859. *Des femmes en Orient.* Zürich: Meyer & Zeller Year.

—. 1859. "La nationalité roumaine d'après les chants populaires" in *Revue des deux mondes,* March 15: 430.

—. 1861. *Peri tōn en tē Anatolē gynaikōn: syngramma.* Athènes: Chrēstou Douka.

—. 1866. "La nationalité albanaise d'après les chants populaires" in *Revue des deux mondes,* May 15: 382.

—. 1865. "La nationalité serbe d'après les chants populaires" in *Revue des deux mondes*, 15 janvier: 315-360.

—. 1867. "La nationalité hellénique d'après les chants populaires", in *Revue des deux mondes,* August 1: 588.

—. 1868. "La nationalité bulgare d'après les chants populaires" in *Revue des deux mondes*, July 15: 319.

—. 1869. *Des femmes par une femme.* Paris: Librairie internationale / A. Lacroix.

—. 1873. "La poésie populaire des Turcs orientaux" in *Revue des deux mondes,* 1 feb: 513-583.

—. 1873. *Gli Albanesi in Rumenia, storia dei principi Ghika nei secoli XVII, XVIII e XIX su documenti inediti degli archivii di Venezia Vienna, Parigi, Berlino, Constantinopoli, etc.*, Francese di B. Cecchetti (tr.). Firenze: Tipografia editrice dell'associazione.

1853. *Les Doinas – poesies moldaves*, J. E. Voïnesco (tr.), Paris: de Soye et Bouchet.

## B. Secondary Sources

Alessandri, Antonio d'. 2007. *Il pensiero e l'opera di Dora d'Istria fra Oriente Europeo e Italia*. Roma: Gangemi.

Alecsandri, Vasile. 1853. *Les Doïnas*, J.-E. Voïnesco (tr.). Paris: Imprimerie de De Soye et Bouchet.

Bolliac, Cezar. 1873. "Doamna Dora d'Istria" in *Trompeta Carpaților*, 22 July and 26 August: 2.

Bordas, Liviu. 2005. "Etnologia ed orientalistica romantica nei nuovi stati Italia e Romania. Angelo de Gubernatis, Dora d'Istria e gli studiosi romeni nella secunda metà dell'Ottocento" in *AION. Annali dell'Università degli Studi di Napoli "L'Orientale"*, Napoli, 65, nr. 1-4: 103-119.

—. 2010. "O insulă exótică a culturii române: Dora d'Istria" in *Revista de istorie şi teorie literară*, n.1-4, IV : 317-328.

Bremer, Frederika. 1876. "La vie dans le vieux monde" in *Operile dómnei Dora d'Istria*, Gregorie G. Peretz (tr.). Bucureşti: Typographia Curţii, vol. I: 364-368.

Cecchetti. B. 1876-1877. "Despre viaţa şi operile principesei Dora d'Istria"in *Operile dómnei Dora d'Istria*, Gregorie G. Peretz (tr.). Bucuresci: Eforiei Spitalelo, vol. I: 3-6.

Ciureanu, Petre. 1954. "Dora d'Istria" in *Revue des Études Roumaines*, n. 2: 169-192; n. 3-4, 1957: 82-110.

Datcu, Iordan. 1988. "Dora d'Istria si unitatea românilor" in *Memoriile sectiei de filologie*, seria IV, t. X: 91-96.

*Dicționarul general al literaturii române*. București: Ed. Univers Enciclopedic, 2004: 719-721;

Fochi, Adrian (ed.). 1968. *Bibliografia generală a etnografiei şi folclorului românesc, I (1800-1891)*. Bucureşti: EPL.

Haan, Francisca De, Krassimira Daskalova and Anna Loutfi. 2006. *A Biographical Dictionary of Women's Movements and Feminisms. Central, Eastern, and South Eastern Europe*. Budapest & New York: Central European University Press.

Herder. Johan Gottfried von. 1943. *Une autre philosophie de l'histoire pour contribuer à l'éducation de l'humanité*, Max Rouché (tr.). Paris: Aubier/Montaigne.

Ionescu, Radu. 1861. "Doamna Dora d'Istria" in *Revista română*, vol. I: 427-448, 783-806 and vol. II, 1862: 17-44.

Iorga, Nicolae. 1932. "Prefaţă", in Magda Nicolaescu Ioan, *Dora d'Istria*. Bucureşti: Cartea Româneasca: 7-8.

—. 1932. "Lettres de Dora d'Istria" in *Revue historique du sud-est européen*, Paris – Bucarest, IX, no. 4-6, April-June: 153.

Jelavich, Charles and Barbara. 1977. *The formation of the national Balkan states*. Washington: University of Washington Press.

Maksutovici, Cristia and Georgeta Penelea-Filitti, 2004. *Dora d'Istria*. Bucuresti: Criterion.

Mazower, Mark. 2002. *The Balkans. From the End of Byzantium to the Present Day*. London: Phoenix Press.

Mladenović, Zivomir. 1999. "Dora d'Istrija i srpska narodna poezija" in *Zbornik Matice Srpske za kwizevnost i jezik*, Beograd, vol. XLVII, n. 2-3: 201-220.

Nicolaescu Ioan, Magda. 1932. *Dora d'Istria*. București: Cartea Româneasca.

Pazacchi, Enrico. 1888. "Dora d'Istria" in *Nuova Antologia*, vol XVIII: 772

Pavlowitch, Stevan K. 1999. *A History of The Balkans*. London: Addison Wesley Longman Limited.

Pop, Vasile Gr. 1876. *Conspect asupra literaturei române*, Bucureşti: Editura Eminescu, vol. 2: 147-148.

Prevelakis, Georgios. 1994. *Les Balkans. Cultures et géopolitique*. Paris: Ed. Nathan.

Ruffini, Mario. 1934. "Il golfo della Spezia nella descrizione di una principessa romena" in *Il Commune della Spezia*, anno XII, n. 4: 3-4.

Thiesse. Anne-Marie. 1999. *La création des identités nationales: Europe XVIIIe- XXe siècle*. Paris: Seuil.

Todorova, Maria. 1997. *Imagining the Balkans*. Oxford: Oxford University Press.

Verdel, Helena and Traude Kogoj (eds). 2003. *Die hundert bedeutendsten Frauen europäischen Ostens*. Klagenfurt: Wieser Verlag.

Wilson, Katharina M. (ed.). 1991. *An encyclopedia of continental women writers*, vol. I. A-K. New York-London: Garland Publishing.

Zaharia, Claudia D.C. 1932. *Dora d'Istria. Viaţa şi opera sa*. Bistriţa: s.n.

Zbuchea, Gheorghe. 2003. *Românii şi Balcanii în epoca modernă*. Craiova: Ed. Scrisul Românesc.

# The Vision of an Equal Nation: Russian-Finnish Author and Feminist Marie Linder (1840-1870)

*Kati Launis*

ABSTRACT This chapter presents an early feminist novel that engaged with a heated debate on women and their position in Finland in 1860s. Marie Linder's *A Woman of Our Time* (1867) deals with the rights of women to study and work, and their possibilities outside the institution of marriage. Linder's novel is connected with the Russian debate on the 'new woman' and classical liberal feminism. It shows how early feminist thinking in Finland included elements of the liberal traditions but was also drawing on Hegel and the nationalist movement. It expresses one alternative in the new way of thinking – a new way of creating a more equal society

THE CREATION OF NATIONAL IDENTITIES WAS one of the main projects of 19th century Europe. The phenomenon was also seen in Finland, which (after the so-called Finnish War, 1808–09) was separated from Sweden and incorporated into Russia as an Autonomous Grand Duchy. From the beginning of the 19th century the intelligentsia – the educated, Swedish-speaking elite of the society – was eagerly constructing a Finnish national identity and spreading the idea of this new kind of cultural identity, Finnishness, among the common folk. "Swedish we are no more, Russian we don't want to be, let us be Finns" is one of the most famous phrases of the time.[1]

In Finland, as well as in other countries, literature was seen as part of the national project, an essential tool for imagining the nation. The most influential of those who advanced this idea in Finland was J.V. Snellman (1806-81), a philosopher and politician whose thoughts were based on the

[1] See Henrik Meinander, *Suomen historia: Linjat, rakenteet, käännekohdat (The History of Finland)*, Paula Autio (tr.), Helsinki: Werner Söderström Oy, 2006: 108-109. I wish to express my warm thanks to Heidi Grönstrand and Viola Parente-Čapková for their valuable comments on this article.

works of German philosopher G.W.F Hegel. Snellman believed that the basis of a national spirit was the national language and a literature written in that language.[2] Works such as the Finnish National epic *Kalevala* (1835, 1849), compiled by the author and doctor Elias Lönnrot, or poems by J.L. Runeberg, who has been called the Finnish national poet, played an important role in the shaping of a Finnish national identity.[3]

During the same decade, the 1840s, when *Kalevala* was published and the national 'awakening' was spreading – in tight connection with the rise of several newspapers, publishers and modern literary genres – female novelists entered the literary field in Finland.[4]

The first Finnish female writers concentrated not on the wars or deeds of the ancient heroes or the descriptions of modest country folk, like their male contemporaries did in the form of epic and poetry; rather, the women's genre was the novel and their focus was mainly on the then present day (or the recent history, like in Fredrika Runeberg's two historical novels) and the private sphere: the home, love, marriage and the possibilities for women in developing society. The female protagonists of their novels – according to the 18$^{th}$ and 19$^{th}$-century plot conventions[5] – fall in love and get married, as in Fredrika Carsten's *Murgrönan. Finskt original* (1840, Ivy: Finnish Original) or in Charlotta Falkman's *Nyårsafton* (1848, New Year's Eve); or commit adultery, as in Wendla Randelin's *Den Fallna* (1848, The Fallen), or they die, as in Falkman's *En Prestgård in N-d* (1847, A Vicarage in N-d). In Fredrika

---

[2] Pertti Karkama, *Kirjallisuus janykyaika (Literature and the Present Time),* Helsinki: Finnish Literature Society, 1994: 56–57.

[3] *Kalevala* is based on the Finnish and Karelían oral folklore and mythology, and the earliest stories in it, collected by Lönnrot from hundreds of runesingers, date back to prehistoric days. In *Kalevala,* Finnishness was defined through its glorious past and ancient, godlike heroes, such as Väinämöinen and the smith Ilmarinen. See Michael Branch, "Finnish Oral Poetry, *Kalevala*, and *Kanteletar*" in George C. Schoolfield (ed.). *A History of Finland's Literature*, Lincoln & London: University of Nebraska Press, 1998: 3–33.

[4] The part played by women was crucial in the development of the novel in Finland, as well as in many other countries too. See Grönstrand, Heidi. *Naiskirjailija, romaani ja kirjallisuuden merkitys 1840-luvulla.* (The Woman Writer, the Novel, and the Significance of Literature in the 1840s.) Helsinki: Finnish Literature Society, 2005. and Launis, Kati. *Kerrotut naiset. Suomen ensimmäiset naisten kirjoittamat romaanit naiseuden määrittelijöinä (Narrated Women: The First Novels Written by Women in Finland Defining Womanhood),* Helsinki: Finnish Literature Society, 2005.

[5] See Nancy K. Miller, *The Heroine's Text: Readings in the French and English Novel, 1722-1782*, New York: Columbia University Press, 1980.

Runeberg's *Fru Catharina Boije och hennes döttrar* (1858, Mrs Catharina Boije and her Daughters), both of these conventional endings, marriage and death, are represented in the fates of two sisters.

This kind of *domestic fiction*, which took its themes and forms from private life, rose to a dominant position in the European novel at the end of the 18th century.[6] In Finland, these early novelists did not have any tradition available: they were producing it in dialogue with existing literature in other countries. Especially inspiring for them were Swedish female writers Sophie von Knorring, Emilie Flygare-Carlén and Fredrika Bremer, who were established writers by the 1830s. Sweden was in many senses an important channel for Finnish literary culture: the Finnish reading public, consisting of a small amount of middle or upper class people, read novels not only in the original language but also the Swedish translations, imported from nearby Sweden.

Thus, it can be said that women writers in the mid-19th century Finland did not, in their novels, concentrate on the "national" in the traditional, mainstream (or malestream) sense of the word. However, the developing literary institution and genre, the novel, offered them the possibility of entering the public sphere and to express their views on issues such as family, women and marriage.[7] In the heated social and political debate of that time, those issues were not only private, they were also public, national issues: family was seen as a basic unit of the nation, as a central political idea, part of the theory of the state from the 1840s on.[8] For women, the forum of for the negotiation of the 'national order' was fiction, especially the novel: other forums of public speech were closed to them, and under the rule of men. Women in other countries were in a similar kind of a situation. According to

---

[6] Armstrong, Nancy. *Desire and Domestic Fiction. A Political History of the Novel.* New York & Oxford: Oxford University Press, 1987:8.

[7] This female viewpoint on nationality – in this case the ideas on family, marriage and women's rights – has often been forgotten in the study of nations, nationalism, and national movements, which have been treated as non-gendered phenomena. See e.g. Linda Racioppi and Katherine O'Sullivan See, "Engendering nation and national identity" in *Women, States, and Nationalism. At home in the nation*? Ranchod-Nilsson, Sita and Mary Ann Tétreault (eds). London & New York: Routledge, 2000:18–34.

[8] Kai Häggman, *Perheen vuosisata, Perheen ihanne ja sivistyneistön elämäntapa 1800-luvun Suomessa* (The Century of Family: The Ideal Family and Bourgeois Lifestyle in the Nineteenth-Century Finland), Helsinki: Finnish Historical Society, 1994: 24.

Ellen Moers, "The novel and the poem were women's only instruments of social action in the early 19th century: literature was their pulpit, tribune, academy, commission, and parliament all in one. 'I want to do something with the pen', said Harriet Martineau, 'since no other means of action in politics are in a woman's power."[9] In the contemporary reviews in Finland, women's novels were seen as a means to define the needs of changing society. They were used to define the ideals of family and womanhood – and in that way they were taken in the service of the national ideology.[10]

I concentrate on one of these 19th century female nation imaginers and builders, the Russian-Finnish Countess Marie Linder (née Mushin-Pushkin, 1840-1870). Her feminist views on women's role in society differ quite radically from those of her contemporary female writers in Finland – worldwide, though, she had many literary sisters. As I will point out, the openly feminist, liberal views Linder expresses in her novel can be connected to the cosmopolitanism of the author: Linder has been included in the 19th century Finnish literary history but she was first and foremost a (female) citizen of the world – a *cultural mediator or agent* through whom the foreign influences, debates and ideas, literary and others, between Finland, Russia and other world travelled. In a similar kind of a way, like, for example a later Finnish-Estonian female writer Aino Kallas (1878-1956), Linder was between different cultures, in no-(wo)man's land, which made it challenging to define her position in the literary field.[11]

These cosmopolitan debates and ideas are present in her novel *En qvinna af vår tid. Karaktersteckning af Stella* (1867, A Woman of our Time: A Character Sketch by Stella) where she focuses on the subjection of women in the patriarchal 19th-century society. Linder stated her aims clearly in the preface, which was, however, left out at the suggestion by the publisher, who

---

[9] Ellen Moers, *Literary Women. The Great Writers*, New York: Oxford University Press, 1976, 1985: 20.

[10] Heidi Grönstrand, *Naiskirjailija, romaani ja kirjallisuuden merkitys 1840-luvulla* (The Woman Writer, the Novel, and the Significance of Literature in the 1840s), Helsinki: Finnish Literature Society, 2005: 107.

[11] Maarit Leskelä-Kärki. *Kirjoittaen maailmassa. Krohnin sisaret ja kirjallinen elämä* (The Krohn Sisters: Lives in Writing), Helsinki: Finnish Literature Society, 2006: 138-142; Kukku Melkas, *Historia, halu ja tiedon käärme Aino Kallaksen tuotannossa* (History, Desire, and the Serpent of Knowledge in the Works of Aino Kallas), Helsinki: Finnish Literature Society, 2006: 61.

thought it to be too defensive. The lines have been preserved in a letter she wrote to her publisher:

> 'A Woman of Our Time' is meant to be the first part of the series treating women's position in the society. Several half elaborated manuscripts will merge into another piece of work, for which the writer is asking in advance the favour of the reading public. The only defence she can offer to the mistakes at every step is that she learned the first words of Swedish seven years ago. She is still working to achieve the perfection of this beautiful and noble language, from which she is still far distant.[12]

My aim is to look more closely at how Linder, as a feminist of the 1860s, saw the relationship between gender and nation. How did she narrate and define the role of female citizens in the developing nation? The central figure in imagining a more equal world is the heroine of the novel, the strong-minded Lady Lucy Suffridge, who is trying to find her own subjectivity and active role in a nation.

## A portrait of "A Woman of our Time"

Marie Linder is a woman who, during her short life[13], crossed several borders, both imaginary and real, including the borders of nations, languages, and also borders between socially constructed gender roles – both in her own life and in a figure of the rebellious heroine of her novel. Linder was born in Russia to an aristocratic family of Mushin-Pushkins, whose close family friends had been, for example, the poet Mikhail Lermontov, the historian

[12] Quoted in Katri Lehto, *Kytäjän kreivitär. Marie Linderin elämä* (The Countess of Kytäjä: The Life of Marie Linder), Helsinki: Otava, 1986: 263, all the translations from Swedish to English in this article are mine.

[13] Marie Linder died when she was only thirty years old and a mother of three children. Her life was full of illness, malady, depression and anxiety, which is obvious when reading her biography written by Katri Lehto. The cause of her death in 1870 is not quite clear – she had fever and cramps, and she used chloroform for her many diseases and pain, but contemporaries spoke more or less directly of suicide. *Ibid.*, 309-310.

Nikolai Karamzin and the most famous member of the family, the poet Aleksander Pushkin.[14]

From the beginning of her life till the end, Linder's other home country was Finland. Her mother, Emilie Stjernvall, was Finnish and her aunt was the well-known Finnish charity patroness Aurora Karamzin, 'Maman Aurora', who took care of Marie after both her parents had died. Finland had thus been familiar to Marie from childhood. Later, she married a Finnish Count Constantin Linder and moved to Finland. According to her biographer Katri Lehto, she was a figure both admired and disapproved of in the society of Helsinki, the capital of Finland – disapproved because of her liveliness and her not-so-conventional behaviour for the wife of a well-known nobleman and the mother of three children. She was keen on acting, discussion, dancing, drinking champagne – and, on top of everything else, writing.[15]

Linder started to write stories for newspapers in 1866. One year later she published her (one and only) novel *A Woman of our Time*. As was typical of the time, she wrote under a pseudonym, even though the author behind it was known, as the reviews indicate. Her pseudonym, Stella, mentioned in the subtitle of the novel, was already familiar to the readers of her stories in newspapers. The novel was written in Swedish, which was the language of the educated classes in Finland until the 1870s, when the Finnish language began to be treated as the language of literature. Swedish was not so familiar to Linder, but she studied it eagerly and was assisted in learning. The novel sold well and was translated into Danish in 1868.[16]

*A Woman of our Time* is the story an English aristocrat, Lady Lucy Suffridge, and her anxiety in a patriarchal 19$^{th}$ century world, under the rule of her despotic, insane father, Lord Robert Suffridge.[17] It narrates the story of

---

[14] *Ibid.*, 39-42, 58; see also Maj Wickman, *Marie Linder. Liv & litteratur* (Marie Linder. Life & Literature), Ekenäs: Ekenäs tryckeri, 2003: 7-18.

[15] Katri Lehto, *Kytäjän kreivitär. Marie Linderin elämä* (The Countess of Kytäjä: The Life of Marie Linder), Helsinki: Otava, 1986: 222-224.

[16] See the database *Women Writers* http://neww.huygens.knaw.nl/. The information about the Danish translation was found in the collections of National Library of Denmark http://www.kb.dk/en/nb/samling/ds/index.html, with the indispensable help from Eeva-Liisa Haanpää from the Finnish Literature Society. The Danish translation is also mentioned in the volume *Biograafisia tietoja Suomen naisista eri työaloilla* (Biographical information on Finnish women in different fields of work), 1896. The Finnish translation by Benita Holopainen came out in 2009.

[17] George C. Schoolfield, "National Romanticism – A Golden Age?" in George C. (ed.). *A History of Finland's Literature*, Schoolfield, Lincoln & London: University of

Lucy's childhood in the gloomy castle of Abbey Hall, an ancient monastery, and her travels to America and France, her love for a Swedish Baron, and finally her difficult choice: should she choose freedom, or marriage to the man she loves. The cosmopolitanism of the settings – England, France, and America – as well as the cosmopolitanism of the author herself, distinguishes Linder's novel from other early novels written by women in Finland. They are mainly situated in Finland or in Sweden, like Fredrika Wilhelmina Carstens's epistolary novel *Murgrönan* (1840, Ivy), which was the first novel published in Finland.

Lucy Suffridge is described in the first chapter of the novel in a letter, which according to the narrator reveals her nature as faithfully as possible. She is described being 'a living mystery' she wants the best for everyone but can be sarcastic and sharp; she is virtuous, almost puritan, but often capricious. In a phrase, she is 'a mysterious woman'. Lucy is also connected with features which are culturally marked as masculine: reason, will, learnedness, courage, rebellion and quest.It is these masculine features that make those who disapprove of her behavior call her 'a bluestocking, a man in a crinoline'.

Lucy's figure is an essential part of the theme of emancipation expressed in the novel. Linder's novel is a comment on women's rights, published in a time when the women's rights movement began to rise in Europe and in the United States. An explicit connection to the movement is Lucy's last name: it is based on the word *suffrage*, which is linked to the strengthening demands for women's right to vote. The name of the heroine could also be an allusion to the historical Lucy S., namely Lucy Stone (1818-1893), who was the founder of the American Woman Suffrage Association, organized in 1869.[18] The central theme of the novel, the subjection of women, occurs right in the heroine's first lines – with the interesting opening word 'no':

---

Nebraska Press, 1998: 332, considers the figure of Lord Suffridge as distantly reminiscent of Sheridan LeFanu's *Uncle Silas*; a Gothic novel which indeed seems to have a great deal in common with Linder's novel.

[18] Leslie Wheeler, "Lucy Stone: Radical Beginnings (1818-1893)" in Dale Spender (ed.). *Feminist Theorists: Three Centuries of Key Women Thinkers*. New York: Pantheon Books, 1983: 124-136. The first women's rights convention in the United States was held at Seneca Falls in 1848; this event has been often seen as the beginning of the movement for women's rights in USA.

> No! A thousand times no! When we have strength, courage and understanding, we should not sit at home like dolls and sew just to have something to do with our hands. (…) I want to be free, free like a lion in the woods![19]

What is central to the portrait of Lucy is that the dominant bourgeois image of a woman as mother and wife, as the 'Angel in the House' – the phrase describing the ideal woman especially in the Victorian cultural imagination – is not for her: she does not want to get married at all, and the narrator explains that taking care of children is not part of her nature. In the novel, the theme of individual freedom transcends the themes of home, family and motherhood. Home is not the 'natural' domain of women – it is closer to a prison, in which the prisoners, women, are buried alive. To Lucy, these women, who devote their lives to the home and its happiness, appear as creatures whose wings have been cut:

> There are people whose souls are without wings; there are other unhappy ones, who, because of their education and unfavourable circumstances, have had their wings cut; let them feel happy in a circle of everyday prose, let them speak of woman's duty to use her skills for the good of domestic happiness. I honour them; but let their virtue not fall like a curse over those who understand life differently, and whose hearts extend their love much longer.[20]

This explicit emancipation demonstrates an important difference compared with earlier women writers in Finland in the 1840s and 1850s. Lucy dreams of studying, working in a profession, and being useful in the public sphere – not just the private family sphere. She admires freedom and America, "the promised land for all lovers of freedom" – a feature which connects Linder's novel with Fredrika Bremer's well-known admiration for the New World.[21] Linder does not focus on the importance of women's role as mothers and wives, as did, for example Charlotta Falkman (1795-1882), a contemporary Finnish woman writer. Charlotta Falkman also used, in one of her four

---

[19] Marie Linder, *En qvinna af vår tid. Karaktersteckning af Stella (A Woman of Our Time: A Character Sketch by Stella)*, Helsingfors: Theodor Sederholms boktryckeri, 1867: 17.
[20] *Ibid.*, 126.
[21] George Schoolfield, "National Romanticism – A Golden Age?": 332.

novels, the pseudonym "en finsk merborgarinna" (a Finnish female citizen), which highlights the gendered nature of citizenship.

Not even the idea of *social motherhood*, according to which unmarried women could work outside the home in the fields of teaching and nursing, is at the core of her novel; this idea was introduced in Finland along with Fredrika Bremer's writings during the 1850s.[22] The central, fundamental idea in "A Woman of Our Time" is the idea of individual freedom, which should concern both women and men. Linder pictures independent, female subjectivity, and imagines a time, when women are "free like a lion in the woods", when "the heavy chains of a prisoner" are broken down, and have access to a proper education and to the professions. This kind of an equal society outlined in the novel is – unfortunately and tragically – in the context of the mid-19th century possible only in dreams, as Linder points out in the extract describing Lucy's thoughts during her trip to the America:

> Several times, when she was alone, she began to laugh at her peculiar thoughts. She forgot herself; she forgot her personality, all those circumstances which bind a person like a slave to conventional laws: she chose herself a profession, she saw herself working in it, but in a moment the illusion was gone – and she was a woman again.[23]

It is notable that the feminist ideal of a new, individual kind of a woman constructed in the novel is an upper class woman. Linder's novel attaches to her own, high social position, but also to the class discourse typical of her own time. In this discourse, the pursuit of independent womanhood was the privilege of middle or upper-class women, and the rights of women were identified specifically with the rights of women of this kind. In 1906, for example, when Finnish women gained the right to vote (as the first in Europe), women were not struggling together to achieve this goal; on the contrary, the gap between women from different classes was wide.[24]

---

[22] Kai Häggman, *Perheen vuosisata. Perheen ihanne ja sivistyneistön elämäntapa 1800-luvun Suomessa* (The Century of Family: The Ideal Family and Bourgeois Lifestyle in the Nineteenth-Century Finland), Helsinki: Finnish Historical Society, 1994: 98-200.

[23] Marie Linder, *En qvinna af vår tid. Karaktersteckning af Stella* (A Woman of Our Time: A Character Sketch by Stella), Helsingfors: Theodor Sederholms boktryckeri. 1867: 27.

[24] Irma Sulkunen, "Suomi naisten äänioikeuden edelläkävijänä (Finland as the Forerunner of Women's Suffrage)" in Irma Sulkunen, Maria Lähteenmäki and Aura

Solutions concerning narration and genre are connected, inseparably, with the central theme of the novel. Marie Linder's novel is written in a form mixing, particularly, the *Gothic novel* – which she uses as a way to criticize the old, unjust world, the core of which is the subjection of women[25] – and the *Sentimental social novel,* in the way that Margaret Cohen has defined the term. The novel focuses on the social suffering of women with conventions drawn from the sentimental, rather than the realist lineage.[26] Cohen studies the novels written by, for example, such French women writers as Caroline Marbouty, Flora Tristan and George Sand, but the same phenomena can be seen in Finland later; and not only in Linder's novel. For example, another female writer of the time, Wendla Randelin, demands a pension fund for handicraftsmen in her adultery novel *Den Fallna* (1848, The Fallen), and Charlotta Falkman criticizes the hard working conditions of needlewomen. These realistic features of women's novels foreshadow the arrival of literary realism (in Finland in the 1880s) and make use of a variety of characters and topics typical of the movement, like adultery, seduction, mental illness, and girls' education.[27]

## Marie Linder as a cultural agent

Literary scholars and historians have, for a few years now, actively searched for new ways to examine literature, to replace the nationalistic view by drawing attention to transnational literary relations. This viewpoint has also brought up a lot of new information on the history of women's writing. In Finland, it has resulted in studies in which, for example, mid-19th century Finnish women writers have been examined in close connection with their

Korppi-Tommola (eds). *Naiset eduskunnassa* (Women in the Parliament), Helsinki: Edita, 2006: 32-68.

25 More closely of the Gothic in Linder's novel see Kati Launis, "'I want to be free!' Marie Linder's Novel *En qvinna af vår tid* as an Early Comment on Women's Rights" in Päivi Lappalainen and Lea Rojola (eds). *Women's Voices. Female Authors and Feminist Criticism in the Finnish Literary Tradition,* Helsinki: Finnish Literature Society, 2007: 22-25; Launis, "From Italy to the Finnish Woods", in press.

26 Margaret Cohen, "Women and Fiction in the Nineteenth Century" in Timothy Unwin (ed.). *The Cambridge Companion to the French Novel: From 1800 to the present*, Cambridge: Cambridge University Press, 1997: 8.

27 Kati Launis, *Kerrotut naiset. Suomen ensimmäiset naisten kirjoittamat romaanit naiseuden määrittelijöinä* (Narrated Women: The First Novels Written by Women in Finland Defining Womanhood), Helsinki: Finnish Literature Society, 2005: 90.

Swedish contemporaries, especially Fredrika Bremer, and Helena Westermarck, the naturalist female writer from the 1880s, in connection with George Eliot.[28]

Marie Linder's case proves, for its part, how important it is to look across the national borders when thinking about the history of women writers. Even though Linder has been included in the 19th century Finnish literary history, she was first and foremost a cosmopolitan, who spoke many languages, including French, English, Russian and Swedish, travelled extensively and moved in literary circles. Linder's position was not local, but cosmopolitan. Neither is her high social status irrelevant here. Cosmopolitan life, travels to European baths, knowledge of languages, and leisure time enabling reading and writing: all this was self-evidently part of a life of an aristocratic woman.

In Linder's novel, cosmopolitanism can be seen (at the thematic level) in such ideologies as liberalism and women's rights. It is particularly notable that she supported the idea of liberalism. She fastened, thus, on the Anglo-American liberal tradition, emphasizing the importance of individuality, not that of communality, which was the core of the Finnish national movement called Fennomania, based on the German Hegelian tradition.[29] Linder was also close to the most radical liberal group in Finland, called "bloodless". These 'radical students' and 'utopians' despised the Finnish national movement and religion. Linder's close friend and the publisher of her novel, Theodor Sederholm, was one of those 'democrats and burgesses' who in his writings opposed the authorities, censorship and class pride. The main organ of liberals, *Helsingfors Dagblad,* published Linder's stories.[30]

New ideas were travelling from one country to another, being transformed into different forms in different cultural contexts. One example of these travelling ideas is the symbolism of slavery Linder uses to describe the subjection of women. In her novel, the bitterness of being a woman is expressed in terms of slavery, martyrdom, and imprisonment:

---

[28] Heidi Grönstrand, "In Fredrika Bremer's Footsteps: Early Women Authors and the Rise of the Novel Genre in Finland" in *NORA. Nordic Journal of Feminist and Gender Research,* vol. 16. 2008: 35-39.

[29] Tuija Pulkkinen, *The Postmodern and Political Agency*, Helsinki: University of Helsinki, 1996: 9-43.

[30] Katri Lehto, *Kytäjän kreivitär. Marie Linderin elämä* (The Countess of Kytäjä: The Life of Marie Linder), Helsinki: Otava, 1986: 229-231.

> Is it not martyrdom, that when you are at the age when you could be useful, you find it to be impossible, that you're whole life is useless? You see other people work and make themselves useful, you try to reach the same goal, but whereever you try to use your power, you feel how the heavy chains of a prisoner bind you to a pillar, from which you can't move more than certain, fixed steps – the pillar is the demands of the society for women – chains are again the education the same society orders to her.[31]

The similar symbols of slavery are used by the central figure of liberalism, John Stuart Mill, who in his *The Subjection of Women* (1869), a thorough analysis of the dependent position of women, several times compares women with slaves: "no slave is a slave to the same lengths and in so full a sense of the word, as a wife is".[32] But symbols of slavery were also common in the novels written by such 19th-century women writers as Fredrika Bremer, Harriet Beecher-Stowe, Charlotte Brontë and George Eliot. Ellen Moers – following Virginia Woolf – calls them the writers of the epic age. What they have in common in their literary works are the feelings of rage and anger due to injustice and oppression[33] – feelings that characterise very precisely Marie Linder's novel too. It is more than probable that Linder knew their works. But more relevant than the question of direct influence is rather the question of *confluence* between these female writers of the same era: not the direct connections, but the shared interest in women's rights as seen in their works.[34] Thus, even though Linder, with her openly feminist novel, is radical in the Finnish context of the 1860s, world-wide she was not an exception or alone: she had literary sisters.

Contemporary critics in Finland were quite harsh towards the theme of women's emancipation expressed in Linder's novel. The reception, if not

[31] Marie Linder, *En qvinna af vår tid. Karaktersteckning af Stella (A Woman of Our Time: A Character Sketch by Stella)*, Helsingfors: Theodor Sederholms boktryckeri, 1867: 182.

[32] John Stuart Mill, *On Liberty. Representative Government. The Subjection of Women. Three Essays by John Stuart Mill*, London: Oxford University Press, 1869, 1971: 463.

[33] Ellen Moers, *Literary Women. The Great Writers*, New York: Oxford University Press, 1976, 1985: 13-18.

[34] On the terms influence vs. confluence, see Carol Hanberry MacKay, "Lines of Confluence in Fredrika Bremer and Charlotte Brontë" in NORA – *Nordic Journal of Feminist and Gender Research* vol 2 (2), 1994:119-129.

totally crushing, was certainly not sympathetic. This is not rare at all when thinking about the reception of women's novels more broadly; George Sand's early novels, for example, were denounced as immoral and anti-matrimonial by several critics in Britain.[35] In Finland, Kaarlo Bergbom, the founder of the Finnish National Theatre, wrote in his review of Linder's novel that the heroine of the novel does not behave as a reasonable woman should, and that emancipation is an already passé view in Europe.[36] One anonymous critic complained of the daring opinions concerning women's position in the novel, and another reviewer made ironic remarks about the 'real women of our time', who wander (like Lucy does) around with Virgil's epic in their hands. According to this review, Lucy is a stupid woman, who does not understand her real responsibilities and homely duties[37] – in other words, her role as a proper female citizen in the service of a patriarchal order, as a mother, a wife, and a dutiful, tender daughter to her ill father.

What is interesting is that contemporary criticism paid attention to the cosmopolitanism of the novel. Kaarlo Bergbom wrote in his review that the novel is cosmopolitan in the very sense of that word:

> This new novel has a unique place among the literature of our country; it proves the totally foreign education of its author. Foreign writers have surely influenced our poets also earlier and, in a way, there is nothing to complain; but this novel of Stella's could have appeared equally well in any other European country as in Finland. The novel is cosmopolitan with regard to its purpose, ideas and style of writing; cosmopolitan also in a sense that though the action claims to take place in England, all its characters and habits show very little of the English character.[38]

---

[35] Kerstin Wiedemann, "Intertextuality and Network Creation: References to George Sand in Novels by Mid-nineteenth-Century German Women Writers" in Hilary Brown and Gillian Dow (eds). *Readers, Writers, Salonnières: Female Networks in Europe, 1700-1900,* Bern: Peter Lang, 2011: 163.

[36] Kaarlo Bergbom, *En qvinna af vår tid. Karaktersteckning af Stella* (A Woman of Our Time: A Character Sketch by Stella) in *Kirjallinen Kuukauslehti* (1), 1868: 22-23.

[37] *Helsingfors Dagblad.* 9.1.1868: 2; *Åbo Underrättelser* 8.2.1868: 2. See the *Historical Newspaper Library* (the digital collection of the National Library of Finland), http://digi.kansalliskirjasto.fi/index.html?language=en

[38] Kaarlo Bergbom, *En qvinna af vår tid. Karaktersteckning af Stella* (A Woman of Our Time: A Character Sketch by Stella) in *Kirjallinen Kuukauslehti* (1) 1868: 22-23.

Bergbom continues by connecting Linder's novel to the French and German novel tradition and its well-known female representatives, George Sand and Ida Hahn-Hahn:

> The heroine, Lucy, for example reminds us much more of French and German examples (e.g. of George Sand's Quintilia Cavalcant or Ida Hahn-Hahn's Ilda Schönholm) than of the female ideals of English or Finnish literature.[39]

This kind of a feminized comparison was a regular custom of the reviewers of the time. Women writers were frequently categorized by comparing them with their foreign counterparts; there are, for example, a number of references to women writers as "the German George Sand" or "the French Hannah More"[40] – or, as in this case, "the Finnish George Sand and Hahn-Hahn". In 19th-century Germany, for example, it was common to compare women writers with Sand; she was a key female figure, an important reference that helped to structure the field of female literary activity.

Linder's biography does not reveal any actual contacts, such as letter writing or visits, with Sand or any other women writers. However, she enters the same discussion about love, marriage and the subjection of women as Sand's early works *Indiana*, *Valentine*, *Lélia* and *Jacques,* and many of the later novels by women writers inspired by them.[41] Sand's works were certainly familiar to Linder: Sand is mentioned in her biography and, moreover, she was enormously popular in Russia from the 1830s on.[42] French was Linder's main language – of course, she had also heard and spoke

---

[39] *Ibid.*

[40] Hilary Brown and Gillian Dow, "Introduction" in *Readers, Writers, Salonnières: Female Networks in Europe, 1700-1900*: 4.

[41] Kerstin Wiedemann, "Intertextuality and Network Creation: References to George Sand in Novels by Mid-nineteenth-Century German Women Writers" in Hilary Brown and Gillian Dow (eds). *Readers, Writers, Salonnières: Female Networks in Europe, 1700-1900*: 165-167.

[42] Sanna Turoma, "Suuret kertojat 1840-1890" (Great Narrators 1840-1890) in Kirsti Ekonen and Sanna Turoma (eds). *Venäläisen kirjallisuuden historia* (The History of Russian Literature). Helsinki: Gaudeamus, 2011: 276.

Russian since her childhood – and French literature was more familiar to her.[43]

Sand was also among the novelists Marie Linder read. She was a passionate reader, which is revealed from in a short biography by the author and historian Zacharias Topelius, her friend and supporter. Among the writers she read were, for example, Victor Hugo, Alphonse de Lamartine, Casimir Delavigne, Aleksander Pushkin, Mikhail Lermontov and English novelists – although Topelius does not specify which.[44] Marie Linder's husband mentions, in his letter to Topelius, that his wife also read Charles Dickens and Fredrika Bremer. Not only Bremer's but also Emilie Flygare-Carlén's and George Sand's novels were, according to her biographer, read aloud in the evenings.[45] However, Linder does not, unlike many of her contemporaries, practice name-dropping in her novel: the only authors she mentions by name are Cervantes (*Don Quijote*) and the ancient Roman poet Virgil, whose epic *Aeneid* she lets her heroine read.

Kaarlo Bergbom's review also shows how well known these two writers, Sand and Hahn-Hahn, were in Finland: he assumes that the readers of the newspaper know them. Even though Sand's works were not translated into Finnish until 1870, when the Finnish translation of the *La petite Fadette* (1849) was published, her works were read in Swedish translations long before that. *Lavinia* and *Pauline,* for example, were published in the Swedish novel series of foreign literature,[46] ordered frequently by the Swedish-speaking readership in Finland. They were also, most probably in Linder's case, read in the original language. Not only translations, but also newspapers were an important medium to introduce foreign literature to Finnish readers. There are several references to Hahn-Hahn and Sand in Finnish newspapers, either articles on them or advertisements of their books. For example Ida Hahn-Hahn is mentioned because of her travel to Sweden to visit Fredrika

---

[43] Katri Lehto, *Kytäjän kreivitär. Marie Linderin elämä* (The Countess of Kytäjä: The Life of Marie Linder), Helsinki: Otava, 1986: 87.

[44] Zacharias Topelius, "Marie Linder" in *Finska qvinnor på olika arbetsområden. Biografiskt album* (Finnish Women in Different Fields of Work. Biographical Volume), Helsingfors: Otava, 1892: 168. A possible connection to Lermontov could be the name of Linder's novel, which reminds us of the title of Lermontov's famous A Hero of Our Time (1840), http://en.wikipedia.org/wiki/A_Hero_of_Our_Time – with the exception that Linder deals in her novel with a *heroine*, not a hero, of our time.

[45] Katri Lehto, *Kytäjän kreivitär. Marie Linderin elämä* (The Countess of Kytäjä: The Life of Marie Linder), Helsinki: Otava, 1986: 133.

[46] See *Helsingfors Tidningar* 13.5.1837: 27; *Borgå Tidning* 29.9.1841: 4.

Bremer, and her book *Ein Reiseversuch im Norden* (1843).[47] Hahn-Hahn is also mentioned as one of the most famous "bluestockings" of the time, while George Sand is described as a "shining star" and, conversely, "a fallen woman", who "smokes [a] cigar like a dandy".[48]

One female 'path' which would be inspiring to trace, but which is left outside the scope of this article, is the connection between Marie Linder's novel and the extensive debate on the *New Woman* in Russia (Linder's country of birth), during the 1860s. The Woman Question (*ženskij vopros*) concentrated on questions regarding the legal, social and cultural position of (aristocratic) women. Such female writers as Nadežda Hvoščinskaja, Julia Žadovskaja, Sofja Stanova and Avdotja Panajeva demanded the right for education and paid labour outside the family, discussing in their novels the issues around this "gendering awakening".[49]

## Conclusion: A liberal-feminist vision of an equal nation

Marie Linder imagines in her novel *A Woman of our Time* a better nation, for which women and men work, together, side by side. It is a nation based on equality, a nation where women can study, work, and have independent agency in the public field. For Lucy, this is a dream, a dear hope, which is not, during the course on the novel, realized. However, this vision glints as a possibility, as an open question. At the end of the novel Lucy hesitates as to whether she should choose freedom *or* marriage to a man she loves – her father is dead and a notable inheritance is waiting for her. Her honorable suitor, the Swedish Baron Oscar Lejonstjerna, affirms to her that she does not have to make the choice: "Together, infusing each other's courage, we shall try, on the golden wings of freedom, to reach the highest goal: *The truth of life*!"[50]

The novel ends with these Oscar's pompous words. The end is left open: the reader does not know what Lucy's final choice will be. But what is clear

---

[47] *Helsingfors Tidningar* 17.6.1843: 2.

[48] *Helsingfors Morgonblad* 18.4.1844: 4; *Åbo Underrättelser* 9.1.1839: 1; *Åbo Underrättelser* 2.6.1841: 1-2.

[49] See Arja Rosenholm, *Gendering Awakening. Femininity and the Russian Woman Question of the 1860s*, Helsinki: Aleksanteri-instituutti, 1999.

[50] Marie Linder, *En qvinna af vår tid. Karaktersteckning af Stella* (A Woman of Our Time: A Character Sketch by Stella), Helsingfors: Theodor Sederholms boktryckeri, 1867: 269.

is that nothing is more important to Lucy than her individual freedom – not even romantic marriage, one of the bourgeois ideals of the time. This urge for freedom stems from the liberal, and more closely the liberal feminist ideas of the time, which, as I have earlier discussed, make up the political context of the novel. Even though Linder, in the Finnish context, can be called an early and quite radical female voice, worldwide she had literary sisters: similar kinds of expressions of injustice and oppression can be read from the works of other female writers of the era. For them, as well as for Marie Linder, the means to imagine an equal nation and show the faults of the present system was the developing genre of the novel.

## Select Bibliography

### A. Primary Sources

Linder, Marie. 1867. *En qvinna af vår tid. Karaktersteckning af Stella.* (A Woman of Our Time: A Character Sketch by Stella.) Helsingfors: Theodor Sederholms boktryckeri.

### B. Secondary Sources

Armstrong, Nancy. 1987. *Desire and Domestic Fiction. A Political History of the Novel.* New York & Oxford: Oxford University Press.

Bergbom, Kaarlo (K. B.). 1868. *En qvinna af vår tid. Karaktersteckning af Stella.* (A Woman of Our Time: A Character Sketch by Stella.) in *Kirjallinen Kuukauslehti* (1): 22-23.

*Borgå Tidning* 29.9.1841. Bokhandels-annoncer: Läsebibliothek (Bookstore announcements), 1840-1841.

Branch, Michael. 1998. "Finnish Oral Poetry, *Kalevala*, and *Kanteletar*". in *A History of Finland's Literature*, C. Schoolfield, George (ed.). Lincoln & London: University of Nebraska Press: 3-33.

Brown, Hilary and Down, Gilliand. 2011. "Introduction". in *Readers, Writers, Salonnières: Female Networks in Europe, 1700-1900.* Brown, Hilary and Gillian Dow (eds). Bern: Peter Lang: 1-9.

Cohen, Margaret. 1997. "Women and Fiction in the Nineteenth Century" in *The Cambridge Companion to the French Novel: From 1800 to the present.* Unwin, Timothy (ed.). Cambridge: Cambridge University Press: 54–72.

Grönstrand, Heidi. 2005. *Naiskirjailija, romaani ja kirjallisuuden merkitys 1840-luvulla.* (The Woman Writer, the Novel, and the Significance of Literature in the 1840s.) Helsinki: Finnish Literature Society.

—. 2008. "In Fredrika Bremer's Footsteps: Early Women Authors and the Rise of the Novel Genre in Finland" in *NORA. Nordic Journal of Feminist and Gender Research.* Vol. 16,46-57.

Häggman, Kai. 1994. *Perheen vuosisata. Perheen ihanne ja sivistyneistön elämäntapa 1800-luvun Suomessa.* (The Century of Family: The Ideal Family and Bourgeois Lifestyle in the Nineteenth-Century Finland.) Helsinki: Finnish Historical Society.

*Helsingfors Dagblad* 9.1.1868. Litteratur (Literature). *En qvinna af vår tid. Karaktersteckning af Stella.*

*Helsingfors Morgonblad* 18.4.1844. Plockgods.

*Helsingfors Tidningar* 13.5.1837. Förteckning öfver Böcker, Musikalier, Kartor, m. m. som finnas till salu hos Wasenius & Comp. i Helsingfors.

*Helsingfors Tidningar* 17.6.1843. Fredrika Bremer.

Karkama, Pertti. 1994. *Kirjallisuus janykyaika.* (Literature and the Present Time.) Helsinki: Finnish Literature Society.

Lappalainen, Päivi. 2007. The Politics of Naturalism: Women and Fiction in the 1880s. In *Women's Voices: Female Authors and Feminist Criticism in the Finnish Literary Tradition.* Lappalainen, Päivi and Lea Rojola (eds). Helsinki: Finnish Literature Society: 35-52.

Launis, Kati 2012. "From Italy to the Finnish Woods: The Rise of the Gothic Fiction in Finland" in *Gothic Topographies – Language, Nation Building and Race,* Mehtonen, Päivi and Matti Savolainen (eds). London: Ashgate, in press.

Launis, Kati. 2007. "'I want to be free!' Marie Linder´s Novel *En qvinna af vår tid* as an Early Comment on Women´s Rights" in *Women's Voices. Female Authors and Feminist Criticism in the Finnish Literary Tradition.* Lappalainen, Päivi and Lea Rojola (eds). Helsinki: Finnish Literature Society: 15-34.

Launis, Kati. 2005. *Kerrotut naiset. Suomen ensimmäiset naisten kirjoittamat romaanit naiseuden määrittelijöinä.* (Narrated Women: The First Novels Written by Women in Finland Defining Womanhood.) Helsinki: Finnish Literature Society.

Lehto, Katri. 1986. *Kytäjän kreivitär. Marie Linderin elämä.* (The Countess of Kytäjä: The Life of Marie Linder.) Helsinki: Otava.

Leskelä-Kärki, Maarit. 2006. *Kirjoittaen maailmassa. Krohnin sisaret ja kirjallinen elämä.* (The Krohn Sisters: Lives in Writing.) Helsinki: Finnish Literature Society.

MacKay, Carol Hanberry. 1994 "Lines of Confluence in Fredrika Bremer and Charlotte Brontë." in NORA – *Nordic Journal of Feminist and Gender Research* Vol 2 (2):119-129.

Meinander, Henrik. 2006. *Suomen historia: Linjat, rakenteet, käännekohdat.* (The History of Finland tr. Paula Autio.) Helsinki: Werner Söderström Oy.

Melkas, Kukku. 2006. *Historia, halu ja tiedon käärme Aino Kallaksen tuotannossa.* (History, Desire, and the Serpent of Knowledge in the Works of Aino Kallas). Helsinki: Finnish Literature Society.

Mill, John Stuart. 1869,1971. *On Liberty. Representative Government. The Subjection of Women. Three Essays by John Stuart Mill.* London: Oxford University Press.

Miller, Nancy K. 1980. *The Heroine's Text: Readings in the French and English Novel, 1722-1782.* New York: Columbia University Press.

Moers, Ellen. 1976, 1985. *Literary Women. The Great Writers.* New York: Oxford University Press.

Pulkkinen, Tuija. 1996. *The Postmodern and Political Agency.* Helsinki: University of Helsinki.

Racioppi, Linda and O'Sullivan See, Katherine. 2000. "Engendering nation and national identity" in *Women, States, and Nationalism. At home in the nation*? Ranchod-Nilsson, Sita and Mary Ann Tétreault (eds). London & New York: Routledge: 18-34.

Rosenholm, Arja. 1999. *Gendering Awakening. Femininity and the Russian Woman Question of the 1860s.* Helsinki: Aleksanteri-instituutti.

Schoolfield, George. 1998. "National Romanticism – A Golden Age?" in *A History of Finland's Literature*, Schoolfield, George C., (ed.). Lincoln & London: University of Nebraska Press: 298-353.

Sulkunen, Irma. 2006. "Suomi naisten äänioikeuden edelläkävijänä" (Finland as the Forerunner of Women's Suffrage) in *Naiset eduskunnassa* (Women in the Parliament), Sulkunen, Irma, Maria Lähteenmäki and Aura Korppi-Tommola (eds). Helsinki: Edita: 10-81.

Topelius, Zacharias. 1892. "Marie Linder" in *Finska qvinnor på olika arbetsområden. Biografiskt album* (Finnish Women in Different Fields of Work. Biographical Volume). Helsingfors: Otava: 162-174.

Turoma, Sanna. 2011. "Suuret kertojat 1840-1890" (Great Narrators 1840-1890) in *Venäläisen kirjallisuuden historia* (The History of Russian Literature), Ekonen, Kirsti and Sanna Turoma (eds). Helsinki: Gaudeamus: 253-347.

Wheeler, Leslie. 1983. "Lucy Stone: Radical Beginnings (1818-1893)" in *Feminist Theorists: Three Centuries of Key Women Thinkers.* Dale Spender (ed.). New York: Pantheon Books.

Wickman, Maj. 2003. *Marie Linder. Liv & litteratur* (Marie Linder. Life & Literature). Ekenäs: Ekenäs tryckeri.

Wiedemann, Kerstin. 2011. "Intertextuality and Network Creation: References to George Sand in Novels by Mid-nineteenth-Century German Women Writers" in *Readers, Writers, Salonnières: Female Networks in Europe, 1700-1900.* Brown, Hilary and Gillian Dow (eds). Bern: Peter Lang: 163-178.

*Åbo Underrättelser* 9.1.1839. Laura, Hertiginna af Abrantes.

*Åbo Underrättelser* 2.6.1841. George Sand (Madame Dudevant).

*Åbo Underrättelser* 8.2.1868. Litteraturbref från Nurijärwi II.

# Selma Lagerlöf, Fredrika Bremer and Women as Nation Builders

*Jenny Bergenmar*

ABSTRACT Departing from Selma Lagerlöf's short story "Mamsell Fredrika", this chapter presents Lagerlöf's discussion of women's tasks in the building of an equal and sustainable nation. She compares men's creation of the State with women's creation of the home, and makes this an absolute prerequisite for the good home in a societal and political sense. This discourse has often been compared to Ellen Key's thoughts on motherhood as a vocation, but closer examination points to a different evaluation of women's work, which is not, in Selma Lagerlöf's view, strictly connected to motherhood in its biological sense, but rather detached from the conventional and instead closely related to writing as another kind of women's work.

SELMA LAGERLÖF'S LIFETIME COINCIDED WITH important changes for women in modern society. When she published her first novel, *Gösta Berlings saga* (1891), and the following collection of short stories, *Invisible Links* (1894), she was employed as a teacher in the town of Landskrona in southern Sweden. She had received her education at the Royal Women's Superior Training College in Stockholm, although her father was reluctant to allow her to leave home. She describes her fears when waiting for approval or rejection of her application to the seminar in the story "Two Prophecies" (1908). The exams had lasted almost a week. Selma Lagerlöf makes her young self into somewhat of a fighter. She has enjoyed the contest and feels quite confident about her achievement, even if her education by a governess at home in the province of Värmland might be less solid than the others, who "have attended proper schools in cities".[1] What really causes her anguish is, instead, the prospect of her life if not accepted to the seminar: "If I fail now, I am finished. I will have to apply for a place as a governess with a salary of

[1] Selma Lagerlöf, "The Holy Night", *Christ Legends,* Velma Swanston Howard (tr.), New York: Henry Holt and Company: 3-11 [1908], 1915: 223.

some hundred crowns, or I will have to go back home and take care of the household".[2] A life as a spinster is her greatest fear, but not because she regrets not being married and having children, but because she wants to be independent. When she finally gets the message that she has passed the exams, she vents her relief in a quiet corner: "I am no longer helpless and dependent. I have a course open to me. I will earn my own living and control my own actions. It will be up to me to reach my own goals".[3]

## Mamsell Fredrika and women as citizens

At the beginning of her authorship, Selma Lagerlöf indicates the strong influence of her predecessor, the writer and feminist thinker, Fredrika Bremer. Selma Lagerlöf's short story "Mamsell Fredrika" was first printed 1891 in *Dagny. Journal For Social and Literary Interests,* one of the most important women's magazines at the time, edited by Sophie Adlersparre, who was also director of the Fredrika Bremer Association, Issue 1–2, published in 1891, was a special edition, honouring Fredrika Bremer (1801-1865) 25 years after her death.[4] In the introduction to Bremer's biography, Sophie Adlersparre stresses her engagement with women who seemed to loose their entire value as human beings when failing, or not wanting, to marry. She cites a letter written by Bremer to the critic Brinkmann, where Bremer describes her view of her duty as an author and as a fellow human being: "How the people need comfort, encouragement, outlook, some light in their lives, and how well could not this be given, how close to the heart and mind of the suffering, in pictures from the everyday life".[5] It was indeed with

---

[2] Selma Lagerlöf, "Två spådomar. Ett stycke lefvnadsteckning" (Two Prophecies) in *Troll och människor. Första samlingen,* Stockholm: Albert Bonniers förlag, 1908: 203–234. On line at the Swedish Literature Bank: http://litteraturbanken.se/#!forfattare/LagerlofS/titlar/TrollOchMann.

[3] Citations in my translation from "Två spådomar" [1908], *Troll och människor,* Stockholm: Bonnier, 1915. When translations to English are available, these will be used in the following: Selma Lagerlöf, "The Holy Night": 228.

[4] All issues of *Dagny* are indexed and available in digital facsimilies at KvinnSam, National Resource Library for Gender Studies, Gothenburg University Library, and used as a source in this article, see http://www.ub.gu.se/kvinn/digtid/

[5] Citations in my translation from Sophie Adlersparre, "En blick på Fredrika Bremer och hennes lifsgärning" in *Dagny. Tidskrift för sociala och litterära intresse.* 1(2), 1891: 5–27, available online at Kvinnsam – National Resource For Gender Studies,

"sketches of the everyday life" that Bremer gained public acclaim and over time became a role model for women writers. 1856 she caused controversy with the novel, *Hertha, or the story of a soul. Sketches from real life,* in which she deals with women's liberation. The main character, Hertha, personally experiences the unjust conditions of women and tells her sister Alma what she would like to say to the king of Sweden, if she had the opportunity:

> They say that King Oscar is noble and just; that he does not refuse their rights to any of his subjects. I should speak to him in this manner (now you are the King and I am your subject): 'Your Majesty, I come on behalf of myself and many of my sisters. We have been kept as children, in ignorance of our human rights and duties, and held as minors, in order that we may not become mature human beings. Both our souls and our hand are in bonds, although God has bade us to be free, and although we demand nothing but what is good and right. In other Christian countries [...] her rights have been determined by law to women at a certain age [...] but in our country, in Sweden, the law ordains, that the daughters of the country shall for all time be under bondage, and declared to be under age, unless they happen to be widows [...]. [6]

As this paragraph shows, *Hertha* is part pamphlet, part novel, and this aesthetic unevenness alongside its political demands was a point of criticism in the reception. The novel lead to a debate about women's right to full independence by the age of 25, and a proposed law on the issue was drafted.[7] It has an incomparable position as feminist forerunner. The fact that the journal *Dagny* took the name *Hertha* in 1914 emphasizes this. After Adlersparre's biographic article about Fredrika Bremer, Selma Lagerlöf's story "Mamsell Fredrika" continues on the same theme. Selma Lagerlöf addresses Fredrika Bremer not only as a fellow female author, but also as an old maid, a 'mamsell'. The story is at once a gender-political statement and a meta-commentary, in the shape of a ghost story. It begins on Christmas Eve.

---

Gothenburg University Library. http://www.ub.gu.se/kvinndata/digtid/03/1891/dagny1891_1_2.pdf)

[6] Fredrika Bremer, *Hertha*, Mary Howitt (tr.), New York: Putnam, 1856: 81–82.

[7] Greta Wieselgren, *Fredrika Bremer och verkligheten. Romanen Herthas tillblivels*, Stockholm: Norstedts, 1987: 97-110; Carina Burman, *Bremer. En biografi*, Stockholm: Bonnier, 2001: 392-393.

Mamsell Fredrika is old and her dead sister Agathe comes to take her to church where the dead are celebrating midnight mass. The dead are old, unmarried women, gathered to honour Mamsell Fredrika, who has changed their fate. Despite being a spinster herself, she has been able to help the poor, the weak, the forgotten – all those who have not had the power to speak for themselves. From the darkness of the church a voice addresses Fredrika and the other women:

> My friends, we shall soon be only a legend. The old Mamsells' measure is full. Death rides about on the road to the church to meet the last one of us. Before the next midnight mass she will be dead, the last old Mamsell.
> Sisters! Sisters! We are the lonely ones of the earth, the neglected ones at the feast, the unappreciated workers in the homes. We are met with scorn and indifference. Our way is weary and our name is ridicule.
> But God has had mercy upon us.
> To *one* of us He gave power and genius. To one of us He gave never-failing goodness. To one of us He gave the glorious gift of eloquence. She was everything we ought to have been. She threw light on our dark fate. She was the servant of the homes, as we had been, but she offered gifts to a thousand homes. She was the caretaker of the sick, as we had been, but she struggled with the terrible epidemic of habits of former days. [...] Her glory has been that of a queen's. She has been offered the treasures of gratitude by millions of hearts. Her word has weighed heavily in the great questions of mankind. Her name has sounded through the new and old world. And yet she is only an old Mamsell. [8]

The voice proclaims the end of the unhappy, despised spinster, deprived of meaningful work. Considered in relation to Selma Lagerlöf's autobiographical accounts, this passage closely resembles a personal act of gratitude, from the young woman who dared challenge the word of her father and leave home to be educated at her own expense. "She has stirred young girls towards the wide activities of life", the voice says of Fredrika Bremer,[9]

[8] Selma Lagerlöf, "Mamsell Fredrika" in *Invisible links* [1894], Pauline Bancroft Flach (tr.), Boston: Little Brown & Company, 1899: 152-153. Online at www.openlibrary.org/books/OL14015398M/Invisible_links.
[9] *Ibid.*, 153.

and Selma Lagerlöf is indeed herself one of those girls. The 23-year old Selma in 'Two Prophecies' knows that it is either the seminar, or the dependent and restricted life of the spinster.

The history of the seminar Lagerlöf attended is also connected to *Hertha*. The debate following the publication of the novel made clear that something had to be done to provide for women thirsting for theoretical education and consequently the seminar was founded.[10] A woman who attended the seminar in 1862 wrote to Lagerlöf in 1909, claiming to have met Fredrika Bremer: "[It] seems to me, that nobody has shown such an understanding of this noble woman, as you do in your beautiful prose-poem", she writes (1909-05-12).[11] Besides opening the path of education for women (which was one of the major themes in *Hertha*), the example of Fredrika Bremer shows the important tasks unmarried women can undertake in society: instead of telling tales to her own children, she has told them to thousands, she has fought prejudice and given her opinion on the important questions of humanity. Selma Lagerlöf is also an unmarried woman, an author-spinster. When she wrote "Mamsell Fredrika" her career was just at its beginning. She had not yet told tales for thousands of children, as she did in *Christ Legends* (1904) and *The Wonderful Adventures of Nils* (1907-1908), neither had she participated in debates or political life. But her position as an author in public became closely associated with the same values that she connects to Fredrika Bremer in this story: social responsibility, an ethical obligation to help those in need and to fight for peace and equality.

## "Home and State" and woman as nation builder

Selma Lagerlöf is often referred to as an author not particularly engaged in politics. She was one of the neo-romantics of the 1890s, and did not have a covert political tendency, as many of the women writers of the 1880s. However, she did participate in both the women's movement and the peace movement, signing pamphlets and writing debate articles in the press. She also wrote several fictional texts about the First World War. In the following, I will focus on the relationship between Fredrika Bremer and Selma Lagerlöf,

---

[10] Annika Ullman, *Stiftarinnegenerationen. Sofi Almquist, Anna Sandström, Anna Ahlström*, Stockholm: Stockholmia förlag, 2004: 34.

[11] Letter to Selma Lagerlöf 1909-05-12. The letters cited have been anonymised for ethical reasons, since the letters often concern personal issues not meant to be public.

discussing the points of contact between these writers' thoughts on women in society, as discussed in letters to Selma Lagerlöf from the public, in women's magazines and in their literary texts.[12]

Selma Lagerlöfs speech "Home and State" is perhaps the most well known of Lagerlöf's political statements. It was held at the Sixth Convention of the International Woman Suffrage Alliance, in Stockholm, June 1911. In this speech, Selma Lagerlöf discusses women's tasks in the building of an equal and sustainable nation. As in "Mamsell Fredrika", she brings to light what is carried out unnoticed in the homes of the nation, namely the work of women. She compares men's creation of the State with women's creation of the home, and makes this an absolute prerequisite: a good home in both the societal and political sense. This speech has been compared to Ellen Key's thoughts on motherhood for society ("samhällsmoderlighet"), but there is one critical difference: in contrast to Ellen Key's idea that woman's nature makes her predisposed for certain societal tasks, Selma Lagerlöf considers womanhood to be a certain experience rather than an essential character. "Mamsell Fredrika", points to a different evaluation of women's work, which is not strictly connected to motherhood in its biological sense, but rather detached from this conventional understanding and instead closely related to writing as another kind of women's work.[13]

The speech is rhetorically built on the opposition between home and state, which is continually deconstructed as a false dichotomy. In Western tradition the concept of 'home' has been used to designate a private sphere, separated from the public arena.[14] But even though the discourses and practices surrounding the home and the state seem to be deliberately set in juxtaposition – one first being feminine, caring and fostering, the other masculine, aggressive and competitive – the underlying thought of the speech is that the state influences the home, and the home ought to be allowed to

---

[12] This article is part of the project "Readers responding to Selma Lagerlöf. The Letters from the Public to Selma Lagerlöf 1891-1940", funded by Riksbankens jubileumsfond.

[13] Lisbeth Stenberg has also argued that Selma Lagerlöf's vision of the state as a good home for *all* citizens differs from Ellen Key's concept of societal motherhood, since Key discusses a chosen *few*, able to raise the superior people of the future. See Lisbeth Stenberg, *I kärlekens namn. Människosynen, den nya kvinnan och framtidens samhälle i fem litteraturdebatter 1881-1909*, Stockholm: Normal, 2009: 313.

[14] Susan Strehle, *Transnational Women's Fiction. Unsettling Home and Homeland*, Basingstoke and New York: Palgrave Macmillan, 2008: 1.

influence the state. To make her speech more convincing, not for the women listeners already fighting for women's right to vote, but for sceptical men, she pretends to have trouble finding good reasons. In doing this she gets the opportunity to mention several strong arguments – the size of the suffrage movement, the fact that women are allowed to take academic exams, that they are entering the labour market on a large scale – but she dismisses these with possible counter arguments. Instead, she uses one statement that cannot be dismissed, even by the most conservative patriarchs: the fact that society is dependent on good homes created by women: "There is no man who claims the honour of the creation of the home [...]. Our gift to humankind has been the home, this, and nothing else."[15] Later, Per Albin Hansson, leader of the Social Democratic Party, continued to emphasize the connection between the home and the state when launching the idea of "the home of the people" in similar words: "We have advanced far enough to begin to furnish the big home of the people. It will be a matter of creating in it a cheerful atmosphere, of making it pleasant and warm, bright and happy and free. For a woman, there should be no more attractive task".[16]

"Home and State" may seem to be a strange statement from an author who, in her autobiographical texts, claims to be uninterested and untalented in managing a household, fears the spinster's conviction to the home, and happily accepts her physical disability, as it disqualifies her from marriage.[17] Strategically, she lets her argument rely, not on exceptional women, like authors such as herself or Fredrika Bremer, but on ordinary women and their experience. It is the unique competence of women traditionally confined to the private, such as Mrs Lagerlöf and Aunt Wennervik who represent female tradition and care in "Two Prophecies", which is brought from the chamber kitchen chamber to the rostrum. The difference from Per Albin Hansson's vision of "the home of the folk", is that Selma Lagerlöf wants women not

[15] Selma Lagerlöf, "Två spådomar. Ett stycke lefvnadsteckning" (Two Prophecies), [1908], in *Troll och människor. Första samlingen*, Stockholm: Albert Bonniers förlag, 1915: 251. On line at the Swedish Literature Bank: http://litteraturbanken.se/#!forfattare/LagerlofS/titlar/TrollOchMann.

[16] Charlotte Tornbjer, *Den nationella modern. Moderskap i konstruktioner av svensk nationell gemenskap under 1900-talets första hälft*, Lund: Studia Historica Lundensia. 2002: 262–263; Helena Forsås-Scott, *Re-Writing the Script. Gender and Community in Elin Wägner*, London: Norvik Press, 2007: 73; Lisbeth Stenberg, *I kärlekens namn. Människosynen, den nya kvinnan och framtidens samhälle i fem litteraturdebatter 1881-1909*, Stockholm: Normal, 2009: 316.

[17] Selma Lagerlöf, *Dagbok för Selma Ottilia Lagerlöf*, Stockholm: Bonnier, 1932.

only to contribute with their ability of making this home pleasant, but with new kinds of work: "You must be present everywhere, you must be assist everywhere, if the state, once and for all, will be loved as a home. Be sure that your labour, now so despised, will be appreciated and in great demand".[18] In this, Selma Lagerlöf's argument bears a clear resemblance to Fredrika Bremer's critique of the conditional freedom granted to women by liberal men in *Hertha.* In one passage, Hertha discusses women's place in society with Judge Carlsson:

> But now a great difference was discovered in the views entertained by Judge Carlson and Hertha. The old lawyer conceded to woman the very highest influence, an influence indeed which would operate upon the whole race, through her action upon domestic life and morals; he would desire to see her developed to her utmost power and extent, for the benefit of the home, husband, children, parents, brothers and sisters, and through the domestic circle, for society at large; but he would not desire to see her education directed to any sphere of action beyond domestic life and its immediate world. He would have public seminars for her, but only with the intention of developing her for that sphere, 'which nature evidently and nature's lord, created her for'.[19]

To this, Hertha replies with a passionate speech, in which she describes women's subjection to men as sinful – if God has created men and women in his image, both has an equal right to freely develop the talents they have been given by him, which requires an equal right to education and work. Anna Sandström, leading profile within reformist pedagogy, writes about Fredrika Bremer in *Dagny* explaining how Bremer called for the liberation of women from other standpoints, than, for example, George Sand and Madame de Staël. Sandström describes Sand's critique of the control of women's sexuality within marriage, and Madame de Staël's discussion of the impossibility of combining the roles of wife and artist.Fredrika Bremer demanded only, writes Sandström, that women too should have the right to develop and find a place in society best suited for their talents. In many cases, this could be the choice of motherhood, but in other cases not.[20] Sandström

[18] Selma Lagerlöf, "Två spådomar. Ett stycke lefvnadsteckning": 260-261.
[19] Fredrika Bremer, *Hertha*: 185.
[20] Anna Sandström, "Fredrika Bremer som personlighet", Föredrag hållet vid 100-årsfesten den 31 oktober, *Dagny,* issue 3, 1902: 58.

also points to Bremer's acknowledgment of the "independent work" of unmarried woman.[21]

The Fredrika Bremer Society adhered to this rejection of the idea that women's nature should decide her purpose in society. Everyone, regardless of gender, or marital status, should have an equal right to self-fulfilment.[22] While Bremer builds her argument in *Hertha* on a religious authority, Selma Lagerlöf refers to a political reality – to save the state that men have failed to sustain and develop, the knowledge and experience of women must be utilized, and their participation in all spheres of society allowed. From an international perspective, Selma Lagerlöf was not alone in pointing to women's potential contribution to society in bringing other experiences and abilities. In connection with the First World War, the mother as the saviour of the state was even more emphasized, and used as an argument for the right to vote. In *La Française,* the leading feminist journal in France, from May 1914, a mother looks at the dead body of a young man next to a smoking cannon and says, "I want to vote . . . so that the wars which murder our sons be prevented".[23] With the outbreak of the First World War, the home became a place to be mobilized for the sake of the nation's wellbeing in Sweden too.[24] But Lagerlöf's vision of a more civilized, equal and ethical state, is not so much about motherhood as letting women choose where their abilities can serve society best.She does not really say anything about woman's nature. Instead, she discusses what they have done in history, and what the may do in the future.

## Selma Lagerlöf in an international context

Given that the women's movement was highly international, it is not surprising that Selma Lagerlöf's standpoint is found elsewhere in the writings

---

[21] *Ibid.*, 63.

[22] Ulla Manns, "Gender and Feminism in Sweden. The Fredrika Bremer Association" in Sylvia Paletschek and Bianka Pietrow-Ennker (eds). *Women's Emancipation Movements in the Nineteenth Century. A Europena Perspective,* Stanford: Stanford UP, 2004:154.

[23] Sandi E. Cooper, "Peace as a Human Right. The Invasion of Women into the World of Higher International Politics" in *Journal of Women's History,* 14 (2), 2002:16.

[24] Charlotte Tornbjer, *Den nationella modern. Moderskap i konstruktioner av svensk nationell gemenskap under 1900-talets första hälft,* Lund: Studia Historica Lundensia, 2002: 201.

of other European feminists. The Austrian feminist Rosa Mayreder was introduced to a Swedish audience in Dagny in 1910. Her portrait was on the cover of the journal, along with a short introduction and a statement from the author herself: "I am the same age as Selma Lagerlöf except for some days, and for 28 years I have lived in the happiest of marriages. Raised in a strict bourgeois family of 13 children, I have since my early youth found within myself all incentives to another evaluation of the female life".[25] An excerpt from the Swedish translation of Rosa Mayreder's *Zur Kritik der Weiblichkeit*, published in English as *A Survey of the Woman Problem,* is also included in the issue.[26] The excerpt published in *Dagny* discusses men's normative ideas of women's place in society as a 'primitive sexual expediency'. In the essay she follows a similar line of argument as Lagerlöf in "Home and State", when she links the crisis of civilization to the lack of women's involvement in public life: "Perhaps the appearance of woman as a social fellow-worker may create a change in that field where the one-sided masculine civilization has failed".[27] Like Lagerlöf, she does not downplay the importance of motherhood for women and society, but she also emphasises the need of all citizens to choose their own calling, consistent or not with societal gender norms. The Swedish translation of *Zur Kritik der Weiblichkeit* was enthusiastically received by Ellen Kleman in a later issue of *Dagny.* Kleman underlined Mayreder's critique of the general assumption of motherhood as woman's destiny.[28]

As the example from Selma Lagerlöf's autobiographical tale "Two Prophecies" shows, Lagerlöf describes how she manages to choose her own calling, that of an unmarried woman of letters. But her authorship is not just an artistic calling but, just like Fredrika Bremer and Rosa Mayreder, a social one. Both Lagerlöf and Mayreder are essentially claiming the same freedom

---

[25] Rosa Mayreder, *Kvinnlighet, manlighet och mänsklighet. Essayer,* Olga Anderson (tr.), Stockholm: Wahlström & Widstrand, 1910, *Dagny* 1910, issue 15: 169-170, my translation.

[26] Notably, the Swedish translation was published two years before the English under the title *Kvinnlighet, manlighet, mänsklighet,* an authorized translation from German by Olga Andersson (1910).

[27] Rosa Mayreder, *A Survey of the Woman Problem*, New York: G.H. Doran, 1913. Online at Harvard University Library: http://pds.lib.harvard.edu/pds/view/2573365; Agata Schwartz, *Shifting Voices: Feminist Thought and Women's Writing in Fin-de-siècle*, Quebec: McGill-Queen UP, 2008:70.

[28] Anna Kleman, "Margrethe Meijboom. Selma Lagerlöfs holländska öfversättarinna" in *Dagny,* 45, 1910: 294-295.

as Bremer did in *Hertha,* but while Bremer underlines the fight for justice, Lagerlöf and Mayreder adds society's need for women's competence in creating a good society. Mayreder was not the only international feminist introduced in *Dagny* in the first decade of the 20th century. There were recurring reports from the women's movement in different parts of Europe and America, and in addition to this, prominent feminists were presented. In several of these, arguments similar to the ones forwarded by Lagerlöf in "Home and State" were promoted.

In connection to the Convention of the International Woman Suffrage Alliance in Amsterdam 1908, Reverend Anna H. Shaw, who was among the Amsterdam Congress most noted and popular personalities, was introduced to the readers of *Dagny* by Anna Kleman, one of the Swedish delegates. When discussing women's right to vote from a Christian point of view, Anna Kleman reports that Shaw stressed that women have great power without responsibility and great responsibility without power.[29] Kleman continues by agreeing with and elaborating this statement: "It is no doubt true, that women have ruled institutions as well as nations, without being publicly responsible, while for every time an unfortunate human being is ruined, it is explained by the fact that she has had a bad mother, yet, this mother hasn't had the slightest power to fight the injustices that perhaps have contributed to or caused the ruin of her child!" (My translations). Anna H. Shaw attracted much attention when, during the Congress in Stockholm in 1911, she gave a sermon in the Church of Gustav Vasa and made the cooperation of men and women in society a major theme.[30]

In a Swedish context, it is not always easy to draw the line between liberal feminists such as Fredrika Bremer, who demanded equal rights on the grounds of an essential similarity between all human beings, and the maternal feminists who emerged at the turn of the century, legitimizing women's political authority by their specific female experiences and/or character.[31] Although Selma Lagerlöf seems to be placing herself in the camp of maternal feminists, her emphasis of the home might be more rhetorical than ideological. There is a significant difference between the statements Lagerlöf

---

[29] *Dagny* 1908, issue 29, 1910: 378.

[30] Vivi Edström, "Selma Lagerlöf och kvinnans rösträtt" in Inge Jonsson Bengt and Ying Toijer-Nilsson (eds). *Selma Lagerlöf-studier 6,* Lund: Selma Lagerlöfsällskapet, 1979: 47.

[31] Karen Offen, *European Feminisms. A Political History,* Stanford: Stanford University Press, 2000: 239.

made in private correspondences and the ones she made publicly. She was, for example, much more critical of Ellen Keys' essentialist feminism in letters, and yet places herself relatively near them in "Home and State".[32] In her private letters, she from time to time provides her thoughts on femininity, strongly criticizing patriarchal society from the perspective of the home. In a letter she describes the real conditions of the spinsters in the house:

> You know, the old gentlemen in the countryside were terribly spoilt in the sixties-seventies. The crowd of women usually present in the homes, and their servants and dependants, were subservient, and this aroused all sorts of despotism and whims. I saw a lot of this in my youth and it made me quite rebellious and drove me to be an enthusiastic supporter of the women's movement.[33]

Considering this experience, the question becomes: is the use of the home as an argument for women's right to vote a strategy, and one made to apply to conservatives who were hard to convince by other arguments? The statement certainly proves what Lagerlöf claims in her speech: it is women who create and sustain the home and these responsibilities should be reflected in power. It is reasonable to align Selma Lagerlöf's standpoint in the question of "home and state" with the liberal feminism proceeding her authorship, of which Fredrika Bremer was a forerunner and Sophie Adlersparre, as leader of the Fredrika Bremer Society, an important representative. In *Väckarklocka* (1941), Elin Wägner further developed the connection between good society and motherhood, or even matriarchy, in Sweden, against the backdrop of the war.[34] In her biography of Selma Lagerlöf, Wägner dismisses Lagerlöf's speech as rhetorically skilful but out-dated, and not as timeless as her literary work.[35]

---

[32] Vivi Edström, "Selma Lagerlöf och kvinnans rösträtt": 47.

[33] Ruben G:son Berg, "Hemma hos Selma Lagerlöf i Falun" in Sven Thulin, (ed.). *Mårbacka och Övralid,* Uppsala: J.A. Lindblads förlag, 1941: 115, my translation.

[34] For a discussion of Elin Wägner in an international context, see Katarina Leppänen, *Rethinking Civilization in a European Feminist Context. History, Nature, Women in Elin Wägner's Väckarklocka,* Göteborg: Acta Univesitatis Gothoburgenis, 2005.

[35] Elin Wägner, *Selma Lagerlöf II. From Jerusalem to Mårbacka,* Stockholm: Bonnier, 1943: 86.

## Read by women, spread by women

Even though these female networks in Sweden and abroad are acknowledged as context of Lagerlöf's authorship, her position within them is only just being explored.[36] As Karen Offen has described in her survey of European feminisms 1700-1950, feminist, international organizations grew increasingly active and visible in the late nineteenth century.[37] In Lagerlöf's case, one might even claim that her international success was, to a large part, dependent on the networks within the women's movement. As is well known, a prerequisite for Lagerlöf's immediate breakthrough in Denmark after her debut in 1891 was an invitation to read from her novel at the Women's Reading Society in Copenhagen. The immediate interest and support from Ida Falbe Hansen and Elisabeth Grundtvig after the reading in Copenhagen in November 1891, lead to a Danish translation of the whole novel, which by their help was made known to the influential critic Georg Brandes, who wrote an appreciating review.[38] The Women's Reading Society also purchased the book for their library, where it was available for national and international guests. Margaretha Meyboom later discovered Selma Lagerlöf's first novel, translated it into Dutch and incorporated it in the Ladies' Reading Museum in The Hague.[39]

In issue 45 of *Dagny* in 1908, Selma Lagerlöf's fiftieth birthday was celebrated, with several articles on her authorship and her home, Mårbacka. Anna Kleman also presents "Margarethe Meijboom. Selma Lagerlöf's Dutch Translator", in a separate article. Kleman writes that "17 years ago

---

[36] Lisbeth Stenberg, *I kärlekens namn. Människosynen, den nya kvinnan och framtidens samhälle i fem litteraturdebatter 1881-1909*. Stockholm: Normal, 2009, focuses mainly on the Scandinavian contexts, but also discusses international points of contact. Anna Bohlin's discussion Lagerlöf's later authorship in relation to the suffrage movement and internationally also to Rosa Mayreder is an important exception. Anna Bohlin, *Läsningar av politik i Elin Wägners Silverforsen, Selma Lagerlöfs Löwensköldstrilogi och Klara Johansons Tidevarvskåserier,* Umeå: Bokförlaget h:ström, 2008.

[37] Karen Offen: *European Feminisms. A Political History*: 213.

[38] Lisbeth Stenberg, *I kärlekens namn*: 259; Helle Hvenegaard-Lassen, *Et andet hjem. Kvindelig læseforeningens historie 1872-1962*, Köpenhamn: Det Kongelige Bibliotek, 2008.

[39] Lizet Duyvendak and Diederik Grit, "Margaretha Meyboom. Not only a Translator" in Suzan van Dijk (ed.). *'I have heard about you'. Foreign Women's Writing Crossing the Dutch Border: From Sappho to Selma Lagerlöf*, Hilversum: Verloren, 2004: 324-330.

Margaretha Meijboom established a reading circle for the purchase and circulation of newly published Swedish books in Danish and Norwegian".[40] This is yet another example of different reading communities taking shape, both on a more institutional level – like The Ladies' Reading Museum – or on a more informal level. The more spontaneous and informal associations are well represented in letters to Selma Lagerlöf, those from abroad increasing during her later authorship. In a letter from California dated 1938, a woman asks permission to translate the short story "The Holy Night", originally published in *Kristuslegender* (1904). The letter-writer, who herself has Swedish origins and knows the language, made the translation so that she could read the story to her sons. She admits to having read it aloud at a Christmas party for academic women: "It is on their request I write this letter, because they think it should be published in one of our monthly journals, so it can be part of our Christmas reading" (1938-10-31, my translation). This letter is typical, exemplifying that translations were individual initiatives by women, often (although not in this case) motivated by need for income. It also shows the unregulated character of the translation business. This letter-writer is obviously unaware of the translation made by Velma Swanston Howard, of *Christ Legends,* in 1908. The letter also highlights two important contexts of Selma Lagerlöf's authorship that have been overshadowed by the more official reception: the way in which her works were read by female reading communities, and the use of her texts as children's literature.

The letters to Selma Lagerlöf are not only from female letter-writers. But the letters from women are of particular interest in displaying contexts normally excluded from, or less visible in, literary history. The women do not necessarily read her texts differently, but they do connect Lagerlöf's work to other contexts. They address her as a teacher, as a participant in the women's movement and as an author writing in the spirit of Fredrika Bremer. The public *ethos* of both Selma Lagerlöf and Fredrika Bremer is, to a large extent, comprised of the same parts: being unmarried, engaged in education, and taking active part in changing women's lives. It is true that Bremer is more outspoken on the subject of women as nation builders. She lets Hertha at length explain the advantages of an equal society, where women are allowed to be independent and make use of their competence. With a few exceptions, such as "Home and State", Selma Lagerlöf's texts need to be interpreted in

[40] Anna Kleman, "Margrethe Meijboom. Selma Lagerlöfs holländska öfversättarinna" in *Dagny,* 45, 1908: 583, my translation.

order to discover the contours of a society acknowledging women's rights and experiences. Judging from the letters, these dimensions of her texts appear more readily to women readers.

In *The Golden Cables of Sympathy* Margaret McFadden uses Harriet Beecher Stowe and George Sand as two cases showing the new spaces of transnational contact growing from the interest in famous female authors. In analysing the impact of these two literary celebrities, she departs from the assumptions that "the community of devoted readers is something real, despite the notorious difficulty of defining and measuring its reality".[41] In the case of Selma Lagerlöf, this need not be an assumption, since empirical evidence of a community of readers is to be found in preserved letters to Lagerlöf. In these letters, it is also obvious that some readers transform into "author-focused enthusiasts – that is 'fans' – who model elements of their lives on the bearing, style, personality, or perceived individuality of the author" (68). Further, McFadden argues that the members of a reading community are, "by virtue of their reading opened to new strategies of mobilization" (68). Although this may not be true for all readers of Selma Lagerlöf represented in the letters, there are certainly some reading communities who take some kind of action after reading – in addition to writing to the author, teachers make suggestions for new textbooks, report how they have read and discussed her texts on certain, sometimes political events, and how these events sometimes lead to a request for permission to translate her texts. Moreover, the parallel reading of important women's magazines, such as *Dagny,* and the letters from the readers to Selma Lagerlöf, gives a glimpse of the 'deep horizontal comradeship' Benedict Anderson holds to be fundamental for imagined communities, even though patriarchal authority makes the real power structure more vertical.[42] But in this case, the comradeship does not come from a shared idea of the nation, but is more adequately described as a common response to the public and political crises brought about by the woman question in its different dimensions, and the two world wars. Just as Selma Lagerlöf describes the story about becoming an author as a prediction ("Two Prophecies") and a heritage from older women (the grandmother, Fredrika Bremer), her texts

[41] Margaret H. MacFadden, *The Golden Cables of Sympathy. The Transatlatic Sources of Nineteenth-Century Feminism,* Lexington: University Press of Kentucky, 1999: 68.

[42] Benedict Anderson, *Imagined Communities. Reflections on the Origins and Spread of Nationalism,* London: Verso, 1983: 16.

also seem to give her readers a sense of connectedness, both to the author and to other readers.

## Select Bibliography

Adlersparre, Sophie. 1891. "En blick på Fredrika Bremer och hennes lifsgärning" in *Dagny. Tidskrift för sociala och litterära intresse.* 1(2), available online at Kvinnsam – National Resource For Gender Studies, Gothenburg University Library: 5-27. http://www.ub.gu.se/kvinndata/digtid/03/1891/dagny1891_1_2.pdf

Anderson, Benedict. 1983. *Imagined Communities. Reflections on the Origins and Spread of Nationalism.* London: Verso.

Berg, Ruben G:son. 1941. "Hemma hos Selma Lagerlöf i Falun" in *Mårbacka och Övralid,* Thulin, Sven, (ed.). Uppsala: J.A. Lindblads förlag: 109-116

Bohlin, Anna. 2008. *Röstens anatomi. Läsningar av politik i Elin Wägners Silverforsen, Selma Lagerlöfs Löwensköldstrilogi och Klara Johansons Tidevarvskåserier.* Umeå: Bokförlaget h:ström.

Bremer, Fredrika. 1856. *Hertha,* (Authorized American Edition tr. Mary Howitt) New York: Putnam.

Burman, Carina. 2001. *Bremer. En biografi.* Stockholm: Bonnier.

Cooper, Sandi E. 2002. "Peace as a Human Right. The Invasion of Women into the World of Higher International Politics" in *Journal of Women's History,* 14,(2):9-25.

Duyvendak, Lizet and Grit, Diederik. 2004. "Margaretha Meyboom. Not only a Translator" in *'I have heard about you'. Foreign Women's Writing Crossing the Dutch Border: From Sappho to Selma Lagerlöf.* Suzan van Dijk (ed.). Hilversum: Verloren: 324-330.

Edström, Vivi. 1979. "Selma Lagerlöf och kvinnans rösträtt, *Selma Lagerlöf-studier 6.* Ek, Bengt, Inge Jonsson and Ying Toijer-Nilsson (eds). Lund: Selma Lagerlöfsällskapet: 27–59.

Forsås-Scott, Helena. 2007. *Re-Writing the Script. Gender and Community in Elin Wägner.* London: Norvik Press.

Hvenegaard-Lassen, Helle. 2008. *Et andet hjem. Kvindelig læseforeningens historie 1872-1962.* Köpenhamn: Det Kongelige Bibliotek.

Kleman, Anna. 1908. "Margrethe Meijboom. Selma Lagerlöfs holländska öfversättarinna" in *Dagny.* 45: 582-3.

Kleman, Ellen. 1910. recension av *Kvinnlighet, manlighet, mänsklighet. Essayer av Rosa Mayreder, Dagny.* issue 25: 294-295.

Lagerlöf, Selma. 1899. "Mamsell Fredrika" in *Invisible links* [1894], (tr. Pauline Bancroft Flach) Boston: Little Brown & Company. online at www.openlibrary.org/books/OL14015398M/Invisible_links

—. 1908. "The Holy Night", *Christ Legends.* (tr. Velma Swanston Howard). New York: Henry Holt and Company: 3-11.

—. 1915. "Två spådomar. Ett stycke lefvnadsteckning" ["Two Prophecies", 1908]. In *Troll och människor. Första samlingen.* Stockholm: Albert Bonniers förlag: 203–234. online at the Swedish Literature Bank: http://littera turbanken.se/#!forfattare/LagerlofS/titlar/TrollOchMann

—. 1915. "Hem och Stat" [1911], in *Troll och människor. Första samlingen.* Stockholm: Albert Bonniers förlag: 247–261. On line at the Swedish Literature Bank: http://littera turbanken.se/#!forfattare/LagerlofS/titlar/TrollOchMann

—. 1932. *Dagbok för Selma Ottilia Lagerlöf.* Stockholm: Bonnier.

Leppänen, Katarina. 2005. *Rethinking Civilization. History, Nature, Women in Elin Wägners Väckarklocka.* Gothenburg Studies in the History of Science and Ideas 18, Göteborg: Acta Universitatis Gothoburgensis.

Letters to Selma Lagerlöf. National Library of Sweden: The Selma Lagerlöf-Collection. L1:100. [*Unpublished.*]

Manns, Ulla. 2004. "Gender and Feminism in Sweden. The Fredrika Bremer Association" in *Women's Emancipation Movements in the Nineteenth Century. A Europena Perspective.* Paletschek, Sylvia and Bianka Pietrow-Ennker (eds). Stanford: Stanford UP: 152-164.

Mayreder, Rosa. 1905. *Zur Kritik der Weiblichkeit. Essays.* Jena and Leipzig: E. Diederichs.

—. 1910. *Kvinnlighet, manlighet och mänsklighet. Essayer.* (tr Olga Anderson). Stockholm: Wahlström & Widstrand.

—. 1913. *A Survey of the Woman Problem.* New York: G.H. Doran. On line at Harvard University Library: http://pds.lib.harvard.edu/pds/view/2573365

McFadden, Margaret H. 1999. *The Golden Cables of Sympathy. The Transatlatic Sources of Nineteenth-Century Feminism.* Lexington: University Press of Kentucky.

Offen, Karen. 2000. *European Feminisms. A Political History.* Stanford: Stanford University Press.

Sandström, Anna. 1902. "Fredrika Bremer som personlighet. Föredrag hållet vid 100-årsfesten den 31 oktober, *Dagny,* issue 3: 51-65.

Schwartz, Agata. 2008. *Shifting Voices: Feminist Thought and Women's Writing in Fin-de-siècle.* Quebec: McGill-Queen UP.

Stenberg, Lisbeth. 2009. *I kärlekens namn. Människosynen, den nya kvinnan och framtidens samhälle i fem litteraturdebatter 1881-1909.* Stockholm: Normal.

Strehle, Susan. 2008. *Transnational Women's Fiction. Unsettling Home and Homeland.* Basingstoke and New York: Palgrave Macmillan.

"Till Rosa Mayreders porträtt" 1910. *Dagny*, issue 15: 169-170.[*unsigned presentation]*

Tornbjer, Charlotte. 2002. *Den nationella modern. Moderskap i konstruktioner av svensk nationell gemenskap under 1900-talets första hälft.* Lund: Studia Historica Lundensia.

Ullman, Annika. 2004. *Stiftarinnegenerationen. Sofi Almquist, Anna Sandström, Anna Ahlström.* Stockholm: Stockholmia förlag.

Wägner, Elin. 1943. *Selma Lagerlöf II. From Jerusalem to Mårbacka.* Stockholm: Bonnier.

Wieselgren, Greta. 1978. *Fredrika Bremer och verkligheten. Romanen Herthas tillblivelse.* Stockholm: Norstedts.

# Decadent Women Telling Nations Differently: The Finnish Writer L. Onerva and her Motherless Dilettante Upstarts

*Viola Parente-Čapková*

ABSTRACT This chapter focuses on the Finnish writer L. Onerva's strategies to construct female subjectivity within the framework of the decadent mode on the one hand, and the 'New Woman discourse' on the other, developed in the context of the Finnish national awakening, in which the late 19th and early 20th century the turn of the 19th and the 20th century Finnish writers lived and operated. L. Onerva was a Finnish language writer, who was supposed to take part, in one way or another, in the 'Finnish national project', but, as one of the most international cultural figures of her generation, producing fiction, poetry, literary and art criticism as well as numerous translations (mostly from French), she was regarded by some as 'too cosmopolitan'. She was concerned with women's emancipation as well as with its problematization, being much closer to the artistic circles enchanted with decadence, Nietzscheanism and other fin-de-siècle trends, accused by many of 'misogyny', than to the mainstream Finnish women's movement, characterized by adherence to patriotism and Christian (Lutheran) moral values.

"WHAT IS THE SO-CALLED FOLK/NATION?",[1] ponders the eponymous protagonist of the Finnish L. Onerva's (1882-1972) novel *Mirdja* from 1908, when she visits a popular festival in the countryside. A decadent New Woman novel, variant of a *Bildungsroman* and an artist novel with a female protagonist, *Mirdja* is a tragic story about an exceptional female individual, clearly inspired, among many other texts, by Germaine de Staël's *Corinne* (1807), George Sand's *Lélia* (1837), and Marcelle Tinaire's *Hellé* (1898),[2] as

[1] The Finnish word "kansa", used in the original, stands for people, folk and nation.

[2] Onerva, who belonged to the first generation of Finnish women writers who were able to study at the university without a "special permit", mentions George Sand in her diploma thesis about female characters in the work of Alfred de Musset ("Musset'n nailuonteet" / "Musset's female characters". Unpublished thesis, Literary Archive of the Finnish Literature Society, 1905). Madame de Staël was a perennial concern for Onerva; she wrote some essays on her at the university, and later, published a small book on the author: *Madame de Staël*, Helsinki: WSOY, 1920. Onerva's translation of *Hellé* by Tinaire was published in 1922.

well as by the Nietzschean idea of the Overman, adapted for a woman; the rich intertextuality endows it with a transnational dimension. Mirdja is a woman of extraordinary intellect and versatile talent, who is, however, unable to love and to materialize her artistic ambitions. As with most decadent texts, the novel is openly intertextual, manifesting numerous other qualities of the decadent art and style: it is self-centred, giving the artist a special role, it adopts particular stylistic poses such as irony and parody, and expresses an acute awareness of decay,[3] all in a very gender specific way. *Mirdja* is fragmentary, mixing dreams, visions and fantasies with reality, abounding in punctuation with, for example, ellipses, exclamation marks, dashes and pauses indicating silences and intermittent speech. The protagonist is a motherless decadent picara figure, raised by her father's brother and other male decadent dilettante bohemian 'philosophers'. As a beautiful young woman, she tests, with the help of various men, the varied roles of womanhood and artistry. She ends up in a childless marriage with a mysterious man, a middle class teacher who writes excessive excerbatedly decadent texts; eventually, old, widowed and mentally ill, she drowns in a bog.

The aforementioned Mirdja's question points to the state of patriotic affairs at the late 19th and the early 20th century. The folk/nation, the 'people', became a puzzle for middle class Finnish patriots (mostly intellectuals, artists, teachers and ministers), who were an active force in the Finnish "national awakening" or "national project",[4] having coined the ideal of "pure Finnishness", embodied in the country folk, "the people". The folk was divinized, as showed in Mirdja's sigh when she overhears a hymn coming from the festival field: "God's feast, God's feast!". She feels an urge to merge with the folk and establish "an extremely close touch with the extremely distant soul of the world or the soul of God (...)"[5] pursuant to the typical *fin de siècle* rhetoric of merging or fusing with a kind of overwhelming, 'liberating' force, from the symbolist longing to 'dissolve in a

[3] Robert Pynsent, "Conclusory Essay: Decadence and Innovation" in Robert Pynsent (ed.). *Decadence and Innovation. Austro-Hungarian Life and Art at the Turn of the Century*. London: Weidenfeld and Nicolson, 1989: 142; see also e.g. Jean Pierrot, *The Decadent Imagination 1880–1900*. D. Coltman (tr.) Chicago & London: The University of Chicago Press, 1981.

[4] Miroslav Hroch, *Social Preconditions of National Revival in Europe: a Comparative Analysis of the Social Composition of Patriotic Groups among the Smaller European Nations.* (tr. Ben Fowkes) Cambridge: Cambridge University Press, 1985: 72-74.

[5] L. Onerva, *Mirdja*. Helsinki: Otava, 1908/1982: 135.

sea of life' to other various, though often convergent ideals. As Robert Pynsent has pointed out, "the Decadent often perceived *his* self as an expression of the history of his nation or of the human race as a whole".[6] However, when the beautiful, delicately pale, fancily dressed Mirdja tries to merge with the common folk, she experiences terror as if being raped, sensing the hatred of the crowd, which, as she perceives it, yearns only for her material well-being. The experience turns into a nightmarish, carnivalesque event, and only when Mirdja gets far away from the festival field, and hears a patriotic song sung by the people, does she again feel that the 'ordinary folk' is the only strong element, the only vital force to be found in humankind. Despite this, after the experience, she herself feels even more alienated, estranged, "proud and lonely".[7]

This scene from *Mirdja* can be read as a reaction to contradictory discourses on the folk/nation during Onerva's life; a reaction which is both ambivalent – as typical of the decadent mode – and profoundly gendered. For the the late 19th and the early 20th century European women writers engaging with decadence (which, in Finland, was often included within the *mélange* of the *fin de siècle* trends and currents, traditionally referred to as 'Neo-Romanticism'), the relationship with nationalism was just one of many contradictions and paradoxes with which they were involved both in their work and in their lives, or, in Biddy Martin's words, in their "(life)styles".[8] Both nationalism and decadence had clearly different meanings in different contexts. Finland, the focus of my attention, was experiencing the culmination of a national awakening at the turn of the late 19th and the early 20th century, incompatible, for many, with the decadent moods of decay, fatigue, sickness, degeneration and egotism. Moreover, decadent individualism was hostile both to the egalitarian ethos, typical of Finnish nationalism, and to the feminist politicization of love and sexuality.[9] Indeed, in the above scene from *Mirdja*, Onerva confronts *fin de siècle* ideas about the "common people", who were, depending on the discourse in question,

---

[6] Robert Pynsent, *Questions of Identity. Czech and Slovak Ideas of Nationality and Personality.* London: Central European University Press, 1994: 110; my italics.

[7] L. Onerva, *Mirdja*: 135.

[8] Martin Biddy, *Woman and Modernity: The (life)styles of Lou Andreas-Salomé.* Ithaca & New York: Cornell University Press, 1991.

[9] Diane Holmes, *Rachilde. Decadence, Gender and the Woman Writer.* Oxford & New York: Berg, 2001: 77.

"healthy and brutish", but also "sick and degenerated", intertwined with the development of a nationalist discourse.[10]

L. Onerva (the pen name of Hilja Onerva Lehtinen),[11] the central topic of my research, is a good example of the contradictions and tensions *fin de siècle* women writers influenced by decadence had to face in the 'awakening' nations on the periphery of Europe. She was a Finnish language writer, supposed to take part, in one way or another, in the 'national project', since the Finnish identity was, at her time, defined as a Finnish language.[12] Onerva was one of the most international cultural figures of her generation, being especially famous for her vivid interest in French culture, acting as a cultural mediator between Finland and France, both in terms of translating and in drawing inspiration from French literature.[13] This activity of hers, highlighted by contemporary translators,[14] had already been recognized by her contemporaries, but not always appreciated: by some, she was considered 'too cosmopolitan', and, allegedly, refrained from treating the "national themes", by which the Finnish critics often meant the topics inspired directly

---

[10] In her articles, Päivi Molarius has discussed the background of the various, often controversial views on the "common folk" in the turn-of the-19$^{th}$-and-the-20$^{th}$-century Finland, mentioning, among others, the way the ideas of Charles Darwin, B. A. Morel, and Hippolyte Taine influenced the literary portrayals of the Finnish *kansa*. See e.g. Päivi Molarius,"'Will the Human Race Degenerate?' The Individual, the Family and the Fearsome Spectre of Degeneracy in Finnish Literature of the Late 19$^{th}$ and Early 20$^{th}$ Century" in Pirjo Lyytikäinen (ed.) *Changing Scenes. Encounters between European and Finnish Fin de Siècle*. Helsinki: Finnish Literature Society, Studia Fennica Litteraria 1, 2003: 121-142.

[11] Before being 'rediscovered' by the feminist literary scholars in the 1980s, L. Onerva used to be famous (similarly to quite a few decadent and *fin de siècle* women writers and artists, e.g. Dagny Juel-Przybyszewska, Laura Marholm, Zinaida Gippius, Lou Andréas Salomé) mostly as the male artists' muse and companion: she was a lover of the major Finnish *fin de siècle* writer and journalist Eino Leino (1878-1926), and her second husband was the notable Finnish composer Leevi Madetoja (1887-1947).

[12] The doctrine of the "monoligual nationalism" was coined by the Finnish "national philosopher" J.V. Snellman (see Kati Launis's article in this volume).

[13] Onerva contributed to the knowledge of the French culture in Finland as essayist, scholar, and translator, having translated extensively from French from Voltaire to Soupault.

[14] H.K. Riikonen (ed.), *Suomennoskirjallisuuden historia I-II.* (*The History of Literature Translated into Finnish*). Helsinki: Suomalaisen Kirjallisuuden Seura, 2007.

by the Finnish folk tradition, regarded, in the Herderian spirit, as the basis of national culture.[15]

L. Onerva was concerned with women's emancipation and labeled a "Finnish New Woman Writer" by feminist literary critics in the 1990s. However, at the beginning of the 20th century, she was closer to the artistic circles enchanted with decadence and Nietzscheanism, accused by many of 'misogyny', than to the Finnish mainstream women's movement, characterized by adherence to patriotism based on Christian (Lutheran) moral values. Though very critical of the church and institutionalized religion, Onerva was, throughout her life, looking for spiritual dimensions and seeking inspiration in religions other than Protestantism, as well as in other spiritual currents like theosophy. Over the course of time, all these complexities proved to be most fruitful when looking at L. Onerva's writing in the context of the the late 19th and the early 20th century Finnish nationalism as well as when testing the transgressive potential of decadent strategies in women's texts. Though there were several Finnish women writers who employed decadent strategies in their texts (e.g. Selma Anttila, 1867-1942; Ain'Elisabet Pennanen, 1881-1945), L. Onerva was the one who used the decadent mode most intensely and innovatively: the novel *Mirdja* (1908) was labeled as the most important representative of the Finnish "Nietzschean decadence" in general.[16]

## Decadent women writers and nationalism – a brief transnational look

The uneasy relationship between the decadent mode and nationalism in the works of women who engaged with it has been explored in various contexts, each case being special due to its context(s). This is why the following cases are mentioned just as examples; a more solid comparative study could be carried out only as a long-term project. The 'racial nationalism' of the American writer and feminist Charlotte Perkins Gilman (1860-1935), the author of one of the most acclaimed decadent texts by women (*The Yellow Wallpaper,* 1892), feels special and controversial in the sense that it highlights "women's reproductive role in crafting the proper (white) national

---

[15] For the importance of the folk oral traditon in the process of creating the Finnish national mythology, see Kati Launis's article in this volume.

[16] See Esko Ervasti, *Suomalainen kirjallisuus ja Nietzsche I.* (*Finnish Literature and Nietzsche I.*). Turku: Turun yliopisto, 1960.

genealogy" and women's work in "building a better society and ultimately reproducing a racially 'pure' nation".[17] The Russian decadent writer Zinaida Gippius' (1869-1945) decadent stylizations, her "utopian life creation" and the attempts to "reconceptualize the body and gender" are, for the most part, inseparable from the utopianism of Russian apocalyptic thought.[18] The spiritual dimension in general, and as well as the religious, is certainly an important element, as in the case of the French poet of English origin, Renée Vivien (Pauline Mary Tarn, 1877-1909), who is often characterised as using the decadent style, and who converted to Catholicism in the manner of other decadent writers and whose open lesbianism was, of course, incompatible with bourgeois nationalism.

The complex relationship of French decadents with nationalism is interesting to trace also in case of Rachilde (Marguerite Eyméry-Valette, 1860–1953), now acclaimed as one of icons of French decadence,[19] whose short stories and novels can be read as mocking the rhetoric of bourgeois patriarchal nationalism, and who shocked the public with her gender masquarades.[20] Recently, some of the *fin de siècle* 'New Women writers' associated with the British Empire, whose oeuvre manifests features of decadence, have been looked at within a broader colonial context, as is e.g. the case of Iveta Jusová's analyses of the approaches of the Anglo-Irish writer George Egerton (Mary Chavelita Dunne Bright, 1859-1945), and the Anglo-Jewish writer Amy Levy (1861-1889).[21] In the case of Egerton, although revealing an oscillating relationship to her own Anglo-Irish 'race', the "selective application of Friedrich Nietzsche's philosophy to an articulation of universal female subjectivity freed the writer, to some extent, from hegemonic attitudes toward evolution and the female body"; Amy

---

[17] Alys Eve Weinbaum, "Writing Feminist Genealogy: Charlotte Perkins Gilman, Racial Nationalism, and the Reproduction of Maternalist Feminism"in *Feminist Studies,* 2001, 27(2): 272.

[18] Olga Matich, *Erotic Utopia. The Decadent Imagination in Russia's Fin de Siècle.* Madison: The University of Wisconsin Press, 2005. 209, 211; see also Temira Pachmuss, *Zinaida Gippius: An Intellectual Profile.* Southern Illinois University Press, 1971.

[19] See Melanie Hawthorn, *Rachilde and French Women's Authorship. From Decadence to Modernism*, Nebraska, University of Nebraska Press, 2001, and Diane Holmes, *Rachilde. Decadence, Gender and the Woman Writer.* Oxford & New York: Berg, 2001.

[20] Cf. Rita Felski, *The Gender of Modernity.* Cambridge (Mass.) & London: Harvard University Press, 1995

[21] See Iveta Jusová, *The New Woman and the Empire*. Columbus: Ohio State University Press, 2005.

Levy, whose identity was seriously threatened by the late-Victorian intensification of xenophobic and eugenic rhetoric, "elevates the personal subjective experience in order to carve out a space for female identity independent of the collective interests of the nation".[22]

Some decadent women writers from the fringes of Europe were even more explicitly international and transnational figures than Egerton and Levy: e.g. Dagny Juel-Przybyszewski (1867-1901), a writer of Norwegian origin living later in Germany and Poland, epitomizing the transgression of boundaries also by being a 'decadent muse', modelling for some prominent *fin de siècle* artists, and a creative author at the same time. The Baltic-German Laura Marholm-Hanson (1854-1928), who also transgressed many boundaries of a different kind, was born in Latvia, later living and working in Germany; in dialogue with Nietzsche and her Swedish-born husband, the decadent writer Ola Hansson, she developed an anti-emancipationalist form of feminism as a possible cure for the decadent disease, streaming towards utopian visions about "new love" and "new man".[23] The Serbian writer Isidora Sekulić (1877-1958), whose difficult reception in being described by contemporary critics as a 'decadent', could be parallelled with L. Onerva's, combined, just like Onerva, a vivid interest in the national project, a cosmopolitan orientation, striving towards "cultural Europeanization", and engagement with gender issues.[24]

---

[22] Heather Miner, "Fragmenting the Female Voice: Restrictive Imperial Discourse and the New Woman Movement" in *Nineteenth Century Gender Studies* 2(2). 2006. Online at http://www.ncgsjournal.com/issue22/miner.htm.

[23] See Ebba Witt-Brattström, *Dekadnesens kön. Ola Hansson och Laura Marholm (The Gender of Decadence. Ola Hansson and Laura Marholm).* Stockholm: Norstedts, 2007 and Kirsti Tuohela, *Huhtikuun tekstit. Kolmen naisen koettu ja kirjoitettu melankolia 1870-1900* (*April Texts. Three Women Writers Encountering Melancholia 1870-1900*). Helsinki: Suomalaisen Kirjallisuuden Seura,2008: 258-268.

[24] See Magdalena Koch, *"Fellow Travellers of a Serbian Woman. Isidora Sekulić or an Overture to Modern Serbian Literature"* in Krystyna Gabrielska, Mirosłava Czarnecka and Christa Ebert (eds), *Die Bilder der 'neuen Frau' in der Moderne und den Modernisierungsprozessen des 20. Jahrhunderts.*. Wrocław: Wrocławskie Wydawnictvo Oświatowe, 1998: 186-196. See also Zoran Milutinović, *Getting over Europe: The Construction of Europe in Serbian Culture.* Studia Imagologica. Rodopi: Amsterdam and New York, 201: 30-31.

## Nationalism and decadence in Finland under the gender lense

As suggested above, nationalism had a different meaning for the big European powers and for the nations on the periphery of Europe, which, at the turn of the century, were experiencing the culmination of their national movements. In France, as well as in Britain, nationalism was associated with the bourgeois philistinism and bourgeois gender models, and defied by decadent artists and writers as such. Antinationalism can be said to be an important element of decadent writing in these countries. The decadents seem almost uniformly to reject the democratic, the secularist, and egalitarian developments of the modern world, preferring instead to seek out the artistocratic and spiritual trappings of an imagined old regime.[25] However, the issue is complex on many levels, since many decadent writers, men and women, changed their stance on nationalism during the course of their careers. As Matthew Potolsky has observed, "decadent writers rejected nationalism from both left and right, and many decadents later became extreme nationalists".[26] However "if, as Timothy Brennan has suggested, the form of the realist novel both mimics and helps produce the form of the nation, decadence might be said to attack the form of the nation, much as it decomposes literary style".[27] Inasmuch as nationalism relies in part on a textual politics that finds the unity of a nation in the unity of its canon, the attention that decadent writers give to language and textuality is less an escapist turn from politics than a critique of the linguistic and textual constitution of the nation.[28] As Matei Calinescu has argued, Paul Bourget's characteristics of decadence as an attribute of a "highly individualistic" society, which is manifested both in the society as a whole and in the 'decadent style' of art and literature with its attributes of fragmentariness, decomposition, etc. means that decadence brings about a clear disadvantage from the point of view of nationalism,[29] as it was felt in Finland, where

[25] L. Denisoff, D. Constable and M. Potolsky, "Introduction" in L., D. Denisoff and M. Potolsky (eds). *Perennial Decay. On the Aesthetics and Politics of Decadence.* Constable, Philadelphia: University of Pennsylvania Press, 1999 : 1-32.

[26] Matthew Potolsky, "Decadence, Nationalism and the Logic of Canon Formation" in *Modern Language Quarterly.* 67(2), 2006: 215.

[27] Ibid. Potolsky is referring to Timothy Brennan's article "The National Longing for Form" in Homi K. Bhabha (ed.), *Nation and Narration*, London: Routledge, 1990: 49.

[28] Matthew Potolsky,"Decadence, Nationalism and the Logic of Canon Formation" in *Modern Language Quarterly.* 67(2). 2006: 244.

[29] Matei Calinescu,*Five Faces of Modernity: Modernism, Avant-Garde, Decadence, Kitsch, Postmodernism.* Durham: Duke University Press:1987.

decadence was 'externalized' by many critics, who argued that it was an inherently non-Finnish phenomenon. The pronouncedly decadent art was labeled as 'foreign', associated with both the Eastern (Russian) and Western (French) features, decay and degeneration, alien to the 'healthy' Finnish mentality,[30] constructed as masculine, similar to the concept of desired "wholeness" (in contrast to the "feminine" fragmentariness).

In other words, in Finland, decadence tended to be "swept under the carpet of the national development", as Pirjo Lyytikäinen put it when analyzing the case.[31] A 'young' nation did not want to have much to do with decay and degeneration, preferring to make use of the organic metaphors of healthy growth, which was also constructed as 'typical' of the very Finnish national culture. If we use the periodization, designed by Miroslav Hroch[32] for the development of the nationalisms of the "small European nations", and adapted by Michael Branch for the Finnish case,[33] Finland was, at the late 19th and the early 20th century, entering the culminating stage of this development. This stage is characterized by mass awareness of the national issue, by looking for the 'right' kind of relationship literature should have with nationalist politics and 'national education',[34] and by seeing political independence as the principal goal (contrary to the earlier stages of the national movement), which was eventually achieved in 1917.

"Entrusted with the responsibility for creating a national language and so laying the foundation for a unique and inalienable national culture, writers place their writing in the service of the nation and the people", Pascale

---

[30] G. Erastoff, "Erotism i dekadens i Rysslands litteratur" ("Eroticism and Decadence in Russian Literature") in *Argus* 15(1), 1908: 3-5.

[31] Lyytikäinen, Pirjo. "Dekadenssi – rappion runous" (Decadence: Poetry of Decay) in Pirjo Lyytikäinen, (ed.). *Dekadenssi vuosisadan vaihteen taiteessa ja kirjallisuudessa (Decadence in the turn-of-the-19th-and-the-20th-Century Art and Literature*) Helsinki: Suomalaisen Kirjallisuuden Seura, 1998: 13.

[32] Miroslav Hroch,*Social Preconditions of National Revival in Europe: a Comparative Analysis of the Social Composition of Patriotic Groups among the Smaller European Nations.* (tr. Ben Fowkes.) Cambridge: Cambridge University Press,1985.

[33] Michael Branch, "The Invention of A National Epic" in Michael Branch and Celia Hawksworth (eds). *The Uses of Tradition. A Comparative Inquiry into the Nature, Uses, and Functions of Oral Poetry in the Balkans, The Baltic, and Africa.* Helsinki, London: SSEES, University of London – Finnish Literature Society, 1994: 195-211.

[34] See Erkki Sevänen, "Kansallisuus valtion suojeluksessa ja valvonnassa" (Nationality under the State Protection and Control) in Lea Rojola,(ed.). *Suomen kirjallisuushistoria 2: Järkiuskosta vaistojen kapinaan*: 245-258.

Casanova wrote.[35] The prototypical writer, was, in this case, a man, just like the prototype of the Finnish citizen, whose principal features were modesty, diligence, perseverance, and proximity to nature – virtues promoted by the Lutheran religion, the dominant religion in Finland from the Reformation, taken as one of the fundamentals of the national identity. Within the nationalist discourse it was contrasted with Orthodoxy and Catholicism, linked by the architects of Finnishness to the 'foreign' and 'decadent' both in the artistic and in the general sense of the word. Only in the last two decades has it been fully admitted that "national" artists, who employed topics from the Finnish oral tradition in their works, led an intense dialogue with the decadent mode and, also only recently, has the work of Finnish writers, who absorbed the decadent inspirations directly from France, been subject to closer attention and thorough examination, also from a gender viewpoint.[36]

What was especially significant and most obviously transgressive from the point of view of the Finnish patriots, was the decadent subversion of gender roles, often at odds with the stereotypization of gender characteristics

---

[35] Pascale Casanova, *The World Republic of Letters*. Cambridge, Massachusetts & London, England: Harvard University Press, 2004, s quoting Milan Kundera's observation on small nation from "The Unloved Child of the Family" (in *Testments Betrayed*, Linda Asher (tr.). New York: HarperCollins, 1995: 193). "A small nation," Kundera has observed, "resembles a big family and likes to describe itself that way (…) Thus in the big family that is a small country, the artist is bound in multiple ways, by multiple cords. When Nietzsche noisily savaged the German character, when Stendhal announced that he preferred Italy to his homeland, no German or Frenchman took offense; if a Greek or a Czech dared to say the same thing, his family would curse him as a detestable traitor." Though Kundera's point is a simplification (including the notorious difficulty to define a 'small nation'), much of it holds for the cases of many coutries on the fringes of Europe in the 19th century, and, indeed, later as well.

[36] See e.g. Lea Rojola, "Oman sielunsa hullu morsian. Mirdjan matka taiteen maailmassa" (A Mad Bride of Her Own Soul. Mirdja's Journey in the World of Art) in Tarja-Liisa Hypén (ed.).*Pakeneva keskipiste. Tutkielmia suomalaisesta taiteilijaromaanista (Escaping Focus. Studies on the Finnish Artist Novel*) Turku: Turun yliopisto, Taiteiden tutkimuksen laitos, 1992, 49-73; Pirjo Lyytikäinen,. *Narkissos ja sfinksi. Minä ja Toinen vuosisadanvaihteen kirjallisuudessa (Narcissus and Sphinx. Me and Other in the Literature of the Turn of the 19th and the 20th Century).* Helsinki: Suomalaisen Kirjallisuuden Seura, 1997; Viola Parente-Čapková, "Decadent New Woman?" in *NORA - Nordic Journal of Women's Studies* 6(1): 1998; and Pirjo Lyytikäinen, "The Allure of Decadence. French Reflections in a Finnish Looking Glass" in Pirjo Lyytikäinen. (ed.). *Changing Scenes. Encounters between European and Finnish Fin de Siècle*. Helsinki: Finnish Literature Society, Studia Fennica Litteraria 1, 2003: 12-30.

typical of national movements,[37] where only certain kinds of "confusions" of masculine and feminine qualities were "allowed", while others were perceived as dangerous and subversive. In societies like the Finnish, where the national issue dominated the scene, women were usually allowed to manifest certain qualities traditionally perceived as masculine, like, for example, courage and perseverance, needed in the process of building the nation. The (male) protagonists of the national movements in European nations undergoing the process of national awakening during the 19th century were often emphasizing the active role of women in this process and using the advanced position of women in their own country, including their participation in creating national literature, as proof of the superiority of the nation in contrast to the "old", "civilized" nations of Europe, whose women were less advanced.[38] However, this "advancement" of (patriotic) women had its rules: the Finnish women were not supposed to refrain from the sacred vocation of motherhood, be it biological or "social".[39] The concept of "social motherhood" was advocated also by the mainstream Finnish Women's Movement, and professed by L. Onerva's history teacher and early role model, the writer and MP Hilda Käkikoski (1864-1912). This "maternal citizenship" can be seen as a counterpart to the prototype of the Finnish masculine ideal citizen: in other words, Finnish women were not excluded from the public arena, but were included on a specific basis.[40] Effeminate men, on the other hand, or male effeminacy in general, were perceived as a

---

[37] See G.L. Mosse, *Nationalism and Sexuality. Middle-Class Morality and Sexual Norms in Modern Europe*. Madison: The University of Wisconsin Press, 1985; and G. L. Mosse, *The Image of Man. The Creation of Modern Masculinity*. New York: Oxford University Press, 1996.

[38] In this respect, the Finnish case is comparable with the Czech one, as analysed by Vladimír Macura, *Znamení zrodu: české národní obrození jako kulturní typ* (The Sign of Birth: Czech National Revival as a Cultural Type.) Praha: H&H, 1995.

[39] See Päivi Lappalainen, "'Äiti-ilon himo'. Naiset ja kansakunnan rakentuminen 1800–luvulla" ("'The Desire for the Joy of Motherhood'. Women and the Nation Building in the 19th Century") in T. Koistinen, P. Kruuspere, E. Sevänen and R. Turunen (eds). *Kaksi tietä nykyisyyteen. Tutkimuksia kirjallisuuden, kansallisuuden ja kansallisten liikkeiden suhteesta Suomessa ja Virossa (Two Ways to the Present. Studies on the Relationship between Literature, Nationality and National Movements in Finland and in Estonia*) Helsinki: Suomalaisen Kirjallisuuden Seura, 1999: 106-129, and Kati Launis's article in this volume.

[40] *Ibid*., 109-113.

subversive element within the patriotic project.[41] Within decadent aestheticism, the situation was, in a certain way, the opposite: the decadent aesthetes despised "physical" femininity (including women's capacity to mother), resented the middle class bourgeois masculinity, and venerated the abstract, artificial femininity, mostly in the form of male effeminacy, epitomized by the decadent dandy.[42]

## Onerva's motherless dilettante upstarts

When discussing the triangle of women/gender – nation (nalism) in L. Onerva's early texts, I will mention several significant elements in her work, all relevant to the relationships within the triangle. All of these elements address the issue of female subjectivity and female creativity, a perennial concern both for Onerva and for the *fin de siècle* women writers in general.

Let us start with L. Onerva's inspirations by the Finnish folk poetry, which, as mentioned above, were, according to some critics, absent from her work. Although only sporadic, there are, in L. Onerva's poetry and prose, to be found inspirations from the imaginary landscapes and the pre-Christian world of Finnish folk poetry, as well as elements inspired by the Finnish folk lyric.[43] This element appears in other decadent women writers' work: in

---

[41] See Eva Buchwald, *Ideals of Womanhood in the Literature of Finland and Russia 1894–1914.* PhD thesis. School of Slavonic and East European Studies. University of London, 1990.

[42] Cf. e.g. A. Sinfield, *The Wilde Century. Effeminacy, Oscar Wilde and the Queer Moment.* New York: Columbia University Press, 1994; and Richard Dellamora (ed.). *Victorian Sexual Dissidence.* Chicago & London: The University of Chicago Press, 1999. For the discussion of the Finnish case, see Viola Parente-Čapková, "Kuvittelija/tar. Androgyyniset mielikuvat L.Onervan varhaisproosassa" ("Fantasy Wo/man. Androgynous Fantasies in L. Onerva's Early Prose") in Päivi Lappalainen, , Heidi Grönstrand and Kati Launis (eds). *Lähikuvassa nainen. Näköaloja 1800-luvun kirjalliseen kulttuuriin (Woman in Focus. Perspectives on the 19th Century Literary Culture).* Helsinki: Suomalaisen Kirjallisuuden Seura, 2001: 216-237.

[43] Traditionally, the Finnish folk lyric has been considered a more 'feminine' than the 'masculine' epic, used by the Finnish revivalists for constructing the national past (cf. *The Kalevala*, the "Finnish national epic", 1835) and thus, within the nationlist discourse of literary history, valued much higher than the lyric, which has been revalued only relatively recently. See Viola Parente-Čapková, 2009 "Decadent Transgressions" in Tiina Mäntymäki, and Olli Mäkinen (eds). *Art and Resistance.* Vaasan yliopiston julkaisuja, Tutkimuksia 290 / Proceedings of the University of Vaasa, Research Papers 290: 39, 2009. The way Finnish male writers engaging with symbolism and decadence explored the epic tradition has been under scrutiny for a long time, see e.g. Pirjo Lyytikäinen, *Narkissos ja sfinksi. Minä ja Toinen*

Rachilde's novel *La Jongleuse* (1900), it is connected with the issue of maternal legacy as an inspiration for female creativity.[44] In Onerva's poems, elements from folk poetry fuse with symbolist and decadent imagery, engaging not in a direct dialogue with the "story of the (Finnish) nation", but in testing the possibilities of the female voice and establishing relationships with other, often imaginary, women and female muses, who, thanks to the metrum, rhythm and imagery typical of Finnish folk poetry, are associated with Finnish folklore. In the novel *Mirdja*, we enter a web of intertextual relations, pointing both to the oral and written tradition, when the old mad heroine, mourning her dead husband, remembers a folk poem about "a dead beloved",[45] echoing a poem by Onerva's contemporary, the aforementioned Eino Leino. Leino's poem was based on a Finnish folk poem and inspired by the rich international tradition of this motif, present both in European folklore and literature (the "Lenore cycle"). Here, Onerva uses the decadent device of foregrounded intertextuality in discussing the identity of an aging widow, a "childless dilettante" without a home country.

Apart from being a biographical element of Onerva's life, childlessness and a complex relationship with the issue of motherhood were one of the author's major concerns in her work. Motherhood, a controversial topic *per se*, used and misused within the nationalist ideologies, acquires complex levels of incompatible unions when associated with decadence, depending, again, on the context in question. For example, Rachilde's heroines reject the institution of motherhood, "in opposition to the dominant ideology both of the Third Republic and of its conservative Catholic opposition".[46] In the case of George Egerton, motherhood, not separated from sexuality, might be appropriated for the decadent version of "constructivist essentialism,"[47]

---

*vuosisadanvaihteen kirjallisuudessa (Narcissus and Sphinx. Me and Other in the Literature of the Turn of the 19th and the 20th Century).* Helsinki: Suomalaisen Kirjallisuuden Seura, 1997.

[44] The heroine of the novel, Eliante, has a black Martiniquaise servant, Ninaude, who sings to Eliante, tells her legends and folktales, enriching Eliante's 'juggling' with the female traditions of songs and folktales, suggesting "another form of creativity". See Diane Holmes, *Rachilde. Decadence, Gender and the Woman Writer*: 141.

[45] L. Onerva. *Mirdja*: 289.

[46] Diane Holmes, *Rachilde. Decadence, Gender and the Woman Write*: 123.

[47] A term coined by Ebba Witt Bratttström to indicate the ways *fin de siècle* women used the icons of essential womanhood for their purposes. See Witt-Brattström, Ebba. "Till modernismens feministiska genealogi – från Narcissus till Eko", "Towards the Feminist Genealogy of Modernism: From Narcissus to Ekho" in *Ur könets mörker. Literaturanalyser.* Stockholm: Norstedts, 2003: 182-196.

irrespective of the discourse of nationalism. One of the most burning issues was, obviously, the relationship between motherhood and (artistic) creativity. On the other hand, Onerva was familiar with transgressive representations of motherhood within the decadent mode, namely the figures of the "fallen" or "prostituted" mother, known from many decadent works of literature and art, from Barbey d'Aurevilly and Gabriele d'Annunzio,[48] to Edvard Munch's painting *Madonna* (1894-1895). In *Mirdja*, the motherless heroine refuses any nationalist genealogy, playing a "gypsy princess" and dreaming about a "stigmatized birth" through her eponymous mother,[49] who was a bohemian wanderer, "as free as a gypsy", and died at Mirdja's birth. Playing with the typically decadent tension between the despised 'real', material, and the highly valued fantastic and immaterial, Onerva's 'real' mother characters in *Mirdja* (a teacher's wife and a Lutheran minister's wife, both mothers of Mirdja's partners) stand for the Finnish petite bourgeois patriotic society with its Protestant ethos, for the "social motherhood", and for the idea of popular enlightenment which suffocates the heroine and impedes her from achieving her artistic ambitions. Much more important are mother figures encountered by the heroine in her dreams or visions, and through works of art. They are nightmarish, but, by a complex interplay between identification and desire, encounters with them allow the author to formulate questions about women's artistic identity.

Having identified with the image of the decadent dilettante, Mirdja attributes it to her sterility, both as an artist and as a woman – again, a quality incompatible with any facet of the patriotic rhetoric. Gradually, Mirdja becomes obsessed with being motherless and childless, and her life ends in a bog, in search of the child she never had. The bog, an intermediate piece of

---

[48] See e.g. Charles Bernheimer, *Figures of Ill Repute. Representing Prostitution in Nineteenth-Century France.* Cambridge, Massachusetts & London, England: Harvard University Press, 1989; and Isabella Nardi, "'Le cattive madri': note sul tema della maternità nei romanzi dannunziani e oltre" in A. Neiger (ed.). *Maternità trasgressiva e letteratura.* Napoli: Liguori, 1993: 79-97.

[49] Deborah Epstein Nord, who has extensively studied the figure of the 'gypsy' in English literature within the "constant, ubiqutous market of otherness", developed analyses of the fantasies of 'lowly' or 'stigmatized' birth as a reversal of Freud's 'family romances'. She sees the fantasy of the being related to 'gypsies' in 19[th] century women writers' works as a sign of longing for otherness, foreigness and escape from femininity, of being released, "if only partially and by association, from the strictures of female destiny and the female plot". See Deborah Epstein Nord, "'Marks of Race': Gypsy Figures and Eccentric Femininity in Nineteenth-Century Women's Writing" in *Victorian Studies* 41( 2), 1998: 189-210.

land with ambiguous connotations, can be seen both as a soulscape and as a decadent version of Mother Earth.[50] At the same time, in the context of Finnish literature, the closing section of *Mirdja* works as ironic re-writing, or a direct parody of Johannes Linnankoski's novel *The Song of a Blood-Red Flower* (1905), a story of a Finnish Don Juan. Olavi, the (male) protagonist of the novel, after having overcome 'decadent' temptations in order to understand life as an aesthetic phenomenon, settles down, has a family and dedicates himself to hard work. He takes part in the "building of the nation" by cultivating a bog, which, in this case, symbolizes the dark forces that used to distract him from his patriotic mission.

Decadent dilettante's sterility was, when discussed by the early Paul Bourget (1852-1935), whose work Onerva knew and translated into Finnish, rather positive. As Richard Hibbitt has shown, in Bourget's early work, namely the *Essais de psychologie contemporaine* (1883), dilettantism, illustrated by the example of Ernest Renan, is a sophisticated position, one of exacerbated self-consciousness, self-analysis, irony, skepticism and nihilism.[51] Its relationship to nationalism is very complex, but, since dilettantism and action appear as mutually exclusive, dilettantism seems mostly antithetical to the process of nation-building. As shown by Hibbitt and others, the concept is, nevertheless, so ambivalent, that it can serve many different purposes; in the work of Bourget himself, it also evolved from a positive to a more negative understanding, and for other decadent writers, it could be unequivocally negative, as it was for Joris-Karl Huysmans. Onerva explores the impossible figure of a woman dilettante, which can be, again, read as protest against the above mentioned patriotic icons of womanhood, as well as against the decadent unequivocal construction of the figure of the dilettante (similarly as that of the decadent dandy) as male. However, it may also be a dangerous trap, given that women were traditionally labelled as

---

[50] Viola Parente-Čapková, "Decadent New Woman?" in *NORA - Nordic Journal of Women's Studies* 6(1), 1998: 6-20. The closing scene of *Mirdja* can be read as an allusion to the death of Kate Chopin's Creole heroine in the *Awakening* (1899), who experiences a kind of a rebirth while fusing with the water element, so often perceived as feminine.

[51] See Richard Hibbitt, *Dilettantism and Its Values. From Weimar Classicism to the* fin de siècle. London: Legenda, Studies in Comparative Literature 9, Modern Humanities Research Association & Maney Publishing, 2006: 88-108.

dilettantes in a depreciatory sense, with regard to their alleged "inborn" imitativeness and the incapacity of original thinking.[52]

A more empowering understanding appears in Onerva's profound interest in the issue of female narcissism, when she uses the figures, images and poetic strategies typical of the decadent mode, but employs them to discuss the problems of creative women, or, directly, 'women of genius'. Onerva's attempt to combine the embodied female beauty and genius is shown, for example, in her intense interest in beautiful women of genius, like Madame de Staël's Corinne. The topic was incompatible both with decadent views on women and with the mainstream discourse of Finnish nationalism. According to the mainstream Finnish women's movement, with its earlier mentioned Christian-patriotic ethos, Finnish woman had to be intelligent, perseverant, courageous and strong, but, at the same time, modest and humble.[53] Unlike e.g. Rachilde, Zinaida Gippius and other decadent women writers, engaging with cross-dressing and constructing themselves as androgynous figures, Onerva, in her works, insisted on exploring various strategies to figure the union of (a pronouncedly feminine) beauty and genius. One of these strategies was an attempt to appropriate the figure of the Nietzschean Overman, present both in *Mirdja* and in Onerva's early poetry and short stories. Again, this allowed the author to ask many important and controversial questions, although the 'heronies' attempts to appropriate the Overman role do not succeed. The heroines who try to elevate themselves to the Overman position end up as variants of a tragic upstart, 'nousukas', a character that Onerva became famous for, namely thanks to the collection of short stories called *Nousukkaita: Luonnekuvia* (*Upstarts / Parvenues: Character Portrays*) from 1911.

The Finnish word *nousukas* can be translated as upstart, parvenue, or social climber, but we have to be careful with its contextualization. All the above mentioned English equivalents sound negative, while the Finnish

---

[52] See Viola Parente-Čapková, "'Kuka, kuka sitoi?' Dekadentti äitiys L. Onervan *Mirdjassa*" ("'Who, Who Bound Me? Decadent Motherhood in L. Onerva's *Mirdja*") in Pirjo Lyytikäinen (ed.). Helsinki *Dekadenssi vuosisadan vaihteen taiteessa ja kirjallisuudessa (Decadence in the turn-of-the-19th-and-the-20th-Century Art and Literature*): Suomalaisen Kirjallisuuden Seura. 1998: 113–117.

[53] See e.g. Riitta Jallinoja,*Suomalaisen naisasialiikkeen taistelukaudet (The Phases of Fight in the Finnish Women's Movement)*. Porvoo – Helsinki – Juva: WSOY, 1983; and Pirjo Markkola,*Synti ja siveys. Naiset, uskonto ja sosiaalinen työ Suomessa 1860-1920* (*Sin and Morality: Women, Religion and Social Work in Finland, 1860-1920*). Helsinki: Suomalaisen Kirjallisuuden Seura, 2002.

notion of *nousukas* is more complex.[54] 'Nousukas' could mean *nouveau rich*, usually referring to a person who became rich during the industrialization of Finland at the second half of the 19th century, but, around the turn of the the late 19th and the early 20th century, literary portrayals of this figure concentrate on the issue of education, which served to "civilize" or "raise" the lower classes of society in the name of a national project, pursuant to J.V. Snellman's patriotic social doctrine of bringing the (in the 19th century, still mostly Swedish speaking) upper classes closer to the (mostly Finnish speaking) people and 'elevating' the common folk by means of education. In this respect, *nousukas* is analogous to the figure of the 'rural student', who comes to the town or city and gets involved in the patriotic enterprise, a figure well known from other Nordic literatures, and, indeed, other European literatures as well. As the Finnish literary critics[55] have pointed out, *nousukas* as a character 'in between classes' becomes a complex cultural trope: it can serve as a kind of a 'strategic hybrid', an ambivalent figure which enabled both the upper and the lower classes of society to meet each other in the name of patriotism, but, at the same time, it maintains the 'natural' order of the society, i.e. gender, class and cultural divisions.

The stories of literary *nousukas* are saturated with failure and feelings of estrangement, alienation, melancholy and shame, and they also reflect contemporary debates on the unresolved conflict of heredity and environment, resulting in conflicting views on degeneration. Onerva's upstarts are, moreover, also typically decadent figures epitomizing an intermediate, 'in-between' state, which might mean a state of transition, but also a state of getting stuck somewhere, without the possibility to return or to proceed. While the majority of the mainstream, canonized literary works at the beginning of the century dealt with male upstarts, Onerva introduces mostly female figures, whose social climbing is very gender specific. Mirdja herself is, clearly, a kind of a *nousukas* figure as well, but I would like to concentrate here on the above mentioned collection of short stories

---

[54] See esp. Kukku Melkas , et al. *Läpikulkuihmisiä. Muotoiluja kansallisuudesta ja sivistyksestä 1900-luvun alun Suomessa* (*Passers-Through. Formulations on Nationality and Culture in the early 20th Century Finland*). Helsinki: Suomalaisen Kirjallisuuden Seura, 2009.

[55] Päivi Molarius, "'Will the Human Race Degenerate?' The Individual, the Family and the Fearsome Spectre of Degeneracy in Finnish Literature of the Late 19th and Early 20th Century" in Pirjo Lyytikäinen,. (ed.). *Changing Scenes. Encounters between European and Finnish Fin de Siècle*. Helsinki: Finnish Literature Society, Studia Fennica Litteraria 1, 2003: 121-142.

*Nousukkaita*. In several of them, Onerva portrays the female upstarts as grotesque figures, who try to 'rise' in the sense of either amplifying or transcending their gender.

The most interesting decadent upstart of the whole collection is a Finnish speaking 'rural student', a woman called Suoma, who wants to progress through means of education, but fails and, as a last hope, tries to enter academic circles by marrying a university professor. The story, called "Naamiaiset" ("Masquerade", or "Carnival"), culminates in a masked ball, a favourite decadent trope, where Suoma's upstart identity is, paradoxically and regardless of her mask, revealed. The ironic narrator, while commenting on Suoma's grotesque efforts, states: "She was too clumsy and stiff for the masquerade" (L. Onerva 1911, 143). The academic circles, ardently patriotic, appear to be the true masked ball, a masquerade, impossible for members of the classes identified with the 'pure' – essential Finnishness, but whose "purity"/"innocence" is, nevertheless, viewed by the elite as clumsiness and a (despicable) lack of sophistication, in the worst case as a brutish primitivity – to break into. The upstart Suoma is denounced as a despicable creature, a dilettante in the negative sense, lingering in-between the classes, no longer belonging to the 'folk', but unable to join the upper, educated classes either. Finally, the whole patriotic discourse as performed by the educated classes is revealed as hypocrisy, a cruel joke at the expense of the *kansa*, i.e. those in whose name the masquerade is being performed. This ironic comment on the Snellmanian ideal of the democratization of the Finnish nation is, as always in Onerva's case, explicitly gendered: at the end, Suoma is shamed in a very gender specific way, when somebody points at her alleged immoral way of life, tolerated in case of the male students, but unforgivable in case of a female student who lives alone in the capital.

The answer to Mirdja's question ("What is the so-called folk/nation"?) appears to be bitterly ironic, as suggested within the wording of the question itself, by using the word 'so-called'. The desire to belong to 'the people', to 'fuse' with an 'authentic', major force like the folk/nation pursuant to the idealist ethos of the Finnish national awakening, is constantly subverted by the decadent feelings of *ennui* and fatigue, as well as by the decadent strategies of ambivalence, fragmentariness, irony, parody, paradox and strong intertextuality, and by the tropes of carnival and masquerade, so popular with the *fin de siècle* writers. Further complexities rise from the gender aspect: on the one hand, there is the obvious wish to participate in the way that the *fin de siècle* questions fixed gender roles, while on the other hand, there is the urge to speak on behalf of woman, to ponder perennial women's issues like motherhood from a pronouncedly female viewpoint, all that *vis à vis* the issue of (women's) artistry. The Decadent New Woman's contradictory identifications and the vivid interest both in the Finnish context and in the international cultural exchange, enabled Onerva to tell (her) nation neither from above nor from below, but from 'in between', in various senses of the expression – aesthetic, political and social – while also engaging with and shaping many elements of the decadent aesthetic.

## Select Bibliography


### A. Primary Sources

L. Onerva. 1908/1982. *Mirdja*. Helsinki: Otava.

—. 1911. *Nousukkaita: Luonnekuvia* (*Upstarts / Parvenues: Character Portrays*). Helsinki: Weilin.

### B. Secondary Sources

Bernheimer, Charles. 1989. *Figures of Ill Repute. Representing Prostitution in Nineteenth-Century France.* Cambridge, Massachusetts & London, England: Harvard University Press.

Branch, Michael. 1994. "The Invention of a National Epic" in *The Uses of Tradition. A Comparative Inquiry into the Nature, Uses, and Functions of Oral Poetry in the Balkans, The Baltic, and Africa*. Branch, Michael and Celia Hawksworth (eds). Helsinki, London: SSEES, University of London – Finnish Literature Society: 195-211.

Buchwald, Eva. 1990. *Ideals of Womanhood in the Literature of Finland and Russia 1894–1914.* PhD thesis. School of Slavonic and East European Studies. University of London.

Calinescu, Matei. 1987. *Five Faces of Modernity: Modernism, Avant-Garde, Decadence, Kitsch, Postmodernism*. Durham: Duke University Press.

Casanova, Pascale. 1999, 2004. *The World Republic of Letters*. (tr. M.B. DeBevoise.) Cambridge, Massachusetts & London, England: Harvard University Press.

Constable, L. Denisoff, D. and Potolsky, M. 1999. "Introduction" in *Perennial Decay. On the Aesthetics and Politics of Decadence*. Constable, L., D. Denisoff and M. Potolsky. (eds). Philadelphia: University of Pennsylvania Press: 1-32.

Dellamora, Richard (ed.). 1999. *Victorian Sexual Dissidence.* Chicago & London: The University of Chicago Press.

Эконен, Кирсти. 2009. *Творец, субъект, женщина: Стратегии женского письма в русском символизме*. (Ekonen, Kirsti, *Creator, Subject, Woman: Strategies of Womens' Writing in Russian Symbolism.*) PhD thesis. University of Tampere.

Erastoff, G. 1908. "Erotism i dekadens i Rysslands litteratur" ("Eroticism and Decadence in Russian Literature") in *Argus* 15(1): 3-5.

Ervasti, Esko. 1960. *Suomalainen kirjallisuus ja Nietzsche I. 1900-luvun vaihde ja siihen välittömästi liittyvät ilmiöt.* (*Finnish Literature and Nietzsche I. The turn of the 19th and the 20th Century and Phenomena connected directly to it*). Turku: Turun yliopisto.

Felski, Rita. 1995. *The Gender of Modernity*. Cambridge (Mass.) & London: Harvard University Press.

Hawthorn, Melanie. 2001. *Rachilde and French Women's Authorship. From Decadence to Modernism*, Nebraska, University of Nebraska Press.

Hibbitt, Richard. 2006. *Dilettantism and Its Values. From Weimar Classicism to the* fin de siècle. London: Legenda, Studies in Comparative Literature 9, Modern Humanities Research Association & Maney Publishing.

Holmes, Diane. 2001. *Rachilde. Decadence, Gender and the Woman Writer.* Oxford & New York: Berg.

Hroch, Miroslav. 1985. *Social Preconditions of National Revival in Europe: a Comparative Analysis of the Social Composition of Patriotic Groups among the Smaller European Nations.* (tr. Ben Fowkes.) Cambridge: Cambridge University Press.

Jallinoja, Riitta. 1983. *Suomalaisen naisasialiikkeen taistelukaudet (The Phases of Fight in the Finnish Women's Movement).* Porvoo – Helsinki – Juva: WSOY.

Jusová, Iveta. 2005. *The New Woman and the Empire*. Columbus: Ohio State University Press.

Koch, Magdalena. 1998. "Fellow Travellers of a Serbian Woman. Isidora Sekulić or an Overture to Modern Serbian Literature" in *Die Bilder der 'neuen Frau' in der Moderne und den Modernisierungsprozessen des 20. Jahrhunderts.* Gabrielska, Krystyna, Mirosłava Czarnecka and Christa Ebert (eds). Wrocław: Wrocławskie Wydawnictvo Oświatowe: 186-196.

Lappalainen, Päivi. 1999. "'Äiti-ilon himo'. Naiset ja kansakunnan rakentuminen 1800–luvulla" ("'The Desire for the Joy of Motherhood'. Women and the Nation Building in the 19th Century") in *Kaksi tietä nykyisyyteen. Tutkimuksia kirjallisuuden, kansallisuuden ja kansallisten liikkeiden suhteesta Suomessa ja Virossa (Two Ways to the Present. Studies on the Relationship between Literature, Nationality and National Movements in Finland and in Estonia*) Koistinen, T., P. Kruuspere, E. Sevänen and R. Turunen (eds). Helsinki: Suomalaisen Kirjallisuuden Seura: 106-129.

Lyytikäinen, Pirjo. 1998. "Dekadenssi – rappion runous" (Decadence: Poetry of Decay) in *Dekadenssi vuosisadan vaihteen taiteessa ja kirjallisuudessa (Decadence in the turn-of-the-19th-and-the-20th-Century Art and Literature*) Lyytikäinen, Pirjo. (ed.). Helsinki: Suomalaisen Kirjallisuuden Seura: 7-15.

—. 1997. *Narkissos ja sfinksi. Minä ja Toinen vuosisadanvaihteen kirjallisuudessa (Narcissus and Sphinx. Me and Other in the Literature of the Turn of the 19th and the 20th Century).* Helsinki: Suomalaisen Kirjallisuuden Seura.

Lyytikäinen, Pirjo. 2003. "The Allure of Decadence. French Reflections in a Finnish Looking Glass" in *Changing Scenes. Encounters between European and Finnish Fin de Siècle*. Lyytikäinen, Pirjo. (ed.). Helsinki: Finnish Literature Society, Studia Fennica Litteraria 1: 12-30.

Macura, Vladimír. 1995. *Znamení zrodu: české národní obrození jako kulturní typ* (The Sign of Birth: Czech National Revival as a Cultural Type.) Praha: H&H.

Markkola, Pirjo. 2002. *Synti ja siveys. Naiset, uskonto ja sosiaalinen työ Suomessa 1860–1920* (*Sin and Morality: Women, Religion and Social Work in Finland, 1860–1920*). Helsinki: Suomalaisen Kirjallisuuden Seura.

Martin, Biddy. 1991. *Woman and Modernity: The (life)styles of Lou Andreas-Salomé*. Ithaca & New York: Cornell University Press.

Matich, Olga. 2005. *Erotic Utopia. The Decadent Imagination in Russia's Fin de Siècle*. Madison: The University of Wisconsin Press.

Melkas, Kukku, et al. 2009. *Läpikulkuihmisiä. Muotoiluja kansallisuudesta ja sivistyksestä 1900-luvun alun Suomessa* (*Passers-Through. Formulations on Nationality and Culture in the early 20th Century Finland*). Helsinki: Suomalaisen Kirjallisuuden Seura.

Milutinović, Zoran. 2011. *Getting over Europe: The Construction of Europe in Serbian Culture*. Studia Imagologica. Rodopi: Amsterdam and New York.

Miner, Heather. 2006. "Fragmenting the Female Voice: Restrictive Imperial Discourse and the New Woman Movement" in *Nineteenth Century Gender Studies* 2(2). Online at: http://www.ncgsjournal.com /issue22/miner.htm [Accessed 1.3.2012].

Molarius, Päivi. 2003. "'Will the Human Race Degenerate?' The Individual, the Family and the Fearsome Spectre of Degeneracy in Finnish Literature of the Late 19th and Early 20th Century" in *Changing Scenes. Encounters between European and Finnish Fin de Siècle*. Lyytikäinen, Pirjo. (ed.). Helsinki: Finnish Literature Society, Studia Fennica Litteraria 1: 121-142.

Mosse, G. L. 1996. *The Image of Man. The Creation of Modern Masculinity*. New York: Oxford University Press.

—. 1985. *Nationalism and Sexuality. Middle-Class Morality and Sexual Norms in Modern Europe*. Madison: The University of Wisconsin Press.

Nardi, Isabella. 1999. "'Le cattive madri': note sul tema della maternità nei romanzi dannunziani e oltre" in Neiger, A. (ed.). *Maternità trasgressiva e letteratura*. Napoli: Liguori: 79-97.

Nord, Deborah Epstein. 1998. "'Marks of Race': Gypsy Figures and Eccentric Femininity in Nineteenth-Century Women's Writing" in *Victorian Studies* 41( 2): 189-210.

Pachmuss, Temira. 1971. *Zinaida Gippius: An Intellectual Profile*. Southern Illinois University Press.

Parente-Čapková, Viola. 2001. "Kuvittelija/tar. Androgyyniset mielikuvat L.Onervan varhaisproosassa" ("Fantasy Wo/man. Androgynous Fantasies in L. Onerva's Early Prose") in *Lähikuvassa nainen. Näköaloja 1800-luvun kirjalliseen kulttuuriin (Woman in Focus. Perspectives on the 19th Century Literary Culture).* Lappalainen, Päivi, Heidi Grönstrand and Kati Launis (eds). Helsinki: Suomalaisen Kirjallisuuden Seura: 216-237.

—. 2009 "Decadent Transgressions" in *Art and Resistance*. Mäntymäki, Tiina and Olli Mäkinen (eds). Vaasan yliopiston julkaisuja, Tutkimuksia 290 / Proceedings of the University of Vaasa, Research Papers 290: 15-46.

—. 1998. "'Kuka, kuka sitoi?' Dekadentti äitiys L. Onervan *Mirdjassa*" ("'Who, Who Bound Me? Decadent Motherhood in L. Onerva's *Mirdja*") in *Dekadenssi vuosisadan vaihteen taiteessa ja kirjallisuudessa (Decadence in the turn-of-the-19th-and-the-20th-Century Art and Literature*) Lyytikäinen, Pirjo (ed.). Helsinki: Suomalaisen Kirjallisuuden Seura: 95-126.

—. 1998. "Decadent New Woman?" in *NORA - Nordic Journal of Women's Studies* 6(1): 6-20..

Pierrot, Jean. 1981. *The Decadent Imagination 1880–1900.* (tr. D. Coltman.) Chicago & London: The University of Chicago Press.

Potolsky, Matthew. 2006. "Decadence, Nationalism and the Logic of Canon Formation" in *Modern Language Quarterly* 67(2): 213–244.

Pynsent, Robert B. 1994. *Questions of Identity. Czech and Slovak Ideas of Nationality and Personality.* London: Central European University Press.

—. 1989. "Conclusory Essay: Decadence and Innovation" in *Decadence and Innovation. Austro-Hungarian Life and Art at the Turn of the Century.* Pynsent, Robert (ed.). London: Weidenfeld and Nicolson: 111-248.

Reed, John. 1985. *Decadent Style*. Athens, Ohio: Ohio University Press.

Riikonen, H. K. (ed.). 2007.*Suomennoskirjallisuuden historia I-II. (The History of Literature Translated into Finnish*). Helsinki: Suomalaisen Kirjallisuuden Seura.

Rojola, Lea. 2009. "Sivistyksen ihanuus ja kurjuus. Suomalaisen nousukkaan tarina" (The Glory and the Misery of Education: The Story of the Finnish *nousukas*) in Melkas, Kukku et al. *Läpikulkuihmisiä. Muotoiluja kansallisuudestaja sivistyksestä 1900-luvun alussa Suomessa* (*Passers-Through. Formulations on Nationality and Culture in the early 20th Century Finland*) Helsinki: Suomalaisen Kirjallisuuden Seura: 10-38.

—. 1992. "Oman sielunsa hullu morsian. Mirdjan matka taiteen maailmassa" (A Mad Bride of Her Own Soul. Mirdja's Journey in the World of Art) in *Pakeneva keskipiste. Tutkielmia suomalaisesta taiteilijaromaanista (Escaping Focus. Studies on the Finnish Artist Novel*) Hypén, Tarja-Liisa (ed.). Turku: Turun yliopisto, Taiteiden tutkimuksen laitos. A 26: 49-73.

Sevänen, Erkki. 1999. "Kansallisuus valtion suojeluksessa ja valvonnassa" (Nationality under the State Protection and Control) in Rojola, Lea (ed.). *Suomen kirjallisuushistoria 2: Järkiuskosta vaistojen kapinaan (The History of Finland's Literature 2: From the Faith in Reason to the Rebellion of Instincts).* Helsinki: Suomalaisen kirjallisuuden seura: 245-258.

Sinfield, A. 1994. *The Wilde Century. Effeminacy, Oscar Wilde and the Queer Moment.* New York: Columbia University Press.

Tuohela, Kirsti. 2008. *Huhtikuun tekstit. Kolmen naisen koettu ja kirjoitettu melankolia 1870-1900* (*April Texts.Three Women Writers Encountering Melancholia 1870-1900*). Helsinki: Suomalaisen Kirjallisuuden Seura.

Weinbaum, Alys Eve. 2001. "Writing Feminist Genealogy: Charlotte Perkins. Gilman, Racial Nationalism, and the Reproduction of Maternalist Feminism" in *Feminist Studies* 27(2): 271-302.

Witt-Brattström, Ebba. 2007. *Dekadnesens kön. Ola Hansson och Laura Marholm* (*The Gender of Decadence. Ola Hansson and Laura Marholm*). Stockholm: Norstedts.

—. 2003. "Till modernismens feministiska genealogi – från Narcissus till Eko" ("Towards the Feminist Genealogy of Modernism: From Narcissus to Ekho") in *Ur könets mörker. Literaturanalyser.* Stockholm: Norstedts: 182-196.

# PART III.

# WOMEN IN NETWORKS

# The Community of Letters and the Nation State: Bio-Bibliographic Compilations as a Transnational Genre around 1700

*Hilde Hoogenboom*

ABSTRACT This comparative study of about one hundred European compilations of women from Italy, France, England, Denmark, Germany, and Russia for the past six centuries proves that, starting around 1700, narratives began to acknowledge women as part of the international debate on nations and their boundaries. The author studies compilations from before 1900 as primary sources that contain both the names and works of writers and additional sources. All this quantitative data about publication and readership reveals the nationalist discourses at work in compilations and literary histories, but also the international networks in which women circulated. The author proves that compilations of women reveal the topography of women's literary history across centuries, like sonar waves.

WOMEN WRITERS CIRCULATED THROUGH MANY SPACES within the international community of letters, including salons, oral culture, letters, poetry, plays, memoirs, treatises, and novels. Compilations of women writers have yet to be fully appreciated for the transnational literary narratives they contain. Women were central to those literary relations that create communal networks between nations. Moreover, they embody the tensions between the inherently nature of the community of letters on the one hand, and nation states on the other. Boundaries are evident in the titles of many compilations of women from the 18th century and later – French women writers, Germany's women poets, Russian women authors, and literary women of England. Yet, although their titles say otherwise, a survey of compilations of women over six centuries from many nations reveals that they have always moved easily across national boundaries. Indeed women and women writers as categories are inherently, generically transnational and relational, about relations between nations.

Compilations from before 1900 are primary sources that contain both the names and works of writers and additional sources, and the name of already one reader: the compiler. Compilations are reception documents, often of other reception documents, alongside translations, reviews, letters, introductions, forewords, library catalogues, and so on. As we reconstruct the international reception of women writers and imagine other literary histories for women, compilations can both supply data and trace the general outlines of those international networks in which women circulated.

My comparative study of about one hundred European compilations of women from mainly Italy, France, England, Denmark, Germany, and Russia for the past six centuries suggests that beginning around 1700, three narratives began to unfold that show women as part of international debates about nations and their boundaries. Compilers created separate collections of women writers by nation and language as representative of a nation's enlightenment. Literary histories of newly envisioned nation states, however, included mainly men, writers in their national literatures. Finally, as literary histories naturally focused on their own literatures, they eliminated the often significant, even overwhelming presence of foreign literatures, mainly novels, many by women writers. Quantitative data about publication and readership reveal the nationalist discourses at work in compilations and literary histories. In a *histoire croisée*, these data can reconfigure the historical relations of women writers through the transnational literary connections between nations through translations, literature in the original languages, and compilations of women writers in Europe.[1]

Beginning in the 14th century, compilations of notable women form an old, cohesive transnational genre that first generated international and then national collections of female worthies, followed by international and national lists of learned women, and by the 18th century, national bio-bibliographic compilations of women writers.[2] Compilers cited each other, as

[1] For a recent study that examines European literature as relational, between England and France, see Mary Helen McMurran, *The Spread of Novels: Translation and Prose Fiction in the Eighteenth Century*. Princeton, NJ: Princeton University Press, 2010.

[2] Lists I consulted include, in English literature, Paula McDowell, "Consuming Women: The Life of the 'Literary Lady' as Popular Culture in Eighteenth-Century England," in *Genre,* 26 (Summer/Fall, 1993): 246-48, and Jane Williams, *The Literary Women of England, including a biographical epitome of all the most eminent to the year 1700 and sketches of the poetesses to the year 1850 with extracts from their works, and critical remarks,* London: Saunders, Otley, 1861: 1-13; in French, "Dictionnaires et listes de femmes célèbres: la liste," SIEFAR: Societé international pour l'Etude des Femmes de l'Ancien Régime, http://www.siefar.org (accessed June 15, 2011), and Joan DeJean, *Tender Geographies: Women and the Origins of the*

they relied on, disagreed with, and often simply used their predecessors' work and thus participated in extensive historical international debates about what constituted notable women. At the end of the 14th century in Italy, Boccaccio completed *Famous Women* (De mulieribus claris, 1361-75), which included women from all nations, mythology, and the Bible, though he excluded contemporary women. Through the 18th century, compilers of notable women continued to reference Boccaccio's *Famous Women*, modeled on Plutarch's *Parallel Lives of the Noble Grecians and Romans* (100 AD), for soon after his work began to circulate in Latin, it was translated into Italian, French, German, Dutch, Middle English, and Spanish, and was also imitated in diverse languages throughout the next two centuries. It is no exaggeration to claim, as does the most recent translator of *Famous Women* into English, that "Boccaccio's compilation is thus the fountainhead of the European tradition of female biography (…)".[3] One of the first responses to Boccaccio's well-known work, which was transmitted through dozens of illustrated manuscripts, was by Christine de Pizan, in *The Book of the City of Ladies* (*Le livre de la cité des dames*, 1405).[4] Her arguments over the merits of illustrious as opposed to famous (and infamous) women throughout history

---

*Novel in France*. New York: Columbia UP, 1991: 219-21; in German, Dorothea Behnke, "*dass weiblichen Geschlechte an Tapfferkeit/Klugheit/Gelehrsamkeit und andern Haupt-Tugenden, gar nichts fehle*": *Lexika zu Schriftstellerinnen aus dem deutschsprachigen Raum*. Osnabrück: Zeller Verlag, 1999; Carl Wilhelm Otto August von Schindel, *Die Deutschen Schriftstellerinnen des neunzehnten Jahrhunderts*. Leipzig: F. A. Brockhaus, 1823-25; repr. New York: Georg Olms Verlag, 1978: xxix-xxxii; Sophie Pataky, *Lexikon deutscher Frauen der Feder. Eine Zusammenstellung der seit dem Jahre 1840 erchienenen Werke weiblicher Autoren, nebst Biographieen der lebenden und einem Verzeichnis der Pseudonyme*. Berlin: Carl Pataky, 1898: xiii-xv; and Elisabeth Friedrichs, *Die deutschsprachigen Schriftstellerinnen des 18. und 19. Jahrhunderts: Ein Lexikon* Stuttgart: J.B. Metzlersche Verlagsbuchhandlung, 1981: ix-xxi; in Italian, Pietro Leopoldo Ferri, *Biblioteca femminile Italiana* Padua: Tipografia Crescini, 1842; and in Russian, A.V. Mez'er, *Russkaia slovesnost' s XI po XIX stoletiia vkliuchitel'no. Bibliograficheskii ukazatel' proizvedenii russkoi slovesnosti v sviazi s istoriei literatury i kritiki*. St Petersburg: Tipografia A. Porokhovshchikova, 1899: 1:16.

[3] Virginia Brown, "Introduction" in Giovanni Boccaccio, *Famous Women*, Virginia Brown (tr.). Cambridge, MA: Harvard University Press, 2003: xxi. For translations, see 257-59.

[4] Christine de Pizan, *The Book of the City of Ladies*, Earl Jeffrey Richards (tr.). New York: Persea Books, 1982. *Famous Women* still exists in 108 complete and partial manuscripts, and 28 known manuscripts that cannot be located. See Virginia Brown, "Introduction": 259.

were kept alive by the long running *querelle des femmes*, which also had its Italian counterpart, through the beginning of the $17^{th}$ century.[5] At this time, the first national compilations of historical women began to appear. Pierre de Bourdeille, seigneur de Brantôme, also looked to Boccaccio for *The Lives of Illustrious Ladies of France in their Time* (1665), which has been in continuous publication, mainly in French but also in translation, in some form for over 300 years, up to 1990.[6]

Yet in the two and a half centuries that separate Pizan's and Brantôme's works, despite their common model and source, a major difference arises between them that leads to the creation of a new category – women writers. Pizan, like Boccaccio, deals with mythological and historical women of the past from all nations, while Brantôme limits himself to historical queens and other noblewomen – female worthies, or *femmes fortes* – of France. Brantôme brings women down to earth, leaving behind Eve and goddesses, which paves the way for women writers. Thus as these compilations become national in content, they give up their international roots in the classics and the ancient world, in the tradition of *translatio studii et imperii.* But as a genre, despite their new national contents, compilations of notable women continued to travel easily from nation to nation in the original and in translation, as the transnational element shifted from the contents to the context.

Given the influence of Boccaccio, it seems natural that the initial compilations devoted to women writers should have appeared first in Italy. The earliest compilation of women writers (as opposed to famous women) that we have identified thus far is from Italy, in 1559, by Lodovico Domenichi: *Rhymes of Some Diverse Noble and Virtuous Women*, in a series of poetry from different Italian cities edited by Gabriel Giolito de' Farrari of Venice.[7] Over a half-century later, Francisco Agostino della Chiesa published *Theatre of Lettered Women and a Short Discourse on the Notability and*

---

[5] For connections between these two texts and earlier medieval catalogs of women, see Glenda McLeod, *Virtue and Venom: Catalogs of Women from Antiquity to the Renaissance*. Ann Arbor: University of Michigan Press, 1991.

[6] Pierre de Bourdeille, Seigneur de Brantôme, *Les vies des Dames Illustres de France de son temps*. Leiden: Jean Sambix le jeune, 1665.

[7] Lodovico Domenichi, *Rime diverse d'alcune nobilissime e virtuosissime donne*. Lucca, Busdrago, 1559. My research assistant Leah Faibisoff assembled a list of sources from those Ferri mentions.

*Perfection of the Female Sex*.[8] At the end of the 17th century, Antonio Bulifon, a French bookseller living in Naples, compiled *Rhymes of Fifty Illustrious Poetesses*, a reprint of Domenichi's collection.[9] Thirty years later, Luisa Bergalli compiled *Compositions of the Most Illustrious Female Rhymers of Every Century*, the first such compilation by a woman.[10] Though all contain only Italian women writers and verses, none of these compilations name Italy, cities, or principalities in their titles, as they would later in the 18th and 19th centuries. Women writers were a category on par with, but not limited by, geography. Domenichi's, Della Chiesa's and Bulifon's compilations became models and sources for 18th-century French and English compilers.[11]

Two widely available French compilations of classical women from the first half of the 17th century were indebted to Boccaccio and likewise became models for the next generation of German, Danish, and English compilers of women writers. In the first of the two, *Encomiums and the Lives of Queens, Princesses, Ladies and Young Ladies Renowned for their Piety, Courage, and Belief*, Father Hilarion de Coste (1595-1661) has 122 alphabetical entries for 113 women from various nations plus nine groups of women from particular places, with three additional tables of contents that select from these women for their "piety", their "courage and valor", and for their "knowledge or for having cultivated literature."[12] The latter category proved

[8] Agostino della Chiesa, *Theatro delle donne letterate con un reve discorso della preminenza, e perfittione del sesso donnesco*. Mondovi: per Giovanni Gislandi e Gio. Tomaso Rossi, 1620.

[9] Antonio Bulifon, *Rime di cinquanta illustri poetesse*, Naples: A. Bulifon, 1695; "Anthologies: Poetry, Early Modern" in Rinaldina Russell (ed.). *The Feminist Encyclopedia of Italian Literature*, Westport, CT: Greenwood Press, 1997: 15.

[10] Luisa Bergalli, *Componimenti delle più illustre rimatrici d'ogni secolo*. Venice: Antonio Mora, 1726.

[11] Antoine Leonard Thomas, *Essai sur le caractère, les mœurs et l'esprit des femmes dans les différens siècles*. Paris, 1772; repr. Colette Michael (ed.). Paris, 1772, repr. Paris, Geneva: Champion-Slatkine, 1987: 37; George Ballard, *Memoirs of Several Ladies of Great Britain Who Have Been Celebrated for Their Writings or Skill in the Learned Languages, Arts and Sciences*. Oxford, 1752, repr. Ruth Perry (ed.). Oxford, 1752, repr. Detroit, MI: Wayne State University Press, 1985: 53.

[12] Hilarion de Coste, *Les eloges et vies des reynes, princesses, dames et damoiselles illustres en pieté, courage & doctrine, qui ont fleury de nostre temps, & du temps de nos pères. Avec l'explication de levrs devises, emblemes, hyerogliphes, & symboles*. 2 vols. Paris: Sébastien Cramoisy, 1630, 2nd ed. 1647.

to be of special interest to the next generation of compilers in Denmark, Germany, and England.

The second internationally influential French compilation of women was by Madeleine de Scudéry (1607-1701). In *Illustrious Women*, she frames twenty encomiums from such renowned ancient women as Cleopatra and Lucretia to such famous men as Mark Anthony and Colatin, respectively, with an argument and an effect. The only women writers among these figures were Sappho and Erinne. Like Scudéry's bestselling tales, her *Illustrious Women* was an international phenomenon, with eight French editions in 25 years (1642-67), two German editions (1654 and 1659), and three English editions (1693, 1714, 1728).[13] In the introduction to the French edition of 1665, she mentions the success of the French translation of a similar Italian volume by Giovanni Battista Manzini (1599-1664), *The Furies of Youth, Rhetorical Exercises*. Manzini's work too was based on Boccaccio's *Famous Women*, and like other such collections of women, was read internationally; it was translated into both French and English.[14]

At the end of the 17th century, two influential compilations of learned women appeared that reengaged not only with Boccaccio's text, but with the 15th and 16th-century texts that were modeled on his. Such lists of learned women, of which there was a large number in the second half of the 17th century, also listed their older Renaissance sources, thus again putting these texts into international circulation. In her study of compilations of learned women, Rang concludes that "these older encyclopedias were extremely important sources for the 17th- and 18th-century authors of collections of learned women's biographies. They were adduced to buttress the claims that Renaissance humanism had already valued female learning".[15] Greatness was still measured by links with the past, but with the Renaissance rather than antiquity; Boccaccio served both purposes.

---

13 Madeleine de Scudéry, *Les femmes illustres, ou les harangues héroïques*. Paris: Chez Antoine de Sommaville & Augustin Courbe, 1642.

14 Giovanni Battista Manzini, *Furori della gioventu esercitii rhetorici*. Geneva: Pietro Auberto, 1647. For example, Francesco Pona, *La Galeria delle donne celebri* Bologna, 1633, translated by François de Grenaille as *La Galerie des dames illustres* (1642).

15 Brita Rang, "A 'learned wave': Women of letters and science from the Renaissance to the Enlightenment" in *Perspectives on Feminist Political thought in European History: From the Middle Ages to the Present.* Akkerman, Tjitske and Siep Stuurman (eds). New York: Routledge, 1998: 50-66.

The first of these influential texts was by Gilles Ménage (1613-92), who at the end of his career was a scholar and member of prominent salons in Paris; he had begun as a lawyer and tutor to Madame de Sévigné and Madame de LaFayette, famed for their letters and novels respectively. He dedicated *The History of Women Philosophers* (Historia Mulierum Philosopharum, 1690) to the most learned woman of his day, Anne Dacier (1654-1720), to whom he had already dedicated two works. His compilation of 65 ancient women was thus part of the *querelle des femmes*, in support of women's erudition, which Molière had mocked in two plays as *préciosité*.[16] Ménage begins his dedication as follows: "So great is the number of women writers that their names alone could fill a large volume, but most of them have pursued such pleasant studies as rhetoric, poetry, history, mythology, or the elegances of letter-writing".[17] Yet women writers in France would not have their own separate compilations for another 80 years, perhaps an indication of the extent to which this abundance of women's talent was taken for granted in France's role as a European cultural power. By second half of the 18th century compilers felt they had to defend women's literary accomplishments. Thus, in addition to other Latin editions and an English translation around 1700, two French translations of Ménage's compilation were published mid-18th century.[18]

Around the same time in Germany, Christian Juncker (1668-1714) attached his internationally famous compilation as an appendix to *A Historical Sketch Concerning the Journals or Diaries of Learned Men Published up to the Present Day in the Renowned Parts of Europe. In an Appendix is Displayed a Company of 100 Women Distinguished by [Their] Learning and Writings, gathered from the above*, dedicated to Ursula Regine Marie von Friesen (1658-1714). Juncker mentions Ménage's compilation, and like him, opposes Molière's depiction of learned women as ridiculous. Their works are complementary because he focused on women since ancient times. Though his main text is in Latin, there are passages in German and extensive quotations in French. As an indication of his influence, aside from Ménage, Juncker lists around a dozen or more sources that his successors in

[16] Gilles Ménage, *The History of Women Philosophers* [1690], Beatrice H. Zedler (tr.). Lanham, MD: University Press of America, 1984.
[17] *Ibid.*, 3.
[18] It was published as an appendix in three Latin editions (Lyons, 1690; Amsterdam, 1692; London 1830), in French (Amsterdam, 1758, 1761), and in English (London, 1702). *Ibid.*, xx-xxi.

Denmark, Germany, and England would borrow from him, beginning with Boccaccio.[19]

By the 18th century, the central transnational theme of these compilations is national preening in the international competition for learned women. This is evident in the national titles of the next wave of compilations. In Denmark, in 1700, the Rector Matthias Henriksen Schacht compiled 36 learned Danish women, *A Sketch Displaying a Sample from the Learned Women of Denmark*, prefaced with a list of seventeen similar Italian and French compilations of women, beginning with Boccaccio's *Famous Women.*[20] On the basis of this compilation of learned women, Pastor Albert Thura published a compilation of 123 Danish women writers, *The Learned Gynaeceum of Denmark, for Women of the Danes, Remarkable for Erudition or Famous Writings, Prefaced with an Introduction Concerning the Bounty of Diverse Women among Literary and Learned Danes, and with, Added to*

---

[19] Christian Juncker, *Schediasma historicum de ephemeridibus sive diariis eruditorum, in nobilioribus Europae partibus hactenus publicatis. In appendice exhibetur Centuria Foeminarum eruditione et scriptis illustrium, ab eôdem collecta.* Leipzig: J.F. Gleditsch, 1692 : 2-3, 12. Among others, Juncker lists: 1) Jacobus Philippus Bergomensis (Jacopo Filippo Foresti). *De claris selectisque plurimis mulieribus* Ferrara, L. de Rubeis, 1497; 2) Giovanni Boccaccio, *Historias de claris mulieribus, recentioribus quidem paucis, plurimis autem illis, que apud veteres gentiles aut vitsis aut virtutibas inclaruere* (1473), Paris, Antoine Vérard, 1493; 3) Giulio Cesare Capaccio, *Illustrium mulierum et illustrium litteris virorum elogia*, Naples: Carlinum et Vitalem, 1608-09; 4) Baptista Fulgosus (Battista Fregoso), *De foeminis quae doctrina excelluerunt*, in *De Memorabilibvs Et Claris Mvlieribvs: Aliqvot Diversorvm Scriptorvm Opera*, Paris, Simon Colinaeus, 1521; 5) Ludovicus Jacobus â Sancto Carolo (Ludwig Jacob), *Gynaecocratia* (Alten Stettin: Starcke, 1676); 6) Gilles Ménage, *Historia mulierum philosopharum, scriptore Ægidio Menagio; accedit ejusdem commentarius italicus in VII sonettum Francisci Petrarcha, a re non alienus* (Lyons: Apud Annissonios, Joan. Posuel, & Claudium Rigaud, 1690); 7) Johann Pasch, *Gynaeceum doctum; sivè Dissertatio historico-literaria vom gelehrten Frauenzimmer*,Wittenberg, Christian Fincel, 1701; 8) Madeleine de Scudéry, *Les femmes illustres, ou les harangues héroiques*, Paris, A. de Sommaville et A. Courbé, 1644; 9) Otto Sperling (1634-1715), *De Foeminis Doctis*, unpublished (The Royal Library, Copenhagen); 10) Jakob Thomasius, *Diatriben academicam de Foeminarum eruditione priorem*, Leipzig, Hehn, 1676.

[20] Matthias Henriksen Schacht, "Schediasma, exhibiens specimen de Eruditis Mulieribus Daniæ," in *Nova Literaria Maris Balthici & Septentrionis*. Lübeck, Böckmann, 1700: 209-19. Schacht lists editions in 1593 and 1598, for which there are no records today. See Virginia Brown, "Introduction": xix-xx, 257-58.

*the End, a Two-fold Index of Persons* (1732).[21] These compilations of learned Scandinavian women arose out of the work of several scholars who shared their work; they are among several such texts, and most, like that of Boccaccio, are in Latin, long a lingua franca of the scholarly world, with an international orientation.[22]

Like these Latin titles, the titles of some texts of this period reveal the hybrid nature of a transition period, from international to national content, yet in a European context. In Germany, in 1715, Georg Christian Lehms compiled the first such German text, in two volumes that contain the new category of women poets as representative of one nation, alongside the traditional compilation in the style of Boccaccio, which mixes notable women of all nationalities, together with an essay on learned women that takes a position in the *querelle des femmes*. The long explanatory title notes the three genres represented in this work: *Germany's Gallant Poetesses with Their Clever and Fine Examples. Together With an Appendix of Foreign Ladies. So that Likewise through Beautiful Poetry They Make Themselves Known to the Curious World, and with a Foreword. That the Female Sex is Just as Suited to Study as the Male Sex.*[23] His two volumes contain 111 German poets and 166 foreign women, the latter much more amply documented, with international sources. While German scholars naturally focus on German writers and ignore the second volume, Lehms's presentation of these European women alongside Germans makes an argument that German women too belong on this international podium.

---

[21] Albert Thura, *Gynæceum Daniæ Litteratum, Feminis Danorum, Eruditione vel scriptis claris conspicuum; præmissa præfatione de feminarum variarum apud danos in litteras et litteratos munificentia, et adjecto ad calcem, una cum appendice duplici indice personarum*. Altona: Apud Jonam Korte, 1732.

[22] Dr. Marianne Alenius, University of Copenhagen, shared her list of sources from a talk, "Scandinavian Learned Women" at the Eleventh International Congress of the Enlightenment of the International Society for Eighteenth-Century Studies (2003). Her list includes several manuscripts by the historian and antiquarian Otto Sperling (1634-1715), who Juncker lists among his sources (13).

[23] Georg Christian Lehms, *Teutschlands galante Poetinnen Mit Ihnen sinnreichen und netten Proben; Nebst einem Anhang Ausländer Dames, so sich gleichfalls durch Schöne Poesien Bey der curieusen Welt bekannt gemacht, und einer Vorrede. Dass das Weibliche Geschlecht so geschickt zum Studieren als das Männliche*. 2 vols. Frankfurt am Main: Anton Heynscheidt, 1714-15. Among Scandinavians, Rang, "A 'learned wave'," 63 (n14) also lists Johannes Eβbergius, *Mulieres philosophantes* (Upsala, 1699), which was a source for Lehms: v. 2 1714: 88.

The first English compilation devoted to women writers appears only in 1752, and is a hybrid text with an emphasis on learned women as writers. Though national in its content, it was international in its outlook. George Ballard published *Memoirs of Several Ladies of Great Britain Who have Been Celebrated for Their Writings or Skill in the Learned Languages, Arts and Sciences*, with 63 women, and a preface that takes a position in the *querelle des femmes* on women's capacity for erudition. In his preface, Ballard voices the new tensions between compilers in the international competition for learned women: "When it is considered how much has been done on this subject by several learned foreigners, we may justly be surprised at this neglect among the writers of this nation, more especially as it is pretty certain that England has produced more women famous for literary accomplishments than any other nation in Europe".[24] He distinguishes both the *quantity* and *quality* of a nation's writers, and these two themes will become dominant in such compilations.[25]

In a letter, Ballard further defends his project by noting the importance of learned women in France, especially Anne Dacier, who was the dedicatee of Ménage's *History of Women Philosophers*, which Ballard lists among his models.[26] For Ballard and other compilers, women writers were a source of national pride in large part because they existed in comparison to those of other nations. Ballard got the idea for his compilation of biographies from one such learned woman, Elizabeth Elstob (1683-1756), an Anglo-Saxon scholar who had also translated Scudéry's *Essay on Glory* (*Discours sur la gloire*, 1671, translated 1708). Ballard's project arose when England imported a third of its literature from France, much of it by such women as Marie-Jeanne Riccoboni (1714-92), a percentage that would decline over the next century as England's women novelists took over the domestic market.[27] The nationalization of England's literary market was a competitive process

[24] George Ballard, *Memoirs of Several Ladies of Great Britain*. 53.
[25] On quantitative compilations, see Hilde Hoogenboom, "Bibliography and National Canon: Women Writers in France, England, Germany, and Russia (1800-2010)," *Comparative Literature Studies* 50(2), 2013: 314-41.
[26] Ballard to Charles Lyttelton, [December 1745], cited in George Ballard, *Memoirs of Several Ladies of Great Britain*: 38-39.
[27] Franco Moretti, *Atlas of the European Novel, 1800-1900*. New York: Verso, 1998 : 151-56; Alan Dugald McKillop, "English Circulating Libraries, 1725-50," in *The Library*, S4-XIV(4), 1934: 477-85 (485).

that occurred together with the elimination of foreign literature and writers, many women, from new literary histories of England.

Like Juncker, these compilers of learned women in Denmark, Germany, and England all provide overlapping lists of their models and sources, some from the 17th century, but others from the 15th and 16th centuries, as they read foreign compilations to justify and create their national compilations. Schacht (1700) listed seventeen works as models, for none could be sources for learned women of Denmark.[28] Lehms (1714) provided extensive footnotes, mostly for the second volume of foreign women, with over a dozen sources.[29]

---

[28] Schacht lists names with some dates: I've added titles where possible: 1) Bergomensis (Foresti); 2) Giovanni Boccaccio, *De mulieribus claris* (1593 and 1598); 3) Capaccio; 4) Francesco Agostino della Chiesa, *Theatro delle donne letterate con vn breue discorso della preminenza, e perfettione del sesso donnesco.* Mondovi: per Giovanni Gislandi, e Gio. Tomaso Rossi, 1620; 5) Coste; 6) Fulgosus (Fregoso); 7) Andreas Fulvius Praenestinus, *Illustrium imagines. Imperatorum et illustrium virorum ac mulierum uultus ex antiquis nomismatibus expressi: et breues tituli cum inscriptionibus appositi per diuersos doctissimos viros: sed pro maiori parte per Andream Fuluium ... emendatum correptumque est totum opus.* Rome: per Iacobum Mazochium, 1517 ; 8) Chatonnière de Grenailles, François de. *La bibliothèque des dames.* Paris: Antoine de Sommaville, 1640 ; 9) Jacob; 10) Cornelius Kyianus; 11) Josephus à Pino (1550); 12) Pinus, Johannes. *De Memorabilibus et claris mulieribus aliquot diversorum scriptorum opera [Plutarchi philosophi de Virtutibus mulierum traductio per alamanum Ranutinum, civem florentinum; Opus Jacobi Philippi Bergomensis de claris mulierius; Divae Catharinae Senensis vita, per Johannes Pinum Tolosanum edits; de Illustribus foeminis opusculum, increto authore; Valenandi Varanii de Gestis Joannae, birginis francae, egregiae bellatricis, libri IV; de Sancta Clotilde; de sancta Genovefa*] Paris: S. Colonaei, 1521; 13) Bernardino Scardeone; *De antiquitate urbis patavii et claris civibus patavinis.* Basel: Episcopium, 1560; 14) Scudéry; 15) Thalamon (1530); 16) Tiraqueau, André *De legibus connubialibus et iure maritale.* Paris, 1513; and 17) Heronymus Tonssatus.

[29] Georg Christian Lehms, *Teutschlands galante Poetinnen Mit Ihnen sinnreichen und netten Proben,* footnotes names, some titles and dates : 1) Pierre Bayle, *Dictionnaire historique et critique.* Rotterdam, 1697; 2) Brantôme; 3) Coste; 4) Fulgosus (Fregoso); 5) Jacquette Guillaume, *Histoire des Dames illustres.* Thomas Jolly, 1665; 6) Juncker; 7) Ménage; 8) Louis Moréri, *Le grande dictionnaire historique, ou le mélange curieux de l'histoire sacrée et profane.* Lyons, 1674; *9)* Pasch; 10) Pietro Paulo de Ribera, *Le glorie immortali de' trionfi, et heroiche imprese d'ottocento quarantacinque donne illustri antiche, e moderne, dotate di conditioni, e scienze segnalate (...) Tra le quali vi sono molte versate in santita, virginita, penitanza, digiuni, vigilie (...) Sonoui alquante inuentrici di varie scienze, e mestieri all'vso humano necessarij (...).* Venice: appresso Evangelista Deuchino, 1609: 11. Pierre Richelet, *Les plus belles lettres françoises sur toutes sortes de sujets: tirées des meilleurs auteurs.* The Hague, 1699; 12) Scudéry; 13) Johannes Ravisius Textor, (ed.). *De Memorabilibvs Et Claris Mvlieribvs: Aliqvot Diversorvm Scriptorvm Opera.*

Ballard (1752) listed thirteen Italian, French, and German works as models, which were of minimal use as sources.[30] Both Schacht and Ballard list Boccaccio – half of their lists overlap – and while they were most likely not aware of each other, they and Lehms had four important immediate common predecessors. Juncker, Schacht, and Lehms all list Scudéry's *Illustrious Women* (1642). Coste's *Encomiums and the Lives of Queens, Princesses, Ladies and Young Ladies Renowned for their Piety, Courage, and Belief* (1647) was a common model for Schacht, Lehms, and Ballard. Both Lehms and Ballard cite the compilations by Ménage and Juncker.

Ballard and his international colleagues also cited other earlier Italian compilations as evidence of the ongoing debates throughout Europe about the merits of women. While largely irrelevant to the actual contents of these French, German, Danish, and English compilations, the 15th through 17th-century Italian sources connected their work to the past and added the weight of the Renaissance to their arguments for women's achievements and talents in the *querelle des femmes*. Like Ballard, 18th-century compilers also became increasingly aware that women were being left out of compilations of writers, which included mostly men, despite the many women writers in France and England.

Despite the two influential 17th-century French models of compilations by Scudéry and Coste, only in 1769 did Joseph La Porte publish a history of 256 French women writers in the form of a collection of letters, with selections from their works.[31] Published under the auspices of the Societé de Gens de

---

Paris, 1521; and 14) Jakob Thomasius, *Diatriben academicam de Foeminarum eruditione priorem*. Leipzig, 1671.

[30] Ballard lists only names; I've added titles where possible: 1) Bergomensis (Foresti); 2) Giovanni Boccaccio, *Libro di m. Gio. Boccaccio delle donne illustri, tradotto per messer Giuseppe Betussi. Con una additione fatta dal medesimo delle donne famose dal tempo di m. Giouanni fino a i giorni nostri*, (tr. Giuseppe Betussi) Venice: Trino di Monferrato, 1545: 3) Capaccio; 4) Chiesa; 5) Coste; 6) Jacob; 7) Juncker; 8) Ménage; 9) (Charles) Pinto; 10) Ribera; 11) Scardeone; 12) Francesco Serdonati, *Libro di M. Giovanni Boccaccio, Delle donne illustri*. Florence: Per Filippo Giunta, 1595; and 13) Petruccio Ubaldini, *Le vite delle donne illvstri Del regno d'Inghilterra, & del regno di Scotia, & di quelle, che d'altri paesi ne i due detti regni sono stato maritate. Doue si contengono tutte le cose degne di memoria da esse, ò da altri per i rispetti loro state operate, tanto di fuori, quanto di dentro de i due regni*. London: Appresso Giouanni Volfio, 1591.

[31] Joseph La Porte, *Histoires littéraire des femmes françoises: ou, Lettres historiques et critiques, contenant un précis de la vie et une analyse raisonée des ouvrage des*

Lettres, according to Joan DeJean in her survey of fifteen compilations containing French women writers, La Porte's *Literary History of French Women* is the first to use the term 'femme auteur', thus announcing a new category in French literary history.[32] La Porte's preface defends women's talents and reason, in the language of the *querelle des femmes*, and without mentioning any examples or other nations, simply states that "It is principally in France that women are able to benefit from these advantages".[33] Soon La Porte's compilation crossed the English Channel as the unacknowledged basis for *Sketches of the Lives and Writing of the Ladies of France* by Ann Thicknesse (1780).[34]

These kinds of compilations traveled quickly from France to England, complete with their lists of sources. It had been preceded by an essay by Antoine Leonard Thomas (1732-85), *Essay on the Character, Manners, and Genius of Women in Different Ages* (1772) that was translated into English (1773), with an additional volume devoted to English women, which drew heavily on Ballard's compilation.[35] This essay treats women from all eras of history and various nations, with a section on women of letters and a list of over 20 earlier such volumes, beginning with Boccaccio,[36] and including many of the same compilers as are listed by Schacht, Lehms, and Ballard, with an additional list of more essays on the merits of women from Italy, Spain, and France, which he viewed as a response to a German treatise by Heinrich Cornelius Agrippa, *On the Nobility and Excellence of the Female Sex* (1529).[37] Thomas concludes that "this opinion or this controversy produced a kind of war among writers otherwise quite obscure, and gave birth to works, responses, and replies that are today similarly unknown".[38] In that warring

---

*femmes qui se sont distinguées dans la littérature françoise, par une société de gens de lettres*, Paris: Chez Lacombe, 1769.

[32] Joan De Jean, *Tender Geographie*: 228, n23.

[33] La Porte, *Histoires*, vi.

[34] Ann Thicknesse, *Sketches of the Lives and Writing of the Ladies of France*. London: Dodsley and W. Brown, 1780. Dr. Suzan Van Dijk (Huygens Institute) made this connection for me.

[35] Antoine Leonard Thomas, *Essai*, 1987; *Essay on the Character, Manners, and Genius of Women in Different Ages*, Mr Russell (tr.). 2 vols. Philadelphia, PA: R. Aitken, 1774. Published in London (1773) first, the translator's introduction makes clear this was meant for a British audience.

[36] Antoine Leonard Thomas, *Essai* : 37-38.

[37] Heinrich Cornelius Agrippa von Nettesheim, *De nobilitate et praecellentia foeminei sexus*. Antwerp, 1529, repr. Geneva: Librairie Droz, 1990.

[38] Antoine Leonard Thomas, *Essai* : 41.

spirit, Thomas thus condemns the list of mainly Italian compilations to oblivion. He summarizes the opposing views of various French critics, none as negative as Boileau: "One notes that in all the verse of Boileau, there is not one name of a single woman of his time".[39] The translator joins in the fray to conclude that "it is just to remark, that few of them deserve to be read (...) Such pedants should be told, that twenty citations will not make a reason".[40] But clearly the citations themselves were an important part of the argument in that they reconstructed, once again, the history of a long, international, cultural debate that had continued to evolve, now to include women writers. Indeed, the translator actually took Thomas's two footnotes,[41] that contained his many citations and inserted them into the main text as a complete section.[42]

Fifty years later, in 1819-20, Russia published its first *femmes fortes* collection, as an addition to the translated popular French compilations by Pierre Blanchard and Girard de Propiac.[43] Both Blanchard's compilation of illustrious men, *La Plutarque de la jeunesse* (1803) and Propiac's compilation of *femmes fortes* (1806) were translated first into German (1806-7) and then into Russian (1816-17), with Propiac's illustrious women from various nations added on to Blanchard's compilation.[44] Anonymous Russian women wrote a collection of biographies of famous Russian women, which was added on two years later. Soon, two new compilations of women writers appeared: an alphabetical library inventory of 97 women by Stepan Russov for an anonymous noblewoman in St Petersburg (1826), and independently in Moscow, a chronological series of 68 bio-bibliographic entries by the editor,

---

[39] *Ibid.*, 1987, 74.

[40] Antoine Leonard Thomas, *Essay*, 1774: 124.

[41] Antoine Leonard Thomas, *Essai* (1987): 37-38, n19 and 41-45, n22.

[42] Antoine Leonard Thomas, *Essay* (1774): 106-24.

[43] *Plutarkh dlia prekrasnogo pola, ili gallereia znamenitykh Rossiianok*, Vols. 5-6. Moscow: Universitetskaia tipografiia, 1819-20.

[44] Catherine-Joseph-Ferdinand Girard de Propiac, *Le Plutarque des jeunes demoiselles, ou Abrégé des vies des femmes illustres de tous les pays, avec des leçons explicatives de leurs actions et de leurs ouvrages*, 2 vols. Paris: Gérard, 1806. Pierre Blanchard, *Plutarque de la jeunesse, ou Abrégé des vies des plus grands hommes de toutes les nations, depuis les temps les plus reculés jusqu'a nos jours.* Paris, Chez le Prieur, 1803-4; *Neuer Plutarch, oder, Kurze Lebensbeschreibungen der berühmtesten Männer aller Nationen von den ältesten bis auf unsere Zeiten.* Vienna: Im Verlage den Anton Doll, 1806-7. Blanshard and Propiak. *Plutarkh dlia prekrasnogo pola, ili zhizneopisaniia velikikh i slavnykh zhen vsekh natsii, drevnikh i novykh vremen*, 4 vols. Moscow: Universitetskaia tipografiia, 1816-17.

Mikhail Makarov, of *Damskii zhurnal* (Ladies' Journal, 1830-33).[45] This small sample gives some sense of the great distances that Italian and later French compilations traveled, via Germany, to Russia, to create in one nation after the next, the category of woman writer.

How and where this category of women writers emerged, the forms it took, and how it traveled from nation to nation are thus questions that compilations reveal and allow us to trace. Compilations demonstrate that around 1700, over a century after the first compilations of women writers in Italy, the category of women writers came into being as both an international and a national phenomenon. Women writers were the generic descendants of female worthies on the one hand, and learned women on the other. Women writers expressed new enlightened notions of nation, an idea that traveled well, and as it moved from nation to nation, compilers looked to each other for sources at the same time as they competed for more and better women writers. Despite the fact that compilations of women writers almost always are limited by a language or a nation, they are generically rooted in transnational debates about the nature of women and the 17$^{th}$- and 18$^{th}$-century competition for learned women.

This brief overview of compilations of women in the tradition of Boccaccio and of women writers as a subset of learned and notable women suggest that a more general internationalization of the category of women occurs well before the 19$^{th}$ century. In her foundational international study, *European Feminisms 1700-1950, A Political History*, Karen Offen begins her discussion around 1700, with the *querelle des femmes*, a debate that she locates in France and England. This genesis of these philosophical debates leads to Offen's main topic, the expanded political debates during the French Revolution, which were a catalyst of the 19$^{th}$ century rise of international feminist movements. Yet, the varied transnational threads of the multiple narratives in compilations significantly push back the beginnings of these

---

[45] Stepan Russov, *Bibliograficheskii katalog rossiiskim pisatel'nitsam*, St Petersburg: Tipografiia meditsinskogo departamenta Ministerstva vnutrennikh del, 1826. M. N. Makarov,"Materialy dlia istorii russkikh zhenshchin-avtorov" in *Damskii zhurnal* 29.1 (1830): 1-5, 29.2 (1830): 17-23, 29.3 (1830): 33-5, 29.7 (1830): 97-102, 29.10 (1830): 145-51, 29.13 (1830): 193-8, 30.15 (1830): 17-20, 30.16 (1830): 33-9, 30.17 (1830): 49-58, 30.18 (1830): 65-76, 30.19 (1830): 81-3, 30.21 (1830): 113-21, 30.25 (1830): 177-85, 31.27 (1830): 1-8, 31.29 (1830): 33-44, 31.30 (1830): 49-55, 31.39 (1830): 193-201, 32.51-52 (1830): 113-20, 35.37 (1831): 161-66, 44.51-2 (1833): 145-50.

debates, back to 1400, and expand the geography to broaden the narrative of the genesis of the political battles over the rights of women.

The transnational genesis of the category of women writers is only one of the many possible stories that bio-bibliographic and other compilations of women more generally can tell us. In her recent article "Narrative and Gender in Literary Histories", Ina Schabert argues that the historiographic function of literary histories has gotten bogged down in their encyclopedic function, and she proposes various possible story lines that bring men and women together in meaningful, productive ways.[46] That warning seems especially apt for compilations. Considered reference works today, in their day they often functioned as literary histories. Indeed, they were initially organized chronologically and only later switched to alphabetical order. Yet *even* these primarily encyclopedic compilations tell stories, contain a variety of narratives, and can be sources not only for information, but also for new stories we may want to tell.

Compilations of women reveal the topography of women's literary history across centuries, like sonar waves: as we go deeper into literary history diachronically and synchronically with the aid of databases, the contents of dozens of compilations *ping* back to us the locations of individuals and groups of women and significantly, where they travel. This European literary history connects larger and smaller nations, the producers and consumers of 'women writers', rather than focusing on just England and France. Compilations contain many dots that need connecting, and in the first instance, the compilations themselves can be connected to other compilations, languages, and nations, in the international community of letters.

---

[46] Ina Schabert, "Narrative and Gender in Literary Histories" in *Comparative Critical Studies*, 6(2), 2009: 149-64. Schabert mentions NEWW's database *WomenWriters* for the international and intercultural connections of women's literary history (154).

## Select Bibliography

### A. Primary Sources

Ballard, George. 1985. *Memoirs of Several Ladies of Great Britain Who Have Been Celebrated for Their Writings or Skill in the Learned Languages, Arts and Sciences*. Oxford, 1752, Ruth Perry (ed.). Detroit, MI: Wayne State University Press.

Bergalli, Luisa. 1726. *Componimenti delle più illustre rimatrici d'ogni secolo*. Venice: Antonio Mora.

Blanchard, Pierre. 1803-4. *Plutarque de la jeunesse, ou Abrégé des vies des plus grands hommes de toutes les nations, depuis les temps les plus reculés jusqu'a nos jours*. Paris, Chez le Prieur.

Blanshard and Propiak. 1816-17. *Plutarkh dlia prekrasnogo pola, ili zhizneopisaniia velikikh i slavnykh zhen vsekh natsii, drevnikh i novykh vremen*, 4 vols. Moscow: Universitetskaia tipografiia.

Boccaccio, Giovanni. 2003. *Famous Women*. Virginia Brown (tr.). Cambridge, MA: Harvard University Press.

Bourdeille, Pierre de. 1665. *Les vies des Dames Illustres de France de son temps*. Leiden: Jean Sambix le jeune.

Bulifon, Antonio. 1695. *Rime di cinquanta illustri poetesse*, Naples: A. Bulifon.

Chiesa, Agostino della. 1620. *Theatro delle donne letterate con un reve discorso della preminenza, e perfittione del sesso donnesco*. Mondovi: per Giovanni Gislandi e Gio. Tomaso Rossi.

Coste, Hilarion de. 1630. *Les eloges et vies des reynes, princesses, dames et damoiselles illustres en pieté, courage & doctrine, qui ont fleury de nostre temps, & du temps de nos pères. Avec l'explication de levrs devises, emblemes, hyerogliphes, & symboles*. 2 vols. Paris: Sébastien Cramoisy, 2nd ed. 1647.

Domenichi, Lodovico. 1559. *Rime diverse d'alcune nobilissime e virtuosissime donne*. Lucca, Busdrago.

Ferri, Pietro Leopoldo. 1842. *Biblioteca femminile Italiana*. Padua: Tipografia Crescini.

Juncker, Christian. 1692. *Schediasma historicum de ephemeridibus sive diariis eruditorum, in nobilioribus Europae partibus hactenus publicatis. In appendice exhibetur Centuria Foeminarum eruditione et scriptis illustrium, ab eôdem collecta*. Leipzig: J. F. Gleditsch.

La Porte, Joseph. 1769. *Histoires littéraire des femmes françoises: ou, Lettres historiques et critiques, contenant un précis de la vie et une analyse raisonée des ouvrage des femmes qui se sont distinguées dans la littérature françoise, par une société de gens de lettres*, Paris: Chez Lacombe.

Lehms, Georg Christian. 1714-15. *Teutschlands galante Poetinnen Mit Ihnen sinnreichen und netten Proben; Nebst einem Anhang Ausländer Dames, so sich gleichfalls durch Schöne Poesien Bey der curieusen Welt bekannt gemacht, und einer Vorrede. Dass das Weibliche Geschlecht so geschickt zum Studieren als das Männliche*. 2 vols. Frankfurt am Main: Anton Heynscheidt.

Manzini, Giovanni Battista. 1647. *Furori della gioventu esercitii rhetorici*. Geneva: Pietro Auberto.

Ménage, Gilles. 1984. *The History of Women Philosophers* [1690]. Beatrice H. Zedler (tr.). Lanham, MD: University Press of America, 1984.

*Neuer Plutarch, oder, Kurze Lebensbeschreibungen der berühmtesten Männer aller Nationen von den ältesten bis auf unsere Zeiten*. 1806-7. Vienna: Im Verlage den Anton Doll.

Pataky, Sophie. 1898. *Lexikon deutscher Frauen der Feder. Eine Zusammenstellung der seit dem Jahre 1840 erchienenen Werke weiblicher Autoren, nebst Biographieen der lebenden und einem Verzeichnis der Pseudonyme*. Berlin: Carl Pataky.

Pizan, Christine de. 1982. *The Book of the City of Ladies*. Earl Jeffrey Richards (tr.). New York: Persea Book.

de Propiac, Catherine-Joseph-Ferdinand Girard. 1806. *Le Plutarque des jeunes demoiselles, ou Abrégé des vies des femmes illustres de tous les pays, avec des leçons explicatives de leurs actions et de leurs ouvrages*, 2 vols. Paris: Gérard.

Russov, Stepan. 1826. *Bibliograficheskii katalog rossiiskim pisatel'nitsam*, St Petersburg: Tipografiia meditsinskogo departamenta Ministerstva vnutrennikh del.

Scudéry, Madeleine de. 1642. *Les femmes illustres, ou les harangues héroïques*. Paris: Chez Antoine de Sommaville & Augustin Courbe.

Schacht, Matthias Henriksen. 1700. "Schediasma, exhibiens specimen de Eruditis Mulieribus Daniæ," in *Nova Literaria Maris Balthici & Septentrionis*. Lübeck, Böckmann: 209-19.

Thicknesse, Anne. 1780. *Sketches of the Lives and Writing of the Ladies of France*. London: Dodsley and W. Brown.

Thomas, Antoine Leonard. 1987. *Essai sur le caractère, les mœurs et l'esprit des femmes dans les différens siècles*. Paris, 1772; Colette Michael (ed.). Paris, Geneva: Champion-Slatkine.

Thomas, Antoine Leonard. 1987. *Essai sur le caractère, les mœurs et l'esprit des femmes dans les différens siècles*, Paris , 1772, repr. Paris : Champion Slatkine.

—. 1774. *Essay on the Character, Manners, and Genius of Women in Different Ages,* Mr Russell (tr.) 2 vols. Philadelphia, PA: R. Aitken.

Thura, Albert. 1732. *Gynæceum Daniæ Litteratum, Feminis Danorum, Eruditione vel scriptis claris conspicuum; præmissa præfatione de feminarum variarum apud danos in litteras et litteratos munificentia, et adjecto ad calcem, una cum appendice duplici indice personarum*. Altona: Apud Jonam Korte.

von Nettesheim, Heinrich Cornelius Agrippa. 1990. *De nobilitate et praecellentia foeminei sexus* (1529), repr. Genève: Librairie Droz.

von Schindel, Carl Wilhelm Otto August.1823-25. *Die Deutschen Schriftstellerinnen des neunzehnten Jahrhunderts*. Leipzig: F. A. Brockhaus; 1978. New York: Georg Olms Verlag.

## B. Secondary Sources

Akkerman, Tjitske and Siep Stuurman (eds). 1998. *Perspectives on Feminist Political thought in European History: From the Middle Ages to the Present.* New York: Routledge.

Behnke, Dorothea. 1999. *Lexika zu Schriftstellerinnen aus dem deutschsprachigen Raum*. Osnabrück: Zeller Verlag.

DeJean, Joan. 1991. *Tender Geographies: Women and the Origins of the Novel in France*. New York: Columbia UP: 219-21.

"Dictionnaires et listes de femmes célèbres: la liste," *SIEFAR: Societé international pour l'Etude des Femmes de l'Ancien Régime*, http://www.siefar.org (accessed June 15, 2011)

Dugald McKillop, Alan. 1934. "English Circulating Libraries, 1725-50" in *The Library* S4-XIV (4) 1934: 477-85 (485).

Friedrichs, Elisabeth. 1981. *Die deutschsprachigen Schriftstellerinnen des 18. und 19. Jahrhunderts: Ein Lexikon* Stuttgart: J. B. Metzlersche Verlagsbuchhandlung.

Hoogenboom, Hilde. 2013. "Bibliography and National Canon: Women Writers in France, England, Germany, and Russia (1800-2010)," *Comparative Literature Studies*, 50(2): 314-41.

McLeod, Glenda. 1991. *Virtue and Venom: Catalogs of Women from Antiquity to the Renaissance*. Ann Arbor: University of Michigan Press.

McMurran, Mary Helen. 2010. *The Spread of Novels: Translation and Prose Fiction in the Eighteenth Century*. Princeton, NJ: Princeton University Press.

McDowell, Paula. 1993. "Consuming Women: The Life of the 'Literary Lady' as Popular Culture in Eighteenth-Century England" in *Genre*, 26 (Summer/Fall): 246-48.

Mez'er, A. V. 1899. *Russkaia slovesnost' s XI po XIX stoletiia vkliuchitel'no. Bibliograficheskii ukazatel' proizvedenii russkoi slovesnosti v sviazi s istoriei literatury i kritiki.* St Petersburg: Tipografia A. Porokhovshchikova.

Moretti, Franco. 1998. *Atlas of the European Novel, 1800-1900.* New York: Verso, 1998.

Russell, Rinaldina (ed.). 1997. *The Feminist Encyclopedia of Italian Literature*, Westport, CT: Greenwood Press.

Schabert, Ina. 2009. "Narrative and Gender in Literary Histories" in *Comparative Critical Studies,* 6 (2): 149-64.

Schacht lists editions in 1593 and 1598, for which there are no records today. See Virginia Brown, "Introduction": xix-xx, 257-58.

Williams, Jane. 1861. *The Literary Women of England, including a biographical epitome of all the most eminent to the year 1700 and sketches of the poetesses to the year 1850 with extracts from their works, and critical remarks,* London: Saunders, Otley: 1-13.

## Anthologies of Female Italian Authors and the Emergence of a National Identity in 19th Century Italy

*Rotraud Von Kulessa*

ABSTRACT During the 19th century, the question of cultural identity becomes more and more important, especially in countries like Italy, where national unity has been created in a somewhat artificial way. The founding works of literary historiography in Italy and France, however, consciously ignore female literary writing, although it existed in both countries. By contrast, ever since the late Middle Ages and Giovanni Boccaccio's *De mulieribus claris* (1361/62), there has been a rich tradition of dictionaries of women as famous authors, amongst other roles. In 19th century Italy, this tradition is in fact particularly lively and serves to define the role of women in the formation of Italy's cultural unity. This chapter focuses on anthologies of famous writers and, more particularly, on the paratexts of these publications, to explain the peculiarities of the Italian context, especially in comparison to France.

THE CONCEPT OF NATIONAL IDENTITY ARISES from a sense of belonging to a historical, cultural, linguistic, geographic and political community.[1] With the formation of nation states in Europe during the 19th century, the question of cultural identity becomes more and more important, especially in countries like Italy, where national unity has been created in a somewhat artificial way.[2] In addition to history and language, the formation of a literary canon is an integral part of a nation's cultural identity. Therefore, the 19th century generally marks the beginning of literary historiography, with exemplary works like *Storia della letteratura italiana* (1870-72) by Francesco de Sanctis, and *L'Histoire de la littérature française* (1894) by Gustave Lanson, in France. Concerning the role played by women in the formation of a 'national' identity, it is significant that these two publications, considered the founding works of literary historiography in Italy and France, consciously ignore female literary writing, even though it existed in both countries. By

[1] Metzeltin, "Die Entstehung der modernen Nationalstaaten" in *Italien 1861-2011: Einheit und Vielfalt. Zibbaldone*, 50/2010: 11.
[2] *Ibid.*, 16.

contrast, since the late Middle Ages and Giovanni Boccaccio's *De mulieribus claris* (1361-62), there has been a rich tradition of dictionaries of women, among others, as famous authors. In 19th century Italy, this tradition is in fact particularly lively, and serves to define the role of women in the formation of Italy's cultural unity.

In this paper, I will first briefly outline the female literary tradition in Italy. I will then focus on anthologies of famous writers, and, more particularly, I will analyse the paratexts of these publications. Finally, I will endeavour to explain the peculiarities of the Italian context, especially in comparison to France.

## The female literary tradition in Italy

As early as the 16th century, Italian female authors excelled in the field of Petrarchan love poetry, and women writers like Vittoria Colonna (1492-1547), Veronica Gambara (1485-1550), or Gaspara Stampa (1523?-1554), are now considered part of the Italian literary canon. In the course of the 17th and 18th century, female voices are less audible, in spite of the fact that, at the end of the 17th century, some women had gained access to universities; Elisabetta Cornaro Piscopia, for example, was the first woman to hold a PhD in philosophy, and in the 18th century, Laura Maria Bassi, who taught philosophy at the university in Bologna, became the first female university professor.[3] In 18th century Venice, there were a number of female journalists and translators, such as Elisabetta Caminer Turra,[4] or Luisa Bergalli Gozzi,[5] who were dedicating themselves to spreading French Enlightenment culture in Italy. Incidentally, with the publication of her *Componimenti poetici delle più illustri rimatrici di ogni secolo* in 1726, Luisa Bergalli Gozzi proved to

---

[3] For Maria Gaetana Agnesi and Laura Bassi, see Andreas Kleinert, "Maria Gaetana Agnesi und Laura Bassi – zwei italienische gelehrte Frauen im 18. Jahrhundert" 26.03.2008, http://www.physik.uni-halle.de/Fachgruppen/history/agbas.htm.

[4] See Rita Unfer Lukoschik (ed.). *Elisabetta Caminer Turra (1751-1796): Una letterata veneta verso l'Europa.* Verona: Essedue, 1999, and Mariagabriella di Giacomo, *L'illuminismo e le donne: Gli scritti di Elisabetta Caminer; 'utilità' e 'piacere': ovvero la coscienza di essere letterata.* Rome: La Sapienza, 2002.

[5] See Rotraud von Kulessa, "Les *Amazones* de Mme du Boccage dans la traduction italianne de Luisa Bergalli Gozzi" in Annie Cointre, Florence Lautel and Annie Rivara (eds), *La traduction du discours amoureux.* Metz : Université Paul Verlaine, 2005: 255-267.

be especially aware of this particular female literary tradition. The work is an anthology of mostly Petrarchan women poets.

During the first half of the 19th century, the literary field in Italy was dominated by the issue of national unity. Literature is thus in the service of the process of national unification. This also applies to the few literary works written by women. Writers like Cristina Trivulzio Belgiojoso (1808-1871) witnessed revolutionary events as journalists and sided with Mazzini. The women's literature of the *Risorgimento* is thus first and foremost of a political nature and seeks to propagate patriotic ideals.[6]

During the second half of the 19th century, following the unification of Italy, there was an effort to return to a more 'aesthetic' literature. With the population becoming more literate, aided by the Riforma Casati, and typography becoming more advanced, a new publishing industry was born to meet the demands of a growing readership. As in France, female authors profited from these developments, as they were encouraged in their literary output, especially in the genre of the serial novel or the popular novel, namely "le roman rose" (*romanzo rosa*).[7] The main themes in female literature were also influenced by the social situation in a post-unitary Italy; in particular, the economic disproportion between the North and the South. Thus, women writers like Matilde Serao, Grazia Deledda, and Maria Messina can be seen as representatives of the Verismo literary movement. They depict the contradictions between the individual needs of women and the expectations of society within the social and economic framework of the islands (Sardinia in Deledda's works, Sicily in Messina's), or of the Mezziogiorno (Naples in the case of Matilde Serao). Other women writers joined the symbolist or decadent movement, like Vittoria Aganoor Pompilj, Contessa Lara or Amalia Guglielminetti. Others devoted themselves to the problems of the proletariat and the issues raised by industrialisation, as did Ada Negri. Finally, a literature dedicated to the feminist question can be observed: In 1906, *Una donna*, by Sibilla Aleramo is hailed as the first novel of this trend.

---

[6] See Christiane Veauvy and Laura Pisano. *Paroles oubliées: les femmes et la construction de l'Etat-nation en France et en Italie (1789-1860).* Paris: Armand Colin, 1997.

[7] Rinaldina Russell, (ed.). *Italian Women Writers: A Bio-Bibliographical Source Book.* Westport/Conn.: Greenwood Press, 1994: XXIV. Antonia Arslan and Maria Pia Pozzato, "Il rosa", in Alberto Asor Rosa (ed.). *Letteratura italiana: Storia e geografia, vol. III, L'età contemporanea.* Turin: Einaudi, 1989:1027-1046.

## Anthologies of famous Italian women writers in the 19th century

The increasing literary production of Italian women writers is accompanied by a growing number of dictionaries about female authors throughout the whole of the 19th century: Ginevra Canonici Fachini's *Prospetto biografico delle donne italiane rinominate in Letteratura* (1824),[8] Eduardo Magliani's *Storia letteraria delle donne italiane* (1885), and *La Donna italiana nelle scienze, nelle lettere, nelle arti. Dizionario biografico delle scrittiri e delle artiste viventi* (1892) by Carlo Catanzaro.

However, even by the 18th century, Luisa Bergalli Gozzi's anthology of women poets (*Componimenti poetici delle più illustri rimatrici di ogni secolo*, Venice, 1726) was relevant to the process of identity formation in Italy. The *Componimenti poetici delle più illustri rimatrici di ogni secolo* was published in two volumes in Venice in 1726, by the editor Antonio Mora. The first volume contains texts by 112 women poets from Antiquity until the year 1575. The second volume, in turn, is divided into two parts; the first part portrays 82 women authors who were already deceased by the time of publication, while the second part presents 55 living authors in alphabetical order. At the end of each volume, there is an alphabetical list of all the poets, followed by a short bio-bibliographical note.

Luisa Bergalli dedicated her work to the Venetian cardinal Pietro Ottoboni (1667-1740), who was considered to be a patron of the arts, especially music and the Academy of Arcadia. There is no evidence of a personal relationship between the author and the cardinal, but the dedication suggests that she deliberately chose a clergyman as patron of her book, hoping to avoid being blacklisted. As such, she invokes the idea of intellectual impartiality: "(…) because thanks to your erudition and sublime mind, the universal prejudice, according to which we women have no talents, is alien to you",[9] and refers to the common homeland Venice.[10] Furthermore, she addresses those who are exempt from prejudice and who concede to

---

[8] This work is available on Google Books. The notes in this dictionary are, however, not included in the online project of the University of Chicago: *Italian women writers*: http://www.lib.uchicago.edu/efts/IWW/

[9] Luisa Begalli Gozzi, *Componimenti poetici delle più illustri rimanatrici di ogni secolo* (1726), available at *Italian women writers*: http://www.lib.uchicago.edu/efts/IWW/

[10] *Ibid.*

women the right to have a literary culture, while at the same time acknowledges the value of their literary productions. To emphasise her statements, Bergalli quotes the fourth canto of the epic poem *Floridoro* (1581) by Moderata Fonte,[11] in which the author calls for equality of the sexes in the literary world: "And in literature and in/printing, both practised by men/women have been and still are so prolific/that they do not have to envy men."She then refers to the long female literary tradition in Venice, a city which has seen the birth of authors such as Cassandra Fedele, Collaltina Collalta, Lucietta Soranzano, Elena Cornaro Piscopia and many others. According to Bergalli, many of these women did not achieve fame, mostly due to their modesty. She ends her preface with acknowledgements of all those who facilitated her access to manuscripts and libraries. Despite its shortness, this preface shows the author's awareness of the problematic authorial status of women. It also implicitly defines a feminist goal, namely the reconstruction of the literary history of women writers within a well-defined cultural context. In fact, Bergalli's endeavour can be seen in the context of the Academy of Arcadia, which was founded in Rome in 1690, by Gian Vincenzo Gravina and Giovanni Mario Crescimbeni. Based on the former *Academia Reale* of Christina of Sweden, the Academy of Arcadia was a literary movement against 'distasteful' baroque literature, and, under the influence of Crescembini its goal was the revival of Italian poetry according to the Petrarchan model. This enterprise also aimed to redefine Italian literature, and was inspired by French literature. Apart from its seat in Rome, the Academy already comprised of 40 bodies in 1726, one of which was the Colonia Animosa, founded in Venice in 1698. Tatiana Crivelli, a Swiss scholar conducting a research project in Zurich, is developing a database that includes all the female members of the Arcadia.[12] Indeed, the Academy of Arcadia was the first Italian academy to accept female members, provided they were active in the literary field.[13]

The first compilation to be published after Luisa Bergalli Gozzi's anthology was the *Prospetto biografico* by Ginevra Canonici Fachini. The

[11] Moderata Fonte is also the author of *Il merito delle donne* which plays an important part in the "querelle des femmes".

[12] http://www.rose.uzh.ch/crivelli/arcadia/donnedetails.php.

[13] Tatiana Crivelli, "L'Arcadia femminile: spazi reali e simbolici du un'interazione culturale" in Gesa Stedman, and Margarete Zimmermann (eds). *Höfe-Salons-Akademien. Kulturtransfer und Gender im Europa der Frühen Neuzeit* Hildesheim/Zurich: Olms, 2007: 241-254.

originality of this work lies mainly in its preface, which is a defence of Italian women andwas addressed to Lady Morgan, an English traveller. It was a response to Morgan's work *L'Italia*, in which the author voices several prejudices about Italian women. In her apologetic response in the form of a letter to her interlocutrice, Fachini refutes the three main theses of Morgan's book, namely the immoral conduct of Italian women, their lack of maternal instincts, and their lack of culture. It is in order to deconstruct the last of the three prejudices that Fachini intends to compile her anthology. This, in turn, is preceded by a short overview of the history of Italian literature and of the position of women from the 13$^{th}$ to 19$^{th}$ century. The anthology itself deals then with the centuries in chronological order, from the 14$^{th}$ to 19$^{th}$, with the latter divided in two parts: one about deceased writers, the other about women who are still alive.

In her preface addressed to her readers, she pretends to have heard of Lady Morgan's travel account through a friend in London who wrote to her, having compiled the passages that harm the reputation of Italian women which encouraged Fachini to refute these unjustified assertions in order to re-establish the honour of Italy and its women.[14]

It is thus possible that Fachini may have taken Lady Morgan's work about Italy, published in English in 1821 and translated into French in the same year, as an excuse to publish her anthology, which surely had been written long before. This allows her to justify her work as a defence of her country's honour and she appeals to her Italian colleagues to re-establish the image of Italian women and that of Italy in Europe:

> I have set my hands to this work with an eagerness that comes from the heart, as it is inspired by a sense of justice, and truth and love and honour of a mother country that is capable to move so much in us. Today, I address you, my valiant female compatriots; I invoke your help, as my own powers are insufficient. I thank you, because not only your genius, but also your austere morals are the most shining proof of

---

[14] "Lady Morgan ha dato alle stampe un libro intitolato L'Italie; descrive il viaggio da esso fatto nella nostra Penisola; vi sono molti articoli che risguardono il vostro sesso, e che non debbono starsene senza confutazione: li troverete qui uniti. E' necessario che pensiate di proposito ad una ben meditata risposta, che risarcisca l'onore del sesso gentile e della Italia nostra." Ginevra Canonici Fachini, *Prospetto biografico delle donne italiane rinominate in letteratura dal secolo decimoquarto fino a' giorni nostri. Con una risposta a Lady Morgan riguardante alcune accuse da lei date alle donne italiane nella sua opera d'Italie*. Venezia, Tipografia Alvisopoli, 1824: 3

> my undertaking to the whole of Europe. I am not looking for glory, but my intention is to defend our honour by praising your maternal piety, your knowledge and that of the women that have preceded you.[15]

Her response to Lady Morgan is written in form of a letter and Canonici Fachini addresses her female English colleague as "Figlia di grande e possente Nazione (…)", while declaring in advance that her own discourse is characterised by the dignity of Italian women, "daughters of the Ancient Roman mothers".[16]

She continues by asking her interlocutrice not to prejudge a whole nation based on a few bad experiences, as: "Families only provide a restricted representation of a great nation".[17] On the contrary, she postulates the ideal of relativity, saying that the character of an individual does not necessarily correspond to that of a nation.[18] Then, she quotes from the translation of Lady Morgan's travel account, citing the latter's first accusation, namely that Italian women behave immorally in their love affairs. In fact, it is the custom of a cavalier servant, a Cicisbeo, that seems to perturb the English traveller. It is true that Fachini's defence lacks fervour, as she herself does not find this custom appropriate for her time. However, according to her, there was nothing dishonourable about this custom originally and she contrasts it with English and French social customs that could be interpreted as being just as dishonourable. Lady Morgan's second reproach concerns the lack of maternal love and especially the habit of giving children away to a wet nurse from the moment of birth. Fachini responds to this assertion through a comparison with England and France, in which countries this custom had only been contested, exactly as it had been in Italy, in the wake of pedagogical reflections at the end of the 18th century. In addition, she mentions as an

---

[15] *Ibid.*, 5-6.

[16] "Figlia di possente e grande Nazione, ora a Voi indirizzo le mie parole, né fra voi e me altro giudice invoco che la verità: niun rancore nel mio cuore s'annida, ch'egli sarebbe oltraggio fra il nostro sesso il parlare sferzando; quindi voi troverete giusto e mite il mio discorso, ma non disgiunto da quella dignità che distingue le Italiane, quali figlie delle auguste prime Romane madri" *Ibid.*, 7

[17] *Ibid.*, 11.

[18] "È ingiusto l'attribuire un vizio ad una Nazione, poiché il carattere nazionale non induce giammai a mal fare colui che al mal costume non è propenso. Il cogitabondo Inglese può divenire buon filosofo, o scellerato politico" *Ibid.*, 11.

example several well-known Italian families, where three generations live under the same roof.[19]

In fact, to Fachini, the most relevant accusation is the apparent lack of education in Italian women, apart from those in Bologna. Lady Morgan adds the cold welcome that Italians give to foreigners, and Fachini is quick to raise the issue of language: as the English only speak English and neither Italian nor French, it is consequently impossible to communicate with them. In this context, she mentions that English, in those days, was not an international language like French, and the fact that the English are not able to speak the latter could very well be interpreted as a lack of education. After having deconstructed Lady Morgan's assertion that there are only learned women in Bologna, Fachini attempts to explain the literary history of Italy to her interlocutrice.

Fachini starts her overview of Italian literary history by summarising the period from the 13th to 15th century, a time that had seen the most important writers of Italy, namely Dante, Petrarch and Boccaccio, and many other illustrious authors. They had mainly imitated antique models, a practice that was not accessible to women, due to the general inability to speak ancient languages. The 16th century, however, had featured a number of important women poets, quite contrary to the 17th century, during which the number of female writers closely related to the decline of literary production in Italy. Instead of writing, women had preferred to excel as painters, a fact that she emphasises by listing 23 female painters of that time. The 18th century suffered from a French influence, namely the denigration of learned women in the style of Molière, which, however, had not stopped Italian women from committing themselves to education towards the end of the century. The ideal Italian woman who is depicted in these pages is thus seen as the mother of the nation's educational formation. To conclude her arguments, Fachini announces her dictionary of Italian women writers, which is intended to serve as a memorial of learned Italian women.[20]

With regard to quantitative analysis, I have counted 11 entries for the 14th century, 36 for the 15th century, 172 for the 16th, 61 for the 18th, and 67 living writers during the 19th century. For the latter, Fachini refers to accounts from her contemporaries in different Italian villages, as well as to scholarly works of her time. The anthology itself subsequently continues with the centuries in

---

[19] *Ibid.*, 27-32.
[20] *Ibid.*, 61.

chronological order, from the 14th to the 19th century, with the latter divided into two parts – one dedicated to dead writers, the other to the those still alive.In each century, the entries are made in alphabetical order and tell the reader the name, first name, birthplace, and, if known, the date of birth and death of each author. Depending on the availability of sources, the bio-bibliographical notes that follow are shorter or longer, and sometimes also mention sources and information concerning the quality of the literary productions. Sometimes they reveal the existence of little known translators. At the end of each note, one can find a list of the author's complete works, without full bibliographical details. All this is followed by an indication of the sources.[21]

This example of Fachini's work is especially significant in the context of the discourse concerning women writers, which was taken up again at the end of the century, when Italian unity was felt to be a failure, and the need to position oneself in Europe's cultural context became virulent.[22] These works often came from little known polygraph writers who doubtlessly fulfilled the requirements of a growing female leadership. As a result, in 1885, Eduardo Magliani[23] published a history of Italian women writers that spanned from the Middle Ages until the 15th century. According to his preface, his self-proclaimed aim was to fill the gaps in literary historiography – I have already discussed the fact that De Sanctis ignores the existence of such a tradition –

---

[21] The most frequently cited are Luisa Bergalli Gozzi, *Componimenti poetici delle più illustri rimanatrici di ogni secolo* (1726), available at *Italian women writers*: http://www.lib.uchicago.edu/efts/IWW/; Giovanni Mario Crescimbeni, *Istoria della volgar poesia.* Lorenzo Basegio 1730/31; Giovanni Fantuzzi, *Notizie degli scrittori bolognesi* (1781). Bologna: Stamperia Tommaso d'Aquino 1794 available on Google Books; Giammaria Mazzuchelli, *Gli scrittori d'Italia, cioè, Notizie storiche e critiche intorno alle vite e agli scritti dei letterati italiani.* Brescia: Bossini, 1753-1763; F.C. Pentolini, *Donne illustri* (1776). Livorno: Vincenzo Falarni, 1783; Luigi Galamini di Recanati, *Racolta di poesie* (Venezia, 1716). Roma: Pellicanolibri, 1992; Girolamo Tiraboschi, *Storia della letteratura italiana di Girolamo Tiraboschi, della Compagnia di Gesù, bibliotecario del serenissimo Duca di Modena.* Modena: presso la Società tipografica, 1772-1782.

[22] To read further about the position of women in the literay field around 1900, see Rotraud Von Kulessa, *Entre la reconnaissance et l'exclusion. La position de l'autrice dans le champ littéraire en France et en Italie à l'époque 1900.* Paris: Editions Honoré Champion, 2011.

[23] Eduardo Magliani, *Storia letteraria delle donne italiane: Le trovatrici – Preludi – Trecentiste – Quattrocentiste – Cinquecentiste.* Naples: Cav. Antonio Morano Editore, 1885.

and to give evidence of the fact that women have contributed to the glory of the Italian nation: "In fact, her intention is to tell an organic history of the Italian female genius and in general, to fill the gaps in literary history by defining the influence of women on the national literary works."[24]

In 1892, Carlo Catanzaro's dictionary *La Donna Italiana nelle scienze, nelle lettere, nelle arti. Dizionario biografico delle scrittrici e delle artise viventi,*[25] which was dedicated to contemporary women, was published. Like other previous works that focused on history, Carlo Catanzaro considers women's writing to have contributed to the glory of the young Italian nation, and discusses the history of Italian customs. The preface, which was revised by Giovanni Manzi, introduces the work in these terms:

> Science adds the enlightenment of thought to these invariable and exquisite feelings. And the Italian women have heard this signal and one only need cast a glance at this meticulous author's biographical dictionary to convince oneself of the large number of studious and even illustrious women in our country. Count and acknowledge yourselves, illustrious and strong-willed women of Italy, you who devote your free hours to an undertaking that honours your sex and country while sitting in the calm of your house near your children's cradle. Become acquainted with each other and join forces to quietly and peacefully reach your goal. The wave of a new life will spread from you, mothers, sisters, governesses into our unstable society that is waiting to be reborn.[26]

---

[24] *Ibid.*, preface.

[25] Carlo Catanzaro, *La Donna italiana nelle scienze, nelle lettere, nelle arti: Dizionario biografico delle scrittrici e delle artiste viventi.* Florence: Biblioteca Editrice della Rivista Italiana, 1892.

[26] "Ai suoi invariati e squisiti sentimenti la scienza aggiunge la luce del pensiero. E questo grande risveglio hanno sentite le Donne d'Italia, si, che ove non paresse, basti dare uno sguardo alla faticosa opera dell'egregio compilatore di questo Dizionario Biografico per convincersi di quante studiose e talora illustri donne possa vantarsi la Patria nostra. […] Contatevi e conoscetevi, illustri e volenteresse Donne d'Italia, che nella queste delle vostre pareti domestiche, presso le culle dei vostri figlioli, consacrate le ore ad un lavoro che onora il vostro sesso e la Patria […] Conoscetevi, e i vostri sforzi concordi vi porteranno a raggiungere tranquillamente, senza scosse, la meta e da voi, madri e sorelle, educatrici, un' onda di vita nuova s'insuerà nella società moderna irrequieta, che attende la sua rigenerazione" *Ibid.*, 5-6.

Indeed, all in all, the volume contains 334 bio-bibliographical notes, mainly of female authors. The appendices add even more women, as well as a list of major works by women writers of the respective period.

Eugenio Comba's[27] mission, by contrast, is different. His dictionary of famous women belongs to the category of educational works, which suggest models of behaviour and appropriate reading for young girls. He explains in his preface to the first edition that his book contributes to the education of the Italian people, a venture in which women play a fundamental role: "But in whatever situation she [the woman] finds herself, there is no doubt that she plays an important part in the people's education (...)".[28] He evokes examples of women writers who should at least be read and consulted, if not imitated.[29] The following editions are continually complemented by notes about contemporary authors. Thus, the 1912 edition presents 65 authors of the 19th century, of which the majority had already died by the end of the century. Apart from these, he mentions others in the appendix, such as the Marchesa Colombi, Ida Baccini, Neera, Ada Negri, Caterina Pigorini-Beri, Emma Perodi, Clelia Bertini Attilj, Luisa Saredo, Maria Cavanna Visconti, and Grazia Deledda.

In his work *Stelle femminile*,[30] Carlo Villani presents 577 bio-bibliographical notes of Italian women, of which 274 are contemporaries who have established a reputation within the cultural field – from Saint Cécile to his own time. In the preface, he explains his undertaking:

> The stars that I unite in this very modest anthology twinkle with all their might in the blue of this very limited and small sky that is our science, literature, poetry and art – our beautiful Italian sky. Doing so, I pay tribute to the woman, who under the endless male tyranny is considered to be inferior to men.[31]

---

[27] Eugenio Comba, *Donne illustri italiane proposte ad esempio alle Giovinette*. Turin/Rome/Milan: Paravia, 1912.

[28] *Ibid.*, 111: "Ma in qualunque condizione ella si trovi, non v'ha dubbio avere la donna parte principalissima nel formare l'educazione del popolo".

[29] *Ibid.*, V.

[30] Carlo Villani, *Stelle femminile: dizionario bio-bibliografico, Nuova edizione*. Naples: Albrighi/Segati, 1915.

[31] "Le stelle invece, che raggruppo in quest'Indice modestissimo, scintillano al loro puro raggio di luce nell'azzurro d'un cielo di gran lunga ridotto e limitato, cielo di scienza, di lettere, di poesia di arti soavi, [...] il nostro bello cielo italico. [...] Si

It is in this respect interesting to see that all these testimonies to a female cultural genealogy contribute to the formation of a national identity, by stressing Italy's belonging to European modernity. Thus, they help to position women within a collective cultural memory in a fundamental way.[32]

## Italy: a special case

Nicole Pellegrin has noted the ambiguity of dictionaries of famous women in 17th century France,[33] on the one hand they contribute "to a democratisation of female celebrity", while on the other hand, they strengthen sexist ideologies by "exemplifying the exception".[34] During the *Troisième République,* and especially at the beginning of the 20th century, there is, in fact, a rise in publications dedicated to the topic of women writers, a phenomenon that Paul Flat calls a 'social fact' in his work *Nos femmes de lettres* (1909). Jean de Bonnefon: *La Corbeille aux Roses ou les Dames de Lettres* (1909); Paul Flat: *Nos femmes de lettres* (1909); Jean de Gourmont: *Muses d'aujourd'hui, essai de physiologie poetique. Ctesse de Noailles, Gérard d'Houville, Lucie Delarue-Mardrus, Marie Daguet, Renée Vivien*, Paris, Mercure de France, 1910; Ernest Tissot: *Les nouvelles princesses des lettres* (1911); Hervé de Broc: *Les femmes auteurs* (1911); Jules Bertaut: *La littérature féminine d'aujourd'hui* (1909) and Ryner Han: *Le massacre des Amazones. Etudes critiques sur deux cents Bas-Bleus contemporains* (s.d.). In general, works like these are written by male authors. Despite the fact that there is a rise in university dissertations by women, only a relatively small number of them write about women writers, most notably scholars like Jean Dorris or Aurel (Mme Alfred Mortier). As opposed to the anthologies

---

facendo, tributo altresì il mio omaggio alla donna, considerata, per eterna tirannia virile, come ineguale all'uomo,[…]" *Ibid.*, XII

[32] For further reading about the concept of 'memory', see Aleida Assmann, Jan Assmann and Christof Hardmeier (eds). *Schrift und Gedächtnis: Beiträge zur Archäologie der literarischen Kommunikation.* Munich: Willhelm Fink Verlag, 1983 and Aleida Assman, (ed.). *Vergessene Texte.* Konstanz: UVK Universitätsverlag, 2004.

[33] Nicole Pellegrin, "Le polygraphe philogyne. A propos des dictionnaires de femmes célèbres au XVIIIe siècle", in Rotraud Von Kulessa (ed.). *Etudes féminines/gender studies en littérature en France et en Allemagne.* Freiburg in Brisgau: Frankreich-Zentrum, 2004:63-79. For a general list of anthologies of famous women in France, see also http://www.siefar.org.

[34] *Ibid.*, 65.

analysed by Nicole Pellegrin, these works position themselves in relation to a scientific discourse in 19th century literary history: "on the one hand with Sainte-Beuve,[35] and on the other hand with the positivist scientism of Brunetière, Auguste Conte and Hippolyte Taine.[36]

By examining works by male authors, it becomes apparent that many of them are polygraphs, practising pseudo-scholarly critique.[37] They adhere to a biological discourse that only serves to cement "eternal femininity" and waver between "praise and exclusion".[38] What Christine Planté says about the 19th century and the time before the *Troisième République* also goes for the Fin de siècle:

> The temptation to define a collective artistic identity connected with the differences of the sexes has known multiple avatars since the 19th century. It was propagated mostly by men, especially writers, critics and intellectuals and always meant to define women as different and thus also inferior. In a time when the intellectual elites consisted mostly of men and equality was at stake, it was really all about defending their status, privileges and social prestige.[39]

It remains to be said that this discourse is portrayed convincingly in a French work that interrupted the debate about female authors for 60 years, namely *L'Histoire de la littérature féminine* by Jean Larnac.[40] Lanarc finished his literary history, that ranges from the Middle Ages to the 1920s, with a chapter called "The drama of the female genius", which is introduced by the

---

[35] See Sainte Beuve, *Portraits de femmes*. Paris: Didier, 1845 and José-Luis Diaz, "Sainte Beuve chez les Muses" in *Romantisme* 77.III. 1992: 77-86.

[36] Géraldi Leroy and Julie Betrand-Sabiani, *La vie littéraire à la Belle Epoque*. Paris : PUF, 1998: 293.

[37] See Margarete Zimmermann, *Salon der Autorinnen. Französische dames de lettres vom Mittelalter bis zum 17. Jahrhundert*. Berlin: Erich Schmidt Verlag, 2005: 19.

[38] See Rachel Sauvé's book on the discourse of prefaces: *De l'éloge à l'exclusion. Les femmes auteurs et leur préfaciers au XIXe siècle*. Vincennes: PU, 2000.

[39] Christine Planté, *La petite soeur de Balzac. Essai sur la femme auteur*. Paris: Seuil, 1989: 15-16. This work analyses the discourse about women writers before the Troisième République. Regarding the discussion, the arguments largely tie in with those of the fin de siècle.

[40] Jean Larnac, *L'Histoire de la littérature féminine en France*. Paris: Kra, 1927. Also cited from Elaine Marks, "Odor di femina", in Denis Hollier (ed.).*De la littérature française*. Paris: Bordas, 1993: 831-836.

following question: "(...) is it normal that women write?"[41] And, after three hundred pages about women writers concludes that it is not. For him, 'normal' women are primarily wives and mothers,[42] and only few women are able to reconcile their duties in the house with literary creation.[43] He proceeds to enumerate famous women writers who had unhappy marriages or became widows early on, such as, for example Mme de La Fayette, Mme de Staël or George Sand.[44] Apparently, for them, literature only served as a "means of replacement":

> For all of them, literature was a way to shift the desires that they had heretofore pursued in vain or allowed them to enlarge the too narrow life they led. It was not a first-rate value, but a substitution. Imagine Mlle de Gournay and Mlle de Scudéry had been beautiful; Mme de la Fayette and Mme de Sévigné perfectly happy with an obliging husband; Mme de Staël and George Sand satisfied with their first love – none of them would have dreamt of becoming a writer.[45]

Elaine Marks places the work within the ideological context of its period – between social Darwinism and nationalism – a time where every change was considered dangerous:

> At the end of the 19th century, all these events contributed to the exacerbation of a literary trend legitimised by social Darwinism, enforced by nationalism and kept up by notions about the degenerated Jews in the West, inferior races and hordes of amazons writing about ineptitudes, endangering the values and the social fabric of occidental civilisation.[46]

[41] Jean Larnac, *L'Histoire de la littérature féminine en France*: 273.
[42] *Ibid.*, 274.
[43] "La polarité entre normalité et anormalité, esquissée dans la première partie, devient la pièce centrale de l'argumentation de Larnac dans la seconde où, s'appuyant sur ce qu'il croit être une théorie scientifique sérieuse, il en vient à son insu à accentuer ce sur quoi ce sont toujours appuyés les condamnations les plus pernicieuses qui décrivent une femme écrivain comme un être dénaturé, singeant les hommes, en bref, une anormale – une femme qui a cessé d'être femme, n'étant ni épouse chérie, ni tendre mère ", Elaine Marks, "Odor di femina": 833
[44] Jean Larnac, *L'Histoire de la littérature féminine en France*: 274.
[45] *Ibid.*, 274.
[46] Elaine Marks, "Odor di femina": 832.

To conclude, one must consider the fundamental differences between France and Italy, when it comes to the impact of dictionaries about famous women writers on the national identity of the two countries. In post-revolutionary France, a discourse develops that is extremely hostile towards women who write, even though from the 17th century a large number of French writers were female. This discourse, which can partly be explained by the emergence of a post-revolutionary bourgeoisie, is supported by positivist theories in the second half of the 19th century that are especially open to biological and essentialist argumentation. Towards the end of the century, this discourse is fuelled even more by growing anti-Semitism, and compares women, especially those trying to express themselves publically to Jews, and regards them as a 'national danger', threatening the social order. In addition to this, there is also a form of literary criticism that adheres to extremely normative, and thus exclusive, values stemming from the 17th century. This trend continues throughout the 20th century, with cultural and scholarly policies advocating canonical works and excluding all kinds of literary production situated at the margin of the literary field.

However, Italian criticism at the end of that century shows a certain acceptance of women's writing.[47] In fact, the discourse about female authors is now considered a part of the process of forming Italy's national identity, affirming the modernity and progress that this young nation has made in education and culture.

---

[47] Rotraud Von Kulessa, *Entre la reconnaissance et l'exclusion. La position de l'autrice dans le champ littéraire en France et en Italie à l'époque 1900*. Paris: Champion, 2011: 305-319.

## Select Bibliography


### A. Primary Sources

Canonici Fachini, Ginevra. 1824. *Prospetto biografico delle donne italiane rinominate in letteratura dal secolo decimoquarto fino a' giorni nostri. Con una risposta a Lady Morgan riguardante alcune accuse da lei date alle donne italiane nella sua opera d'Italie*. Venezia, Tipografia Alvisopoli.

Catanzaro, Carlo. 1892. *La Donna italiana nelle scienze, nelle lettere, nelle arti: Dizionario biografico delle scrittrici e delle artiste viventi*. Florence: Biblioteca Editrice della Rivista Italiana.

Comba, Eugenio. 1912.*Donne illustri italiane proposte ad esempio alle Giovinette*. Turin/Rome/Milan: Paravia.

Crescimbeni, Giovanni Mario. 1730/31. *Istoria della volgar poesia*. Venezia: Lorenzo Basegio.

Fantuzzi, Giovanni. 1794. *Notizie degli scrittori bolognesi* (1781). Bologna: Stamperia Tommaso d'Aquino.

Galamini di Recanati, Luigi. 1992. *Racolta di poesie* (Venezia, 1716). Roma: Pellicanolibri.

Magliani, Eduardo. 1885. *Storia letteraria delle donne italiane: Le trovatrici – Preludi – Trecentiste – Quattrocentiste – Cinquecentiste*. Naples: Cav. Antonio Morano Editore.

Mazzuchelli, Giammaria. 1753-1763. *Gli scrittori d'Italia, cioè, Notizie storiche e critiche intorno alle vite e agli scritti dei letterati italiani*. Brescia: Bossini.

Sainte Beuve, *Portraits de femmes*. Paris: Didier, 1845

Pentolini, F.C. 1783. *Donne illustri* (1776). Livorno: Vincenzo Falarni.

Tiraboschi, Girolamo. 1772-1782. *Storia della letteratura italiana di Girolamo Tiraboschi, della Compagnia di Gesù, bibliotecario del serenissimo Duca di Modena*. Modena: presso la Società tipografica.

### B. Secondary Sources

Arslan, Antonia and Maria Pia Pozzato, "Il rosa", in Alberto Asor Rosa (ed.). 1989. *Letteratura italiana: Storia e geografia, vol. III, L'età contemporanea*. Turin: Einaudi: 1027-1046.

Assmann, Aleida, Jan Assmann and Christof Hardmeier (eds). 1983. *Schrift und Gedächtnis: Beiträge zur Archäologie der literarischen Kommunikation*. Munich: Willhelm Fink Verlag.

Assmann, Aleida, (ed.). 2004. *Vergessene Texte*. Konstanz: UVK Universitätsverlag.

Crivelli, Tatiana. 2007. "L'Arcadia femminile: spazi reali e simbolici du un'interazione culturale" in Gesa Stedman, and Margarete Zimmermann (eds). *Höfe-Salons-Akademien. Kulturtransfer und Gender im Europa der Frühen Neuzeit* Hildesheim/Zurich: Olms: 241-254.

Diaz, José-Luis. 1992. "Sainte Beuve chez les Muses" in *Romantisme* 77.III: 77-86.

Giacomo, Mariagabriella di. 2002. *L'illuminismo e le donne: Gli scritti di Elisabetta Caminer; 'utilità' e 'piacere': ovvero la coscienza di essere letterata*. Rome: La Sapienza.

Kleinert, Andreas. 2008. "Maria Gaetana Agnesi und Laura Bassi – zwei italienische gelehrte Frauen im 18. Jahrhundert". Online at http://www.physik.uni-halle.de/Fachgruppen/history/agbas.htm.

Larnac, Jean. 1927. *L'Histoire de la littérature féminine en France*. Paris: Kra.

Planté, Christine. 1989. *La petite soeur de Balzac. Essai sur la femme auteur.* Paris: Seuil.

Leroy, Géraldi and Julie Betrand-Sabiani. 1998. *La vie littéraire à la Belle Epoque*. Paris : PUF.

Marks, Elaine. 1993. "Odor di femina" in Denis Hollier (ed.). *De la littérature française.* Paris: Bordas: 831-836.

Metzeltin. 2010 "Die Entstehung der modernen Nationalstaaten" in *Italien 1861-2011: Einheit und Vielfalt. Zibbaldone* 50/: 11-16.

Pellegrin, Nicole. 2004. "Le polygraphe philogyne. A propos des dictionnaires de femmes célèbres au XVIIIe siècle", in Rotraud Von Kulessa (ed.). *Etudes féminines/gender studies en littérature en France et en Allemagne*. Freiburg in Brisgau: Frankreich-Zentrum: 63-79.

Russell, Rinaldina (ed.). 1994. *Italian Women Writers: A Bio-Bibliographical Source Book*. Westport/Conn.: Greenwood Press.

Sauvé, Rachel. 2000. *De l'éloge à l'exclusion. Les femmes auteurs et leur préfaciers au XIXe siècle*. Vincennes: PU.

Unfer Lukoschik, Rita (ed.). 1999. *Elisabetta Caminer Turra (1751-1796): Una letterata veneta verso l'Europa*. Verona: Essedue.

Veauvy, Christiane and Laura Pisano. 1997. *Paroles oubliées: les femmes et la construction de l'Etat-nation en France et en Italie (1789-1860).* Paris: Armand Colin.Villani, Carlo. 1915. *Stelle femminile: dizionario bio-bibliografico, Nuova edizione*. Naples: Albrighi/Segati.

von Kulessa, Rotraud. 2005. "Les *Amazones* de Mme du Boccage dans la traduction italianne de Luisa Bergalli Gozzi" in Annie Cointre, Florence Lautel and Annie Rivara (eds). *La traduction du discours amoureux.* Metz : Université Paul Verlaine: 255-267.

—. 2011. *Entre la reconnaissance et l'exclusion. La position de l'autrice dans le champ littéraire en France et en Italie à l'époque 1900*. Paris: Editions Honoré Champion.

Zimmermann, Margarete. 2005. *Salon der Autorinnen. Französische dames de lettres vom Mittelalter bis zum 17. Jahrhundert*. Berlin: Erich Schmidt Verlag.

# Histories of Women, Histories of Nation: Biographical Writing as Women's Tradition in Finland, 1880s-1920s

*Maarit Leskelä-Kärki*

ABSTRACT This chapter deals with women's biographical traditions in Finland in the late 19th century and early 20th century – at a time when Finnish literature started to flourish in connection with the construction of a national identity. It focuses both on short collective biographies written about women (mostly by the women's movement) and on biographies written about one individual life-course. In Finland, women started writing individual biographies from the 1890s onwards, as seen with two early biographers Helena Westermarck and Helmi Krohn. Their work can be seen as pioneering in the early Finnish tradition of biographical writing. We will discover what kind of nationality and national history these women biographers promoted in their writings

IN 1915 THE FINNISH AUTHOR, TRANSLATOR AND JOURNALIST Helmi Krohn (also known as Helmi Setälä, 1871-1967),[1] published a biography on the Swedish modernist author Victoria Benedictsson, under the title *Siipirikko. Erns Ahlgren kirjailijana ja ihmisenä* (*Broken-Winged. Ernst Ahlgren as a writer and a person*).[2] After publishing six novels and working as a

[1] http://neww.huygens.knaw.nl/authors/show/3625

[2] Ernst Ahlgren was the pseudonym of Victoria Benedictsson, and Krohn used this pseudonym throughout the book; only when discussing her childhood did she use the name Victoria. Benedictsson and her realist novels had already made an impact on the young Helmi Krohn, who described her views to her friend Maila Winter, the future novelist Maila Talvio, in 1889. Krohn was ambitious in writing this biography, since a full-length biography on Benedictsson had not yet been written. At the turn of the 1910s she spent a lot of time in Copenhagen and Stockholm gathering material for her work; she also met the famous Scandinavian modernist literary critic and theorist Georg Brandes, who had been Benedictsson's great love. The biography became a study of a woman artist and explored the possibilities open to women writers, for them to claim their own subjectivity. See more on the process of writing the biography in Maarit Leskelä-Kärki, *Kirjoittaen maailmassa. Krohnin sisaret ja*

professional in different literary fields, Krohn had started to publish biographies, and *Broken-Winged* was her second. The reception of the biography was favourable, and in the *Woman's Voice* magazine it was received as an important, encouraging and exemplary book for women:

> We, especially we women, have a particular reason to thank Helmi Krohn for this rich book. It is a valuable addition for those books we read, not only alone, but together, not only to forget them tomorrow, but to empathize with them in our thoughts, and to draw recreation and courage from them.[3]

The book was one of the first biographies on Benedictsson; only one had been published before. It is also worth noticing that the meaning of the book for the women's collective cause is pointed out in the review. This short review and Helmi Krohn's work as a biographer is a good example as to how biographical writing and the genre of biography has played an important part in building national history and also women's history; it has been a way to construct a gallery of important people. British historian Alison Booth argues that, in fact, the biographical form has been vital for the whole formation of the modern, national subject. Referring to Benedict Anderson's ideas on the construction of national communities, she points out that for young, emerging nations "The selected lineage of life narratives helps to constitute 'imagined communities'".[4]

Historical literature has been and is partly made outside the academic genre of historical writing, and is seen in fiction, public speeches, museums, audiovisual representations etc. Biography is one particular field where history has been – and is being – constructed. In this article, I will view beyond the national canon of biography, a genre that has mainly dealt with statesmen, male politicians, and leading (male) national artists.[5] I search for

---

*kirjallinen elämä*. Helsinki: SKS, 2006: 554-562. See also: http://neww.huygens.knaw.nl/authors/show/527.

[3] Hilja Riipinen's critique of Helmi Krohn's *Siipirikko*. See Maarit Leskelä-Kärki, *Kirjoittaen maailmassa*: 192

[4] Alison Booth, *How to Make It as a Woman. Collective Biographical History from Victoria to the Present.* Chicago and London: The University of Chicago Press, 2004: 12.

[5] In the Finnish context, this gendered canon of biography could be interpreted (for example) in the anthology *Yksilö ja yhteisö* first published in 1994, where articles concerning biographical writing and biographical tradition from the 1930s onwards

the tradition of women's biographical writing and observe how women have used and developed this genre within the particular national context of Finland. I will further consider the European context in which these women acted and wrote in order to highlight the interconnections between biographical traditions in Europe. The article relates to discussions concerning the history of historiography, the history of women's history and the history of women's literary practices.[6] I will look for feminist impulses and the ways in which women have used the genre to build up their own history, as well as commenting on national history.

## Women's early input in historical writing

Biographical writing has been one important genre where non-academic women writers have taken part, constructing the national history and traditions of historical research in different European countries, and a history of women. At a time when women were not allowed to pursue scholarly ambitions or write inside the academic world, they took part in writing history in other genres. For example, Bonnie G. Smith, who has studied the early professionalisation of historical research and women historians, points out how professionalisation deepened the hierarchy between amateur and professional writers of history. Women acted outside the professional field, but took part in the writing of social and cultural history outside academic professionalism. The consequence of this hierarchy has meant that the texts these women produced have been left aside – only professional and academic

---

were collected. None of the articles addressed biographies on women and most of them dealt with biographies on politicians and statesmen. When reprinted in 2006, they responded to my critique and published two of my articles on Helmi Krohn and the methodological practices of biography.

[6] See Mary Spongberg et al., *Companion to Women's Historical Writing*. Palgrave: Macmillan, 2009; Angelica Epple and Angelika Schaser (eds). *Gendering historiography. Beyond National Canon*. Frankfurt/New York: Campus Verlag, 2009; Mervi Kaarninen and Tiina Kinnunen, "'Hardly any women at all.' Finnish historiography revisited" in *Storia della Storiografia* (46) 2004: 152-170; Maarit Leskelä-Kärki. *Kirjoittaen maailmassa. Krohnin sisaret ja kirjallinen elämä. (Krohn sisters: Lives in Writing)* Helsinki: SKS, 2006; Ritva Hapuli & Maarit Leskelä-Kärki. "The public and private worlds of writing." in Johnson, Bruce and Harri Kiiskinen (eds). *They Do Things Differently There: Essays on Cultural History*. Turku: K&h-kustannus, 2011.

writing has been considered as important.[7] The Swedish critic Anna Nordenstam has also pointed out that the writing of women's history has very much happened outside the academic field – as was, for example, the case in writing the history of women's literature in Sweden. The first women's literary histories were produced in the journal Tidskrift för hemmet.[8] It has also been noticed in Finland that women first started to develop ways of constructing historical knowledge outside the academic field during the 19th century and early 20th century, when they were not allowed to enter academic studies.[9] Official academic research into women's history started long after Second World War, more precisely during the 1960s, and it has, until now, forgotten the early pioneers of the 19th and early 20th century.[10]

Women's participation in writing historical texts and producing historical knowledge was, of course, related to their education. Before the 1840s, girls (and mostly upper-class girls) were taught history in some private schools, and only in 1843 was a new law of school order introduced, allowing girls to receive a grammar school education. But, as Eva Packalén concludes, an education in history and the overall historical knowledge of girls was quite scarce even in the mid-1800s.[11]

In Finland, women started to be active in different literary fields in the early decades of the 1800s – of course, they did not number very many, but did start to publish poetry in the 1830s, and, as in many other countries, were among the first to publish novels and historical novels in Finland, starting in

---

[7] Bonnie G. Smith, *The Gender of History. Men, Women, and Historical Practice.* Cambridge, Massachusettes & London: Harvard University Press, 1998.

[8] Anna Nordenstam, *Begynnelser. Litteraturforskningens pionjärkvinnor 1850-1930.* Stockholm/Stehag: Brutus Östlings Bokförlag Symposion, 2001: 122-127.

[9] In Finland, this was gradually made possible from the 1880s onwards, but only in 1901 were women not forced to ask for special permission to enter universities.

[10] Elina Katainen, Tiina Kinnunen, Eva Packalén, Saara Tuomaala, "Naiset historiankirjoittajina. Akateeminen marginaali ja uuden tiedon tuottaminen." ("Women as producers of historical knowledge in Finland of the early and mid-1800s.") in Elina Katainen, Tiina Kinnunen, Eva Packalén ja Saara Tuomaala (eds). *Oma pöytä. Suomalaiset naiset historiankirjoittajina.* (Desk of One's Own. Finnish women as writers of history). Helsinki: Suomalaisen kirjallisuuden seura, 2005: 14. See also Anna Nordenstam, *Begynnelser*: 114-135.

[11] Eva Packalén, "Naiset historiallisen tiedon tuottajina Suomessa 1800-luvun alkupuolella ja puolivälissä." in Elina Katainen, Tiina Kinnunen, Eva Packalén ja Saara Tuomaala (eds). *Oma pöytä. Suomalaiset naiset historiankirjoittajina*: 52-54.

the 1840s.[12] These first novels were written in Swedish, as the first literary works in the Finnish language were published only from the 1860s onwards.[13] Among these early literary women was the most well-known author Fredrika Runeberg,[14] who was a pioneer in writing historical novels; she also published autobiographical texts, which were only much later compiled as a book *Min Pennas Saga* [The Story of my pen]. Her historical novels *Fru Catharina Boije och hennes döttrar* (1843/1858) and *Sigrid Liljehjolm* (1862) can be interpreted as women's histories, as they were based on historical happenings and people from the early 1700s.[15] Runeberg herself pointed out how she would have liked to create 'a history of women', but the plan was too difficult to achieve because of a lack of time and sources, which were hard for women to attain.[16] In fact, Fredrika Runeberg was among the first women writers about whom other women writers in Finland started to write biographies at the turn of the 1900s. As the wife of the national poet Johan Ludvig Runeberg, yet pursuing her own career as a novelist, she was seen as exemplary in the generation of women who started their careers as writers in the 1890s and early 1900s. Both Helena Westermarck and Helmi

---

[12] Women who wrote the first novels in Finland were Fredrika Wilhelmina Carstens, Charlotta Falkman, Maria Kraftman, Wendla Randelin, Fredrique Blum, Marie Linder. They all published only one novel. Heidi Grönstrand, *Naiset, romaani ja kirjallisuuden merkitys 1840-luvun Suomessa.* [Women, the novel and meaning of literature in Helsinki of the 1840s] Helsinki: SKS, 2005, and Kati Launis, *Kerrotut naiset. Suomen ensimmäiset naisten kirjoittamat romaanit naiseuden määrittelijöinä.* (*Women narrated. The first Finnish novels written by women as definers of womanhood*) Helsinki: Suomalaisen kirjallisuuden seura, 2005, were the first to analyse their production in their PhD theses in 2004.

[13] Thedolinda Hahnsson was the first woman writer to publish her texts in Finnish, she also translated the works of, for example, Heinrich Hoffman, Fredrika Bremer and Daniel Defoe. Marjaliisa Hentilä, "Ensimmäinen suomenkielinen naiskirjailija ja ympäristönsä tarkkailija Theodolinda Hahnsson" in Elina Katainen, Tiina Kinnunen, Eva Packalén ja Saara Tuomaala (eds). *Oma pöytä. Suomalaiset naiset historiankirjoittajina*: 98-99.

[14] See *Women writers database*: http://neww.huygens.knaw.nl/authors/show/1223. See also a portrait at the *Women Writers Portraits of Authors* http://www.womenwriters.nl/index.php/Fredrika_Charlotta_Runeberg

[15] Other early women writers used many european genres in writing their novels, such as the adultery novel, epistolary novel etc. See more on these early novelists in Heidi Grönstrand, *Naiset, romaani ja kirjallisuuden merkitys 1840-luvun Suomessa*; Kati Launis, *Kerrotut naiset.* . See more also in Eva Packalen,"Naiset historiallisen tiedon tuottajina Suomessa 1800-luvun alkupuolella ja puolivälissä".

[16] Elina Katainen, Tiina Kinnunen, Eva Packalén ja Saara Tuomaala (eds). *Oma pöytä. Suomalaiset naiset historiankirjoittajina*: 35.

Krohn wrote about her, and Helmi Krohn also gave public lectures on Runeberg's work. The later distinguished biographer Tyyni Tuulio wrote about Runeberg and her contemporaries in the 1970s, and also started translating her historical novels in the 1980s.

Sara Wacklin[17] was Runeberg's contemporary and one of those early women writers who depicted the lives, histories and habits of certain areas in Finland, especially in her book *Hundrade minnen från Österbotten (Satanen muistelmia Pohjanmaalta*, 1844-1845/*Thousand memories from Pohjanmaa*). She used many genres in her writing, and her book can be seen as fiction, history and documentary. At the end of the 19th century, more women started to enter the public literary sphere, and more women were active in writing in different genres and literary professions, as, for example, translators and journalists. Although they did not number very many, there were also a few women writers interested in historical novels, such as Betty Elfving, who wrote about the wars of 18th century in two of her novels and a play.[18]

When analysing the literary institution and the different literary genres in 19th century Finland, it is important to point out how the whole field of history writing was very heterogenous and the idea of dividing writers into categories of professional – amateur is not, perhaps, valuable. The borders between fiction, literature of fact, and academic literature etc. were also vague and under constant negotiation during this period. Furthermore, it is important to notice that amateur writing and the vague borders between literary genres did not only involve women– many of the amateur history writers, and biographers, were also men.[19] This perspective also opens up the plurality of the history of historiography, that is, as Maria Grever points out:

---

[17] Online at http://neww.huygens.knaw.nl/authors/show/3865.

[18] Her texts were connected to the political upheavals of the turn of the 20th century, when Finland was under pressure from the Russian regime and nationalist tendencies were strong. On Elfving see Tiina Koski, *Puoliksi mustepullossa: kirjoittaminen, arkipäivä ja historia Betty Elfvingin (1837-1923) teksteissä*. [Writing, everyday and history in Betty Elfving's texts] MA-thesis, Dept. of Cultural History, University of Turku 2013.

[19] Marja Jalava "Isien äänen äärellä. Paavo Virkkusen Agathon Meurman" , in Tiina Kinnunen. Marja Jalava, Irma Sulkunen (eds). *Kirjoitettu kansakunta. Sukupuoli, uskonto ja kansallinen historia 1900-luvun alkupuolen suomalaisessa tietokirjallisuudessa.* [Gender, Religion and National History in early 20th century Finnish non-fiction literature] Helsinki: SKS, 2013: 269-306.

"an open, contingent, and unpredictable process in which other transformations with other outcomes were possible".[20]

## Heyday of biographical compilations

As in many other countries, for instance in Sweden, Finland experienced a boom in biographical writing from the early 1800s onwards.[21] Connected to rising nationalism, biographical accounts of important men and their achievements were being published from the 1820s on. In many other countries with a longer history in producing biographies, such as Great Britain, there were tens of volumes of collections of famous or scandalous lives published, as well as several dictionaries – such as *Biographica Britannica* (1747-66), which had already been published in the 18th century.[22] Finland, like many other small countries encountering a nationalist boom, only entered this field in the early 19th century. In 1778, a four-part bio-bibliographical compilation was published by vicar Georg Gezelius. Finnish historian Matti Klinge, who has studied these early traditions of biographical writing (in particular these compilations), names *Otawa* as the first Finnish biographical book. It was compiled by G.A. Gottlund and published in three parts, and consisted of several longer biographies about "famous and distinguished Finnish men, [--] such as lawyers (Civile), priests, soldiers, merchants, craftmen – and even farmers (landowners)". The first part of *Otawa* consisted of six biographies and the third part had seventeen short biographies.[23]

---

[20] Maria Grever, "Fear of Plurality: historical culture and historiographical canonization in Western Europe" in Angelica Epple and Angelika Schaser (eds). *Gendering historiography. Beyond National Canon*: 53.

[21] About Sweden see Lisbeth Larsson, *Sanning och konsekvens. Marika Stiernstedt, Ludvig Nordström och de biografiska berättelserna* (*Truth and consequence. Marika Stiernsted, Ludvig Nordström and biographical stories).* Stockholm: Nordstedts. 2001.

[22] See Hermione Lee, *Biography. A Very Short Introduction.* Oxford: Oxford University Press. 2009: 64-65. Following the hagiographical tradition which flourished in the Middle Ages, biographical writing became much more diverse in England in the 17th century. The word 'biography' came into general use in the late 17th century England. *Ibid.*, 19-38.

[23] Matti Klinge, *Muistamisen arvoiset.* (*Worthy of remembrance*) *Kansallisbiografia* (*National biography electronic document.*) 2010. Online at http://www.kansallisbiografia.fi/kb/?p=18

As we can see, so far the tradition of these bio-bibliographical compilations in Finland has been about men. This continued, when the Finnish Historical Society started publishing a compilation called *Biografinen nimikirja* (Biographical name's book) in the 1870s. There had already been an attempt to publish biographical compilations of historical persons during the 1850s, but these short leaflets, which aimed to show the history of ordinary men working in different professions (such as doctors, priests etc.) under the title *Finland minnesvärde män* (Finland's noteworthy men), were criticised, and soon ended. Matti Klinge points out that the first important landmark of the Finnish biographical tradition was the publication of *Biografinen nimikirja* between the years 1879-1883 (altogether 844 pages).[24] This was an important achievement, but it must be noted that Klinge does not even mention the input women had started to make in this area, during the 1880s. Thus, much work needs to be done on the tradition of gendering historical writing, and in particular highlighting women's achievements in this area.

It is possible to argue that early women activists wanted to criticise this biographical compilation of important *men* by starting to publish their own biographical compilations on women. *Suomen naisyhdistys* (Women's Association in Finland) was the first women's association in Finland established in 1884. It aimed at 'enlightening women' and enhancing women's possibilities both economically and in society.[25]

An important part of the activities of this association was looking into the past and finding examples for their own female contemporaries. Collecting women's biographies was one important part of this endeavour, and the Finnish Women's Association published its first biographical compilation in 1890. This was called *Biografisk Album med 13 porträtter i ljustryck utgifvet af Finsk qvinnoförening*, published by G.W. Edlund, Hfors in 1890 [Biographical album with 13 portraits published by the Finnish women's association]. The texts were compiled from different authors, and some names are pseudonyms with only initials. Thus, we cannot know for sure if

---

[24] Matti Klinge, *Suomalainen ja eurooppalainen menneisyys*. (*Finnish and European Past*). Helsinki: Finnish Literature Society, 2011: 204-206.

[25] After several turbulent years, some of the younger members decided to establish a new association Women's League Union (Suomen naisasialiitto Unioni). They felt they had not been heard inside the Women's Association and that the older, and more conservative women headed the association. Minna Hagner and Teija Försti, *Suffragettien sisaret*. (*Sisters of Suffragets*), Helsinki: Unioni naisasialiitto, 2006: 14-46.

all the writers were women. Each of the biographical portraits was ca.10-20 pages long, and while some are based on secondary sources (not mentioned) others are based on the writer's own face-to-face encounters with these women. Only two of the women are Finnish: Emma Irene Åström, the first woman to achieve her university degree in Finland in 1882, and Aurora Karamzin, who was originally Finnish but married a Russian, and became a great benefactor of women's education by establishing a school for deaconesses in Helsinki in the 1870s. The other eleven women in the *Biografisk Album* were forerunners in education, women's activism, and socialist movements in Sweden (Ellen Key), Norway (Ragna Nielsen), Denmark (Mathilde Fibirger), Russia (Nadeschda Dmitrijewna Hwostschinskaja), Hungary (Janka Zirzen), Germany (Lina Morgenstern), France (Isabelle Bogelot), Great Britain (Caroline Ashurst Biggs), United States (Elizabeth Cady Stanton and Susan B. Anthony) and India (Pundita Ramabai). With the exception of Ramabai from India, these women represented the Scandinavian, Middle-European and Anglo-American women movements. Alexandra Gripenberg (1859-1913), who wrote the texts on Stanton, Anthony and Ramabai, was one of the most important and powerful leaders of the Finnish women's movement at this time, and was very international. She was an active writer and closely associated with international women's movement. One of her main works is a four-volume *Naisasian kehitys eri maissa* (The development of women's question in different countries).[26]

In 1892, the Association published a compilation *Finska qvinnor på olika arbetsområden* [Finnish women in different professions], and included biographies of 16 Finnish women working in the fields of art, literature, school and nursing. These were writers Fredrika Runeberg, Marie Linder, Wilhelmina Nordström, Augusta Wallenius (Lundahl), Augusta Pipping and Hedvig von Numers, singer Johanna von Schoultz, painters Fanny Churberg and Alexandra Såltin, the founder of the Finnish theatre Emilie Bergbom, pedagogue Elisabeth Blomqvist, educator of teachers Charlotte Lydecken, pedagogue Ida Godenhjelm, Finland's first deaconess Amanda Cajander,

---

[26] It was first published in Swedish (*Reformarbetet till förbättrande av kvinnans ställning)* in 1893-1903, and then in 1905, 1906, 1908 translated into Finnish by Tilma Hainari. Tiina Kinnunen has written an extensive article on Gripenberg's work, see Tiina Kinnunen, Historia "herätyksenä naisasian suurempaan harrastukseen." Alexandra Gripenberg Suomen naisten menneisyyden tulkkina, in Tiina Kinnunen, Marja Jalava, Irma Sulkunen (eds). *Kirjoitettu kansakunta:* 189-229.

pedagogue and developer of deaconess education Charlotta Molin, and nurse Anna Broms. Thus the focus was shifted to Finnish women and their input in developing Finnish society and culture. It was the start of a focus on national examples and tradition. In the foreword of the book it is noted:

> When men's work usually is situated at the public sphere, it has not been so difficult to scketch these men and their life-work. The situation is totally different, when looking at women and their input in cultural work. The fields of activity for women have so far been very limited.[27]

As in others, the foreword emphasizes the gratitude of the younger generation towards the older generation. It also considers the gap in the history of women's early input because of a lack of useful biographical material, but hopes that in the future these gaps will be filled.[28] As Elina Katainen, the first critic in Finland to gather information about these compilations, has noticed, these compilations emphasize certain aspects of women's position and identity in Finland: women's activity and energy in different fields was highly appreciated from early on, and certain women, such as writers Sara Wacklin, Fredrika Runeberg and Minna Canth or politician Miina Sillanpää, started to constitute the biographical canon of Finnish women.[29]

In this compilation, most of the writers were women, and mostly from inside the women's movement, in fields of education and literature. Some of the writers were, however, men, such as the professor in history and novelist Zacharias Topelius. The compilation included women who were already well remembered and appreciated, such as Fredrika Runeberg or Elisabeth Blomqvist, but many of the women had already been forgotten. Some of the writers also notice how the women of these early generations were forced into situations where they could not immediately choose their future careers. This is how Charlotta Molin's indented and manifold career path is described by Hilda Käkikoski:

---

[27] *Finska kvinnor på olika områden* 1892, företal [foreword].

[28] *Ibid.*

[29] Elina Katainen, Tiina Kinnunen, Eva Packalén ja Saara Tuomaala (eds). *Oma pöytä. Suomalaiset naiset historiankirjoittajina*: 290. See also about the compilations Tiina Kinnunen: "Mainioita naisia – pienoiselämäkerrat autonomian ajan historiapolitiikassa". [Biographical compilations in the history politics of autonomous Finland], *Historiallinen Aikakauskirja* 4/2012: passim.

> Charlotta Molin is not a character who would have been an example for future generations by her clear professional aims. They are hardly ever to be found among women at that time, when the 'weaker sex' was doomed at living on civilization's scraps that were falling from the tables of the more fortunate. The hard collecting of these scraps has often paid a lot of expensive time for these women, and lot of energy has thus been vanished. A more systematic education would be crucial so that these skills could be developed for the common good of the whole nation.[30]

The next compilation entitled *Kalenteri Suomen naisen työstä* [Calendar of the work of Finnish women, 1894] was followed up by a more detailed compilation *Biografisia tietoja Suomen naisista eri työaloilla* [published in 1896, Biographical information on Finnish women in different professions] that was meant to add to the information provided in the earlier book. The foreword emphasised that this book was not about complete biographies on famous women, but was meant to give some biographical information on Finnish women in different fields in the format of a handbook. The book wanted to reveal women's input in spheres that had been previously been unnoticed. It was also noted that the book included such fields that had previously been ignored by researchers, and this new information was regarded important for its cultural historical value. The Women's Association had also asked for suggestions as to which women they could present in this book in newspapers, but they had not received many answers to their call. In the foreword it was humbly noticed that this was only a 'test' version, and it was compiled because of "the gratitude for both those women of past generations, whose work had been done in silence and had not been recognised, and for those contemporary women who work in different fields for the common cause of the fatherland".[31]

The book consisted of 198 women who had worked in different fields of culture and society in Finland from the 15th century onwards. There were, for example, religious women (such as lay preachers), nuns, pedagogues, artists, writers, musicians, craftswomen, gardeners, women active in societal questions, politics and business, upper-class benefactors. Women were presented in alphabetical order, and the information consisted of their family

---

[30] Hilda Käkikoski, "Charlotta Molin", *Finska kvinnor på olika områden*: 135.

[31] *Biograafisia tietoja Suomen naisista eri aloilla* , Suomen Naisyhdistys. Helsinki, J. Simeliuken perillisten kirjapaino osakeyhtiö, 1896: first pages (without number.

background, possible education, marriage, other personal relations, professional achievements, publications etc. On some occasions the descriptions were longer, and also somewhat poetic, describing the economic difficulties, sickness, and other hindrances these women encountered during their lives.[32]

There is an interesting historical change seen in the four compilations The Finnish Women's Association published during the 1890s. They started by introducing exemplary women figures, mostly from abroad and mostly from inside the women's movement. Gradually the compilations covered a larger field of women's input, and the last compilation covered the lives of those women who worked in quite local surroundings and were not, as such, famous. There can also be seen an aim to cover the history of Finnish women's activities in various fields of society over several centuries. Short and detailed biographical portraits offered an effective means to depict the already vast field of women's activity. Biographical form showed its power in constituting history, tradition and meaning for societal discussion, and these compilations tell of the importance of tradition, foremothers and historical knowledge in the work of the early women's movement.

The Finnish Women's Association certainly had many examples to follow, as the tradition of collective biographies had lasted for centuries in other European cultures. Even if the tradition of women's collective biographies on other women was extensive, it has been said that Christine de Pizan's *Le livre de la cité des dames* (The book of the city of ladies) from the early 15th century would be the first biographical input of a woman about another woman.[33] The case of Finland tells of a small nation starting to construct its national and cultural history with very little input – the quantity of works is entirely different when analysing the tradition of collective biographies in larger countries.[34]

---

[32] *Biograafisia tietoja Suomen naisista eri aloilla,* 1896. Many biographical texts are also to be found in the presentations and speeches women gave: e.g. the activist and international figure Alexandra Gripenberg gave a speech on Elizabeth Cady Stanton and women's activism in 1896. *Elizabeth Cady Stanton och kvinnosaksarbetet: föredrag hållet i Stockholm,* hotel Continentals sal, d. 30 maj 1896, it was also published in Stockholm.

[33] Alison Booth, *How to Make It as a Woman*: 1.

[34] For example, Alison Booth, who has written about the tradition of collective biographies of women (written by both women and men) in Britain, has a bibliography of 900 collective biographies from the 19th century. *Ibid.*, 2-3.

## Changing biographical field

The Women's Association did not pursue publishing compilations, but the heyday of compilations was not over. A new series of Kansanvalistusseura (Association for the enlightment of the people) started publishing a biographical series in 1900. This series would publish biographies on both foreign and Finnish men, and as Mervi Kaarninen points out, the series was meant to strengthen the cult of great men in an era of strong nationalist aspiration. Although writer Maila Talvio was asked to write the first biography on poet J.L. Runeberg, there were no female names on the list of candidates. Later, there was discussion about a female candidate, which would have been Queen Elisabeth I, but it was not published. The series was popular, and between 1900-1918 it published 29 biographies in total.[35] At the same time, biographical compilations aimed at children were popular, and one pioneering female biographer, Helmi Krohn, published such books. Further to this, the genre of individual biographies (biographies written on one person) began to be developed.

At the end of the 19th century, the production of ambitious, research-based biographies telling the lives of one individual person began. One of the first to be written was by a female author. Lucina Hagman (1853-1946) was a school-teacher for girls and distinguished pedagogue, who also published a few biographies. In 1886 she published a biography of 264 pages about the Swedish writer Fredrika Bremer entitled *Fredrika Bremer: kuvaus vuosisatamme alkupuolelta* [Fredrika Bremer: Description of the early 1800s]. Although active in Sweden for almost her entire life, Bremer was Finnish by birth, and her influence in the Finnish women's movement has been seen as pioneering, which can also be seen from the biography of Hagman. Lucina Hagman published her other biography on the modernist female writer Minna Canth. The first part was published in 1906, and the second in 1911.

The biography was given a prize from the Finnish Literature Society. As a comparison, one can note that Eliel Aspelin Haapkylä, professor of aesthetics and literature, first published biographies on artists Johannes Takanen and Werner Holmberg in 1888 and 1890. During the 1890s, several biographies

---

[35] Mervi Kaarninen : "'Pitäisi olla puoleksi runoilija voidakseen kirjoittaa historiaa…' Kirjoittavat naiset ja isänmaan historia nuorisolle. [Women Writing the History of Nation to the Youth], in Tiina Kinnunen, Marja Jalava, Irma Sulkunen (eds). *Kirjoitettu kansakunta. Sukupuoli:* 149-188.

on important 19th century men were published.[36] Biographies became more and more popular quite quickly during the first years of the 1900s. So far, Hagman's book is recognised as the first biography on woman published in Finland.[37] Thus, it can be observed that women were at the forefront in developing the genre of biography in Finland, and saw the opportunities biography could offer as a form of depicting the lives of women and their input in culture.

Women did not stop being active in this field, and Helena Westermarck started her future career as a pioneering biographer in the early 1890s. She was also a novelist, painter and women's activist, and published her first biography in 1894 on George Eliot *(George Eliot. En literär studie*). She worked with the source material in British Library beside her brother, the famous anthropologist Edward Westermarck. After that, she was among one of many to write an early piece on Fredrika Runeberg in *Fredrika Runeberg. En literär Studie* (1904). Many of Westermarck's biographies deal with Finnish women painters, who belonged to the same generation of painters as she did. She wrote, particularly, on women painters who stayed in the margins of Finnish art history for a long time, and who were rediscovered from the 1980s on. Westermarck wrote on the first Finnish female painter Mathilda Rotkirch (*Mathilda Rotkirch. Finlands första målarinna. En kulturbild,* 1926), and on three of her close colleagues: Fanny Churberg, Maria Wiik och Sigrid af Forselles in *Tre konstnärinnör. Fanny Churberg, Maria Wiik och Sigrid af Forselles* (1937).

Her biographies include works on women acting in different professional fields, often as pioneers. These include her biography on Elisabeth Blomqvist, *Elisabeth Blomqvist: hennes liv och gärning. En biografisk studie, enligt brev och dagboksanteckningar I-II* (1916-17), one of the early influential school-teachers for girls, as well as the female activist and journalist Adelaïde Ehrnrooth, *Adelaïde Ehrnrooth. Kvinnospår i finländskt kulturliv* (1928), and the first Finnish female doctor Rosina Heikel, *Finlands första kvinnliga läkare Rosina Heikel. Kvinnospår i finländskt kulturliv*

---

[36] Marja Jalava, "Isien äänen äärellä. Paavo Virkkusen Agathon Meurman", in Tiina Kinnunen, Marja Jalava, Irma Sulkunen (eds). *Kirjoitettu kansakunta*: 269-306.

[37] Elina Katainen, Tiina Kinnunen, Eva Packalén ja Saara Tuomaala (eds). *Oma pöytä. Suomalaiset naiset historiankirjoittajina*: 291; Minna Hagner, "'Naisasian tarkoitus on ihmiskunnan sopusointuinen kehitys'. Porvarillisen naisliikkeen tuottamat kertomukset naisten historiasta." *Ibid.*, 291.

(1930).[38] *Kvinnospår. Kulturbilder från 1800-talets förra del* (1913) was a study on women's education based on the correspondence between lieutenant Samuel Möller and his daughter Eva Sophia at the end of the 18th century and early 19th century. Westermarck was a versatile writer. She had started her career as a writer of novels, and these literary works can also be depicted as women's history and the everyday life of the upper- and middle-class women in Finland.[39]

## The case of Helmi Krohn: crossings between nationality and gender

Helmi Krohn was, like Helena Westermarck, one of the early pioneers in this literary field. Krohn wrote in the Finnish speaking literary sphere, and Westermarck in the Swedish. Although Krohn was very skilled in languages, and must have known about the books produced in Finland, it is interesting that there seems to have been no connection between Westermarck and Krohn on a personal level. This tells us something about the separate language fields and the political debates around language issues that were ongoing for a long time at the turn of the 20th century.

Most of Krohn's biographies and biographical compilations dealt with figures from Finnish national history, and a certain double strategy can be seen in her literary works – she was active in constructing the national/ist history of Finland at a time when Finland was still a part of the Russian Empire. But, simultaneously, many of her biographies can be interpreted as a particular women's history project.

Helmi Krohn's work as a biographer gives a fruitful example on the ways biography could be used in the construction of nationality. This can most vividly be seen in the several compilations she wrote over many decades. Many of these compilations were originally published in children's magazines and other cultural journals. Compilations such as *Kun suuret olivat pieniä* (1911) [When great ones were little] dealt with the childhood of

---

[38] Git Claesson Pipping, *Men arbetet! Mitt arbete! Identitet och berättandet i Helena Westermarcks yrkeskvinnobiografier*. Stockholm: Makadam, 2008.

[39] See more in Minna Hagner, "'Naisasian tarkoitus on ihmiskunnan sopusointuinen kehitys'. Porvarillisen naisliikkeen tuottamat kertomukset naisten historiasta" in Elina Katainen, Tiina Kinnunen, Eva Packalén ja Saara Tuomaala (eds). *Oma pöytä. Suomalaiset naiset historiankirjoittajina*: 100-118.

26 artists and writers. All of them were Finnish, and most were men, but there are several women, such as singers Emmy Achté and Maikki Järnefelt-Palmgren, as well as the actress Ida Aalberg and painter Maria Wiik. A compilation entitled *Suomen suuria miehiä* (1915) [Great men of Finland] dealt with only nationalist statesmen, soldiers, politicians, writers and academics such as Mikael Agricola, Daniel Juslenius, Henrik Gabriel Porthan or Zacharias Topelius, and *Pikkupojista sotaherroiksi* (1935) [From little boys to soldiers] was about Finnish soldiers and politicians. In 1924, she published a book about Finnish theatre directors and actors called *Kulissien takaa* (1924) [Behind the scenes], in which quite a few female actors were presented.

In a compilation about the mothers of great men (*Merkkimiestemme äitejä,* 1937), she wrote articles on the mother of the sculptor Walter Runeberg (Fredrika Runeberg) and of her own grandmother Julie Dannenberg. In a book published as late as 1957, *Lapsesta elämä alkaa [Life begins from children],* she wrote not only on the childhood of Finnish artists, but also on foreign artists (Genoveva, Marco Polo, Giotto di Bondonen, Hans Holbein, Jacques Amyot, Bartolome Murillo, Molière, Isaac Newton, J.W. von Goethe, Ludwig van Beethoven, Franz Schubert, Alexander Dumas, Aleksander Petöfi, Louisa May Alcott), in which only few women can be noticed. In 1945, Krohn had published a compilation book entitled *Ystäviäni kirjeittensä valossa* (1945) [My friends in the light of their letters]. This included small biographical portraits of people she had met and known personally. They included texts on both foreign men and women, people Krohn was personally acquainted with: Georg Brandes, P.E. Pavolini, Laura Kieler, Lucie Hörlyk, Ananda Comaraswamy as well as Erkki Melartin, Jalmari Finne, Ida Alberg, Wihtori ja Ester Peltonen, Arvid Järnefelt, J.H. Erkko.

Helmi Krohn's first individual biography dealt with the first Finnish woman poet, Isa Asp, in 1912, and the second, as mentioned at the beginning of this article, with the Swedish modernist writer, Victoria Benedictsson. It seems that her interest was very much in the field of literature at this point. She gave public speeches on several writers, such as Juhani Aho and Minna Canth during the early 1910s, and these literary speeches inspired her to start writing. Her biography of Benedictsson was only the second to be written about the author; a total outsider, who had not known Benedictsson personally, had written the first.[40] Krohn did some interviews and communicated with the Swedish public by writing newspaper articles outlining her interpretations of Benedictsson. The proceeding biographies, at the end of the 1910s and early 1920s, dealt with women in the worlds of theatre and opera (Emilie Bergbom, the founder of Finnish theatre; acctress Hedvig Raa Winterhjelm; opera singer Jenny Lind; opera singer Emmy Achté). In 1918, Krohn published a book called *Naisia* (Women), which was based on short biographical portraits published earlier, in a literary magazine called *Valvoja*. These texts are idealising, popular biographical descriptions of interesting, mostly literary, but also other, already partly forgotten women.[41]

With her biographical works, Helmi Krohn took part in the nationalist project with which she was intensely connected in multiple ways, as the daughter of the nationalist poet and professor Julius Krohn and the wife of the nationalist linguistic and politician Eemil Nestor Setälä. It is possible to trace elements of education and enlightenment in her work, but also the foundations of the cultural history of Finland through a gallery of important men and women. Her biographies, and especially her compilations written for children, reveal the picture of a young nation starting to negotiate a place for itself. She describes the lives of important women and men working in the field of art, literature, and theatre, who were constructing a nationalist ethos in the early 20th century, before independence. But the picture is not that clear, or at least is not without fractures. It is also possible to find a special feminine voice[42] in her biographical production. With her biographies on women in the Finnish theatre (such as the founder Emilie Bergbom or actor Hedvig Raa) or opera (Emmy Achté), it is possible to see that she was also

---

[40] Krohn was one of the first ones in the upcoming long list of biographers of Benedictsson. See more on the tradition of Benedictsson biographies in Lisbeth Larsson: *Sanning och konsekvens* and *Hennes döda kropp. Victoria Benedictssons arkiv och författarskap.*

[41] The list is as follows: Camilla Collet, Goethe's young admirer Bettina von Arnim, the singer and lover of Ivan Turgenejev Pauline Viardot, actress Helena von Racowitza, Norwegian writer Amalie Skram, "the women of Richard Wagner", the writer and hostess of the literary salon Rahel Varnhagen, and writer Malwida von Meysenburg.

[42] I would not call Krohn's literary work feminist, as she was very much outside the women's movement, and, all in all, feminism is an anachronistic term when we are talking about society in the early 20th century. I prefer to see some of Krohn's work as devoted to the women's cause and gender imbalance in society and nationalist history.

looking for a place for women in this nationalist project. Some of her critics noticed this, saying how she had "chosen to depict the lives and work of those noteworthy women, who had sacrificed their lives for the cause of Finnish civilization". A particular international dimension is seen in her biographies on Victoria Benedictsson and in the compilation *Naisia*, where she analyzed exemplary women from different European countries.

Although it is possible to argue that there is a certain specific focus on women and the gendered system in Krohn's biographical production, one must be careful of the interpretation. Many issues influenced her literary work, such as the economic situation, her family and professional networks, and the family situation.[43] However, something of Krohn's aims and role as a biographer can be interpreted from a review she wrote on Lucina Hagman's biography of the writer Minna Canth. In this review, Krohn pointed out how the most important value of a biographer was the ability to forget oneself and only let the object of the biography talk. Krohn saw that Hagman had put too much of her own ideas and beliefs into the biography of Canth, and used it for her own feminist purposes. In Krohn's opinion, biography should give an objective, clear picture of the person depicted, "this might be ungrateful as a job, especially for a person like Lucina Hagman who has herself been involved in the same battle [for women's cause], that she describes in the book. But even then, one should not mix one's own personality and one's own opinions in the depiction that aims at giving a clear, objective picture of a certain person and her life's work".[44]

Helmi Krohn saw that Hagman had forgotten these ideals while writing her book. Hagman saw Canth only as a part of the women's movement, and Krohn was very critical towards Hagman's emancipatory tone and contempt of men, believing that she had used Canth to put forward her own opinions, to promote the female cause. This had, in Krohn's opinion, produced a situation where Canth's artistic and literary worth came second. When it came to biographies, Hagman's position was very different to Krohn's. Krohn aimed to diminish herself and her opinions, and wanted her

---

[43] See more in Maarit Leskelä-Kärki, "Narrating life-stories in-between the fictional and the autobiographical" in *Qualitative Research*, special issue Liz Stanley (ed.). 2008 (8): 325-332.

[44] Helmi Setälä's critic on Lucina Hagman's work on Minna Canth in *Valvoja* magazine, ref. in Maarit Leskelä-Kärki: *Kirjoittaen maailmassa*, 2006, 190-191.

protagonists to speak through the use of (for example) letters and other personal materials.[45]

After reading this critic, one can be sure that Helmi Krohn did not want to actively promote feminist issues in her production. This does not, however, suggest that there was no specific, gendered tone to her production. As a writer and a professional in different literary fields, she was an early pioneering women writer, and was interested in the input of women in the culture and history of Finland. Thus, it is possible to interpret a certain double-strategy in her biographical work: she created places for women in the national history and also took part in developing the genre of biography, by not only writing about them, but also by acting as a critic. It can also be argued that Helmi Krohn looked for examples and ideals for her own work as a literary professional.

## "Bleak winter sunrays"

Both Helena Westermarck and Helmi Krohn have been forgotten as the early developers of the biographical genre. They both acted in various literary fields at a time when the whole Finnish literary institution and various literary genres were only just developing. They contributed to the biographical genre at the moment it was developing. Looking at their production, and the earlier Finnish compilations produced during the 1890s, we can notice an important connection between biography, history and nationalism. Biography offered a serious, and also a popular, genre in which writers could take part in the discussions about how to build up a gallery of nationally important men and women.

In the reception of the work of Helmi Krohn, her ability to write was noticed, but she was not seen as a professional writer: she wrote biographies, but was not a researcher. She was seen as the writer of big audiences, and as an educator of young people, as the mediator of ideal cultural historical and national values. She did not write "historically profound biographies or thorough academic research",[46] and neither was it seen that her work would consist of "deeper independent and academic ground work like a true biography analyzing an artist character or artistic lifework would have to

[45] *Ibid.*, 132-135.

[46] *Sisäsuomi* 14.10.1927, in Maarit Leskelä-Kärki, *Kirjoittaen maailmassa*:189.

have".[47] She was not a true professional, but a "lay person" (amateur).[48] Thus her work was connected intensely to the building of a national Finland and to the role of the educated class in promoting national values.

The Finnish Women's Association and the forthcoming women biographers pioneered in the genre of biography and saw the advantages of this genre very early on. They took examples from other countries and from the women's movement. These compilations also tell us something about the international character of the women's movement, where examples from many places (not only Finland) could be found. This also suggests something about the history of the young nation, and a very similar trend can be seen in other smaller countries as well. For example, Katja Mihurko Poniz has pointed out the meaning of foreign exemplary figures in a country such as Slovenia, in which there were no early women figures. A Slovenian magazine, Women's World (*Ženski svet*), had a special column between 1923-33 called "Faces and souls" that depicted the lives of important European women from different fields of art and politics. In presenting these biographies, as Ponzi suggests, the magazine opened up a "transnational perception of women's history".[49]

In the Finnish context, the importance of national history, and the role of women within it, became visible in the compilations of the 1890s and in the works of Helena Westermarck and Helmi Krohn. Simultaneously, Westermarck and Krohn were international figures also writing about other non-Finnish women (like George Eliot and Victoria Benedictsson), and balancing between the national and transnational. In the works of these female biographers, biography gave room for women who were, as Alexandra Gripenberg describes when referring to Camille Collet, "bleak winter sunrays, that appear in January predicting the forthcoming Spring –

[47] *Tampereen Sanomat* 13.10.1927, in Maarit Leskelä-Kärki, *Kirjoittaen maailmassa*:189.

[48] *Aamulehti* 11.2.1924, in Maarit Leskelä-Kärki: *Kirjoittaen maailmassa*: 189.

[49] Katja Mihurko-Poniz, "Biographical Discourse in the Slovenian Magazine 'Women's World'". Paper presented at *Women's biographical traditions across Europe. IABA Europe 2011 Trajectories of (Be)longing: Europe in Life-Writing* (Tallinn University. 18-20 May 2011). Regarding the heroic biographical tradition of the women's movement, see also Ellen C. Dubois, "Making Women's History: Activist Historians of Women's Rights, 1880-1940." in Leon Fink, Stephen T. Leonard and Donald M. Reid (eds). *Intellectuals and Public Life. Between Radicalism and Reform*). Ithaca and London: Cornell University Press. 1996; Lisbeth Larsson, *Sanning och konsekvens*: 402-410.

who by their intelligence and their gifts foretell new and richer possibilities for their sex".[50] Gripenberg notices that these women have been everywhere and in all nations, and have sometimes been forgotten (like Augusta Wallin, whom she writes about), but the genre of biography makes it possible to give them life again.

[50] Gripenberg's article in *Finska qvinnor på olika arbetsområden* 1892, 119, orig. in Swedish.

## Select Bibliography

### A. Primary Sources

*Biografiskt album med 13 porträtter i ljustryck*. 1890. Utgifven af Finsk Kvinnoförening. G. W. Edlund, Helsingfors

*Finska qvinnor på olika arbetsområden*. 1892. Biografisk album utgifven af Finsk Kvinnoförening. Fölagsaktiebolaget Otava: Helsingfors.

*Biograafisia tietoja Suomen naisista eri työaloilla*. 1896. Suomen Naisyhdistys. J. Simeliuken perillisten kirjapaino osakeyhtiö. Helsinki.

### B. Secondary Sources

Booth, Alison. 2004. *How to Make It as a Woman. Collective Biographical History from Victoria to the Present*. Chicago and London: The University of Chicago Press.

DuBois, Ellen C. 1996. "Making Women's History: Activist Historians of Women's Rights, 1880-1940." in *Intellectuals and Public Life. Between Radicalism and Reform*. Fink, Leon, Stephen T. Leonard and Donald M. Reid. (eds). Ithaca and London: Cornell University Press.

Epple, Angelica and Schaser, Angelika (eds.) 2009. *Gendering historiography. Beyond National Canon*. Frankfurt/New York: Campus Verlag.

Grever, Maria. 2009. "Fear of Plurality: historical culture and historiographical canonization in Western Europe." Epple, Angelica and Schaser, Angelika (eds). in *Gendering historiography. Beyond National Canon*. Frankfurt/New York: Campus Verlag: 45-62.

Grönstrand, Heidi. 2005. *Naiset, romaani ja kirjallisuuden merkitys 1840-luvun Suomessa*. Helsinki: SKS.

Hagner, Minna. 2005. "'Naisasian tarkoitus on ihmiskunnan sopusointuinen kehitys'. Porvarillisen naisliikkeen tuottamat kertomukset naisten historiasta." in *Oma pöytä. Suomalaiset naiset historiankirjoittajina*. Toim. Elina Katainen, Tiina Kinnunen, Eva Packalén ja Saara Tuomaala (eds). Helsinki: Suomalaisen kirjallisuuden seura, 2005.

Hagner, Minna and Försti, Teija. 2006. *Suffragettien sisaret*. (*Sisters of Suffragets*) Helsinki: Unioni naisasialiitto.

Hapuli, Ritva and Leskelä-Kärki, Maarit. 2011. "The public and private worlds of writing." in *They Do Things Differently There: Essays on Cultural History*. Johnson, Bruce and Harri Kiiskinen (eds). Turku: K&h-kustannus: 185-210.

Hentilä, Marjaliisa. 2005. "Ensimmäinen suomenkielinen naiskirjailija ja ympäristönsä tarkkailija Theodolinda Hahnsson." in *Oma pöytä.*

*Suomalaiset naiset historiankirjoittajina*. Katainen, Elina, Tiina Kinnunen, Eva Packalén ja Saara Tuomaala (eds). Helsinki: Suomalaisen kirjallisuuden seura: 98-99.

Jalava, Marja. 2013. "Ihanteellista seurustelua jaloluontoisten ihmisten kanssa – Kansallisuus, kansallinen kapitalismi, kristillisyys ja miehisyys Paavo Virkkusen *Agathon Meurman*-elämäkerrassa." [Nationality, national kapitalism, Christianity and masculinity in the biography of Agathon Meurman by Paavo Virkkunen] in *Kirjoitettu kansakunta. Sukupuoli, kansallisuus ja historiakirjoittaminen 1800-1900-lukujen Suomessa*. Kinnunen, Tiina, Marja Jalava, Irma Sulkunen (eds). Helsinki: SKS: 269-306.

Kaarninen, Mervi and Kinnunen, Tiina. 2004. "'Hardly any women at all.' Finnish historiography revisited." in *Storia della Storiografia* (46): 152-170.

Kaarninen, Mervi. 2013. "Suomen historiaa kaikelle kansalle." [History of Finland for all.] in *Kirjoitettu kansakunta. Sukupuoli, kansallisuus ja historiakirjoittaminen 1800-1900-lukujen Suomessa*. [Gender, nationalism and historical writing in the 19th and 20th century Finland] Kinnunen, Tiina, Marja Jalava, Irma Sulkunen (eds). Helsinki: SKS:149-188.

Katainen, Elina, Kinnunen, Tiina, Packalén, Eva ja Tuomaala, Saara (toim.) 2005. *Oma pöytä. Suomalaiset naiset historiankirjoittajina.*Helsinki: Suomalaisen kirjallisuuden seura.

—. 2005. "Naiset historiankirjoittajina. Akateeminen marginaali ja uuden tiedon tuottaminen." in *Oma pöytä. Suomalaiset naiset historiankirjoittajina*. Katainen, Elina, Tiina Kinnunen, Eva Packalén ja Saara Tuomaala (eds). Helsinki: Suomalaisen kirjallisuuden seura: 11-49.

Klinge, Matti. 2010. *Muistamisen arvoiset.* Kansallisbiografia http://www.kansallisbiografia.fi/kb/?p=18.

—. 2011. *Suomalainen ja eurooppalainen menneisyys.*] Helsinki: Finnish Literature Society.

Koski, Tiina. 2013. *Puoliksi mustepullossa: kirjoittaminen, arkipäivä ja historia Betty Elfvingin (1837-1923) teksteissä*. [Writing, everyday and history in Betty Elfving's texts] MA-thesis, Dept. of Cultural History, University of Turku.

Krohn, Helmi. 1915. *Siipirikko. Ernst Ahlgren kirjailijana ja ihmisenä.* Helsinki: Otava.

Larsson, Lisbeth. 2001. *Sanning och konsekvens. Marika Stiernstedt, Ludvig Nordström och de biografiska berättelserna.* Stockholm: Nordstedts.

—. 2008. *Hennes döda kropp. Victoria Benedictssons arkiv och författarskap.* Weyler.

Launis, Kati. 2005. *Kerrotut naiset. Suomen ensimmäiset naisten kirjoittamat romaanit naiseuden määrittelijöinä.* Helsinki: Suomalaisen kirjallisuuden seura.

Lee, Hermione. 2009. *Biography. A Very Short Introduction.* Oxford: Oxford University Press.

Leskelä-Kärki, Maarit. 2006. *Kirjoittaen maailmassa. Krohnin sisaret ja kirjallinen elämä. [*Krohn sisters: Lives in Writing] Helsinki: SKS.

—. 2008 "Narrating life-stories in-between the fictional and the autobiographical." in Qualitative Research, special issue Stanley,Liz (ed.). (8):325-332.

Mihurko-Poniz, Katja. 2011. "Biographical Discourse in the Slovenian Magazine 'Women's World'". Paper presented at *Women's biographical traditions across Europe. IABA Europe 2011 Trajectories of (Be)longing: Europe in Life-Writing* (Tallinn University. 18-20 May 2011).

Nordenstam, Anna. 2001. *Begynnelser. Litteraturforskningens pionjärkvinnor 1850-1930.* Stockholm/Stehag: Brutus Östlings Bokförlag Symposion.

Packalen, Eva. 2005. "Naiset historiallisen tiedon tuottajina Suomessa 1800-luvun alkupuolella ja puolivälissä." in *Oma pöytä. Suomalaiset naiset historiankirjoittajina.* Katainen, Elina, Tiina Kinnunen, Eva Packalén ja Saara Tuomaala (eds). Helsinki: Suomalaisen kirjallisuuden seura.

Pipping, Git Claesson. 2008. *Men arbetet! Mitt arbete! Identitet och berättandet i Helena Westermarcks yrkeskvinnobiografier.* Stockholm: Makadam.

Smith, Bonnie G. 1998. *The Gender of History. Men, Women, and Historical Practice.* Cambridge, Massachusettes & London: Harvard University Press.

Spongberg, Mary; Curthoys, Ann and Caine, Barbara. 2009. *Companion to Women's Historical Writing.* Palgrave Macmillan.

# Early Women's Press (Three Female Magazines): A Challenge for the 19th Century East and Greece

*Sirmula Alexandridou*

ABSTRACT Abstract: This chapter interrogates the notion that the publication of magazines for women and by women represented a male public discourse during the second half of the 19th century. The publication of three female literary magazines did not only mark indelibly the broader area of Hellenism, but also contributed to the emergence of a female consciousness and identity. The anxiety to conserve Greekness and secure national identity, a common characteristic of all three magazines, as well as the use of purist Greek as the only language that could ensure continuity with the past and the ancient Greek language, appears to have suffocated the dynamic emergence of the female press.

BY 1845, THE YEAR OF PUBLICATION OF THE FIRST GREEK women's literary magazine in Istanbul, Greece had already been an independent state for fifteen years. The newly-founded state was small, and significant areas inhabited by Greeks still lay within the borders of the Ottoman Empire, or were under English control. A close-knit Greek community, that in 1843 numbered 120.000 people out of an entire population of 450.000, lived in the Ottoman capital of Constantinople. Due to the strong economical and intellectual growth of this area, in addition to political favourable conditions, Constantinople was the ideal location for women authors to excel.[1]

---

[1] Efrosini Samartzidou was to settle in Constantinople with her husband during the year of 1845. The Greek Revolution that broke out in 1821 lasted until the year of 1827 and ended with the establishment of independent state .The independence of the Greek state was ratified by the London Protocol in 1830 and the London Convention in 1832. See Basil Kremmidas, *Modern History Greek and European.* Athens: Gnosi, 1984, and Nikos Svoronos, *Histoire de la Grèce Moderne.* Paris: P.U.F., 1972. The London Convention in 1832 ratified that the newly independent state would include the Peloponnesus, the Cyclades, the island Euboea, the islands nearby Peloponnesus, the North Sporades and the Mainland Greece to limit Pagasitikos- Amvrakikos Bay. Under the terms of the London Convention in 1832, Thessaly, Epirus, Macedonia,

The liberation of these areas, and the widening of the nation state's boundaries, was the object of national foreign policy and diplomacy until 1922, and constituted the ideological framework,[2] whilst encouraging restructuring of the state and its cultural development. From 1834, the spiritual radiation emitted Athens, as the new capital of the Greek kingdom,[3] (Athens' influence) did not only cease in formal education policies, including the organisation of formal education for boys in the founding of primary and secondary schools – the basis for which had been developed under the government of the first Prime Minister of the newly-founded state, Ioannis Kapodistrias, from 1828 to 1831[4] – but was also reflected in intense publishing activity (newspapers and magazines). For example, during the period 1830-1846, 53 magazines were published, of which 39 were within

---

Thrace, the islands of North Aegean , Crete and Dodecanese would still lie within the borders of the Ottoman Empire and the Ionian under the English control.

[2] As it was difficult for the boundaries of Hellenism to be defined and for the national ambitions of the newly Greek state to be moderated – the idea of national liberation identified with the rising of the Byzantine Empire and concerned the 'Great idea' that constituted the ideological framework until 1922 and dominated the foreign policy of Greece, see Nikos Svoronos, *Histoire de la Grece Moderne*: 80-82, 84-86 and 97-99 (Athens 1985, with a rich bibliography guide written by Spiros Asdrachas); Richard Glogg, "The formation of Greek Nation, the Big Idea and the National Division" in *A Concise History of Greece*. Cambridge: Cambridge University Press, 1992: 49-103 (Athens 1995); George Castellan, *Histoire des Balkans,* Paris: Libraire Artheme Fayard/ Athens: Govosti, 1991: 409; Douglas Dakin, *The Unification of Greece 1770-1923, London, Ernest Benn Limited 1972.* Athens: Cultural Foundation of National Bank, 1972.

[3] During the Greek Revolution, Nauplia was ratified as the first capital of the Greek state. The year 1834, after numerous intense consultations, Athens was selected as the new capital for historical and political reasons. In this period, Athens was a small town with a population of approximately 5000 inhabitants, but in the following years, population growth, the recovery of the economy and the reconstruction did not reflect its poor past at all. See Basil Kremmidas, *Modern History Greek and European.* Athens: Gnosi, 1984; P. Stefan Papageorgiou, *The Greek State (1821-1909).* Athens: Papazisis, 1998: 130; Martha Karpozilou, *The Greek Family-Literary Magazines (1847-1900).* Ioannina: Scientific Annals of the Department of Education, University of Ioannina, 1991: 42.

[4] Paul Petridis, *Greek politics and social history 1821-1940*, Thessaloniki: Paratiritis, 1986: 69-70. Helen Koukou, "The education from 1828 to 1831" in *The History of Greek Nation.* Athens: Ekdotiki. *Ibid.*, vol. 12, 1975: 589- 593.

the borders of the Greek state and 14 were abroad, published by Greeks in the Greek language, reaching as far north as Paris.[5]

Although this rich expression of speech touches on a variety of issues of interest to a wide readership, it does not appear able to satisfy the needs of the Greek family, and as a result, from 1847, more specialized family-literary focused magazines were published.[6] Neither are the interests of women covered until 1845, when they were introduced into the magazines' editorial notes and contents.

In 1845, the publication of *Kypseli* in Istanbul, by Efrosini Samartzidou, challenged male-dominated journalistic circles, not only for Greeks within the nation state, but equally in the East.This challenge highlighted two issues: *Kypseli* was the first Greek female magazine that dared to come into the 'spotlight', to articulate the reasoning that revealed main aspects of women's issues, such as education and their position in the society (and address women). Thus, it is considered a pioneering and bold venture. It was published in an era that Samartzidou considers favourable in the East because of the 'Enlightened' Sultan, who was in favour of all actions that improved the education of citizens of the Ottoman Empire.[7] However, given the social conditions of the 19th century, the majority of the Greek nation was, in fact, illiterate, and not only Greeks within the nation state, but also those in the East[8]. Desires to expand the Greek kingdom and the education of the male

---

[5] Martha Karpozilou, *The Greek Family-Literary Magazines (1847-1900)*. Ioannina: Scientific Annals of the Department of Education, University of Ioannina, 1991: 40-42.

[6] *Ibid.*, 30.

[7] Abdul Metzit (1839-1861), when he became Sultan, founded the reforms with the passage of the Tanzimat (1839) and Hatti Humayun (1856). It was important for unredeemed Greeks as they were then considered equal with the Muslims of the Ottoman Empire. In the year 1845, Resint Pasha prepared an educational reform plan for Ottoman Muslim citizens. George Castellan, *Histoire des Balkans*: 377-380; Basil Kremmidas, *Modern History Greek and European*: 199-200.

[8] Although the founding of primary schools was continuing, this did not necessarily mean anything. Until the Second World War, the percentage of the illiterate was higher among other industrial European countries. In 1840, this percentage was 87,5% for men, but is unknown for women. In 1870, the year *Eurydice* was published, the percentage of illiterate people was 71, 38% for men and 93,70 for women. The statistics are better for secondary level of education, but only for the men, because the percentage of women that go to secondary schools is about 3,5-6 % during the 19th century. See more Konstantinos Tsoukalas, *Dependance et reproduction. Le role social des appareils scolaires en Grece*. Athens: Themelio, 1975 and 1992: 392-403, 470-47; Helen Varika, *The revolt of the Ladies: The birth of a feministic*

population were the priorities of the newly-founded Greek State. On the other hand, formal education for females was considered by the Greek government, an 'unnecessary luxury'. For secondary education, there were only Private girls' schools.

Wealthy parents chose Private schools for their girls or preferred to tutor them at home. The Educational Company was the most important private organisation for secondary education. In 1861, the Greek government recognized the girls' school of the Educational Company as the only senior school to train teachers. The government and municipalities, not only from the Greek State but also from the enslaved Hellenism, sent female scholarship students to study there and to become teachers.[9]

Simultaneously, the educational system in the enslaved Hellenism was organized on a private, community and church basis.[10] The publication of *Eurydice* in 1870 coincided with an intense educational movement in the areas of enslaved Hellenism. *Eurydice* monitored and recorded the establishment of Girls' Schools across the areas that still lay within the borders of the Ottoman Empire through a wide network of correspondents,

---

*consciousness in Greece 1833-18370.* Athens: The Foundation of Research and Education of Emporiki Bank of Greece, 2004: 76-77.

[9] For secondary education, there were three private Girls' School in Athens, during the half past of 19th century: The Girls' School of Hill (1831), the Girls' School of Volmerange (1835-1852), the Girls' School of the Society for the Friends of Education "Arsakeion" (1837) and the Girls' School of M. Korck (1842-1859), Ziogou S. Karastergiou, *The Secondary Girl's Education in Greece 1830-1890.* Athens: IAEN. 1986: 110-124; Helen Koukou, "The Education from 1828 to 1831": 592.

[10] I will indicatively mention only the most famous Girls' Schools in Constantinople and Smyrna. In Constantinople: The "Byzantine" School Girl (1847). In 1850 was established the Girls' School of 'Peran', that in 1864 renamed as 'Central Girls' School of Stavrodromi' and became one of the most important among the others of this period: The Girls's School of Filomousos Company, 'Pallas', an ancient name of the goddess' Athena (1874) and the Girl School 'Zapeion' (1875). Kalliopi Kechagia, a teacher and a writer, was the directrice of it. In Smyrna: "Agia Fotini Central School" (1841). Sapfo Leontias was the directrice of it for two periods: 1863-1877 and 1886-1891. The other one was the "Greek Girl School" (1881): Ziogou S. Karastergiou, *The Secondary Girl's Education in Greece 1830-1890*: 250-252; Kyriaki Mamoni, *The life and the activity of the enslaved Greeks, History of Greek Nation.* Athens: Ekdotiki of Athens, 1975, vol.13: 376-377.

and the founders of the girls' schools were considered to be the benefactors of religion, the nation and the country.[11]

Thus, using the year 1845 as a starting point, my research focuses on the Greek literary magazines that address women of the 19th century. Fourteen magazines covering the second half of the 19th century, specifically from 1845 to 1899, were identified. Their content leads to two categories, as follows:

a) Magazines published by women, for women.
b) Magazines published by men and addressed to women.

This double discrimination will lead to further concrete considerations. Concerning the magazines published by women, we may ascertain that an initially small percentage of well-educated women from the middle or upper class, which widened progressively, skating over significant social and political barriers, promoted the women's movement, some with more progressive ideas and others more disguised. The women writers focused on revolutionary claims, that education ought to be a common good for both men and women, and that gender discrimination at the level of formal education must be lifted in order to upgrade women's education, promote social justice, equality in the family, a dynamic role and presence in the progress of the nation, recognition and reward in new roles, such as directorship of girls' schools.[12] The political issue of women's right to vote in parliamentary elections had not yet been asserted because it was judged to be too advanced for 19th-century society, even by the journal *Magazine of*

---

[11] Konstantinos Tsoukalas, "The secondary education", "Some conclusions", "The education among the Greeks living abroad" in Konstantinos Tsoukalas, *Dependance et reproduction*: 397-403, 423-429 & 449-48. From the journal *Eurydice* I indicatively mention: *Eurydice*, (21)1871: 14-15, (26) 1871: 55, (6) 1872: 103. For the general private initiative of the Benefactors in Greece, during the 19th century, see more: Konstantinos Tsoukalas, *Dependance et reproduction* : 483-495; K. Xanthopoulos, *A Concise of the intellectual development of Modern Greek*. Constantinople: Voutiras, 1880: 42-47.

[12] For K. Parren, literature is the best way to persuade Greek society that the 'new' women are morally and spiritually equal to men and worthy of freedom. Helen Varika, *The revolt of the Ladies: The birth of a feministic consciousness in Greece 1833-18370:* 281; Demeter Stamiou, "The Feminist Movement in Greece (1860-1890)" in E. Leontidou and Sigrid R. Ammer (eds). *The Greece of Women.* Athens: Enallaktikes Ekdoseis/ Gaia. 1992: 57-59 and Efrosyni Samartzidou, "Editorial notes" in *Kypseli*, Konstantinople (1)1845: 12-13.

*Ladies* (1887-1917), published by Kalliroe Parren seventeen years after the publication of *Eurydice.*[13]

In the second category, we find magazines published by men for women. Their style is not feministic, nor is their tone disconcerting, as far as women's demands and female achievements are concerned. The few voices supporting the rights of women and equal access to education, or pose the issue of the political role of women, are 'notable' exceptions, which not influence the conservative framework of 19th century ideas.[14]

These magazines mainly address the middle-class daughter or woman, who could include light literary information, for pleasure, among their topics of interest, on the topic of knitting, needlecraft, fashion and beauty, savoir-vivre. The model of the woman cultivated by these magazines is, without doubt, a woman outside the sphere of political and social activity, in accordance with the stereotypical image of the woman accepted by wider society at the time. This image is certainly far from that of the woman who attempts to form a new identity for herself, as a responsible, forthright and collaborative entity.

By contrast, the magazines published by women invite their readers to leave the introversion imposed by 'the confinement' and 'safety' of the private sphere of the home, and to 'come out', with the help of the Press, in support of the women's cause as a collective female identity, in various ways.[15] Moreover, they highlight the intense demand for women to take part

---

[13] Demeter Stamiou, "The Political Rights of Women (1864-1952)" in *Mnimon.* (12) 1989: 161-172.

[14] P.D. Iliopoulos, "Conversations" in *Artemis*, Athens: (1)1866: 4-8. See Demeter Tzanaki, *Slave and Lady. Aspects of Nationalism: roles and behaviours in Greece of the Romantics Years 1836-1897.* Athens: Savalas, 2007: 123-131. In his article from the newspaper *Neologos*, and addressed to the writer and teacher in Constantinople, Alexandra Papadopoulou, Stavros Voutiras, outlined the views of the majority of Greek society in the 19th century: return to your housework, because women were born for the home and man for science and society. To J .Papakostas, Alexandra Papadopoulou: the first Greek novelist, newspaper *To Vima*, 2 of March 2006 .

[15] "So, because of these favourable conditions, the lovely and fair sex should follow us", Efrosini Samartzidou "The East" in *Kypseli*, (2)1845: 51. An anonymous collaborator wrote to *Eurydice*: "The women in Europe are working for the intellectual emancipation by establishing associations or editing newspapers and magazines. Thus, this is what *Eurydice* is trying to achieve, to take a step further. The Greeks "writers" ought to contribute too", K, "The women writer", *Eurydice*, (2) 1871: 30-31. See Helen Varika, *The revolt of the Ladies: The birth of a feministic consciousness in Greece 1833-1870*: 280-282 .

in what appears to be a social and national mission: "the enlightenment of womanhood", is, for *Kypseli*; to be an intellectual, dealing with the rights, duties, mission and women's relations in family, society and nation, for *Thalia*; "the development, the progress, the spiritual and intellectual rebirth of our sisters in the East", for *Eurydice.*[16] Thus the editors, not only, saw the work of journalism with great respect: "to the sacred struggle of journalism"; "journalism is the noblest and, also the hardest work"[17] and, as depicted in the foreword, the editor of *Eurydice* will try to stand up to "the laborious and high work of journalism", but also considered their mission sacred: "thanks to the sacred purpose, of this beneficial idea for the nation".[18]

On the basis of the image promoted by female literary magazines, we come to the realisation that they propose a special relationship between women and the nation: to take action, instead of submitting; to distinguish themselves through education, instead of accepting rigid racial differences; and to establish a clear goal with regards to the services they offer to the nation, with a rounded personality. We will follow up this relationship on three levels: language, upbringing, and education.

Katharevousa was the name given to the official language of the free Greek State. Katharevousa, being the continuation of the ancient Greek language and, also, the chosen language of literature, was established for national reasons, as the only viable option in the minds of educated citizens. This is especially the case for those in the circle of Fanariotes, surrounding the Patriarchy, residents of the 'Fanari' area.[19] They sought to enhance national pride, historic continuation, and strengthen national identity and unity. It was for this reason that not much attention was paid to the variety of local dialects, a fact that was ridiculed by column writers and literary writers of the time. However, the spiritual life of the Heptanes (The Ionian islands) was overlooked. The language of the School of the Heptanes was a demotic (folk) language, mainly represented by the later-to-become national poet of Greece, Dionysius Solomos, a glorious follower of the Cretan Renaissance

---

[16] Efrosini Samartzidou, "Dedication to Her Majesty the Queen Mother of the Sultan" in *Kypseli*, (1)1845: 6, Penelope Lazaridou, "Program"in *Thalia*, (1)1867: 1, Emilia Ktena – Leontiadou, [without title], *Eurydice*, (1)1870: 1-2.

[17] Efrosini Samartzidou, "Editorial notes"in *Kypseli*, (1) 1845: 16.

[18] Emilia Ktena – Leontiadou, [without title] in *Eurydice*, (1)1870: 2.

[19] Roderic Beaton, *An introduction to Modern Greek Literature*. Oxford: Clarendon Press, 1994(Athens: Nefeli. 1996): 51-53; Mario Vitti, *Storia della litteratura neogreca*. Athens: Odisseas. 1978: 116-119.

(1560-1669) and of Vitsentzos Kornaros's "Erotokritos".[20] This choice, as one among many instruments of language for the nation, caused a rift in the spiritual world on many occasions. The opinions expressed, the texts written, the struggles that took place, are all part of the so-called "language issue".[21]

Katharevousa was consequently the language of the intellectual elite, of those representing the Romantic era and of poetic competitions.[22] It was the language taught in schools and used in school manuals. The choice of this language by female publishers also served the same aforementioned national demands and simultaneously reflected their education and the spiritual environment of their upbringing, as well as their social roots.

The use of katharevousa (morphology and vocabulary) varies significantly among the articles of the three magazines being considered: the language is rich in *Kypseli,* in terms of the use of words, and enriched by the personal style and education of Efrosini Samartzidou. There is an ancient–inspired language, a kind of katharevousa, similar to Ancient Greek in terms of its morphology and words, and used by Penelope Lazaridou in *Thalia.* There is also the language used by Emilia Ktena – Leontiadi, publisher of *Eurydice*, which is a simple katharevousa, moving towards an ancient language. It is used by her and her colleagues, allowing some space for demotic language in a few children's poems by the educator, Sapfo Leontias, who was a sister and colleague of the publisher.

Penelope Lazaridou strengthens the yearning for the nation in one of her texts entitled "proper expression and judgement on talking" in the 4th issue of *Thalia*, which emphasises the need for women to learn "our lovely native language".[23] This aims to encourage Greek women to employ the correct use

---

[20] Linos Politis, *History of Modern Literature.* Athens: Cultural Foundation of National Bank, 1980: 138-151 and 152-167; K. Dimaras, *History of Modern Greek Literature.* Athens: Ikaros, 1975: 227-243.

[21] Linos Politis, *History of Modern Literature.* Athens: Cultural Foundation of National Bank, 1980: 11-15, an introduction of all the history of the language's issue. For more information see the chapters in the same book entitled: "The end of the Age of Enlightenment and the language issue" and "The language issue and Psicharis", 94-100 and 208-214. See Roderic Beaton, *An introduction to Modern Greek Literature.* Oxford: Clarendon Press, 1994: 369- 427 (Athens: Nefeli. 1996), where the writer examines thoroughly the language issue.

[22] Linos Politis, *History of Modern Literature.* Athens: Cultural Foundation of National Bank, 1980: 168-179; K. Dimaras, *History of Modern Greek Literature.* Athens: Ikaros, 1975: 338-341.

[23] P. Lazaridou, "About women's propriety: a. proper expression and judgment on talking" in *Thalia*, (4)1867: 59-61.

of katharevousa, attesting to their good education and fine upbringing, as opposed to the use of "barbaric and vulgar words of [the] demotic (folk) language", which she entirely rejects.[24] An equally ardent supporter of hers is Sapfo Leontias, who during a speech as director of the female school Saint Fotini in Smyrna, suggested that the language spoken by people at home was wrong and corruptible. Thus, she proposes educational reforms, arguing that language (katharevousa) should be taught 1-2 hours daily in schools.

The publishers, self-evidently interested in language, aspired to its cultivation through education, but did not highlight it independently thereafter, instead discussing it in combination with the other two issues mentioned earlier (upbringing and education). They considered it to contribute equally to the strengthening of the national identity, as long as Greek daughters, "as prudent breeders of the future generation, and bearing in mind their Greek identity (…), embellished respectfully with morality and Greek beliefs," were also brought up well.[25]

Thus, in adopting the basic mode of thought, also shared with men, that mothers with a strong sense of morality and a good upbringing bred good citizens, they adopted the logic established as a national claim: "Who can ennoble the family better and through this ennoblement also the nation? The woman?"[26] However, they did not restrict themselves to this opinion, but also covered it with an idealistic content: "women hereafter should decorate society by being prudent, loyal and caring wives, and decent mothers".[27]

Synergy between the spiritual forces of men and women was necessary to achieve this goal. Thus, the way was cleared to broaden and upgrade the quality of education offered; it was unthinkable that upbringing could be improved without the help of education. Sapfo Leontias, the director and educator of the girls' school, Parthenagogio Saint Fotini in Smyrna, strongly supported the idea that education should always and at all costs promote and strengthen good upbringing. Supporting the same view, an anonymous correspondent from Heraklion of Crete (perhaps a teacher or director of girls' school there), wrote to *Eurydice* that they greatly emphasise the courses schedule and the choice of teachers, determined to "give our daughters the

[24] *Ibid.*, 60.
[25] Anonymously, "Examinations in Smyrna" in *Eurydice*, (12) 1872: 187-190.
[26] *Thalia*, (1) 1867: 5.
[27] *Kypseli*, (6) 1845: 182.

necessary upbringing and education and to make our Girls' School capable of playing this role as far as possible".[28]

As a result, young age is a crucial point of reference and thus, through a 'correct' and healthy upbringing, emphasises the whole philosophy that aims to form a girl's character. In most articles of the three journals, Kypseli, Thalia and Eurydice, especially with the pedagogic content that is published in these periodicals, the view that it would be ideal if girls could arm themselves with moral values that would prevent them from imitating foreign patterns, fashion and clothing, is strongly supported.[29]

The tendency towards learning foreign languages, taking care of themselves and having an interest in luxury, is considered 'ill thought', and an obstacle to the efforts invested in securing their pure and solid Greek character.[30] The woman should stay focused on reality, not tending towards day-dreaming, through the reading of foreign novels. The latter (among them those of Alexander Dumas and Paul Feval) are considered unsuitable readings.[31] In order to replace them, Greek original novels with moral and educational content are introduced, like *Fiakas*, a Greek theatrical comedy with a didactic moral tone written by Misitzi, and published in five continuations in *Eurydice.*[32] Introducing the publication of the later comedy in her periodical, Amilia Ktena Leontias wrote that parody the charlatanism and propensity of many young people to cheat the young girls. This also lampooned the anti-Greek and foreign upbringing that some families chose for their daughters, which the editor considers shameful, and harmful to the Greeks. In the last scene of the second part, Evanthia, the person about to be married, Fiaka, exclaims in delight when she unmasks the charlatanism of Fiaka. She believes that her imagination has been carried away by reading foreign novels, and points out the negative consequences of a frivolous and imperfect upbringing. And the moral of this comedy: Evanthia hopes her

---

[28] Anonymously, "Private correspondent" in *Eurydice*, (35) 1871: 125.
[29] I identically mention: "Education and upbringing" in *Kypseli*, (4) 1845: 103-105. Anonymously, "Private correspondent" in *Eurydice*, (39) 1871: 160. Sapfo Leontias, Opinions on women's education, in *Eurydice*, (8) 1872: 133.
[30] P. Lazaridou in *Thalia*, (2) 1867: 29. Z. Ypandreumenos, "Zinovia" in *Eurydice*, (5) 1870: 56-58. Sapfo Leontias, "On Women's Call" in *Eurydice*, (5)1870 : 49-52.
[31] I indicatively cite Anonymously, "The consequences of luxury" in *Eurydice*, (32) 1871 : 102 ; Aristaia L.B., "Eurydice and women" in *Eurydice*, (9) 1871: 100-101 ; D. K. Misitzis, "Fiakas" in *Eurydice* (11)1872): 172-175.
[32] D. K. Simitzis, "Fiakas". Issues of *Eurydice*: 6, 7, 8, 9-10 & 11, 1872 : 100-103, 116-117, 128-133, 153-156 and 172- 175.

misfortune will be a lesson to young Greek women and encourage them to engage with 'healthy' and ethical literature. Thus, it was expected, that correct and pious thinking would be interwoven with 'living with morality and virtue'. Only then could young ladies, worthy of the hopes of their home country, aspire to a bright future, as a 'correct' upbringing would equip them with "a fortune brighter than all the diamonds of the world".[33]

This idealistic approach, expressed in the words of Efrosini Samartzidou, bridged class differences and strengthened incentives for education, but it was not able, at the same time, to conceal the problems of education, and the gap between the official educational policy of the Greek kingdom and the private initiative. However, neither magazine, *Kypseli* and *Thalia*, touch such topics directly, instead approaching educational issues either philosophically or realistically. Philosophically, under the creative influence of the ideas of the Enlightenment, such as those of Efrosini Samartzidou in *Kypseli*, which demonstrate the meaning of education as being of the highest value: "The enlightened cities of London, German, Paris show to the whole land that the inevitable way for global happiness is the way of Education",[34] and with more emphasis on the text entitled "The East": "What are we really without enlightenment? What are we on earth without education? Do we live? (...) Do we have a sense of real happiness on earth? Certainly not!"[35] However, this is also realistic, with a strong critical spirit; E. Samartzidou and P. Lazaridou see women's education in its true colours. The most critical position to the whole content of *Kypseli* is expressed by E. Samartzidou in the editorial notes:

> The male gender believed that being a woman was by nature inferior to man, thus she could live only under his dominance, as an insignificant being in the human population. Because of this opinion they deprived her of the right to equality, they deprived her of all social rights, but the worst of all, they deprived her of Education, with its moral up-bringing![36]

---

[33] E. Samartzidou, "Virtue saves societies" in *Kypseli*, (4) 1845: 126.

[34] E. Samartzidou, "Editorial notes" in *Kypseli*, (1)1845 : 10-11

[35] E. Samrtzidou, "The East" in *Kypseli*, (2)1845 : 50.

[36] E. Samartzidou, "Editorial notes": 13. Penelope Lazaridou has also written about the prejudices of women's education: "Many people have always supported and continue, unfortunately to date, to support the disastrous idea that female gender is superfluous great education", P. Lazaridou, "About the necessity of the great up-bringing and education of the female gender" in *Thalia*, (1)1867 : 5.

In the 25 years between the publication of *Kypseli* (1845) and *Eurydice* (1870-1873), many things were reformed and the picture, as described up to now, changed. The presence of the magazine, and the opportunities it offered as a forum for anyone to publish his or her opinions, was utilized by a significant number of women writers. The column of the journal entitled "Reports of Eurydice" or "Correspondence of Eurydice", which began in the first issue, built up a wide network of correspondents, demonstrating the support for Hellenism beyond the borders of the Turkish and Greek state.[37] Thus, this network connecting the journal and the town of Constantinople with the outside world, was 'the eyes and the ears' of the journal.

The establishment of female schools (always sponsored by private initiative and philanthropic organisations or benefactors), the speeches during their opening ceremonies or at the end of the school year, and public lectures about female education and upbringing presented in literary clubs, invite female readers to send in their reports, mainly anonymously (using their initial monograms or just their first-names).[38] The female writers take this opportunity to state their personal points of view. It is considered "unfair and un-Hellenic to keep woman uneducated or to educate her in a faulty semi-literate environment."[39]

Concern about the nation overrides everything the female writers openly show in relation to it, and is presented clearly and courageously. This is

---

[37] The correspondents sent their reports from various places: areas of the East (Smyrna, 40 Churches, Kydonies) or from the many suburbs of Constantinople (such as Peran, Diplokionion, Xaskioi), areas of the Greek independent state (Athens), from the unredeemed Greeks (Jeanine, Crete, Xanthi), areas from other places in the Balkans (Filippoupoli, Braila) and beyond the borders of the Greek state (Trieste, Boston, Florence).

[38] Many correspondents sent their reports to *Eurydice* anonymously or using their initial monograms or pseudonyms: L, *Eurydice*, (8) 1871: 88, K..., *Eurydice* , (2) 1872: 31 and 38, Helen, *Eurydice*, (6) 1872: 92, Zoi, *Eurydice*, (35)1871: 115, Penelope, *Eurydice*, (7) 1872: 120. Vosporis was one of the seven pseudonyms that the writer Alexandra Papadopoulou used, to avoid all those who wanted to criticize her articles in newspapers and magazines : see K. Papakostas, "Alexandra Papadopoulou". Kalliroi Parren used the pseudonym Eva Prenar, not only at first but as editor of her journal, the *Ladies' Journal* (1887-1917) and used the pseudonym Maia for publishing her first novel "The Emancipated", while continuing to issue her own journal: see Angelika Psarra, *The Emancipated.* Athens: Ekati, 1999: 428-431. On this subject, see also Irini Rizaki, *The Greek female "writers"(Notes for the women's intelligentsia of the 19th century.* Katarti: Katarti, 2007: 143-165; Virginia Woolf, *A Room of One's Own.* Athens, Odisseas, 2005: 74-77.

[39] *Ibid.*

partly due to the fact that the editing of *Eurydice* came after the Cretan revolution (1866-1869) and its unfavorable outcome for the Hellenic nation, which meant the continuation of Turkish rule. In the meantime, the Bulgarian Church was becoming independent from the Patriarchy, the Greek Orthodox Church in Constantinople, and founded the Bulgarian Exarxato.[40] The rise of Bulgarian nationalism caused great concern among Greeks, especially in the areas of enslaved Hellenism. This entire situation had an impact on educational policy, but particularly in the curricula of girls' schools, where, as always, the idea of the Nation and Orthodoxy came first.The Bulgarians were now the new enemy, not overtly named, but implied. It aimed to raise the Greek spirit, and the continuous reference to the nation aspires to support Greek learning and education in order to save "the nice and valuable character of women".[41] Education is further reinforced by the constitution of female literary clubs, acting on several fronts in favour of the nation "we cordially hope to announce the constitution of clubs which can help with new forces and courage Hellenism".[42]

This curriculum is to be found in Ancient Greek literature, as well as in orthodox religious documents. The education provided in female schools is religious and national, as is stated "in our times and in our Greek orthodox nation".[43] Ancient writings are considered to be the only appropriate and beneficial option, for ethnic reasons. Thus, ancestor worship, as an influence on school curricula, and as a basis of ideology in Greek scholarship, is hidden, as "only useful for the salvation and the prosperity of our nation", or more characteristically, "without being afraid of being accused of ethnic pride, if the human mind does not study Greek literature, mainly the masterpieces of Homer, Plato, Sophocles, Euripides, it cannot be developed".[44]

---

[40] For more information see D. Dakin, "The second liberation struggle: The first phase of the Cretan Revolution 1866-1869" and "The beginning of the Bulgarian issue" in Douglas Dakin, *The Unification of Greece*: 168-184 and 188-190. See also G. Kastellan, "The Bulgarian issue 1840-1876" in George Castellan, *The Histoire des Balkans* : 432-439.

[41] Anonymously, "Clerical voice in favour of Greek women" in *Eurydice*, 9.(10) 1872: 148.

[42] Aimilia Ktena-Leontidou: as editor, a comment on the clerical voice, in *Eurydice*, 9-(10) 1872: 147.

[43] Anonymously, "Exams in Smyrna" in *Eurydice*, (12) 1872: 189.

[44] Anonymously, "Private Correspondence of Eurydice" in *Eurydice*, (35) 1871: 125.

While we realize that the ratio of female gender to the nation was redefined relatively easily through education, the basic notion about the woman and her role in society remained unchanged. The triptych wife-mother-housewife was common, and showed the utilitarian value of education, as well as the goal of women's upbringing, as we have already demonstrated. No one claims that education is a unique necessity for women, but it always depends on her role in the family.

The idea of morality formed the appropriate sophism, for obedience and the acceptance of gender roles to appear as natural. As a result, moral formation of the man was to do with his character, whereas for the woman it was to do with her destiny, which was the family: "but what education? The one equivalent to her destiny and to the role she is destined to play (…) She must be educated for moral reasons".[45] This fact defined the character of the magazines, especially *Eurydice*, because it hosted collaborators that demonstrated significant ideological variation – and opinions ranking from progressive to rather conservative – on the female issue. However, women's education was generally upgraded, and hopes were born for a promising continuation.

In closing, we could say that women's incorporation into the nation curbed the expression of a more dynamic and independent attitude towards womens' issue and formed a common female identity through the national identity. Consequently, apart from any contradictions raised and discernable in the material and character of the magazines, female speech was not only critical in the face of gender discrimination and female inferiority, but was also asserted. They asserted a right to the authority of the intelligentsia, to participation in public life, to activity in the public sphere. The texts were also against the men in charge of female schools and, again, asserted this position in strong tones. In an anonymous article, entitled 'Our Girls School', a female writer describes how the girls' school of Constantinople was reduced to a terrible position, estimating that among the various causes the most serious was the bad management of men. It expressed the view that in order for the work of the Education Committee established in Patriarchy to be effective, in addition to the former, another Commission ought to be appointed, by educated and experienced Greek women, as they know better than men what their sex needs. To finish, the hope that all those who have set themselves the task of overseeing the Girls' School, "our national

[45] Anonymously, "The Girls' School in Xalki" in *Eurydice*, (47)1871: 219.

establishment", will entrust it to adequate women furthering females' gender interests, is expressed.[46]

With the establishment of "*The Ladies' Journals*" (1887-1917), seventeen years after the publication of *Eurydice*, a new era was dawning for those wanting to assert the above-mentioned demands. The long life of the journal and the fighting editorial line contributed to the formation of a more autonomous female identity and to the birth of the feminist movement in Greece.

---

[46] Anonymously, "Our Girls School" in *Eurydice*, (2)1873: 24-25.

# APPENDIX 1.

***MAGAZINES* PUBLISHED BY WOMEN**

| /A | TITLE | SUBTITLE | PLACE-PUB. YEAR | DIRECT.-PUBLISHER |
|---|---|---|---|---|
| 1. | *Kypseli* | Writing Female Magazine | Istanbul, 1845 | Efrosini Samartzidou |
| 2. | *Thalia* | Writing Magazine of womanhood every month with special section | Athens, 1867 | Penelope Lazaridou |
| 3. | *Eurydice* | Women's Weekly Review post patterns | Istanbul, 1870-1873 | Emilia Ktena-Leontias |
| 4. | *Ladies' Journal* | | Athens, 1887 – 1917 | Kalliroe Parren |
| 5. | *Family newspaper* | Section of Ladies Newsp. | Athens, 1893 | Kal. Parren-Siganou |
| 6. | *Family* | Weekly Female Magazine (B' period) | Athens, 1897 | Ann Serouiou |
| 7. | *Pleias* | Magazine of The Ladies Ergani-Athena | Athens, 1899- 1902 | Association of Ladies Ergani-Athena |

*MAGAZINES* PUBLISHED BY MEN

| /A | TITLE | SUBTITLE | PLACE-PUB. YEAR | DIRECT.-PUBLISHER |
|---|---|---|---|---|
| 1. | *Artemis* | | Athens, 1866 | P.D.Iliopoulos |
| 2. | *New Penelope* | - | Athens, 1888 | Th.F.Ksenakis |
| 3. | *Guide for handiwork* | - | Athens, 1892 | Fragoulis-Dimitriadis |
| 4. | *Handiworks* | - | Athens, 1892 | Sotiris Christidis |
| 5. | *Handiworks Magazine* | | Athens, 1893-1895 | I. Kalfoglou |
| 6. | Athena | Family Magazine for all Greeks | Athens, 1893-1895 | Sotiris Christidis |
| 7. | *The Family* | Magazine Leaf Published for Families | Athens, 1893 | PChrisanthakopoulos |
| 8. | *Refined Penelope* | Magazine of Handiwork And Fashion for all Greeks | Athens, 1897-1920 | Al. Alexiadis |

## Select Bibliography


### A. Primary Sources

*Artemis.* 1866. Athens.
*Eurydice.* 1870-1873. Konstantinople.
*Kypseli.* 1845. Konstantinople.
*Magazine of Ladies.* 1887-1917. Athens.
*Family.* 1897-1898. Athens.
*Thalia.* 1867. Athens.

### B. Secondary Sources

Beaton, Roderic. 1994. *An introduction to Modern Greek Literature.* Oxford: Clarendon Press. (Athens: Nefeli. 1996)

Castellan, George. *Histoire des Balkans, Paris, Libraire Artheme Fayard, 1991* Athens: Govosti. Chapter 12.

Dakin, Douglas. 1982. *The Unification of Greece 1770-1923, London, Ernest Benn Limited 1972.* Athens: Cultural Foundation of National Bank.

Dimaras, Alexis. 1988. *The Educational Reform has not been, Athens: Hermes.* (1): 1821-1894.

Dimaras K., 1975. *History of Modern Greek Literature.* Athens: Ikaros.

*Encyclopedia of the Greek Press 1784-1974.* 2008. Athens: Modern Greek Research Intitute – National Research Foundation. (1).

Glogg, Richard. 1993. *A Short History of Modern Greece.* Cambridge University Press 1979. (In Greek), Athens: Kardamitsa.

—. 1992. "The formation of Greek Nation, the Big Idea and the National Division" in *A Concise History of Greece.* Cambridge: Cambridge University Press. (Athens 1995). 1831-1922.

Karastergiou, Ziogou S. 1986. *The Secondary Girl's Education in Greece 1830-1890.* Athens: IAEN.

Karpozilou, Martha. 1991. *The Greek Family-Literary Magazines (1847-1900).* Ioannina: Scientific Annals of the Department of Education, University of Ioannina.

Koukou, Helen. 1975. "The Education from 1828 to 1831" in *History of Greek Nation.* Athens: Ekdotiki. Vol.12.

Kremmidas, Basil. 1984. *Modern History Greek and European.* Athens: Gnosi. Chapters 8, 9.

Mamoni, Kyriaki. 1975. *The life and the activity of the enslaved Greeks, History of Greek Nation.* Athens: Ekdotiki of Athens. vol.13.

Papageorgiou, P. Stefan. 1998. *The Greek State (1821-1909).* Athens: Papazisis.

Papakostas J. 2006. "Alexandra Papadopoulo: the first Greek novelist", in *To Vima*, (2 of March 2006), A 58/ Nees Epoches.

Petridis, Paul. 1986. *Greek Politics and Social History 1821-1940.* Thessaloniki: Paratiritis.

Politis, Linos. 1980. *History of Modern Literature.* Athens: Cultural Foundation of National Bank.

Psarra, Angelika. 1999. *The Emancipated.* Athens: Ekati.

Rizaki, Irini. 2007. *The Greek female "writers"(Notes for the women's intelligentsia of the 19th century.* Katarti: Katarti.

Stamiou, Demeter. 1992. "The Feminist Movement in Greece (1860-1890)" in *The Greece of Women.* E. Leontidou and Sigrid R. Ammer (eds). Athens: Enallaktikes Ekdoseis/ Gaia: 57- 63.

—. 1989. "The Political Rights of Women (1864-1952)", in *Mnimon.* (12): 161-172.

Svoronos, Nikos. 1972. *Histoire de la Grece Moderne.* Paris: P. U. F. (Athens 1985, with a rich bibliography guide written by Spiros Asdrachas) .

Tsoukalas, Konstantinos. 1992. *Dependance et reproduction. Le role social des appareils scolaires en Grece.* (Paris, 1975) Athens: Themelio.

Tzanaki, Demeter. 2007. *Slave and Lady. Aspects of Nationalism: roles and behaviours in Greece of the Romantics Years 1836-1897.* Athens: Savalas.

Varika, Helen. 2004. *The revolt of the Ladies: The birth of a feministic consciousness in Greece 1833-18370.* Athens: The Foundation of Research and Education of Emporiki Bank of Greece.

Vitti, Mario. 1978. *Storia della litteratura neogreca.* (Torino 1971) Athens: Odisseas.

Woolf, Virginia. 2005. *A Room of One's Own.* Athens, Odisseas.

Xanthopoulos, K. 1880. *A Concise of the intellectual development of Modern Greek.* Constantinople: Voutiras.

# Connecting People, Inventing Communities in Faustina Sáez de Melgar's Magazine *La Violeta* (Madrid, 1862-1866)

*Henriette Partzsch*

Abstract Faustina Sáez de Melgar was one of the leading women writers in the Spain of Queen Isabel II. Extremely well-connected to the neo-Catholic establishment of her day, she worked on consolidating her position by venturing into an ambitious enterprise, the publication of La Violeta. By exploring the different (and sometimes dissonant) voices brought together in La Violeta and its commitment to abolitionism, this chapter discusses how the enterprise confronted the delicate task of moving between international and nationalistic allegiances, as well as domestic ideologies, in the highly volatile period leading up to the revolution of 1868. It will show that in the process, it created a network with local, national and international dimensions and a dynamics of its own, which did not only regularly clash with the very tangible limitations of the existing national infrastructure but also, in the end, with the gendered and class limitations to political commitment outside the pages of a magazine.

In his seminal book, *Imagined Communities,* Benedict Anderson famously highlights the importance of the press in the process of nation-building: by creating 'imagined linkage' among its consumers, the press significantly contributed to "that remarkable confidence of community in anonymity which is the hallmark of modern nations".[1] While each individual reader peruses the current edition of a newspaper on his own, he is nevertheless aware that he participates in a daily ritual shared by thousands or even millions of other readers. Although Anderson does not discuss the gendering effects of this process, his evocation of a male newspaper reader to illustrate his argument goes beyond an unreflected use of the pronoun 'he' for the purpose of generalisation; it can be understood as a trace of the power relations that shaped European societies in the very period which also saw the

[1] Benedict Anderson, *Imagined Communities: Reflections on the Origins and Spread of Nationalism.* London, New York: Verso, 2006 [1983]: 36.

rise of the periodical press. The image of the male reader therefore reminds us of the need to analyse how access to cultural institutions is regulated and how privileging, tolerating, ignoring or excluding certain groups can shape a community and its self-awareness. In the specific context of the press we therefore have to ask the following, very basic questions: "[G]iven the emphasis on print technology and literacy as essential for nation-building and the diffusion of national myths, how were print media disseminated and consumed; to whom and by whom were they disseminated?"[2] As a matter of course there can be no universally valid answer; rather, this approach requires the carefully contextualised study of specific periods, cultures and cases, which will provide in turn material for broader comparisons. In the present article I will focus on the ways in which women in mid nineteenth-century Spain engaged with the press, and in particular how the literary circle around Faustina Sáez de Melgar[3] (1834-1895) used the publication *La Violeta* [The Violet] to create their own community.

## Women and the press in mid 19th-century Spain

The national daily newspapers are at the centre of Anderson's argument about the creation of imagined linkage at a national level; however, extremely few women contributed to these big enterprises in mid nineteenth-century Spain, and when they did, their work usually did not appear in the section with political news and opinions. Although I cannot provide a systematic overview of women's participation in the Spanish press during the 1850s and 1860s, it seems that in addition to publishing individual poems,[4] women wrote in daily newspapers mostly as translators, sometimes authors, of serialised novels. An outstanding example is Joaquina García Balmaseda[5] (1837-1883), who was responsible for the *roman feuilleton* in the newspaper

---

[2] Linda Racioppi and Katherine O'Sullivan See, "Engendering Nation and National Identity." in Sita Ranchod-Nilsson and Mary Ann Tétreault (eds). *Women, States, and Nationalism: At Home in the Nation?*, London, New York: Routledge. 2000: 29.

[3] See online at http://neww.huygens.knaw.nl/authors/show/3423

[4] Lisa Surwillo, "Poetic Diplomacy: Carolina Coronado and the American Civil War." in *Comparative American Studies* 5(4): 2007 : 409-422, has shown how the well established poet Carolina Coronado attempted to influcence Spanish public opinion regarding the Civil War in the US by a sophisticated use of this possibility.

[5] See online at http://neww.huygens.knaw.nl/authors/show/3412

*La Correspondencia* between 1864 and 1883.[6] This limitation reinforces the strong association of the (serialised) novel with women.[7] Women are thus relegated to the the margins of the newspaper-reading community, both in terms of production and consumption; the space assigned to them, the serialised novel, is separated by a black line from the actual news, a symbolic barrier which cordons off the body politic.

This situation did not prevent women from working for the periodical press, but they did so rather in the context of the more cultural, *i.e.* not directly political publications. Appearing less often than the newspapers, these magazines contained miscellaneous texts aimed at providing entertainment and instruction. Some of them, such as the illustrated *Museo de las familias* (1843-1870), were extremely well received and survived for a long time in the volatile Spanish print market. *Museo de las familias* could count on contributions by three firmly established women writers from the romantic generation, Carolina Coronado (1821-1911), Gertrudis Gómez de Avellaneda (1814-1873) and Fernán Caballero (1796-1877).[8]

The main space of activity, though, were educational and women"s magazines, which were written increasingly not only for but also by women.[9]

---

[6] María del Carmen Simón Palmer, *Revistas femininas madrileñas*. Madrid: Artes Gráficas Municipales – Área de Régimen Interior y Personal. [Ciclo de Conferencias: El Madrid de Isabel II; 8], 1991: 284.

[7] María Cruz Seoane and María Dolores Saiz, *Cuatro siglos de periodismo en España. De los avisos a los periódicos digitales*. Madrid: Alianza, 2007: 113, point out that information about serialised novels were usually addressed to "las lectoras", i.e., explicitely to the female readers. Given that serialised novels were usually printed at the bottom of the first page, I wonder how many women used the opportunity and read the main poltical news as well – unless it was cut out.

[8] Hemeroteca Digital de la Biblioteca Nacional de España, *Museo de las familias*, permanent URL http://hemerotecadigital.bne.es/datos1/numeros/internet/Madrid/ Museo de las familias/1843/184301/18430125/18430125_00000.pdf (accessed 2 March 2012). See online http://neww.huygens.knaw.nl/authors/show/3277; http://neww.huygens.knaw.nl/authors/show/126; and http://neww.huygens.knaw.nl/ authors/show/1277. The three writers also published in *Semanario Pintoresco Español*, among other publications. See María del Carmen Simón Palmer, *Escritoras españolas del siglo XIX: Manual bio-bibliográfico*. Madrid: Castalia, 1991. On the romantic generation of women writers see Susan Kirkpatrick, *Las Románticas: Women Writers and Subjectivity in Spain, 1825-1850*. Berkeley, Los Angeles, London: University of California Press, 1989.

[9] For information about women's press in Spain see María del Carmen Simón Palmer, *Revistas femininas madrileñas*; Inmaculada Jiménez Morell, *La prensa femenina en España (desde sus orígenes a 1868)*. Madrid: Ediciones de la Torre, 1992 ; Mercedes

Due to a rate of female illiteracy which in 1860 amounted to more than 80%, low wages for working women, the cost of living and the prices of subscription, they mainly catered for a small readership of affluent higher and middle-class women.[10] In comparison to the daily newspapers, women's press was therefore clearly a niche market. If we follow Anderson's argument about the role of the press in nation-building, it becomes clear that women (especially poorer and working women) were at the time only marginally involved in this specific mechanism of creating imagined linkage at a national scale. However, some women nevertheless used periodical publications to connect people and invent communities – partly overlapping, partly colliding with hegemonic discourse formations about the Spanish nation and women.

## Faustina Sáez de Melgar's magazine *La Violeta*

One example of this kind of initiative is the weekly cultural magazine *La Violeta* [The Violet]. It appeared between the end of 1862 and the end of 1866, towards the turbulent last years of Queen Isabel's II reign, and was mostly (but not exclusively, as we will see) addressing a female readership. It belonged to the range of publications in which women played an important role in the production process, holding its ground in a difficult market where many women's magazines did not survive beyond their first year.[11] *La Violeta* therefore seems particularly suited to our current purpose: it was not too short-lived to create a complex network with local, national and international dimensions, while the total number of 209 published issues still allows to achieve a good overview of the magazine in its entirety. Furthermore, it can be argued that the trajectory of the magazine showcases the tensions and anxieties called forth by the changes to women's roles in Spanish society. *La Violeta* enjoyed the official endorsement by the highest

---

Roig Castellanos, *La mujer y la prensa: Desde el siglo XVII a nuestros días*. Madrid: self-published, 1977; and Isabel Segura and Marta Selva, *Revistes de dones (1846-1935)*. Barcelona: Edhasa, 1984.

[10] Inmaculada Jiménez Morell, *La prensa femenina en España (desde sus orígenes a 1868)*: 21.

[11] One of the most remarkable exceptions was *El correo de la moda* (1851-1893). Incidentally, when *La Violeta* ceased publication at the beginning of 1867, the remaining subscriptions were transferred to *El correo de la moda* (*Diario oficial de avisos de Madrid*, 11 January 1867).

authorities of the state; from 1865 onwords, it could even proudly display on the title page the information that the publication had been declared by royal decree textbook for Girls' Schools and the formation of female primary teachers.[12] Nevertheless, the dynamics developed in the magazine through the interaction with its readers and the broader public sphere finally clashed with the barriers which circumscribed the political commitment of middle-class women in mid 19$^{th}$-century Spain.

## Connecting people: The network

At the very heart of this publishing enterprise stood its director and proprietor Faustina Sáez de Melgar, who was, together with Pilar Sinués de Marco (1835-1893) and Ángela Grassi (1823-1883),[13] one of the most active and successful female participants in the publishing market of the time.[14] Her name and function appear in prominent place on the title page of *La Violeta*, backed by the royal arms and the dedication of the entire magazine to Queen Isabel of Spain. This presentation clearly assigns a central, authoritative role to this at the time well-known woman writer.[15] Interestingly, the other half of the story is hidden away in the small print at the very end of the magazine. Only on its last page the readers were reminded that Valentín Melgar, Sáez's husband, was the proprietor and editor of the magazine and therefore financially and legally responsible for the publication. The very layout of *La Violeta* thus reflects the contradictory legal position Spanish women held at the time. Although they could become owners of intellectual property, their possibilities of entering binding legal and financial contracts were limited by

---

[12] This status gave the publication a clear competitive edge because it allowed institutions for the formation of female primary teachers and higher schools for girls to take out subsciptions payed for by the school budget. Íñigo Sánchez Llama, *Galería de escritoras isabelinas: La prensa periódica entre 1833 y 1895*. Madrid: Cátedra, 2000: 192-93, explains this success by the personal connections of the Melgar couple.

[13] See online at: http://neww.huygens.knaw.nl/authors/show/3426; and http://neww.huygens.knaw.nl/authors/show/3415.

[14] See for instance Íñigo Sánchez Llama, *Galería de escritoras isabelinas*; and Alicia A. Andreu, "Arte y consumo: Ángela Grassi y el *Correo de la moda*" in *Nuevo Hispanismo* (1)1982: 123-135.

[15] For a discussion of Sáez de Melgar's staging of authorship in *La Violeta* see Partzsch (in print).

the legal dependence on their fathers or husbands.[16] Even publications which were run by women were always legally backed by a man.[17] Given the tight regulation of the press and the required monetary guarantees for periodical publications, it is therefore difficult to imagine how Sáez de Melgar could possibly have created *La Violeta* without the active support of her husband – although there are no hints in *La Violeta* that he took further interest in the enterprise.

This situation points at the strategic importance of the immediate local level of the network in order to face the challenge of founding and running what was a complex and financially all but safe business. Its geographic centre was from January 1864 the editorial office in the street Concepción Jerónima 13, close to the old town square of Madrid. When the magazine tried to expand into advertisement, several businesses in the immediate neighbourhood of the editorial office would seize the opportunity and advertise their services, for instances the boutique *Las Novedades* in Concepción Jerónima 5, which tried to attract customers through the detailed information about the arrival of new stock in August 1864.[18] The importance of proximity and personal connections also shines through in the reports about prestigious social occasions, a section in which the magazine clearly profits from Sáez de Melgar's access to the better society of Madrid. At the same time it promotes cultural initiatives in which contributors to the magazine were personally involved, such as the soirées at the *Liceo Piquer*. At this local level, the connection between the magazine and its readers included the possibility of personal encounters, not only in the streets, salons and theatres of Madrid, but also at the editorial office, where readers could purchase at a special discount most of the works written by Sáez de Melgar. The local distribution of the magazine was further supported by several

---

[16] Cristina Enríquez de Salamanca, "The Question of the Political Subject in Nineteenth-Century Domestic Discourse." in José Colmeira et al. (eds), *Spain Today: Essays on Literature, Culture, Society*. Dartmouth College: Department of Spanish and Portuguese, 1995: 103-112. Cristina Enríquez de Salamanca, "La mujer en el discurso legal del liberalismo español" in Catherine Jagoe, Alda Blanco and Cristina Enríquez de Salamanca (eds), *La mujer en los discursos de género: Textos y contextos del siglo XIX*. Barcelona: Icaria, 1998: 219-252.

[17] This becomes very clear when thumbing through the technical descriptions of the women's periodicals studied by Inmaculada Jiménez Morell, *La prensa femenina en España*.

[18] *La Violeta* (89): 14 August 1864.

booksellers in Madrid who stocked the publication and facilitated subscriptions.

However, the readership of *La Violeta* was by no means limited to the capital; the printed communications of the magazine to individual subscribers and some agents give ample evidence of a distribution effort that reached even the more remote parts of provincial Spain, including the islands, Ceuta in Africa and British Gibraltar. Furthermore, the magazine had agents in the Spanish colony of Cuba, as well as in Lisbon and Argentina. If *La Violeta* was a niche publication, in the sense I have discussed above, it was one with a truly national readership and a distribution even beyond the borders of the Spanish state.

This distribution network was impressive as well as extremely fragile, due to Spain's unreliable infrastructure. Complaints are constant and create a high level of frustration. Subscribers who claim missing copies are routinely informed that the fault lies with the postal services, not the magazine. The issue worst hit by bad postal service seems to have been number 117 (1865): the clearly embittered secretary of *La Violeta* had to explain to angry readers that most of its copies had never left the post office in Madrid because its employees had been too busy celebrating Carnival.[19] The difficulties of getting the product to the customers are mirrored by the complications which accompany money transfers from individual subscribers to the editors, a problem that might have contributed to the demise of the publication at the end of 1866.

We have seen how *La Violeta* drew on its local connections in Madrid; however, at least of equal importance for the success of the business were its connections in Paris, where it sourced the all-important fashion drawings and sewing patterns. Information about the latest Parisian fashion and detailed instructions which allowed readers to make their own dresses and accessories were necessary for the survival of any periodical mainly aimed at a female readership.[20] Importing this coveted information directly from Paris meant that the editors of the magazine had to rely on the still very new and sometimes temperamental railways, another factor that could cause

[19] *La Violeta* 121: 26 March 1865.

[20] Incidentally, the section on fashion is the only one in *La Violeta* which was always written by a woman, whereas all other sections and genres were sometimes signed by male, sometimes by female names.

disruptions to the smooth working of the business by preventing the punctual delivery of the drawings (*La Violeta* 96).[21]

## Inventing a community

In order to understand the ways in which *La Violeta* tried to create in its pages a sense of community among this disperse readership, it is necessary to complement our short overview of the commercial geography of the magazine with a brief analysis of its self-representation. Rather predictably, *La Violeta* sees itself from the very first number as a publication rooted in the domestic sphere. Saez de Melgar imagines her readers, male as well as female, old as well as young at home, perusing and enjoying the magazine:

> Our aim is that readers of all ages and sex will find in it agreeable recreation, as well as solid instruction. It will therefore contain moral stories and sage advice for children, those beautiful angels who tomorrow will be called to solve the intricate problems that agitate us; articles about fashion, needlework, education and morals for young women and mothers; theatre reviews, travel writing, scientific discoveries; articles about customs and manners, history and agreeable entertainment to make the white-haired old man in his study forget for a moment his voluminous tomes and amuse his fatigued mind with light and pleasant information.[22]

Conspicuously absent from those readers are the men at working age, presumably occupied with more serious issues away from their families. Nevertheless the outside world reached into the space of the home: after all, the 'beautiful angels' who study the offerings of *La Violeta* would grow up to confront the problems of society, and the old man in his study, converted into an amused reader, belonged earlier in his life to the missing demographic segment, the active, middle-class male adult, reader of the daily newspapers and thus, unlike our women writers, a full and undisputed member of the imagined national community.

---

[21] In the early 1880s, Sáez de Melgar and her two surviving daughters relocate to Paris while her husband works as a civil servant in Cuba. In the French capital the writer will embark on new publishing enterprises. See Virginia Seguí Collar, *Gloria Melgar (1859-1938)*. Madrid: Ediciones del Orto, 2002: 22-24.

[22] *La Violeta* 1 (7 December 1862): 1-2 (my translation).

The domestic nature of the readership is mirrored by the self-representation of the magazine. Paradoxically, it relies heavily on the public staging of personal relationships, relationships which are not established through work or a shared interested in a commercial enterprise but through personal, private contacts. The impression of listening in on a circle of friends and acquaintances is for instance created by the publication of dedicated poems of friendship, literary texts inspired by the death of Sáez de Melgar's second son, as well as poems speaking to her surviving child Gloria. Indeed, if we are to believe an enthusiastic encomium by Sáez de Melgar, the whole enterprise is only viable thanks to her friendship with the Andalusian woman writer Rogelia León (1828-1870),[23] who certainly contributes an astonishing number of texts, especially during the periods in which her friend is prevented from looking after the magazine.

*La Violeta* presents itself as rooted in a real network of personal relations, a network that seems to invite the reader to become a part of it. *La Violeta* performs thus the function of a kind of bridge: on the one side, it reaches into the homes of the subscribers to the magazine; on the other, it indirectly connects its readers to some of the public figures in the capital. Above them all shines reassuringly the name of the Queen herself; however, if we have a closer look at the names that are cited in the reports about social events, alongside some of the female contributors, we find among them decidedly political, definitively non-domestic players, such as the future president of the first Spanish Republic, the director of the influential daily newspaper *La Iberia* or a writer of anti-clerical best-sellers with socialist undertones. This continuum from the private to the public does not appear as contradictory: although the magazine clearly favours texts which do not go beyond what is perceived as suitable for women, there are enough essays and literary contributions that deal with topical themes which agitate contemporary society. A very good example is the reaction to a cholera epidemic that swept through Spain. Readers were treated to a tragic love story in which the illness plays the central role, while medical advice to prevent contagion appeared in the section with miscellaneous information. When catastrophic flooding strikes Valencia, readers are encouraged to contribute to a charitable subscription for the victims. The donors' names appeared in the following issues of the magazine, thus strengthening the sense of belonging and, what is more, of working together towards the same goal: a better, more charitable

[23] See online at http://neww.huygens.knaw.nl/authors/show/3520

Spain based on Christian/Catholic sentiments. It is this attitude that opens the possibility of intervening as women in society, thereby shaping the face of the nation.

## The politics of charity

Woman's close association with charity was of course a commonplace, so widely accepted that it usually passed without notice. However, if the commonplace is taken seriously and developed in a consequent and coherent manner, the results can reach surprisingly subversive dimensions. This is exactly what happened when *La Violeta* turned its charitable attentions towards the abolition of slavery, a hotly contested issue with very direct implications for Spanish society and indeed the Spanish economy through the plantations in Cuba and, to a lesser degree, Puerto Rico.[24] Following an appeal to the ladies in Madrid by several British women's abolitionist organisations, in December 1865 *La Violeta* openly took up the cause by actively supporting in its pages the planned foundation of a female branch of the (of course male) Spanish Association for the Abolition of Slavery, recently founded in the capital.[25] The widely publicised meeting of the Association, celebrated with the intention of solemnly formalising the new female additions to the ranks of its official activists, raised considerable interest among the public, an interest reflected in the detailed reports and close scrutiny in a broad range of political newspapers. Women's activism had suddenly come to the attention of the national community of newspaper readers, and especially the more right-wing papers like *La Esperanza* did not like at all what they saw. *La Esperanza* neatly rejected this new development of women's activism by reminding their readers that a woman's agreement to the statutes of an association was not binding, given that her father, husband or brother could revoke it at any time (*La Esperanza* [12 December 1865]: 2). Apparently, there was a clear boundary which the abolitionist women had

---

[24] The final abolition of slavery in Cuba was only achieved in 1886. A standard work on abolitionism is Corwin (1967). For a detailed analysis of the involvement of *La Violeta* with abolitionsim see Henriette Partzsch, "Violets and Abolition: The Discourse on Slavery in Faustina Sáez de Melgar's Magazine 'La Violeta'" (Madrid, 1862-66), in *Bulletin of Spanish Studies*, 89,6, 2012: 859-875.

[25] On the Association, see Christopher Schmidt-Nowara, *Empire and Antislavery: Spain, Cuba, and Puerto Rico, 1833-1874*. Pittsburgh: University of Pittsburgh Press, 1999: 100-125.

tried to blur: women, especially from the middle and upper classes, were of course expected to contribute to the relief of human suffering; however, founding an organisation to maximise their effort and thus its impact on society was definitively a step to far.[26] Predictably, it did not help that the initiative targeted an extremely sensitive political issue, although the economic consequences and the possible link to decolonialisation were not discussed.

The hostile reactions after the meeting forced the group around *La Violeta* to clarify and indeed develop its position. This task was immediately taken up by Rogelia León, in a rhetorically very forceful piece titled "A las piadosas señoras de todos los países que trabajan con ardor por la emancipación de los esclavos".[27] Its common denominator is precisely international female solidarity, the idea of mutual support to defend a morally unobjectionable cause. Its addressees are, as the first line shouts, "Dear sisters! My (female) friends! Women with a compassionate heart and a great soul!", who are encouraged to rally in order to confront the common enemy, impervious to the oppression and sarcasm meted out by men to those women who dared to undertake a great and indeed heroic enterprise. For León, there is no contradiction between making a man's happiness, being the angel of the house as well as a loving mother and wearing the laurel crown of heroism, a heroism that is not redefined as self-effacing sacrifice and happy resignation but emulates the example of militant women of the past: the biblical Judith, Joan of Arc, Charlotte Corday and, closer to home, the legendary heroine of the war against Napoleon, Agustina de Aragón. Later in her argument, León will step up her game even further by invoking the mother of Christ and Saint Theresa, doctor of the Church: linked through emotional and family ties to the *patria*, the fatherland, it is a woman's duty to speak out against such a horrible crime as slavery, precisely in her role as woman.[28] León does indeed speak out: she uses the grand style of nineteenth-century oratory in her

---

[26] Interestingly, *The Times* in London makes the same point (albeit more explicitly) against Fredrika Bremer's appeal to create an international women's peace alliance to fight the sufferings caused by war. See George Dodd, *Pictorical History of the Russian War 1854-5-6 with Maps, Plans, and Wood Engravings*. Edinburgh and London: W. and R. Chambers, 1856 : 69.

[27] "To the pious Ladies in all countries who work passionately for the emancipation of the slaves" (my translation), *La Violeta* 160 [24 December 1865]: 615-618.

[28] Another well-known and well-connected Spanish woman writer, Carolina Coronado, will follow a much more low-key strategy : Lisa Surwillo, "Poetic Diplomacy: Carolina Coronado and the American Civil War": 409-422.

article, with exclamations, rhetorical questions, a carefully constructed speech rhythm and the exalted register of the conventional sublime.

After the rather disastrous meeting in the real world, where even the mute participation of a considerable number of women (the list of speakers was all male) was sufficient to produce a profound unease that interrupted the proper functioning of discourse in the public sphere, the author from Granada thus transforms *La Violeta* into a tribune of her own, which allows her to appropriate the political discourse and to re-phrase the opposition against slavery in gendered terms.[29] Suddenly, the domestic niche publication shows that it can become a public space in its own rights, invoking an imagined international community whose linkage is based on gender and Christian convictions, in opposition to the male professionals of the Spanish public sphere who are, in the eyes of *La Violeta*, blinded to the greater good by the interests of their respective political allegiances. This last point is not only made by León, but also three months later by another regular contributor to the magazine, Leandro A. Herrero. He laments in his two-part article "La ley de la perfectibilidad" [The law of perfectibility][30] the fragmentation and divisions of societies: "In one word, we are divided in the world of politics by mundane interests which enact an eternal antagonism." The only way of vanquishing this situation, the only real progress can be achieved through the development of the human soul and the spread of charitable sentiments towards all human beings. Herrero does not spell out the consequences; however, if we think about the other claims made about the nature and realm of women in the magazine, the conclusions are clear: the male domain of politics can only embrace partial and conflicting interests, thus becoming an obstacle to the real progress of mankind instead of a solution to its problems. Women, by contrast, have access to a more universal perspective. They can thus become the vanguard of real progress; as angels and examples of virtue, they can guide not only a specific society but mankind in general towards a

[29] Isabel Morales Sánchez has pointed out the importance of this mechanism: "Even though many characteristics assigned to their sex were predominant in nineteenth-century women writers, many women intellectuals sought and found other 'platforms' to express their worries, thus showing their active implication in society. These areas were mainly the essay, the press and literature", Isabel Morales Sánchez, "El orador sin tribuna: Damas, política y literatura en el siglo XIX." in José Antonio Hernández Guerrero et al. (eds). *Oratoria y literatura*, Cádiz: Universidad-Ayuntamiento, 2004: 95-96 (my translation).

[30] *La Violeta* 168 and 169 [24 and 28 February 1866].

more perfect state. The political daily newspapers feed on struggles, division and conflict, the imagined linkage they create will help to introduce those elements into the very heart of the nation, the public space. In its reflections on the place of women in society, *La Violeta* experiments with a different kind of imagined community, one in which the connection between public and private sphere is never completely severed because the standpoint rooted in domesticity and at a prudent distance from the battlefields of politics cannot be ignored by society. If considered from the right angle, it becomes indeed a vantage point that enables the "women with a great heart and a compassionate soul" to see were the real interests of society lie, for instance in the abolition of slavery. However, this different narrative about the Spanish nation, based on common places about woman and gaining momentum and edge especially in the context of the fight against slavery, remains only the possibility of a counter-narrative. Public perception sees the questions raised by the abolitionist women as an incursion into politics, not the emergence of a kind of alternative way of articulating society. Although the consistent and sincere commitment of many Spanish women writers to abolitionism are unequivocal, the linkage between them was not strong enough to create a durable, functioning organisation.

## Select Bibliography

### A. Primary Sources

*Diario oficial de avisos de Madrid*, 11 January 1867. Madrid: Imprenta de Frías y compañía.

*La Esperanza*, 12 December 1865. Madrid: Imprenta de la Esperanza a cargo de D. A. Pérez Dubrull.

*La Violeta: Revista hispano-americana*, 1862-1866. Madrid: Imprenta de M. Rojas; A. Pérez Dubrull; R. Vicente.

Dodd, George. 1856. *Pictorical History of the Russian War 1854-5-6 with Maps, Plans, and Wood Engravings*. Edinburgh and London: W. and R. Chambers.

### B. Secondary Sources

Anderson, Benedict. 2006 *Imagined Communities: Reflections on the Origins and Spread of Nationalism*. London, New York: Verso. [1983].

Andreu, Alicia A. "Arte y consumo: Ángela Grassi y el *Correo de la moda*", in *Nuevo Hispanismo* (1)1982: 123-135.

Corwin, Arthur F. 1967. *Spain and the Abolition of Slavery in Cuba, 1817-1886*. Austin, London: The University of Texas Press for the Institute of Latin American Studies.

Cruz Seoane, María and Saiz, María Dolores. 2007. *Cuatro siglos de periodismo en España. De los avisos a los periódicos digitales.* Madrid: Alianza.

Enríquez de Salamanca, Cristina. 1995. "The Question of the Political Subject in Nineteenth-Century Domestic Discourse." in *Spain Today: Essays on Literature, Culture, Society*, Colmeira, José et al. (eds). Dartmouth College: Department of Spanish and Portuguese: 103-112.

—. 1998. "La mujer en el discurso legal del liberalismo español." in *La mujer en los discursos de género: Textos y contextos del siglo XIX*. Jagoe, Catherine; Alda Blanco and Cristina Enríquez de Salamanca (eds). Barcelona: Icaria: 219-252.

Jiménez Morell, Inmaculada. 1992. *La prensa femenina en España (desde sus orígenes a 1868)*. Madrid: Ediciones de la Torre.

Kirkpatrick, Susan. 1989. *Las Románticas: Women Writers and Subjectivity in Spain, 1825-1850*. Berkeley, Los Angeles, London: University of California Press.

Morales Sánchez, Isabel. 2004. "El orador sin tribuna: Damas, política y literatura en el siglo XIX." in *Oratoria y literatura*. Hernández Guerrero, José Antonio et al., (eds). Cádiz: Universidad; Ayuntamiento: 93-102.

Partzsch, Henriette. "Violets and Abolition: The Discourse on Slavery in Faustina Sáez de Melgar's magazine *La Violeta* (1862-1866)." in *Bulletin of Spanish Studies*. (Forthcoming).

—. "Autorschaft auf Raten: Gender, Öffentlichkeit und Presse im Spanien des 19. Jahrhunderts am Beispiel von Faustina Sáez de Melgar." in *Strategien von Autorschaft in der Romania: Zur Neukonzipierung einer Kategorie im Rahmen literatur-, kultur- und medienwissenschaftlich basierter Geschlechtertheorien*. Grohnemann, Claudia, Tanja Schwan and Cornelia Sieber (eds). Heidelberg: Universitätsverlag Winter, in print.

Racioppi, Linda and O'Sullivan See, Katherine. 2000. "Engendering Nation and National Identity." in *Women, States, and Nationalism: At Home in the Nation?* Ranchod-Nilsson, Sita and Mary Ann Tétreault (eds). London, New York: Routledge: 18-34.

Roig Castellanos, Mercedes. 1977. *La mujer y la prensa: Desde el siglo XVII a nuestros días*. Madrid: self-published.

Sánchez Llama, Íñigo. 2000. *Galería de escritoras isabelinas: La prensa periódica entre 1833 y 1895*. Madrid: Cátedra.

Schmidt-Nowara, Christopher. 1999. *Empire and Antislavery: Spain, Cuba, and Puerto Rico, 1833-1874*. Pittsburgh: University of Pittsburgh Press.

Seguí Collar, Virginia. 2002. *Gloria Melgar (1859-1938)*. Madrid: Ediciones del Orto.

Segura, Isabel and Selva, Marta. 1984. *Revistes de dones (1846-1935)*. Barcelona: Edhasa.

Simón Palmer, María del Carmen. 1993. *Revistas femininas madrileñas*. Madrid: Artes Gráficas Municipales – Área de Régimen Interior y Personal. [Ciclo de Conferencias: El Madrid de Isabel II; 8].

—. 1991. *Escritoras españolas del siglo XIX: Manual bio-bibliográfico*. Madrid: Castalia.

Surwillo, Lisa. 2007. "Poetic Diplomacy: Carolina Coronado and the American Civil War." in *Comparative American Studies* 5(4): 409-422.

# Part IV.

# Women Looking Elsewhere

# Overpassing State and Cultural Borders: A Polish Female Doctor in 18th-Century Constantinople

*Joanna Partyka*

ABSTRACT Regina Salomea Pilsztyn, doctoress of medicine and ophthalmologist, is the authoress of a diary in Polish, characteristically entitled *The practice of journey and my life's adventures*. An outcast in Poland because of her independence, excessive enterprise, eloquence, education, but also her inadequate fulfilment of the role of mother and wife, she found her place on earth far away from her homeland, in the world of Islam. In Turkey, she was primarily a stranger, but she was accepted by the culturally different community. Regina Salomea's diary, unpublished until the 20th century, is an interesting itinerary abounding in rich cultural observations and comments.

THE DIARY OF REGINA SALOMEA PILSZTYN, "Doctoress of medicine and ophthalmologist", completed in 1760 and prepared by the author for the printers, was published on the basis of the manuscript only in 1957, with a brief and not too valuable commentary. But this does not mean that Regina's diary was not in circulation during her own time: it was, but in the form of a manuscript which probably circulated in Poland until it reached the Princes Czartoryski Library in the middle of 19th century. There is an inscription in the first page of the diary: *Ex Cathalogo Librorum Joannis de Witte Colonelli Art[illeriae] Reg[imentum]*. De Witte (1709-1785) was a Polish[1] military engineer (of Dutch descent) and he kept a wide correspondence with the Turkish *pashas,* as well as with Regina's son Stanislaus Pichelstein who was an interpreter and Polish diplomat in Turkey. De Witte loved literature, and was possibly the first to read Regina's diary. She prepared the diary for printing but the plan failed we do not know why. The book was finally printed in 1957. However the diary was published as a manuscript by

[1] See online at http://en.wikipedia.org/wiki/Poland.

copying it, a very popular way of 'publishing' books in Poland in 17th and 18th centuries.

While historians of literature and historians of medicine are aware of the diary, very little has been written about it thus far. It is frequently treated as a kind of a curio, and some people go even so far as to be ironic, as seen in this characteristic example:

> Salomea Regina neé Rusiecka Pilsztyn had very clear literary ambitions. Good fate was at least partially favourable to those ambitions: when after two hundred years of lying in manuscript the diary was published in print, the editors brought out the book in such an exquisite outfit that the beauty of the congenially matched illustrations and enticing cover totally obscured a tentative reflection that that female ophthalmologist was after all *an ignorant woman* and her diary inadvertently reflects it.[2]

Without stopping to discuss the clumsy style of the author and without going into a semiotic discussion as to the notion of 'an ignorant woman', used by the Polish critic cited above, I shall treat the diary of the 18th-century female doctor and traveller who crossed state and cultural borders as observations, that related to her experiences of alienation and otherness as well as her sense of place and space.

Yi-Fu Tuan, in his classic book entitled *Space and Place: the Perspective of Experience*, makes a distinction between the latter two important categories – space and place – notices that open space is a domain of unrestricted movement and adventure, while that which is closed and humanized becomes a place which, as a quiet centre of set values, provides a human being with the sense of safety and stability. To live, a human being needs both space and place: he/she becomes attached to his/her place, but also desires freedom offered by open space. Such ambivalence, or sometimes even a dilemma, accompanies any travel, especially when crossing state borders which often involves overpassing cultural borders.[3]

It is exactly the case of the 18th-century Polish woman who, having deliberately relinquished her due place in her native country, negotiated

---

[2] Andrzej Cieński, *Pamiętnikarstwo polskie XVIII wieku*. Wrocław: Ossolineum, 1981: 153-154.

[3] Yi-Fu Tuan, *Space and Place: The Perspective of Experience*. Minneapolis/London: University of Minnesota Press, 2001: 74-75.

thousands of miles in order to settle down – socially, economically and culturally – in the space of a Muslim world, measuring out a small part of it for herself. The process of becoming accustomed to that space is multidimensional: upon entering the alien world Pilsztyn overcame linguistic, religious, conventional and professional barriers. She was successful as a woman-doctor, but failed as a wife and mother. Writing her diary with an intention to publish she confessed in the foreword that:

> Insults, disdain shown by husbands, children and neighbours, and also my servants – those drove me out of my country and it is nicer for me to live here in the desert in peace, to the Lord's glory, than in Poland.[4]

The diary was written using travel notes and remained the sole source of knowledge of the life and adventures of Pilsztyn. We learn from it that she was born in 1718 in the environs of Grodno, in the territory of today's Byelorussia (land that then belonged to Poland), most probably in a bourgeois family. She married twice. Her first husband was doctor Jakub Halpir. It was with him that she went for the first time to Istanbul, shortly after the wedding, where Halpir was given the position of 'physician and ophthalmologist'. Regina was allowed to look after the 'dispensary', and when her husband was absent she used to give medical advice, apparently quite successfully. She was widowed at the age of 17, although the marriage had grown apart earlier; from the diary, onelearns it happened because of religious differences – Halpir was Lutheran (perhaps even of German descent) and Regina was Catholic – but also because her husband wanted to return to the country, whereas his young wife had become well accustomed to the new conditions and had no desire to go back. The widow continued her husband's practice, primary in ophthalmology. An Italian doctor taught her how to write out prescriptions in Latin and presented her with unknown medical books. She had already treated some patients successfully when she decided to leave Istanbul for a short time in order to buy out her Turkish friends from Russian captivity. However, various types of business kept her away from Turkey for much longer, a total of 15 years. In the meantime she travelled a lot. Her itinerary included Ljubljana, Sofia, Bucharest, Petersburg and Vienna. Several times she returned to Poland, making longer stopovers in

---

[4] Regina Salomea Pilsztynowa, *Proceder podróży i życia mego awantur*. Pollak, R. (ed.). Kraków: Wydawnictwo Literackie, 1957: 35.

Lvov, Kiev, Przemyśl and Kamieniec. Each time, however, she sought a pretext to go away, as if travel was the objective in itself. She considered settled life to be like slavery, which she clearly stated in her diary: "I would like to tear myself free from that land [Poland]".[5]

In 1739, during her successive sojourn in Poland she was married again to a gentleman she had bought out from Turkish captivity two years before, an ensign of the Imperial army, Józef Fortunat Pichelstein (she polonized his name to Pilsztyn). They were protected by a Lithuanian magnate, Michał Kazimierz Radziwiłł, known as 'Rybeńko', at his landed estate at Nieśwież. Regina worked there as a household physician, and her husband was nominated officer of the Lithuanian army. Pilsztyn turned out to be a lecherous and prodigal man. After four years of conflict Regina managed to free herself from him. It is not known whether he died, or whether the couple got a divorce. Now a wealthy woman and a mother of three children, Regina decided to get involved in another, this time informal relationship with an unknown 'amorat', a lover, who was primarily interested in her money. She fled from him to Istanbul to fill the position of the court lady physician in the harem of sultan Mustafa III. The fate of the diary authoress after 1760, which is mentioned as the date the diary was being prepared for the printers, is unknown, but according to on her frequent declarations she certainly had no intention of going back to Poland.

It would be interesting to discover why the author of the diary failed to find in her native country a peaceful, sheltered *place of set values,* which would be a *safe haven* for her – to quote Yi Fu-Tuan. The vicissitudes of her life, the choices she made, seem to indicate that she detested exactly those *values,* which she would have to abide by should she remain in Poland. She felt in no way attached to her family (to the extent that she never mentioned them in her diary), or the land where she was brought up (during her later journeys she must have travelled across her native land many times, but she never mentioned it). She was given away to be married as a very young girl, most probably against her will. Neither could she herself decide whether to follow Halpir to Istanbul, or wait for him in Poland. One may wonder what the life of the author would have been like had she stayed in Poland. In the first half of the 18th century the ideal Polish woman was a caring mother, frugal housewife, docile and devout wife. The physical place for women was the home, or otherwise the church. That situation lasted in Poland until the

[5] *Ibid.*, 152.

mid eighteenth century. Women were not allowed to enter into legal transactions, and after the death of a husband they and their children were assigned a legal guardian. They were frequently married against their will. A systematic and comprehensive education for women was a totally new subject. An entrepreneurial spirit was valued in women provided it was related to running a household and raising children. Historians of culture have many written sources (treatises, sermons, manuals of bringing up children, as well as letter, diaries, judicial documents etc.), which could serve as proof of the status of women in the Polish-Lithuanian Commonwealth.

Women living in cities were frequently involved in crafts, commerce or small service businesses. However, like the milieu of the gentry, they were not usually valued for their ingenuity. A woman who had her own interests and ambitions, presented broader intellectual horizons and ventured to criticize accepted values, usually did not find her place in society and was treated as an iconoclast.Giving her promptly away to be married was at that time a "rescuing procedure", since there was a chance that in being subordinated to her husband, obliged to behave decently and morally as a wife and mother, the individualist would agree to observe the accepted values and deny her own "person".

The majority of women in Europe were in a similar predicament.[6] Although female humanists were already active in Italy during the Renaissance, and female intellectuals organized cultural life in 17th-century France by setting up literary salons, in the mid-eighteenth century women at large were still deprived of the right to decide their own fate. For centuries men forced the thesis that women were intellectually inferior, and considered their education to be pointless. It was even believed that learning could spoil a woman's nature. In Poland, such attitude towards women lasted for an exceptionally long time. A devout, moral and obedient woman usually could

[6] Linda Timmermans, *L'Accès des femmes à la culture (1598-1715). Un débat d'idées de Saint François de Sales à la Marquise de Lambert.* Paris: Honoré Champion, 1993; Katherine Usher Henderson, Barbara F. McManus, *Half Humankind: Context and Text of the Controversy about Women in England 1540-1640.* Urbana: Univ. of Illinois Press, 1985; Pamela J. Benson, *The Invention of the Renaissance Woman. The Challenge of Female Independence in the Literature and Thought of Italy and England.* Pennsylvania: Pennsylvania State Univ. Press, 1992; Marylin Williamson, *Raising Their Voices. British Women Writers, 1650-1750.* Detroit: Wayne, 1990.

not write. In the words of an highly regarded Jesuit, Piotr Skarga: "Schooling does not become females, [they benefit more] from prayer and work".[7]

Pilsztyn is clearly is out of accord with such an ideal of a woman. Perhaps she was married early because her family wanted to curb her temperament or subdue her aspirations? Perhaps her parents wanted to get rid of her from their home as quickly as possible, and she was willing to part with the family she had no feeling for? Perhaps she already knew before the wedding of the plans to Istanbul and deliberately accepted it, anticipating that this way the world would open for her and she would be able to find a place for herself. And it proved thatin Istanbul, the doctor's wife turned out to be a woman who was energetic, enterprising, to some extent independent (also financially) from her husband, bravely fighting for her rights as a woman and a physician.

There are a lot of indications that Pilsztyn indeed had a talent for curing people as well as a lot of intuition, as she made a career for herself in Istanbul as an outstanding ophthalmologist (she successfully removed cataracts) and commanded fair fees for treatment. If necessary, she knew how to bargain. At that time, a woman with a doctor's status was an exceptional phenomenon in Poland. It was true that the services of various women herbalists and quacks were used, but usually by poor people, who could not afford the services of a doctor or a barber. Moreover, men ridiculed women who wanted to compete with male doctors.

In a foreign country, Regina Pilsztyn was accepted more readily and without reservation. It was also considered natural that she charged a fee for her services. Neither had she to go to a patient on her own – a carriage was sent for her. In this respect the 'doctoress' would not accept anything less. 'Spoiled' by the Turks, while on a visit in Poland she refused to treat Cracow's chatelain Jerzy Mniszech because she did not care to go on foot, and he did not send a carriage for her. While he was astonished by her behaviour, the magnate kindly forgave her misdeed.

Pilsztyn could not be a 'hushed mouse' as the then female savoir-vivre prescribed. Listing 'maiden duties', one 17th-century Polish philosopher and physician, Sebastian Petrycy of Pilzno, emphasised in his *Commentaries* to *Aristotelian Politics* (Kraków 1605), in the chapter, "How parents are to raise their daughters", that: "Boys' games are different, as how to study, rule,

---

[7] Piotr Skarga, *Żywot ś. Katarzyny*, as cited in Andrzej Wyrobisz, « Staropolskie wzorce rodziny i kobiety – żony i matki » in *Przegląd Historyczny,* 1999, 3: 20.

trade, soldier, and so are those of girls – how to spin, sew, stitch and embroider".[8] He claimed also that apart from "religiousness, modesty and obedience to her parents" a girl should remember "to remain silent when a man was present".[9] Reticence was also valued in married women. In the Muslim world, Pilsztyn paradoxically was allowed to speak in public, although a Muslim woman could not stay in the company of men who were not related to her, not to mention engage in conversation with them. Conversely, a Polish lady doctor daringly makes it clear to a Turkish captain: "I am free to talk to both women and men, because here and now I am talking to you".[10]

Ignoring European and Muslim recommendations of silence in the company of men, Pilsztyn engaged in heated religious disputes with Muslims, Jews and members of the Orthodox Church, putting forward arguments in defence of "the true Roman Catholic faith". These disputes clearly pleased both sides, since they are described as follows: "And so we [were talking about religion] atour leisure, he [Hasan] one day about the Turkish one, and on another day I about Christ and other articles of faith".[11] Pilsztyn travelled in a carriage, but frequently, sporting a janissary outfit, she mounted a horse. She bought 'the Turkish male clothes' for comfort and safety. She was extremely astonished when she was recognised on the road by a Balkan highway robber, who exclaimed: "Good morning, Madam Doctor." "I am not a Madam Doctor – she warded off – I am a man";[12] but it was to no avail. She was clearly a 'public' figure, well known even in the circles of robbers prowling the Balkan mountains.

Pilsztyn treated both women and men. If one believes her own words, she had a great success. She was held in high esteem by the Turks, showered with money and expensive gifts. "For the entertainment to meet some people" she attended dinners given by envoys of foreign states, embassy interpreters and merchants.[13] She conversed with them in their own languages – she definitely spoke Russian and Turkish, she could also communicate with the Germans

---

[8] Sebastian Petrycy of Pilzno, "Jako rządzić mają rodzice córki swe" in Stefan Wołoszyn (ed.). *Źródła do dziejów wychowania i myśli pedagogicznej.* t.1. Warszawa, PWN, 1965: 306.

[9] *Ibid.*, 306.

[10] Regina Salomea Pilsztynowa, *Proceder podróży i życia mego awantur*: 42.

[11] *Ibid.*,184.

[12] *Ibid*,. 58.

[13] *Ibid*,. 204.

(her second husband was from Carinthia). When she visited Russia she apparently had an opportunity to personally meet two czarinas – Anna and Elizabeth; in Wroclaw she was received by Frederick II of Prussia. Thus, she was a woman of the world and she took a pen to commemorate her vicissitudes and unbelievable adventures. But she did it to please a reader, to entertain him or her, not to immortalize her merits. She shared all her experiences with the reader, weaving into the narration psychological observations and elements typical of a travel narrative. Some parts of her diary are like a pastoral novel, others like a romance with robbers, attacks, duels and disguises. Apparently the author of the diary was familiar with popular romance literature of that time, although there is no direct evidence in the text.

The diary of a Polish 'lady doctor' abounds in interesting, almost ethnographical observations of her itinerary, revealing her talent as an observer and 'researcher'. The author was determinedly engaged in what today's ethnographers would call participant observation. Frequent journeys provided an excellent opportunity to collect various true-life stories. Pilsztyn always very conscientiously noted down whether she herself personally witnessed the events, or whether it was related to her: "I heard, but I did not see it", "I saw it myself", "I asked, I dare say...", "what I've written here I heard from..." In this way she protected herself against possible charges that she was repeating unbelievable stories. One discerns sincere interest in the culture and religion of the countries she visited. She is particularly interested in people, observing them with patience, asking them questions in their own language and with a big dose of tolerance, trying to understand their point of view. She is fascinated by the culture of Muslim women having the possibility to meet with them and freely talk to them (for example in the bath, where "they see one another, and they enjoy beeing together, they eat and drink, and they can sing and dance there")[14] Pilsztyn is accepted by these women, she visits them in their homes, and makes friends with them.

An avid traveller supporting herself by offering medical treatment, a diarist with literary and ethnographical aspirations, an enterprising and independent woman, fighting for her rights, boldly engaging in discussions with men, seems to be a prototype of the nineteenth-century liberated woman. In the time she happened to live, however, she was not an example to be followed. She was not a silent and obedient woman, who had no

[14] *Ibid.*, 54.

opinions of her own, whose world was limited to four walls of a household, and the only trip she made was to church. This is probably why she was looking for a distant world: to be free from all the biases of Polish (European) society.

Pilsztyn could also not adjust herself to the role of a wife and mother. This strong woman was totally helpless in her relationships with men, who took advantage of her enterprise and money. In personal matters she was not a liberated woman, as she refers to male views regarding the female sex admitting that she was merely an imperfect, impatient woman of simple heart. Pilsztyn had three children. However, she did not create a family home for them; she was not a proper other to them. She used to leave them with casual guardians and set out for another journey. One of her sons paid for this with his life at the age of 9, being treated badly, even starving, while waiting for his mother to be back home. Her daughter stayed with her step-father Pilsztyn for a long time. She had almost no contact with her mother. From the diary it is also apparent that the authoress had a son-in-law, although earlier there is not a single mention of her daughter's wedding or any courtiers asking for her hand. She was deeply hurt by her elder son who, sent by the guardian to join her in Istanbul, declared that he had no intention of staying with her there. It was a genuine shock and it is probably one of the reasons why she started a diary. It did not make her return to her native country, however. Turkey had already become her homeland. She experienced distress almost exclusively in Poland: "Oh, my God, how this world and golden Polish freedom has pressed me!"[15] Such exclamations are reiterated throughout the diary. "I could never win anything with our Polish gentlemen, which filled me with great sorrow reminding myself that in foreign countries I enjoyed both esteem and benefits (...)", reads another passage.[16] Conversely, by remaining in Turkey, she could count on many friends. It is significant that her returns to the Turkish Empire were always linked with a feeling of relief, with a sense security, with undisguised joy, as if she had returned home. She was always welcomed there as a human being.

The 'doctoress of medicine and ophthalmologist', who felt lost and cheated in her native country, found her *place* in the Turkish world. In Poland she was not accepted, because she was different – too enterprising, too eloquent, too educated in her profession, too liberated and independent.

---

[15] *Ibid.*,193.
[16] *Ibid*,. 215.

She was not able to settle into the role of a wife, she failed in her duties as a mother – she openly fought for her right and won.

In Turkey, she was not different – she was foreign. The categories of foreignness and difference are not subject to the same criteria of judgment. That is why it was easier for her to be accepted there. She was accepted as a foreign woman practicing a male profession.

In the Muslim world, the division between priviledges due for men and what is related to femininity have always been very precisely defined, perhaps until more recently. Being a very keen observer, Pilsztyn noted down in her diary the differences she discerned between the status of European and the Muslim women. She was struck that Muslim women "tie kerchiefs round their faces",[17] that they are not allowed to be seen in the company of unrelated men, and the fact that "it is not becoming for women to go out of their homes"[18] seems to her absolutely unacceptable. (One can imagine what would it mean for our traveller to be locked within the four walls of a home). The following fragment of her diary is very telling in this respect:

> There is a place in Istanbul, Eski Saray, that is where wives and servants of the first emperors live, and those are true slaves in the world, because they have to stay there until they die.[19]

This comment suggests that Regina needed not only a *place* to live, but also a *space* around it, since only in the open space is it possible to feel the qualities of a place intensely, as Yi Fu-Tuan outlines. Her numerous journeys (at the end of the diary onelearns about a planned 'entertainment' trip to Egypt and Jerusalem) perhaps provided her with a feeling of security, in being rooted in the space she had chosen in Istanbul. But she did not reject her Polish identity, proudly referring to it on different occasions – although any attempt to return to her homeland ended in one more escape. Instead she found her land somewhere else, feeling in her homeland not only rejected but also misunderstood.

Looking for her *place*, Regina went very far – figuratively and literally. In taking advantage of the fact that she had been accepted by the Turkish world she grabbed for herself a space normally due to men. She encroached it and

---

[17] *Ibid.*,244.
[18] *Ibid.*, 228.
[19] *Ibid.*, 227.

settled there, creating a ‘spot of quietude’ she could not experience in her own country, where she was different.

## Select Bibliography

Benson, Pamela J. 1992. *The Invention of the Renaissance Woman. The Challenge of Female Independence in the Literature and Thought of Italy and England.* Pennsylvania: Pennsylvania State Univ. Press.

Cieński, Andrzej. 1981. *Pamiętnikarstwo polskie XVIII wieku.* Wrocław: Ossolineum.

Petrycy of Pilzno, Sebastian. 1965. "Jako rządzić mają rodzice córki swe" in *Źródła do dziejów wychowania i myśli pedagogicznej.* t.1. Wołoszyn, Stefan. (ed.). PWN,Warszawa.

Pilsztynowa, Regina Salomea. 1957. *Proceder podróży i życia mego awantur.* Pollak, R. (ed.). Kraków: Wydawnictwo Literackie.

Timmermans, Linda. 1993. *L'Accès des femmes à la culture (1598-1715). Un débat d'idées de Saint François de Sales à la Marquise de Lambert.* Paris: Honoré Champion.

Tuan, Yi-Fu. 2001. *Space and Place: The Perspective of Experience.* Minneapolis/London: University of Minnesota Press.

Usher Henderson, Katherine, McManus, Barbara F. 1985. *Half Humankind: Context and Text of the Controversy about Women in England 1540-1640.* Urbana: Univ. of Illinois Press.

Williamson, Marylin. 1990. *Raising Their Voices. British Women Writers, 1650-1750.* Detroit: Wayne State University Press.

Wyrobisz, Andrzej. 1999. « Staropolskie wzorce rodziny i kobiety – żony i matki » in *Przegląd Historyczny,* 3: 20.

# Between National Myth and Trans-national Ideal: The Representation of Nations in the French-Language Writings of Russian Women (1770-1819)

*Elena Gretchanaia*

ABSTRACT At the turn of the 18th century, when a positive image of a frenchified Russian began to be developed, and when Russian specificity was also emphasized, women began to contribute to the discourse on the Russian nation and its place among other nations. In this chapter, the author studies the contributions of francophone Russian women writers to the discourse, including that of Empress Catherine II, Julie de Krüdener, Princess Ekaterina Dashkova and Princess Zinaida Volkonskaya. Each of these women succeeded in offering a more balanced view of the nation.

IT WAS NOT UNTIL THE TURN OF THE 18th century that Russia, a country which had long placed itself in opposition to Europe by its Orthodox religious orientation, took to the European stage. This entry into the European family of nations, stimulated and guided by Peter the Great, raises questions about the place of Russia among other nations. The opinions expressed by Russian writers of the 18th century are generally polarised: some (Lomonosov, Golikov), following the lead of French philosophers such as Fontenelle and Voltaire, supporters of the 'Russian mirage'[1] welcomed the European orientation of their country, while others (Shcherbatov, Boltin) claimed the singularity of Old Russia and accused Peter the Great of having corrupted the nation.

French, the European *lingua franca*, and from the second half of the 18th century the language of the nobility and intellectual elite was used as a vehicle in the establishment of a dialogue with Europe and to promote different visions of the Russian nation. It is in this context that Russian

[1] See Sergei Karp and Larry Wolff (eds). *Le mirage russe au XVIIIe siècle*. Ferney: Voltaire. CIEDS, 2001.

francophone poets, including Count Andrei Shuvalov and Prince Aleksandr Belosel'skii, developed a positive image of a frenchified Russian perfectly at home in the European context, while Vasilii Naryshkin in his *Ressouvenirs sur la Russie, écrits entre Aix La Chapelle et Spa* (*Remembrances on Russia written between Aachen and Spa*, 1791), emphasises Russian specificity[2] the 'individual character' and 'value' of the nation which must distance itself from Western reality.[3] These two perceptions of Russia were, as we know, to be developed and consolidated in the following century by the Westernisers and the Slavophiles,[4] within which women did not occupy a significant place. However, women did contribute to the discourse on the Russian nation and its place among other nations.

While men wrote about the Russian nation in both French and Russian, women's contributions to this discourse appear more often in French. Female-authored Russian-language texts have not yet come to light. Women's texts, most of which are poems, are generally limited to declarations of patriotism and attachment to the official religion.

## Defence and representation of Russia

It was during the second half of the 18th century that women entered the debate about the nation. Members of the social elite, when they took up the pen in both published and manuscript texts, more often than not addressed themselves to European readers. Empress Catherine II (1729-1796) was a key figure amongst these women.[5] From the moment that German-born Catherine II came to power in Russia, she established herself at once as an enlightened sovereign, follower of Montesquieu and Voltaire, and as a Russian patriot, the mother of the nation. She considered Russia to be part of Europe, and its people as no different to the rest of humanity. She defended the Russian people with a maternal zeal, regularly opposing the representation of Russia

---

[2] Elena Gretchanaia, *"Je vous parlerai la langue de l'Europe (...)". La francophonie en Russie (XVIIIe-XIXe siècles)*. Bruxelles: P.I.E. Peter Lang, 2012: 51-72, 81-4.

[3] Alexey Naryshkin, *Ressouvenirs sur la Russie, écrits entre Aix La Chapelle et Spa*, Riga [Johann Friedrich Hartknoch], 1791: 4.

[4] See Nicholas Riasanowsky, *Russia and the West in the teaching of the Slavophiles*. Goucester Mas: P. Smith. 1965; and Vera Tolz, "The West" in William Leathebarrow and Derek Offord (eds). *A History of Russian Thought*. Cambridge: Cambridge University Press, 2010: 197-216.

[5] See online at http://neww.huygens.knaw.nl/authors/show/201.

as an uncivilised country, and also expressed inflexible opposition to the alleged superiority of French culture. The dispute with the West that emerges in letters from the Empress to her French correspondents, reached its height in *Antidote*, published anonymously in French in St Petersburg in 1770 and in Amsterdam between 1771 and 1772. This was a virulent critique of the Abbé Chappe d'Auteroche's *Le Voyage en Sibérie* (*A Journey into Siberia*, 1768), which depicts a vision of Russia that the Empress found unacceptable. Catherine II defends her country and people in terms reminiscent of one of her letters to Voltaire. On 31 March 1770, the year of publication of *Antidote,* she wrote to Voltaire: "When Europe becomes better acquainted with this nation, many misconceptions and prejudices about Russia will be reviewed."[6] The same assertion is central to *Antidote*: "There is no nation extant, which has been abused with more falsity, absurdity, and impertinence than the Russians."[7]

In her attempt to confute Chappe d'Auteroche, the Empress mocks the "nation that is guilty of showing arrogance towards all that is unlike it." In denigrating the French, it is from Voltaire that she borrows the term "Welches":

> Russia has been a barrier to the domination of the Welches, and as they cannot prevent it, they can only revenge themselves by shewing it in a false light. Poor, pitiful, mean revenge! what can be expected from it?[8]

Towards the end of her book the Empress abandons the mocking tone that has been her weapon of choice and breaks off very seriously, evidently addressing her conclusion to the whole of Europe:

> Whatever [Chappe] says, we are not and will never be cruel or barbaric. [...] Let us continue to cover ourselves with glory and to disregard the envious. It is better to be envied than pitied.[9]

---

[6] Alexandre Stroev (ed.). *Voltaire-Catherine II. Correspondance, 1763-1778*. Paris: Non-lieu, 2006: 114 (my translation of all quotations).
[7] Hélène Carrère-d'Encosse (ed.). *L'Impératrice et l'Abbé : Un duel littéraire inédit entre Catherine II et l'Abbé Chappe d'Auteroche*. Paris : Fayard, 2003: 334.
[8] *Ibid.*, 335.
[9] *Ibid.*, 563.

Princess Ekaterina Dashkova (1743-1810)[10] takes up a similar position to Catherine II in her defence and representation of Russia. In her memoirs entitled *Mon Histoire* (*My History*; written between 1804 and 1805),[11] she depicts herself travelling across Europe as a shining representative of Russia, a country which, in her opinion, is in no way inferior to Europe and, in certain areas, even surpasses it.[12] As an example, Dashkova argues that "Learning had travelled from Greece to Kiev much earlier than it had to many a European nation now so quick to saddle the Russians with the name of barbarians."[13] Russia, as Dashkova notes, was not actually in need of the reforms of Peter the Great, who wanted to bring his Empire 'closer to Europe' because, she says, "when a mass as great as my homeland is well governed, all that it could wish for is drawn to it."[14] While she highlights Russia's rich culture and the fact that the country was a force to be reckoned with long before the advent of Peter the Great, the Princess does not deny the benefits of European civilisation to which Catherine II had 'gently'[15] introduced Russia. Dashkova especially holds in high esteem the achievements of British civilisation, and in her character portraits presents a favourable image of her English, Scottish and Irish acquaintances.[16] She is proud that her son was educated at Edinburgh University and was able to share the fruits of British civilisation with his compatriots on his return to Russia.

[10] See online at http://neww.huygens.knaw.nl/authors/show/202

[11] Published for the first time in 1840 in English translation, and in 1881, in French: Ekaterina Dachkova, "Mon histoire" in *Arkhiv kniazia Vorontsova*. Bd. 21. Moscou: V. Gote, 1881.

[12] Dans ses articles de presse rédigés en russe, elle proteste énergiquement contre la gallomanie : "O smysle slova vospitanie" ("Ce que signifie le mot éducaion"), in *Sobesednik*, 1783, partie 2 : 12-28 ; "K gospodam izdatelam *Novyh ejemesiachnyh sochineniy*" ("Aux Messieurs les éditeurs de *La nouvelle revue mensuelle*"), in *Novye ejemesiachnye sochinenia*, 1792, n° 78 : 3-5; "Pismo k izdatelu *Russkogo vestnika*" ("Lettre à l'éditeur du *Messager russe*") in *Russkiy vestnik*, 1808, n°2 : 227-232.

[13] Ekaterina Dachkova, "Mon histoire" in *Arkhiv kniazia Vorontsova*. Bd. 21. Moscou: V. Gote, 1881: 124.

[14] *Ibid.*, 220.

[15] *Ibid.*, 221.

[16] *Ibid.*, 133-135, 170-171, 174-176.

## The emergence of the Russian myth

Francophone Russian women were active participants in the creation of national mythology. In the writings of the Slavophiles, the 19th century saw, as we know, the constitution of a providential image of Russia. The country was invested with a special and highly spiritual, even messianic, role to play among other nations.

It was the trials endured by Russia as well as its victories in the war against Napoleon that inspired Varvara-Juliana de Krüdener (1764-1824),[17] the spiritual guide of Emperor Alexander I, to suffuse the Russians with a legendary aura. But even before the Napoleonic era, she depicted Russians in an unusual light, cloaking them in mystery while at the same time declaring her predilection for France, a country that she considered to be "*her* true homeland."[18] She also begins her semi-autobiographical novel *Algithe* (written between 1802 and 1805) with the following statement: "I cannot say precisely to which nation I belong (...)".[19] Krüdener's reflections on French language and culture, which she spares the usual criticism, can be found in her manuscript of *Algithe*. She appears to share the opinion voiced by Louis-Antoine Caraccioli that "the Frenchman, without his frivolity, would not have charmed and seduced Europeans (...)":[20]

> Manners in France have benefited from courtesy itself, from elegance and delicacy [...]. The French, who have acquired, I do not know why, the reputation of the world's most frivolous people, have in both their tastes and pleasures, a solemnity that does not exist outside France. They detest what is grotesque and exaggerated; it is by more noble means we will contrive to please them.[21]

---

[17] See online at: http://neww.huygens.knaw.nl/authors/show/431.

[18] Julie de Krüdener, Letter to Mme de Staël of 29 July 1802, in Francis Ley, *Bernardin de Saint-Pierre, Madame de Staël, Chateaubriand, Benjamin Constant et Madame de Krüdener (d'après des documents inédits)*. Paris: Editions Montaigne, 1967: 124.

[19] Julie de Krüdener, *Autour de Valérie. Œuvres de Mme de Krüdener*. Michel Mercier, Francis Ley and Elena Gretchanaia (eds). Paris: Champion, 2007: 261.

[20] Louis-Antoine Caraccioli, *L'Europe française, par l'auteur de la Gaieté (...)*. Turin, et se trouve à Paris, chez la veuve Duchesne, 1776 : 265.

[21] Julie de Krüdener, *Algithe and different notes* in Russian State archives (GARF), fund 967, inventory 1, n° 19, f°37 v-38.

Her love for France does not, however, prevent Krüdener from composing, in 1797, a story promoting the Russian nation. In her text *Alexis, ou l'histoire d'un soldat russe (Alexis, or the history of a Russian soldier),*[22] the Russians, despite their reputation as 'dull-witted', are represented as possessing a share of "delicacy, generosity and virtue."[23] The narrator remarks of a Russian Count encountered in Italy: "[He] had a gentleness of character that was visible in his features and even in his voice. It seemed strange to me that an inhabitant of a harsh climate had nothing of its ruggedness."[24] The author draws attention to the rapid progress of civilisation in Russia: "I wondered that in a nation barely civilised, there were men enriched by the Enlightenment and progress for which the centuries had prepared the way so slowly in Europe."[25] The author criticises the French who know only the "courage and selfless devotion in battle" of the Russians, and ignore "the progress of other nations, and even their most common features."[26]

Krüdener's text presents a religious image of Russia that was soon to become an essential feature of the Russian myth. Alexis is a native of Vera (which in Russian means 'faith'), a village located on the banks of the Volga. The villagers are Old Believers (*Raskol'niki*) and religion is central to their lives: "sobriety, love of work and hospitality are their distinguishing features."[27] This image of provincial Russia contrasts with stereotypes formed under the influence of works such as Chappe d'Auteroche's *Voyage en Sibérie*: the people are remarkable for their "gaiety, grace, the spontaneous and sublime impulses that drive them, and that account for their never thinking of danger, and always coming to the aid of others".[28] A "spark" of imagination "exists in these eyes that are reminiscent of the peoples of the East".[29] The women "are svelte, slender as birches [...] a charming grace animates their features [...] their voices are melodic and entrancing".[30] Patriotism unites the people of this Russia, everything 'binds' the people to

[22] Published in 1834 in Odessa (Russia), in the French-language review *La Quêteuse*.
[23] Julie de Krüdener, *Alexis, ou l'histoire d'un soldat russe* in Russian State archives. GARF, fund 967, inventory 1, n° 18, f° 4.
[24] *Ibid.*, f° 3.
[25] *Ibid.*
[26] *Ibid.*
[27] *Ibid.*, f° 8.
[28] *Ibid.*, f° 4.
[29] *Ibid.*, f° 16.
[30] *Ibid.*

their homeland: "manners, customs, religious views, and even their harsh winters".[31]

The local colour presented in Krüdener's text is consistent with the widespread representation of Russia, but shows it in a positive light: superstitions ("they carefully avoid spilling salt, because this is a sinister omen"),[32] are seen as exotic and innocent and go hand in hand with hospitality and a desire to aid the destitute. Russian baths, that were the object of many caricatures depicting them as a place where the two sexes mix,[33] are represented as places of modesty.

Following the story of *Alexis* comes *Fragment,* which was clearly written at about the same time (the same Russian Count reappears; having travelled through part of Europe, he returns to his homeland with 'wise projects' to improve the lot of his peasants; some of the ideas in *Alexis* are repeated here).[34] Following in the footsteps of Voltaire and Diderot, Krüdener dedicated this text to the glory of Catherine II.

Catherine is depicted as patron of the arts and a wise legislator that works to improve the savage manners of her people. At the end of *Fragment*, Catherine II's attention is 'fixed' on Greece, and, alluding to the 'Greek project',[35] the conquest of Constantinople and the liberation and regeneration of Greece, Krüdener describes her as "full of indignation **against the** barbaric race that covers this earth."[36]

Krüdener's text shows her thorough knowledge of Voltaire's works on Russia and his correspondence with Catherine II which was revealed to the public on the eve of the French Revolution. In addition, *Alexis* and *Fragment* attest to her comprehension of the importance of national mythology and her desire to contribute to it with the help of the French language.

Krüdener's essay *Le camp de Vertus (Camp of Vertus)*, was composed on the occasion of the military parade of the Russian army which took place in

---

[31] *Ibid.*, f° 6 v.

[32] *Ibid.*, f° 8.

[33] See Galina Kabakova Alexandre Stroev, "Les vouyageurs aux bains russes", in *Revue des études slaves*, 1997, n° 64/4: 505-518.

[34] A particular passage worthy of comparison with the one in *Alexis* cited above: "She [Catherine] had spread Enlightenment and knowledge for which the centuries had prepared the way so slowly in Europe (...)"; "a nation barely civilized", Julie de Krüdener, *Alexis*: f° 27 v-28.

[35] See Hugh Ragsdale, "Evaluating the Tradition of Russian Aggression: Catherine II and the Greek Project" in *Slavonic and East European Review*. 66(1) 1988: 91-117.

[36] *Ibid.*, f° 28 v.

Champagne in September 1815. Published in Paris, it is dedicated to victory in the war against Napoleon. Krüdener emphasises the fact that it is religious sentiment which inspires a providential mission in the Russians, namely that of ensuring their salvation, as well as that of others: "And from this distant land, that we knew only in fable, came simple people [...] who had not yet abandoned the God that saved them."[37] Russian victory is interpreted "as the introduction of the Universe in other times, and as a living preface to this sacred history that must lead to universal regeneration."[38] *Le camp de Vertus* was published at a time when Krüdener was enjoying great fame in both Europe and Russia. Emperor Alexander I was in constant contact with her in Paris and she hosted many politicians and men and women of letters at her Paris salon.[39]

Her mysticism is in turn seen as a manifestation of Russian religion, especially because commitment to religion becomes an increasingly essential feature to the image of Russians. Germaine de Staël particularly emphasises this trait in her book *Dix années d'exil (Ten Years' Exile*) written in 1812/13 and published in 1818. In one of her letters of October 1815, she calls Krüdener "the harbinger of a great religious era that is preparing for the human race."[40] The French language used by Krüdener permits her to deploy throughout Europe the enigmatic and powerful spirituality of a country too long unknown.

Probably about 1817/18 she writes a type of hymn preserved in her archives, where she urges, in French, Russia and its people to bless and praise the Lord. She gives here a poetic overview of different regions of this vast empire (steppes of Crimea, marshes of Finland, Caucasus mountains, snows of Siberia) and invokes its people (Russians, Kalmyks, Kyrgyzs, Tatars, Circassians) to become, like David, inspired cantors.[41] All these vast lands give Russians an exceptional spiritual strength and excite them "not to be deterred and running in ways pleasing to the Lord."

---

[37] Julie de Krüdener, *Le Camp de Vertus*. Paris: Le Normant, 1815 : 3-4.
[38] *Ibid.*, 7.
[39] See Francis Ley, *Madame de Krüdener. 1762-1824. Romantisme et Sainte Alliance.* Paris: Honoré Champion, 1994.
[40] *Ibid.*, 337.
[41] Julie de Krüdener, [*Religious writings*], in GARF, fund 967, inventory 1, n° 49: f° 51 52 v.

## For the union of nations

The desire for fusion of different cultures marks the writings in French of the Princess Zinaida Volkonskaya (1789-1862)[42] who receives a brilliant European education, has great interest in the history of Russia and finally converts to Catholicism, lives and dies in Italy. before ending her life in Italy One of Volkonskaya's poems, probably written in 1812, is addressed to Germaine de Staël, whom the Princess knew and apparently met in August of the same year in St Petersburg, as evidenced by a letter from Staël to her.[43] In this poem, the Princess follows the author of *Corinne* in depicting the opposition of the South and North, uses the European stereotype of the cold climate of Russia and deploys great enthusiasm for Italy. The stereotypical view of Russia, as not favorable to the arts, contains, however implicitly, the suggestion that its inhabitants are sensitive to poetic harmony and are able to cultivate the flowers of poetry:

I salute you, beautiful Italy! you whose adornment
Meets every donation disheveled in nature,
And consists alternately
In flowers of remembrances, regrets and love!
[...]
I have not, like you, experienced the noble influence
Of these enchanting edges,
In the bosom of frosts passed my childhood.
For us the Sun is not the God of poetry,
Lute languishes without harmony.
Thus the flower blooming in the middle of winter
Exhales in vain a breath of life.[44]

In 1819, Princess Volkonskaya published in French in Moscow *Quatres nouvelles (Four stories)*. In the years preceding this publication, she travelled to Europe where her musical and artistic talents were highly recognised, lived in Paris and returned to Russia in the spring of 1817.

---

[42] See online at http://neww.huygens.knaw.nl/authors/show/1352.

[43] Bayara Aroutunova, *Lives in letters. Princess Zinaida Volkonskaya and her correspondence*. Columbus (Ohio): Slavica Publishers. Inc., 1994 : 43-48.

[44] "À Madame de Staël en lui renvoyant Corinne" ("To Madame de Staël sending back Corrinne to her"), in *Archives d'Apollon* [album manuscript of the baron Alexander Stroganov], 16, Tomsk State University Library, Department of manuscripts and rare books.

Three of her 'four stories', 'American', 'African' and 'Asian', are written in the mode of exoticism, and present innocent savages. The fourth 'European story?, *Laure*, describes the worldly life in Montpellier (Volkonskaia made a trip in the south of France in 1816), where "three distinguished travelers" arrive.

The author shows a perfect harmony that unites a Parisian, an Englishman and a Russian despite the difference in their characters that bear the imprint of their nations. The Parisian cultivates literature, arts and gallantry. The author reveals his "noble thoughts, his natural manners, his heart unable to feel a great passion."[45] The Englishman is concerned about the affairs of his parliament. The Russian "inspires the greatest curiosity",[46] and gives place to a stereotypical vision, at least in the French province, of his country and its inhabitants:

> The Russian name has the advantage of producing even in the nineteenth century, in the south of Europe, the same curiosity that occurred two centuries earlier: they consider there that the Russians have something unique and somewhat barbaric, which awakens attention.[47]

According to common saying, "Russia is a country that is covered with ice during the twelve months of the year."[48] Unlike the two other friends, the Russian is designated only by his first name (apparently so as not to clutter the French text with Russian names deemed too complicated for the French ear), and is called Count Vladimir.The count wants to be Russian. But in so doing he adopts the stereotype of Russian warriors present in European consciousness:

> He was struck by the ridicule that some of his compatriots were leaving the warrior and simple manners which are natural for them, and copying strictly the ways of one or another nation. He suffered to see them this assignment which contrasted so strongly with the Russian national character, and told them they had become caricature of those they wanted to emulate. [...] Vladimir had kept the simple

[45] Zinaida Volkonskaya, *Quatre nouvelles. Par Mme la princesse Zénéide Volkonsky, née P[rince]sse Béloselsky*. Moscou: de l'imprimerie d'Auguste Semen, 1819: 68.
[46] *Ibid.*, 75.
[47] *Ibid.*
[48] *Ibid.*, 76.

> manners of a soldier, he had sought to embellish and not to disguise them, convinced that imitation is below the dignity of man.[49]

If Count Vladimir wants to keep 'the Russian national character', he also demonstrates his spontaneous and natural insertion, outside 'servile imitation', in the French cultural context. The Montpellier society hoped "to find in him a meeting of all the tribes of Siberia",[50] but he was "amiable, gay, somewhat contentious, and more Parisian than the Parisians themselves for the urbanity of his language".[51]

Concerned with the idea of the meeting of Russian and European cultures, Princess Volkonskaya writes in French *Tableau slave du cinquième siècle (Description of Slavs in the fifth century)*, published in Paris in 1824 anonymously. It is a kind of historical novel based on Karamzin's *History of the Russian State*. In her preface, the author insists on the novelty of her representation of the Slavs. She shows "in a simple framework what has survived of their occupations, their customs, their manners and their worship."[52]

The author wants to find in the past the traits that make up the image of her countrymen, and one of these essential features becomes "attachment to religion."[53] Volkonskaya recalls that the Slavs and other nations in Europe have Asia as a common cradle, and that the Slavs have throughout history gone through the same evolution of morals as other people enjoying the progress of civilization. Wild tastes of 'Slavs of the forest', who were shy and knew nothing but "fight, conquer, steal",[54] are eventually replaced by the gentle manners, the delicate feelings and sociability of 'Slavs of the plain' who embodied the European civilization outside of Europe.

*Tableau slave du cinquième siècle* had several reviews that prove the author's name did not remain unknown to French critics.[55] It is mentioned in Stendhal's report published in *Courrier anglais* on 1 July 1824, which is not benevolent. Stendhal criticizes mercilessly the novel (though he considers it

---

[49] *Ibid.*, 69-70.
[50] *Ibid.*, 81
[51] *Ibid.*, 69.
[52] Zinaïda Volkonskaia, *Tableau slave du cinquième siècle*. Paris : chez la Veuve Renard, libraire, 1824 : vj.
[53] *Ibid.*, ix.
[54] *Ibid.*,177.
[55] N.V. Saykina, *Moskovskiy literaturnyi salon kniagini Zinaidy Volkonskoy (Princess Zinaida Volkonskaya's literary salon in Moscow)*. Moscou: Naouka, 2005: 26-30.

curious) by linking its defects with the savagery that he considered to be a typical characteristic of the Russians.[56] In a report published in the *Journal encyclopedique* Marc-Antoine Jullien is more lenient towards the author of *Tableau slave* whose name he also knew and regretted he could not name. He appreciates "the delicacy and freshness of the style, always pure, elegant, harmonious" saying that this "foreign lady" is "the worthy rival of our French ladies most practiced in the art of writing."[57] In reports published in *Drapeau blanc*, *Diable boiteux* and *Gazette de France*, the novel of Princess Volkonskaya is also appreciated.[58] In 1825 the Russian translation appeared, and in 1826, a Polish adaptation of *Tableau slave* was published.[59] In 1824, Volkonskaya's salon in Moscow became a meeting place for writers, artists and musicians of Europe and Russia. She was called the Corinne of the North, and was encouraged to take the vacant place of the Russian woman writer. Despite publishing some poems in Russian, she did not fill this position and remains best known as a salon hostess.

## Conclusion

The Russian women's francophone writings participate in presenting Russia to foreign readers and contribute to reflections on the position of this country in the concert of nations. Patriotism and contribution to the formation of national mythology do not lead, as it is often the case in men's writings, to distrust of the Western model.

This distrust is expressed openly in the letters of the playwright Denis Fonvizin written in Russian during his trip to France in 1777-1778, in a travel diary (1783-1786), written in Russian and French, by Alexey Bobrinski, natural son of Catherine II, in the mentioned Naryshkin's *Ressouvenirs sur la Russie*, or in the *Memoir on Ancient and Modern Russia* (1811) written in Russian by Nikolay Karamzin. Karamzin addressed his manuscript *Memoir* to Alexander I, and its numerous copies circulated in Russia (it was only

[56] Stendhal. "Tableau slave du cinquième siècle" in *Courrier anglais. New Monthly Magazine*. vol. 2. Paris : Le Divan, 1935: 182-3.

[57] Marc-Antoine Jullien, "Tableau slave du cinquième siècle" in *Revue encyclopédique, ou analyse raisonnée des productions les plus remarquables dans les sciences, les arts industriels, la littérature et les beaux-arts*. vol. XII, 1824: 709.

[58] N.V. Saykina, *Moskovskiy literaturnyi salon kniagini Zinaidy Volkonskoy*: 27-30.

[59] *Ladovid i Miliada, czyli początek Kijowa. Obraz Słowian piątego wieku*, Warszawa, 1826, in *Ibid.*, 37.

published in 1988). Before, in his *Letters of a Russian traveler* (1791-1792), Karamzin, a sentimentalist writer who advocated the feminization of the literature of his country,[60] presents himself as a 'Russian European' who reconciles patriotism with admiration for Europe. He seems to follow the example of the French cultural model, which reserved an important role in the creation of a harmonious atmosphere within society for women in his *Letters of a Russian traveler* In 1803, as the official historian, Karamzin gradually adopts a more rigid position and takes the side of those thinkers who value Russia before opening to Europe, as Alexander Shishkov, author of the famous essay against the use of foreign words by Russians (*Treatise on the Old and New Styles of the Russian Language*, 1803).

We can conclude that women first represent themselves in their writings as Russian Europeans, and this position remains theirs later on. Sensitive to the often fierce criticism of Russia by European writers, particularly the French, Catherine II and Princess Dachkova defend the Russian nation without claiming its exclusivity and consider it as equal to other European nations. They adopt the Enlightenment universalist project and the valorization of their country and its young civilization outlined by philosophers such as Fontenelle and Voltaire. Describing the 'barbaric' people as a healthy nation animated by a real faith, and for that reason alone able to regenerate the whole of Europe, Varvara-Juliana Krüdener does not abandon her love for France and the French, whose national specificities she defines with sympathy. The desire for the union of nations is especially evident in the texts of ZinaidaVolkonskaya who, like other Russian women, uses largely national stereotypes, adopting and transforming them into a vision of the united and cognate nations. Based in her *Tableau slave du cinquième siècle* on the *History* of Karamzin, she does not insist on the particular way of Russia, but showing the progress of civilization, anticipates the movement of Westernism, which unlike Slavophilism, saw Russia as a country that pursued the same way as other European countries. The francophone Russian women have succeeded well, relying in part on the writings of men, to offer a more balanced view on nations.

[60] See Judith Vowels, "The 'Feminisation' of Russian Literature: Women, Language and Literature in Eighteenth-Century Russia" in Toby W. Clyman and Diana Greene (eds). *Women Writers in Russian Literature*. Westport, London: Praeger, 1994: 35-60; and Gitta Hammarberg, "The Feminine Chronotope and Sentimentalist Canon Formation" in Anthony G Cross and Gerald S. Smith (eds). *Literature, Lives and Legality in Catherine's Russia*. Nottingham: Astra Press, 1994: 103-120.

*Translated by Emilie Murphy, Lucia Bergamasco, Elena Gretchanaia*

## Select Bibliography

### A. Primary Sources

*Antidote, ou Examen du mauvais livre superbement imprimé, intitulé Voyage en Sibérie*. 1770. Saint-Pétersbourg: [imprimerie de l'Académie des sciences]. Amsterdam: chez Marc-Michel Rey, (1771/72).

Bobrinskiy, Alexey. 2003. *Dnevnik [Diary].* in Kozlov, Sergei. *Russkiy puteshestvennik epokhi Prosveshcheniia [Russian Traveler at the age of Enlightenment]*. Saint Petersburg : Istoricheskaya illustratsiia. vol. 1: 356-447.

Caraccioli, Louis-Antoine. 1776. *L'Europe française, par l'auteur de la Gaieté (...)*. Turin, et se trouve à Paris, chez la veuve Duchesne.

Dachkova, Ekaterina. 1881. "Mon histoire" in *Arkhiv kniazia Vorontsova*. Bd. 21. Moscou: V. Gote.

Fonvizine, Denis. 1995. *Lettres de France (1777-1778)*. Grosse, Henri, Jacques Proust and Piotr Zaborov. (eds). Paris : CNRS-éditions; Oxford: Voltaire Foundation.

Jullien, Marc-Antoine. 1824. "Tableau slave du cinquième siècle" in *Revue encyclopédique, ou analyse raisonnée des productions les plus remarquables dans les sciences, les arts industriels, la littérature et les beaux-arts*. vol. XII.

Krüdener, Julie de. 1815. *Le Camp de Vertus*. Paris : Le Normant.

—. *Alexis, ou l'histoire d'un soldat russe*. in Russian State archives (GARF), fund 967, inventory 1, n° 18.

—. *Algithe and different notes*. In Russian State archives (GARF), fund 967, inventory 1, n° 19.

—. Letter to Mme de Staël of 29 July 1802, in Francis Ley. *Bernardin de Saint-Pierre, Madame de Staël, Chateaubriand, Benjamin Constant et Madame de Krüdener (d'après des documents inédits)*. Paris: Editions Montaigne, 1967: 124.

—. [*Religious writings*]. In GARF, fund 967, inventory 1, n° 49.

[Naryshkin, Alexey]. 1791. *Ressouvenirs sur la Russie, écrits entre Aix La Chapelle et Spa*, Riga [Johann Friedrich Hartknoch].

Pipes, Richard. 1959. *Karamzin's Memoir on Ancient and Modern Russia: A Translation and Analysis (Russian Research Center Studies; 33)*. Cambridge, MA: Harvard University Press.

Stendhal, 1935. "Tableau slave du cinquième siècle" in *Courrier anglais. New Monthly Magazine*. vol. 2. Paris : Le Divan.

Volkonskaya, Zinaida. 1819. *Quatre nouvelles. Par Mme la princesse Zénéide Volkonsky, née P[rince]sse Béloselsky*. Moscou: de l'imprimerie d'Auguste Semen,

Volkonskaia, Zinaïda. 1824. *Tableau slave du cinquième siècle*. Paris : chez la Veuve Renard, libraire.

—. 1865. *Œuvres choisies de la princesse Zénéide Volkonsky*. Paris and Carlsruhe : W. Hasper.

Stroev, Alexandre (ed.). 2006. *Voltaire-Catherine II. Correspondance, 1763-1778*. Paris: Non-lieu.

## B. Secondary Sources

Aroutunova, Bayara. 1994. *Lives in letters. Princess Zinaida Volkonskaya and her correspondence*. Columbus (Ohio): Slavica Publishers, Inc.

Carrère-d'Encosse, Hélène (ed.). 2003. *L'Impératrice et l'Abbé : Un duel littéraire inédit entre Catherine II et l'Abbé Chappe d'Auteroche*. Paris : Fayard.

Gretchanaia, Elena. 2012. *"Je vous parlerai la langue de l'Europe (...)". La francophonie en Russie (XVIIIe-XIXe siècles)*. Bruxelle: P.I.E. Peter Lang.

Hammarberg, Gitta. 1994. "The Feminine Chronotope and Sentimentalist Canon Formation" in Cross, Anthony G. and Gerald S. Smith (eds). *Literature, Lives and Legality in Catherine's Russia*. Nottingham: Astra Press: 103-120.

Karp, Sergei and Larry Wolff (eds). 2001. *Le mirage russe au XVIIIe siècle*. Ferney: Voltaire. CIEDS.

Krüdener, Julie de. 2007. *Autour de Valérie. Œuvres de Mme de Krüdener*. Mercier, Michel, Francis Ley, and Elena Gretchanaia (eds). Paris: Champion.

Ley, Francis. 1994. *Madame de Krüdener. 1762-1824. Romantisme et Sainte-Alliance*. Paris: Honoré Champion.

Ragsdale, Hugh. 1988. "Evaluating the Tradition of Russian Aggression: Catherine II and the Greek Project." in *Slavonic and East European Review*. 66(1): 91-117.

Riasanowsky, Nicholas. 1965. *Russia and the West in the teaching of the Slavophiles*. Goucester Mas: P. Smith.

Tolz, Vera. 2010. "The West" in Leathebarrow, William and Derek Offord (eds). *A History of Russian Thought*. Cambridge: Cambridge University Press: 197-216.

Saykina, N.V. 2005. *Moskovskiy literaturnyi salon kniagini Zinaidy Volkonskoy* Moscou: Naouka.

Vowles, Judith. 1994. "The 'Feminisation' of Russian Literature : Women, Language and Literature in Eighteenth-Century Russia" in Clyman, Toby W. and Diana Greene (eds). *Women Writers in Russian Literature*. Westport, London: Praeger: 35-60.

# Regina Maria Roche and Ireland: A Problematic Relationship[1]

*Begoña Lasa Alvarez*

ABSTRACT At the end of the 18th century, when Ireland was treated as a colony, Irish women writers had to negotiate a problematic context when producing their literary works and tackling Irish themes. This is the case of Regina Maria Roche: her Gothic fiction shows the writer's eagerness to offer her audience a positive vision of Ireland, while also using relevant, historical facts which affected Europeans, and, by extension, Irish and British society. The aim of her contribution was to familiarise British and other foreign readers with what was happening in Ireland.

A CONTEMPORARY OF THE IRISH NOVELIST Regina Maria Roche, the well-known German writer Johan Gottfried Herder, argued that "every nation is one people, having it's own national form, as well as it's own language [sic]".[2] At the end of the 18th century, when the idea of nation started to be considered a necessary social, political and historical entity, Ireland had been dispossessed of what Herder deemed to be the inherent features of a people that were considered necessary for constituting a nation. On the contrary, it was treated as a colony. Irish writers, particularly Irish women writers, had to negotiate this problematic context when producing their literary works, and principally when tackling Irish themes.[3] Novels in particular usually express and help to describe a nation, and although it is often only vaguely sensed by the readers, "novels are the source of some of our most influential ideas and

---

[1] This paper has been possible thanks to the research project "O papel da muller na prensa inglesa no inicio da idade moderna: estudo sincrónico e diacrónico" (PGIDT07PXIB212149PR), funded by the Galician Government (Xunta de Galicia). This grant is hereby gratefully acknowledged.

[2] Johann Gottfried Herder *Outlines of a Philosophy of the History of Man*. T. Churchill (tr.) (1784), New York: Bergman Pub, 1966: 166. First published in London in 1800.

[3] Clíona Ó Gallchoir, *Maria Edgeworth. Women, Enlightenment and Nation*. Dublin: University College Dublin Press, 2005.

expressions of national identity [...and] play a key part in the transmission and dissemination of national images, memories, and myths".[4] Roche illustrates this fact. She had to deal with these issues in the narratives she set in her homeland, and although they are not discussed in depth, the main social, political and economical concerns of her country are present – namely, the consequences of Protestant ascendency. But in the case of this particular writer, there are other aspects to bear in mind, mainly those that related to her apparent financial difficulties.

Very little is known about Roche's life. However, one of the few records we have indicates that she had to ask for support from the Royal Literary Fund. In our opinion, this fact suggests that she wrote for bread, like many other women writers before her, such as Aphra Behn and Frances Sheridan, or her contemporaries, such as Charlotte Smith and Mary Wollstonecraft. Consequently, Roche appropriated the most popular genres and topics of her time in order to gain the attention of publishers and also readers' affection, which she got in her time, as the wide circulation of her novels demonstrates.[5] This obituary published in *The Gentleman's Magazine* illustrates this: "This distinguished writer had retired from the world and the world had forgotten her. But many young hearts, now old must remember the effect upon them of her graceful and touching compositions; and imagination once excited by her skill will yet acknowledge her loss with melancholy feeling of regret".[6]

---

[4] Patrick Parrinder, *Nation & Novel. The English Novel from Its Origins to the Present Day*. Oxford: Oxford University Press, 2006: 1, 6.

[5] Begoña Lasa Álvarez, "Regina Maria Roche, an Eighteenth-Century Irish Writer on the Continent and Overseas." in Marisol Morales Ladrón and Juan F. Elices Agudo (eds). *Glocal Ireland: Current Perspectives on Literature and the Visual Arts*, Newcastle upon Tyne: Cambridge Scholars Publishing, 2011: 51-61.

[6] Natalie Schroeder, "Regina Maria Roche, Popular Novelist, 1789-1834: The Rochean Canon" in *Papers of the Bibliographical Society of America* (73) 1979: 462. Taking into account that Regina Maria Roche is one of many women writers who enjoyed enormous popularity in their time, but nowadays have fallen into oblivion, it might be interesting to mention briefly some aspects of her life. Regina Maria Roche was born in Waterford, in the south of Ireland in 1764. She moved to Dublin as a child, where she later married Ambrose Roche around 1794, and the couple moved to England. Her two most successful novels, *The Children of the Abbey* (1796) and *Clermont* (1798), were issued at the end of the 1790s. However, she interrupted her literary career for seven years, probably due to financial difficulties, since she asked the Royal Literary Fund for economic aid, which she received. She then published eleven novels set in Ireland, such as *The Munster Cottage Boy* (1820), *Bridal of*

As a consequence, and if she really wanted to please her readers, her obvious option was Gothic fiction. However, Roche's novels are better defined as Gothic romances, a particularly alluring genre in this period which has been mainly connected with those who borrowed books from circulating libraries – in particular, that is, unsophisticated and undemanding readers. Critics were extremely belligerent with respect to the detrimental effects of circulating libraries on readers, as can be observed in the periodical press of the period, which considered the reading materials of these libraries to be "lumbering trash".[7] Moreover, their position was even more aggressive regarding women readers, given their fragility and delicacy: "books are instructive, they teach [young girls] how to avoid the wicked arts of men. But by no means suffer them to go to the Circulating Library, rank poison is to be found by every girl who subscribes to it".[8] However, the emotional appeal of Gothic fiction was unavoidable, a fact that put this genre ahead in relation to another fashionable genre among readers during the second half of the eighteenth century: the sentimental novel. This mixture of genres "provides opportunity for projected fears and wishes, for fantasies that bear indirectly yet powerfully upon the emotions of women," while at the same time, "also affords the security of a rational and moral frame that appeals to its audience's ideal of delicacy and reinforces the feminine acceptance of patriarchal ideals".[9] Curiously enough, a similar conservative aim was exhibited by the Minerva Press, the printing house where Roche published most of her narratives,[10] in a prospectus from

---

*Dunamore, and Lost and Won. Two tales* (1823), *The Tradition of the Castle* (1824), *The Castle Chapel* (1825), and *Contrast* (1828). She died in her home town of Waterford in 1845.

[7] *World*, Saturday, October 12, 1793.

[8] *Public Advertiser*, Saturday, August 25, 1787.

[9] Bette B. Roberts, *The Gothic Romance. Its Appeal to Women Writers & Readers in Late Eighteenth-Century England.* New York: Arno Press, 1980: 35.

[10] Although Irish, Roche published her fictional texts in London, as did many other Irish writers, as the publishing industry was in clear decay in Ireland. Rolf Loeber and Magda Stouthamer-Loeber point out two main causes for this decline, the 1798 rebellion and the Act of the Union between England and Ireland three years later. These two events affected Irish economy in general and also particularly the printing business. In the *Dublin Magazine; or, a General Repository of Philosophy, Belles-Lettres, and Miscellaneous Information* 1 (1820), this fact is stressed, even mentioning the very publishing house where Roche's novel was published: "Previous to the year 1800, printing flourished in Ireland […] sufficiently to afford us native productions […] [but since then] printing presses are no longer used in Ireland, except for the use of newspapers, or parish and county documents […] [Instead], Minerva

1784. The editor, William Lane, not only displayed in it every formal quality and merit of the texts issued from his presses, but also affirmed that "we have never introduced any subjects but such as are founded on the basis of virtue, and have tended to improve the understanding, and to amend the heart".[11]

The plots in Gothic fiction have conventionally been set in far-away and exotic places, like Ann Radcliffe's fiction, which is set in France, Spain or Italy. Nevertheless, Roche, unlike her contemporary, with whom she has often been compared,[12] sets most of her novels in Britain. She chooses not to leave her homeland and to demonstrate to her readers that similar risks and perils to those which Radcliffe's heroines are confronted with abroad may be experienced in their own society. This fact is clear in one of her most famous novels, *The Children of the Abbey*, which has been already been explored.[13] However, it is remarkable that in a novel entitled *The Tradition of the Castle; or, Scenes of the Emerald Isle*, which the reader would expect to be located exclusively in Ireland, the hero moves abroad, to France and Spain, a journey which occupies the first volume of the novel. Consequently, we are going to take this text, published in 1824, as the object of our analysis, focusing

---

Presses, vending every species of pernicious productions, will rise on the ruins of the honourable and independent publishers [...]" (qtd. in Loeber, Rolf and M. Stouthamer-Loeber, Magda. "The Publication of Irish Novels and Novelettes, 1750-1829: A Footnote on Irish Gothic Fiction" in *Cardiff Corvey: Reading the Romantic Text* 10 June 2003. Online at http://www.cf.ac.uk/encap/corvey/articles/cc10_n02.html. Likewise, Norman Vance adduces economic causes for this matter, arguing also meaningful consequences regarding Irish authors' writings: "The permanently depressed Irish economy and social structure could not fully sustain local writers at this period, so successful Irish writers needed to appeal to essentially the same British audience and British taste as their English and Scottish contemporaries", NormanVance, *Irish Literature since 1800*. Harlow: Longman, 2002: 47, a circumstance that deeply affected many Irish writers' literary career.

[11] Dorothy Blakey, *The Minerva Press 1790-1820*. London: The Bibliographical Society, 1939: 18.

[12] Natalie Schroeder, "*The Mysteries of Udolpho* and *Clermont*: The Radcliffean Encroachment on the Art of Regina Maria Roche" in *Studies in the Novel*. 12 (2). 1990: 131-143; and Anthony A. Mandal, "Revising the Radcliffean Model: Regina Maria Roche's *Clermont* and Jane Austen's *Northanger Abbey*" *in Cardiff Corvey: Reading the Romantic Text* 3 (September 1999). Online at http://www.cf.ac.uk/encap/corvey/ articles /cc 03_n03.html.

[13] Begoña Lasa Álvarez, "*The Children of the Abbey* (1796): A Nineteenth-Century Bestseller" in Susana Mla Domínguez Pena, Margarita Estévez Saá and Anne MacCarthy (eds). *Ireland in the Coming Time: New Insights on Irish Literature / Nuevas Incursiones en Literatura Irlandesa*. Weston, Florida: Netbiblo. 2006: 33-41.

chiefly on the role Roche's homeland plays in it. The choice of this novel among the literary works of the writer is quite obvious. In brief, the protagonist, Donaghue, a young man of Irish origin but brought up in England, shares the prejudiced view of the English against Ireland. However, once in his native land, thanks to love and his concern towards his fellow country people, he becomes a true Irishman. Anyone familiar with the fiction of this period set in Ireland will find this plot very similar to *The Wild Irish Girl. A National Tale* (1806), written by Sydney Owenson, better known as Lady Morgan, or to some of the novels by Maria Edgeworth, such as *Ennui* (1808) and *The Absentee* (1812). Both these authors are considered the founders of a female-authored genre named after the subtitle of Morgan's novel, the national tale, which shows an "explicitly public and political orientation".[14] Here, there is one of the influences present in Roche's text, but the hero's journeys abroad, as well as certain descriptions, allow her to handle other appealing aspects for her audience, such as castles and ruins, very much in line with Robert Maturin's *Melmoth the Wanderer* (1820). As we will see, both these trends significantly marked the way Roche tackled her native country in this novel.

It is, firstly, interesting to note the presence in the novel of a relevant historical fact which affected Europeans, and, by extension, Irish and British society, profoundly: the Napoleonic Wars, a topic that also relates to Roche's understanding of nation. As Derek Hand maintains, the motif of travel and journeying is a key feature in the Irish novel of the period.[15] This journeying happens not only in Ireland, and between Britain and Ireland, which might be expected in these narratives, but also includes travel abroad. Donaghue, the male protagonist of *The Tradition of the Castle,* travels abroad after various disappointments and takes a commission for Foreign Service, which allows Roche to explicitly allude to the war atmosphere on the Continent: "there being at this time a constant demand for fresh troops for the Continent".[16] As an officer, Donaghue takes part in the battle of Waterloo, where he is a witness to the horrors of war: "Never could Donaghue forget the dismal

---

[14] Ina Ferris, "The Irish Novel 1800-1829" in Richard Maxwell and Katie Trumpener (eds). *The Cambridge Companion to Fiction in the Romantic Period*. Cambridge: Cambridge University Press, 2008: 236.

[15] Derek Hand, *A History of the Irish Novel*. Cambridge: Cambridge University Press, 2011: 49.

[16] Regina Maria Roche, *The Tradition of the Castle; or, Scenes in the Emerald Isle*. London: Printed for A.K. Newman and Co, 1824: I, 276.

howlings, the dreadful screams, the shrieks of madness and despair, that here resounded round him".[17] During the battle, a meaningful episode takes place: Donaghue observes a British dragoon fighting against two French soldiers and he comes to his aid, and together they are able to defeat the enemies.[18] In her seminal work, *Britons. Forging the Nation 1707-1837*, Linda Colley has emphasised that Britishness as a national identity was forged with respect to the Other, particularly in response to conflicts.[19] Accordingly, the Napoleonic wars – when life is at stake – provide the adequate scenery where British and Irish soldiers might feel the necessity of being united to defeat a common enemy, that is a common Other.[20]

With this dramatic scene, Roche is implicitly alluding to the benefits of a union between Britain and Ireland, which in fact took place in 1800, when the Act of Union was passed. This transcendental moment in the history of Ireland, however, is explicitly mentioned at the very beginning of the novel. In this particular episode, as in the war scene, Roche seems to be in favour of the union of both countries, when Donaghue's parents argue about the Act of Union of Ireland and England, which has been passed. Mr O'Brien, Donaghue's father, has supported 'the glorious bill', as he calls it, since, in his opinion, Ireland requires to be taken under the paternal wing of England.[21] Mrs O'Brien is not so sure about the benefits of the union, and she expresses her apprehensions to her husband.[22] Later on, the main reason for her anxieties is explained: O'Brien, "like too many of his countrymen, had given himself up so totally to habits of indolence"[23] and is going to abandon his home and lands in Ireland in order to live in London. Thus, the character that embodies the viewpoint endorsing the union, Mr O'Brien, is not a

---

[17] *Ibid.*, 283.
[18] *Ibid.*, 279.
[19] Linda Colley, *Britons. Forging the Nation 1707-1837*. London: Pimlico (1992) 2003: 6.
[20] Religion was also crucial in forging the British identity, the Other being Catholicism, against which the British nation reinforced its distinctiveness: *Ibid.*, 7. In *The Tradition of the Castle* this antagonism is also present. Roche takes the protagonist and the novel plot to Spain during two chapters, which allows her to describe perilous inquisitorial rites and ceremonies, and to express her opinions on Catholic faith.
[21] Regina Maria Roche, *The Tradition of the Castle; or, Scenes in the Emerald Isle*. London: Printed for A.K. Newman and Co, 1824: I, 2.
[22] *Ibid.*, 4.
[23] *Ibid.*, 31.

positive character at all, a fact that undermines the favourable view of the union, since, apart from being indolent, he also loses all his possessions through gambling, before dying in strange circumstances. Mr O'Brien is also compared to his wife, a much more sensible character, who is capable of seeing both sides of the question and who is also closer to Ireland and the Irish and wants to inculcate these ideas to her son. In this regard, it is quite remarkable that such assumptions are voiced by a woman precisely at a moment when the active participation of women in political issues was barely admitted as a possibility,[24] even though she expresses her opinion at home and to her husband. By means of this episode, Roche might tell her audience to consider more attentively women and women's opinions, even about those issues which were out of their own sphere. However, Clíona Ó Gallchoir argues, in line with this, that precisely the lack of an Irish nation, after the Union, and the situation in which Ireland was placed facilitated the entrance of women into the public sphere as writers.[25] They became visible, as in the case of Maria Edgeworth and Lady Morgan, but also in the case of other less renowned writers, such as Roche. Thus, as writers they were given the opportunity to express their own opinions and also to be the voice of many women, who did not have the opportunity to express their ideas in public and who, like Mrs O'Brien, had a more accurate view of the circumstances of their country.

Interestingly, it is Mrs O'Brien who also brings up an important social issue at that time in Ireland, absenteeism, since, contrary to her husband, "it struck her that the continuance of the landholders on their estates was absolutely essential to the interests of the country".[26] In an earlier novel, *The Children of the Abbey*, the Irish novelist also referred to this matter (Roche *The Children* II, I, 4), explaining it and even offering an answer, the necessity of the landlords' presence in Ireland and particularly of their revenues.[27] In *The Tradition of the Castle*, Roche quotes the words of "a patriotic nobleman" to refer to the causes that have produced the impoverishment of Ireland:

---

[24] Clíona Ó Gallchoir, *Maria Edgeworth. Women, Enlightenment and Nation*. Dublin: University College Dublin Press, 2005: 4-5.

[25] *Ibid*,. 8.

[26] Regina Maria Roche, *The Tradition of the Castle; or, Scenes in the Emerald Isle*: I, 30.

[27] Begoña Lasa Álvarez, "*The Children of the Abbey* (1796): A Nineteenth-Century Bestseller": 38-9.

> It is calculated that about three-fourths of the landed proprietors of Ireland live out of it, to whom six millions of money are annually remitted; how, then, can it be said, that it is the same thing to the labouring poor, their landlords living on their states or in London! [...] their presence [in Ireland] would keep their tenants together, and thus frustrated the wicked schemes of those wretches, who are prowling about to take advantage of the idle and discontented. (1824: I, 40-1)

Curiously enough, Roche uses the word 'indolent' to define Mr O'Brien, a word used by Edgeworth years before to refer to Glenthorn, the protagonist of *Ennui* (1812), and even employing the same definition for this special feature in a person's character, that is, an indolent person is someone who does not think or act by oneself.[28] This clearly shows Edgeworth's influence on Roche, at least regarding this particular topic, which is not only present in this novel, but also in *The Absentee*, where Lord Colambre travels to his estates in Ireland to find the mismanagement caused by unscrupulous agents. Taking into consideration the distinction made by Ina Ferris,[29] between two models of nation in the novels of the period: the political and economical model, defended by Edgeworth, and the cultural model, more in line with Lady Morgan's narratives. Roche is closer to Edgeworth's reformist notions regarding the Irish estate. Nevertheless, in other elements of *The Tradition of the Castle*, where exoticism and Gaelic features are more relevant, it is obvious that Lady Morgan's texts, particularly *The Wild Irish Girl*, are in Roche's mind. Although the transfer of the legislature to London increased absenteeism and weakened the Irish economy, Roche and Edgeworth seem to envisage hope in their texts and, moreover, trust younger generations. Both writers' readers are introduced to a hero, who, as usually happens in the novels of this period, is a "cosmopolitan, non-Irish (usually English) character, whose progress westward, towards an acquaintance with Ireland, provides the main basis for plot and incident".[30] Particularly, the protagonist of *The Tradition of the Castle*, Donaghue, who has spent his youth in

[28] Maria Edgeworth, "Castle Rackrent" in *Tales and Novels by Maria Edgeworth*. London: Printed for Baldwin & Cradock, 1832, vol. I: 1.
[29] Ina Ferris, "The Irish Novel 1800-1829" in Richard Maxwell and Katie Trumpener (eds). *The Cambridge Companion to Fiction in the Romantic Period*, Cambridge: Cambridge University Press, 2008: 239-40.
[30] Joep Leerssen, *Remembrance and Imagination. Patterns in the Historical and Literary Representation of Ireland in the Nineteenth Century*. Indiana: University of Notre Dame Press and Cork: Cork University Press, 1997: 36.

England, is initially reluctant to move to Ireland since he shares the prejudices of fashionable English people against his native land, "representing it as a place from which every person of respectability had fled since the union".[31] However, he accompanies his mother to take care of their possessions there and when he arrives at his destination in Altoir-na-Greenie the amazing scenery throws him off his guard.

Roche takes the opportunity here to include some nuances of Gothic fiction. Thus, Donaghue's ancestral home is a castle because, as J.M.S. Tompkins[32] points out, it was simply felt to be a suitable home for a hero. Part of this mansion is in ruins, another favourite feature of these novelists, who in some way wanted "to combine in their architecture the attractions of tyrannous strength and of melancholy".[33] Accordingly, the ruins of Altoir-na-Greenie and the emotions they inspire are thus described:

> Yet, on these ruins, the eye, perhaps, rested with more delight, from the pleasing exercise they gave the imagination, that it would have done on the most magnificent structure of modern days; for in every breeze that sighs amidst these decaying piles, we seem to hear the voice of other days; and where is the soul that feels not a pleasing dread at the idea?[34]

The longing for the past mentioned in this quotation is related to another important feature of the Irish novel from this period: antiquarianism – that is, the inclusion of multiple allusions to Ireland's Gaelic past, which made this land an exotic place for foreign readers, particularly the British, to whom these novels were primarily addressed. This is why Irish fiction of this period, especially post-Union fiction, has been defined as explanatory.[35] The Irish writers themselves were aware of this fact, as Maria Edgeworth verbalizes in the preface to *Castle Rackrent* (1800). In this paratext she explains that she writes "to those who are totally unacquainted with Ireland", that is, to the "*ignorant* English reader", and consequently, she has included

---

[31] Regina Maria Roche, *The Tradition of the Castle; or, Scenes in the Emerald Isle*: I, 48.

[32] J.M.S. Tompkins, *The Popular Novel in England 1770-1800*. London: Constable & Co 1932: 265.

[33] *Ibid.*, 267.

[34] Regina Maria Roche, *The Tradition of the Castle; or, Scenes in the Emerald Isle*: I, 59.

[35] Joep Leerssen, *Remembrance and Imagination*: 33.

some notes.[36] The same strategy was used by Lady Morgan in *The Wild Irish Girl*, but in a more intense way, to the point that some scholars have considered the notes as the real interest of the novel.[37] Roche's *The Tradition of the Castle* does not enlighten the reader with paratextual elements, but it shows the writer's concern to offer to her audience a positive and nice vision of Ireland, although not such an explanatory one.

Donaghue's attitude in the novel and his progressive change from contempt to real affection towards his native land is decisive and clearly contributes to this positive view of Ireland. Interestingly, Donghue's view of Ireland gets even better when he meets the heroine of the novel. This young woman is called Eveleen Erin, a name that significantly refers to Ireland. As is known, both in English and Irish writings and representations, Ireland as a nation has frequently been allegorized as a woman.[38] The obvious conclusion is that Miss Erin might be the embodiment of Ireland in the novel. She is described as a flawless girl and Donaghue feels attracted to her from the first time they meet, but his vanity makes him treat her with contempt and when he proposes she rejects him. After being rejected, Donaghue leaves Ireland, but when he comes back he feels differently and has changed his mind completely. He arrives in Dublin harbour with various English visitors, with Ireland being an attractive alternative destination for tourists from the rest of the kingdom and even Europe at the time, and he realises that his country is unjustly regarded as a place "where there was hardly civilization".[39] As a consequence, he decides to make amends, focusing mainly on the improvement of the peasants' condition. Finally, after countless tribulations, as was expected of the genre, everything ends well, and Donoghue and Eveleen Erin get married. Thus, the implicit symbolic meaning is simple: if, due to his upbringing and education, Donogue represents English values, these are considered positive for Ireland, as long as Englishness does not mean superiority and accommodates Irish necessities, and Ireland, despite even in spite of all its merits and virtues, can benefit from them. This journey is not be an easy one, but the ending is worth it. As has been mentioned before, Lady Morgan's *The Wild Irish Girl* offers a similar plot, with an

---

[36] Maria Edgeworth, "Castle Rackrent" in *Tales and Novels by Maria Edgeworth*. London: Printed for Baldwin & Cradock, 1832, vol. I: xii.
[37] Joep Leerssen, *Remembrance and Imagination*: 55.
[38] C.L. Innes, *Woman and Nation in Irish Literature and Society 1880-1935*. Athens: The University of Georgia Press, 1993: 10.
[39] Regina Maria Roche, *The Tradition of the Castle*: II, 91.

allegorical union at the end of the novel between Horatio and Glorvina, who, like Donoghue and Eveleen, could stand for England and Ireland. The characterisation and development of both couples is analogous. Surprisingly, in both novels the female character does not have to change, while the male does. After closer observation and a better understanding, both men learn their lesson and achieve a more favourable view of the country. Consequently, in being represented as possessing a sound character, Ireland is a superior nation if compared to England, which is compelled to change; however, there is also a possible imperial reading of this idea, since, according to postcolonial theories, the Irish might also be viewed as passive, while the British are active.[40]

The concept of audience is also of crucial importance in such societies like that in Ireland, which has been touched by colonialism. Moreover, in the latter half of the eighteenth century "Ireland was invented as a response to certain British needs at a particular moment of the history of its imperial development",[41] and novels, in particular, provided an appropriate location for this invention. Accordingly, the Ireland described in these texts is heavily dependent on English notions of Irishness. What, then, does Roche offer as an image of Ireland as a nation in her novel? The message is quite clear. As other Irish women writers such as Lady Morgan or Maria Edgeworth did in this period, Ireland appears adorned with many positive features, it is a nice, beautiful, exotic, learned, sensible, spirited, but mistreated and misunderstood country, which requires to be managed and protected, but in the right way. Ireland has to be approached, appreciated and valued without prevailing prejudices. In addition, the recipient of the message is also relevant in a political and social context such as the one which emerged after the Act of Union. Accordingly, for a mainly British audience, what better is there than a man of Irish origin with an English upbringing like Donaghue to do so? Although the beginning of this particular relationship between the embodiments of Britain and Ireland is not easy, the Union is fruitful because both nations need each other. The colonial assumption is clear and the sad consequences are known. Maria Edgeworth herself was conscious of that

[40] Derek Hand, *A History of the Irish Novel*: 76.

[41] Gerry Smyth, *The Novel and the Nation. Studies in the New Irish Fiction*. London & Ann Arbor: Pluto Press, 1997: 44.

issue and even admitted that "Ireland loses her identity by a union with Great Britain",[42] a very significant assertion at that time.

Roche's readers did not choose to read *The Tradition of the Castle* or any of her novels because of this cause, and they were more interested in the protagonists' romantic fortunes and misfortunes; but, the subliminal political message is there. At that time, this national element did not receive much attention with regards to Roche's novels or indeed the texts of other Irish authors, such as Maria Edgeworths', which dealt with these issues more explicitly. However, these writers and the wide circulation of their texts, with numerous editions and translations, possibly did more than the discourse of politicians to familiarise British and other foreign readers with what was happening in Ireland.

[42] Maria Edgeworth, "Ennui" in *Tales and Novels by Maria Edgeworth*, London: Printed for Baldwin & Cradock. 1832, vol. VI: xiii.

## Select Bibliography

Blain, Virginia; Patricia Clements and Isobel Grundy. 1990. "Regina Maria Roche." In *The Feminist Companion to Literature in English*. London: B.T. Batsford Ltd.

Blakey, Dorothy. 1939. *The Minerva Press 1790-1820*. London: The Bibliographical Society.

Colley, Linda. 2003. (1992). *Britons. Forging the Nation 1707-1837*. London: Pimlico.

Edgeworth, Maria. 1812. "The Absentee" in *Tales of Fashionable Life*. Vols. V & VI. In six volumes. London: Printed for Johnson & Co.

—. 1832. "Castle Rackrent" in *Tales and Novels by Maria Edgeworth*. In eighteen volumes. Vol. I. London: Printed for Baldwin & Cradock.

—. 1832. "Ennui" in *Tales and Novels by Maria Edgeworth*. In eighteen volumes. Vol. VI. London: Printed for Baldwin & Cradock.

Ferris, Ina. 2008. "The Irish Novel 1800-1829." in *The Cambridge Companion to Fiction in the Romantic Period*, Maxwell, Richard and Katie Trumpener (eds). Cambridge: Cambridge University Press: 235-249.

Hand, Derek. 2011. *A History of the Irish Novel*. Cambridge: Cambridge University Press.

Herder, Johann Gottfried. 1966. (1784). *Outlines of a Philosophy of the History of Man*. (tr. T. Churchill. *Ideen zur Philosophie der Geschichte der Menschheit*) First Published in London in 1800. New York: Bergman Pub.

Hodinott, Emma. "A Biography of Regina Maria Roche" in *The Corvey Project at Sheffield Hallam University*. Online: Internet (02/02/2004) http://www.shu.ac.uk/schools/cs/corvey/corinne/Corinne%20authors71 Roche/Roche%20biography.htm.

Innes, C.L. 1993. *Woman and Nation in Irish Literature and Society 1880-1935*. Athens: The University of Georgia Press.

Lasa Álvarez, Begoña. 2006. "*The Children of the Abbey* (1796): A Nineteenth-Century Bestseller" in *Ireland in the Coming Time: New Insights on Irish Literature / Nuevas Incursiones en Literatura Irlandesa*. Domínguez Pena, Susana Mla., Margarita Estévez Saá, and Anne MacCarthy (eds). Weston, Florida: Netbiblo: 33-41.

—. 2011. "Regina Maria Roche, an Eighteenth-Century Irish Writer on the Continent and Overseas." in *Glocal Ireland: Current Perspectives on Literature and the Visual Arts*, Morales Ladrón, Marisol and Juan F. Elices Agudo (eds). Newcastle upon Tyne: Cambridge Scholars Publishing: 51-61.

Leerssen, Joep. 1997. *Remembrance and Imagination. Patterns in the Historical and Literary Representation of Ireland in the Nineteenth Century*. Indiana: University of Notre Dame Press and Cork: Cork University Press.

Loeber, Rolf and M. Stouthamer-Loeber, Magda. 2003. "The Publication of Irish Novels and Novelettes, 1750-1829: A Footnote on Irish Gothic Fiction" in *Cardiff Corvey: Reading the Romantic Text* 10 (June 2003). Online: Internet (14/12/2010) http://www.cf.ac.uk/encap/corvey/articles/ cc10_n02.html.

Mandal, Anthony A. 1999 "Revising the Radcliffean Model: Regina Maria Roche's *Clermont* and Jane Austen's *Northanger Abbey." in Cardiff Corvey: Reading the Romantic Text* 3 (September 1999). Online: Internet (30/10/2010) http://www.cf.ac.uk/encap/corvey/articles/cc03_n03. html.

Maturin, Charles. 1992. *Melmoth the Wanderer*. Grant, Douglas (ed.). Oxford: Oxford University Press.

Ó Gallchoir, Clíona. 2005. *Maria Edgeworth. Women, Enlightenment and Nation*. Dublin: University College Dublin Press.

Owenson, Sydney (Lady Morgan). 1999. *The Wild Irish Girl. A National Tale*. Kirkpatrick, Kathryn (ed.). Oxford: Oxford University Press.

Parrinder, Patrick. 2006. *Nation & Novel. The English Novel from Its Origins to the Present Day*. Oxford: Oxford University Press.

Roberts, Bette B. 1980. *The Gothic Romance. Its Appeal to Women Writers & Readers in Late Eighteenth-Century England*. New York: Arno Press.

Roche, Regina Maria. 1796. *The Children of the Abbey, A Tale*. In four volumes. London: Printed for William Lane, at the Minerva Press.

—. 1824. *The Tradition of the Castle; or, Scenes in the Emerald Isle*. London: Printed for A.K. Newman and Co.

Schroeder, Natalie. 1979. "Regina Maria Roche, Popular Novelist, 1789-1834: The Rochean Canon." in *Papers of the Bibliographical Society of America*. (73): 462-468.

—. 1990. "*The Mysteries of Udolpho* and *Clermont*: The Radcliffean Encroachment on the Art of Regina Maria Roche." *Studies in the Novel.* 12 (2): 131-143.

Shteir, Ann B. 1987. "Regina Maria Roche." in *A Dictionary of British and American Women Writers*, Todd, Janet (ed.). London: Methuen & Co: 272-273.

Smyth, Gerry. 1997. *The Novel and the Nation. Studies in the New Irish Fiction*. London & Ann Arbor, Mi: Pluto Press.

Todd, Janet, ed. 1989. "Regina Maria Roche." in *Dictionary of British Women Writers*. London: Routledge: 578-579.

Tompkins, J.M.S. 1932. *The Popular Novel in England 1770-1800*. London: Constable & Co.

Vance, Norman. 2002. *Irish Literature since 1800*. Harlow: Longman.

# Amor Vincit (R)Om(A)Nia: Reshaping Identities in Romanian mid 19th-Century Culture

*Carmen Beatrice Dutu*

ABSTRACT The novel phenomenon in Romania had been '*foreign*' par excellence from the very start, being imported (and eventually translated and adapted) from French culture. Within this context, the exponential demand of women readers for sentimental novels triggered an array of reactions in the public sphere, most of them negative, and generated by the trespass of women on traditional barriers within the private realm. This chapter aims to offer an imagological analysis on how the impressive body of women readers of mid 19th-century novels played a crucial role in shaping the new Romanian (trans)national identity.

FEMINIST RESEARCH IN ROMANIAN CULTURE IS today only hosted by social and political sciences, whereas in literature studies this is still considered trivial. Recently, doctoral research has generated a new wave of interest among young researchers who have started examining the Romanian literary phenomenon from the more generous perspective of Cultural Studies. This does not, however make for the resistance of the Romanian academia against women's and gender studies. There is, of course a set of reasons to explain this situation, ranging from the lack of expertize and theoretical resources in the field, to the very fear of approaching themes which are subject to prejudice. Last, but not least, we should take into account the fact that gender studies methodology itself is today the terminus point of a long line of theories in feminist literary study, many of which have proven contradictory.

Therefore, at this point one must ask oneself, even rhetorically: can gender be accepted as a valid category of analysis for Romanian literature? There are at least two valid reasons for these question, both residing in our historical past.The more recent history has proven that ideology was the main tool which made totalitarian censorship possible; and feminism/ gender studies/ women's studies, are overtly ideological approaches to literature, being concerned with:

> [...] woman as the consumer of male produced literature, and with the way in which the hypothesis of a female reader changes our apprehension of a given text, awakening us to the significance of its sexual codes...Its subjects include images and stereotypes of women in literature, the omissions of and misconceptions about women in criticism, and the fissures in male-constructed literary history.[1]

Based on the grounds of such social memory, gender discourse in Romanian literature may not easily find sympathy in the Romanian academia; not to mention the fact that gender studies subversively militate for the deconstruction of existing canons. However, things are not as grim as they may seem: Virgil Nemoianu, Adrian Marino and other reputed Romanian scholars have signaled the necessity of introducing gender in the Romanian literary theory and criticism as a valid and, by all means, necessary category of analysis. Their arguments are synthetized below.[2]

1. value is relative, being determined by the historical moment in which a literary work occurs;
2. traditional hierarchies must be reconsidered periodically, this process being not only legitimate, but also necessary;
3. popular literature, second-hand texts must be reconsidered
4. literary canon also needs reconsidering from a gender perspective
5. cultural globalization triggers different means of literary reception, which involves the deconstruction of existing traditional canon.

The above principles may, therefore, constitute the grounds for legitimizing the gender approach to early modern Romanian literature. Consequently, we will examine how the adapted texts of the early modern

---

[1] Elaine Showalter, "*Towards a Feminist Criticism*" in Catherine Belsey and Jane Moore (eds). *The Feminist Reader. Essays in Gender and the Politics of Literary Criticism*, London: Macmillan, 1997: 238.

[2] I am referring here to Adrian Marino's ideas from *Biografia ideii de literatura. (The Biography of <the idea of Literature>), 4th vol. 20th Century (2nd part)*, Cluj –Napoca, Dacia, 1997, and Virgil Nemoianu's ideas from "*Batalia canonica – de la critica americana la cultura romana*" ("*The canonical 'querelle' – from the American critique to the Romanian culture*") in *Romania Literara*, XXXIII, 41, 11th Oct. 1990: 13-18.

Romaniannovels were built on the grounds of a domestication process of imported Western (French) modernity which contributed to a true cultural paradigm shift, eventually determining the making of a new modern Romanian identity discourse. The evolution of this phenomenon is even more dramatic, considering that once triggered, the synchronization occurred in a few decades! For the purposes of this paper, I have taken into account the research in the field which situates the scope of the early-modern Romanian novel roughly between 1848 and 1860. However, considering that the whole importing-translating-adapting process is a broader phenomenon, I will further follow the argumentation of Paul Cornea's extensive research[3] on the early to mid 19th century romance novels audience, from translations to *domestication* of the imported formula.

The scenography of receiving French influence in Romania has been thoroughly studied in Romania. Starting with Pompiliu Eliade, as revealed in his *De l'influence française sur l'esprit public en Roumanie: Les Origines* (1889)[4] (*The French Influence over the Public Mindset in Romania*), moving towards Paul Cornea and Mihai Zamfir, with their *Introduction* to *Gandirea romaneasca în épоca paşoptistă (1830-1860)*[5] *(The Romanian Thought in the Mid 19th Century)*, and ending with more recent works such Stefan Cazimir's *Alfabetul de tranzitie*[6] *(The alphabet of Transition)* (2006), these Romanian scholars (and others) have pointed out the fact that the replacement of the

---

[3] See Paul Cornea, *De la Alecsandrescu la Eminescu (From Alecsandrescu to Eminescu)*, Bucharest: EPL, 1966; also, "*Cerere şi ofertă în determinarea profilului traducătorilor de la jumătatea veacului trecut*" ("*Demand and offer in determining the profile of translators at mid 19th century*") in *Oamenii începutului de drum (Literary pioneers)*, Bucharest: Cartea Românească, 1974: 45-67; "*Constituirea unui gen. Între 'romance' şi 'novel': romanul românesc în secolul al 19-lea*" ("*Establishing a genre. Between 'romance' and 'novel': the 19th century Romanian novel*"), in *Regula jocului (The Rule of the Game)*, Bucharest: Eminescu, 1980: 32-46; "*Instituţionalizarea culturii: cadru şi preocupări*" ("*The institutionalization of culture: framework and interests*"), in *Originile romantismului românesc* (*The Origins of Romanian Romanticism*), Bucharest, Cartea Românească, 2008: 81-107.

[4] Pompiliu Eliade, *Influenţa franceză asupra spiritului public în România. Originile. Studiu asupra stării societăţii româneşti în vremea domniilor fanariote (De l'influence française sur l'esprit public en Roumanie: Les Origines*). Aurelia Dumitraşcu (tr.), Bucharest: Institutul Cultural Român, 2006.

[5] Paul Cornea and Mihai Zamfir (eds.). *Gândirea românească în epoca paşoptista (1830-1860) (Romanian thought in the mid 19th century)*. Bucharest: EPL, 1969: 33-34.

[6] Ştefan Cazimir, *Alfabetul de tranziţie (The alphabet of tranzition)*. 1st ed., Bucharest: Cartea Românească, 1980. 2nd ed., Bucharest: Humanitas, 2006.

dominating Oriental influence in the first part of the 19th century, with the French influence within a few decades, was the effect of combined factors. One should have in mind the social, linguistic and cultural conditions that formed the basis for the French influence in the Romanian culture: towards the end of the 18th century, the elites had rediscovered the ideas of Latinity and national rebirth, based on the seismic effects of the French Revolution, further carried by the 1848 Revolution. The illustrious French model – a modern, Latin people, with a classical and encyclopedic culture was bound to stir the admiration of the Romanian intellectuality at the beginning of 19th century. In fact, the history of French influence in the Romanian culture is prior to this period; it had already started in the 18th century, with the Greek Fanariot rulers, being made possible by means of the ever increasing presence of the French teachers in the Fanariot ruler's courts; this situation was followed by the Tsarist army occupation which propagated a French lifestyle within the local aristocracy, especially via gallant officers socializing at the court, and becoming involved with local beauties. Eventually, the beginning of the 19th century witnesses the fashion of sending one's rich offspring to study in France, and Romanian students' number increased exponentially.

All these realities reflected into all social strata and in all aspects of daily life, including the practice of reading sentimental novels. The erotic inheritance of Western courtly love penetrates the heavy traditional Eastern mentality with a conquering force. "Visiting cloisters and aristocracy libraries, not once have I been puzzled by the number and type of French books that I found there" stated N. Iorga,[7] one of the most prominent Romanian scholars of the early 20th century. Thus sentimental novels come to the forefront in the daily life of the aristocracy, and, in a few decades, of the entire bourgeoisie. According to Iorga, French novels became the preferred genre, among which, *La Nouvelle Héloïse*, *Paul et Virginie*, *Die Leiden des JungenWerther* (in a French version), probably Richardson's works, so popular at the time, of Restif de la Bretonne and Mme de Staël's, where the most common in private libraries. Regarding the popularity of *Corinne* (Madame de Staël, 1807*)*, an interesting detail is revealed by Kosmali, a foreign traveler from the end of the Fanariot period. He recorded that he had

---

[7] N. Iorga, *Istoria literaturii romanesti. Introducere sintetica.* (*The history of Romanian literature. A synthetic introduction*). Bucharest: Editura Librăriei Pavel Suru, 1929: 125.

found Madame de Staël's book in an aristocratic home, annotated by the mistress of the house, a passionate of sentimental literature;[8] also, a certain Marieta Cantacuzino, a young woman from the aristocracy had in her personal libraryLouvet de Couvray's*La vie et les amours du chevalier de Faublas* (14 volumes!) before 1821.[9] It was only natural that after the Revolution in 1848, translators became professionalized, specializing predominantly in sentimental novels translations, which met the public's increasing demand for this genre.

The analysis of the early-modern Romanian sentimental novel from a gender perspective may not ignore the mediation, and, respectively, catalyzing role which translations played in the Romanian culture, under the influence of the French one. According to Cornea, the genre repartition of these translations reveals the ever increasing importance the sentimental novel gained around the 1860s: the translations from French novels increase to 400% comparing to 1840, and with 250% compared to 1850.[10] Examining the list of the translated authors, we notice that the general thematic of these texts is sensational and erotic romance, among which "a privileged spot is owned by Paul de Kock, with his novels".[11] This situation is the more interesting when it reveals the fact that censorship had no echo with the public. Noticing the overwhelming presence of the novel as a genre, in his statistics on the translation phenomenon form 1780 to 1860, Cornea points out the fact that the relationship of the local translator with the foreign text can be characterized by the classical *traduttore-tradittore*:

> These translators allowed themselves to tamper with the original texts, omitting some passages, interpolating others, rationalizing the composition; thus the Romanian reader met less of the original text itself, and more of its interpretation.[12]

---

[8] A.D. Xenopol, *Istoria romanilor (The history of Romanians)* 10th vol., Iasi, Tipo-Litografia H. Goldner, 1988: 209-210.

[9] See G. Calinescu, *Istoria literaturii romane. De la origini pana in prezent*, (*The History of Romanian Literature. From its Origins up to the Present Time*) 2nd ed. Al. Piru (ed.). Bucharest: Minerva, 1986.

[10] P Cornea, *Traduceri si traducatori in prima jumatate a secolului al 19-lea (Translators and translations in the first half of the 19th century)*, in *De la Alecsandrescu la Eminescu*: 60.

[11] *Ibid.*, 61.

[12] *Ibid.*, 55.

In the mediation process, our translators delivered a *meta-reading*, the translation being, obviously, a first act of reception of the imported literature. Defenders of public morality raged against these dangerous reading practices, here, as elsewhere. The only difference is that in the Romanian culture, the reason for rejecting the so-called *belle littérature* was not triggered by aesthetic reasons, as in the case of French Classicism, for instance. In our case, the reason resides purely in morality, with the same effects, however. Consequently, due to the very lax notion of intellectual property and to the concern of not frightening the reader with unusual ideas, translators would frequently and blatantly tamper with the text: they would suppress details, soften the tone, and add their own commentaries and sometimes entire passages to the 'translated' text, because "(...) the novel was suspected of circulating subversive ideas, French ones in particular, of propagating a dubious morality, triggering, eventually, the deconstruction of traditions and stirring of senses."[13] Consequently, translators as intermediaries are very much aware of their audacity: all Romanian versions are, with no exception, perfectly salubrious with their moralizing discourses, and politically correct attitude towards social hierarchy and moral precepts. The fact that Cornea's statistics reveal that out of the impressive body of translators[14] active between 1780 and 1860, only 20 were womencan be explained when viewing men as the defenders of morality. It is symptomatic that these translations are overwhelmingly dealing with the theme of love, as it is portrayed in the Western culture, where the erotic discourse is blatantly opposed to *Agape*, the one type of love professed by the obsolete confessional literature.Once established, this type of literature consumption becomes the dominant fashion. Alecu Russo reveals in 1840 how powerful this feminine fashion is over the entire society:

> Following the elegant and fashionable women, the second class aristocracy will only speak of Balzac and Soulie, Lamartine and Hugo, Kock and Dumas; especially Paul de Kock – they adore.[15]

The statistics revealed by Paul Cornea[16] (and later on developed by his disciples IoanaDragan and LiviuPapadima),[17] evidenced an exponential

---

[13] *Ibid.*, 88.
[14] *Ibid.*, 301.
[15] Al Russo, *Scrieri alese (Selected works)*. Şerban, Geo (ed.). Bucharest: Albatros, 1970: 73.

interest of the feminine public for the 'cheap', paperback, *dime-a-dozen* type of literature, with no intrinsic value (according to Cornea): from 18 translations in the 3rd and 4th decade of the 19th century, and 29 in the 4th and 5th decades, to 73 titles between the 5th and 6th decades. Further on, Cornea unequivocally asserts that:

> After 1860, due to the progresses in education, urbanization and rapid development of economic life, the number of literate people and, intrinsically, of the potential audience emerging form the lower levels of society, is constantly increasing. It is this very small and unpretentious bourgeoisie audience, lacking any solid education, among which women represent a significant percent [s.n.] that stimulates translations from widely accessible novels, namely 'sentimental' novels.[18]

Unfortunately, the above studyfails to give an account of the names of the translators and their works, as well as a more in depth analysis of statistical data. A more recent research in the field, *The repertoire of Romanian translators from French, Italian and Spanish,*[19] provides us a more in detailed picture of the same 1830-1865 period investigated, revealing the following:

- 92 translated sentimental novels;
- 14 women translators;
- 26 foreign novels written by female authors translated into Romanian;
- 5 novels written by foreign women authors translated by Romanian women.

---

[16] P. Cornea, *Regula jocului*: 282.

[17] See Liviu Papadima, *Literatura si comunicare. Relatiaautor-cititor in proza postpasoptista* (*Literature and commnunication. The author-reader relationship in the mid 19th century prose),* Iasi: Polirom, 1999; Ioana Dragan, *Romanul popular in Romania. Literar si paraliterar (The popular novel in Romania Literary and paraliterary).* Cluj : Casa Cartii de Stiinta, 2001.

[18] P. Cornea, *Regula jocului*: 282. There is a slight error in Cornea's analysis: from the correspondence and diaries of the early 19th century we find that the fashion of reading romance novels was initially embraced by the elite of the day, propagating itself later on to the other social strata.

[19] Georgiana Lungu Badea (ed.). *Repertoriul traducătorilor români de limba franceză, italiană, spaniolă din secolele al XVIII lea şi al XIX-lea. Studii de istoria traducerii (I),* (*The repertoire of Romanian translators from French, Italian, Spanish cultures in the 18th and 19th centuries. Studies in the history of translations (I)*). Timisoara: Universitatea de Vest Publishing House, 2006.

- 9 novels written by foreign men authors translated by Romanian women.

The fact that our own statistics reveals that out of the impressive body of translators (92) active between 1840 and 1865, only 14 were women, can be explained when viewing men as the defenders of morality.

It is significant that the demand of the feminine public stimulated this type of translations; eventually the production of domesticated formulas came as the natural solution to satisfy both the censorship of the traditional morality and the public demand. How can one explain this collective and sudden demand of the feminine audience for a type of literature whose pivotal theme is erotic love? Cornea proposes (1974) a motivation which calls for social psychology reasons:

> Obviously, this kind of audience, finding itself on the first steps of literary literacy, but being driven by the heart's impulses and the games of fantasy, as any young public, favored comedy, vaudeville, and melodramas, as well as the sentimental novella with a happy ending and sensational narratives, and, by-and-large, was interested in what was being said in a story, not how it was being said.[20]

Although pertinent and realistic, I would contend that the audience's drive for sentimental novels may not be fully explained within Cornea's terms. One should not omit the fact that the public was predominantly feminine, which leads us to believe that there was a certain inner motivation which triggered this sudden urge for massive consumption of a *certain* type of literature. To be more accurate, other Romanian critics have noticed the determining relationship between the imported formula of the sentimental novel and women's reading practices, as revealed by Stefan Cazimir (1973):

> The reception of foreign novels by the Romanian audience of the time might trigger an interesting study of social psychology, based on literature's accounts, especially. [...] the attitude towards novels becomes a frequent issue within the novels themselves, in order to reveal the gap between generations and between the sexes, the old people's panic , men's corky attitude, women's high receptivity ("we

[20] P. Cornea, *Oamenii inceputului de drum*: 162.

owe it to women the beginning of civilization- said V. Alecsandri [a reputed 19th century Romanian poet, n.n.].")[21]

The above critics in fact claim the necessity of applying the *reader-response critique* to the early 19thcentury sentimental novel. Consequently, the research of the mechanics of women's demand for setimental novels in particular reveals new connotations of the Romanian context. In fact this demand perfectly illustrates Pierre Bourdieu's theory from which shows that reading, as well as writing, involve aspects which display the power conflict between individuals, as long as any book contains in its subsidiary the potential to meet the reader's horizon of expectation.[22] This new type of reception became active in the Romanian culture within the public's reading practices; a feminine public *par excellence* – according to its traditional characterization – with very little critical thinking education; a public which did not make any connection whatsoever with the literary past and present of the Romanian culture; moreover, these readers barely made any distinction between fiction and reality; in other words, they did not have any sense of *literarity*, of distancing themselves from the text. After examining the *importing-translating-adapting* phenomenon up to 1860, Cornea's overall conclusion is that reading practices will eventually determine a certain individual pattern of behavior. The act of reading demands assuming a modified self-image, which eventually triggers a modified role of the individual, within the couple and within society.[23]

Within this context, the Romanian early novel wasadapted on the ground of a codified discourse, a new phenomenology of love, the text being romance, and its sub-text eroticism and sexuality. It is by all means symptomatic that the core theme of allsentimental novels adapted form the French models revolve around the theme of love. The fight for gender dominance is transferred in the agora of literature as revealed by the fact that the 'devastating' consequences of women's reading practices became a topos,

---

[21] Stefan Cazimir (ed.). *Pionierii romanului romanesc* (*The pioneers of Romanian novel*), Bucharest: Minerva, 1973: VII-VIII

[22] Erwin Koppen, "*Hat die Vergleichende Literaturwissenschaft eine eigene Theorie? Ein Exempel: Der literarische Einfluss*" in Horst Rüdiger (ed.). *Zur Theorie der Verghleichenden Literaturwissenschaft*, Berlin: der Gruyter, 1971: 43, apud Dan Grigorescu, *Introducere în literatura comparată. Teoria (Introduction in the Theory of Comparative Literature)*. Bucharest: Universal Dalsi, Semne, 1997: 95.

[23] Pierre Bourdieu, *Regulile artei (The rules of art)*. Laura Albulescu and Bogdan Ghiu (tr.), Bucharest: Art, 2007.

transgressing reality and becoming a recurrent literary theme, involving issues such as what, and especially, who should decide what women should read, as revealed by one of the authors of the time:

> You'd rather read French romances, claiming that this is true reading and, perhaps, to learn how to fulfill your duties as mistresses. But this is hilarious! You are not even able to take advantage of this situation! I know you: you even lack the ability to love properly![24]

The virulence of this masculine character is specific to almost all Romanian early sentimental novels; a natural attitude, considering that there "the novel is written by men, and read by women!"[25] In the particular case of the Romanian culture, the fact that up to mid 19th century there is no female authorship in the classical sense (i.e. writer who produces a more or less original work), places the *woman-as-a-reader* in pivotal position in Elaine Showalter's terms, this perspective being concerned with:

> [...] woman as the consumer of male produced literature, and with the way in which the hypothesis of a female reader changes our apprehension of a given text, awakening us to the significance of its sexual codes...Its subjects include images and stereotypes of women in literature, the omissions of and misconceptions about women in criticism, and the fissures in male-constructed literary history.[26]

During the dual process in which women were encouraged and eventually, they encouraged the production of sentimental novels, the image of modern women was constantly overlapped with the novel, which triggered the vehemence against this genre and the constant attempt to push it towards the margins, in order not to contaminate the centre. As stated before, the fictional code was practically inexistent and, consequently, male writers used literature as a vehicle for their ideas and moralizing principles.

---

[24] Mihail Kogalniceanu, *Soirées dansantes (Adunari dantuitoare) (Dancing soirees)*, in *Opere I (Works I)*, (introduction and notes by Dan Simonescu) Bucharest: Academiei R.S.R., 1974.

[25] P. Cornea, *Regula jocului*: 264-165.

[26] Elaine Showalter, "*Towards a Feminist Poetics*": 238.

However, if we apply a contrapuntal reading to these early novels, in E. Said's terms,[27] we may witness a puzzling phenomenon: the attempt to exclude women of the public sphere is obviously undermined by women's emancipation, fact confirmed (among other documents) by testimonies of foreign travellers on Romanian territory. Still, how was it possible that the connection between women, sentimental novels became a vector of modernity, especially given the negative reactions to their reading practies? Applied to our study, Said's theory is relevant for us because it allows a better understanding of this oxymoronic relationship between women and the novel. As Said explains "The point is that contrapunctual reading must take account of both proceses, that of imperialism and that of resistance to it."[28] Within this context a Romanian critic (Ibraileanu, 1979) noticed that love as a theme and preoccupation plays a subversive role, which women perceived (often unconsciously) as a breach into the traditional system of values, no longer corresponding to their (and the overall society's, for that matter) lingering need for emancipation.:

> In the love affairs from these novels we may, in fact, witness the solidarity between women in the higher society and the youngsters: women have become modernized sooner than men – a fact noticed by Alecsandri himself, and confessed by Ion Ghica. Alecsandri clearly states that women could no longer get along with their men, therefore erotic adventures, divorces. The same thing in Bolintineanu's novels: emancipated youn men love high society women, who understand them. We need to take into consideration the fact that women were the first to embrace modernity when they first came into contact with the Western civilization.[29]

Women and their lifestyle, especially their reading practices worked as a phenomenon of alterity in Virgil Nemoianu's terms (*A theory of the Secondary,* 1997) which, he claims: "[...] appears as a guiding nucleus, or a fortuite, but ferm option within this floating, "slushy" mass of information

[27] Edward Said, *Culture and Imperialism*. London: Vintage, 1994.
[28] *Ibid*., 23.
[29] Garabet Ibrăileanu, *Opere VIII (Works VIII),* Rodica Rotaru and Al. Piru (eds). Bucharest: Minerva, 1979: 364.

and, as a thunderrod, attracts incipient noise and starts building a world with a certain structure".[30]

Within the sentimental novel we can detect this phenomenon of alterity which triggered an intrinsic erosion of the gender roles within the couple, with irreversible consequences, a reflex adopted by the domesticated novels: here we may witness a dramatic shift of the erotic imaginary, form the display of feminine and masculine bodies, to new gender roles within the couple, and a reorganizing of space itself around this gender shift. The imported mentality comes to change the status quo and quickly incorporates the existing reality. Indeed, most 19th century foreign traveller's accounts on the Romanian society gravitate around common issues, such as beauty, manners and education, social roles, gender relations (family, the couple), entertainment practices ; what is more, with no exception, these writings make reference to Romanian women's ability to receive and promote modernity, at least at the level of their dressing code and flirting methods.[31] In the high society clubs of the capital city, the elite ladies reveal their splendor, and everyone would follow their example. "Around this ravishing elite, around these opulent women, there flourished the arts and letters, being encouraged by tchem".[32]

The imported framework has produced, in a very short time, a new content: new values, new morality. Symptomatically, the Romanian sentimental novel is abundent in examples of this new positioning of gender roles, separately and in relationship; here is what a Romanian student to Paris finds when returning home after fiveyears in the French capital (a recurrent theme in the early novel formula) in Pantazi Ghica's *A Romanian bohemian* (1860):

> As for the morality, the world is upside down. Elderly men supporting young women, and elderly women supporting young men who were [...](the characterization would be too harsh) to sell themselves. A

---

[30] Virgil Nemoianu, *O teorie a secundarului. Literatură, progres şi reacţiune (A theory of the secondary. Literature, progress and reaction)* Livia Szasz Câmpeanu (tr.) Bucharest: Univers, 1997: 172.

[31] See N. Iorga, *Istoria românilor prin călători*; Nicolae Isar, *Publicişti francezi şi cauza română* (*French publicists and the Romanian cause*) 1834-1859. Bucharest: Academiei, 1991.

[32] V. Diculescu, *Viaţa cotidiană a Ţării Româneşti în documente 1800-1848, (Daily life in Tara Romaneasca in documents. 1800-1848)*, Cluj-Napoca, Dacia, 1970: 238.

> very lucrative preoccupation! [...] Lack of affection, trust support, family ties. Venal marriages, concluded for the dowary, lacking any love. An overall disorder.[33]

Another narrator (Bolintineanu, 1855) reveals the fundament for this'underground' revolution triggered by women's emancipation, when complaining that women's behaviour had occured to the detriment of national literature: "They will not speak into their beautiful Romanian language; they write, speak, read everything in a foreign language."[34] The writer reveals today the breach created by women – via their reading practices – within the Romanian cultural space. Once secondary social actors, women come to the forefront of the modern existence, with their frivolous preoccupations: reading romances, erotic display, love for luxury and entertaining: "The most oppulent luxury here (in Bucharest, the capital, n.n.) lies here in the elegance of the carriages, number of servants, wealth of apartments and ladies clothing [...]".[35] These mechanisms of change were created practicly over night, due to a certain horizon of expectation which made change possible, fact also proven by the striking phenomenon of the public request for translations from French sentimental novels. The fact that this public was predominantly feminine and was present thorughout all social classes lead us to the conclusion that the sentimental novel was one of the triggering factors of Romanian women's emancipation in the 19th century, and consequently, of the entire society modernization. The theme of love, is evidently a synecdoche for gender relations, the translated and adapted novels representing a powerful subversive, informal means to introduce modern mentality in Romania. The shift in gender relations occurred in these novels was, thus, but a local adaptation of the broader network of mentalities emerging in the entire modern European space. The "transformation of intimacy"[36] had occurred!

---

[33] Pantazi Ghica, "Un boem român" ("A Romanian bohemian") in Stefan Cazimir, *Pionierii romanului românesc.* (The pioneers of Romanian novel). Bucharest: Tipografia Jurnalului Naţional, 1860: 145.

[34] D. Bolintineanu, *Manoil*, in *Opere V (Works V)*, Iasi, Tipografia oomano-franceza, 1855: 72.

[35] *Ibidem.*

[36] I am referring here to Anthony Giddens' theory from his *The Transformation of intimacy. Sexuality, Love and Eroticism in Modern Societies*, Cambridge: Polity Press, 1992. The theory reveals the larger context of the changes ocured in gender

## Select Bibliography

Al Russo. 1970. *Scrieri alese (Selected works)*. Şerban, Geo (ed.). Bucharest: Albatros.

Bolintineanu, D. 1855. *Manoil*, in *Opere V (Works V)*, Iasi, Tipografia romano-franceza.

Bourdieu, Pierre. 2007. *Regulile artei (The rules of art)*. Laura Albulescu and Bogdan Ghiu (tr.), Bucharest: Art.

Calinescu, G. 1986. *Istoria literaturii romane. De la origini pana in prezent*, (*The History of Romanian Literature. From its Origins up to the Present Time*) 2nd ed. Al. Piru (ed.). Bucharest: Minerva.

Cazimir, Stefan (ed.). 1973. *Pionierii romanului romanesc* (*The pioneers of Romanian novel*), Bucharest: Minerva.

—. 1980. *Alfabetul de tranziţie (The alphabet of tranzition)*. 1st ed. Bucharest: Cartea Românească. 2nd ed. Bucharest: Humanitas, 2006.

Cornea, Paul. 1966. *De la Alecsandrescu la Eminescu (From Alecsandrescu to Eminescu)*, Bucharest: EPL.

—. and Mihai Zamfir (eds.). 1969. *Gândirea românească în epoca paşoptista (1830-1860) (Romanian thought in the mid 19th century)*. Bucharest: EPL.

—. 1974. "Cerere şi ofertă în determinarea profilului traducătorilor de la jumătatea veacului trecut" ("Demand and offer in determining the profile of translators at mid 19th century") in *Oamenii începutului de drum (Literary pioneers)*, Bucharest: Cartea Românească: 45-67.

—. 1980. "Constituirea unui gen. Între 'romance' şi 'novel': romanul românesc în secolul al 19-lea" ("Establishing a genre. Between 'romance' and 'novel': the 19th century Romanian novel") in *Regula jocului (The Rule of the Game)*. Bucharest: Eminescu: 32-46

—. 2008. *"Instituţionalizarea culturii: cadru şi preocupări" ("The institutionalization of culture: framework and interests")*, in *Originile romantismului românesc* (*The Origins of Romanian Romanticism*), Bucharest, Cartea Românească: 81-107.

Diculescu, V. 1970. *Viaţa cotidiană a Ţării Româneşti în documente 1800-1848, (Daily life in Tara Romaneasca in documents. 1800-1848)*. Cluj-Napoca, Dacia.

relations in the 19th century in Europe, based on the evolution of modern capitalism and democratic societies.

Dragan, Ioana. 2001. *Romanul popular in Romania. Literar si paraliterar (The popular novel in Romania Literary and paraliterary)*. Cluj : Casa Cartii de Stiinta.

Eliade, Pompiliu. 2006. *Influenţa franceză asupra spiritului public în România. Originile. Studiu asupra stării societăţii româneşti în vremea domniilor fanariote (De l'influence française sur l'esprit public en Roumanie: Les Origines*). Aurelia Dumitraşcu (tr.), Bucharest: Institutul Cultural Român.

Giddens, Anthony. 1992. *The Transformation of intimacy. Sexuality, Love and Eroticism in Modern Societies*, Cambridge: Polity Press.

Ghica, Pantazi. 1860. "Un boem român" ("A Romanian bohemian") in Stefan Cazimir, *Pionierii romanului românesc. (The pioneers of Romanian novel).* Bucharest: Tipografia Jurnalului Naţional: 145.

Grigorescu, Dan. 1997. *Introducere în literatura comparată. Teoria (Introduction in the Theory of Comparative Literature).* Bucharest: Universal Dalsi, Semne.

Ibrăileanu, Garabet. 1979. *Opere VIII (Works VIII),* Rodica Rotaru and Al. Piru (eds). Bucharest: Minerva.

Iorga, N. 1929. *Istoria literaturii romanesti. Introducere sintetica*. (*The history of Romanian literature. A synthetic introduction*). Bucharest: Editura Librăriei Pavel Suru.

—. 1991. *Istoria românilor prin călători*; Nicolae Isar, *Publicişti francezi şi cauza română* (*French publicists and the Romanian cause*) 1834-1859. Bucharest: Academiei.

Isar, Nicolae. 1991. *Publicişti francezi şi cauza română* (*French publicists and the Romanian cause*) 1834-1859. Bucharest: Academiei.

Kogalniceanu, Mihail. 1974. *Soirées dansantes (Adunari dantuitoare) (Dancing soirees),* in *Opere I (Works I)*, (introduction and notes by Dan Simonescu) Bucharest: Academiei R.S.R.

Lungu Badea, Georgiana (ed.). 2006. *Repertoriul traducătorilor români de limba franceză, italiană, spaniolă din secolele al XVIII lea şi al XIX-lea. Studii de istoria traducerii (I),* (*The repertoire of Romanian translators from French, Italian, Spanish cultures in the 18th and 19th centuries. Studies in the history of translations (I)*). Timisoara: Universitatea de Vest Publishing House.

Marino, Adrian. 1997. *Biografia ideii de literatura. (The Biography of the idea of Literature).* Cluj –Napoca, Dacia.

Nemoianu, Virgil. 1990. "Batalia canonica – de la critica americana la cultura romana" ("The canonical 'querelle' – from the American critique to the Romanian culture") in *Romania Literara*, XXXIII, 41, 11th Oct: 13-18.

—. 1997. *O teorie a secundarului. Literatură, progres şi reacţiune (A theory of the secondary. Literature, progress and reaction).* Livia Szasz Câmpeanu (tr.) Bucharest: Univers.

Papadima, Liviu. 1999. *Literatura si comunicare. Relatiaautor-cititor in proza postpasoptista (Literature and commnunication. The author-reader relationship in the mid 19th century prose),* Iasi: Polirom.

Said, Edward. 1994. *Culture and Imperialism.* London: Vintage.

Showalter, Elaine. 1997. *"Towards a Feminist Criticism"* in Belsey, Catherine and Jane Moore (eds). *The Feminist Reader. Essays in Gender and the Politics of Literary Criticism.* London: Macmillan.

Xenopol, A.D. 1988. *Istoria romanilor (The history of Romanians).* Iasi, Tipo-Litografia H. Goldner.

# Women's Nation from Ottoman to the New Republic in Fatma Aliye and Halide Edip Adıvar's Writing

*Senem Timuroglu*

ABSTRACT This chapter presents the works of Fatma Aliye and Halide Edip Adıvar, two cornerstones of women's writing in Turkey. They were witnesses of the transition between the Ottoman and Republic modernization, but also of the lack of change in the patriarchal mentality that dominated both periods. The author focuses on how this transition, from a multicultural, multilingual and poly-ethnic empire that encompassed a vast geography for centuries, to a nation-state based on a monolingual, mono-religious and mono-ethnic society, has been experienced by these two women writers.

"In Turkey, we have a saying, 'Women are all one nation'" [1]

WOMEN'S FREEDOM HAS BEEN ONE OF THE COMPONENTS of the nationalist movement in Turkey; their demand for rights took place at the same time as the national fight for democracy. Women were allowed to be active in the national independence fight so long as they put the country's interests first, and were cast out as soon as they vocalized their demands for rights and freedoms more loudly than usual. Turkish nationalism, which started to develop at the end of 19th century and took a crucial step forward with the founding of the New Republic in 1923, had a different, more paradoxical quality than Balkan and Middle East nationalisms as a result of its similarity to European allies as a colonizer and ideal model. Another difference is the way in which it defined itself in opposition to the Ottoman legacy, not consisting entirely of Turkish ethnicity.

We aim to analyze works of Fatma Aliye and Halide Edip Adıvar, two cornerstones of women's writing in Turkey and witnesses of the transition

[1] Halide Edip Adıvar, *Conflict of East and West in Turkey.* Jamia Millia Extension Lectures. Lahor: S.M.Ashraf, 1963: 193.

between Ottoman Empire and Republic of Turkey, by focusing on how this transition from a multicultural, multilingual and poly-ethnic empire that encompassed a vast geography for centuries, to a nation-state based on a monolingual, mono-religious and mono-ethnic society, has been experienced by these two women writers.

The works of these two women capture the continuation between Ottoman modernization and Republic modernization, and the lack of change in the patriarchal mentality that dominated both periods. The experiences of these two writers show us that male-dominated history only mentions women if their demands are in-keeping with society's goals. If they compromised their movement, they would be cast aside and left out. Halide Edip was more visible in male-dominated history than Fatma Aliye inasmuch as she valued patriotism over the women's movement; however, she was marginalized when she expressed her opinions on the issue.

Ottoman modernization, which began in the military in the 17$^{th}$ century, gained momentum with reforms that transformed politics, law, education and social life and continued until the end of the 19$^{th}$ century. As a result, the Turkish Republic was founded in 1923. However, to do so, the republic had to sever ties with the past and negate everything it was. It crowned its legitimacy with a severance rhetoric. The most important outcome of Mustafa Kemal's (the founder of New Turkey), revolution was the severance from Islam. This meant that the figures of Islam and Ottoman were unable to reach the present day.

The first woman writer of modern Ottoman Islam literature, and the first female philosopher and historian, well-known in her time both nationally and internationally, was Fatma Aliye (1862-1936).[2] A generation after her was Halide Edip Adıvar (1882-1964) female representative of the Turkish Republic's literary canon, known as the Turkey's Jeanne d'Arc. Both were the victims of the Republic government's arbitrary acceptance and exclusion politics, and each adopted different ideologies as a result of the tendency to form cliques in politics, and lose their individual voices in the process. Undoubtedly, this was also caused by the ideological views of male intellectuals who drowned out women's voices. Both practiced self-censorship or could not make choices according to their own views. Fatma

[2] Although Zafer Hanım's 1877 novel Aşk-ı Vatan was published before Fatma Aliye's first work, Aliye still holds "the first woman writer" title since she created a larger body of work in her career than Zafer Hanım.

Aliye, as a result of the influence of her relationship with her father, Ahmet Cevdet Pasha, a well-known Tanzimat era historian, barrister and politician, as well as Ahmet Mithat Efendi (1844-1913), a popular writer of the day and her mentor, could not be straightforward. Neither could Halide Edip, who had a relationship with Mustafa Kemal and married Adnan Adıvar, the first scientist in Turkish Republic history.

We will examine these two women, whose voices were drowned out by the official history and misreported by the canon. We shall claim that an alternative history of this geography, which went through a dramatic transformation from an empire to a republic, was written by them, and showcased their resistance in opposing grand male narratives in their texts. We will further claim that the identities imposed upon them should be subject to interrogation.

## Fatma Aliye, the first Ottoman feminist

Fatma Aliye became the subject of a new dissociation in the polarization between conservatives, who are the pioneers of the present-day Islamic intellectuals descending from the Ottoman modernization, and Westernists who are the pioneers of present-day Kemalists, when she was chosen as the face of the new 50 TL banknotes in the transition to new Turkish Lira on January 1, 2009. The main objection was the claim that the Fatma Aliye banknotes did not fulfill the criteria that portraits on banknotes should belong to people internationally well-known and representative of the national identity. Some academics contended that Halide Edip Adıvar was a more suitable choice. This argument is significant in that it shows the popular opinions of Fatma Aliye and Halide Edip. While Fatma Aliye is imprisoned into an Islamic identity opposed to the Republic, Halide Edip is ingrained into the social memory as a representative of the national and Republican identity. Fatma Aliye's feminism is questioned in academia, and her struggle for women's rights and emancipation is found to be insufficient, as there is an inclination to see her in the light of present-day Islamic ideology and thus interpret her as Islamic, conservative and reactionary.

When she died on July 13 1936, Fatma Aliye had been living as a recluse for a long time in her houses in Beyoğlu and Pangaltı. Even back then, her death was publicized as "The Death of the Forgotten Litterateur"[3] in the press. It was known that her illness, which came on after 1885, and her daughter's conversion to Christianity and move to Europe, had worn her down. Her writing had also become sparse and irregular. In the article announcing her death, Turhan Tan emphasised that political reform had driven Fatma Aliye into reclusion and oblivion, the fame that came before the new literary school Edebiyatı Cedide was about to burn out in the face of Halide Edip's writing, which he believed should not result in Aliye's exclusion from literary history. Clearly, even in her own time, Halide Edip was pitted against Fatma Aliye. As yet, I do not have any information about whether these two women interacted with each other. I know from conference documents that they presented papers at the same female societies; however, from her two volume autobiography and the lecture that she gave in India on Turkish Women and Turkish literature, we can see that Halide Edip did not show the same solicitude to the women's movement as Fatma Aliye, andonly mentioned the names of two women intellectuals, and briefly talked about women's struggles. One of these women was not Fatma Aliye but her sister Emine Semiye, who was also a writer, and the first woman member of the Committee of Union and Progress. I know that Fatma Aliye supported her contemporary women writers and poets, and wrote about their work in a women's newspaper. It is possible that Halide Edip saw her predecessor as a rival and consciously chose to be silent about her.

As her mother, Adviye Rabia, let her take lessons from her French teacher in her headscarf, and her father, Ahmet Cevdet Pasha, allowed her to have an education until she got married, Fatma Aliye who was born in Istanbul in 1862, was allowed to have a multicultural education until the age of 17. While taking private lessons in Qur'an, history and philosophy, she learned French on her own. Belonging to the generation before Halide Edip, Fatma Aliye was widely read; her work *The Muslim Women* (1892), which she wrote to correct European women travelers' misconception about Eastern women, and consisted of three chapters – On Concubines, On Marriage and Polygamy, On Fashion and Music – attracted fame both nationally and internationally.[4] Nevertheless, after fifteen books, countless articles and

---

[3] Tan Turhan, "Unutularak Ölen Edip" in *Cumhuriyet* (4371), 15 July 1936: 5.
[4] See online at http://neww.huygens.knaw.nl/authors/show/2490.

various social activities, she was condemned to be a recluse, even while she was still alive.

Of course, Fatma Aliye was not the only victim of this elimination as a result of political strategies. The New Republic condemned the women that had come before it to silence. As Zehra Toska wrote in her paper "Cumhuriyet'in Kadın İdeali: Eşiği Aşanlar ve Aşamayanlar", although the pioneering women of the Ottoman women's movement adopted and supported the Republic, wanting to sever its ties with the past and raise its own citizens according to Republican ideals, the new political regime chose the 'Anatolian woman' as its ideal woman. This ideal stereotype goes back to pre-Islamic nomad Turkish society. The devoted Anatolian woman who was equal to her husband in every aspect was held superior to the Ottoman woman who represented the 'city women'. Indeed, the Ottoman women's movement was criticized for neglecting the presence of Anatolian women in the fight for freedom. Embracing this criticism, Ottoman women continued their activities after the founding of the new Republic, commented on new laws, and even founded the political organization Kadınlar Halk Fırkası (Women's Political Party) before the first political party of the Republic was founded in 1923. The founder of the party, Nezihe Muhittin, was a woman who had the experience and qualification of being involved with the past women's movement and she was still in touch with its leaders. Founded in order to achieve political rights, this party was not officially approved by the government and was turned into an association with an article promising to grant political rights. However, in 1927, this article was removed and Nezihe Muhittin and some board members were estranged from the administration. Nezihe Muhittin died in a mental institution after continuing her life in seclusion writing novels. It is possible to argue that she was the last bridge between women's movement of the past and the Republic. As a 'city woman' with her roots in the previous women's movement, Halide Edip went to Anatolia with Mustafa Kemal to found the new Republic and became the ideal Republic woman, thus severing her ties with Istanbul women. However, the Republic declared her a traitor when she refused to conform to its rules and dismissed her from the Republican family.

The Republic regime made history by being the only political body to acknowledge women's rights and freedoms; however, it also made this very difficult when it converted the national language into the Latin alphabet. As a result of this, the second feminist movement in Turkey that kindled after 1980 was unaware of the feminist movement that had come before. However, after 1990, feminist researchers rediscovered the Ottoman women's movement in the archives via old publications for women such as journals and newspapers. After 1993, all of Fatma Aliye's work was brought to life again by the translations from the Arabic alphabet into the Latin alphabet. Despite this, Fatma Aliye is known in the present day and popular memory as a writer of questionable feminism, religion, patriotism and progressionism/ reactionism.

When she became active in the literary world, the Ottoman Empire was going through many changes. The failure of the 2nd Vienna Siege, lost wars, and the development of the modernity project in the world transformed and divided the Ottoman Empire. Although the modernity project was universal, it was seen as westernization from the point of view of the East.As modernization symbolized the transition from eastern to western, it caused an identity loss syndrome. Consequently, there was resistance against westernization as a part of the Ottoman modernization.

Fatma Aliye was the daughter of the historian, barrister and important politician Ahmet Cevdet Pasha (1822-1895), who represented the traditionalists of the Tanzimat era (1839-1876). Cevdet Pasha was against the lifestyle changes modernity required; moreover, he was against the modernization of law. He claimed that private life should be secluded and thereby protected the laws that it concerned by writing Mecelle with a committee he established himself. The popular inclination to articulate Fatma Aliye into Islamic feminism comes from her reformist Islamic thinker and barrister father. However, Fatma Aliye not only objected to the Westernist viewpoint that women had fallen behind because of Islam, but also objected to the views of traditionalist male intellectuals on the subject, due to the legitimate platform created by the Tanzimat edict, which accepted all subjects as equals in front of law.

In the time period between Tanzimat and the founding of II. Meşrutiyet (The second constitutional Era) (1839-1908), progressive reforms were made for women in education and law. Midwife courses opened in the Medical School in 1843, marking the first occupational education intended for women. In 1859, industrial schools for girls were opened to develop young women's manual skills and create a source of income for them. In addition to the middle schools for girls, which opened in 1859, the Teacher Training College for Girls was opened in 1869 to educate young women as teachers for girls, which was the occupational extent that Tanzimat allowed for women. In 1876, elementary education became mandatory for both boys and girls. In 1880, the first high school for girls was opened. The government was in a state of confusion in the Tanzimat era, which was essentially a transition period between Islamic law and Western law: in1874, concubines and slaves were freed, in the 1858 land laws, women had the same rights as men when it came to their deceased parents' estates.

Fatma Aliye was both supported and limited by the men around her. The support of these men was induced by their wish to control her creativity and zest for learning, both of which they found out of the ordinary, or their desire to stop her lust for learning and writing, and to call her success as their own. As an author of almost two hundred books on education, law, history, philosophy, economy, maths, and a writer of popular novels, Fatma Aliye's mentor, Ahmet Mithat, wrote a biography on her in 1893 called *Fatma Aliye Hanım yahut Bir Muharrire-i Osmaniyenin Neşeti.* This pioneering biography was the only biography written about her in the 19th century and informs about Fatma Aliye's education from childhood to adulthood, and her unstoppable thirst for knowledge. However, Ahmet Mithat's Fatma Aliye biography is essentially a very narcissist text, though it provided her with a transition into the public sphere.[5] Although Ahmet Mithat claimed that he was aiming to tell the story of a Muslim woman becoming a writer in the Ottoman Empire, he tried to show that Fatma Aliye was an avid reader of his own works, and that this reading made her a writer. The adult Fatma Aliye is non-existent in this biography; her adult body and maturity, her thoughts and feelings after she married are absent.

When she entered the literary world, there was no female novel tradition, and as opposed to Western literature at the time, male writers were also writing their first novels. The novel genre emerged in the Ottoman era as an extension of Westernization. Therefore, Fatma Aliye's novels are also some of the earliest Ottoman novels. Male writers' novels also dealt with family issues and relationships. While male writers supported the idea that the family institution required some changes, they suggested that these changes should be limited, traditional morality maintained, and that women should change only in a way that made men happy and that meant that their children were better educated. The change was to better patriarchal society.

A while before Fatma Aliye published her work, the First Constitutional was founded in 1876, thanks to the favour of modernization by the New

---

[5] Adak Hülya, "Gender-in(g) Biography: Ahmet Mithat (on Fatma Aliye) or the Canonization of an Ottoman Male Writer" in *Querelles*, vol.10, May 2005: 189-204.

Ottomans. Indeed, II. Abdülhamit had been crowned only with the promise that he would declare the First Constitutional. However, he closed down parliament in 1878 indefinitely and it stayed closed till the founding of The Second Constitutional in 1908. Fatma Aliye published her work during a time when Ottoman oppression and reforms were dominant. Schools for girls were opened, and the longest running publication by women *Hanımlara Mahsus Gazete* (1895-1908), of which Fatma Aliye was the head writer, began to be issued during this time. During the First Constitutional and the period of tyranny, male Tanzimat intellectuals were of the same opinion that women needed to be educated for the Ottoman to be saved. Future generations, that would shape the coming days, could only be raised well by educated mothers. Eve so, a woman type that had not been approved by either the Westernists or the traditionalists had emerged: a woman type who copied the Western life-style completely and ignorantly – an impostor. This type was used as a trump by traditionalist intellectuals against Tanzimat reforms. For example, according to the traditionalist intellectual, these reforms were not to be allowed because women would lose the essence that made them Ottoman women if they were to learn foreign languages, go to school, and be present in public sphere just like non-Muslim women.

In order to both counter this belief that not only hindered reforms for women but also the whole society, and to resist Western modernizations and nationalism and thereby protecti their identity, Tanzimat intellectuals resorted to the method of re-creating the past.New Ottomans claimed that they found the support and inspiration they needed in the early days of Islam to re-create Asr-ı Saadet (the happiest time of Islam). Women resorted to the same method against these traditionalists, suggesting that the opposition was based on religion. Fatma Aliye discussed women's rights in terms of Islamic law, and continuously noted that women in this era of Islam, which was not tainted by other cultures, had many freedoms in the public sphere. However, she drew a different, unique and original Muslim woman profile compared to the 'new woman"'idea Tanzimat era male intellectuals conceptualized. Although she limited her discourse on women's rights in her columns to the period's atmosphere, in her fiction she was striving to be an individual. While she had been a girl who was the work of her father and mentor in her early days in the literary world, she became an adult woman by creating continuity with the previous generation women, and planting the first seeds of a feminist history of women in this geography. In order to show her standing, in her

"Beware of the Bluestockings" article that was published in *Hanımlara Mahsus Gazete*'s[6] second issue, Fatma Aliye said:

> We shouldn't be the followers of bluestockings! We should follow our famous Muslim ancestors and women! We shouldn't take Bluestockings as examples when we have our grandmothers, their legacy.[7]

However, in the same article while explaining who the 'bluestockings' were, she mentioned Madame Mary Montagu's name, describing her as a very important person and indicating that she was planning to talk about Lady Montagu in subsequent articles. After this, she was asked to write about famous Muslim women, upon which she wrote Fatma Bint Abbas' biography who taught men in the early days of Islam. According to Fatma Aliye, Iran's influence on Ottoman culture resulted in the loss of women's rights and freedoms. Fatma Aliye created a form of Ottoman feminism by trying to find a feminism that was outside of Europe for Muslim women.

Her article "Ta'lim ve Terbiye-i Benat-ı Osmaniyye", she was upset that girls memorized the life stories of Jeanne d'Arc, Hachette, Madame de Stael, Madame Sévigné, and George Sand but were not aware of the existence of women Muslim poets.[8] She also claimed that "what was really important was a good sense of morality, which could exist both in the European and the Eastern".[9] Fatma Aliye showed that she was well educated on both Islam and Christianity in *Nisvan-ı İslam* (1891-92), which she wrote for the European women who visited her. As a host who was an example of the self-created 'Muslim woman' type that was a master of French and sharia at the same time, she showed both European and Ottoman women how the Muslim Ottoman woman should be. However, what was striking in this article was Fatma Aliye's defense of Islamic law over Christian law, while still professing her admiration for her European female guests, without religious discrimination. After spending a day with her European guest, who was an astronomy and geometry scientist, Fatma Aliye was entranced by her education and morals and described her as an example of the ideal woman

---

[6] *Hanımlara Mahsus Gazete*. İstanbul: Kadın Eserleri Kütüphanesi ve Bilgi Merkezi Vakfı, 2009: 30.
[7] *Ibid.*. 30.
[8] Fatma Aliye, "Ta'lim ve Terbiye-i Benat-ı Osmaniyye": 135.
[9] *Ibid.*, 133.

type she envisioned, even though she was of another religion and nation, by saying that "only superior morals and education could create such a mature person".[10]

While in *Nisvan-ı Islam* (Muslim Women) she claimed that she found polygamy far better than the illegitimate relationships in Europe, arguing that women had the right to divorce in Islamic polygamy, whereas women in Europe did not, in her novels her characters did not tolerate polygamy. On the contrary, her female characters divorced their husbands when they were forced into polygamy and went on to find jobs to free and support themselves. It seems that Fatma Aliye kept her real thoughts to her fiction. In *Refet*, and *Udi*, she claimed that women needed to work to find their feet. The underlying message in all her novels was that women should choose their own husbands. She even suggested divorce for unhappy marriages. While the female characters in her contemporary male writers' work were well-educated, happy and submissive, Fatma Aliye's women were well-educated but unhappy. Fatma Aliye showed that the 'educated, good wife, good Muslim and mother' stereotype created by male writers was a fantasy and unrealistic. In Fatih Kerimi's interview with her, she said that in the process of writing *Ünlü Islam Kadınları* (Famous Islam Women) she had some reservations about its publication in Turkish. Her words show that she practiced self-censorship and indicated the reasons behind it:

> If it was published in Turkish, it would be obtained by anyone, qualified to read it or not. Unfortunately, our men are very intellectually deprived when it comes to the issue of women and family. They would attack me. I have received threats, anonymous letters and insults about my papers before. Our men study at European universities, become professors, become philosophers like Kant and Auguste Comte; however their minds don't change about two subjects: the veil and their wives. No matter how modernized they become, they don't compromise on giving Muslim women their freedom and rights.[11]

This confession shows that the modernization made by nationalist elitists could not result in freedom for women; even in new reforms women's freedom was constrained. In the letters of Fatma Aliye and her mentor Ahmet

---

[10] *İslam Kadınları*. İstanbul: İnkılab Basım Yayın, 2009: 60.
[11] Fatih Kerimi, *İstanbul Mektupları*. İstanbul: Çağrı, 2001: 265.

Mithat, which were published under the name *Fazıl ve Feylosof Kızım* (My philosopher Daughter), it can be seen that Ahmet Mithat's ideological sympathies were a source of oppression for Fatma Aliye, as Ahmet Mithat told her that he was loyal to the Sultan and she had to "choose if she would love Young Turks or himself".[12] In order to support her father, Fatma Aliye wrote a biography titled *Ahmet Cevdet Paşa ve Zamanı* (Ahmet Cevdet Paşa and His Time) (1915) at a time westernization supporter Mithat Pasha was applauded and her father was attacked because of his views. In this biography she was bold enough to defend The Second Constitutional and parliamentary system despite her father's constitutional monarchy-opposing views, and criticize II. Abdülhamid for closing parliament. She believed that Tanzimat was a reform that would ensure freedom for the people and it is evident that she was aware of a new emerging regime, and showed that she was supporting the new Republic and Mustafa Kemal in a letter she wrote to him. However, since the biography was published at a time when Fatma Aliye's fame had subsided, this biography did not gather enough attention. After this period, she wrote less frequently and maintaining an approving silence in Republic era.

The source of the ambivalent situation Muslim women of the Ottoman Empire found themselves in related to global modernization and the transformation of Ottoman society, as colonized lands rose in rebellion. While Fatma Aliye was fighting her position as the outcast of her patriarchal culture, a colonial position, she was also fighting the patriarchy of the new culture: modernity's patriarchy. As a result of the fight with these two forces, her discourse also appeared ambivalent. Fatma Aliye's feminism had national reflexes, in accordance with that period's conditions, and was not Islamic feminism. She used the same strategy New Ottomans used by re-creating the past as a standing point for the reforms they envisioned while she was demanding rights and freedoms for women. Islam's focus on the New Ottoman was taken over by Turkish nationalists by switching the focus to the Turkish past; while writing the Turkish history in 1914, Ziya Gökalp defined Islam, Turkish nationalism and modernity together with an emphasis on Turkish nationalism. As Elif Ekin Akşit put in her paper "Hanımlara Mahsus

[12] Ahmet Mithat Efendi, *Fazıl ve Feylosof Kızım.* Istanbul: Klasik Yayınları: 2011: 385.

Milliyetçilik: Fatma Aliye ve Erken Milliyetçi Stratejiler",[13] Fatma Aliye was writing in a transition period between these two ideologies.

Fatma Aliye developed her theory under the influence of her father Ahmet Cevdet Pasha, because despite representing the traditionalist wing in Tanzimat, Ahmet Cevdet Pasha paved the way for nationalist ideologist ideas in his work. While writing about the beginning of the 19th century Ottoman history, Cevdet Pasha attributed the fortitude of Ottoman Islam to its Turkish roots. After his work, research proving that the Ottomans had descended from Turkish ancestry surfaced, and Yusuf Akçura supported this historical approach with political principles, claiming that Turkism was the most appropriate political form for the Ottoman Empire in his paper Three Policies, which dealt with Ottomanism, Islamism and Turkism. Later, the term Turk evolved into a word, denoting race.

After 1908, Turkism gained momentum with Young Turks. In 1908, the next generation following the New Ottomans, educated in Europe, and the Young Turks of the Committee of Union and Progress managed to declare The Second Constitutional after 30 years of tyranny full of Abdülhamit oppression and reforms. Women such as Fatma Aliye's sister Emine Semiye and Gülistan İsmet Hanım supported the Committee of Union and Progress in this fight against Abdülhamit's autocracy. They exhibited a more radical stance compared to women of their past generation who were much more in accord with authority.

Fatma Aliye found democracy and feminism in Islam's early days and developed this ideology in her papers and in *Nisvan-ı Islam*. As Aksit suggested, this method was to be continued by the Republic's building stone Turkists, including Halide Edip.

## Halide Edip Adıvar, the first feminist of republique

More rights and freedoms were promised under the rule of The Second Constitutional. However, the Committee of Union and Progress moved slowly, and to quicken the process they founded many female societies

[13] Elif Ekin Akşit, "Hanımlara Mahsus Milliyetçilik: Fatma Aliye ve Erken Milliyetçi Stratejiler" in *Kebikeç* (30), 2010: 64. Online at http://80.251.40.59/politics.ankara.edu.tr/aksit/hmg.html.

between 1908-16, after the first society was founded by Fatma Aliye in 1897. Among these was Teali-i Nisvan (the society for the elevation of women) founded by Halide Edip Adıvar in 1908, which required its members to speak English, taught them English, was in contact with English suffragettes. These societies supported girls in their education, collected money for wounded soldiers and their families during the 1912 Balkan War.

This time, the discourse that pointed to the early days of Islam was switched to the nomadic Turks. These demands all centered on women's rights, and freedom became the factor that bonded Turkist feminists and Ottomanist feminists; nationalist Nezihe Muhittin claimed Fatma Aliye and paid her respect in *Türk Kadını.*[14] Halide Edip, on the other hand, did not even mention her name, and adopted the rupture myth of the new Republic's strategy and chose to bury her in silence. However, when the works of Fatma Aliye and Halide Edip, and the woman utopia they adopted, are examined, it is clear that there was a continued women's movement from the empire to the Republic.[15]

It can be observed that these biographies, which do not include female adulthood, and woman's relationship with her body, are an extension of the half-biographical half-autobiographical pioneering text *Fatma Aliye or the Birth of an Ottoman Woman Writer*. As Adak said, since the adult self could not speak because of self-censoring, and only childhood and adolescence could be described, periods that collided with the Ottoman's late period, there was a writerly emphasis on continuation between Ottoman and the Republic, which created a political strategy against official history.

Halide Edip Adıvar did not mention the women writers who had come before her in her autobiographies and work, nor did she mention the freedom fight of women from different ethnic backgrounds, which created the illusion that she was the only woman writer of the time. This illusion was carried further perpetuated by the official literary canon.

---

[14] Ayşegül Baykan and Belma Ötüş-Baskett, *Nezihe Muhittin ve Türk Kadını, 1931*. İstanbul: İletişim Yayınları, 2009.

[15] Hülya Adak says in her paper "Suffragettes of the empire, daughters of the Republic: Women auto/biographers narrate national history (1918-1935)", this can also be seen in the autobiographies of the transition from the empire into the nation-state, despite the official history's rupture myth. Halide Edip's Memoirs of Halide Edip (1926), The Turkish Ordeal (1928) and Nezihe Muhiddin's Türk Kadını (Turkish Woman-1931), are examples of this.

As Gregory Jusdanis suggests in his book *Belated Modernity and Aesthetic Culture: Inventing National Literature,* "building a nation requires collective narratives, homogenizing the technical differences and making sure that the citizens embrace the ideology of a fantasy community".[16]

Textbooks and anthologies have been the main tools in creating the right citizen model during the process of founding the nation state. With the purpose of developing the national identity, this approach called for texts that told the stories of love of the country, heroic feelings, enemies, others, and war against these others, literature.[17]

As Ayşe Durakbaşa suggests in her *Halide Edip, Turkish Modernisation and Feminism,* in Turkish public opinion, Halide Edip had two personas: "Exemplary Turkish woman, a pioneer in the women's independence, and a demonic character with ambitions of power, who betrayed Atatürk reforms".[18] While some praised her and her texts for her work on the fight for national independence, the others accused her of being a traitor for suggesting an American mandate. This accusation was made for the first time in the 26 hour long talk by Mustafa Kemal in the Grand National Assembly, which was later published under the name *Nutuk.* In textbooks, she is largely portrayed as originally suggesting the mandate but later changing her mind. Her derogatory discourse against official ideology was censored by her will in official Turkish history and Halide Edip was mainly portrayed with regards to her national independence and her novels. However, Halide Edip claimed in the second volume of her autobiography *Turkish Ordeal,* which she chose to write in English as a willing exile following the tension that had arisen between her and Mustafa Kemal, that she did not want to be forgotten or remembered only as the writer of official history:

> I would try to recreate that period of Turkish history by preserving a faithful record of my experiences during that great ordeal. I would try

---

[16] Gregory Jusdanis, *Belated Modernity and Aesthetic Culture: Inventing National Literature (Theory and History of Literature).* Minnesota, Univ of Minnesota Press, 1991.

[17] Reyhan Tutumlu analyzed 21 text books, 6 of which did not include any women writers, in her work "Women Writers in Anthologies and Literature Text Books", and it can be seen in this research that while Fatma Aliye was only mentioned once in a 1934 Turkish Literature textbook, Halide Edip Adıvar has been included in 11 books from 1930 to today.

[18] Ayşe Durakbaşa, *Halide Edip, Türk Modernleşmesi ve Feminizm.* İletişim: İstanbul, 2009: 152.

> to tell the story of Turkey as simply and honestly as a child, that the world might some day read it – not as a historical record nor as a political treatise, but as a human document about men and women alive during my own lifetime; and I would write it in a language far better fitted to reach the world than my own.[19]

Although her husband Salih Zeki was a progressionist and modern man, he told Halide Edip he wanted a second wife. Halide Edip refused and, as a result, she divorced him in 1910. After this, she published her work under her father's name Halide Edip. Also in 1910, she published *Seviyye Talip,* in which she discussed the marriage problem. She joined the Turkish Unions in 1911, which was a nationalist club of Young Turks. She was influenced by Panturkism, which had been conceived by Ziya Gökalp and Yusuf Akçura in order to confederate all the Turks in the world. In addition to Ziya Gökalp's nationalist ideal, she followed feminist ideas that suggested that women should have freedom in pre-Islam Turkish societies. When she went to London for the second time in 1911, she wrote her novel *Yeni Turan,* in which she described her Turkish state utopia.

Halide Edip exists in the literary canon only with her nationalistic novels; her early romantic novels are not well-known. These novels, just like those by Fatma Aliye, bear autobiographical qualities. As opposed to pioneering strong, self-sufficent women making their own decisions and shaping their own lives, like Fatma Aliye, Halide Edip conceived her novels around male characters. However, her male characters are different from those of the male writers. As Hülya Adak argued in her paper "Otobiyografik Benliğin Çok-Karakterliliği: Halide Edip'in ilk romanlarında Toplumsal Cinsiyet", Halide Edip transformed the 'evil' that was the bad influence of women on men as a result of their sexual appeal, into the ideal woman whose only 'evil' influence on men was a result of her well-built character, education and intellect.[20] Men would lose their strength in front of these women, and even lose themselves, choosing love above their cause. Halide Edip wrote these novels during a dark period of her life, after Salih Zeki told her that he was thinking about marrying a second wife. She might have used the effect of

[19] Halide Edip Adıvar, *The Turkish Ordeal*. New York –London: The Century, 1928: 132.

[20] Hülya Adak, "Otobiyografik benliğin çok-karakterliliği: Halide Edib'in ilk romanlarında toplumsal cinsiyet" in Sibel Irzık and Jale Parla (eds). *Kadınlar dile düşünce: edebiyat ve toplumsal cinsiyet*. İletişim, Istanbul, 2004: 170.

'stripping' her male characters of their powers as therapy for herself. Although Halide Edip's father and her first husband Salih Zeki were liberal and progressionist men who supported women's education and progression, they were still very conservative, as Fatma Aliye said, when it came to polygamy. The distress caused by her father's polygamous marriage resulted in her creating male characters that did not tolerate polygamy in her novels. The ideal woman characters in Halide Edip's early work are a continuation of Fatma Aliye's Islamic woman archetype. These women were educated according to European ideals but were still loyal to Muslim culture; they did not see westernization only in modal terms, they were immersed in both cultures and managed to find a harmony between the two. In *Rafik'in Annesi* (Raik's mom) one of the male characters describes the ideal woman as:

> She can speak foreign languages, even three of them, but she shouldn't bargain in French in Beyoglu. She shouldn't embrace fake laughter, strange rubbing of hands, nodding, walking as if jumping just to imitate French women. She shouldn't fake mock surprise at every meaningless occurrence. She shouldn't say 'oh! mon per' when she sees her father, or 'oh! Mondiyö' when afraid. She should believe in god and go to the mosque every once in a while.[21]

*New Turan*, which she wrote in England, is a transition from her more individualistic early work, incorporating characters who abandoned their personal desires and dedicated their lives to national independence. Writer of a Turkist and Islamist utopia with the influence of Ziya Gökalp and Yusuf Akçura whom she met at Turkish Unions, Halide Edip had an idea of nationalism that was not racist and hostile, that she defended her whole life and had a difference of opinion about with Committee of Union and Progress. The protagonist of this novel, Oğuz, appealed to Kurds, Arabs, Armenians and Greeks living in the Ottoman Empire for the Turan ideal, not only Turks. Thus, Halide Edip distanced herself away from the Panturkism, which aimed to bring Turkish race together. In *Memoirs of Halide Edip*, she underlined that she was misunderstood in being portrayed as the "representative of Committee of Union and Progress's nationalist views". In her answers to the comments she received in this way, she expressed her discontent of Committee of Union and Progress's current situation:

---

[21] Halide Edip Adıvar, *Raik'in Annesi*. Istanbul: Atlas Kitabevi ,1967: 21.

> It looks forward to a New Turkey where a chastised and matured Union and Progress has taken the reins of power, where women have to vote, and where women work with the qualities of head and heart which characterize the best Turkish women. The simplicity and the austerity of their lives have become different since the magnificent days of the Ottomans, with the unhealthy luxury and parasitic tendencies of a class of women which only a high but degenerate civilization like the ottoman creates.[22]

The Ottoman woman criticized here is not the Istanbul woman with whom she identified. When asked by Grace Ellison how English women could contribute to the Turkish women's movement, she replied by saying: "in order to eradicate the term harem that is full of misunderstandings and talk about the women in Turkish households, this questioned should be asked them".[23] Just like Fatma Aliye, Halide Edip wanted to correct the misunderstanding in the Western world that the lifestyle in the Ottoman palace existed in all Turkish households. Therefore, the woman type who enjoys make-up, extravagance and appearances can be found in the palace. As she said in *New Turan*, she wanted a culturally nationalist but politically liberal and democratic Turkey, the administrative system of which was not chauvinistic.[24] She faced a difference of opinion with the Committee of Union and Progress on Armenian relocation and conversion for Armenians living in the Empire in 1915, although this idea culminated in Turkism, with an ideal of one ethnicity and one language. She wrote her opinions of Armenian relocation in her memoirs, a part she did not include in the Turkish translation. According to her memoirs, she had discussed the Armenian problem and nationalism in Turkish Unions, which angered Unionists and Talat Pasha, who made the relocation decision, wanted her to be punished for it. Although Talat Pasha criticized her and her party's political moves, he said that "she serves her country in the way she believes", "let her speak her mind, she is sincere".[25] Halide Edip commented on Armenian relocation in her English memoirs:

---

[22] *Memoirs of Halide Edip*, Piscataway, Gorgias Press, 2005: 332.
[23] *Ibid.*,17.
[24] *Ibid.*, 332.
[25] *Memoirs of Halide Edip*: 388.

> There are two factors which lead man to the extermination of his kind: the principles advocated by the idealists, and the material interest which the consequences of doing so afford certain classes. The idealists are the more dangerous, for one is obliged to respect them even if one cannot agree with them. Talaat was of that kind.[26]

She was disappointed about the nationalism:

> I who had dreamed of a nationalism which will create a happy land of beauty, understanding and love, I have seen nothing but mutual massacre and mutual hatred; I have seen nothing but ideals used as instruments for creating human carnage and misery.[27]

In the first volume of her autobiography, which was translated into Turkish as *Mor Salkımlı Ev* (House with Wisteria), Halide Edip wrote that she grew up with Circassian, Albanian, Roman, Kurdish, Greek and Armenian ethnic identities and religious views, and to her, leaving this household, which was a small model of the empire's multi-ethnic identity, represented her transition from childhood innocence to the real world, and ultimately the demise of the Ottoman Empire. For the little Edip, these different ethnicities, languages and religions were a part of a whole:

> She had not entered yet that narrow human path where religion and language as well as racial differences make human beings devour each other. The little girl was still in a world where the joy of life is heart fusion and natural existence.[28]

The innocence of childhood was also underlined in the story of the founding of New Turkey in *Turkish Ordeal,* with the words: "I would try to tell the story of Turkey as simply and honestly as a child".[29] Halide Edip's account is different from the heroism of the official history. Historical characters are portrayed with positive and negative attributes. She was forced to leave her country and language because she could not find the freedom for herself, although she fought for its independence. While she was a model Turkish woman overseas, she was declared a traitor in her own country. However,

---

[26] *Ibid.*: 387.
[27] *Ibid.*: 376.
[28] *Ibid.*: 27.
[29] Halide Edip Adıvar, *The Turkish Ordeal*: 132.

because she wrote her work in English, she managed to demolish the Eastern women stereotype in Western patriarchy, and made Turkish women a voice of world history by freeing herself from the narrow discourse of the Turkish official history. Her independence narrative is a polyphonic, anti-militaristic text that tells the story of women left out of the official history, their experience of war, people from different ideologies, and the other side of the war.

The pioneer of Turkey's feminist literature, Fatma Aliye was the first woman who dreamed of a free world for women of her country, and suggested solutions within her novels and papers. She presented women with examples, telling them that their situations were not their destiny, and giving them strength and courage to voice their demand for freedom; she became the first feminist historian of Turkey. Halide Edip followed and continued her ideals, although she did not mention the writer's name or works in her texts (strangely she did mention her sister Emine Semiye). In the "Turkish Women" chapter of her work *Conflict of East and West in Turkey* she attributed the history of Turkish women to Fatma Aliye's perspective, pointing to the fact that there was a feminist atmosphere in the early days of Islam, an idea that had been conceived and nurtured by Fatma Aliye, which is one of most important examples of Halide Edip's attendance to Fatma Aliye's ideals: "We see in the early days of Islam a host of women working as teachers, poets and preachers some even enlisting as soldiers".[30]

Following the traces of Fatma Aliye and Halide Edip's lives and works shows that no matter what the regime, women must always face the different guises of patriarchy in governments. The feminist consciousness that was born into the nationalist project and tried to vocalize itself in the Ottoman and the Republic era, showed continuity among the nationalist views that clashed, excluded and finally severed ties.

[30] Halide Edip Adıvar, "Turkish Women" in *Conflict of East and West in Turkey*: 201.

## Select Bibliography

### A. Primary Sources

Aliye, Fatma, 2009. *Hanımlara Mahsus Gazete*. İstanbul: Kadın Eserleri Kütüphanesi ve Bilgi Merkezi Vakfı.

Edip Adıvar, Halide, 1928. *The Turkish Ordeal*. New York –London: The Century.

—, *Conflict of East and West in Turkey*, 1963. Jamia Millia Extension Lectures. Lahor: S.M.Ashraf.

—, *Raik'in Annesi*, 1967. Istanbul: Atlas Kitabevi.

—, *Memoirs of Halide Edip*, 2005. Piscataway, Gorgias Press.

Turhan, Tan, 1936. "Unutularak Ölen Edip" in *Cumhuriyet* (4371), 15 July.

### B. Secondary Sources

Baykan, Ayşegül and Belma Ötüş-Baskett, 2009. *Nezihe Muhittin ve Türk Kadını, 1931*. İstanbul: İletişim Yayınları.

Durakbaşa, Ayşe, 2009. *Halide Edip, Türk Modernleşmesi ve Feminizm*. İletişim: İstanbul.

Ekin Akşit, Elif, 2010. "Hanımlara Mahsus Milliyetçilik: Fatma Aliye ve Erken Milliyetçi Stratejiler" in *Kebikeç* (30). Online at http://80.251.40.59/politics.ankara.edu.tr/aksit/hmg.html.

Hülya, Adak, 2005. "Gender-in(g) Biography: Ahmet Mithat (on Fatma Aliye) or the Canonization of an Ottoman Male Writer" in *Querelles*, vol.10, May.

Jusdanis, Gregory, 1991. *Belated Modernity and Aesthetic Culture: Inventing National Literature (Theory and History of Literature)*. Minnesota, Univ of Minnesota Press.

Kerimi, Fatih, 2001. *İstanbul Mektupları*. İstanbul: Çağrı.

Mithat Efendi, Ahmet, 2011. *Fazıl ve Feylosof Kızım*. Istanbul: Klasik Yayınları.

## Notes on Contributors

SIRMOULA ALEXADRIDOU is a teacher of Greek Literature. Her basic studies and MA (*The allegorical dimension of the "Dam" on the novel of Spyros Plaskovitis*) was in Modern Greek Literature from the Faculty of Philosophy, at the Aristotle University of Thessaloniki. She is engaged in an ongoing doctoral dissertation dealing with the edition of magazines by women and for women in Greece and East (Constantinople) during the second half of the 19$^{th}$ century, a Her current research interests are in the areas of women's writing and education during the 19$^{th}$ century.

NADEZHDA ALEXANDROVA is an assistant-professor at the Faculty of Slavic Studies at Sofia University "St. Kliment Ohridski", Bulgaria. Her interests are focused on the 19$^{th}$ century women's periodicals and literature, as well as on the history of education and emancipation in Southeastern Europe. After publishing her monograph *Robini, kukli i chelovetsi: Predstavi za zhenite vuv vuzrozhdenskata publitsistika i prozata na Ljuben Karavelov* (Slaves, dolls, individuals: Representations of women in nineteenth-century Bulgarian periodicals, and in Lyuben Karavelov's fiction) in 2012, she has published articles and book reviews in English, French and Turkish in international journals. Dr. Alexandrova is a board member and co-secretary of *The European Association for Gender Research, Education and* Documentation (ATGENDER), a co-editor of "Teaching with Gender" book series, and a member of the *Women Writers Network*. She has participated in a number international research projects, concerning gender mainstreaming in education, mobility and belonging, and women's literary history.

NIEVES BARANDA is expert in Medieval and Early Modern Spanish women writers, as Professor at the Universidad Nacional de Educación a Distancia (UNED), in Madrid. She is leader of the research project BIESES, *Bibliography of Spanish Women Writers*, (http://www.bieses.net), a database with over 11.000 references on these writers' works, lives, reception, contemporary mentions and present critical studies and editions, and first Vice-President of the U.S.A. association *GEMELA*, as well as Manager collaborator for the nation-wide evaluation of Humanities Research Projects, Ministry of Economy. She has publications on women's education, readings, autobiographies, and writers' social conditions or paratexts.

JENNY BERGENMAR, born 1973, has a PhD in Comparative Literature and Senior and is a Lecturer at the Department of Literature, History of Ideas and Religion at the University of Gothenburg. Her fields of research include the history of reading, reception studies and the digital humanities. She is currently finishing the research project Readers Responding to Selma Lagerlöf. The Public's Letters to the Author 1890–1940, and starting a new project: *Swedish Nineteenth Century Women Writers on Export.*

SUZAN VAN DIJK is a specialist in French literature and senior researcher at the Huygens Institute for the History of the Netherlands (KNAW Royal Dutch Academy of Arts and Sciences). She is particularly interested in women's authorship (18th and 19th century), the reception of women's writing and international connections between women authors. In this field she initiated and chaired a series of international projects, funded by NWO, COST, CLARIN-NL and HERA.

BILJANA DOJČINOVIĆ is associate professor at the Department for Comparative Literature and Literary Theory at Faculty of Philology, University of Belgrade. Her fields of study include modernism, literary theory, women's writing, digital humanities, with the works of Henry James, James Joyce, Virginia Woolf, John Updike, Jelena Dimitrijević in the focus of her research. She is author of six books and director of the research project *Knjiženstvo, theory and history of women's writing in Serbian until 1915* www.knjizenstvo.rs, and editor-in-chief of the electronic journal *Knjiženstvo*. For further information see http://www.fil.bg.ac.rs/katedre/op-sta/BB%20Biljana.html.

CARMEN BEATRICE DUTU, born 1974 in Bucharest, Romania, obtained her PhD at Bucharest University in 2010. She is an Associate Professor of Comparative Literature and Theory of Criticism at *Dimitrie Cantemir* University in Bucharest, Romania, where she held the management position of the *Institute for Intercultural Studies and Research* from 2011 to 2012 and the Dean position of the Faculty of Foreign Languages and Literatures from

2012 to 2013. She conducted her doctoral and postdoctoral research in the Netherlands, at the *Aletta Institute for women's studies* (Amsterdam, 2009) and the *Huygens Institute of the Royal Academy of Arts and Sciences* (The Hague, 2011). Currently, she is a Visiting Lecturer at Ercyies University, Kaisery, Turkey where she teaches Cultural Studies and Contemporary Critical Theory at graduate and postgraduate level. Her field of research includes gender studies (her doctoral thesis investigated masculinity and femininity identity construction in Romanian mid 19th century sentimental novels), cultural studies, and more recently, citizenship and education as identity formation factors, contributing to an encyclopaedia in the field.

HENRIETTE GOLDWYN is Professor of French Literature at New York University and the Director of New York University in Paris. A specialist of early modern France, her research and publications focus on narrative fiction in the 17th century, early modern women writers, polemical journalism, religious discourse and exilic studies. She has written extensively on Mme Du Noyer and edited her *Mémoires.* She is now co-editing a five-volume anthology of early modern women playwrights from the Renaissance to the end of the 18th century and is preparing a volume on the culture of prophecy in France following the Revocation of the Edict of Nantes.

ELENA GRETCHANAIA is professor of Comparative Literature at the University of Orléans (France). Her research focuses on French-Russian cultural interactions, French-language Russian literature, French and Russian poetry, and autobiographical texts. Publications: *Interactions littéraires franco-russes et le contexte religieux (1797-1825)* (Moscou, 2002) ; *"Si tu lis jamais ce journal...". Diaristes russes francophones. 1780-1854* (Paris, 2008, with Catherine Viollet) ; *"Je vous parlerai la langue de l'Europe..." : la francophonie en Russie (XVIIIe – XIXe siècles)* (Bern, 2012).

ALEJANDRO HERMIDA DE BLAS, born in 1971, is a professor of Slavic philology at the Complutense University of Madrid, where he obtained his PhD in 1998. He completed his studies at the Comenius University of Bratislava (Slovakia) and the Masaryk University of Brno (Czech Republic). He has written numerous studies on Czech and Slovak texts, their relationship with Spain, and the theory and history of translation regarding these languages. He has contributed to collective works such as *History of Slavic Literatures* (Madrid 1997), *Spain and the Slavic World* (Madrid 2002),

*Iberian and Slavonic Cultures: Contact and Comparison* (Lisbon 2007), and *Historical Dictionary of Translation in Spain* (Madrid 2009). Alejandro Hermida is one of the editors of *Eslavística Complutense*, the first scientific journal devoted to the Slavic languages and cultures in Spain. He is also a translator of Slovak and Czech literatures.

HILDE HOOGENBOOM earned a PhD in Slavic languages and literatures from Columbia University (1996) and is an assistant professor of Russian in the School of International Letters and Cultures at Arizona State University, specializing in nineteenth-century Russian literature, women writers, noble culture, Russian francophone writing, and comparative and quantitative literary studies. She has published a collection of archival letters by Nadezhda Khvoshchinskaia and her sisters Sofia and Praskovia (2002), the Russian Bronte sisters, and has translated Catherine the Great's memoirs from French for the Modern Library (2005). She is completing a monograph on foreign literature in nineteenth-century Russia, *The Rise of Russian Novels: Sentimentalism, Noble Culture, and the Literary Marketplace.* Her work is supported by fellowships from the National Humanities Center (2000-1), the Social Science Research Council (2001-2), and over a dozen travel grants for archival research in Russia. She is past president of the *Eighteenth-Century Russian Studies Association* (2006-8), and currently on the Board of the *Association for Women in Slavic Studies* (2014-16).

MADELEINE JEAY is professor emerita at McMaster University (Hamilton, Canada), specializing in medieval literature. Her more recent book, *Le commerce des mots*, deals with the poetics of lists in XII-XVIIth centuries. She currently works on a study of the poet's name in medieval poetry. Interested in writings related to women, she has written on the *Evangiles des Quenouilles* (*The Distaff Gospels*), a XVth-Century compilation of popular beliefs presented in the boccacian frame of old women gatherings. Medieval mystic women are also one of her interests: she has published with Kathleen Garay an English translation of the *Life of Douceline de Digne* by Felippa Porcellet.

ROTRAUD VON KULESSA is professor of French and Italian Literature at the University of Augsburg. Her fields of research are French and Italian women's literature from the 18th to the early 20th century. Publications include: Françoise de Graffigny, *Lettres d'une Péruvienne.* Edition annotée et commentée (Paris, 2014) ; *Entre la reconnaissance et l'exclusion. La position de l'autrice dans le champ littéraire en France et en Italie à l'Epoque 1900* (Paris, 2011), and the notions of game and Querelle in literature: "Das Wissen von der Liebe als Spiel. Pietro Bembo: *Gli Asolani*", in *Nobilitierung vs. Divulgierung? Strategien der Aufbereitung von Wissen in Dialogen, Lehrgedichten und narrativer Prosa des 16.-18. Jahrhunderts* (München, 2011) and transcultural literature of the 21th century: "La letteratura migrante tra testimonianza ed impegno" in *Letteratura italofona* (Würzburg, 2013).

BEGOÑA LASA ALVAREZ teaches in the Faculty of Education at the University of A Coruña. She has two Bas, in Spanish and English Studies, and a PhD on the reception in Spain of eighteenth-century English novels by women. Her academic interests focus on eighteenth-century women writers and the reception of British literature and culture in Spain, and she has published several articles on these topics. Some of her most relevant publications are: *The Children of the Abbey (1796): A Nineteenth-Century Bestseller* (Florida, 2006), *From Britain to Spain via France: Amelia Opie's The Father and Daughter* (Oxford, 2007), *Titles in Translation: Some Eighteenth-Century Examples* (Aveiro, 2009), *Reviewing Women in the Long Eighteenth Century* (Madrid, 2010), *Regina Maria Roche, an Eighteenth-Century Irish Writer on the Continent and Overseas* (Newcastle, 2011). *Viajeros británicos en la prensa española de principios del XIX: La Biblioteca británica de Olive* (Bern, 2013).

KATI LAUNIS is a Postdoctoral Research Fellow in and Adjunct Professor of Finnish Literature at the University of Turku, Finland. Her main areas of research are nineteenth-century women writers and the figure of child in Finnish literature. Dr Launis is the author of *Narrated Women: The First Novels Written by Women in Finland Defining Womanhood* (2005, in Finnish) and numerous articles on nineteenth-century female writers, working-class writers and Gothic fiction.

MAARIT LESKELÄ-KÄRKI, PhD, Adjunct professor, works currently as a University Lecturer at the Department of Cultural History at the University of Turku, Finland. Her PhD-thesis (2006) dealt with the cultural history of women's writing and the correspondence of three literary sisters. She has edited books on epistolary practices and literary history, and published on gender history, biographical research and autobiographical sources. Her current research relates to the traditions of biographical writing in Finland during the 20th century as well as the methodological questions of historical biographies.

ILEANA MIHAILĂ, born 1959 (Bucharest, Romania), MA 1982, PhD 1995, is Assistant Professor at the University of Bucharest, where she teaches Eighteenth Century French Literature, and Senior Researcher at the Institute of History and Theory of Literature of the Romanian Academy. She is a specialist in eighteenth- and nineteenth-century French and Romanian literature, Gender Studies, Comparative Literature and Franco-Romanian cultural relations. She is the author or co-author of several studies and books on these subjects. For further information see www.unibuc.ro/prof/mihaila_i/.

KATJA MIHURKO PONIŽ is associate professor of Slovenian Literature at School of Humanities, University of Nova Gorica. Her research interests include early Slovenian women writers, especially Zofka Kveder, the history of women's movement in Habsburg monarchy, the digital humanities and the relations between Slovenian and German literature. She is author of three books and editor of the critical edition of the Collected Works of Zofka Kveder (three volumes of the collection have been published so far).

INÊS DE ORNELLAS E CASTRO is Professor at Faculty of Social and Human Sciences – University Nova of Lisbon, where she has been teaching Latin since 1991. She received a PhD in Latin language and culture (2007) with the thesis *De la table des dieux à la table des hommes. La symbolique de l'alimentation dans l'Antiquité romaine* (Paris, 2011). She is a Principal Researcher and coordinator at the Institute of Literature and Tradition's Studies (UNL) and collaborates with various national and international research networks. Apart from publishing translations of Greek and Latin texts, she is the author of several articles on the cultural history of food and the body, on female writing and on Renaissance medical texts.

MARÍA JESÚS PANDO-CANTELI is Associate Professor in the Department of Modern Languages and in the Department of Communication, University of Deusto, Bilbao, (since 1996) where she teaches graduate and undergraduate courses in English Literature, European Studies, and Media and Gender studies. She received her doctorate degree in Languages and Literatures in 2001, and has also taught at the University of the Basque Country (UPV) and at Santa Clara University (USA). She has been a postdoctoral Fulbright fellow at Stanford University, Department of English, (2008-2009), and at the Folger Shakespeare Library, USA (2007). Her current research interests are women in early modern cultures, and gender and media studies. Her recent publications in early modern studies include "*Tentando Vados.* The Martyrdom Politics of Luisa de Carvajal y Mendoza" in the *Journal of Early Modern Cultural Studies* (2010).

IVANA PANTELIĆ is born in 1977. BA Contemporary History, Faculty of Philosophy, University of Belgrade. MA Social and Cultural Anthropology, Faculty of Philosophy, University of Belgrade. Ongoing doctoral dissertation dealing with public perception of Jovanka Broz, Yugoslav's president Josip Broz Tito wife. Currently employed as research assistant at the Institute of Contemporary History in Belgrade. Among her recent publications: *Female Partisans as Citizens: Social Emancipation of Female Partisans in Serbia, 1945-1953* (Belgrade, 2010) and *Two parts of Remembrance: Partisan Diaries as a Source of Second World War History* (Belgrade, 2013).

VIOLA PARENTE-ČAPKOVÁ is a Researcher at the Department of Finnish Literature, School of History, Culture and Arts Research at the University of Turku and an Associate Professor/Docent in Theory of Literature at Charles University, Prague. Her research interests are Decadence and Modernism, gender studies, women writers in transnational/European perspective with a focus on Finland, mimesis, studies of nationalism and post-colonialism, and theoretical issues in literary history. She is currently working in a Collaborative Research Project *Travelling Texts: The Transnational Reception of Women's Writing at the Gringes ot Europe*, financed by HERA, Joint Programme Cultural Encounters.

JOANNA PARTYKA is an anthropologist and historian of literature, associate professor in Cultural Studies at the Faculty of "Artes Liberales" (University of Warsaw), and researcher at the Institute for Literary Research, the Polish Academy of Sciences. Her main field of interest is the Mediterranean culture of the 16th and 17th centuries analyzed from a comparative perspective. In her research she explores paraliterary texts, such as penitencial books, itineraries, encyclopedias, moral and pedagogical treatises, letters, household books, diaries, etc. She is interested in the history of women, especially their active and passive participation in European culture. She has published two books and above 60 articles in Polish, Spanish and English. She also translates from Spanish to Polish.

HENRIETTE PARTZSCH has worked at the Universities of Basle and Geneva (Switzerland), after receiving her PhD in Spanish Studies at the Technische Universität Berlin (Germany. Since 2008 she has been a Lecturer in Spanish at the University of St Andrews. From July 2014, she will join Hispanic Studies at the University of Glasgow. A member of the European COST Action *Women Writers in History: Toward a New Understanding of European Literary Culture*, she has published in recent years on women, the press and authorship in nineteenth-century Spain. She is the project leader of the HERA-funded collaborative research project *Travelling Text 1790-1914: The Transnational Reception of Women's Writing at the Fringes of Europe (Finland, the Netherlands, Norway, Slovenia, Spain)* (Sept 2013-Aug 2016).

AMELIA SANZ is a Professor in the French Department of the Philology Faculty at the Complutense University of Madrid. Since 2001 she has led the research group *European Literatures from Text to Hypermedia* (LEETHI). She began her career studying comparative literature, specifically the relationship between France and Spain in the seventeenth and eighteenth centuries, and also the transfers of French women writers. In her books she has developed theoretical reflections on key twentieth-century concepts such as intertextuality, interculturality, transliteratures and hypercolonialism.

FRANCESCA M. SCOTT is a lecturer at Amsterdam University College. She has been a member of the COST Action *Women Writers in History* since late 2011, and will be collaborating with the subsequent HERA *Travelling TexTs* project as a postdoctoral researcher at Huygens ING. She completed her PhD, *The Fuzzy Theory and Women Writers in the Late Eighteenth Century,* at the University of Warwick, and her research interests include women's writing in the long eighteenth century, the history of childbirth, midwifery and women's health, and a number of fields in the medical humanities. Forthcoming publications include *Picturing Women's Health* (2014).

SENEM TIMUROĞLU graduated from the Francophone private high school Notre Dame de Sion in 1995. In 1999, she received her Bachelor's degree at the Turkish Language and Literature Department of Mimar Sinan University. In 2002, she completed her Master's thesis in Paris, at Eastern Languages and

Civilisations Institute (INALCO). In 2006, she received her second MA at Bilkent University, Turkish Literature Department. Currently, she is doing her PhD at Sorbonne Paris IV, working on a dissertation on *Transnational Perspectives on 19th and 20th Century Ottoman and French Women Literatures*. She has been teaching at Özyeğin University since 2009. Her articles and translations are published in various journals. Her areas of research are 19th and 20th century women's literature, feminist literary theory, gender, transnationalism, poststructuralism and postcolonial theory. She is the mother of Mert Deniz.

## INDEX

**Literary genres**

**Writing literary history**



**Proper Names**

CPSIA information can be obtained at www.ICGtesting.com
Printed in the USA
LVOW07*0313281214

420587LV00005B/81/P

9 789042 038707